Emily Post's

ETIQUETTE

17th Edition

Also from The Emily Post Institute

Emily Post's The Gift of Good Manners

Emily Post's Wedding Etiquette, 4th edition

Emily Post's Wedding Planner, 3rd edition

Emily Post's Entertaining

Emily Post's The Etiquette Advantage in Business

Essential Manners for Men

Emily Post's The Guide to Good Manners for Kids

Emily Post's

ETIQUETTE

17th Edition

PEGGY POST

HarperResource
An Imprint of HarperCollinsPublishers

EMILY POST'S® ETIQUETTE (SEVENTEENTH EDITION). Copyright © 2004 by The Emily Post
Institute, Inc. All rights reserved. Printed in the United States of America. No part of this book may
be used or reproduced in any manner whatsoever without written permission except in the case of
brief quotations embodied in critical articles and reviews. For information, address HarperCollins
Publishers Inc., 10 East 53rd Street, New York, NY 10022.

HarperCollins books may be purchased for educational, business, or sales promotional use. For information, please write: Special Markets Department, HarperCollins Publishers Inc., 10 East 53rd Street, New
York, NY 10022.

Book Design by Ralph Fowler
Illustrations by Martie Holmer

Library of Congress Cataloging-in-Publication Data

Post, Peggy
    Emily Post's Etiquette.—17th ed. / Peggy Post.
        p.   cm.
    Includes index.
    ISBN 0-06-620957-9
    1. Etiquette.   I. Post, Emily, 1873–1960. Etiquette.   II. Title.

BJ1853.P6 2004
395—dc22

                                          2004040508

05 06 07 08   WB/QW   10 9 8 7 6 5 4 3

With gratitude, I dedicate this book to the thousands
of individuals who have shared their etiquette dilemmas with me,
demonstrating that they truly care about being considerate and respectful;
and to Emily Post, my great-grandmother-in-law, whose
compassionate spirit and timeless advice serve as solid foundations
for courtesy in today's busy world.

Acknowledgments

So many people have been generous with their time and knowledge as they've helped me with the creation of this book. It is with deep appreciation that I would like to acknowledge the following for their contributions:

Martha Hailey and Fred DuBose for their invaluable insights, creative talents, and hard work throughout this entire project—they have been my right and left arms, from start to finish!

Cindy Post Senning, Elizabeth Howell, and Peter Post at The Emily Post Institute, and Katherine Cowles, our agent, for their steady support, ideas, and assistance.

Toni Sciarra, Greg Chaput, Diane Aronson, and Nick Darrell of HarperCollins, whose editing skills have been essential to the completion of the book, and Bill Ruoto, Leah Carlson-Stanisic, and Karen Lumley for their design and production expertise. Stephen Hanselman, Mary Ellen Curley, and the entire HarperCollins team for their constant support and creative ideas.

Alexis Flippin, Kathy Schwarz, Lynn Ferrari, and Anna Post, who have been a formidable research team; their efforts have helped me to assure the accuracy and completeness of the book.

Manners and customs vary from region to region and culture to culture. The following people were gracious in sharing their knowledge of various regions, cultures, and religions: Himi Akdag, Dr. Parveen Ali, Dr. Shaukat Ali, Robert Barnett, Sister Janet Baxindale, Andrew Benko, Hilton Caston, Mustafa Gundogan, Naomi Krauss, Father Nektarios Morrow, Father James G. Moskovites, Theo Nicolakis, Harold and Ilana Rabinowitz, Thomas A. Ranieri, Wanda Vasquez, Ersin Yazicioglu, and Erhan Yildirim.

Etiquette covers so many aspects of our lives and relationships that I have found myself drawing information from a myriad of people who had important contributions to the advice offered herein: Kimi Abernathy, Richard Bailey, Sarah Buchwald, Ashley Dixon Burns, Harriett Temple Caldwell, Josette Caruso, Evelyn Christman, Barbara and Allan Converse, Diana Dixon, Polly DuBose, Hope Egan, Royce Flippin, Steve and Cathi Fowler, Sue Beasley Fryer, Vera Gibbons, Joseph Gonzalez, Allegra Holch, Peter Hopkins, David Kornacker, Eileen Leong, Deborah Leslie, Amy Lin, Kevin Mack, Kalinda Matthews, Kathy Maycen, David Miner, Bob Moore, Karen Nelson, Megan Newman, John Parker, Angela Ponce, Casey Post, Teresa Reagan, Matthew Reagor, Kelly Regan, Barbara Richert, Eric Rutz, David Shields, Cindi Smith-Walters, Ph.D., Fay Spano, Evan Spingarn, James F. Sporrer, Kate Stark, Mark Teague, Ginger Van Wagenen, and David Walkinshaw.

And, finally but not least, I thank my family, who has always supported me in more ways than I can express: My father, Ferd Grayson; my parents-in-law, Bill and Libby Post; and the person who has always encouraged me and patiently understood my long hours at the computer and on the telephone while working on this book, my husband, Allen Post.

Contents

Part Three

Children and Teens

Getting children off on the right (and mannerly) foot . . . Greetings, introductions, and other manners for the young . . . Dressing and grooming choices . . . Host and guest etiquette, from birthday parties to sleepovers . . . Sportsmanship, table manners, and mall manners . . . Developing and honing speaking and writing skills. . . . Teen dating from every angle . . .

Part Four

Communication and Protocol

Proof that the art of letter writing lives on . . . Should you handwrite that note? . . . The return of social cards . . . Ways to become well-spoken . . . Conversational blunders to avoid . . . Responding to nosy questions . . . The exemplary e-mailer . . . Manners in cyberspace . . . Our love/hate relationship with the cell phone . . . Titles, forms of address, official protocol, and displaying the flag. . . .

Part Five

Dining and Entertaining

The truth about table manners . . . Eating difficult foods with ease . . . Keeping the fun in eating out . . . Six major faux pas at restaurants . . . Relaxed dinner parties and cocktail parties . . . Smart advice for hosts and houseguests . . . Surviving the social whirl, from casual get-togethers to formal dances . . . Trouble-free toasting, with sample toasts aplenty. . . .

Part Six

Celebrations and Ceremonies

Do's and don'ts for baby showers, coming-of-age celebrations, and birthday and anniversary parties . . . Reaffirming marriage vows . . . The ABC's of gift giving . . . The last word on gift registries and regifting . . . Offering condolences in times of sorrow . . . The changing funeral service . . . On-line memorials . . . Behavior in your own house of worship and those of other faiths. . . .

Part Seven

Weddings

Making the engagement "official" . . . Keeping wedding plans from spinning out of control . . . Is a "destination wedding" a good idea? . . . Invitation styles and timing . . . Six invitation mistakes to avoid . . . Gift registries and their alternatives . . . The personalized ceremony and reception, including same-sex unions . . . The good guest . . . Marrying again (and again?) . . . Breaking with tradition. . . .

Part Eight

You and Your Job

Getting along with coworkers and supervisors . . . Dealing with workplace dilemmas . . . Cubicle etiquette . . . Keeping meetings running smoothly . . . Business meals, office parties, and other entertainments . . . Relationships between the sexes. . . .

Part Nine
Travel and Leisure

The new airplane etiquette... Rules of the road... Smooth sailing on cruises... Adjusting your cultural lens overseas... Your tipping questions answered... The ubiquitous tip jar... Audience etiquette... Hiking, camping, and boating do's and don'ts... good sportsmanship for tennis players and golfers, skiers and skaters... Staying on your toes at fitness centers and athletic events. ...

Contents

[xii]

A Note to Readers

What a pleasure it is to bring you an all-new, completely rewritten edition of a book that has been a staple of American life for eighty-two years! Times are changing so rapidly it's a challenge for most of us to keep up, but I'm happy to assure you that helping people adapt has been a mainstay of the Emily Post philosophy from the beginning.

Emily knew when she wrote *Etiquette: The Blue Book of Social Usage* (1922) that it was time for a reappraisal of the Victorian rules of etiquette. As a result, her revolutionary book discounted manners as rigid rules, tied them instead to ethics and values, and saw them as belonging to people from all walks of life. She also stressed that manners should be *fluid,* adaptable not only to the times but to the situation at hand. The same is true today. Considering the stuffiness of the etiquette books that had gone before, my great-grandmother-in-law would probably have told her readers to "lighten up!" had the phrase been around in her day.

As Victorianism gave way to the Jazz Age, the more informal approach to things foreshadowed the casualness that infuses virtually every aspect of life in the twenty-first century, from the way we communicate to how we dress. Where does today's more "anything goes" attitude leave etiquette? Given the pressures of modern life, more in demand than ever! The many letters I receive through my monthly columns in *Good Housekeeping* and *Parents* magazines—not to mention the e-mails sent to the Emily Post Institute Web site—suggest that Americans are very much interested in the basic courtesies and want to deal respectfully and courteously with others. They clearly want answers for ways to get along with one another, even if the answers are sometimes complex.

Those many questions about etiquette are also an indication that Americans are increasingly worried about what they see as declining standards of civility. Statistics bear out their concerns. A comprehensive 2002 national study from Public Agenda with support from The Pew Charitable Trusts (*Aggravating Circumstances: A Status Report on Rudeness in America*) found that seventy-nine percent of Americans believe that a "lack of respect and courtesy is a serious problem for our society"; forty-one percent admitted that they themselves had behaved in rude and disrespectful ways. Other studies support these findings. On a purely anecdotal level, just mention "courtesy" or "civility" or "etiquette," and listen to the tales filled with examples of bad manners that people have recently seen or experienced.

New Century, New Book

WHILE MANY PEOPLE AGREE that good manners may be needed more than ever, just what etiquette *is* often leaves them scratching their heads. Sometimes it seems that the word itself has more definitions than a formal place setting has forks. To many people, etiquette is nothing more than a tired set of no-longer-relevant rules after everyone wised up and started "doing their own thing." To others, it's an affectation of the upper crust, with little meaning for anyone else. (In fact, one theory holds that the word derived from the signs [*etiquettes*] requesting that the courtiers at Louis XIV's palace of Versailles keep off the grass—but that was another time, another place.) Adding to the confusion is the fact that what is considered good manners often varies from region to region and from ethnic group to ethnic group.

Such uncertainties about what etiquette *means* and why it's important explain why I've rethought and rewritten this book, the seventeenth edition of *Etiquette*. The book defines etiquette in today's real-life terms and brings it down to earth. An all-new section, "Everyday Etiquette," features a whole chapter on coping with rudeness, while other chapters take into account modern-day concerns—from confusions about e-mail etiquette to handling "road rage" to living cheek-by-jowl with our neighbors in an increasingly crowded world. In another new section, "Children and Teens," I offer advice to parents on how to raise respectful and self-confident young men and women, even in the midst of hectic lives and challenges all around. The "You and Your Job" section is an up-to-date guide to dealing with the kind of workplace pressures that previous generations could have hardly imagined.

Can You Make a Difference?

MY ANSWER TO THE QUESTION of whether individuals can contribute to a more civil society is an emphatic "yes!" Courtesy tends to be contagious; in fact, a seemingly small act of consideration can have a tremendous impact. Smiling and saying "thank you" to a harried waitress in a restaurant may remind her that most of her customers appreciate her efforts. Saying "excuse me" when brushing past a stranger on a crowded sidewalk might, in just a fraction of a second, encourage that person to be a little kinder to his fellow workers that day. A little kindness goes a long way.

Etiquette *must be active.* It isn't enough to know what to do. Courtesy matters only when it is translated into everyday behavior—not just put on for show when it's convenient. The rewards of an active commitment to everyday courtesy are myriad, though not often tangible. (See Chapter 1, "Guidelines for Living," pages 3–6) There are also important personal rewards that some people may not even be aware of, including the self-confidence that comes from knowing what to do in new or difficult situations; a positive reputation with others; and personal relationships that are more congenial, even in times of stress, because the people involved treat one another with respect.

Finally, courteous people enrich their own spirits by making other people feel good. The special feeling that comes from being kind may well be the most powerful incentive to remember and practice everyday courtesies, as delineated in this all-new edition of Emily Post's American classic.

Peggy Post
Summer 2004

Part One

Everyday
Etiquette

Chapter One

Guidelines for Living

THE WORLD IS TOO MUCH WITH US," Wordsworth wrote in 1807, and his phrase has taken on a whole new meaning in the twenty-first century. In fact, the old boy would probably be running for cover if a time machine whisked him to streets full of people rushing about as though there were no tomorrow—many of them yelling into small metal objects held to their ears.

It would be easy for us to sympathize with him. While scientific and medical advancements have made life easier over the years, the stresses and strains that have come with population density, technological advancements, all-pervasive news and entertainment media, and a redefinition of the family have resulted in a whole new set of challenges. People behave no worse than they used to (rudeness and other social offenses are nothing new), but the pressures of modern life make it all the more difficult to stay civil.

What's needed for this day and age? New guidelines for courteous behavior, especially in a time when it often seems that "anything goes." It's true that a more casual approach to dressing, communicating, and entertaining has taken hold, but that's hardly something to be concerned about. The history of human interaction is one of change, and manners by their very nature adapt to the times. Today's guidelines help steer our behavior as we move through our daily routines—no matter what difficulties we face, how informal the occasion or event, or which surprises are sprung. In fact, it can be said that we need manners more than ever to smooth the way.

Although today's manners are more situational, tailored to particular circumstances and the expectations of those around us, they remain a combination of common sense, generosity of spirit, and a few specific "rules" that help us interact thoughtfully. And as fluid as manners are (and always have been), they rest on the same bedrock principles: respect, consideration, and honesty.

Respect. Respecting other people means recognizing their value as human beings, regardless of their background, race, or creed. A respectful person would also never treat a salesperson, a waiter, or an office assistant as somehow inferior. Respect is demonstrated in all your day-to-day relations—refraining from demeaning others for their ideas and opinions, refusing to laugh at racist or sexist jokes, putting prejudices aside, and staying open-minded.

Self-respect is just as important as respect for others. A self-confident person isn't boastful or pushy but is secure with herself in a way that inspires confidence in others. She values herself regardless of her physical attributes or individual talents, understanding that honor and character are what really matter.

Consideration. Thoughtfulness and kindness are folded into consideration for other people. Consideration also encapsulates the Golden Rule: Do unto others as you would have them do unto you. Being thoughtful means *thinking about* what you can do to put people at ease, while kindness is more about acts. Taken together, these qualities lead us to help a friend or stranger in need, to bestow a token of appreciation, to offer praise.

Honesty. Honesty has more to do with ethics than etiquette, but the two are intertwined. What could be more unmannerly than being deceptive? Honesty ensures that we act sincerely and is also the basis of tact: speaking and acting in ways that won't cause unnecessary offense.

A tactful person can say something honest about another person without causing great embarrassment or pain. In other words, tact calls for both empathy and benevolent honesty: "I like the other bathing suit on you better" is honest, while "That bathing suit makes you look fat" may be equally true but amounts to an insult.

Two Other Essential Qualities

GRACIOUSNESS AND DEFERENCE are also part and parcel of mannerly behavior. Graciousness is the ability to handle situations with aplomb and flexibility, while showing deference can be as easy as removing one's hat in a place of worship.

The mark of a gracious person is his ability to put people at ease and spare them any embarrassment. (You're being gracious when someone forgets your name during an introduction and you say, "Oh, please don't feel bad! I'm always drawing a blank when I try to remember names.") It's easy to forget that "gracious" is the adjective form of "grace," which dictionaries variously define as "good will; favor"; "thoughtfulness toward others"; and "a sense of what is right and proper." By any definition, grace is a quality anyone should strive to achieve.

Deference is primarily a means of recognizing a person's experience and accomplishments. Courtesies like standing when an older person enters a room, giving a senior executive the head seat at a conference table, and addressing authority figures by their titles and last names (unless they specifically request otherwise) do not demean anyone. Far from it. Deferring politely reflects well on the person who defers by demonstrating that he values other people for their achievements.

Misconceptions about etiquette and the need for it abound, which makes it necessary to list four things that etiquette is most certainly *not*:

A set of rigid rules. Manners change with the times (something Emily Post emphasized from the beginning) and today are more flexible than ever before. Etiquette isn't a set of "prescriptions for properness" but merely a set of guidelines for doing things in ways that make people feel comfortable.

Something for the wealthy or well-born. Etiquette is a code of behavior for people from all walks of life, every socioeconomic group, and of all ages. No one is immune to having his life enhanced by good manners.

A thing of the past. Sometimes it seems that yesterday's standards have gone out the window, but today's more casual approach to things is something that sits on the surface. The bedrock principles of etiquette remain as solid as they ever were.

Snobbishness. Little violates the tenets of etiquette more than snobbery—which, more often than not, is just another name for pretentiousness. A person who looks down on others shows himself not as superior but small—the kind who's anything *but* respectful and considerate.

Actions Express Attitude

PEOPLE WHO REALLY PAY ATTENTION to others have little trouble translating what they see and hear into courteous behavior. Courteous people are *empathetic*—able to relate emotionally to the feelings of others. They listen closely to what people say. They observe what is going on around them and register what they see. A self-centered person might say, "I know exactly how you feel" to someone in a traumatic situation and then immediately start describing his *own* experiences. An empathetic person is more likely to say something like, "I can't know how you feel right now, but I can understand your grief [or anger or sadness]. And if you want to talk about it, I'm here to listen."

This concern for others leads to another characteristic of courteous people: They are *flexible*—willing to adjust their own behavior to the needs and feelings of others. This doesn't mean that well-mannered people are pushovers or lack strongly held principles. But courtesy means understanding that nobody is perfect. Courteous people aren't so concerned about forms (using the right fork or introducing people in the correct order) that they would embarrass or denigrate others for simple breaches of etiquette. Courteous people would never use another person's mistakes as an excuse to react with callous words or cruel acts.

Why Etiquette Matters

GROUNDED AS IT IS in timeless principles, etiquette enables us to face whatever the future may bring with strength of character and integrity. This ever-adaptive code of behavior also allows us to be flexible enough to respect those whose beliefs and traditions differ from our own. Civility and courtesy (in essence, the outward expressions of human decency) are the proverbial glue that holds society together—qualities that are more important than ever in today's complex and changing world.

Chapter Two

Greetings and Introductions

Greetings and introductions are like chemical catalysts—they get things going. It's hard to imagine daily life without friendly greetings and introductions to bring people together in a spirit of goodwill. These courtesies are observed in all societies, though the forms differ. From the most casual wave to the most formal presentation, greetings and introductions are as basic to civilized interaction today as ever.

This chapter is devoted to the etiquette of artful greeting and meeting, and the first lesson is to *do it*—say "hello" even when you feel a bit grumpy or shy, and make introductions even when you aren't quite sure of the fine points of who is introduced to whom. Every greeting and introduction is a chance to show your respect for others and to create a favorable impression of yourself.

The Essentials of Greeting Others

A GREETING IS AN ACKNOWLEDGMENT of someone else's presence. For most people, greeting others is so ingrained that they hardly notice doing it. Yet when people fail to greet someone they know, the omission may cause hurt feelings and misunderstandings. If a normally courteous person doesn't wave at her neighbor or say "good morning" to coworkers, they may feel snubbed or think that the person is behaving oddly. Such failures happen for a variety of reasons—the person is preoccupied or distracted, she's late for an engagement, she forgot her glasses and just doesn't see someone she knows—and can usually be corrected with a warm greeting the next time around. But such failures demonstrate the first essential of good greeting manners: taking notice of other people.

Informal Greetings

An informal greeting may be spoken, gestured, or both. These days, the classic spoken greetings in the United States are "hello" and "hi" (or "hey" in some regions), accompanied by the person's name if you know it and said with a pleasant smile. "Good morning," "good afternoon," and "good evening" are still commonly heard, though they may be more popular in some regions than others. Children and teenagers have their own greeting lingo, but they should be discouraged from using the current slang with people outside their circle of friends.

Saying "hello" doesn't obligate you to stop and chat, so don't hesitate to greet someone just because you're in a rush. If the person wants to talk, explain your hurry ("Hi, Brenda. I wish I had time to talk, but I'm on my way to the dentist's office") and part graciously. It's only right to be courteous to people in general, so don't forget to greet people who serve you—salespeople and repair people, cashiers, receptionists, food service and hotel/motel employees. Good manners often earn good treatment in return.

Sometimes a spoken greeting isn't possible, as when someone is too far away to hear or when a greeting would disturb others. A smile and a nod or wave will do in public places such as a theater, concert hall, or restaurant. But if any gesture is likely to indicate lack of attention or to distract others (as waving and nodding might during a religious service, lecture, or live performance), it's polite to smile and save your greeting for later.

Formal Greetings

In certain situations, the ritual of greeting is more formalized. The language is often the same as or similar to an informal greeting—"Hello, Mr. Carpenter" or "How do you do, Mrs. Ramirez?"—but the greeter's general demeanor tends to be less casual, often much less. In business environments, coworkers may greet one another casually but treat their bosses with considerable deference. In a formal receiving line, even people who know each other well will often shake hands or exchange social kisses, make a polite comment, and then move on in order not to hold up the line. The elements of a formal greeting include what is said ("hello" is preferable to "hi"), tone of voice, and posture. Formal greetings tend not to be effusive but should always be pleasant and genuine.

∼ Greetings at Home ∼

The best place to cultivate the greeting habit is in the home. Yet how often do busy family members actually say "good morning" to one another at the start of the day? How frequently is someone welcomed home from work with only a curt "dinner's ready" or "the dryer's broken again"? It takes just seconds to acknowledge the people we live with, making humdrum days far more pleasant and setting a good example for everyone.

Standing . . . or Not

Rising to greet someone who just entered a room is a time-honored display of respect. However, there are times when standing up is either difficult—you're holding something in your lap—or inconvenient, as when coworkers pop in and out of one another's offices or cubicles.

In general, stand whenever you can, especially when the person you're greeting is older than you, someone you're meeting for the first time, or someone who is traditionally shown special respect (a religious leader, for instance, or a person of high rank). Hosts and hostesses should rise and go to greet all arriving guests at social events, but once the party is under way, it's unnecessary to stand every time someone enters a room. When someone leaves the table during a dinner party or restaurant meal, the other diners need not stand when he returns. You have to judge the situation: If standing in a crowded restaurant or theater will disturb other patrons, stay seated. But standing and offering your scat to an elderly or infirm person on a crowded subway or train is both courteous and humane.

Old rules about males rising while females remain seated have gone by the wayside; women today often stand and put out their hands when greeting others.

Handshaking

Ritual handshaking dates back at least to ancient Egypt and Babylon and may be older than recorded history. The theory that men extended their open right hands to show that they were not bearing weapons may explain why women didn't follow the custom until fairly recently. Today, a handshake symbolizes both welcome and good faith, as when people seal a deal by shaking hands, and either sex may offer a hand first.

In most places people appreciate a firm grip—neither limp nor bone-crunching—and shaking that is perceptible but not pumping. It's generally best to release your hold after a few seconds or as soon as you feel the other person relax his hand or pull away. If you favor a really strong grip, be alert and adjust to the pressure you feel from the other person. If you extend your hand but the other person doesn't respond, just assume that he or she didn't see your gesture; lower your hand and forget the shake, even though offering your hand is correct.

By being attuned to others, you can sense when handshaking is appropriate. Shaking will inconvenience a person who is carrying things in both hands or has a hand, arm, or shoulder infirmity. In some cultures, touching hands is offensive or may be prohibited between men and women. (See Chapter 45, page 793: "Basic International Courtesies.")

Kissing, Hugging, and Other Affectionate Gestures

It's natural for close family members and very good friends to kiss or hug when they meet, if that's their custom. However, kissing, hugging, and any physical contact beyond handshaking with casual acquaintances raises several questions.

When outdoors, does a person have to remove his gloves when shaking hands? By the way, where we live, the winter temperature is often below freezing.

Shaking hands doesn't mean risking frostbite, so when you meet someone on the street in the dead of winter, you can leave your gloves on. In warmer weather, people normally remove their right glove to shake hands. People wearing heavy or soiled work gloves and padded sport gloves, like ski mittens, may simply forgo handshaking. Except for very formal occasions and receiving lines, gloves are removed indoors.

Everyday Etiquette

[10]

Should you kiss, hug, or touch? Comfort levels regarding physical greetings vary greatly, so rushing forward to kiss or hug a casual or new acquaintance might cause the person real discomfort. In a diverse society, it's also difficult to know the many cultural and religious traditions and prohibitions involving physical contact—including restrictions based on gender. It's wise to limit touching to the offer of your hand unless you're absolutely sure a person will welcome more intimate gestures. Other than handshaking, touching of any sort in business situations—especially between men and women and between superiors and subordinates—can be misinterpreted as harassment and have serious repercussions. Some people may regret the demise of the friendly pat on the back or arm around the shoulder among colleagues, but in today's world, it's better to be safe than to risk reputation and career.

How do you avoid bumping heads when greeting with a kiss? There is a simple guideline for dodging a collision when greeting with a kiss: Go for the person's right cheek. But this orderly right-side procedure is not widely known, which accounts for the frequency of bumped heads. Usually if you make it a point to go directly to the other person's right cheek, he will instinctively follow suit, and you'll avoid the awkward bobbing of heads.

How does the two-cheek, or European, kiss work? Kissing both cheeks is a traditional greeting in much of Europe, in cultures influenced by European traditions, and in the Middle East (where kissing and other physical contact in greeting is limited to people of the same gender). Kissing is usually accompanied by an embrace, which may be close or involve only arm touching. While they are facing and hugging, each person turns his or her head a bit and offers one cheek, then the other. Usually, warm words are exchanged during the greeting.

What is an "air kiss," and how is it done? When air kissing, two people merely touch or brush cheeks but kiss into the air—avoiding lipstick smudges and possibly swapping germs. There are no rules for air kissing, which isn't the same as a real kiss,

Greetings in Other Cultures

The meeting and greeting customs of the rest of the world are enormously varied and can be complex. For example, using the well-known German greeting "*Guten Tag*" is a social gaffe in Bavaria, where "*Gruess Gott*" is the standard, but either greeting is acceptable in Austria and Switzerland. Extending a friendly hand is regarded as impolite in Japan, where bowing is customary.

Before traveling or entertaining foreign visitors, do some research. A keyword search of the Internet (country name plus "etiquette" or "greetings") should produce the information you need to put yourself and others at ease. You may make mistakes, but your effort to be respectful and do the right thing will show that you're a well-mannered and thoughtful person.

---

but the usual procedure is to put your cheek to or near the other person's cheek, "kiss" the air, then pull back. The process may be repeated with the other cheek. To keep their balance, participants often touch arms or place their hands on the other person's shoulders. An air kiss is accomplished quickly.

What about hand kissing? You may encounter hand kissing on occasion, though it's not customary in the United States. Traditionally, a woman extended her hand palm down, and a man held it lightly, bowed, and kissed quickly just above the hand—without lip-to-hand contact.

How do you signal that you don't want to be hugged or kissed? You can extend your hand with a fairly stiff arm, shake, and then take a step back. Most people will respect the space you create with your body language. This technique may also work with someone who, while not a "toucher," tends to stand too close. Sometimes you can't avoid the contact, and it's best to grin and bear it; backing away a bit once the person has released you should signal your feelings. If the effusive greetings of someone you see frequently really make you uncomfortable, you may have to explain your feelings. Be tactful; let the person know that you enjoy his or her company but that physical displays are difficult for you or contrary to your culture or religion.

A Graceful Exit

When a greeting is followed by some conversation, departing requires more than a brusque "bye" or "see you." The traditional parting is still "good-bye," normally said with some pleasantry that winds the conversation down. ("It's been so good to see you." "I wish I had more time to visit, but I'll call you next week.") If a person appears reluctant to continue chatting, you should finish what you're saying and bring the meeting to a courteous conclusion.

The How-to's of Introductions

PEOPLE OFTEN WORRY ABOUT the forms of introductions, but the only truly unforgivable breach of etiquette is the failure to attempt an introduction when people who don't know each other are in your presence. Making errors in order, forgetting or mispronouncing a name, giving an incorrect courtesy or professional title—these embarrassments are minor (and easily corrected) compared to the discourtesy of expecting people to be sociable when they have no idea who the other person or people are.

The Forms of Introductions

The purpose of an introduction is, first, to convey names, and, second, to promote a sense of comfort and ease between or among strangers. Most introductions are casual, and very few people will take it as a slight if you make an error. If you catch yourself making a mistake, the best advice is to keep going. Stopping in the middle of an introduction and trying to correct yourself will only confuse everyone.

Control what you can. For example, if you're planning to entertain and introductions will be required, be sure to brush up on pronunciations and correct titles before the party. If you're attending a meeting at which you are likely to be introduced, you might get an advance list of the participants and familiarize yourself with names and titles.

The following guidelines for making introductions and being introduced are intended to make the process go as smoothly as possible for both parties.

When you are making the introduction . . .

➤ Look first at the person to whom you're making the introduction, then turn to the other person as you complete the introduction. In other words, when introducing Mr. Green *to* Miss Brown, look at Miss Brown. Admittedly, this can be difficult when you're introducing a number of people at once, but it is much easier to understand and remember a name when we both see and hear it spoken.

➤ Speak clearly. A muffled or mumbled introduction defeats the whole purpose.

➤ State your introductions courteously. The basic language is well established, as the examples in this chapter illustrate. It is considered impolite to make an introduction in the form of a command such as "Harry, shake hands with Mr. Malone" or "Ms. Benson, come here and meet Mr. Simpkins."

➤ Try to introduce people by the names and titles they prefer. It's often appropriate to present people by first and last names in casual settings and if the people are near in age and status. ("Judy, this is Tom Akira. Tom, this is Judy Miles.") You can use a nickname if you know a person prefers it. When there's an obvious age difference and in more formal situations, it's usually best to use courtesy titles and last names ("Mrs. Miles, I'd like you to meet Mr. Akira") and then let the people request use of their first names if they want. Unless an adult specifically asks you to use his or her first name when introducing children, teach children to use adults' titles and introduce children to adults as: "Mrs. Miles, this is my nephew Benji Rose." (For more on introduction etiquette for children, see Chapter 13, page 165: "Greetings and Introductions.")

➤ When you share last names, introduce your spouse and offspring to adults by first names only. ("This is my husband, Ron"; "I'd like to introduce our children, Rita and Simon.") But include last names when married people use different professional names and children or stepchildren have a different last name. No matter how casual the situation, don't use terms like "my old lady" or "the brats" that may be funny within the family but will seem strange, even demeaning, to strangers.

➤ Introduce other family members by their full names unless they request otherwise. The relationship between the introducer and the family member is often mentioned, as in "Uncle Jonas, I'd like you to meet Matt Winnett. Matt, this is my great-uncle, Jonas Quinn." (For information about introducing in-laws, see Chapter 9, page 109: "Good Relations With In-laws.")

➤ Don't repeat names unnecessarily. "Mrs. Jones, this is Mrs. Smith. Mrs. Smith, Mrs. Jones" is redundant. But repeating names that may be difficult to pronounce or remember is a kindness to both parties. ("Mrs. Chimileski, I'd like to introduce Mrs. Jones. Sally, this is Margaret Chimileski.")

➤ When introducing someone to a group, name the group members first. This is a practical suggestion. Naming the people in a group of three, four, or more calls their attention to the introduction. ("Louise, June, Will, I'd like to introduce Curtis Tyler. Curtis, I'd like you to meet Louise Oliver, June Weaver, and Will LaGasse.") Otherwise, people in the group may continue chatting without realizing that introductions are being made.

➤ Start some conversation. The most polite introduction will fall flat if the person making the introduction doesn't initiate conversation. Try to find some topic the people have in common. ("Jane's daughter is transferring to your old alma mater next fall"; "Roger is a vintage car buff, so he might like to hear about the Studebaker you restored, Sam.") In social situations, hosts and hostesses should take the time to jump-start some chat between people they've just introduced before moving on to other guests.

When you are being introduced . . .

➤ Listen carefully, be attentive, and focus on names. If the person doing the introduction makes a mistake, let it pass. Concentrate on the name and try to say it in conversation: A polite "It's nice to meet you, Liz" is an excellent way to start cementing the name in your memory. If you didn't understand a name, ask. Saying "I'm sorry, but I didn't get your last name" or "Could you please tell me your name again?" is a courtesy.

➤ Respond graciously. After a formal introduction, the traditional response is "How do you do?" But "hello" and variants of "I'm very glad to meet you" may sound less stilted and are acceptable in formal and casual situations. Using the person's name adds warmth to a response—as does speaking in a tone that conveys sincere interest.

➤ Use the names by which people are introduced. If someone is introduced as "William," don't call him "Bill" unless he says to. Always avoid familiar or sexist terms such as "sport," "buddy," "pal," "sweetie," and "honey." Also, it's rude to ask a question like "What kind of name is that?" If you're curious about the origin of a person's name, wait until you know her better to inquire.

➤ Correct any mistake as soon and as graciously as possible. Should the person you've just met call you "Mark" instead of "Mike," it's simple to say, "It's Mike," with a smile. The longer you delay correcting a name, title, or pronunciation, the harder it becomes. If someone repeatedly introduces you by the wrong name or a nickname or a title you don't like, take the person aside and tell him the problem as nicely as possible. ("I use *Michael* now. Would you mind introducing me that way?")

➤ Listen for conversational cues. Something may have been said in the introduction (an identification such as "my neighbor" or a professional title) that provides an opening for conversation. If the person who made the introduction doesn't start the conversation, you should speak up. Something as seemingly banal as a comment about the weather or current events can lead to more interesting talk.

➤ Wait until all introductions are complete before conversing. Sometimes one person in a group jumps the gun and begins talking before others in the group have been introduced. This mistake is entirely avoidable if everyone pays attention to the introducer and allows him or her to name everyone.

When someone forgets to introduce you . . .

The scenario: You're talking with someone when a third person approaches. The person with you greets the new arrival, so it's obvious they're acquainted with each other. But no introduction is made, the other two are talking, and you are feeling left out and ignored.

Chances are, the person who fails to introduce you assumes that you know the third person. Or she may have blanked on your name and is desperately hoping you will speak up. When there's a little break in the conversation, address the newcomer with a pleasant "hello" and your name. Problem solved for everyone.

The Order of Introductions

Who to introduce to whom is one of those issues that many people seem to agonize about needlessly. Traditionally, the person who is *named first* is being shown a degree of deference based on seniority or prominence, and the order of introduction can be crucial in the high-stakes worlds of diplomacy and politics and in some business situa-

Most introduction mistakes are the result of normal—and forgivable—memory lapses or nervousness. But the foul-ups below result primarily from insensitivity and tactlessness.

Looking away. People who look over shoulders and around the room while involved in introductions are saying in every way but words that they really don't care very much.

Making too-personal comments. Divorces, bereavements, job losses, illnesses, rehab history, and the like are not fit subjects to raise in the course of social and business introductions.

Interrupting. When people are engaged in serious conversation or obviously occupied, don't break in to introduce someone else. Wait for a more convenient moment.

Deferring to one person at the expense of the other. Be sure that both parties are included in any conversation that follows a polite introduction.

Gushing. Most people are embarrassed by overly enthusiastic introductions. A note to would-be matchmakers: While you may think that two eligible people would be a perfect couple, avoid exaggerated praise when you introduce them.

tions. But few people will take offense if you make an error in everyday introductions. In most circumstances, these four basic guidelines will see you through:

➤ A younger person is introduced *to* an older person. ("Aunt Ruth, I want you to meet my roommate, Mimi Jackson. Mimi, this is my aunt, Mrs. Cox.")

➤ A person of high rank or special prominence is named first and receives the introduction. ("Bishop Gordon, may I present my husband, John?") A savvy employee will make a special effort to name bosses and supervisors first when introducing them to anyone of lower rank. ("Ms. Gentry, I'd like you to meet Ralph Clayburgh, who just came on board as an associate account manager. Ralph, this is Ms. Gentry, our director of Research and Development.")

➤ When introducing others to family members, the other person's name is generally said first ("Raoul, I'd like you to meet my brother, Carl Michaud") if the people being introduced are of roughly the same age and rank. But as a sign of respect, an older family member is named first ("Gran, I'd like to introduce Mr. Jonathan Fox. Jonathan, this is my grandmother, Mrs. Josephson").

➤ Traditionally in social situations, men are introduced *to* women. ("Mrs. Barrett, I'd like to introduce Mr. Hirsch.")

Self-introductions

It may take a little courage to approach someone you don't know, but introducing yourself is really one of the easiest kinds of introductions. After all, you only have to remember your own name. Even in formal settings, self-introductions are relatively casual. If the person is by herself, a friendly "Hello, I'm Justin Vail" is usually enough to start. The person will probably reply along the lines of "I'm Maria Fuentes. It's nice to meet you, Mr. Vail." And you can begin a conversation.

Someone attempting a self-introduction may blurt out, "What's your name?" while forgetting to say his own. But asking for the other person's name first can seem abrupt and rude. It's more graceful to ask the person's name only *after* saying your own and giving her the chance to reply.

When introducing yourself to a group of people, wait for a natural break in their conversation. "Hello" and your name may be enough, or you may want to explain your interest in the group. ("Hi, I'm Justin Vail. This is my first Historical Society meeting, and I was wondering about tonight's agenda.") Asking for assistance or information can be an effective way to enter a group.

At large social events, it's often impossible for the hosts to introduce everyone, so be prepared to introduce yourself, especially if you see someone who is alone.

Standing and Shaking Hands

The greeting etiquette for standing and shaking hands (see page 9: "Handshaking") applies as well to introductions. An additional point regards standing when you are introducing or being introduced to someone who is seated. While it is nice to meet on an equal level—all parties on their feet or seated—this often isn't possible or practical, as when meeting someone in a restaurant. If you're standing, keep a little distance so

∽ How to Introduce "Significant Others" ∽

The English language may contain more words than any other, but it has yet to supply satisfactory designations for people in intimate relationships other than "husband" and "wife" and the French *fiancé* and *fiancée*. So begin with the introduction basics: a gracious exchange of names. Spelling out relationships in an introduction can be a distraction and may make some people uneasy.

For couples of the opposite or same sex, terms such as "partner," "live-in," and "roommate" can be confusing and easily misinterpreted. "Boyfriend," "girlfriend," and "special friend" seem childishly inappropriate for couples in their thirties and older. And "significant other" and "domestic partner" can sound stilted and legalistic. The euphemisms "my good friend" and "my close friend" may or may not be understood, depending on the circumstances. If you decide to explain your personal relationship, it's more natural to do so in conversation after exchanging names.

you don't tower over the seated person. Bending forward a bit will help everyone hear the introduction in a noisy setting. Be observant before offering your hand to a seated person; reaching across a dinner table, for example, may risk knocking over glasses. Let common sense be your guide.

Handling Mistakes

THOUGH IT MAY BE EMBARRASSING to get a name wrong or draw a complete blank (it happens to the best of people), such lapses are not rude—just very human.

If you can't remember a name . . .

Don't panic. Embarrassing as it may be to stumble over a name, don't fail to attempt an introduction. If the person is attentive, he may see your hesitation and cover for you by introducing himself. If the person is wearing a name tag, you might take a quick peek. Otherwise, you should apologize quickly and say that you've suddenly forgotten the person's name. Do the same if you aren't sure of someone's last name. ("I'm sorry, Aileen, but I don't know your last name.") The person should fill in the blank for you. There's no need to continue apologizing for your lapse.

If you get a title wrong . . .

It's easy to forget that a friend prefers the title "Ms." since her divorce or that Captain Beaton is now Major Beaton. If you use an incorrect title, the person may make the correction during the introduction or tell you later. Frankly, it's not a big deal either way. But make an effort to remember the title in the future.

If you mispronounce a name . . .

Rather than mangling the name of someone you've just met, it's all right to ask him or her to say it in an introduction. ("I'd like you to meet our new neighbor, Charles. Charles, would you please say your last name? I'm afraid I'll mispronounce it.") When you mispronounce a name you should know, apologize when the mistake is pointed out and then practice to avoid repeating the error. When you know that you'll be expected to introduce a person whose name you aren't sure how to pronounce, you can ask someone who does know or the person himself ahead of time.

Chapter Three

When Out and About

THE WORLD MAY NOT BE WAITING to see how you act as you go about your everyday pursuits, but most people won't fail to notice when you disrupt the order of things, no matter how slightly. Most Americans still stick to the premise that there's a time and a place for everything, and doing what's appropriate and practicing the standard courtesies makes things go better for everyone.

One person might be unfailingly polite to those he's with but think of his commute to work as a contest with other drivers. Another may extend help to the frail and infirm at every opportunity but barrel her way through able-bodied pedestrians. While nobody's perfect, staying observant and thoughtful when you're out and about means you'll be able to handle virtually anything in an appropriate way.

Standard Courtesies

SIMPLY GETTING WHERE YOU'RE GOING every day raises a few questions for the manners-minded, starting with opening and entering doors—an example of how chivalry is no longer something just for men.

"After You, Sir"

Today it only makes sense that men and women open and hold doors for each other, depending on who arrives there first. The traditional door-opener, however, might want to give the woman a choice—"May I get the door for you?" She could reply either "Thanks!" or "No thanks, I've got it" if she gets to the door first.

When you and a stranger of either sex approach a door at the same time, it's polite to open and hold the door—especially if he or she is elderly, carrying a package, or managing small children. Most important, don't ever let a door close on the person behind you after you've just walked through.

What about revolving doors? Men traditionally entered a revolving door first if it wasn't moving, but women went first if it was already in motion. (This old bit of etiquette was based on the notion that women needed help to push the door.) Today, the person in front enters first and pushes.

In an Elevator

The rules for entering and exiting an elevator are much the same—whoever's in front goes first. After pushing the floor button once you're inside, move as far to the back of the elevator car as possible. If the car's so crowded you can't reach the button, ask someone else to push it for you—adding a "please," of course.

If an elevator you want to enter is already jammed with people, don't squeeze your way inside, even if you've waited a long time for it to arrive. Likewise, be patient when you find the door closing as you approach. Although it's always a nice gesture for a passenger to hold the door for you or push the "door open" button, it's equally thoughtful of you to allow the passengers already aboard to go ahead and get to their floors without delay.

While in transit up or down, don't stare at others, smack your gum, speak on your cell phone, or sing along with your cassette player. If there's a mirror or reflective wall in the elevator, resist the kind of grooming best performed in a restroom.

If you see someone you know on an elevator, say, "Hello." Say, "Hot enough for you?" Say, "Have a nice day." But be careful about going further unless you're the only two people aboard. A brief chat is fine, but a gabfest complete with laughter may annoy fellow passengers, trapped as they are for the length of the ride. Whispering isn't the answer, because in the presence of others (strangers included), it is rude. As for cell phone calls, make them only after you've exited the car.

The old-style elevator operators nattily attired in a jacket with gold braid may be a vanishing breed, but any operator is always due a "please" and "thank you" when you request a floor and disembark.

Riding Escalators

Keep to the right on an escalator so that other people can walk past you. If you're the rider who needs to get past, politely say, "Excuse me"—but only when riders are few and far between. On crowded escalators, the only choice is to be patient and stay where you are.

When stepping off an escalator, don't stop to survey the scene. Move out of the way immediately so that you don't cause a logjam.

On the Sidewalk

WALKERS SHOULD STAY to the right on city sidewalks—but the odds of their actually obeying this rule are about the same as an alien craft landing on the block. In bustling cities, sidewalk etiquette is all about bobbing and weaving as expertly as possible— which means maneuvering past others without jostling or exasperating them.

Allow other pedestrians as much space as possible and give the corners of buildings a wide berth to avoid a collision should another person round the bend. Keep your elbows in and make sure briefcases or backpacks don't bump others. If you accidentally brush or hit someone, say, "I'm sorry." The person who bumps into someone and doesn't even look back brands himself as a boor.

Try your best not to tailgate in crowds. You could not only clip the heel of another person's shoe but could collide with her if she were to stop without warning. When cutting in front of another pedestrian, allow about three steps' worth of space.

As you wait for lights, don't stand off the curb; when a turning car forces you to step back, you'll have to jump into the knot of people behind you. When it comes to jaywalking, use common sense. Even if jaywalking is legal in your locality, it still can be dangerous—especially on one-way streets, where you might not notice a speeding bike messenger or delivery person going the wrong way.

Umbrella Tips

When using an umbrella, handle it in such a way that you disrupt things as little as possible.

> ➤ Always unfurl an umbrella in the vertical position—and wait to do it outdoors, not indoors.

> ➤ Raise your umbrella straight up when passing shorter pedestrians and lower it as you pass those who are taller.

> ➤ Don't tip your umbrella so far forward that it blinds you to oncoming foot traffic. (Clear plastic umbrellas make it possible to see where you're going.)

> ➤ When walking under construction scaffolding, close your umbrella unless the structure is dripping; if it is, take special care not to bump others' umbrellas in this tighter space.

> ➤ Discard any umbrella with any spokes exposed, since bare spokes are just waiting to poke someone on an overcrowded sidewalk.

> ➤ Before walking into a dry space—say, the foyer of a building or the stairs to a train station—"fluff" the umbrella back and forth a few times to shake off raindrops, taking care not to spray anyone nearby. Then fold your umbrella, secure the spokes around the handle with the fastener, and hold it vertically at your side.

> ➤ When carrying a closed umbrella on the street, hold it vertically, not tucked under your arm horizontally. Don't swing it around by the strap when the sidewalk is crowded. A closed "walking" umbrella (the long kind) is traditionally held like a cane.

They don't really mean to annoy, but some pedestrians are so sealed in their own little worlds that they forget they're sharing the sidewalk with others. The more crowded the sidewalk, the more aggravating their inattentiveness or poor personal habits become.

The Juggernaut. The person who charges down a congested sidewalk becomes an unstoppable force when armed with a baby stroller or a rolling suitcase. Pedestrians should remember that they're taking up at least twice their usual space when pushing or pulling anything large and heavy.

The Yakaholic. There's just something about a pedestrian who's loudly gabbing away on a cell phone that rubs most people the wrong way, possibly because he also barely looks where he's going. (Since two people chatting don't elicit the same response, the resentment must be based on the long-standing belief that there's a time and a place for everything.) Pedestrians who keep a call as quiet as possible will go a long way toward deflecting those angry stares.

The Sudden Stopper. Foot traffic is moving smoothly, then the person in front suddenly stops dead in her tracks. She may not cause a pile-up, but at the very least she's thrown the sidewalk rhythm out of synch. If a pedestrian needs to stop for any reason, she should first ease her way out of the stream of walkers.

The Meanderthal. This pedestrian might also be dubbed the Veerer, since he often suddenly decides to walk diagonally rather than straight ahead. His more common trait is walking slowly and aimlessly while everyone about him is keeping to a faster pace.

The Phalanxers. A modern definition of *phalanx*: a line of clueless pedestrians who walk abreast and make it impossible for anyone to pass. When people are walking together, they should be sure not to block anyone who's trying to get by. A group on crowded sidewalks should walk in single file.

The Stationary Schmoozers. It's amazing how many people plant themselves in the middle of the sidewalk to chat, seemingly oblivious to other pedestrians. When crossing paths with friends and deciding to talk, pedestrians should move to one side so as not to impede the flow of foot traffic, whether they're a group of two or twenty.

The Spitter. It goes without saying that spitting on the pavement is nasty, unhygienic, and rude. Spitting into the gutter is no less disgusting to those who witness the act or spot the spittle.

Joggers, Skaters, and Bikers

Jogging or skating on a suburban neighborhood sidewalk is permissible so long as the sidewalk is relatively empty and you give a wide berth to everyone. Crowded city streets are another matter, although you wouldn't know it from the kind of jogger who plays dodge-the-pedestrian as he sprints through the crowd.

Bicycles are meant for streets, not sidewalks, so stay on the road as a general rule. An early morning ride down an empty suburban footpath may do no harm (if it's legal), but riding a bike on a crowded city street riles pedestrians and has proved time and again to endanger them. (See also Chapter 48, page 842: "Cycling.")

Walking the Dog

People who walk their dogs on urban streets should always see that the leash (compulsory by law in most cities) doesn't block traffic or, worse, trip someone. Use a leash no more than six feet long and avoid retractable leashes in areas where you're likely to encounter skaters, joggers, or cyclists; such leashes' thin lines can become almost invisible from a distance and trip anyone who's coming on fast.

If your dog is a barker, don't leave him tied to a parking meter or lamppost while you shop or get a bite to eat. Constant barking will disturb both passersby and the patrons in the adjoining establishments.

All dog owners are obligated to remove their dogs' droppings with a pooper-scooper or plastic bag. (It's the law in most urban municipalities.) Even if you're in a hurry, leaving your dog's "calling card" for other pedestrians to dodge is a serious shirking of responsibility.

Before letting your animal socialize with another dog, always ask the owner's permission first. The same goes twice over for children. Before allowing your dog any physical contact with kids, ask the parent, "May my dog say hello to your son?" Make sure the dog doesn't jump on, bounce off, or nuzzle the child.

Adults and children alike can be wary of dogs, so don't assume that everyone feels comfortable with your sweet little Misty. Ask those who will be around your dog even briefly if they're okay with it; then tell them a little about your pet: "She barks at first, but she's really gentle."

On Public Transportation

WHETHER YOU LIVE in a large city with a rapid-transit system that's usually stuffed to the gills or a small town where you're sure to find a seat at any time of day, you can help keep things running smoothly—which, as often as not, means *not* doing certain things.

If you've taken a seat on a bus or train car that starts filling up, don't leave a bag, backpack, or any other object on the seat next to you. A polite rider also always offers her own seat to anyone who seems to need it more—a pregnant woman or a parent with young children, an elderly passenger, a mother holding a baby, a passenger who is loaded down with packages, or one who looks frail or extremely tired.

~ Echoes of Tradition ~

The old rules for the ways for men and women to walk together and go through doors may have faded, but there are still plenty of people who prefer the traditional way of doing things, particularly on social occasions. Here's a rundown:

> ➤ On the street, a man traditionally walks on the curb side—a custom born of the idea that women needed to be shielded from the potential hazards posed by the passing horse-and-buggy parade.

> ➤ A woman precedes a man through a door, on an escalator (unless she needs help getting on or off), or through a narrow outdoor passageway.

> ➤ The man precedes a woman down a steep ramp or a slippery slope, on rough ground, and through crowds, taking her hand as necessary.

> ➤ In times gone by, a man regularly offered his arm to a woman. Today, he usually does so only if he is an usher at a wedding, the woman is his partner at a formal dinner, he's walking with an elderly woman, or he's assisting a woman wearing high heels over broken pavement or down stairs.

When standing, move toward the middle of the bus or train car (or the back, depending on where the doors are) to make room for the boarders at the next stop; don't wait for the driver or conductor to ask you to move. Make sure you've maneuvered your way to a door by the time you reach your stop.

Backpacks are a real source of frustration on crowded buses and trains, taking up more room and easily bumping other passengers. A courteous rider unstraps his backpack and carries it at his waist.

Keep any conversation quiet. Shouting over the noise of the bus or train car to a friend across the aisle annoys others. Be careful of what you say; fellow passengers won't appreciate foul language or conversations of an intimate nature.

On a rainy day, don't rest a wet umbrella on an empty seat or the overhead rack, where it could drip on other passengers. Instead, keep the umbrella under your seat or flat on the floor at your feet, making sure it doesn't stick into the aisle.

If eating is allowed on public transportation in your city or town, do it only if there's no chance of offending the other passengers. A candy bar is okay, but filling the bus or train car with the smell of greasy fries is not.

Riding the Bus

When more than three people are waiting to board a bus, form a line; then wait your turn no matter how packed the bus may be. Have your change or fare card ready so you won't hold others up as you rummage through your purse or pockets. If there are plenty of seats available, leave those at the front for passengers who may be elderly or disabled, even if they're not designated as such.

Bus riders are usually subjected to more cell phone abuse than train passengers because many rail systems run underground where cell phones can't get a signal. The stories are legion of passengers who've broken into applause when the bus driver tells a cell phone user to pipe down. Such reports suggest that cell phones and buses don't mix.

On Subways and Other City Trains

When a city train (subway or above-ground) pulls into the station, *stand aside as passengers disembark*. No one should have to fight his way through a knot of people, but blocking doors still ranks as one of the most common discourtesies. Door-blockers all too often make a stand inside the train car as well: Passengers inside the train who plant themselves in front of the doors while the train is moving and then fail to move aside when others try to board are guilty of rudeness that borders on the aggressive. When you're standing by the doors and people are streaming off, step outside the train car to give them plenty of room. You'll have more than enough time to step back on before the doors close.

If, when the doors open, you see that riders are packed in tight, wait for the next train. Shouldering people aside to squeeze in may be the most obnoxious offense of all.

Don't hold doors for someone rushing to make the train, which will delay its departure. Nor should you pry open doors as they begin to close or jam them with a briefcase or other object. (If you try the last ploy, your briefcase may leave with the train while you're left standing there on the platform.)

On Commuter Trains

Unlike airline passengers, rail travelers can use their cell phones and other electronic devices to conduct business or call friends. Even on train lines that limit cell phone use, using phones can be an issue.

The most thoughtless passengers have a way of spreading out papers and tapping away on a laptop when taking a break from a seemingly endless call. But other passengers should be understanding of anyone who uses a cell phone for a valid reason and tries her best not to disturb others.

Keep your voice down when chatting with a seatmate. Many commuters enjoy reading their newspaper on the train, and keeping things relatively quiet makes the trip more pleasurable for everyone.

Resist the temptation to put your feet on the empty seat opposite you, and don't leave anything behind—newspapers, coffee cups, the brown bag that held your snack. You'll be doing a favor both for the next person who uses the seat and for the transit authority cleaners.

In Your Car

IN THE 1945 EDITION of *Etiquette*, Emily Post contemplated the ways of the typical motorist: "How often have we noticed . . . that John Citizen, who is courteous in all

How you present yourself in public is part and parcel of your persona, from your appearance to your personal habits. Most often, it's the personal habits that offend, so give some thought to how you're perceived by those around you.

Keep your voice volume to a reasonable level. Public places are noisy by nature, but don't add to the din by talking louder than you must. Think of keeping your voice volume down as a personal form of public service.

Go easy on the cell phone. It's not the act of using a cell phone in public that upsets those who are held captive to it but the way you go about it. In short, be sure your conversation intrudes as little as possible on those around you.

Keep your language clean. Curse words that may not faze a friend may offend those who overhear—and it's hard for people not to overhear on public transportation and sidewalks. Save your more colorful language for a private place.

Let your grooming wait. Quickly combing your hair or freshening lipstick won't offend, but performing your morning grooming routine on public transportation—or, more dangerously, in your car—is something to avoid.

Chew gum unobtrusively. Cracking gum, smacking it, or chomping away in a mechanical rhythm can be disturbing or distracting to many people, especially in close quarters. In public, chew gum discreetly and dispose of it in a waste receptacle—never on the ground.

Save the passion for later. In public, holding hands and exchanging pecks on the cheek with your significant other can be charming, but prolonged and passionate embraces and soul kisses are always inappropriate.

Take care if you're a smoker. On crowded sidewalks, make sure your lit cigarette doesn't brush anyone. Don't flick butts onto the street; they may be small, but they still qualify as litter. Cigar smokers should smoke outdoors only in uncrowded places so that people who want to escape the smell can easily do so.

Don't be trashy. Throw all trash or debris into the nearest waste receptacle. That includes cups, flyers and newspapers, wrappers, wads of chewing gum, and cigarette butts (which must be completely out no matter how you dispose of them). If you don't see a wastebasket nearby, hold the trash till you find one.

Practice ATM etiquette. Stand back and don't try to get a peek at whatever transactions the person ahead of you is making. Be patient and don't complain if someone is taking more time than you think necessary. At drive-up ATMs, never honk or flash your lights at anyone using the machine.

his contacts with people, becomes suddenly transformed into a bad-mannered autocrat when driving his car!" Back then, when driving fifty miles per hour was considered speeding, rude behavior by drivers was a prime concern. In today's world, rudeness compromises safety in more ways than one, as evidenced by the growing number of aggressive drivers and what has become known as road rage.

Good Manners = Safety

Any discussion of manners and driving should be prefaced by two reminders: (1) Always wear your seat belt and insist that your passengers do so as well. (2) Never drink and drive. Not actually manners per se, these safeguards are nonetheless the most thoughtful acts of all.

Besides those two essentials, the guidelines for safe driving in cities and towns are much like those for driving on the highway (see Chapter 45, page 778: "When You're the Driver"). Drivers must pay utmost attention to the task at hand—propelling an extremely heavy and potentially dangerous machine down the road. Putting on makeup, snacking, or chatting on a cell phone (which in some localities is not only hazardous but illegal) takes your mind off what you're doing and interferes with your ability to respond physically and mentally. If you must eat, groom, or talk on the phone, pull off the road to a safe spot.

Using your turn signals when you're about to turn a corner or move to another lane is another must. Two other cautions are equally obvious: Stay at or under the speed limit (though not driving so slowly that you start a rush for other cars to get around you) and never tailgate another driver.

Road Rage

Some precautions are more important than ever. In the 1980s, the mounting pressures of daily life gave rise to road rage, confrontations over perceived on-the-road slights that escalated to violence and sometimes injury and death. Aggressive driving and its counterpoint, defensive driving, are par for the course these days, but road rage is something else: behavior that crosses the line to criminal. To avoid putting yourself in a situation that could spin out of control, *never* do the following:

➤ Tailgate another driver, especially at high speed
➤ Make eye contact with an aggressive driver
➤ Make an obscene gesture of any sort
➤ Lay on the horn and not let up
➤ Block the passing lane for more than a reasonable amount of time

You have to keep your own house in order, too. No matter how badly your day has gone, how many traffic jams you've suffered, and how many cars have almost clipped yours as they abruptly changed lanes, keep reminding yourself not to take traffic problems personally. Never focus your generalized anger on a single incident, which could become the flash point for a dangerous confrontation.

Stay Courteous!

Your car horn should be used as a warning, not as an expression of your displeasure. When a pedestrian doesn't see you coming or you need to avoid any other danger, honk only as much as is necessary. Otherwise, use a few horn taps to communicate with drivers—say, when you're stopped at a red light and the driver in front of you is rummaging through his glove compartment and hasn't noticed the light turn green. Three other things for drivers to remember:

➤ When driving on blocks with an unbroken line of traffic, let a car trying to exit a parking lot or driveway enter the line by waving them on. If several cars are waiting to exit, you needn't wait for every one; instead, count on the politeness of the drivers behind you to let the cars into the traffic stream one or two at a time.

➤ Don't slow to a crawl to see what's happening at any attention-getting activity—be it a film shoot, a protest rally, or an accident. If you must rubberneck, pull over and park your car.

➤ If you encounter a funeral cortege (signaled by a line of cars with headlights or flashing hazard lights on), it's respectful to pull over to the side of the street until the cars have passed. Waiting at a green light while a cortege passes is also expected, even if someone behind you is honking for you to proceed.

Keeping Your Cool at Intersections

Traffic lights and stop signs are there to be obeyed, not to be outfoxed—so don't try to race through a yellow light. If you're coming to an intersection and the block ahead is congested with traffic, don't cross over until you know there's no chance of blocking everyone once the light turns red.

At four-way stops, wait your turn; the drivers proceed in the order in which they arrive at the stop signs. (If it's a tie, the driver on the right goes first.) Flashing red lights at an intersection are treated as a four-way stop.

Don't block pedestrian crosswalks. If people don't have room to walk between your car and the one behind it, they'll have to walk in front—which might force them so close to passing traffic that they put themselves in danger. Also, don't block the right-hand turning lane in states where it's legal to turn right at red lights. If possible, move to the center lane so you won't hold up those in the right-turn lane.

Parking Lot Etiquette

In parking lots, go slow and pay attention to signs and the traffic flow. Don't drive down a row in which cars are parked in the opposite direction, and do use extra caution if driving through an open space in a row to get to the other side; it's hard for other drivers to see you coming through. Center your car in a marked space, and don't even think of trying to cram an SUV or other large vehicle into a space reserved for compacts.

At the Gas Pump

At multi-island gas stations, drive slowly and carefully to accommodate people who are standing at the pumps or walking back and forth to the store. When possible, pull up to the gas pump that will allow other drivers easy access to unused pumps. Pay special attention to any "Cash Only" or "Credit Card Only" signs on the pumps so that you won't waste others' time by having to move from one pump to the other.

Shop for items or attend to any other business inside only if you've parked your car in a parking spot (leave it at the pump only when paying your bill inside). Remember, too, that you're in a potentially hazardous environment. Avoid danger by turning off your engine before pumping gas and waiting until later to light a cigarette, cigar, or pipe.

The Ins and Outs of Carpooling

KEEPING TRAFFIC DOWN BY SHARING rides in cars or vans helps conserve both energy and the money in the carpoolers' wallets. It's been shown that ride sharing can save commuters as much as $3,000 a year on gas, repairs, parking, and insurance. Carpooling also lessens the stress of being behind the wheel every day.

∼ At the Drive-through Window ∼

Today, you can drive up to a window and get money, food, prescriptions, dry cleaning, and auto parts with minimum hassle. The drive-through window has been around for a long time, but more retailers are now offering this convenience to customers who want their service fast. Courtesy will make the drive-through easier for everyone.

First, be patient; window service is quick but not instantaneous. If you go at a busy time, expect a wait. Don't crowd the car ahead of you, and don't honk, blink your vehicle's lights, or shout if the person in that car is taking more time than you think he should. Pay attention to other cars, and never pull out of line without checking what's behind you.

When ordering over an intercom system, speak clearly; turn off the car radio or tape/CD player and ask anyone else in the car to be quiet. (If the intercom is difficult to hear, politely report the fault when you get to the window.) Try to pull as close to the drive-up window as you can so the employee doesn't have to strain to hand you your items. Have your money or items like prescription or bank deposit slips ready.

Check your order or items before driving away, and never back up to the window if you discover something missing; a packet of ketchup isn't worth having a fender-bender with the car behind. If there's a real problem, it's best to park, go inside, and speak with a supervisor. Don't litter the area as you drive off.

Above all, be courteous to the people on the other side of the window. They'll appreciate a pleasant "hello" and "thank you."

Making It Work

The key to a smooth-running car pool is having everyone agree on the rules, with three considerations in the forefront:

> ➤ Share expenses equally. If drivers rotate, there's no reason to worry about reimbursements. But if the car pool depends on a particular driver, the driver should be reimbursed for fuel, maintenance, and parking costs. Figure out a fair fare for each carpooler and how often it should be collected—usually weekly or monthly.

> ➤ Decide in advance how you'll proceed when a driver is ill or his car has mechanical problems. Make sure everyone has the home, work, and cell phone numbers of all the other riders so you can come up with a backup plan.

> ➤ So that everyone gets to work on time, decide on the maximum time you will wait for passengers. Five minutes is standard in most car pools.

More Tips for Carpoolers

No matter how friendly you are with your fellow carpoolers, don't request a stop along the way; picking up a quart of milk or your dry cleaning is something you do on your own time. A few other things to remember:

> ➤ Ask the other passengers before you open or close a window.

> ➤ Apply perfume or cologne sparingly so you won't risk bothering any of the other passengers.

> ➤ Watch your personal habits. Tapping your fingers, humming along with the radio, or chatting incessantly is eventually going to annoy your fellow passengers.

> ➤ Set your alarm a few minutes early so there's no chance that you'll keep the other carpoolers waiting.

In Taxis and Limousines

EVERY MUNICIPALITY HAS ITS OWN regulations for taxis. In smaller cities and towns, taxis are summoned with a phone call and then pick you up at a certain address. In large urban centers, taxis are more often hailed on the street or engaged at depots or taxi ranks, where they wait in line and take passengers by turn. When hailing a taxi on the street at a busy time, it's unforgivably rude to jump in front of anyone who has been waiting longer.

Once you're in the taxi, give the driver clear directions up front, letting him know if you want to go a certain route. Otherwise, if he takes Eighth Avenue when you think he should've taken Tenth, it's too late to complain. Saying at the outset, "Do you think Tenth Avenue will be faster?" beats grumbling, "But I wanted to go up Tenth!"

When long lines of traffic have to merge, I make a point to let one car in front of me. But then other drivers peg me as a pushover and try to cut in. Is there anything I can do? This kind of tactic makes me not want to give any driver a break!

It's frustrating when people take advantage of a roadway courtesy—but it's often best to give way to those rude drivers. First and foremost, stay calm and collected. If you let your anger affect your judgment and try to keep the second car from cutting in, you could risk causing an accident. In fact, it's been shown that hostile or aggressive drivers can be as great a hazard on the road as those who lack driving skills. The bottom line? Use common sense to judge whether letting a car cut in is worth the risk.

Make sure you have small bills in your wallet in case the driver isn't able to make change; although it's the driver's responsibility to be able to change at least a $20 bill, there are no guarantees. Tip according to service. A comfortable ride, a clean cab, and a courteous driver should be taken into account when deciding how much to tip.

Limousine Hires

If you hire a limousine to take you to the airport or elsewhere, don't act as if you're "riding high." Even if you love the idea of being chauffeured, be amicable and do not condescend to the driver. You're not expected to develop a friendship, but occasional small talk shows you as thoughtful and might improve service in the bargain.

If you hire a driver for several hours and your destination is a remote location with no services, see that a driver who has to wait for two or three hours is given a snack and drink. (For tipping, see Chapter 46, page 805: "In Taxis, Private Cars, or Limousines.")

The Art of Shopping

THE SALESPEOPLE YOU'RE HAPPY to encounter are likely to look you in the eye and greet you, devote their attention to you (not to the coworker with whom they're chatting), and thank you just as you thank them. But don't forget that keeping things civil when shopping is a two-way street. Salespeople hardly deserve all the blame for customer service problems, and it's essential that customers treat salespeople with respect. Say "hello," "please," and "thank you" and your dealings will run all the more smoothly. The more courteous customers are, the more likely salespeople are to respond in kind—and vice versa.

Don't hold salespeople responsible for things beyond their control. It's not their fault that the shirt you want is out of stock, that the price seems too high, or that you have to make an exchange instead of getting a refund. If you want to complain, either ask to speak to a manager or write a letter of complaint to the store. (See also Chapter 17, page 245: "Letters of Complaint.")

Smart Shopping

A pleasant shopping experience is about more than just your interaction with the salesperson, with three things of particular concern to the manners-minded:

➤ At the cash register, don't wait until the total is rung up to get your money, checkbook, or credit card out and at the ready. People who waste time searching through their purses or pockets are especially frustrating to the customers waiting to be served.

➤ Keep children under control. If a child has a habit of being disruptive when you shop, make arrangements to leave him at home whenever possible. At the very least, shop with children when they're not too hungry or tired—something that's kind not only to others but also to your child.

➤ Keep cell phone use to a minimum and the volume on a cassette player or radio low enough so that others can't hear the music through your headphones. Adding to the noise level in stores as you shop is annoying to others. *Never* talk on a cell phone when you're paying for your purchases at the cash register; it says to the cashier that, in your eyes, she's "not there."

Grocery and Home Store Do's and Don'ts

In the minds of supermarket and home store shoppers, who's the champion cheater at the checkout? The shopper in the express lane who ignores the ten-to-fifteen-items rule and unloads a cartful of goods. Vying for the title is the queue jumper, the last person in line who rushes to grab the first spot in the new one, even though everyone else has been waiting longer.

A well-mannered person won't commit such thoughtless acts and will deal with people who do in a calm and measured way, if at all. Following are things to avoid while shopping in a grocery store, home store, or most anywhere. (See also Chapter 4, page 39: "How to React?")

Do follow the express lane rules.
Do let those ahead of you in line go first when a new checkout line opens up.
Do return an item you've decided you don't want to its proper place instead of leaving it at the counter or stashing it on the nearest shelf.
Do bag your own items if the store is busy and no assigned employee is bagging at your counter. This enables the cashier to go straight to the next customer and allows you to leave the store faster.
Do make your items as accessible to the cashier as possible.

Do place the divider on the conveyor belt once you've unloaded all of your items.

Do tell an employee if you drop a food jar that breaks instead of just hurrying away from the mess.

Do treat the cashier respectfully. Don't, for instance, get angry at him if the register scans the wrong price; if he can't rectify the discrepancy, see someone at the customer/courtesy desk who can.

Do take special care when pushing the large carts designed for shoppers with small children. Some, designed like toy cars, are big enough to be very disconcerting when they come hurtling around a corner.

Don't block traffic by parking your cart on one side of the aisle while you study the items on the other side; stand behind your cart instead.

Don't get halfway through the checkout and remember you forgot something. It's better to finish checking out and go through the line again than to keep everyone else waiting.

Don't push the items of the person who's checking out in front of you aside on the conveyor belt. The rule is hands off other people's things, and not abiding by it could result in crushed loaves of bread and similar damage to someone else's goods.

Don't put your money, credit card, or coupons on the conveyor belt, even when it's stationary; you never know when it may start up again.

Don't use a cell phone to communicate at length with whoever makes the shopping list back home. Also avoid long phone chats while in the aisles and the checkout line.

Don't leave your shopping cart in a parking space in the parking lot; it goes in the spot designated for carts.

Shopping Short Takes

Treating employees with respect and interacting courteously with other customers are things shoppers should do as a matter of course, and the following tips will make a shopping excursion more enjoyable:

In Department Stores

If a salesperson is nowhere to be found, go to the nearest available register and politely ask where you might find one. If the cashier doesn't know, you could go to the manager. If, at the other extreme, a salesperson latches onto you and hovers as you browse the merchandise, shake him as politely as possible. So that he won't be concerned about losing a commission on a sale, just say, "Thanks, but I'd rather just look on my own right now. If I decide to buy something, I'll find you before I take my things to the register."

In Clothing Stores

Make an effort to get in and out of a fitting room as quickly as possible, especially if other customers are waiting. If a salesperson tells you a particular garment "looks fabulous" on you and you're not sure you agree, thank her for her help and go your way with "Thanks so much! I'll let you know if I decide to buy something."

When you're finished in the dressing room, put clothing back on the hangers, not in a heap on the floor. Then, depending on store policy, either leave the clothes inside or just outside the dressing room or put them back on the sales racks.

In Drugstores

If your prescription medicine is expensive, your copayment has increased, or you didn't realize that your deductible has yet to be met, don't take out your frustration on the person serving you; all of these decisions are made by the drug and insurance companies, not by the pharmacist or the sales clerk.

Unless you're prepared to wait, call in or drop off a prescription in advance. Pharmacists also have to deal with incoming calls from doctors and patients while giving prescription-filling the attention it deserves, and that takes time.

At Beauty Salons

Be sure to arrive on time for a beauty salon appointment; being late can slow things down for other customers for the rest of the day. If you want to cancel, calling ten minutes before an appointment may well cost your hairdresser money.

If you're not happy with your cut or color, let your stylist or the salon know as quickly as possible, since it could possibly be fixed the next day. A thornier problem comes when you decide to switch stylists (especially one you've had for a long time), whether at the same salon or elsewhere. The solution is to be benevolently honest. Most stylists say they want to know why a client leaves, but try your best not to make them feel insulted. Tell your stylist that you appreciate all her efforts to please you and that you've enjoyed getting to know her (if true), but you just want to try someone else. "I just feel I'm in a rut and would like to try one of Mr. Vic's crazy haircuts" or "As you know, I haven't been happy with the color the last few times, so I've decided to try someone else. But I do appreciate your efforts." What you should never do is simply disappear.

At Spas

A spa is by nature a relaxed place, but that doesn't mean you can be late for your appointment. Beyond that, it's fine to talk quietly while having a massage or other treatment, but it's equally okay to remain silent. Do, however, give the therapist feedback on your comfort and any trouble areas she should know about. Remember that spas should remain child-free, since quiet and relaxation are essential to the experience.

At Yard Sales

Comply with any requests for "no early birds!" Don't arrive while the seller is still setting up just to make sure you get the best bargains—considered "dirty pool" in yard-sale circles. Though a sale may start as early as 7:00 AM, the neighbors may not yet be awake—so forgo loud conversation or laughter. Don't block a neighbor's driveway with your car.

Leave the displays as you found them, not in disarray. A little bargaining is often expected, but don't haggle aggressively over prices. Carry small bills and plenty of change. The seller doesn't have the resources of a regular store, so don't be surprised or annoyed if he can't change a $20 bill when you're paying for a $1 item.

Chapter Four

Dealing with Rudeness

FOR A WORD OF ONLY FOUR LETTERS, "rude" has more than its share of meanings, ranging from in-your-face aggressiveness to insults so subtle they don't hit you until hours later. But the source of rudeness is always the same: a simple lack of courtesy and respect.

A speeder tailgates you on the freeway. An acquaintance asks about your salary. A man you've just met makes suggestive remarks about your figure. The woman at the cash register fails to even acknowledge your presence, much less say "thank you." On the surface these acts are very different, but at bottom they all qualify as rude.

To understand rudeness, you need to see through its many guises. It's worth noting the myriad ways that people get under one another's skin.

Aggressive rudeness. Intentional, no-holds-barred, no-bones-about-it rudeness is designed to punish you for something you've done (you're screamed at after accidentally bumping into a passerby), to put you in your place (a coworker unfairly criticizes you for "thinking you're so smart"), or to exact revenge (on the road, you're purposely slowed down by a driver who feels you cut him off).

Casual rudeness. Often unconscious on the part of those who practice it, casual rudeness isn't directed at you personally but drives you crazy nonetheless. Falling into this category are such acts as disturbing the peace by loudly yakking away on a cell phone, rushing from the back of a line to the front of a newly opened one, and blocking a busy sidewalk by standing smack-dab in the middle to chat with friends.

Rudeness in disguise. Some rudeness comes clothed in kid gloves. The perfect example is the back-handed compliment: "Love that new haircut! You look so much better than you did with long hair!"

Unwitting rudeness. Poor table manners and talking at high volume because of a hearing problem are among the behaviors that are unintentional but are often spoken of as rude.

Bottom-of-the-barrel behavior. Some behaviors are not only rude but also repellent. Among these never-evers are spitting on the sidewalk, belching at the table, blowing your nose on anything but a tissue or handkerchief, and using hair-curling obscenities in public, especially around young children.

While surveys have shown that almost three-quarters of Americans think that rudeness has increased in the last few decades, it's also true that people have believed the same for centuries. (A book that took the English to task for a boom in bad behavior was written in 1405!) Still, modern life has spawned a whole new set of stress-builders, all of which contribute to bad behavior.

Media and entertainment are often blamed for undermining civility, and there's plenty of ammunition for the critics. On TV and in film, grossness and disrespect are often portrayed as humorous; in music, foul language is part of the package in certain genres; and in video games, the victorious are often the most violent.

Sociologists also cite our obsession with self as a cause—good old American individualism gone wild, with people convinced that things should happen *their* way. We also feel the need to pack as much as we can into a twenty-four-hour day, and the technological revolution of the last two decades has made it possible to do just that. The price is a barrage of intrusions, from the nonstop cell phone chorus to e-mail in-boxes crammed with spam.

Overlay it all with overcrowding in sprawling cities and suburbs and the need to do everything *fast*, and it's no wonder that stress-induced rudeness seems to spring forth from all corners and at every turn.

∾ All the Rage ∾

It says a lot about life in the twenty-first century that "rage" is tacked onto words almost as frequently as "-gate" is attached to scandals. Road rage, a term coined to describe terrible—even fatal—confrontations on the streets and highways, spawned front-page reports of air rage on planes. Stressed-out white-collar workers soon got into the act with desk rage. Now there's no shortage of contrivances—cell phone rage, biker rage, rink rage, surfer rage, and so on. In a reported incident of "grocery store rage," a woman in Massachusetts expressed her anger at an express-lane violator by taking a can of whipped cream out of her cart and topping the man with everything but a cherry.

The new buzzword status of "rage" reflects the mounting frustrations of life in the modern world. And who knows? It might even contribute to the common good. The more people are reminded of the risks and dangers inherent in the loss of self-control, the more likely they are to think twice before angrily confronting a fellow human being.

The Art of Responding

SOMETIMES AN AFFRONT HAPPENS so quickly you have no chance to respond. For instance, someone on a crowded sidewalk accidentally whacks you with a briefcase, then continues on his way without so much as a look back. But we're more often faced with the decision of whether to let it go or respond.

Most people are loath to challenge rudeness because they're fearful that even a minor confrontation might easily escalate; in fact, a national survey conducted by Public Agenda showed that most of those who've been offended just walk away.

How do you go about speaking up if you're determined to take a stand? Very carefully. Responding in kind (i.e., answering with something just as bad) serves only to spur more unacceptable behavior, which can then spin out of control. There's also the safety issue to consider, even with someone you know. Getting into a tangle with a person prone to violence could put you in real danger.

The lesson here is to kill 'em with kindness. By keeping your cool, you're teaching by example, much as a parent does for a child. Good behavior is catching; the more you display it, the more it spreads. This doesn't mean becoming a doormat; it does mean you can defuse a situation without wrangling over who's right or wrong.

Sometimes, sympathizing with the other person—just expressing your understanding of why an incident occurred—is all it takes. On an airplane, for example, you politely tell a parent that his youngster is kicking the back of your seat and the parent comes back with an angry retort. Your calm response: "Please don't shout. I know the space is tight and kids will be kids, but your daughter has been kicking my seat since we boarded. I'd really appreciate it if you would ask her to stop. Thanks!"

Other things to consider when someone has been rude to you:

Don't automatically take it personally. Sometimes the offender has had a terrible day or is simply in a bad mood. Give him the benefit of the doubt by imagining what he might be going through—the sting of a recent confrontation with someone, a family problem, trouble at work, the illness of a loved one.

Size up your annoyances. Sometimes it's best to let things go. Will making a point to the person who's using her credit card in a line with a too-big-to-miss sign over the cash register saying "Cash Only" accomplish anything, or will it be a waste of your emotional energy?

Take responsibility for your own actions. Ask yourself whether you did something to provoke the treatment. If you speak sharply to a bank teller because you've had an awful day at work, it's no wonder that you won't get the best service.

Mentally count to ten. Whenever someone else's behavior makes you angry, forget about them and focus on yourself or something else for a few seconds. Take a few deep breaths and ask yourself, "Is it really worth blowing my stack over this?"

Use humor. Countering a friend's comment that "you look terrible" with a sarcastic retort like "How kind of you to say so!" is preferable to "Well, you look pretty bad yourself." Another tactic is to laugh it off—literally. Just chuckle and change the subject. Just smile or even chuckle (eye-rolling optional); then change the subject.

Phrasing and Tone

How you phrase a response to rude behavior can make all the difference. "Stop talking so loudly! You're driving everyone crazy!" will raise the offender's hackles, while "Many of us are trying to read, so would you mind lowering your voice? Thanks!" is more likely to spur him to stop. Likewise, your tone of voice can make the exact same words sound either innocent or angry. "Would you please sit down so I can see?" is a simple request, while "Would you *please* sit down so I can *see*?!" is a challenge.

Taking It Higher

Sometimes the best solution is not to confront the rude person herself but to take it to a higher level. If you've been treated rudely at the rental car counter (the agent has not only served you a large portion of attitude but was disrespectful and condescending to other customers as well), write a letter of complaint to the agency manager or company headquarters. The same goes for dealing with a problem caused by another patron in a store, restaurant, or theater. Usually, the best solution is to take it to the manager in charge, not to deal with the culprit directly.

On the other hand, you can do your part to make things better by commending people who are particularly courteous and helpful. If a parking attendant charged your dead battery or a sales clerk went the extra mile to track down and order an out-of-stock item for you, write an appreciative letter to his employer. It's been said that the courtesy bug is contagious, and a letter of praise or similar "official" act may help it spread all the faster (see Chapter 17, page 244: "Letters of Commendation.")

Accept Responsibility

You grab an empty shopping cart you assume to be free, only to be told "That's mine!" by a person who left it unattended. You dash down the hall at work with a cup of hot coffee and collide with a coworker who rounds the corner. When you inconvenience someone else, whether unwittingly or because of carelessness, accept responsibility for the act, apologize immediately, and make amends if possible. Often, a simple explanation can calm the situation—as when you hold up a line at a store checkout because the clerk is getting a price. Most people will understand if they see the problem and realize that you're aware of it, too. Getting defensive and angry when you're perceived as rude is precisely the wrong thing to do, since it could lead to flared tempers or a confrontation.

If every American were asked to vote on today's rudest public behaviors, the following would doubtlessly rank near the top:

➢ Telling racist or ethnic jokes, which not only insults the listener's intelligence but smears entire communities

➢ Using four-letter words and other obscenities in public without any reservations—especially in the presence of children

➢ Doing the "cell yell"—conducting a cell phone conversation so loudly that those around you wonder if your phonemate is hard of hearing

➢ Treating a salesperson, food server, or any other service provider as someone who's beneath you

➢ Letting kids run wild or make constant noise in restaurants, supermarkets, theaters, or any other public or private place

➢ Endangering others on a busy expressway by playing NASCAR wannabe: zipping from one lane to the other while driving like a maniac and not even bothering to signal

➢ At a youth sporting event, abusing the referee, coach, or opposing team's players because your child's team has suffered what you consider a wrong

➢ Fouling the sidewalk with spit, trash, or pet poop left unscooped

➢ On public transportation, staying planted in your seat when an elderly, pregnant, or disabled person obviously needs it more

➢ Charging thoughtlessly through crowds—especially when skating, riding a bike or electric scooter, or pushing a baby stroller

➢ Butting in, whether jumping into a checkout line in a store or taking a parking space that someone else is clearly waiting for

➢ Lighting up to smoke tobacco in a roomful of nonsmokers—and adding insult to injury by not asking permission beforehand

Dealing with Rudeness

How to React?

HOW SUCCESSFULLY you keep your dignity after you've been insulted depends on how you react. Whether you've been on the receiving end of a diatribe or someone brazenly breaks in front of you as you wait in line, the politely delivered riposte is your best tactic, should you choose to respond.

Following are typical instances of rudeness and how you might go about dealing with them.

When Shopping . . .

All the checkouts at a grocery store have people waiting in line—perhaps the reason the person before you in the express lane is breaking the ten-items-or-less rule and unloading a small mountain of groceries.

It's safest to wait patiently, then pay a visit to the manager after you've checked out. While he may have instructed the staff to accommodate rule-breakers because "the customer is always right," the store may change its policy if enough people complain. If you do choose to speak up, give the person the benefit of the doubt by saying, "Excuse me, but I guess you didn't realize this is the express lane. I'm just letting you know for future reference." If the person reacts negatively, don't give in to the temptation to talk back.

You're next in line at a counter where service is as slow as molasses. When another one opens up, the person behind you rushes to get there first.

Unless the cashier has motioned to the last people in line, say, "I'm sorry, but I've been waiting longer than you. Would you mind if I go first?" If the person doesn't yield, let the matter drop then and there: You've got a lout on your hands, and he may be spoiling for a fight. You could also mention the problem to the manager, suggesting that henceforth a salesperson who opens a new line say, "May I help the next person in line?"

The grumpy salesperson who's checking you out says only, "How do you wanna pay?"—no "Thank you," no "Have a nice day," no "Bye, now." You could understand if he were serving an unbroken string of customers, but he's not.

Do you *really* want to express your displeasure, or would you rather say nothing? If you choose the former, simply look the person in the eye, smile, say "Thanks!" and wait for a reply. If he doesn't respond, you can either decide that you're not going to let it get under your skin or let the manager know that the person manning Lane 4 is ignoring the basic courtesies.

At Work . . .

Come lunchtime, the guy in the next cubicle frequently microwaves broccoli in the kitchen, then eats it as his desk. The smell is so strong that it lingers for up to an hour.

This is one problem that lends itself to a lighthearted response: "Stephen, are you trying to drive us all away so you can have a quiet lunch? The smell of that broccoli just may do the trick."

You regularly overhear a coworker unjustly trashing a workmate she doesn't like as she socializes with a small group in the office lunchroom.

First of all, speak up only if you couldn't help but overhear; as an eavesdropper, you would have no grounds for complaint. Say something like, "Theresa, I don't mean to butt in, but if you're going to speak ill of Virginia, don't you think you should do it someplace more private? You never know when she might walk in." If her accusations are false, you could calmly point that out to her as well.

A workmate asks you what your college-age son has chosen as a major. When you answer, "Philosophy," she draws back, widens her eyes, and says, "How on earth is he ever going to make a living with that?"

Talk about a rude reply! It's a shame when an education is seen as nothing more than the ticket to a high salary, but this is unfortunately often the case. One way to squelch such remarks is to say, "Like me, Jimmy thinks the real reward comes from loving what you do, not how much you make—and I couldn't be prouder of him."

When Out in Public . . .

You're walking down a street in your neighborhood when a man and his young son throw their empty paper cups to the ground—and they're no more than ten feet away from a trash bin.

Walk over and pick up the cups and deposit them in the trash bin—your way of teaching by example. Don't do it ostentatiously and don't glare at the litterers. The silent message you're sending is strong enough to make your point.

A slouching passenger on the subway is taking up three seats—and you're extremely tired and you want to sit down.

If you feel comfortable enough to speak up, do so with a calm "Excuse me. Would you mind if I sit down?" If he refuses to make room for you, don't force the issue. Some seat-hoggers are just waiting to be challenged; in the interest of safety, the last thing you want to do is rile them.

On a bus, two teenagers are engaged in a rollicking conversation filled with four-letter words, loudly enough for everyone to hear.

Draw on your intuition before saying anything. If the youths seem to be baiting the passengers, ignore them as well as you can. If they seem like otherwise decent people, you can quietly venture a suggestion: "Excuse me, but I'm not sure you noticed that there are children on the bus. Could you please watch your language?" If they react negatively to your remark, let the matter drop; it's unlikely they'll cease and desist.

Phone Provocations . . .

At an upscale restaurant, the man at the next table has been yelling into his cell phone for ten minutes, sharing his brilliant deal-making talents with everyone within earshot.

If the look of surprise you direct to the offender does nothing to stop the racket, discreetly ask the manager or maitre d' to intervene. It's always better to allow someone at the establishment to make such a request rather than to risk a patron-to-patron confrontation.

I was recently driving my elderly mother and my brother to a restaurant when my brother lit a cigarette in the car, even though my mother and I don't smoke. After I left them at the door and parked, I found them seated in the smoking section. I fairly shouted, "First you smoke is my car—and now this?" We moved to nonsmoking, but my brother was cool to me during dinner and on the way home. Did I overreact?

Your brother was undoubtedly rude, but you threw fuel on the fire. As inconsiderate as he was, a calmer statement—"Robert, I assumed you smoked in the car so you wouldn't need to in the restaurant. Would you mind if we moved to non-smoking?"—would probably have gotten the same result without putting a damper on the occasion.

You've left several voice mail messages for the information officer of an organization, and he hasn't returned your calls.

Try once more before giving up: "Mr. Johnson, this is Jane Stewart, the freelance garden writer who called you about the new 'Polly Marshall' tea rose. I'm worried about meeting the deadline for my article, so could you please give me a call? Again, my number is 800-555-6543. Thanks." If Mr. Johnson still doesn't respond, you might want to contact someone else at the organization to politely explain the problem and ask for help. Or, if the information is available elsewhere, simply write Mr. Johnson off and try the other source.

Chapter Five

Dress and Grooming

I<small>T'S NO SECRET</small> that in twenty-first-century America, casual has trumped more formal ways of dressing. Emily Post no doubt would have approved of this shift in
style; she was very practical and favored using common sense to make everyday life a
little easier. But even in this go-go world, "casual" should never be sloppy or inappropriate. The clothes we wear and the way we groom ourselves represent how we
choose to present ourselves to others and *reflect the importance we attach to the occasion.*
The more significance we assign to an event or activity—whether a worship service, a
night at the theater, or a last-minute get-together with friends—the more thought we
should give to dressing. Individuality and personal expression have their place, but the
principles of respect and consideration for others, plus a healthy dose of common
sense, should underlie all dressing and grooming decisions.

Dressing with consideration is also rooted in respect for cultural, religious, and regional customs. A teenager who wears well-pressed jeans to church may look presentable, but some worshipers might feel that jeans are inappropriate in that particular
setting. This attitude may seem unfair to some, but it's reality. The *message* that clothes
can send often matters more than the clothes themselves.

What's Happened to Tradition?

C<small>ASUAL</small> *IS* <small>THE AMERICAN NORM</small> today, yet traditional dress survives. In fact, the
move toward casualness (though not comfort) has slowed, and in some cases, reversed
direction. There's a growing feeling among many that casual attire has been misinterpreted to mean "sloppy" and contributes to laxity—especially in the workplace. Be
prepared to adapt, adjusting what you wear for each situation. If you're selling a con-
cept to the board of directors, your appearance should reflect the same attention to
detail as your presentation. On the other hand, if you meet with a client at a media
company where jeans and body piercings are the norm, dressing too conservatively
could create the wrong impression.

With casual clothing and accessories, the important concern is *not* to cross the line into bad-taste territory. Some things to avoid are

Sloppy

➤ Shirttail out
➤ Hem ragged
➤ Mismatched shoes or socks
➤ Stains on clothing
➤ Wrinkled clothing
➤ Worn-looking or frayed clothing

Inappropriate

➤ See-through blouses
➤ Low-cut cleavage or mesh tank tops at the office
➤ Barefoot and topless men, other than at the beach
➤ Children dressed provocatively beyond their age
➤ Teen or adolescent girls in clingy tops or with cleavage exposed
➤ Stiletto shoes at work

Tacky

➤ White socks with dress clothing
➤ Slacks, jeans, or shorts with the waistline so low that massive bare skin is exposed
➤ Women in curlers in public
➤ Jogging suits in fine-dining restaurants
➤ Torn jeans in the workplace

Utterly Clueless

➤ Wearing sneakers or boat-style shoes with suits
➤ Men and boys wearing hats in restaurants or at dinner tables
➤ Men, women, teens, and children wearing baseball caps in restaurants or at dinner tables
➤ Tank tops in a business situation
➤ Wearing ill-fitting clothing, such as a suit that's too tight
➤ A man wearing dressy lace-up shoes with jeans

Traditional-versus-casual dress questions come up in social situations as well. For example, anything more casual than a sport jacket or any kinds of nice dress may be inappropriate for a cocktail party, while shorts and flip-flops might be fine for a backyard cookout.

Tradition does hold its own most firmly with formal wear. That's because the tuxedo, cocktail dress, and evening gown might very well satisfy our hunger for traditional elegance.

What's Appropriate?

KNOWING WHAT TO WEAR in every situation can be a challenge, but common sense and consideration for others come into play. Trust your instincts. Your knowledge about a situation is just as effective as—and more important than—any rules about style. By thinking first and asking for guidance when you aren't sure, you'll almost always make the correct clothing decisions. Even fashion mistakes tend to be minor when the wearer makes a genuine effort to do the right thing.

Dressing appropriately often means toning down a look out of regard for the sensibilities of others. In unfamiliar situations and around new people, it's usually wisest to err on the side of conservatism. When in doubt, under-dressing can be safer than over-dressing.

Appropriateness is also governed by local and regional tastes and customs, so observe how others dress and be guided by what you see. It's not as if you have to wear black in New York or tropical colors in Miami, but try not to stick out like the proverbial sore thumb—donning shorts and a T-shirt, say, for an event where something dressier is the local norm.

Accessories in General

AS BASIC AS A TIE, as showy as jewelry, as ephemeral as cologne, accessories can dress up an outfit, dress it down, make it seem expensive, or make it seem cheap. Like garments, accessories change character according to the situation.

Hats

Hats are not the essential article of clothing they once were but are still worn by both sexes for fashion and for function. Knowing when to remove a hat is as important as wearing the right hat for the occasion. This chart shows when it's fine to wear a hat and when it's not.

Men	Women
Hats can be left on . . .	**Hats and nonbaseball caps can be left on . . .**
Outdoors	In a home and other dwellings (with the exception of winter headgear)
At athletic events (indoors and out)	
On public transportation	At luncheons, weddings, garden parties, and so on
At religious services, as required	
In public buildings (post office, airports, etc.)	At religious services
In office and hotel lobbies	In a theater, movie, auditorium, or other large gathering place if the view of those behind is not blocked
On elevators	
	When the national anthem is played
Take hats off, including baseball caps . . .	When the flag of the United States passes by, as in a parade
In a home	
Indoors at work, especially in an office (unless required for the job)	**Take hats off . . .**
	Indoors at work, especially in an office (unless required for the job)
At mealtime, at the table	Anywhere hats may block others' view
In restaurants and coffee shops	
At a movie or any indoor performance	**Remove baseball-style (unisex) caps . . .**
When the national anthem is played	In a home
When the flag of the United States passes by, as in a parade	Indoors at work, especially in an office (unless required for the job)
	At mealtime, at the table
	In restaurants and coffee shops
	At a movie or play
	When the national anthem is played
	When the flag of the United States passes by, as in a parade

Jewelry

Whether costume or the real thing, jewelry is an adornment and ought not overpower your total look. In business settings, avoid going overboard with rings, bracelets, and other ornamentation. Always consider the occasion and the sensitivities of others. For instance, a courteous person won't wear religious jewelry when attending services of another faith.

Jewelry shouldn't be noisy. In social and public settings, shut off watches that beep or chime. Jingling bracelets and earrings, beaded necklaces that rattle and clank, and bells on anything can cause considerable discomfort for others—especially in places like the theater and at public lectures where silence is golden.

Jewelry should be cleaned routinely; a dirt-encrusted ring or a frayed watchband can ruin an otherwise well-groomed appearance. Checking bands, chains, clasps, clips, and earring backs and studs for any damage or breaks will spare others the bother of searching for your lost or broken accessories.

Piercings and Tattoos

The truth about body piercings and tattoos is that one person's adornment can be regarded by others as mutilation. Though ear piercing is acceptable, more extreme forms of piercing and tattooing can be distracting and literally make some people feel queasy. Piercing may lead to skin infections, which can be treated easily but are unpleasant to see. Call them narrow-minded, but some people just think that body piercing and tattoos are tacky.

Many employers regard the display of tattoos and piercing as unprofessional. So important is this issue that career counselors frequently advise job applicants to avoid wearing piercing jewelry other than earrings (a pair for women, a single one for men) and to cover visible tattoos, if possible, for job interviews. A good rule of thumb: When in doubt, especially in the business world, don't wear it or show it.

Eyewear

Keep your lenses clean, smudge-free, and in good condition overall. Regardless of your glasses' style, emergency repairs are just that—for emergencies. Though you may have to fasten a broken frame with a safety pin or tape a broken nosepiece for a day or two, don't let a temporary fix become permanent.

Remove sunglasses when indoors (unless the lighting is very harsh or glaring) because they interfere with direct eye contact. Except when there's a medical need, wearing sunglasses either indoors or at night may be regarded by others as pretentious, attention-grabbing, or secretive.

Briefcases, Laptop Cases, and Handbags

For business, choose a briefcase of good quality, preferably in soft leather. For a simple sheaf of papers, a leather envelope or folder carried under the arm is an option. Briefcases made of plastic or aluminum may be fine in some fields but might look unprofessional in more traditional ones.

Laptop cases are generally made from microfiber fabrics; keep your case clean and neat. Worn-looking or discolored cases can make you seem inattentive to basic details.

Purses and handbags should be appropriate to the occasion. You wouldn't go to a business meeting with a big straw bag, for example. The old rule that bags and shoes must match is gone. Specific color rules—"Never wear black accessories with a blue

"Black tie optional." "Smart casual." These and other terms on party invitations are intended to tell the recipient what is appropriate to wear for the occasion, but they are just as likely to raise questions. For hosts and hostesses, the more thoughtful approach is to stick with the standard categories (business casual, semi-formal, black tie, and white tie) and to use ambiguous terms (sport casual, smart casual, and dressy casual) only when an explanation is supplied. This chart includes traditional as well as current dress notations:

White Tie

Men. Black tailcoat, matching trousers with a single stripe of satin or braid, white piqué wing-collared shirt with stiff front, white vest, and white bow tie; white or gray gloves; black patent shoes and black dress socks

Women. Formal evening gown

Black Tie

Men. Black tuxedo jacket, matching trousers, formal (piqué or pleated-front) white shirt, black (silk, shiny satin, or twill) bow tie, black cummerbund to match tie, dressy suspenders to ensure a good fit (optional); black patent shoes and black dress socks; no gloves. In summer or on a cruise: may have white dinner jacket, black tuxedo trousers, plus other black tie wardrobe

Women. Formal evening dress or short, dressy cocktail dress

Black Tie Optional

Men. Either a tuxedo (see "Black Tie" above) or dark suit with white shirt, conservative tie

Women. Formal evening dress; short, dressy cocktail dress or dressy separates

Creative Black Tie

Men. Tuxedo combined with trendy or whimsical items, such as a black shirt or a matching colored or patterned bow tie and cummerbund; black patent or dressy black leather shoes and black dress socks

Women. Formal evening gown, dressy cocktail dress or dressy separates; any of these accessorized with items such as an ostrich-feather boa, a colorful brooch, or an elegant shawl

Semiformal

Men. Dark, dressy business-type suit (usually worsted wool), with or without a matching vest, white shirt, conservative tie; dressy leather shoes and dress socks

Women. Short afternoon or cocktail dress or long, dressy skirt and top

Festive Attire

Men. Slacks, seasonal sport coat or blazer in color of choice, open-collar shirt, perhaps a holiday-theme tie

Women. Short cocktail dress or long, dressy skirt and top or dressy pants outfit

Dressy Casual

Men. Slacks, seasonal sport coat or blazer, open-collar shirt

Women. Street-length dress, skirt and nice top, or dressy pants outfit

Business Casual

Men. Khakis or slacks, seasonal sport coat or blazer, open-collar shirt

Women. Khakis or slacks, skirt, open-collar shirt or knit shirt, sweater

Sport Casual

Men. Khakis or jeans; nice tee, polo, or casual button-down-the-front shirt

Women. Khakis or jeans; nice tee, polo, or casual button-down-the-front shirt

Beach Casual

Men. Khakis or shorts (cargo or Bermuda), knit shirt, sport jacket optional

Women. Sundress or khakis or shorts (cargo or Bermuda), open-collar shirt or knit shirt, lightweight jacket or sweater

Holiday Casual

Clothing is the same as for "Business Casual" with some holiday colors or designs. Just be careful not to overdo.

A QUESTION FOR PEGGY

My boyfriend and I were out for dinner last night with another couple. When my contact lenses started hurting while we waited for dessert, I changed them at the table. Later, my boyfriend said I should have done it in the ladies' room. Is he right?

Yes, he is. What is a simple process for the contact lens wearer can be quite unpleasant for other people to watch, especially during a meal. Even if your fellow diners are close friends, they deserve the same lens-changing courtesy you'd extend to someone you've just met. (There are exceptions. If you have an emergency and must remove lenses immediately, that's okay. Just be discreet.)

Anytime you need to change your lenses in public, go to a private spot—a *clean* restroom, a deserted foyer or lobby, or beyond the edge of the crowd at an event.

outfit," for instance—are likewise passé, and women no longer feel compelled to have a purse to match every outfit. Handbags should be as roomy as you need, but an outsized bag can inconvenience others in crowded places.

Backpacks

The cardinal rule of backpack etiquette is this: In crowded places, whether a bus or a shoulder-to-shoulder outdoor concert, remove the pack and carry it at your side or front. A strapped-on backpack can knock into people when you're pivoting in a crowd or walking down the aisle of a train, plane, or bus.

Perfume and Cologne

Scents have been used throughout history to disguise body odor, but cleanliness remains the best solution. When you use perfume or cologne, take a "moderation in all things" approach. In close quarters, heavy scents can irritate others and cause some people to have allergic reactions. Mixing scents—scented deodorant, hair, and bath products in addition to cologne or perfume—can also be disagreeable.

The composition of scents differs. *Perfume* is heavier and generally richer in fragrance than *toilet water*, and *cologne* is the lightest mix. Because bodies react differently, try a sample and wear it for a day or two before buying a new scent.

Hairstyles

An extreme hairstyle can be a turnoff to some people. Oftentimes a wild hairdo is simply unbecoming. Unless you're in the hairstyling business, an extreme style is generally not a wise choice in the workplace.

The Importance of Grooming

THE PEOPLE YOU'RE WITH can be extremely uncomfortable if you become lax about the condition of your clothing or about your personal hygiene. Paying attention to grooming demonstrates respect for yourself and for others.

Your Wardrobe

No matter how expensive or stylish your clothing, if it's messy or ill-fitting, then style and cost mean little. Remember that clothes send a message about how you want others to see you.

Clean clothes. Don't be tempted to wear anything with spots or stains or that is just plain dirty (even if the problem doesn't show). You'll be doing yourself and others a favor if you keep an eye out for dirt and odors on your clothes. Ignoring problems can be inconsiderate. Especially at work, clothes should be spotless at the start of each day; soiled work clothing reflects on both the wearer and his or her employer.

It's not that difficult to stay clean. Many of today's blended fabrics, those for exercise and sport clothes included, allow easy care, including frequent washing. Even clean clothes, though, may not be as fresh as they appear. When dressing, apply the sniff test. Items that have hung in the closet or been stored for some time can take on a musty smell. That jacket you wore yesterday may have picked up odors from the environment or retain perfume scents. If the smell is strong, washing or professional cleaning is probably necessary before you wear the garment again.

Neatness. A neat appearance tells others that you care enough about yourself, and them, to organize and to attend to details. Often, neatness can compensate for clothing that is not as new or stylish as you'd like. If neatness isn't your strong suit, take heart. Neat and tidy habits can always be learned and improved on. A good mirror in a well-lighted place is a practical starting point.

Hair. Keep hair clean; greasy-looking, unkempt, or poorly maintained hair can sink the snazziest look. Dandruff can also negate a clean, streamlined look, so keep a lookout for flakes.

Nails. Check your nails often to see if they need cleaning or filing. Long, long nails—especially those with bright colors, painted designs, or extra-long stick-ons—can be out of place in many business environments. The basics of nail care for women and men include neatly manicured nails and cuticles. (A note to nail-biters: Keep your nails clipped short to prevent them from looking ragged.) If you wear polish, maintain it regularly.

Breath. To keep breath fresh, brush your teeth after lunch as well as in the morning and at night. Regular flossing, plus brushing the back of the tongue, helps control odor, and breath mints can help.

My coworker has body odor so intense that people joke about him behind his back. I like him and want to help. Is there a tactful way to broach the subject?

Your sympathy is commendable, but it's not sufficient reason to risk humiliating or angering your coworker. If you aren't really good friends, don't broach the subject. And it doesn't sound as if you're a supervisor who needs to discuss a possible obstacle to his advancement. This is a very personal area. His problem might be caused by a medical condition or his preference to go deodorant free.

Only if your friendship is close, take him aside and delicately say, "I've noticed you have a problem with perspiration. I hope you don't mind my mentioning it, but I really want to help you if I can." You may be able to recommend something that has worked for you. Assure him that the discussion about his problem will stay private, and be sure that it does.

Body odor. A daily bath or shower is the best defense against body odor. *Deodorants* mask odor, while *antiperspirants* block sweat. Combination deodorant-antiperspirants do both. Don't apply these products so thickly that the perfumy scent is obvious.

Men's Clothing and Grooming

THE ANSWER TO WHAT men should wear used to be easy: a suit and tie at the office and a hat outdoors, slacks and a sport coat for casual wear, and a tuxedo or dinner jacket for anything formal. Today, it may seem that the sky's the limit. But expanding your sartorial horizons doesn't mean abandoning appropriateness. You won't compromise self-expression when you show respect by wearing a tie or removing your baseball cap.

No matter what your dressing style, be sure you follow the basic tenets of grooming etiquette. If you're in the dark about the appropriate attire for a situation, be observant. Given the ebb and flow of fashion, it pays to become a trend-watcher of sorts—not to keep up with the latest thing but to gauge the degree of casualness suited to various situations. What are well-dressed men wearing to work? To indoor concerts? To religious services? When you aren't sure, ask someone who knows. If you're going to a party, call the host. If visiting a business, call the receptionist or human resources department and ask what the men usually wear.

What of the Suit?

The suit remains an essential, if only for weddings and funerals. The suit also has two undeniably positive attributes: It shows respect, and it makes almost any man look his best. But the pluses are wiped out if the suit hangs sloppily or is dirty.

When choosing a suit, make sure the weight of the fabric suits the season: for spring and summer, gabardine, cotton, or microfiber; for fall and winter, worsted wool. A subtle color (dark gray, navy, or black) in a fabric of the right weight is the ideal. When you buy a suit, think less of making the latest fashion statement than of finding something that fits well, feels comfortable, and fits in.

Men's Accessories

THE FINISHING TOUCHES to a man's wardrobe can speak as loudly as his garments and footwear. Think about how well an accessory complements your overall look, and then tone it down if necessary.

Ties, scarves, and handkerchiefs. Neckties and scarves allow for personal expression. Bright colors and flashy designs may be fine at times, but your choice should be in keeping with the occasion. All neckwear should be scrupulously clean (dry-clean ties).

A dress, or chest-pocket, handkerchief is for show only, not for use. The dress handkerchief is appropriate with a suit jacket, casual blazer, or sport jacket and can be included with or without a tie.

Jewelry. Two words sum up the well-dressed man's use of jewelry: minimal and subtle. A wedding band and a watch aren't quite the limit, but they're close. Keep anything else on the hands and wrists to a simple ring and cuff links. Showy chains, especially those with pendants, are not suitable in most workplaces. Bracelets of any kind may be frowned on in conservative businesses, although thin and smartly designed ID bracelets are usually fine.

Wallets. Wallets should be thin enough not to cause an obvious bulge in your back pocket. You might want a very thin wallet for a few credit cards and a money clip for bills, kept in a pants pocket.

Hats. Men's hats nowadays offer ways to express your individuality—a radical shift from the conformity of times past. The choice of hat makes a statement (the fedora says retro; the panama, resort), but every man should know when to take a hat off (see page 46: "Hats Off?").

The baseball-style cap has become entrenched in the wardrobes of millions of men. The billed cap covers the head and shades the eyes from sun and glare. It's relatively connotation-free, unlike the Stetson (appropriate for ranchers and cowboys) and the English sport cap (with its all-things-tweedy overtones). A cap should come off at work (unless it's normally worn on the job), at mealtimes, at the table, in restaurants, and anytime the national anthem is played.

Formal Wear for Men

THERE'S SOME ROOM FOR VARIATION when dressing for a formal event, but in most cases, personal expression is best saved for other occasions (see also page 48: "Invitation Terms"). Putting your own stamp on formal attire more or less defeats the purpose. Events are formal so that a certain tone will prevail; introducing a jarring note that calls attention to itself is what the French call *déclassé*. The following can serve as a checklist of mistakes to avoid when going formal:

At formal occasions, avoid . . .

- Boots or loafers (An exception might be a black-tie affair with a Western or Old West theme.)
- Cuffed pants
- Wearing a cummerbund upside down (The rule is *pleats up*, dating from Henry VII's time, when pleats were turned up to catch bread crumbs.)
- White dinner jackets in cold-weather months, except when you're on a cruise in a hot climate or visiting the tropics
- Puffy or frilly shirts, unless the invitation says "Creative Black Tie"
- Tieless shirts (banded collar or turtleneck), unless the invitation says "Creative Black Tie"
- A pocket handkerchief worn with a boutonniere

If you're a groomsman, avoid . . .

- A top hat worn with anything other than a cutaway for a morning wedding
- Attire dressier than the groom's (a tailcoat when the groom is wearing a tuxedo)
- Shoes that miss the mark: too informal, dirty or scuffed, or vastly different from those of the groom or other groomsmen

Well-groomed Hair

AT ITS MOST BASIC, well-groomed hair is clean, odor free, and untousled (see pages 51–52: "The Importance of Grooming").

Facial hair. Neatness counts, so keep beards and moustaches trimmed. Long or straggly beards or moustaches and extreme styles—Fu Manchus and handlebars—are out of place in many work environments.

Five o'clock stubble. This can be a problem if you have very dark hair or heavy stubble. An electric shaver will spiff you up for a late-afternoon meeting or an early evening out, so keep one handy if you need it.

Wearing clothes that are clean and in good condition is one thing, but style choices are another. Don't shy away from personal expression, but avoid these missteps:

➤ Poorly fitted clothes—too baggy or too tight

➤ Shoes in bad condition

➤ Sandals with a suit

➤ Socks worn with sandals

➤ Socks that show when you're standing, shins that show when you're sitting (due to short socks)

➤ A tie with a short-sleeved shirt

➤ Too much jewelry—heavy on the chains, rings, and bracelets

➤ Dandruff flakes on dark garments

Nose and ear hair. Check regularly to see if your nose hairs need clipping (special blunt-end scissors are made for the purpose) or your earlobes need tweezing. A barber can take care of the ear hair; otherwise, tweeze at home, not in the restroom at work.

Dressing and Grooming for Women

TODAY'S FASHION TRENDS tend to reflect what women really *want* to wear. As women have entered more professions, business attire has evolved to meet the needs of the workplace. Sportswear and casual clothing now constitute a major portion of women's wardrobes, expressing the modern taste for active, informal, and health-conscious lifestyles. Interest in ethnic diversity has broadened dressing options. The advent of unisex dressing has blurred the traditional dividing line between male and female styles, freeing women from many of the restraints of the past.

The etiquette of dressing and grooming now involves few rules but a great deal of emphasis on doing what helps people feel comfortable in their interactions, whether casual or formal. Self-respect and consideration for others are the underlying principles. Respect for religious traditions and for regional and cultural customs also plays an important role in contemporary dressing choices.

Instead of focusing on fashion rules, women's dressing and grooming decisions should begin with evaluation: What is the occasion—a casual get-together, a business event, a fancy party? Who will be there, and what are their general expectations about any dress code for the event? What will make *you* feel good about your appearance?

White can be worn 365 days a year. The old rule about wearing white only between Memorial Day and Labor Day is a thing of the past. Today the question of wearing white applies to the *weight* of fabrics—not the color. Lightweight fabrics (cotton, linen, organdy, and the like) in white and pastels are worn in the warm and hot months, and heavier fabrics known as "winter whites" (woolens, heavy cottons and corduroys, suede, satin, and so forth) are worn in the cool and cold months. Since the country includes such varied climate zones, the times for switching between summer and winter whites will depend on the weather where you are. In January, a woman might board a flight in New York wearing a white wool pantsuit, then change into a white linen outfit after arriving in Los Angeles—and be fashionably correct on both coasts. When going abroad, check local customs and weather forecasts before packing.

What about a guest who wants to wear white at a wedding? It's okay as long as the outfit doesn't compete with the bride's. (For more on wedding attire, see Chapter 40, page 709: "Guest Attire.")

Dressing for the Occasion

THOUGHTFULNESS ABOUT DRESSING IS COMPOUNDED of both self-interest ("Will I look good and make a favorable impression?") and respect for others ("Is my look in keeping with the general standards of the people who will see me?"). Whatever the occasion, a considerate person does not dress in a way that will make other people feel embarrassed, uncomfortable, or socially inadequate.

Dressing by Request

Invitations that include dress instructions are intended to be helpful by indicating the *general* nature of attire that is expected for the event. (See page 48: "Invitation Terms.") When a social invitation doesn't mention dress, the event is usually one that you'll know how to plan for. When in doubt, check with the host or someone else attending. Be attentive to other dressing information on invitations: If you're invited to a masked ball, wear a mask; if the invitation says "pool party," take a bathing suit if you want to swim.

Consider the time of the event. An invitation to a midday barbecue probably means choosing a somewhat more casual outfit than an invitation to an alfresco supper at 6:00. Invitations to business-related functions often don't include dress notations, especially when guests come directly from work and are not expected to change from their normal daytime attire.

How Much Flesh?

"Decorum" is an old but apt word for the ability to do what is fitting and in good taste. Though most Americans seem to welcome the new casualness in dress, they do not confuse freedom of choice and self-expression with an inappropriate display of skin. It may not be fair, but most people will harshly judge a woman, of any age, who reveals too much.

Decorous dressing means knowing that the exercise of personal taste carries with it the responsibility to show concern for the feelings of other people, whatever the situation. Is your neckline attractively décolleté, or does it plunge into lewdness? Will anyone pay attention to your ideas if you wear that stunning see-through blouse to the town meeting? Is a beach outing with parents and children really the place for an itsy-bitsy bikini? Ask yourself questions like these, and common sense will probably supply the courteous answers.

Makeup

TYPES AND DEGREE of facial makeup are matters of personal taste, but the most attractive makeup choices are based on circumstances. Sparing use of cosmetics for a clean, natural look is usually preferable for work and daytime activities, with a bolder look for nighttime social events.

Etiquette issues relate primarily to the application and use of makeup around others. There is a difference between applying makeup, which should be tended to in privacy, and touching up, which can often be handled discreetly around others. Sometimes, it's permissible to freshen lipstick in public if you can do so without being obvious. Be guided by the situation; it's hard to be discreet when dining at a deluxe restaurant or sitting next to your boss in a business meeting. But among friends at a casual occasion, it's fine to make a quick application of lipstick right after a meal. When in doubt, retreat to a restroom or other private place. Applying powders, blushes, and scents; brushing and combing hair; and tending to dental care needs are never done at the table or in public. For any of these health and beauty procedures, excuse yourself and go to the restroom (see also page 51: "The Importance of Grooming").

Women's Accessories

ACCESSORIES CAN BE a woman's best friend—adding interest to a plain outfit or giving day wear a dressier evening look. An elegant hat or a pretty scarf can make the wearer feel more attractive. But too much accessorizing can defeat the purpose by overwhelming both the clothes and the woman wearing them (see also page 45: "Accessories in General").

Can I wear fashion sandals to a formal Valentine's Day dance? If sandals are okay, should I wear stockings?

If you mean dressy, strappy, open-toed party shoes, then yes. Sandal-look high or low heels in leather, suede, satin, or other kinds of textured material are often worn with formal and semiformal winter outfits. You might want to wear stockings (a personal choice) since this is a formal, winter occasion, but make sure no hosiery seams are visible at toes or open heels. If you do wear stockings, be sure they're the sandal-toed kind.

For the Valentine's Day event, take a pass on casual flat sandals. These are generally limited to warm weather, when legs are apt to be bare, and to sporting situations.

Hats

Fashion hats have made something of a comeback in recent years. When a hat is part of a woman's outfit, it may be worn indoors (except in an office). But a large or flamboyant hat should be removed anytime it might obscure other people's view—at the movies or a performance, for example—or is very distracting.

Head coverings worn for religious and cultural reasons are generally not removed indoors. If you are attending a religious service in a tradition outside your own, check with someone of that faith about appropriate headwear for visitors.

Head gear that is part of outerwear—caps, scarves, rain cover-ups, and so on—is normally removed as soon as a woman comes indoors, unless it's part of an outfit. Baseball-style caps are regarded as unisex outerwear, not fashion accessories. They should always be removed indoors. When the national anthem is played at an event, women should take off their caps as a gesture of respect, though traditionally, fashion hats need not be removed (see page 46: "Hats Off?").

Gloves

Like hats, gloves may be part of a fashion look or worn strictly as outerwear. Winter gloves and mittens are removed and tucked away in a pocket or purse as soon as they're no longer needed.

Gloves are often worn for formal and semiformal parties, social luncheons and teas, and special civic and religious ceremonies. Gloves are kept on when going through or standing in a receiving line. As fashion accessories, gloves can be worn until any food or beverages are served, but are always removed for eating and drinking. At a seated dinner, you can lay your gloves on your lap (under your napkin) and then put them on again, if you want, after the meal.

A good mirror is your best friend when it comes to spotting and correcting most of these common fashion flaws:

➢ Clothing that is too tight, too short, or too revealing for the occasion

➢ Dandruff flakes on dark garments

➢ Visible stocking-foot seams with open-toed shoes

➢ Buttoned garments that gap and show skin or underwear better left hidden

➢ Overly dressy or too-high heels with casual clothes like jeans

➢ Wearing a dress meant for evening during the day

➢ Jewelry that jingles or clangs so much that others are annoyed

➢ Torn hems and linings that show

The length of gloves is generally a matter of personal taste and tradition, though mid-length and full-length fashion gloves are usually reserved for dressier affairs. Jewelry, including watches, is worn underneath gloves.

Corsages

A corsage is generally a gift for a special occasion, and the giver may consult with you about flower and color choice. If asked, try to provide several options. Should you be allergic to certain flowers, by all means say so.

When a corsage is worn at the shoulder, it's pinned so that the flowers face upward, just as they grow in nature. Corsages may also be worn at the waistline, positioned in the most attractive manner. If a corsage is a surprise and doesn't flatter your outfit, be gracious and wear it if you can. A good solution in a case like this might be to pin the flowers to your purse.

Wristlets are corsages with elastic bands and are worn like bracelets. Although fairly popular with teenage girls, wristlets are not often worn by women past school age. If you receive a wristlet, you may pin it to your outfit (clipping off the elastic makes this easy) or attach it to your purse.

Part Two

Relationships

Chapter Six

Dating

Oনce upon a time, he asked her out and then paid for everything. She followed his agenda with dewy-eyed appreciation. Males were chivalrous; females were demure and coy. That was the ideal back in the *Ozzie and Harriet* 1950s, when dating was regarded as the first step in a natural progression toward marriage and family.

What a long way we've come! Dating by the rules has given way to more casual encounters and laissez-faire relationships. Women can ask men out and pay for the date; men can be courted with the open fervor that was once their exclusive province; and marriage is no longer the immediate objective for all single people.

Whether today's casual dating is an improvement is a matter of ongoing debate. Just mention dating among single people, and reactions will range across the full spectrum of emotions. Lots of singles complain that it is harder than ever to meet potential partners who share their interests. Others opt out entirely, saying that their busy careers don't leave time for the dating rat race. And across the country, single people express their longing for clear-cut standards and expectations—something between the strict dating rules of their parents' and grandparents' day and the seeming free-for-all confusion of modern dating.

In the process of striving for balance in their relationships, many single people are discovering that good manners are one of the most effective ways to bridge the gap between too many restrictions and too few. Commitment to the principles of respect for oneself and others, consideration, and integrity won't guarantee success in dating, but it can make the process a lot more enjoyable.

Begin With Some Self-appraisal

Whether you've been dating fairly routinely or you're returning to the dating scene, it's a good idea to take stock of your own attitudes. Ask yourself how you define a date. Your expectations will probably change over time. For example, the dating customs of high school or college may not be suitable for dating in the career-building years. And those getting back to dating after a number of years often need to readjust their thinking.

When two people approach a date with widely differing expectations, the way is open for misunderstandings and hurt feelings. So consider your goals. What do you want from dating? Do you think of a date as a pleasant interlude, or are you hoping for a lasting relationship?

Honestly appraising your own attitudes—and evaluating past experiences, good and bad—should enable you to be more sensitive to others and their needs. Here are some basic guidelines that can help make virtually every date pleasant (at minimum) for both parties.

Treat people as individuals. Stereotyped thinking ("All men are afraid of commitment"; "All women are fickle") is a monumental barrier to successful dating. There's a good adage to remember: A person is not his or her group; it's not possible to judge individuals before you know them.

Be realistic. There's no perfect man or woman, so when setting standards, don't place the bar so high that it's impossible for anyone to leap. If you expect every date to be Mr. or Ms. Right, you're sure to be disappointed.

Communicate. No date should be expected to read minds, so participate in dating decisions. When questions about objectives come up, be honest and straightforward. A partner deserves to know whether you want to go out for the sheer fun of it or your goal is a long-term commitment.

Show respect. Courteous manners speak volumes about your attitudes toward the people you go out with and your own self-respect (see page 71: "The Etiquette of a Date").

Adapt to change. The willingness to adapt to new or different dating mores expands your opportunities for friendships and more personal relationships. Problems may arise from differences in customs among regions and cultures. For instance, a person from a conservative community may find the customs of big-city dating more spontaneous than he or she is used to.

Be gracious. There's no reason to make another person feel uncomfortable or inadequate because a date doesn't go as you hoped. When a date turns into a disaster, the blame rarely lies with one person alone.

Where People Meet

INTRODUCTIONS THROUGH FRIENDS AND COLLEAGUES are still the favored way of meeting other singles. Group dating (which may mean going out with a mixed group of unattached people or pairing off within a group) is very popular. Double-dating and matching single people at dinner parties are good ways to "set up" friends without the awkwardness many adults associate with blind dating. A surprising number of singles report happy introductions made by family members, so don't be too quick to dismiss a parent's or sibling's suggestions.

There are lots of places to meet—work, school, special-interest clubs and volunteer organizations, places of worship, cultural events, sporting venues, the health club. Bars and coffeehouses show up in surveys of the dating population, though the bar scene is more attractive to young adults. Internet dating services and personal ads have made inroads, in part because they allow people to get to know each other behind a veil of anonymity (see page 66: "On-line Dating Tips").

Professional matchmaking services use modern methods to pair up clients according to interests and objectives. Religious and social groups have entered the dating fray by providing opportunities for singles to meet. There are innovations such as "speed dating"—a combination of the old-style college mixer and musical chairs, in which a room full of singles talk one-on-one for a limited time, then move on to the next person under the stopwatch.

In other words, the ways to meet other singles are almost endless. But it's up to you to make the most of your opportunities, and the following advice is offered as a good starting point:

Go out. It's easy to get stuck in the home–job–home-again rut. To meet other people, you have to go where they are—not to hunt for dates but to seek out places where people like you gather and participate in activities that interest you.

Be observant. A lot of chances to meet are thrown away simply because people fail to notice a nice smile or a pleasant comment.

Introduce yourself. It's a scene from a movie: Two strangers strike up a conversation. There's more than a spark of interest. They part. And when it's too late, they realize that they didn't exchange names. What might have been the romance of the century is brought down by a breach of fundamental etiquette. (See Chapter 2, page 16: "Self-introductions.")

Take reasonable risks. No one should ever drive off to a secluded location with a person they just met, but a cup of coffee at a close-by restaurant might be the perfect way to extend your conversation. It's not advisable to give your home phone number or address to a stranger, but you might give a work number that goes through a switchboard, your cell phone number, or e-mail address. Exercise rational caution, but also be open to follow-up when a first meeting seems propitious.

An important caveat: When using personal ads, on-line matching services, and other types of introduction services, keep private any information you receive from someone who contacts you. It is unethical to share names (real names, pseudonyms, or Internet "handles") and addresses with anyone else.

On-line Dating Tips

On-line dating can begin with chance contacts in chat rooms and on message boards. But these electronic meeting places can pose dangers since the information that chat partners provide is unscreened and often untrue. As a result, millions of people are turning to commercial on-line dating services, which function much like the computer dating services of the 1980s. For a fee, singles submit personal profiles and photos, and the service matches its clients based on its set of criteria (age, education, location, work, personal interests, physical characteristics, etc.). Clients receive the profiles and pictures of other clients whom they might like to contact. Identities are confidential, and it's up to the client to decide whether to pursue the contact and arrange a face-to-face meeting. The largest on-line services are open to anyone who pays their fee. Other commercial services are more exclusive and usually more expensive, with memberships limited to people in special groups—ethnic, religious, professional, and so forth.

Despite the promised securities, on-line dating services are quite new, and safety measures and client etiquette can still be regarded as "under construction." The following suggestions should help service users get the most for their investment of time and money:

➤ Use a reputable on-line dating service. Check it out before you sign on.

➤ Be honest when you write your profile, and post an up-to-date photo. Proofread your profile carefully.

➤ Respond when someone contacts you, even when you aren't interested—just a quick message expressing thanks and a courteous regret will do. If you're no longer available, say so, but don't use this excuse if you continue to use the service and your cybername.

➤ If someone uses inappropriate or offensive language, you shouldn't reply. If the approaches continue, notify your service.

➤ Protect yourself by not giving out any personal information—last name, home address, phone number, e-mail address, or office address and number.

➤ Arrange first meetings in a public place and limit their duration. An hour should be long enough to decide if you want to meet again. It's advisable to tell a friend or family member where you'll be and how long you expect the meeting to last.

Some services are better than others at screening out undesirable contacts, and a smart user will take other people's profiles with a grain of salt. It's human to exaggerate one's good points, and especially easy on the anonymous Internet. If you're interested in a person but not quite sure about his or her claims, you can save messages and then look back for inconsistencies that indicate a lack of honesty. Trust your instincts and back away from any contact that seems odd or makes you uncomfortable.

"Setting Up" Friends and Acquaintances

A woman at work shares an interest with your good buddy and you think they'd enjoy meeting. How can you set up a meeting that doesn't sound like the dreaded blind date? First, ask yourself if the two people are likely to be compatible; consider their total personalities, not just a single common interest. If you think they'll get along, try to arrange a meeting that includes more than just the two people. Include them in a group get-together, plan a double date, or ask them both to lunch and see what happens. If you can't organize an introductory meeting, ask if they'd like to exchange phone numbers, but don't give out numbers until both agree. However you go about it, avoid overselling with exaggerated descriptions ("She's absolutely gorgeous" or "He tells the funniest stories ever"). Your goal is to introduce two people you like, not to play marriage broker.

Asking and Answering

IN THE PAST, the man almost always initiated a date, and exceptions were few and far between. Times have changed, but perhaps not as much as many people think. Surveys and studies of contemporary dating habits indicate that men still like to do the asking and women still enjoy being asked. But like so many dating customs today, the issue of who asks is largely situational, and a woman is certainly free to ask out a man.

Our times may be more relaxed, but good manners are still one of the most effective means to assure that you make a good impression.

Choose a convenient time to ask. Try to find a time when the person isn't too busy or engaged with other people. If you phone, calling very early in the morning or very late at night probably wouldn't be convenient. Calling the person at work might be a problem, so keep the conversation brief.

Ask straightforwardly and give the necessary information. "What are you doing after work on Wednesday?" is too general. Instead, say, "Would you like to go to dinner with me Wednesday night? I thought we might try that new Indonesian restaurant." This invitation politely gets to the point and gives the person a clear idea of what the date will entail. Even for last-minute invitations, a date needs to know what you plan to do and at what time.

Discuss the arrangements. Where will you meet? If in a public location, agree on a definite spot. Will you be paying or is it a Dutch treat date? (See page 69: "The 'Who

67

Dating

Pays?' Dilemma.") Will you take your date home? You might give some information about what to wear. Also, alert your date if you'll be meeting a group of friends.

Call back and confirm. A quick call to confirm the details of an imminent date shows concern and prevents embarrassments like showing up at the wrong time or the wrong place. A confirming e-mail is okay, if you think it will be read.

Accept a "no" without argument. Chances are that a turndown is not a personal rejection, but even if it is, there's no reason to quiz the other person about his or her motives or demand an explanation. Be attuned to the person's attitude and tone. An astute observer of social cues often gets a sense of whether the person would like another opportunity to go out; if you sense real interest, try again later.

However you ask, language matters. If you say, "I'd like to take you out," most people will interpret you to mean that the date is your treat. Saying "Maybe we could meet for lunch" is more open-ended and could mean going Dutch. Be aware of current terms that have double meanings. To many people, "hooking up" simply means getting together, but to others it could have sexual connotations. Be cautious, avoid ambiguous language, and say what you really mean.

Saying "Yes" or "No"

The decision to accept a date or not is totally personal. Whatever your answer, it should be said with respect and grace. Accepting and refusing should include a "thank you." Though the invitation may be stated a little awkwardly or shyly, the person is saying that you're special and he or she wants to spend some time with you. Regardless of your opinion of the person, that's a high compliment.

If you can't reply on the spot but would like to say "yes," explain the difficulty (like a tentative commitment to do something else or a possible work conflict) and tell the person that you will get back to him or her. It's rarely necessary to take longer than a few hours to check your schedule and call back. However, if changing or canceling existing plans will inconvenience others (for example, backing out of a dinner party or leaving houseguests on their own), then you should definitely say "no" to the date.

If you want to accept but have a prior commitment, explain. It's fine to suggest a future get-together. ("I have to work on the Hayes project all weekend, but maybe we could get together next week.") You might be able to agree on a rain-check date, but if not, you'll have signaled your interest.

What about someone who can't take "no" for an answer? Most people will get the message after a couple of rejections. But if they're persistent, you need to be firm—not cruel. Make your feelings clear: "It's flattering that you want to go out with me, Ned, but I'm not interested in dating you." When there's a specific, truthful reason, state it: "I've made it a rule never to date anyone I work with" or "I'm seeing someone exclusively." Avoid any remark that might give the person false hope. ("I'm so busy working on my thesis that I can't go out with anyone right now" may lead to more unwanted offers in the future.)

Deciding whether to accept a date is not an excuse to grill the person who asks. Digging for details about his or her finances is out of place. So are prying inquiries about employment and family background. Be careful when asking questions such as "Where are you taking me?" and "Who else is going to be there?" Such queries are often innocent but can imply (especially if you don't know the person well) that your interest is only in being seen in the "right" places with the "right" crowd. You should ask reasonable questions, but subjecting anyone to a cross-exam is hardly gracious.

Whatever you say, don't stoop to personal insults or make up excuses that will come back to haunt you. If you discuss the invitation and/or the person with others, be positive. Demeaning a person who asked for a date goes beyond discourtesy; it's mean-spirited and immature.

The "Who Pays?" Dilemma

MUCH OF THE CONFUSION about today's dating customs revolves around the question of who pays. There's fairly widespread acceptance of the notion that women can pay, but it's not universal. In some cultures and regions, the "man always pays" rule is strictly observed, especially on first dates and in the early stages of a relationship. Older men and women who grew up with the "man pays" rule might find it hard to conform to the new attitude. There are egos to consider: A woman who makes an issue about picking up the check because she earns more should probably take a few lessons in the dynamics of male–female relationships.

Following are some helpful guidelines based on sensitivity to other people's feelings and plain common sense.

> ➤ For a first date at least, the person who asks should pay unless both parties agree in advance to share expenses. By saying that you want to "take out" or "treat" someone, you make it clear that you intend to pay.

> ➤ If the person who isn't paying suggests doing something in addition to or more costly than the original plans—for example, going to a club after the other person has already paid for a nice dinner and concert tickets—then she or he should offer to pay or split the extra costs.

> ➤ When a date "just happens" and you aren't sure who asked whom, it's reasonable to suggest sharing the costs. This doesn't always mean splitting everything straight down the middle. He might pay for dinner, and she could get the movie tickets.

Dating

➤ If you really aren't sure who'll pay, be prepared by taking cash or credit cards. You can offer to cover your share, but don't make an issue if the other person clearly intends to pay.

➤ Paying for a date does not obligate the other person to do anything in return. To expect or demand any kind of intimacy because you picked up the check is totally out of bounds.

Paying in a group. When people go out as a group, it's generally accepted that each person pays for himself. Couples within the group might pool their funds or pay separately, or one might pay for both. The point is to settle the question before the occasion—and certainly before the check arrives. Nothing can spoil a fun time faster than quibbling over the bill.

If you're new to a group, follow the lead of established participants. If the group customarily divides the food and drink check evenly, you shouldn't demand separate checks or a to-the-penny accounting of your costs—unless you don't want to be included again. But if you regularly meet with an established group and you routinely order less than the others (for example, you drink water and they drink wine), it's fine to ask for a little relief. When a group pools money for tips, it's usually easiest to divide the amount equally based on the entire bill, even if one or two people consumed a little less. Such expenses usually even out in the long run.

Breaking a Date

AS WITH ALL SOCIAL INVITATIONS, once you've agreed to a date, it is unacceptable to break it except for illness, medical emergency, a death in the family, or an unexpected and unavoidable business or family conflict. If your job is on the line unless you agree to work overtime, you have a legitimate excuse. An academic conflict, like a research paper, might pass muster if it came up at the last minute. For single parents, any emergency involving their children must take precedence. But changing one's mind or getting a "better" offer is no excuse.

If you must break a date, quickly get in touch with the person and explain the problem. A personal call is best, but you might have to leave a message or use e-mail if your date is difficult to reach. If the person offers to help (say, driving you to the hospital to see a sick relative), you can agree if it's comfortable for you. Otherwise, tell the person that you'll get back to him. You might reschedule the date, but when that's not possible—as when you're dealing with illness or a family emergency—you should call or e-mail the person at some point and alleviate any worries he or she may have.

It is inexcusable to stand anyone up. Should you be genuinely unable to notify the person (as might happen in a serious family situation), get in touch just as soon as you can, explain, apologize, and do what you can to make amends.

There are bad dates, and there are people who date badly. Don't be surprised if you recognize at least some of the thoughtless and self-absorbed types in the categories below.

"My way or the highway" dates. These petty dictators have to be in control. The person who asks usually has something in mind, but a willingness to consult and compromise shows genuine respect.

Abandoners. Treating dates like hot potatoes by leaving them to fend for themselves at social gatherings is a dating felony. Being attentive to a date and making introductions to others is common decency.

Social show-offs. The guy who thinks it's suave to bully a head waiter, the gal who drops the names of celebrities as if they were her dearest friends—these show-offs are rude and boring.

Outrageous flirts. Noticing other people is natural. But ogling every man or woman in the room shows disrespect for one's date. The outrageous flirt sends a message as obvious as a neon sign: "I'm out for myself. Don't trust me."

Touchers. In public and private, they treat dates like cuddly toys—stroking, hugging, squeezing, and hanging on when the touches aren't welcome. Lacking all sense of personal space, touchers apparently never learned the difference between a comfortable physical gesture and incessant grabbing, grasping, and groping.

Dates who live in the past. Her last boyfriend was a control freak. His first wife ran off with the pool man. Interesting . . . to a point. But their endless remembrances of relationships past hardly flatter the person who is with them. Dull, dull, dull.

Promise-breakers. Some troglodytes still end a date by promising to call when they have no intention to do so. It's such an easy promise to make, and so deeply hurtful when it's false.

The Etiquette of a Date

THE RULES OF DATING MAY have changed, but not the fundamental courtesies. The etiquette basics that you probably learned in high school still apply, but it never hurts to review these key points before starting out.

Be on time. Arrive when you said you would. Five minutes late may be okay, but if you're going to be any longer, call and give your date a reasonable idea of the length of the delay.

When your date is picking you up, be ready to go. Expecting a date to entertain himself or herself for a half hour while you dress is like saying that your time is more valuable than theirs.

When you're meeting at a place other than home, call if you're unavoidably delayed. If you can't catch the person at home or work and if he or she doesn't have a cell phone, you may be able to call a restaurant or theater box office and get a message delivered. But relaying messages is unreliable—and impossible when you're meeting in a busy public place like a park or outside a theater. So be serious about punctuality, and don't let this fundamental courtesy slide after you've had a few dates or the relationship becomes steady.

Go to the door. When picking up dates at their houses or apartments, don't park at the curb and honk or call on your cell phone to let them know you're waiting. This behavior is acceptable only if you and your date have agreed in advance. If you're meeting at a workplace, let your date know that you've arrived and wait patiently (and inconspicuously) if she or he must finish some final tasks. If you initiated the date and you're meeting in a public place, try to arrive a few minutes early, so you can greet your date.

Review your plans. On a first date, reviewing plans can be a conversation starter. On any date, it's respectful to discuss any changes in the original plans. If you asked your date out for an Italian dinner and decided at the last minute that you'd rather have Thai food, bring it up as an option. Your date may agree, or you may be able to settle on a compromise choice. If you or your date is responsible to others—young children, elderly or ill relatives—be sure that they and/or their caregivers know where you're going and how to reach you.

∼ A Good, Old-fashioned Courtesy ∼

When you arrive at a date's home, be prepared to graciously meet and greet anyone else in the household—parents, siblings and other family members, roommates, children. Be especially attentive to a date's children; they need to feel that their mother or father is going out with a nice person. Don't go overboard; just a few minutes of chat shows real interest in others.

Don't be offended by personal questions. Call on your tact, common sense, and good humor if the questions are too personal. Should you be asked about a prior marriage, for instance, you might say, "My ex is a fine person, and the divorce was best for both of us." Then change the subject.

When someone is coming to your home, you have the obligation to introduce the person to others. Even if you aren't quite ready to go, meet your date at the door, make introductions, and help get some conversation started.

On the Date

Good manners on both sides can go a long way toward making even a so-so date more enjoyable for both people.

Transportation. The person who makes the date is normally responsible for transportation. If you're driving, be sure your vehicle is clean inside and out, gassed up, and in good running order. If you'll be taking cabs, have the phone number(s) of one or more reliable taxi companies at hand. If you use public transportation, it's a good idea to check schedules in advance; also be sure you have the necessary change, tokens, or tickets.

Conversation. People naturally worry about what to talk about on a first or second date, and you'll probably keep it light until you get to know one another. Don't think you have to be a brilliant conversationalist or avoid obvious topics. There's nothing wrong with commenting on the weather, which seems to interest many people these days, or asking about her job or his hobbies to get a conversation going.

Wit and erudition may be great, but the key to successful small talk is *listening*. Focus on what the other person is saying—not what you plan to say next. Listen for clues to your date's interests and cues for new topics. Your comment about the rain might elicit the fact that he's canceled a couple of camping trips because of the inclement weather. Now you know that he's a fan of the outdoors.

Keep up your end of the conversation. Good conversation is like a tennis volley: The only way to sustain it is for both people to return the ball. The usual advice is to "just be yourself"—a good plan, unless being yourself means monopolizing the con-

~ JUST COMMON SENSE ~

Opening Doors and Holding Chairs

Whether a man should open doors and hold chairs for a woman depends largely on whether the woman will appreciate these gestures. (It's fair to say that most younger women today are not inclined to sit in a car while a date walks around to open the door.) The man's best bet is to ask: "May I get the door for you?" or "Can I hold your chair?" By leaving the choice to her, he doesn't have to guess about her preference. The woman should respond politely ("Yes, thank you" or "No, but thank you. I can manage it"). Like so many matters of modern etiquette, a little communication between the people involved is the logical way to resolve the problem.

Opening doors at a restaurant or cinema—or entering revolving doors and turnstiles—is generally a matter of who gets to the door first. If the man is encumbered or has a physical limitation, a thoughtful woman will hold the door, just as she would for anyone.

versation or, conversely, failing to take part or respond to your companion. (See also Chapter 19, page 280: "The Basics.")

There are some topics that are best to steer clear of at first:

> **Personal money matters.** Asking about a date's income is out of line. So is disclosing your own financial status, particularly in an effort to impress.

> **Previous romantic relationships.** Talking about the wonderful or awful qualities of past loves is very annoying because the person you're with is likely to feel that he or she is being compared to old flames.

> **Gossip.** It's one thing to talk about the latest antics of a pop star but quite another to tell tales on mutual acquaintances. A person who complains too much about coworkers and bosses risks being perceived as a whiner.

> **Politics and religion.** These subjects aren't off-limits but are better when eased into. A first date is the last place to campaign, preach, or proselytize.

Dining. Surveys show that most dates involve some kind of meal. Whether it's a leisurely dinner at a fine restaurant or a quick bite at the local deli, good table manners will make a good impression.

People usually place their own orders in restaurants, but if your date is familiar with the menu or cuisine and you're not, you can ask for recommendations. When the place is pricey, thoughtful dates stick to the middle price range unless their dates do the ordering. When it's Dutch treat, order what you can afford. If you'd like wine with your meal, don't feel that you have to be an expert; the wine steward or your waiter can make suggestions based on your food choices and your budget.

Both people should speak up if they have real problems with or aversions to certain foods or cuisines. A vegetarian or a person with religious restrictions or food allergies should let the other person know when he or she accepts a dinner or lunch date. No one should ever make negative comments about a date's food choices.

When you accept a date that includes a meal—at a restaurant or prepared by your date—make the effort to eat. If you're on a diet or normally eat light meals, tell your date, so you don't hurt his feelings by eating nothing or very little.

Bringing It to a Close

When you ask someone out, it's your responsibility to see that she or he gets home safely, and the best way is to escort your date to the door. People may just go their separate ways, but a considerate person will see that his date has a ride or will wait with her until her transportation arrives. The fact is that women on their own are more vulnerable to violence, especially at night, so a man should normally see a date to her car or escort her through dangerous or poorly lighted areas such as parks, parking lots, and streets. Don't allow a date who is intoxicated to drive or wander off on his or her own.

In some circumstances, it makes sense to call a date later and be sure he or she got home in one piece. Tell the person that you'll be calling or ask him to call you. It may

The emergence of HIV/AIDS in the 1980s and the increase in other sexually transmitted diseases (STDs) have transformed the issue of disclosing and discussing sexual histories with a potential intimate partner. What was once an extremely embarrassing discussion is now a matter of life and death. Despite advances in AIDS treatments, the disease cannot be cured, and many STDs have lifelong health consequences.

Admittedly, it's not easy to raise the subject, but it is absolutely essential whenever a relationship is likely to include sex. There are ways to approach the subject. With someone you've only recently met, it's perfectly okay to say, "I'm sorry, but until we know each other better and feel comfortable talking about sex, we just can't get involved in a sexual relationship. There's too much at stake." If the other person feels insulted, he or she may need more time and better education about HIV/AIDS and STDs. If a person tries to pursue sexual intimacies without revealing his or her sexual history, he or she doesn't have your best interests at heart. Your life and health aren't worth the risk.

Honest discussion isn't a matter of prying; there's no reason to name names or give the intimate details of other relationships. The purpose is to disclose everything that can affect a partner's health and life. Both people should be willing to have blood tests and medical checkups and to exchange the results. For a number of reasons, people may lie about test results, so a literal exchange of records is not only reasonable but advisable.

Men and women are both responsible for condom use, and each partner has the right to insist that condoms are worn. A woman should never hesitate to provide condoms if her partner is unprepared.

seem as if you're acting like a parent, but imagine how you would feel if something happened and you could have helped but didn't.

Whether the date has been a success or not, both people should express their thanks graciously. But unless you really intend to get in touch again, don't make any promises you can't keep. Remember that a person with integrity won't discuss the personal details of any date with anyone else.

Dating and the Workplace

THESE DAYS, THE WORKPLACE IS an obvious place for people to meet and personal relationships to bloom. But before starting an office romance, workers should check their employers' fraternization policies. Many businesses don't have problems with employees dating other employees, but difficulties can arise if the relationship interferes with work or causes conflicts with other employees. Ask your supervisor or human resources department for information. (Though it is not nearly so common as people may think, there may be severe penalties for office romance, including transfer or dismissal.)

Depending on the circumstances, dating a person you work with can be problematic even if there's no official policy. Dating a superior can raise issues of favoritism and unfair promotion. The situation can be trickier for the superior, who may risk running afoul of sexual harassment and discrimination policies and laws. A recent survey by the American Management Association found that sixty-seven percent of respondents (managers and employers) okayed dating among coworkers, but less than twenty-five percent approved of dating between superiors and subordinates.

In general, the etiquette of dating a coworker is to keep the relationship low-key when at work. It's fine to let people know, if you want, but avoid displays that are distracting or offensive to others (customers as well as clients) and can reflect poorly on the business and its management. Maintain a professional attitude until the workday is over. (See also Chapter 44, page 766: "About Sexual Harassment")

Sending Gifts to the Office

The date was great, and you want to send something that says, "I had a wonderful time." Is it appropriate to send a bouquet of roses or balloons to her or his workplace? The answer is: maybe. It depends on how such gifts will be regarded by the employer. Some places have fairly strict rules about displaying personal items, and some discourage non-work-related deliveries to employees. Can a large item be accommodated in the workplace? A person with a private office or cubicle probably has space for a vase of flowers, but someone on a retail floor or in an assembly area may have no more than a locker or cubby. If you aren't sure about workplace policies or accommodations, have flowers and the like delivered to the person's home or send something smaller. A nice card with a personal message can be just as impressive as a large bouquet because each says that you enjoyed the date and you're a thoughtful person.

Breaking Up

ENDING A RELATIONSHIP IS HARD. Ending it well may seem impossible, but it can be done if both people stay true to the principles of respect, consideration, and integrity. When the decision is mutual, breaking up can be more wistful than painful. But when one person ends the relationship, he or she is responsible for giving the news in a manner that shows genuine concern for the other person. No matter how uncomfortable the situation, there are certain decencies that must be observed.

Meet personally. Someone you've been close to is owed a face-to-face meeting. Don't use anyone else as an intermediary. Don't resort to a "Dear John" or "Dear Jane" letter. Don't e-mail or fax or send a text message. Phoning may be necessary when time and distance are a problem, but don't leave a brush-off message or voice mail. If ending the relationship is your choice, face up to it.

Meet privately. To deliberately stage a breakup in a place where other people are close by—hoping that the presence of others will keep things calm—is cowardly.

Get to the point. Don't try to ease the blow by taking the person out for a nice time, then dropping the axe at the last minute. The person will probably feel that he or she has been made a fool of.

Avoid blaming. Neither party will benefit from cutting reviews of their faults and failings. Blaming or hurling insults is childish and cruel. So is presenting phony or superficial excuses. The other person may say hurtful things, particularly if the breakup is a shock, but you don't have to respond in kind.

See to the other person's well-being. Be sure that he or she is reasonably in control before leaving. A person who is extremely upset or angry is not in the best shape to drive or go off on her own. A breakup may be volatile, but it doesn't excuse ignoring concerns for another human being's safety and welfare.

The details of a breakup should be kept private. What's past is over, and talking disrespectfully about a former partner will reflect on the one who does the talking.

Getting Back to Dating

FOR SOMEONE WHO HAS LOST a spouse through divorce or death or experienced the breakup of a long-standing, steady relationship, it can be very difficult to begin dating again, and people often put their social lives on hold. There are many reasons not to date for some time—to adjust to the single life and avoid "rebounding," to heal old wounds and rebuild trust after a failed relationship, to get established as chief wage earner and head of household. Widows and widowers need time to grieve the loss of a beloved spouse and may feel that going out with someone else is a kind of betrayal.

But sooner or later, most people decide it's time to take a chance and reenter the dating pool. When that time comes, it can be helpful to consider the following do's and don'ts:

   Do give yourself permission to enjoy yourself and the companionship of other adults. Dating per se is not a lifelong commitment. It's an opportunity to get to know someone else, do something that may not be routine for you, and have fun for a few hours.
   Do understand that times have changed. If you're nervous about the new dating rituals, talk with some of your contemporaries who date to get a clearer picture of how things are done in your social group. Dating customs can vary considerably among regional, cultural, and age groups, and you'll feel more confident when you know what to expect.
   Do set fundamental standards for yourself and your dates. Decide what you hope to gain from dating—friendship or something more. Think about the

qualities you look for in potential companions or partners and evaluate your own assets. You'll probably discover that your expectations of others have changed radically since your earlier dating days and that you have a lot more to offer than you were aware of.

Don't be embarrassed to express your feelings and preferences and to ask questions of a date. If you're more comfortable sharing expenses, say so. Be willing to offer suggestions and alternatives when someone asks what you'd like to do or suggests an activity that you'd rather not do. If a date proposes seeing a movie that you've already seen, speak up. A person who asks you out wants you to have a good time, not to suffer in silence.

Do tell dates about your family responsibilities. If you have children (whether you're the custodial or noncustodial parent) or if you're the caregiver for a family member, it's only fair to tell anyone you date about your responsibilities. Besides, it's better to know at the outset whether someone is or isn't interested in a relationship that comes complete with a family.

Do let your children know you're dating and introduce them to your dates. Be aware that children—of any age—naturally have questions stemming from concern for their parent or worries about how a new relationship could affect the family. Children need a lot of reassurance, but also need to be helped to understand that their parent has a right to a social life.

~ Committed Relationships ~

When dating seems to be leading to something more serious—a monogamous or live-in relationship or an engagement—it's essential that both people are in agreement about the course they're taking. Open communication is the only way to go.

In close relationships, people too often make the mistake of *assuming* that their own feelings are shared. She assumes that because she isn't seeing anyone else, he isn't either—until she sees him with another woman. Or he assumes that because he wants to live together, she does, too—only to learn that she won't give up her independence without marriage. Such misunderstandings are too common, yet they're preventable if people will talk with one another.

Taking another person's feelings for granted violates the fundamental principles of respect and consideration. These basics apply to all aspects of a committed relationship, including good manners. Just because people have become close, they shouldn't forget to be considerate and courteous to one another. If the relationship is to thrive, it will be firmly planted in the Golden Rule: *Treat the person you care about as you want to be treated.*

Chapter Seven

Separation and Divorce

WHEN EMILY POST was writing her groundbreaking book *Etiquette* in the early 1920s, divorce was so unusual that it was rarely mentioned in polite company. In the U.S. today, about forty-five percent of all first marriages end in divorce, as do an even larger percentage of remarriages. This increase in the occurrence of divorce has not made marital breakups any less hurtful for the participants, but divorce and separation no longer carry the social stigma they did in Emily's day. Still, the decision to end a marriage is perhaps the most stressful a couple can make, particularly if they have children, and the process can be heartbreaking for everyone. Good manners may seem like a minor concern, but attending to important details and taking time to nurture other relationships can truly help both during and after the painful passage from married to single.

Separation

A SEPARATION MAY BE EITHER a legal decision, spelled out in writing, or a private, less structured choice made by a married couple. In either case, the goal is often to live apart while working out problems in hopes of reconciliation. Usually one spouse moves out of the family home. (He or she will take personal belongings, but the couple's home and possessions are not altered except by mutual agreement.) Their children normally remain in the home with the parent who stays, though there are situations when separated spouses continue to live under the same roof.

Whatever the living arrangements, a separation is an upheaval and can be traumatic for the couple and especially for their children. Together, if possible, parents need to explain what's happening before one parent leaves the home. Children tend to equate separation with divorce—and the end of life as they know it. Parents shouldn't encourage false hopes, but it's essential to be honest. Avoid involving children in issues they can't understand, and never expect a child of any age to act as a go-between or to favor one parent over the other.

Try to maintain as normal a schedule as possible; the absent spouse should not be an absentee parent. Like divorce, a separation threatens a child's sense of stability, so his ties with grandparents and other close adults can be especially important and should be nurtured. Separated parents also need to be alert to other life changes that occur during a separation or divorce; a family breakup is likely to be doubly stressful for a child who is entering day care or first grade or a teenager who is applying to or preparing to leave for college.

The Etiquette of Separation

The following etiquette issues frequently arise during a separation.

Telling others. A separation is not publicly announced. A couple should explain the situation to family and close friends, and word will spread. If the couple reunites, there is no public announcement.

Names and rings. The wife continues to use her husband's name (if she has taken it), and both spouses usually continue to wear their wedding rings.

Change of address. If the separation is lengthy, the spouse who moves out of the home should give his or her new address and phone number to anyone who needs to know, such as an employer.

Social invitations. The couple usually refuses any invitations addressed to "Mr. and Mrs." If they do attend the same social or business functions, they should behave as normally as possible and not draw others into their problems. Most adults make accommodations for separated couples by not inviting them both to the same social events. So don't get upset if mutual friends fail to include you in a party to which your spouse has been invited. Chances are, the friends are not choosing sides but are trying to avoid a difficult situation for everyone. Your time will probably come.

∾ Dating During a Separation or Divorce ∾

During a separation or the process of divorcing, spouses are free to carry on their social lives. Dating and serious relationships outside the marriage, however, should be carefully considered. Until the divorce decree is handed down by the court, the couple are still married and should show respect for one another. Questionable personal behavior during any period of separation can also have serious legal, financial, and custodial repercussions. Divorce laws differ from state to state, so it's important to consult with a knowledgeable lawyer before doing anything that may jeopardize your situation. If dating might cause problems, you can attend social and public events on your own, with other couples, or with a group of friends. Explain the situation to anyone who wants to arrange a date for you to social activities.

Divorce

DIVORCE IS AN EMOTIONAL EARTHQUAKE; the shock waves extend far beyond the couple at the center and continue long after the original break. While there's no way to generalize about feelings or predict behaviors, it's common for individuals who are divorcing to become introspective, sometimes forgetting about the impact of their decision on the people who love and care about them. Yet thinking about and acting on behalf of others can be a kind of release that opens a path out of self-absorption, pain, and regret.

Children must come first. A divorce means not just that their parents are no longer living together but that the secure world children have always depended on is shattered (see "Separation," above). Divorce challenges other close relationships, notably those with family and friends. Most people genuinely want to be helpful, but they need guidance from the divorcing spouses. Consideration for other people includes not overburdening them with your problems, showing at least some interest in their lives, and not expecting them to choose between you and your spouse. Despite your best efforts, however, some friendships may not survive, but this is one of the unfortunate side effects of divorce.

Telling the Children First

When a family breaks apart, children feel anxiety, loss, and perhaps guilt. Even when a marriage has been volatile or abusive, most children still want their parents to stay together. Although studies show that the long-term consequences of divorce may not be as damaging as once thought, the best results are achieved when parents are willing to set aside personal animosities and cooperate in all their decisions about and dealings with their children.

Children of any age must be the first to hear of their parents' separation or divorce, and the news should come directly from the parents. Loving parents will not delegate

～ Wedding Rings and Gifts ～

Spouses do not continue to wear wedding rings after a divorce, and many remove their rings when it's clear that the marriage cannot be saved or when legal proceedings are initiated. Some divorced people transfer their wedding rings to the right hand. A wife's engagement ring belongs to her, not to the former husband. Often engagement rings are stored away and later passed on to children. It's also acceptable to wear an engagement ring on the right hand or to have the stones reset and worn in other jewelry.

Divorced couples do not return wedding gifts. However, if a marriage is annulled and the couple never lived together, gifts should be returned.

this responsibility to anyone else. It's best if the couple can talk with their children together and reassure them that Mom and Dad love them as much as ever—and always will. One conversation won't be enough. Young children, teens, and even adult children need preparation for a breakup and plenty of time to adjust. Parents must answer their questions as fully and honestly as possible, remembering that even young children probably already have a sense of the friction between their parents and need lots of opportunities to talk about their feelings and fears.

Parents should also inform anyone who cares for their child, including relatives, child-care workers, teachers, and the parents of a child's friends. People in frequent contact with a child or adolescent can often spot problems (acting out and other unusual behaviors, depression, and the like) that parents who are dealing with divorce might miss.

When Older Couples Divorce

Statistically, the average age for first divorces in the United States is thirty-five for men and thirty-three for women. But older couples divorce, too, and the social etiquette is the same. One issue deserves special attention: telling grown children. No matter how old they are or how far away they live, children should be informed first—in person, if feasible, or by personal correspondence. A couple with grandchildren should then consult with the parents about the best way to tell younger generations. Even when relations between older parents and grown children are not close, the news of a divorce can be disturbing and saddening, and regardless of age, a child shouldn't be the last to know.

Informing Others

IN GENERAL, THE PEOPLE WHO matter most to you should be told of the divorce in person whenever possible. These conversations can sometimes be difficult, but you will be glad you made the effort. Family and good friends can provide invaluable support, encouragement, and counsel during a divorce and later, when you face the world on your own.

Parents and Family

Although parents and close family members are often aware of trouble within a marriage, they need to be told of concrete changes such as a separation or impending divorce. Generally, husband and wife will speak to their relatives on their own. Your family may immediately come to your defense, or they may be more circumspect. A person who is divorcing wants allies, but it's wrong to set family members against the other spouse or to turn what is a personal decision between two people into a family feud or worse.

The spouse with physical custody of the children should do nothing to interfere with the children's relationships with the grandparents and close relatives on the other side of the divorce. Feelings between spouses and in-laws are often strained during

After my divorce six months ago, I moved to a new city. I haven't seen my former in-laws, with whom I was quite close, since the divorce. But we still communicate fairly often by phone and e-mail, and I want to keep my relationship with them. Is it appropriate for me to send them birthday and Christmas gifts this year?

Since you remain friendly with your former in-laws, then, yes, you can send gifts if you want. It would be wise to select less expensive items than you did when you were married. This will avoid any implication that you are trying to compete with your ex-spouse.

If your former in-laws don't seem to expect to exchange gifts, then cards with personal messages arc appropriate. Staying on good terms with former in-laws is wonderful, so long as you and they understand that the relationship is now different and that the pattern of your contacts will inevitably change.

and after a divorce, but children need the comfort and security of extended family when their nuclear family is broken.

Talking to Friends

Very good friends should hear the news from you—not through the grapevine. Usually this means a personal conversation, but you might write to friends who live elsewhere. Try to avoid going into intimate details or a full-blown negative account, and don't expect friends to take sides. Everyone needs sympathy at such a painful time, but someday, you and your friends may look back with regret on things that were said if discussions became hateful.

You can ask close friends to tell others about the breakup and then let the news travel. Be aware, though, that not everyone will hear. When meeting someone who doesn't know, you'll have to tell with tact. When asked, "How's Marie?" you might answer along these lines: "We're divorced now, but I talked to her recently, and she's doing well." Avoid remarks such as "Didn't you know? We're divorced" that make an acquaintance feel bad because he didn't know. Don't make negative remarks about an ex that will put the person in an uncomfortable position.

When a friend or acquaintance first hears about a divorce, the natural response is "I'm sorry." Take the remark in stride. The person may mean that she's sorry your marriage failed, but it's just as likely she's expressing regret that you have gone through a difficult experience. Instead of becoming defensive, you can say something like, "Thank you. It was for the best, and I'm getting on with my life." A reasonably sensitive person will follow your lead and not pry into past events.

Forget the Party

Letting others know about a divorce should be done with *tact* and *sensitivity*. Announcing the news of a divorce is *not* a time for any behavior that demeans a former spouse. A recent fad (fortunately, not widespread) is to celebrate a new divorce in a public way by holding "independence parties" and sending "funny" divorce announcements and greeting cards. Such tactics should be avoided. Treating an ex-spouse as an object of ridicule is cruel. It's in bad taste and, in the long run, isn't likely to make anyone feel better. Mean-spirited jabs at one's ex can cause real pain for children who are dealing with difficult adjustments in the aftermath of a divorce. Such callous parties and announcements can easily backfire, making the "celebrant" appear cold-hearted and insensitive.

Coworkers and Business Associates

Tell those to whom your divorce will make a difference. Your employer and any immediate supervisor should probably know. You might also tell a few close coworkers and ask them to discreetly inform other colleagues, if this approach makes sense in your situation.

Discretion is the better part of valor in the workplace. If someone asks a tactless question, try to keep your responses neutral and brief, especially if fellow employees also know your spouse. Don't test other people's loyalties or spend work time dwelling on your personal situation.

Very difficult or messy divorces can affect a person's productivity, and even amicable breakups may require taking extra time off for meetings with lawyers and court appearances. The sympathy of coworkers will probably not stretch as far as taking on a colleague's responsibilities, so plan carefully for your absences.

The Practicalities of Making Changes

The practical aspects of divorce include making some necessary changes.

Names and courtesy titles. Men don't change their names unless they adopted a double, hyphenated surname during the marriage. Mr. Jacob Haynes-Curtis may keep the double name or go back to Mr. Jacob Curtis.

Women have more decisions to make. A divorcée can keep her former husband's last name, but not his given name. Today, many divorced women will opt for the courtesy title "Ms." Others, particularly when there are children from the marriage, prefer to retain "Mrs." Some will return to use of their maiden name. When a marriage is annulled, the ex-wife always resumes her maiden name because an annulment signifies that the marriage never existed. The chart below indicates the most common options.

～ Responding to the News of a Divorce ～

Or, seven remarks not to make to a person who is going through—or recently got—a divorce.

➤ "Oh, no wonder you look so stressed and tired!"

➤ "Was she (he) having an affair?"

➤ "Well, I hope you take him (her) for every penny."

➤ "I really feel bad for your children, poor things. It's going to be just awful for them!"

➤ "I guess you'll be selling the house now."

➤ "I always thought he (she) was a jerk."

➤ "I'm surprised it lasted this long."

Questions and comments of this sort run the gamut from presumptuous to downright mean. Though there's no all-purpose response to the news, try to say something that shows concern without prying, such as "Thanks for letting me know. I wish you the best."

How should a divorced or separated person reply to thoughtless comments? With a large grain of salt. Without being rude, you can ignore or defuse the re-mark ("It's all for the best" or "I really don't discuss it") and turn the conversa-tion in another direction.

Married surname	Ms. Andrea Bronson
	Mrs. Andrea Bronson
Hyphenated married surname	Ms. (Mrs.) Andrea Sloan-Bronson
Maiden and married surnames	Ms. (Mrs.) Andrea Sloan Bronson
Maiden name only	Ms. (Miss) Andrea Jane Sloan

Professional titles. Professional, religious, and academic titles do not change, al-though a woman may keep her married surname or resume her maiden name (Dr. Sarah Schwartz, Dr. Sarah Fletcher-Schwartz, or Dr. Sarah Fletcher).

Addresses. Mailing addresses, phone numbers, and e-mail addresses must reflect alterations in living arrangements. When one or both of the couple move from the former family home, they should be sure that the address and name changes are regis-tered with the postal service and telephone company as soon as possible. To head off e-mail foul-ups like receiving an ex's personal communications, close joint accounts and start over individually with new user names and passwords. You'll also want to have stationery, calling cards, business cards, checks, and the like reprinted as soon as you possibly can.

Important notifications. There are numerous people and institutions that must be told about your change of status—usually the sooner the better. Often this is a simple matter of filling out change-of-address forms or making a few quick calls.

- ➤ Landlords and leasing agents, building superintendents, and doormen
- ➤ Banks, mortgage companies, credit and billing agencies, investment firms, and other financial institutions (Be sure to change any joint accounts.)
- ➤ Government agencies, including the U.S. Post Office, motor vehicle department, and voter registration office, that require changes of name and address (Contact the State Department about revising passport information for you and your children.)
- ➤ Utility companies and any businesses with which you have charge accounts
- ➤ Accountants and tax preparers, lawyers, health care providers, insurance companies
- ➤ Schools, child-care providers, and organizations that care for your children (Talk directly to administrative officials and be sure that the information in your child's file is brought up to date. Clarify who is authorized to pick up your child at school and activities.)
- ➤ Your place of worship and any clubs and organizations you belong to

Difficult Situations

THERE'S A SAYING THAT DIVORCE never really ends. Months, even years, after a marriage has been dissolved, situations arise that require former spouses and their families to communicate and cooperate with tact, courtesy, and sensitivity. In circumstances such as the following, the goal is to do what's right—not to open old wounds or replay the past.

An Ex-spouse Who Won't Move On

When one spouse was a reluctant participant in a divorce, he or she may harbor thoughts of reconciliation. Ex-spouses are sometimes guilty of sending mixed signals—telling a former mate that he or she must "move on" while continuing to initiate contacts (other than necessary ones regarding the children). It's important to spell out the exact nature of post-divorce relationships and stick to the limits you set. (No dropping by unexpectedly or calling an ex-spouse for help when the water heater breaks.) Whatever your custody and visitation arrangements regarding children, honor your agreements. Show consideration for your ex-spouse by having children ready for visits and returning from visits on time and by discussing necessary schedule changes well in advance.

When an Ex-spouse Remarries

Whatever your feelings may be, guard what you say. There's no excuse for making cutting remarks about a former spouse or his or her new marriage partner or showing any signs of disrespect.

If you are invited to a former spouse's wedding, attending is a personal decision, though it's better to decline the invitation. Even when relations between exes are cordial, it's rare for one to attend the other's wedding, because his or her presence would likely make the others there feel uncomfortable. Do be sure to reply. Be sensitive with your selection of a wedding gift; choose it as you would for any couple—no joke gifts or painful reminders of the past. (For information about the roles of divorced parents when their children marry, see Chapter 34, page 571: "Planning the Big Event," and Chapter 39, page 688: "Seating the Families and Special Guests"; page 699: "The Receiving Line.")

However you feel about your ex-spouse's new wife or husband, don't convey negative feelings to others, especially your children. If there is competition and jealousy between former and current spouses, children are caught in the middle. The adults should work together to anticipate and solve problems. A typical issue involves how children should address a stepparent. A more serious concern relates to authority—when and how a stepparent should discipline. How well the adults, especially the ex-spouses, resolve such questions will profoundly affect their children's happiness (see Chapter 8, page 90: "Stepfamilies).

[87]

A QUESTION FOR PEGGY

My ex-husband brings his new girlfriend to my son's soccer games, and it makes me very uncomfortable. My son doesn't mind, but should I be subjected to this woman's presence? Isn't my ex being disrespectful of my feelings?

Whatever your former husband's motives, it is your son's feelings that particularly matter. His father is taking an active role in his life, and whether your ex-husband attends games on his own or with a date, he is *involved* with his child. You may be uncomfortable, but for your son's sake, you should keep your feelings to yourself. Life goes on after a divorce, and sooner or later, divorced parents must face up to the fact that their former spouses will likely form new romantic attachments. If the current situation really is intolerable for you, you and your ex might agree to attend games alternately if this won't disappoint your son. For one-time special events such as a championship game or school play, both of you should make the effort to attend (with or without dates) and to behave with dignity. You can sit separately and focus on your child's participation in the event.

The end of a relationship between unmarried companions or domestic partners can be every bit as difficult as the end of a legal marriage. If children are affected, they will feel the same painful emotions and need the same loving attention as children in a divorce. A partner may not be a biological or adoptive parent, but if the bond between that adult and a child is strong, the loss of the adult is no less traumatic. If you're in an established relationship, a breakup should be handled much like a divorce in terms of explaining to children and telling others. There are no real rules, but a relationship that began in love ought to end with as much mutual respect as possible.

The Death of a Former Spouse

Even people who have been divorced for many years can feel grief and sadness when a former spouse dies. Expressing those feelings requires delicacy and consideration, particularly when the person's survivors include a current wife or husband and children.

Generally, a divorced spouse stays in the background. A note of sympathy is usually called for. An offer of help may be included, but only if you know it will be welcome. A donation to the deceased's designated charity may be preferable to sending flowers. It's usually best not to attend the visitation.

A divorced spouse can attend the funeral as long as his or her presence won't cause discomfort for the family. A divorced spouse doesn't sit with the family unless asked to, as may happen when the divorced couple's children are young. If graveside services are limited to family, a former spouse should not attend unless specifically invited.

Rarely does a divorced person speak at an ex-spouse's funeral or memorial, but it may be appropriate if the deceased had no other living family, if his or her survivors make the request, or if it was the wish of the person who died. An ex-spouse should not attempt a eulogy unless he or she can pay genuine tribute to the deceased.

Chapter Eight

Today's Families

Wʜᴀᴛ ɪs sᴛɪʟʟ ɢᴇɴᴇʀᴀʟʟʏ ʀᴇꜰᴇʀʀᴇᴅ as the "traditional family" (wage-earning husband, wife at home with the children) is a fairly modern invention— a product of the Industrial Revolution and the growth of the middle class. Today's families, however, can look very different.

By the end of the twentieth century, only a little over twenty percent of American married couples fit the definition of "traditional," and the majority of households, more than sixty percent, now do not include children. Large families were once the norm; today, two or three children are most common. In two-parent families, both adults are likely to be wage earners. A growing number of young people are delaying marriage and children until their late twenties and their thirties. About a third of all children are born to unmarried mothers. Single people and same-sex couples are creating their own nuclear families through adoption.

Population statistics reflect what most people already know from experience. Chances are, you have a least one or two family members or friends who are raising children on their own. You may know unmarried couples who are living together with or without children, married couples who have chosen not to have children, and people who are perfectly happy living alone. While some people literally have no living family members (people related to them by blood, marriage, or adoption), there are many who widen their definition of *family* to include close friends and others with commonly held beliefs.

In practice, families are self-defining and seem almost infinitely varied in their size, structure, and complexity. Today's "ideal" family is found anywhere that love grows, respect is nurtured among individuals, and kindness and consideration flourish.

Family Values, Family Manners

ꜰᴏʀ ᴀʟʟ ᴛʜᴇɪʀ ᴅɪᴠᴇʀsɪᴛʏ, today's American families tend to share basic values, including mutual affection and respect, commitment to the well-being of other family members, personal responsibility and integrity, and loyalty to the family unit. These

If you've ever wondered why the "families" portrayed in advertisements look so similar, there's a reason. Those commercial families represent the country's largest group of real-life buyers. In the United States, married couples account for about half of all households but about two-thirds of all consumer spending. They purchase more houses, cars, and household products. They buy food, clothes, toys, and college educations for their children. Advertisers, news sources, TV programmers, and filmmakers direct their messages to this powerful demographic group. But media images have a way of creating "norms" that don't reflect reality.

This image can affect manners by distorting perceptions. If people perceive the "media family"—Mom, Dad, and two adorable kids, whose lives seem to revolve around laundry detergent and breakfast cereal—as typical and ideal, then they may regard other family arrangements as somehow less than correct. This can lead to stereotyping, prejudice, and unkind and ill-mannered treatment of families that are regarded as "different."

values are passed on from generation to generation in part through behaviors that demonstrate core values in everyday interactions.

Respect for our own families should logically engender respect for other families, whatever their makeup. Yet different family structures also create special needs and concerns, and this chapter highlights some of the key etiquette issues facing today's families and the people around them. The following categories are not all-inclusive and often overlap in complex ways, but the fundamentals of courtesy apply to all.

Stepfamilies

Stepfamilies are primarily the product of combining households through remarriage after divorce or the death of a spouse. The partnership of unmarried adults, when one or both have children, may also create a stepfamily-type relationship. Stepfamilies often include the mutual child or children of the couple in addition to stepchildren, and multiple remarriages can create a maze of relationships that are hard for even immediate family members to keep straight.

"Blended" is a new way of labeling stepfamilies, but it should be noted that the term isn't universally accepted. Critics object that "blended" implies an easy process in which individuals can be folded together like the ingredients in a soufflé. In fact, building familial relationships is generally a lengthy process requiring difficult adjustments by everyone. To speak of "blended families" also leaves out the natural, or biological, parent who isn't part of the stepfamily unit. Current use of the word "blended" may be an effort to overcome "wicked stepmother" stereotypes, but people in step relationships know that their lives aren't fairy tales, and many prefer the conventional terminology.

To achieve stable, loving, enduring relationships, stepfamilies need the support of other family and friends. Grandparents and close family members can be of great help by welcoming stepchildren wholeheartedly and treating all the children in the newly formed household equally. This isn't always easy when the bonds between natural family members have been very tight. But caring adults will curb the impulse to show favoritism and respect the individuality of every child.

It's equally important to respect new stepparents and biological parents and to avoid comparisons between a child's natural parent and stepparent. Children in stepfamilies often suffer from divided loyalties, and no adult should do or say anything that indicates or implies that one parent is "better" than another. When a former son- or daughter-in-law remarries, for example, there may be little contact between his or her new spouse (or partner) and former in-laws. But when children are involved, it's very important to speak of and treat the new spouse (and his or her children if this is the case) respectfully—whatever the custodial arrangement. No matter what family members may think of ex-in-laws and their new spouses, it is unkind and uncaring to sow seeds of doubt in the minds of children.

A few more recommendations for the families and friends of stepfamilies follow:

Be considerate of custodial and visitation arrangements. A child's need for time with a noncustodial parent overrides other schedules. If your grandchild, niece, or nephew can't attend a family gathering, confine yourself to a normal expression of regret and don't complain. You don't want a child to feel that he or his noncustodial parent has caused a problem that is, in reality, a minor inconvenience.

Include stepparents in family discussions. While stepparents (other than those who adopt stepchildren) are generally not legal custodians, they should be involved in family discussions and decisions about children. Whether the issue is something simple like asking for a child to visit you or a major concern about discipline, try to include parent and stepparent when you raise an issue.

Be available to listen. Children adjusting to a stepfamily may turn to an adult other than a parent to talk about their feelings and problems. Don't push children into discussions, but be attentive to their cues. You may be able to offer suggestions, but don't be drawn into criticism of or quarrels among others in the stepfamily.

Avoid overindulging children in stepfamilies. Recent research indicates that over time, most children in stepfamilies fare as well as those in first-marriage families. But the stereotyped view of children in stepfamilies as fragile and somehow "damaged" can lead others to indulge youngsters out of misguided sympathy. All children need an abundance of love balanced with limits, guidelines, and discipline.

Adoption

A recent national survey (conducted for the Dave Thomas Foundation for Adoption and the Evan B. Donaldson Adoption Institute) found that nearly two-thirds of Americans had experienced adoption either in their families or among close friends. More than three-quarters of respondents expressed their belief that adoption should be encouraged. This positive attitude reflects dramatic changes that have occurred over the last half century.

Adoption is no longer a secretive and mysterious process. Parents and children alike generally welcome the new openness, but attitudes vary and people outside the immediate family should take their cues from each family. Above all, remember that children who are adopted have exactly the same status as biological children and should always be treated as such. The following points, gathered from adoptive families, will help guide other family members, friends, and acquaintances.

Realize that adoptive parents are parents, not saints. Adoptive parents want children for the same reasons as biological parents. But when others imply that adoptive parents are unusually selfless or have somehow "saved a child," the results can be to place an especially heavy burden on the parents and to create feelings of guilt in the adopted child. No one can measure up to perfection.

Understand that adopting is a process that is usually lengthy and can be disappointing. Respect the feelings of adopting parents as they go through the process. Unless you've had a similar experience, don't be too quick to give advice or to criticize the system. If the adoption isn't completed, the hopeful parents will need time to grieve. Comments such as "You can always try again" trivialize their loss.

Wait for the adoptive parents or child to discuss their individual adoption story. Just as it would be thoughtless to ask about a biological child's conception and birth, it's rude to ask for the details of individual adoptions (for example, whether the adopting parents were present at the birth of a child). The choice to share personal information is theirs alone.

Don't inquire about a child's biological parents. This is a private matter and should not be broached by others. If the subject is raised by the adoptive parents or child, avoid using the term "real parents," which implies that the adoptive parents are not real. "Birth parents," "biological parents," and "genetic parents" are all correct; in conversation, you can usually pick up the term preferred by the family.

Most adoptive parents are happy to provide information about the adoption *process* to people who are genuinely interested. If you're considering adopting or want information for a family member or friend, it's fine to ask procedural questions (how to begin, what's involved in a home visit, what kind of lawyer to hire, and so forth).

We adopted our only child three years ago, when he was one, and he's the joy of our life. But he is of a different race, and I'm getting really sick of people who make obnoxious comments. The other day, I ran into a friend whom I hadn't seen in years, and when she saw Tommy, she asked me, "Whose little boy is this?" I said that he is my son, and then she asked if I have any children of my own! I try not to get upset, but my child now understands what people are saying, and I worry about his feelings.

Your friend obviously spoke without thinking, and there's little you can do except hold your temper and make a polite reply (something like, "No, we don't have other children. Tommy's our only child and our greatest joy"). Your son's feelings are your most important concern. You can't shield him from tactless people, but you and your husband will be his models for handling other people's ignorance and lack of common sense.

You should be able to stop thoughtless remarks by introducing him as soon as you meet people who are unfamiliar with your family. "I'd like you to meet our son, Tommy" will satisfy most people's curiosity. If someone persists with inappropriate remarks, you can try to change the subject. But if necessary, you may have to be firm that matters such as your child's background or why you chose interracial adoption are personal and not open to discussion.

Single-parent Families

Today, record numbers of single parents are raising children and in most cases doing a fine job of it. Single-parent families may result from divorce, death of a spouse, or the choice of the parent, but those outside the family are cautioned against assuming that every family has the same story. A single parent might be a grandparent or other relative, a legal custodian, an adoptive parent, or a foster parent.

Single-parent families often have more difficulties than two-parent families, particularly when the adult must be both breadwinner and full-time parent. (Recent U.S. Census figures reveal the vast economic gap between families headed by women—the majority of single-parent families—and those headed by men and married couples. Median, annual household incomes at the beginning of this century were approximately $28,000 for female-headed families, $42,000 for male-headed families, and $59,000 for married-couple families.)

The single parent must maintain a constant and precarious balance between nurturing her or his children and supporting them financially. Family members, friends, neighbors, employers, and coworkers can help by valuing these families and doing nothing that will add to their everyday stresses.

Avoid saying or doing anything that casts doubt on a single parent's competence or parenting skills. A casual remark such as "It's too bad your mother has to work and can't come to your ballgames" is like salt in a wound for a child who already knows that his parent isn't as available as he'd like. If you think a child needs something or you're concerned about his welfare, talk privately with the parent. Just be sure you make it clear that you want to alert the parent to a possible problem, not criticize her parenting.

Do not criticize a single parent around your own or other children. A seemingly inoffensive comment by an adult about a single parent's lifestyle can quickly be translated into cruel teasing on the playground.

Be considerate of a single parent's primary obligations. Part of a single parent's balancing act is setting priorities, and making time for the family will almost always take precedence. Employers who routinely expect late hours and excessive overtime place an enormous burden on all parents. Pressing a single parent to chair a committee or volunteer for school- and sports-related activities (and being critical when the parent declines) is thoughtless. Even if a single parent hasn't been able to accept social invitations in the past, friends will continue to ask.

Offer genuine help. You may be able to take a child to school and social events or pick her up at day care or after-school when the parent is occasionally late from work. Sometimes, just telling a parent that you're available in emergencies is the greatest assistance. You may never be called on, but your offer can bring peace of mind.

Don't expect tit-for-tat return of favors. Single parents may not have the time or resources to reciprocate for every nice thing you do. Remember the Golden Rule, and try not to feel resentful if you seem to host all the sleepovers or do more than your share of carpooling. Most single parents try not to expect too much of others, but if you feel that a parent is imposing on you, explain your feelings to the parent (who may be unaware of your limitations). Don't complain to a child.

Same-sex Families

The children of same-sex couples may be the biological offspring of one parent (sometimes adopted by the other adult) or adopted. Whatever their feelings about same-sex relationships, adults should never make negative comments to or around the child of a same-sex couple, other children, or anyone else. Children learn prejudice as much from the offhanded remarks of their elders as from calculated indoctrination.

Avoid questioning children about the relationships in their family. Whether Bobby's "uncle" is a blood relative or a parent's partner is really no one's concern, and no child or adult should be put on the spot to satisfy idle curiosity.

Describing the relationships among same-sex parents and their children is another matter, especially in introductions. Does Bobby really have two mommies or daddies? Instead of assuming, ask the parents how they wish to be addressed. Pay attention

Understanding family relationships often requires knowing a complicated web of state laws and judicial practices—starting with some basic definitions of terms:

Parental custody is normally decided during the legal divorce process. A custodial parent has physical custody of a child. Noncustodial parents usually have visitation rights, set out in custody agreements. "Joint custody" means that parents share legal custody.

Adoption ends all legal rights and obligations of birth parents. In law, adoptive parents are the child's parents in every respect, and no distinction is made between adopted and biological children.

Open adoption involves legal agreements giving a birth parent some personal access to an adopted child and spelling out the nature of the contact. State laws vary greatly, but violation of an agreement does not invalidate a legal adoption.

Guardianship and legal custody are arrangements whereby guardians, named by courts, assume responsibility for a child. But birth parents may seek reinstatement of custody. Some states also provide for "standby guardianship," in which a designated caretaker assumes guardianship under specified circumstances, as when a terminally or chronically ill parent becomes incapacitated and unable to care for the child.

Permanent guardianship is granted by courts, usually when it is determined that a parent or parents should not have physical custody of a child.

Foster care involves temporary placement of children with caregivers appointed and approved by legal authorities, usually a state office of children and family services. Foster families may be unrelated to the child or may be family members. Foster families often receive financial compensation, but not always. The length of a foster arrangement can range from a day to many years, with the goal of either reuniting a family or finding a permanent home for the child. At any one time, there are more than a half-million American children in foster care.

when you're introduced to same-sex couples (with or without children) and follow their lead. If you really don't know the family's preferences, you'll probably be okay saying "Bobby's parents" or "Bobby's family."

Empty Nesters

Parents whose children have grown and left home make up a rapidly expanding portion of United States households. It was once generally believed that reaching the end of one's active parenting days was a sad time for parents, mothers especially. But today's empty nesters are more likely to feel pride in their accomplishment and a renewed sense of personal freedom.

Changes in family names are most common with remarriage and adoption. An adopted child receives the last name of his new parent or parents, though a change in first name is often limited to infants and young toddlers. Divorced mothers may resume their maiden names, but unless there is a very good reason, children normally retain their biological father's last name. In stepfamilies, changing the names of biological children is generally done only if the child is adopted by the stepfather, the child has the mother's maiden name and takes her married name, or the child clearly wants to make the change.

A person's name is an integral part of his or her identity, so changes should be undertaken with great sensitivity. Children ought to be consulted from the outset, and their wishes given top priority. Depending on the situation, it's sometimes preferable to delay changing the name of a very young child; even a toddler just learning her own name may later become resentful when she learns that her surname was changed.

The biological parent and other family members—grandparents in particular—also deserve consideration. Unless handled with great kindness, tact, and reassurance, changing a child's last name can be taken as rejecting the family members whose surname is dropped. It's the responsibility of the parent—not the child—to inform close family of the change as soon as the decision is made and, for the child's sake, to encourage the continuation of existing family relationships.

Name changes after a divorce, remarriage, or the marriage of a single parent are not generally announced publicly, though a parent may want to write personal notes to family and close friends. It's a good idea to tell the parents of the child's friends and ask them to explain to their children. Anyone responsible for a child—preschool teachers, schoolteachers and school officials, coaches, pediatricians and other health care providers—should be informed as soon as a legal change is made. Also, make the name change in wills, trusts, financial accounts, insurance policies, and other documents relevant to the child.

The adjustment can be hard, however, in the early weeks and months when parents often feel "homesick" for their children. You may be at loose ends for a while, but be careful not to impose on others. Rather than constantly bemoaning your circumstances (even close friends will tire of it quickly), try to focus on positive things you can do with your new independence.

Some people just love to show sympathy to empty nesters, so it's usually best to cut them off with a graceful or humorous response that will, hopefully, turn the conversation in another direction.

When someone says: "What do you do with yourself now that the children are gone?" *You might reply:* "Everything I haven't had time for in the last twenty years. Did you know that I've started my own business?" (Or some other activity that will redirect the conversation.)

When someone says: "I guess you'll be moving to a smaller place now."
You might reply: "Actually, I'm thinking about redecorating." (If and when you "downsize" is your business. If you're considering a move, it's best to keep it to yourself until the decision is made.)

When someone says: "You'll feel better when you have grandchildren."
You might reply: "That will be nice if it happens, but of course it's a personal decision for our children."

Singles and Childless Couples

People who live on their own and couples without children now constitute the largest number of households in the United States. Although many are older couples and widows/widowers or divorced people with grown children, a substantial number of today's singles and childless couples have chosen the independent lifestyle. These include young adults in their higher education and career-forming years, older adults who are delaying marriage and children, and people who don't want to marry or become parents.

The days when people pitied the spinster or confirmed bachelor should be over, but some people still have trouble realizing that "alone" doesn't automatically mean "lonely." And "unmarried" isn't a polite way of saying "on the prowl." Single women, for example, now enjoy the social freedom once limited to men, so it's no longer necessary to arrange a dinner companion for a female guest, though you can ask if she'd like a partner for the event. Likewise, there's no reason to exclude singles and childless couples from occasions that include children.

Expressing disapproval of a person's chosen lifestyle is presumptuous and rude. On the other hand, singles and childless couples should try not to become defensive when subjected to thoughtless comments. You may be able to use good humor to fend off a friend bent on matchmaking or promoting the virtues of parenthood. If you must be more direct, be kind ("You and Sal have a great marriage, but that's not the right choice for me") and avoid getting into a lifestyle debate.

Respecting Families

RESPECT MEANS LITTLE unless it is demonstrated on a daily basis. The following etiquette issues involve common courtesies and consideration, not only within families but also for outsiders.

Names and Introduction Manners

The courtesies related to names might be tricky when family relationships are as complicated as they are in this day and age. But respecting the preferences of the people involved and using common sense—plus tolerance on everyone's part when mistakes are made—will smooth the way.

Stepfamilies. Forcing a reluctant child to refer to step-relatives as "mother/ father," "sister/brother," and "grandmother/grandfather" can damage the growth of trust and affection. It's usually best to let children and teens decide how they want to introduce a stepparent. A child may be comfortable saying "my stepmom, Bonnie" (*or* Bonnie O'Brien if the last names are different), or "my mother, Bonnie," or simply "Bonnie O'Brien." The same is true for stepsiblings and other relatives.

However, children should not be allowed to address or introduce any family members in a rude or disparaging manner. Research shows that adolescents tend to experience the most difficulty adjusting to a stepfamily. But no matter how angry a preteen or teen may be, introducing or speaking of a stepparent as "my father's other wife" or a stepsibling as "my mother's husband's kid" is unacceptable when the tone makes it obvious that the words are intended to cause pain and embarrassment.

Grown children are often uncomfortable referring to an older parent's new spouse as "mother" or "father," even when the marriage itself is welcome. Conversely, older stepparents may be hesitant to call a spouse's adult children by any variant of "daughter" or "son." It's common for adult children and their stepparents to address each other by first name. As long as an introduction is warm, it's respectful for an adult to say, "I'd like you to meet Louis Strayhorn, my mother's husband" or "Ginny Alvarez, my husband's daughter."

Adoptive families. Adopted children are introduced just as biological children are. Unless there is a specific reason (for instance, introducing the child to a health care provider who will be taking a family medical history), there's no reason to comment on the relationship. Adopted children generally call their parents by some form of "mother" and "father," though older children may prefer first names or nicknames.

Guardianships. Relationships need not be spelled out in introductions, but if you're the guardian of a relative, you would include the family relationship and your relative's last name if different from yours ("I'd like you to meet my niece, Cecelia Jernigan.")

When introducing a child in foster care, consider the situation before announcing the relationship. There are times when an explanation is needed, as when introducing a child to school officials, but always think of the child first. Should someone ask if the child is yours, you can respond, "No, Ricky is our foster son," if the child prefers. But

∽ Adoption Announcements ∽

Sending adoption announcements to family and friends is a wonderful way for families to share their joy with other family members and friends. Adoption announcements are appropriate for older children as well as infants and may also be sent when a stepparent adopts a spouse's biological child. (For examples, see Chapter 18, page 277: "Adoption.")

it's just as easy to say something like "No, Ricky is staying with us for a while, and we're so happy to have him."

Former spouses. When introducing a relative's or friend's ex-spouse, it's rarely necessary to mention the nature of the relationship. Though well meant, remarks such as "Chris was my niece's first husband, but I still think of him as my favorite nephew" tend to put people outside the family on the spot by implying negative feelings toward, in this case, the niece (who divorced such a paragon) and her new spouse (who is seemingly not up to standard).

Domestic partners. Introducing domestic partners can be problematic because there are really no universally accepted terms, as yet, to denote intimate relationships outside marriage (see Chapter 2, page 16: "How to Introduce 'Significant Others' "). Consult the people involved about how they prefer to be introduced and then respect their wishes even if you are not wholly comfortable with the designation. In a pinch, you can always say, "I'd like you to meet Jacob Green and his friend Caroline Knight." Parents are introduced as parents ("This is Harry's father, Jacob Green"), whatever their domestic arrangements.

Addressing Correspondence

The most important concern when addressing invitations, holiday cards, and other correspondence is to get all names and addresses correct. Questions may arise when nuclear family members have different last names, as in many stepfamilies and single-parent families. The best approach is to list children by first and last names (following the parent's or parents' names). If there's more than one child, list their names separately and in order of age, beginning with the eldest. Don't distinguish between stepchildren and mutual children.

If you're inviting a parent or parents and their young children, you would normally include the children in the parent's invitation. When a child doesn't live with the parent you're inviting, send a separate invitation to the child at her *home* address. This is a courtesy to the custodial parent, who may have to rearrange schedules and transport his or her child to your event.

∼ A Memory Device ∼

For those who have trouble remembering names, dates, and familial relationships, a good memory device is the old-fashioned address book or its electronic counterpart. When you receive wedding invitations and birth and adoption announcements, take a minute to update your address book, add new names, and check spellings. Party invitations and holiday cards can also give information such as the names or nicknames people prefer to go by. Jotting down a person's name and relationship ("Aunt Laura's stepson") can help etch the details on your memory.

A sample address for a formal invitation to a stepfamily including children's full names:

Mr. and Mrs. Roger W. Hamilton
Miss Charlotte Mary Compton [*eldest: mother's biological child*]
Miss Ann Marshall Hamilton [*middle child: father's biological child*]
Roger W. Hamilton, Junior [*youngest: couple's mutual child*]

An informal invitation:

Mr. and Mrs. Roger Hamilton
Charlotte Compton, Ann Hamilton, and Chip Hamilton

Though you might address a very casual invitation to "The Hamilton Family" or "Rog and Peg Hamilton and family," it's thoughtful to list all names so that the young people will feel truly included.

Invitations to single-parent families follow the same form, as this address to a divorced mother and her daughter:

Dr. Harriet Ransom Bennett
Miss Eleanor Jane Sykes

When unmarried couples live together intimately, you can address a single card or invitation to both, putting the woman's name first. However, if you're not sure about and can't ascertain the nature of the relationship, you should send separate invitations.

When different sets of adults—parents, adult children (single or married), older or younger relatives, roommates—reside at the same address, send separate invitations to each set or individual. Separate holiday cards are also preferable, but if you address holiday cards to the entire household, be sure to add a personal message that clearly

---

Introduction Etiquette to the Rescue

Judging by appearances is one of the straightest roads to manners blunders. An adult and a child who do not look alike may be biological kin, step-relatives, related by adoption, or unrelated. Couples may be married, engaged, dating seriously or casually; they might be family members, professional colleagues, or just acquaintances. There are so many possible combinations . . . and consequently so many chances for error.

The most basic introduction etiquette comes to the rescue: Don't assume and don't guess. Give people you meet the opportunity to identify their relationships. Listen very closely to introductions. (Courteous listeners should quickly learn that, for example, the young man with a friend's daughter is not her boyfriend but her business associate.) When you make introductions, include relationships when necessary to prevent confusion and avoid embarrassment all around.

includes everyone. You don't have to send cards to people you don't know, even though they reside in the same household.

Older Parents

The trend toward delaying marriage and childbearing has produced a not infrequent sight—parents in their late thirties, forties, and fifties with very young children. People may jump to the conclusion that a fifty-year-old woman and the five-year-old

~ Those "Once Removed" Cousins ~

Betty and Bob are sister and brother. But what are their children to one another, and who is "once removed"? The answers lie in the generations. It begins with siblings. The children of siblings are first cousins because they are the first generation of cousins. The children of first cousins are second cousins to one another. And so on through the generations.

"Once removed" doesn't indicate that a cousin was ever banished from the family—just that the cousins are separated by a generation. So your parent's first cousin is your first cousin once removed. And vice versa: You are first cousin once removed to your parent's first cousin. By the time Betty and Bob reach grandparenthood, most people in their family will probably be introducing one another simply as "cousin," which is both polite and correct.

Generation	Family member(s)	Relationship to . . .	Family member(s)
First	Betty	sibling	Bob
Second	Betty	aunt	Bob's children
	Betty's children	first cousins (same generation)	Bob's children
Third	Betty	great-aunt	Bob's grandchildren
	Betty's children	first cousins once removed (one generation apart)	Bob's grandchildren
	Betty's grandchildren	second cousins (same generation)	Bob's grandchildren
Fourth	Betty	great-great-aunt	Bob's great-grandchildren
	Betty's children	first cousins twice removed (two generations apart)	Bob's great-grandchildren
	Betty's grandchildren	second cousins one removed (one generation apart)	Bob's great-grandchildren
	Betty's great-grandchildren	third cousins (same generation)	Bob's great-grandchildren

with her are grandmother and grandchild, and when the mistake is corrected, everyone is embarrassed.

To prevent such misunderstandings, older parents should promptly introduce their children by name and relationship. ("This is my daughter, Francesca.") If you forget to clarify and the person you're meeting misinterprets, explain as quickly as you can. ("Actually, Francesca is my daughter.")

If you're the one who made the mistake, apologize when you are corrected but don't be too embarrassed. Just be careful not to compound the error by making remarks such as "Was she a surprise?" that are prying and insensitive.

Families Under Stress

In times of stress and crisis, people outside a family should not assume that family members' reactions can be predicted by their literal family connections. Family members often have close (or distant) relationships that have little to with their places on the family tree. For example, people not aware of a family's dynamics may assume that stepchildren or adopted children need less comfort than biological children when a parent dies. Such behavior can happen on joyful occasions as well. It's not uncommon for stepparents and stepchildren, noncustodial parents, and domestic partners to be treated with little more than polite indifference by guests at weddings, christenings, and coming-of-age celebrations.

Blood is not the only tie that binds families. Family relationships should always be honored, regardless of the composition of the family. Even when you know that family members are not close, good etiquette requires that you treat every family member with respect and dignity.

Chapter Nine

The Thoughtful
Family Member

THE BONDS OF FAMILY are so fundamental that "family" is defined as the basic unit of all human society. Family is where we learn to love and be loved and to temper self-interest with respect and kindness to others. Family members grow up and move away, but the bonds are not easily broken. In the modern world with all its distractions, however, family members often have to work harder at maintaining contact and being thoughtful of one another. Good communication, whether over the back fence or across thousands of miles, promotes understanding and consideration. Communication and the essential principles of etiquette—respect, consideration, and honesty—make up the foundation that holds families together through the best of times and the worst of times.

Spouses and Children

Marriage was once regulated by strictly defined social and gender roles—the male as breadwinner and the female as homemaker—from which neither spouse drifted too far. Today's marriages and domestic partnerships are much more flexible. Yet the nucleus of the family remains the people at its center, and when couples treat each other with respect, courtesy, civility, and integrity, they'll be setting the tone for all their family relationships.

➤ Couples should not make joint social arrangements without consulting each other. When accepting invitations or hosting social occasions individually, talk with your spouse or partner in advance and be sure that your plans will be convenient. Anticipate conflicts: If your husband is an avid golf fan, the weekend of the Masters Tournament is probably not the best time to hold a baby shower at your home.

➤ In private and public, show the utmost respect for one another. For the sake of the relationship and the sensibilities of everyone you know, don't discuss intimate matters with others. Avoid put-downs ("You are so inept!"). In the confines of home, showing respect (or disrespect) for each other is the model that your children will carry into their adult relationships.

➤ When speaking about shared relationships, responsibilities, and possessions, recognize the other half of your family unit. The first-person plural expresses closeness and mutual respect: "*We* have three children." "*We're* so excited about *our* new house."

➤ Some things aren't shared, and considerate couples won't invade one another's privacy. Neither partner should open mail addressed to the other (or anyone else), read personal writings or private correspondence, or listen in on phone calls or private conversations. Nor should anyone expect a spouse or partner to *automatically* share all of his or her opinions and attitudes.

➤ Respecting each partner's right to a reasonable amount of alone time is often a core value in successful marriages. Allowing one another time off and supporting individual interests reinforces the trust essential to an enduring partnership.

Considerate Children and Teens

One's offspring are most likely to become considerate themselves when their adult role models consistently expect and model thoughtfulness and good manners. (This subject is covered in depth in Part III, "Children and Teens.") To be thoughtful, a young person has to *think* about others, and in this sense, thinking is learned and refined with practice. Parents of young children begin the process by appealing to youngsters' burgeoning empathy and helping them understand that other people have feelings like their own. When reason kicks in, around age six (sometimes before), you can explain the why's of considerate behavior and put thoughtful actions into context. Family life presents daily opportunities for lessons in thoughtfulness: "We carry our dirty dishes to the kitchen so that we share in the cleanup." "Please turn the music down, so we can hear each other."

In adolescence, most young people begin to pull away from family, and some may seem to turn into thoughtless heathens almost overnight. This is part of the process of growing up, though it tests virtually every parent's patience. Still, it's an excellent time to promote thoughtfulness by engaging preteens and teens as often as possible in negotiation, letting them exercise their thinking skills, and respecting their opinions even when you disagree. Not every family discussion will be a success, but don't give up. Through the give-and-take of discussing issues such as participation in family activities, teens learn to value the needs and ideas of others and to think about the consequences of their own actions. Be alert to a young person's thoughtful deeds and be generous with your unconditional support and praise.

Whenever we get together with family, our fifteen-year-old insists on wearing grungy jeans and T-shirts. I've told him that dressing presentably is a sign of respect for us and others, but he says it's his style and I should leave him alone.

Your son is old enough to understand that his grungy clothes are out of place in certain settings, but he's at an age when dress style is one of the ways that teens assert their independence. You probably don't want to make too much of an issue, especially just before seeing your relatives, when he's likely to be most obstinate. Talk with him at a calmer time. Let him know that you're grateful that he attends family gatherings. (It's not uncommon for teens to balk at family activities, since they prefer being with their friends.) But remind him that you generally don't interfere with his clothing choices. Listen to his ideas and work together to find a compromise that satisfies him and you. Perhaps jeans, but without holes in the knees, will do. He may be more inclined to dress appropriately for family occasions when he sees that you respect his independence and want to negotiate solutions with him.

Gathering the Family Together

EXTENDED FAMILIES OFTEN get together for religious and national holidays, birthdays, and family reunions. When they live close, the regular family meal may be a valued tradition. The following courtesies should help make every family gathering a low-stress, fun occasion:

Spread the responsibilities around when possible. Offer to help when a family member holds a get-together. If you live near one another, alternate locations for events. Share child-watching duties among the adults.

Follow the hosts' lead and adapt to their style of entertaining. Your sister may enjoy preparing and serving every morsel by herself, while Cousin Lily prefers a potluck and Uncle Lee insists on taking everyone to his favorite restaurant. Relax and enjoy the variety.

Avoid bringing family problems to the gathering. This is not the time to air grievances. Negative talk about anyone who isn't present will probably get back to them and cause hurt feelings.

Indulge the family storytellers. When the tales aren't at the expense of someone else, stories of past and present are often the means by which younger generations and new in-laws learn the family's history.

Accept one another's quirks. As long as no one is being hurt by a relative's actions and words, be open-minded about harmless idiosyncrasies.

Remembering Milestones

Birthdays, weddings, anniversaries, religious holidays, graduations—every family has its milestones and its own ways of observing them. These occasions celebrate the event and the family, and it's worth the effort to attend if you can.

Giving gifts can be problematic, however. Some family members can afford to send gifts for every holiday and birthday or make a splash with expensive presents, but overdoing can cause hurt, resentment, or confusion when others aren't so fortunate. Gift exchanges that began within the limits of a nuclear family can get out of control when the family grows to include dozens of sisters- and brothers-in-law, aunts, uncles, and cousins. People often have different ideas about the appropriate occasions for gifts. For example, in many families, Mother's Day and Father's Day are observed with phone calls, visits, greeting cards, and gifts. Other families regard these days as commercially inspired and barely give them a nod.

When deciding when to give and what to select, consider the family norm. You don't have to do exactly what everyone else does, but do think about the wishes of the recipient and the general nature of the gifts from other family members. If a relative has made it clear that he or she doesn't want birthday gifts, respect the request and consider alternatives—a card, a personal note, and perhaps a donation to the relative's favorite charity. If gift giving within the family has gotten out of hand, the adults need to consult about other options such as drawing names and setting spending limits; restricting annual gift exchanges to Christmas, Hanukkah, or another special occasion; and giving gifts to children only. When family members agree to limitations, everyone should stick to the bargain.

Relatives as Houseguests

For years, it was the norm for grown children and their children to travel to visit their parents and grandparents. Nowadays, older relatives are just as likely to be the travelers. The following etiquette essentials of staying with relatives of any age are grounded in mutual respect:

Establish convenient dates for visits. Invitations to visit are usually casual, but it's important to consider your hosts' schedule and responsibilities. Consult about plans well in advance.

Avoid surprises Don't drop in for the weekend without notice. Leave pets at home or in a boarding facility unless your hosts *insist* that your animal come along.

Be conscious of the hosting family's capabilities and tailor visits to their needs. If Aunt Maggie recently sold her five-bedroom house and moved to a small condo,

My husband and I married last June, and now my parents and his parents have invited us for Christmas. Unfortunately, we all live hundreds of miles apart. We don't want to hurt their feelings, but to visit with both families means spending most of our holiday on the road or in airports. We both work and have only a few days off at Christmas.

This is a common dilemma when families are separated by distance. First, you and your husband must decide what *you* want to do. You might visit one family this year and the other next year; flip a coin if you need to avoid any appearance of favoritism. Another option is for you to host Christmas for both sets of parents, though a large gathering of out-of-town guests may be difficult with your work responsibilities. Or you might spend your first Christmas on your own and visit with your families at less busy times. Since it's unlikely that either set of parents wants your holiday to be an endurance test, they'll surely be sympathetic to your choice when they know your situation and your feelings. If you decide not to travel, call your parents on Christmas at times when you can have more than a hurried conversation.

it's unlikely she can accommodate you, your spouse, and children. Staying at a nearby hotel or bed-and-breakfast would be considerate.

Set days and times to arrive and depart. Avoid impositions of the "We'll be there Thursday or Friday—Saturday at the latest" kind. If you can't pin down an arrival time, it's better to stay overnight at a motel rather than arriving on a family member's doorstep at three in the morning.

Be a considerate host and gracious guest. When relatives stay in one another's homes, the etiquette is no different from any houseguest occasion (see Chapter 26, page 468: "Guidelines for Guests"). A thank-you note and a gift for the hosts are always nice. But if you visit frequently, notes and gifts aren't required for every visit, though saying "thank you" is a must.

Allow yourself to be entertained. Be adaptable. If your relative plans activities, participate with enthusiasm. If there is something you can't do—a walking tour of the city's historic district, for instance, may be too much for an elderly relative or small children—explain without complaining. It's fine to suggest one or two activities, but don't expect your host to accommodate your every desire.

Participate in the hosts' household routine. Volunteer your help and pitch in with daily chores. Be neat.

Leave on time. If you must delay your departure, be sure that doing so isn't going to inconvenience your host. You might move to other lodgings if an extended stay is likely to cause stress and strain.

Staying in Touch

GRANDMOTHER AND GRANDFATHER have moved to a retirement community in the Sun Belt. Daughter, her husband, and children live in the East. Son is at college on the West Coast. One sister lives in a nearby town, but another works for an international conglomerate in the Far East. Cousins are scattered across the continent and around the globe.

Sound familiar? Today's family is likely to be far-flung, and maintaining family ties can seem difficult. Though some family members may see each other nearly every day or regularly on holidays, others often pass months or years between visits. But we live in an age when technology facilitates frequent contact. Here are a few easy ways to say that you care:

> ➤ Pick up the phone or send a quick e-mail. Many of today's older generation are computer savvy and love staying in touch via the Internet.

> ➤ Send pictures of your family: photos, digital images via the Internet, homemade videos.

> ➤ Pass on newspaper and magazine articles that a distant relative might enjoy. Communicate about interests you share—the Super Bowl, the stock market, a hobby.

∽ JUST COMMON SENSE ∽

Using a Family Member's Home

A member of your family offers her vacation home for your next holiday. Or she suggests you stay at her house or apartment while she's away. Some families "trade" houses in order to experience different locales. Whatever the situation, living temporarily in a family member's home is a responsibility. When it comes to making messes and offending neighbors, family shouldn't be expected to be more tolerant than strangers. If you request to use a family member's dwelling, make a serious offer to pay rent. If your family member asks you to house-sit, be sure you both understand the terms of the agreement. (Will you be paid or reimbursed for household expenses? What are the house rules, including the owner's policies about entertaining other guests?) Treat a relative's home with care; leave behind a clean house, a warm note of appreciation, and perhaps a house gift.

- Give a globe-trotting relative a prepaid calling card (a nice gift for relatives in military or diplomatic service overseas); when you travel, send picture postcards, especially to young relatives.
- Encourage children to become pen pals with faraway relatives of their age.

Good Relations With In-laws

WHEN A COUPLE MARRIES, they are endowed with "instant parents." What's more, two sets of relatives, who may be little more than strangers to one another, are brought together as extended family. Each family has its own customs, traditions, and

∾ Ten Behaviors That Drive Families Wild ∾

There's a saying that family are the people who have to take you in when no one else will. But they don't always have to like it. Following the Golden Rule with family should help you avoid the following mistakes:

- Taking advantage of family members: dropping by without notice; expecting relatives to babysit on the spur of the moment; borrowing money, cars, and other possessions; not returning borrowed items; not offering to reciprocate a relative's generosity
- Criticizing or being condescending to family members in their presence or gossiping about them to others
- Embarrassing family members by telling personal stories, blurting out private information, or treating one's spouse or children disrespectfully
- Wasting family members' time by failing to communicate plans for a visit or consistently being late
- Treating family occasions as business opportunities or expecting relatives to provide free professional advice, service, or goods
- Failing to offer to help at family gatherings or playing the martyr by refusing assistance when one is the host
- Displaying poor table manners, interrupting, dominating conversation, and other behaviors that a person wouldn't think of indulging in around people who aren't relatives
- Failing to discipline one's children and not allowing host family members to enforce their house rules when children visit; allowing one's child to tease or bully the children of other relatives
- Boasting excessively about one's child or frequently drawing comparisons between children in the family
- Insisting that children be included in occasions for adult family members

expectations, which may differ widely. Even when family cultures are similar, they aren't the same, and everyone must be prepared to make adjustments.

Probably the best way to establish and maintain harmonious relationships is for couples and their in-laws to follow a policy of noninterference. In spite of the mother-in-law jokes, interference can come from both generations and genders. A person's motives may be laudable, but too much advice and criticism can fracture family relationships. In most instances, the wise course is to be tolerant of and show respect for differences. Try to avoid reading hidden meanings into everyday remarks. Listen politely to unsolicited advice, clear up any major misunderstandings quickly and courteously, and don't hesitate to apologize when you're in the wrong. Make every effort to put a problem behind you, and don't carry a grudge.

In-law Intrusions

There are times when parents-in-law must tread with extra care. One involves who should attend the birth of a grandchild. The mother may wish her own mother in the delivery room but not her mother-in-law. Another example involves the naming of a child (or appointing godparents). These are intimate family matters, and in-laws should always wait to be asked for their input. Even when asked for advice, be careful that your suggestions don't sound like demands or expectations, and never use guilt to try to get your own way.

How to Address In-laws

Should you call your new mother-in-law "Mom" or "Harriett" or "Mrs. Turner"? Is your father-in-law to be "Dad" or "Pop" or "Matthew"? The question often troubles engaged and newly married couples and sometimes couples who've been married for some time, but it needn't. If your parents-in-law haven't broached the subject, ask

∼ Who Is an In-law? ∼

When a couple legally marries, each becomes a member of the other's family, and the relatives of your husband or wife become your in-laws—mother-in-law, father-in-law, brother-in-law, and so on. However, the husbands and wives of your in-laws are not technically related to you. Your husband's sister is your sister-in-law. Her husband is the brother-in-law of your husband, but not you. He is simply your sister-in-law's husband. Their children, on the other hand, would be your nieces and nephews.

Such technicalities can muddle even a genealogist, and most people just do what's comfortable. "In-law" is generally reserved for a spouse's nuclear family (parents and siblings)—but rarely used for grandparents, aunts, uncles, and cousins. If you introduce your husband's sister's husband as your "brother-in-law," don't fret. Consider it a term of family endearment.

My former sister-in-law and I have known each other since high school and remain good friends although she is now divorced from my brother. But we both wonder how we should make introductions to people who aren't aware of our family history.

Unless there's a reason to indicate the past relationship, simply introduce each other (and other members of your families) by first and last names. If your surnames are the same, you might simply say, "This is my friend I've known since high school, Ashley McNamara." If someone asks if you are related, you can truthfully say "no," or you can briefly describe the relationship ("We used to be in-laws, but we've always been friends") and then steer the conversation in another direction. Without going into the divorce, it's your choice how much or how little you wish to explain. Using the term "former sister-in-law" as you do is generally considered friendlier than "ex."

them how they want to be addressed, give them time to consider their options, and then respect their decisions. The same consideration applies to grandparents, aunts, uncles, and cousins.

Parents-in-law and other in-laws should be aware that many people feel that intimate terms of address indicating actual blood relationships should be reserved for biological or adopted family. If your new son- or daughter-in-law is uncomfortable with any variation of "mother" and "father," don't force the issue. These days, in-laws often prefer to address one another by first names, which is both convenient and a recognition of the adult nature of their intergenerational relationship.

Adult Children in the Home

GROWN CHILDREN WHO RETURN to or never leave the family home are often referred to today as "the boomerang generation" because they come back. They range from high school graduates who remain at home while working or attending college to adults in their thirties or older who return to the parental home for reasons including the unavailability of reasonably priced housing, divorce, and financial difficulties.

This trend has been growing for several decades, and recent U.S. Census figures indicate that nearly a third of all young adults aged eighteen to thirty-four live with their parents. Many parents and their adult children now regard living under the same roof as a practical stepping-stone to independence, and most parents are willing to assist their grown children through difficult times.

For the relationship to be successful, parents and children should understand their individual responsibilities and expectations. Even when everyone is in agreement, situations will almost surely arise that test patience and fray tempers. To keep little ir- ritations from becoming major problems, open and ongoing communication is essen- tial. Remembering that everyone is now an adult, parents and grown children might begin with mature conversations about these fundamental issues.

Determine a time frame for the arrangement, if possible. Work together to estab- lish a future date when the adult child will leave home and assume full independence.

Clarify financial arrangements. A child who is still in school may be almost en- tirely dependent on parents, but adult children who are earning income need to con- tribute to the family coffers as much as they can. This might include paying rent, providing for their own transportation, sharing expenses, including food, and paying for a separate phone line and phone service. (It's wise to talk to your insurance agent about health and disability coverage for an adult child who isn't covered by a group policy.)

Discuss household duties. An adult who expects a parent to make his bed, prepare his meals, and wash his clothes needs reminding that he's a guest in his parents' home.

Determine arrangements for sharing. Discuss issues such as having meals to- gether—or not—telephone and television privileges, and use of a family car. Decide on schedules—who can use what and when—and agree on means to communicate changes in schedules.

Be very sensitive to privacy issues. Everybody must remember the manners learned in childhood—knocking on closed doors before entering, no eavesdropping on private conversations, no rummaging through personal possessions, no borrowing another person's things without permission, and no snooping.

Agree on policies about entertaining other guests at home and going out. Grown children don't need curfews. They can be expected to check with parents be- fore bringing friends home and to inform parents when they go out for the evening and where they can be reached if they are away for a day or longer. Negotiate guide- lines about overnight guests and respect parents' feelings about acceptable sexual be- havior in their home.

When an adult child has children, it's critical that the adults cooperate to set boundaries and agree on disciplinary issues. To give children the stability they need— especially during a separation or divorce—and to avoid the conflicts that occur when authority figures send mixed signals, the parent and grandparents must be in accord on the basic standards of child rearing.

When Parents Move In

For many pragmatic reasons not related to health, a growing number of active, older adults are moving in with their grown children. The "in-law addition"—separate living quarters within a house or on the property—is making a comeback, and the arrangement can be beneficial for all, so long as certain courtesies are observed. Those involved should agree on the ground rules, which can be similar to those for boomeranging adult children (above), and accept that living in close proximity is not an excuse for interfering or expecting too many favors. (A grandparent who lives in the same house is not an automatic babysitter or housekeeper.) Before deciding on personal responsibilities, it helps to discuss two core principles that may seem, at first glance, irreconcilable. First, the people involved are all independent adults and their individual rights must be honored. Second, a certain degree of interdependence is required for peace and harmony. Communal living is most likely to succeed when built on a foundation of mutual understanding and respect.

Caring for Elderly Parents and Relatives

WHEN ELDERLY PARENTS OR RELATIVES become ill, disabled, or unable to maintain their past lifestyle, families often find themselves making difficult decisions about medical care and living arrangements. There are numerous options available, including assisted-living facilities, nursing homes, and hospice care for the terminally ill. But the high costs, both financial and emotional, of long-term care can be devastating, and many elderly people and their families choose at-home care in the person's home or the home of a close relative, often a daughter or son.

Whatever the arrangement, everyone in the family has responsibilities to the elderly relative, which begin with respect and ongoing communication. (See also Chapter 11, page 132: "Advice for Caregivers"; page 135: "Visiting the Sick at Home.")

A QUESTION FOR PEGGY

My wife's parents, who are retired, invite us out for a nice restaurant dinner every two months or so. But they always pay, and this makes me feel awful because they live on a fixed income and both my wife and I are well-paid professionals. My wife says it's their choice, but I know that treating us is a sacrifice for them. Should I insist on picking up the check?

Although the cost may be a strain on your in-laws' budget, they apparently enjoy treating you. Getting together probably means much more to them than the financial outlay. Since they issue the invitation, you are their guest and do not pay. You can always reciprocate by inviting them out. You and your wife might also suggest a family meal at your home as an occasional alternative to a restaurant. Look for ways to share their company without challenging their independence or dampening their pleasure in being your hosts. When your in-laws do pay, show your gratitude and don't feel guilty.

Visit, write, or call regularly. One-on-one visits are wonderful, but phone calls, cards, and letters will also boost spirits and communicate that you care. Try to be regular with calls and visits; if a visit must be delayed or canceled, call immediately and speak directly to your relative if you can. When you visit, let your relative set the pace. Every visit doesn't have to be a talkathon; sometimes just your presence is the greatest comfort.

Encourage children in the family to stay in touch. Include your children in visits when you can. Prompt young children to create pictures or cards for their relative. If you live too far away for visiting, older children and teens can write and call. Talk with your children about what is happening. Without clear and age-appropriate explanations, youngsters may become scared, imagine that the situation is worse than it really is, or feel that they are somehow at fault. Honesty is essential, and adults should never convey false optimism when a relative (of any age) is chronically or terminally ill.

Treat the person as an adult and an individual. Unless an elderly relative is mentally incompetent, he or she should be listened to and taken seriously, especially about decisions that affect his or her life and health. Physical disabilities shouldn't be equated with intellectual or psychological incapacity. Since the natural consequences of aging can be frightening for younger people, it's a good idea to do some serious research and, if possible, talk with a gerontologist or a physician who specializes in care for the elderly.

If your relative is in a health care facility, talk with the staff about his or her condition and progress. Ask what you can do to assist. Treat all staff members with respect and courtesy, but be observant. If you see or hear something troubling, raise the issue with senior staff or administrators as well as other family members.

Keep family members informed. A family "phone tree"—a plan by which people are assigned names to call—is useful when news, such as a change in your relative's condition, needs to be communicated quickly.

Chapter Ten

The Good Neighbor

FROM THE HIGH-RISE COMPLEXES of bustling urban centers to the sprawl of suburban developments to the smallest rural communities, good neighbors are, in the words of Thomas Jefferson, "a very desireable thing." Yet in a country of such great variety and unpredictability, is there a "typical" good neighbor?

There is. A good neighbor may be the quiet person who is rarely seen and heard or the sociable person who is always Johnny-on-the-spot with good cheer and a helping hand. Whatever the style, the "typical" good neighbor is one who adheres to the Golden Rule.

What good neighbors share is the awareness that their everyday behavior affects the people who live around them. They understand that the core of neighborliness is the willingness to exercise self-restraint and sometimes give up what they want in order not to inconvenience or impose on others. Without compromising their principles, they live up to their responsibility to promote peaceful, cordial relationships among neighbors. Day in and day out, good neighbors "do unto others" by applying neighborly manners that are grounded in consideration, sensitivity, flexibility, and a good deal of compromise.

When New Neighbors Move In

IN TODAY'S HIGHLY MOBILE SOCIETY, it's not so unusual for people to move into a neighborhood almost without being noticed. Even so, being hospitable to newcomers is a time-honored tradition in the U.S. and one that will, hopefully, always be valued.

Meeting New Neighbors and Giving Welcome Gifts

Calling on new neighbors is one of those rare instances when dropping by unannounced is good manners. Initial meetings are usually casual and brief. If you see your new neighbor in his yard, go over and say "hello." Or knock on his door and introduce yourself, whether or not you bring a gift. You might be invited in, but don't expect a long visit. The goal is simple: to extend a warm welcome and exchange names and perhaps telephone numbers, not to get a new neighbor's life history.

Appropriate welcome-to-the-neighborhood gifts differ from housewarming presents because they're not based on the tastes of the recipients (unless you already know the newcomers) and aren't costly. Typical welcome gifts will brighten the newcomers' day and ease the hassle of settling in—a plate of cookies, a bouquet of garden flowers, or an extra telephone book in case theirs hasn't been delivered. If you aren't at home when neighbors move in, you might leave your gift and a note in a safe place or put a note of welcome in their mailbox when you have a chance.

There's no statute of limitation on meeting neighbors. If you become aware of newcomers weeks or even months after they move in, you can still knock on the door and introduce yourself. No excuses are necessary, but if you wish, you can explain if your work or travel schedule or circumstances like a family illness took you out of the loop for a while. You needn't give a gift if the neighbor is clearly settled in.

Offering to Help

Offers of assistance require sensitivity to a new neighbor's actual needs and time constraints. If the house is full of movers or decorators, just extend your welcome and promise to come back at a less harried time. In most cases, you're a stranger to new neighbors, and some may not feel comfortable accepting your well-intentioned offer until they know you better.

Suggestions for help that people might need, especially when they are moving into an area that is unfamiliar, include the following:

Lending a hand. Some new neighbors would love a little help arranging furniture or unpacking boxes. It's often best to say when you will be available and what you can do (don't, for example, volunteer to "move a few boxes" if you have a bad back) and then let your new neighbors take you up on the offer if and when they really need assistance.

Providing information about your locality. Schools and places of worship; restaurants, grocery stores, and good places to shop; reliable service providers, and the like: Let new neighbors know you're happy to share information, answer questions, and give directions.

Babysitting, if you feel comfortable with the responsibility. An hour or two of child-minding will provide relief for parents who are in the midst of unpacking and settling in.

What Doesn't Help

It isn't helpful to impose on a neighbor's time, gossip about others, or in any way denigrate the neighborhood. Even in good humor, it's presumptuous to make comments about a newcomer's background. (If you once lived in the city your new neighbor moved from or work for the same company, wait to know each other much better before cracking jokes.) Only inconsiderate neighbors would use a first meeting to proselytize for their religion, political party, or favorite cause.

When You're the New Neighbor

WHO SHOULD MAKE the first contact when someone moves into a neighborhood? It really doesn't matter who takes the first step. When you see a neighbor clipping her hedge or fetching the mail, introduce yourself. If you recognize a person from the neighborhood when you're out, take a few moments to identify yourself. ("Hello. I'm Lynn Kovak, and we just moved to Hilltop Road. I believe we're neighbors.") In multi-unit dwellings, communal areas—elevator, laundry, exercise room—offer opportunities to say "hi" to a neighbor you haven't met and initiate a little pleasant conversation. Meeting and greeting is a fundamental of good manners regardless of who makes the first move.

~ JUST COMMON SENSE ~

The Manners of Moving Out

Moving is notoriously stressful, but the neighbors you're leaving behind will remember you fondly when you give them advance notice of your move and then practice these basic moving-day manners:

➤ Schedule moves at low traffic times. Moving trucks and movers can cause major congestion, so if possible, avoid early morning and late afternoon.

➤ Be sure that moving vehicles and equipment don't block neighbors' driveways, sidewalks, alleys, or pedestrian access to any buildings.

➤ Keep the noise down. If your movers are blasting music, politely ask them to lower the volume.

➤ Clean up on your way out. Leave the exterior of your old house presentable by disposing of any trash and sweeping paths and driveways. If you live in an apartment, don't pile boxes and bags of junk in the hallways.

Whether your movers are professionals or friends recruited for the day, they'll appreciate having plenty of drinks available (cold water, soda, coffee, but nothing alcoholic). Be ready to treat friends to lunch or supper. Confine pets to a room or the garage, or take them to a boarding facility for the day; this courtesy will lower everyone's blood pressure, including your pet's. (For the etiquette of tipping movers, see Chapter 46, page 811: "Movers.")

Establishing Your Boundaries

WHEN YOU MOVE into a new neighborhood, you may want to establish your willingness or unwillingness to participate in neighborhood activities. Not everyone wants to join the homeowners' association or sign up for Neighborhood Watch. When asked, don't make up excuses, but if you have a good reason, state it. ("We moved here to be closer to my mother, who's ill. I'll be spending so much time with her that I can't commit to anything else right now.") If group activities just aren't your thing, be honest without being rude. You may be able to contribute something other than your time; a financial donation to the local firefighters or rescue squad would be welcome.

Do try to attend one-time or occasional activities such as block parties and street fairs if you can. You'll meet people, and your neighbors will appreciate your presence. Look for everyday opportunities to show interest without joining formal groups. Buy lemonade from the children who set up a stand on the corner. Take a few minutes to admire a neighbor's roses.

Housewarmings

A HOUSEWARMING PARTY—especially casual affairs such as backyard barbecues—is an excellent opportunity to introduce neighbors to your family and old friends. Some people worry that neighbors will feel awkward amid strangers, or they're unsure about extending an invitation that generally calls for a gift. But these are minor concerns compared to the goodwill that can be lost by excluding close neighbors. No one expects you to invite the entire neighborhood, but it's nice to include next-door neighbors and anyone you see regularly. Be sure your neighbors meet everyone, and as for gifts, leave that up to your guests. (For housewarming ideas, see Chapter 27, page 478: "Housewarmings.")

The Neighborly Basics

GOOD NEIGHBORS DON'T IMPOSE. But what exactly is an imposition? The definition varies from household to household. Some people enjoy casual, over-the-fence contact; others want their neighborhood relationships more structured. The following neighborly behaviors are basic but not written in stone; as you get to know your neighbors, you'll learn their preferences. By paying attention to individual lifestyles, customs, and social cues, good neighbors are rarely guilty of imposing.

Be considerate of neighbors' schedules. Don't waylay neighbors in the hall or on the street when you know that they're heading to or returning from work and social engagements.

Roommates might be described as mega-neighbors. They live as near as the next room or, in situations like college dorms, the next bed. Yet they aren't family, and you may be barely acquainted. To keep relations amicable, roommates have to establish basic rights and responsibilities up front. Be aware that problems can arise as roommates settle in; circumstances can alter dramatically when a roommate changes jobs or work schedule, becomes engaged, or enters a permanent relationship.

Respect roommates' privacy and personal property. A roommate's bedroom or sleeping area, clothing, bed and bath linens, cosmetics and personal hygiene products, private storage spaces, personal papers, computers and/or electronic files, and phone conversations should be inviolate. *Make it a rule never to borrow a roommate's possessions without permission.* Return borrowed items on time and in the same condition as when you borrowed them.

Live up to your financial obligations. Make rent and utilities payments on time. Agree on payment schedules and divide shopping chores. Contribute promptly to shared expenses, and don't expect a roommate to do all the shopping for food and household supplies. If you or a guest of yours causes damage to property or runs up phone bills, you are ethically responsible for the costs.

Be fair. One roommate might have a bigger bedroom or better facilities (like a private bath or more closet space) or use more services (as when one roommate monopolizes a shared phone). To be fair, the person who has or uses more should pay more, so negotiate in advance. If the inequity arises after you begin sharing, talk it over and make adjustments. When a boyfriend or girlfriend moves in with one roommate, rent and all other expenses should be renegotiated; a live-in should be regarded as a roommate with the same responsibilities as everyone else.

Keep shared spaces clean and neat. Don't clutter common spaces with your clothing, shoes, sports equipment, makeup, and other personal items. Determine how you'll share housework. The kitchen and bathroom are obvious problem areas if roommates don't clean up. The refrigerator is also a shared space, so throw out leftovers before they smell or grow mold.

Don't abuse entertaining privileges. Notify roommates when you will have a guest or guests, and don't subject roommates to a constant flow of your friends. If you want to give a party, clear your plans with roommates first—and be sure to invite them. When you entertain on your own, you're responsible for the costs and cleanup and for protecting your roommates' privacy. Don't expect roommates to disappear whenever you entertain, and don't use guests as an excuse to violate house rules, like no smoking or no loud music on weekend mornings.

A final roommate tip— Do the thoughtful thing: Post a note, send an e-mail, or leave a message on the answering machine when you'll be unusually late or plan to be away for even a day. You might leave a number where you can be reached. Roommates aren't family and may not be best buddies, but they care about your safety.

[119]

The Good Neighbor

Call ahead before visiting. Some neighbors happily pop in and out of each other's homes without warning, but don't assume that all neighbors enjoy this custom. Call and ask if it's convenient for you to stop by.

Limit visits to a reasonable amount of time. Be attuned to what your neighbors are doing, and leave at the first hint that they're ready for the visit to end.

Don't take advantage of a neighbor's expertise or talent. Living on the same street as a doctor, lawyer, mechanic, or anyone with special skills doesn't entitle neighbors to ask for free consultations or services.

Ask for help only when necessary, and say thanks for any favors. Don't constantly expect neighbors to provide free babysitting and fix-it services.

Enjoying Differences

Neighborhoods today are far more likely to be culturally, racially, and ethnically heterogeneous than in the past. Lifestyles vary widely, and old majorities no longer hold sway. (See Chapter 8, page 89: "Family Values, Family Manners.") It was once common to describe this country as a "melting pot" in which all differences were boiled away. But we're learning that "stew" is the more apt metaphor—a blend of differences that makes life more flavorful and interesting. Respecting and enjoying diversity often begins in one's neighborhood.

A QUESTION FOR PEGGY

We have a neighbor who drops by and never calls first. I like her, but she shows up so often that I've started closing the curtains and pretending that I'm not at home when I see her coming. There must be a better way to handle the problem.

It sounds as if you haven't discussed the dropping-in with your neighbor, so she probably thinks that you enjoy her unannounced visits. You have to let her know that you want to be called first. Do it with tact and patience. One approach is subtle: The next time she shows up, you can say something like "I'm glad to see you, Kathy, but I'm really busy right now. I'll call you later and make a time to get together." Follow up by calling and making a date for a specified day and time. Do this a few times, and she should get the message. A more direct approach is to bring up the subject of visits. You could say, "Kathy, would you mind calling me before you stop by? I enjoy our get-togethers so much, but it will work much better for me if we call first to make sure the timing is good." By expressing enthusiasm about your visits with your neighbor, you can keep your friendship going, but in a more manageable way.

When neighborhood conflicts arise from ethnic, cultural, or lifestyle differences, some people choose not to get involved. But reticence can often be mistaken for agreement when people are intent on ganging up on someone perceived as different.

Your attitude can be influential, so be sure that neighbors understand your feelings. If neighbors engage in hateful conversation, don't give any appearance of taking part. If you do discuss differences, be certain you know what you're talking about. Keep conversations generalized and don't allow talk to degenerate into personal attacks. Make an effort to meet your "different" neighbors, and as long as they agree, introduce them to others. Prejudices often melt away when people get together in low-pressure situations. You can't change diehard bigots, but by your example, you may be able to facilitate tolerance and encourage neighborly relations.

Avoid making judgments based on stereotypes. Categorizing individuals by their group is rude at best and can be dangerous. Good neighbors *work* at being open-minded. They don't form opinions until they've gotten to know someone well enough to have an opinion.

Steer clear of pejorative language. A person doesn't have to be politically correct to know that labels can cause pain. It's impolite to automatically describe or single out people by their race, national origin, religion, political affiliation, or physical or mental condition. (A person is a "neighbor," not "the foreigner across the hall" or "the lady with the handicapped child.")

Be interested and ask polite questions. There's no better way to dispel myths and stereotypes than by asking people about lifestyle differences. No one is obligated to explain or defend himself, but when the situation is comfortable and questions are posed out of genuine interest, people often enjoy talking about the way they live and the history of their traditions.

Show respect. A classic example of disrespect is any attempt to "convert" neighbors or hint that their way of living is open to debate. Another is thoughtlessly expecting neighbors to worship on the same days or observe the same holidays in the same ways. Lack of respect is often the result of ignorance. An occasional slip is usually forgivable; repeating the error is not.

Respecting Privacy and Property

Neighbors in close quarters need to be attentive in order not to be intrusive. For example, it's all too easy to overhear conversations in hallways, on elevators, or around the pool, so *not* eavesdropping requires some mental effort. Not repeating what is accidentally overheard is just common decency.

Everyone ought to know what bad gossip is: spreading false or unsubstantiated rumors, revealing information that should be kept private, breaking confidences, and generally dishing the dirt on people who aren't around to defend themselves. But all gossip is not inherently evil. Tapping into the neighborhood grapevine can be a good way to learn important news—the arrival of a new family, an upcoming vacation, a neighbor's illness. Good gossip is informative, bad gossip is hurtful, and common sense will signal the difference.

Living around others is easier and more pleasant if neighbors are alert to privacy and property issues and make conscious efforts not to step over the line. Communicating with neighbors is essential, as is honoring the general standards in a neighborhood.

Everyday Etiquette

FROM ESTABLISHED NEIGHBORHOODS to transient communities such as college housing and singles apartments, the common good is served when residents think about how their behaviors may affect neighbors. Even the local sourpuss might loosen up when his or her neighbors observe the following everyday basics:

Greet neighbors whenever you see them. A smile, a wave, and a pleasant "hello" are probably the easiest ways to show neighbors that they matter to you. If you don't know a neighbor's name, ask.

Have an occasional chat. There's a lot you can learn through casual conversations. It's nice to discover a neighbor who shares your taste in books or your allegiance to the local college team.

Dress considerately. You have the right to dress as you like in your own home. But when neighbors are likely to see, it's thoughtful to dress in a way that will not cause embarrassment. A special concern is sunbathing and swim attire, or lack thereof. Very skimpy clothing and nudity should be reserved for totally private places.

Keep garbage and junk neat and secure. Bag garbage and stash it in tightly lidded containers. Take containers to the curb shortly before scheduled collection times and retrieve them as soon as you can. Bag or box used clothing and bundle and tie newspapers and other items to prevent scattering.

Be careful about lighting. When you install outdoor lighting, including holiday lights, consider your neighbors' point of view. Aim spotlights so they won't shine in neighbors' windows. Use timers that turn off exterior lights at a reasonable hour. If your interior lights, TV, or computer screen could bother anyone in a neighboring apartment, draw the drapes or close the blinds.

Controlling Noise

Few neighborhood problems generate as much bad feeling as excessive noise. Unlike unkempt lawns and peeling house paint, noise goes into the hearts of other people's homes and is nearly impossible to escape. Uncontrolled noise has become such a nuisance that it's considered a form of environmental pollution increasingly subject to legal regulation. In closely populated urban neighborhoods, people may think their noise can't be heard above the sounds of the city, but it can. To gauge how far your sounds travel, step outside your home and *listen* when the stereo is on or an appliance is running.

Determine hours for noisemaking with neighbors in mind. When your next-door neighbor comes home with a new baby, it's time to quiet late-night music sessions and perhaps purchase a set of earphones.

Limit use of lawn mowers, blowers, power tools, and the like to reasonable times. You may love the smell of freshly cut grass in the morning, but the roar of a lawn tractor at 6:00 AM is unlikely to thrill anyone else.

In apartments, duplexes, and condos, try to place noisemaking equipment and appliances away from shared walls. Even commonplace noises like a ringing phone or grinding food blender can shatter a neighbor's peace.

Be considerate about live music. Your youngster may be a budding Louis Armstrong, but the sound of his bleating trumpet can be tolerated for only so long. Try to hold practice sessions in sound-dampened areas, and be especially cautious with amplified instruments.

Ban boom boxes on residential streets. Cranking up portable and vehicular stereos should be confined to wide-open spaces. Since young people are the most likely offenders, parents have to exercise control.

Borrowing and Lending

It's neighborly to be generous, but frequent borrowers soon become neighborhood pests. While it's preferable not to borrow from neighbors, follow these etiquette principles if you do:

Ask for the item but don't persist. If your neighbor says "no" or seems at all reluctant, drop the matter with a polite "I understand."

Give a time when you will return the item, and be punctual. If the lender says she needs the item back by a certain time, don't abuse her trust.

If lessons in consideration start early, most children will have a fairly good understanding of what is off-limits by the time they reach school age. But parents must remain vigilant. Youngsters can easily forget their manners and the rules of safety when they're curious or caught up in play.

Teach children where they can and can't go. Children shouldn't cross a neighbor's property, play on driveways and in yards without the owner's permission, enter closed gates, or play with pets unless the owners are present. Teach youngsters that fences mean "stay out."

Curb the noise. Youngsters need to learn and respect "quiet times." Parents should be conscious of other annoyances such as a basketball or tennis ball bouncing off walls and floors. If your child loves to stomp and jump, teach him to tread softly on communal stairs, in halls, and on floors above neighbors.

Go slow around others. Children and teens on bikes, skates, skateboards, and in riding toys can be hazardous to others. In general, parents should restrict riding to safe places, including driveways, designated bike trails, and riding and skating areas in parks. Teach children to slow down whenever they see someone approaching on a sidewalk and to walk their vehicles around blind corners.

Put away outdoor toys. To prevent injuries to others (see page 127: "Swimming Pools and Other 'Attractive Nuisances'"), give youngsters a place to park riding toys. See that toys and equipment, including buckets, digging tools, and pup tents, are put away safely after each use. Be especially careful to empty wading pools and cover sandboxes.

Relationships

| 124 |

Return the item in at least as good condition as when you borrowed it. Refill the tank before you take the mower back. When "borrowing" a carton of milk or a can of motor oil, replace it exactly—same brand and quantity.

Repair, replace, or pay for anything that's damaged, broken, or lost. Don't just tell your neighbor what happened (or worse, ignore the whole thing) and expect him to let the matter slide.

Soliciting Neighbors

Many neighbors will try to help out when a neighbor, especially a child, asks that they buy an item or make a donation for a fund-raising event. But no one should be subjected to endless solicitations, no matter how worthy the cause. Be considerate of your neighbors' patience and budgets; limit solicitations and never use high-pressure tactics.

Outside solicitors—salespeople, people seeking employment, religious groups,

I don't mind lending things to people, but I have one forgetful neighbor who never brings anything back on time. At the moment, he has my electric weeder and my daughter's bicycle pump. How can I get my possessions back without hurting his feelings?

Approach your neighbor in a friendly way and tell him that you need your weeder and pump. It's best to avoid saying anything that may embarrass him, but you don't have to apologize for asking. A request along these lines should produce results: "I'm working in the garden, and I just realized you still have my weeder. While I'm here, I can get Missy's bike pump, too."

If he can't comply at the moment, give him a specific time when you'll come back for the items. Occasional forgetfulness may be excusable, but since your neighbor makes it a habit, you might turn down his requests in the future. Without singling him out, tell him that your family has lost so many things that you've made it a policy not to lend to anyone.

charitable and political canvassers, and census takers—generally have legitimate motives, but it's wise to be cautious. Even if you've checked a solicitor's credentials and are certain that he or she is legitimate, don't offer referrals or give out any information about your neighbors.

Keeping an Eye Out

There's a big difference between being nosy and being observant. Good neighbors watch out for one another and do what's appropriate if they see something that seems amiss—newspapers piling up on a doorstep, strange people at a neighbor's home when the neighbor is known to be away, children playing in an unsafe area. No one should be offended if a neighbor inquires about a worrisome situation. Assume you're being asked out of genuine concern. There may be a logical explanation—you canceled the paper and didn't realize it was still being delivered—or you may need to take action.

Watching out for neighbors also involves informing them of any activity that may cause them inconvenience. Home renovations create noise and dirt problems that can go on for weeks. A large party may bring parking and noise problems. Neighbors are usually understanding if you tell them about your plans in advance and ask for their tolerance.

You'll probably recognize at least some of these neighborhood nuisances. They're not bad people—just unthinking, careless, inconsiderate, and rude.

Messy Mike. His litter always lands on his neighbor's property.

Smelly Shelley. An apartment dweller's nightmare, she cooks with garlic and onions, burns incense, and smokes, but she never cracks a window or flips on the exhaust fan.

Lead-foot Larry. When he walks, the earth trembles. His favorite activity is doing step exercises just over his neighbors' heads.

Slamming Sidney. Front door, back door, closets, cabinets. Windows and drawers, too. His incessant slamming has his nearby neighbors coming unhinged.

Curious Connie. She looks in mail slots, checks packages left in the hall or on the doorstep, and, at her worst, peeks at her neighbors' trash.

Know-it-all Nate. Wash the car, paint the shutters . . . and Nate's radar goes off. Not that he offers to lend a hand; unsolicited advice is his stock-in-trade.

Garage-sale Gertie. Mindless of local ordinances, she runs a permanent bazaar in her yard or garage. Her bargain-hunting customers have few qualms about tramping over lawns or blocking driveways to get a good deal.

Bellowing Bob. He can't go find his children or whistle for his dog. Morning, noon, and night, he likes to step outside and shout at the top of his lungs.

Outdoor Etiquette

OVERGROWN LAWNS AND GARDENS are unattractive, can adversely affect property values for an entire neighborhood, and may pose health and safety hazards. Considerate homeowners will, at the least, regularly maintain that part of their property—including house exterior, garage, and any outbuildings—that is visible to others. Start by stowing away eyesores like an overabundance of garden supplies, used appliances, and old tires. Trim back ground covers and low-hanging limbs that can cause falls on walkways or block vision at corners and intersections. Inspect yards routinely for broken glass, rocks, and metal pieces that can be stepped on or become projectiles when hit by a mower.

Good neighbors accept that taste is individual. So long as neighbors maintain their property, there's no call to criticize their fondness for garden gnomes. When something unavoidable (an illness or injury, a death in the family) prevents a neighbor from doing outdoor chores, kind neighbors will often pitch in to mow and water until the person can make permanent arrangements.

Smoke and Odors

While those grilled steaks or kebabs may be delicious, the smoke and cooking odors aren't appealing to people in your vicinity—especially on hot days when there's not a breeze to dissipate the air pollution. Smoke from balcony and patio grills can collect in apartment hallways, covered walkways, and other residents' flats. Many apartments and condominiums offer communal areas where outdoor cooking is properly ventilated. Be conservative with fire-starting chemicals (or your neighbors will think they're living next to a diesel pump).

Outdoor burning of leaves and other materials is generally regulated by state and municipal law. When burning is allowed, considerate neighbors are cautious about the materials they burn. Even treated wood may be toxic. Check with your fire department or state environmental agency before burning anything. Whether cooking or burning, have a water source and fire extinguishing equipment at hand; watch out for drifting sparks.

Be conscious of other possible odor producers, including garden fertilizers, insect repellents, and compost piles. Wash and disinfect outdoor trash containers regularly.

Blowing Leaves

Autumn brings crisp days, cool nights, and tons of dead leaves. You are responsible for leaves that fall from your neighbors' trees and land in your yard. It's up to you to dispose of leaves on your property no matter where they originated. Neighbors can make autumn cleanup easier by blowing or piling leaves away from property lines. If your collection does blow into a neighbor's yard, it's thoughtful to offer to clear it away.

Power leaf blowers are so noisy that many municipalities regulate their use or ban them outright, and some impose hefty fines on offenders. Be considerate: Choose a low-decibel model and limit use to times when neighbors are least likely to be bothered.

Swimming Pools and Other "Attractive Nuisances"

In law, an "attractive nuisance" is any object or condition on a person's property that is both attractive to and dangerous for children. Under the theory that children are neither as rational nor as responsible as adults, anything from a backyard trampoline or swing set to a swimming pool or construction materials can be an attractive nuisance. A property owner who doesn't take reasonable steps to prevent injuries to children can be held liable. (A competent adult who enters your property without permission is a trespasser, and the law generally takes a case-by-case approach to teens.)

Apart from the law, common sense and consideration mean that you should do everything you can to protect others. What seems harmless to an adult—a trickling water feature in the garden, a broken place in a fence large enough to trap a small head or arm—can be deadly for a child. Look at your property from a child's viewpoint; be sure any hazardous objects are locked away and dangerous areas (including pools, hot tubs, garages, tool sheds, and building sites) are secured.

About Rover and Kitty

Dogs can be wonderful companions but terrible neighbors if their owners are irresponsible. In cities and towns, owners should know and obey local collar, leash, "pooper-scooper," and other health laws as well as any residential restrictions. Cleaning up is a fundamental because dog waste is smelly, hazardous for pedestrians, and a genuine public health problem. Dogs should be well trained in basic commands and under control whenever other people or animals are around. Experts recommend that owners *introduce* their dogs to people before allowing any direct contact. Be extremely cautious about allowing a dog to approach children.

In suburban neighborhoods and rural areas, dogs enjoy considerably more freedom, but owners are responsible for following local laws and keeping dogs from invading other people's physical and psychological space. A lot of goodwill is sacrificed when dog owners allow their pets to dig in neighbors' gardens, defecate on their lawns, paw

∼ Four Ways to Complain Politely About Pets ∼

Your neighbors' cat stalks the songbirds in your yard. Or their dog buries anything that isn't nailed down. What can you do? Begin by understanding that a pet owner can't control a situation that he or she isn't aware of. A one-on-one conversation is the ideal place to start.

Have a polite word with your pet-owning neighbor. Take a calm, tactful approach and try to frame your complaint as concern for the pet and the owner. ("I'm sure you want to know that Fluffy has been getting out of your house while you're away. I'm afraid he might get into traffic.")

Write a courteous note if you can't catch your neighbor in person. Avoid any language that could be construed as insulting or threatening to the owner or pet. Neighborhood petitions may seem like a good idea but are very intimidating, especially if the owner doesn't know about the problem.

Ask for help from building owners/managers or homeowners' associations. A pointed but confidential letter from a higher authority will remind a negligent pet owner of the rules he or she is expected to follow. This can be a reasonable approach if you don't know the pet owners or they have a history of disregarding individual complaints.

As a last resort, take the problem to public officials. It may help if several neighbors band together to talk with local authorities. An official letter of warning (detailing the problem but not naming the complainants) may do the trick. If you suspect that a pet is being abused or neglected or that an animal poses a physical threat to others, courtesy is less important than reporting before any harm is done.

through garbage, or bark and yowl all day and night. If a neighbor's dog barks incessantly while the neighbor is at work, inform him and ask for some relief (See page 128: "Four Ways to Complain Politely About Pets.)

The independent feline is not governable like a dog, but cat owners are equally obligated to observe local health and safety ordinances and to protect neighbors against invasive cat behavior. Cat litter—all pet litter—should be bagged and sealed before it's put out with the trash.

Every owner should learn as much as possible about his pet's species and breed and its habits. Neutering and spaying of cats and dogs is a public service.

Parking Problems

When communal parking is limited, the rights of neighbors should come first. Problems often arise when someone entertains and fails to make adequate arrangements for guest parking. Most neighbors will simmer quietly when they're inconvenienced, but their resentment is justified. The following suggestions can help both guests and neighbors enjoy your special occasions:

Hire parking attendants for large gatherings. Attendants can direct the traffic flow so that cars don't clutter streets, block drives, or overflow onto neighbors' yards.

Arrange off-site parking, if necessary. You might be able to use a church or business parking lot. If the lot isn't within walking distance, you can provide shuttle service.

Reserve parking. When on-street parking is difficult, you might reserve space for your guests' cars in a convenient commercial parking center.

Handling Difficult Situations

YOUR NEXT-DOOR NEIGHBOR builds his new toolshed three feet over your property line. The house down the street has been empty and overgrown for a year, and it's attracting vermin. You suspect that a neighbor's children are neglected or that teens in the neighborhood are forming a gang. There are some problems that require more than neighborly forbearance.

While it's usually best to try to negotiate a reasonable solution, this isn't always possible. In some cases, you may be dealing with a landlord or management company rather than someone you know. In other cases, directly involving yourself in a situation such as drug trafficking, gang activity, or domestic violence is likely to put you in physical danger.

Getting Help

If you have a homeowners' or apartment association or co-op board, start there. Or talk with other neighbors and perhaps form an ad hoc group to approach property owners and/or public officials. In cases of suspected violence or abuse, you should report to police or family/children's services as quickly as possible.

You may need to consult an attorney about individual problems like property-line disputes. Rather than rushing to file a lawsuit, it's important to know whether you have a case. Some municipalities offer neighborhood mediation services, often administered by the civil courts. For the sake of maintaining neighborly relations, settle differences as civilly as possible; don't ask others to take sides in a private matter.

❧ Neighborly Advice for People ❧ Who Work at Home

These courtesies should help keep the peace between people with home businesses and their neighbors.

➤ Tell neighbors that you work at home. Most people will respect your schedule if you explain your work hours and what you're doing.

➤ Obey local laws. Municipal and county ordinances usually address at least some of the issues that may cause conflict with neighbors, including zoning, licensing, parking, business hours, and signage.

➤ Be tasteful with signage. If you hang out your shingle, be sure it's in keeping with the aesthetic standards of the neighborhood.

➤ Provide parking for employees, clients, and customers. Be sure that people who come to your home don't block access or hog on-street parking.

➤ Inform delivery services where to leave packages and envelopes when you're away. Avoid constantly asking a neighbor to accept or bring in your business deliveries. An occasional request may be okay.

➤ Be very careful about selling to neighbors. Unless they volunteer, don't impose on neighbors to attend or host sales presentations or buy products they don't want or need.

Chapter Eleven

Illnesses and Disabilities

ANY ETIQUETTE SURROUNDING a minor illness is fairly straightforward. We know to be careful not to spread anything contagious—the common cold included—and whenever we're in the company of someone who's under the weather in any way, we offer sympathy: "Sorry to hear you've been sick with the flu. I hope you're feeling better."

A more serious illness, including the recovery period after an operation, calls for a get-well card, flowers, or perhaps a visit. And dealing with a debilitating or terminal illness makes more demands on loved ones and friends, all of whom want to make such difficult days as comfortable for the patient as possible.

When You're the One Who Is Ill

UNTIL SCIENCE FINDS that elusive cure, the one sickness no one can escape is the cold. Running a close second is influenza, or the flu.

If you're like most people, you go about your routine activities when you come down with a cold—but if that includes shopping and going to work, you're not doing the people around you any favors. Colds are contagious during the first five days of infection, and it's common sense to stay home as much as possible during that period. To lessen the risk of passing on a cold, you should wash your hands several times a day (hand contact passes the virus to anything you touch) and sneeze into a handkerchief or tissue. (Think of a sneeze as an aerosol spray of infectious saliva and mucous particles.)

The flu generally confines you to bed for a few days but still can spread easily. Flu is infectious for three to five days after symptoms first appear, so isolate yourself as much as possible. For children, the infectious period is a couple of days longer, something to take into account before sending them back out into the world.

Serious Illnesses

Colds and the flu pale in comparison to an extended illness of any kind, be it a recovery from persistent infection, a bout with mononucleosis, or an illness much more serious. When you expect to be incapacitated and confined at home for a few weeks or longer, there's more to consider.

First, you and your caregiver(s) should agree that you'll have your own space, both literally and figuratively (see "Advice for Caregivers," below). Explain to family members and friends that there will be times when you need to be alone and other times when you feel like being sociable. Stress that no one should be offended when you want privacy; at times, solitude can be just the right medicine.

Because the primary caregiver in your family will often deal with health care professionals, good communication is essential to prevent conflicts or misunderstandings between you, the caregiver, and any other care providers. So that your caregiver won't receive mixed signals, make sure he or she fully understands your wishes. Write everything down, including notes on discussions with doctors, which medications and other treatments have been prescribed, and any questions to ask your doctors.

While you're incapacitated, other family members will have to take over your household tasks. Be flexible; no one who's helping you will ever do things exactly the way you do, whether it's choosing groceries or putting away the dishes. If you tend toward perfectionism, make a concerted effort to be both grateful and gracious.

When you start to feel well again, be aware of how your transition can affect your family. Do things gradually. If you're resuming certain responsibilities that have been taken on by others, bear in mind that this is the reverse of what happened when you fell ill (now *you're* the one who's changing the way things are done). Be considerate as you take back your tasks and be thankful for the efforts made by others.

Advice for Caregivers

IF YOU FIND YOURSELF CARING for someone with a prolonged illness, it's extremely important to let the person have his own space so that he can feel as independent as possible. Everything he needs should be close at hand—a telephone, radio and television, reading material and a good light, and so on. If the person is confined to bed, provide a bell, intercom, or some other way of calling when help is needed; shouting takes precious energy.

So that the patient can follow his own schedule, he should have a room or area away from where the spouse or partner sleeps. This way, if he's having trouble sleeping at night, he'll be able to read, watch television, or do whatever he wants without disturbing anyone. A separate space also allows him to get away to rest during the day.

Screening phone calls for the sick person is a good idea when he doesn't feel like talking. Use the answering machine or have another person in the home take messages and field calls with a prearranged line like "I'll check to see if he's awake."

If the caregiving falls on one family member, a friend or relative might give her a periodic break. This "respite care" will allow the caregiver time for herself—perhaps to run errands or visit friends. Health care professionals say that respite care is vitally important for the mental health of the caregiver and the family as a whole.

An important note: Take care not to hover over someone who is sick, reminding yourself that there's such a thing as being *too* solicitous.

Debilitating Diseases

When the illness is as serious as cancer, severe cardiovascular disease, or Alzheimer's, caregivers have more concerns and worries—starting with what to say. Family and friends alike may struggle for the right words for someone who has a debilitating or terminal disease, but just listening to the patient is often preferable to talking. No matter how you word the thought, "I'm here for you" will reassure the person of your love and support and will help her to open up.

Acts of kindness for people with a debilitating disease can range from shopping to bookkeeping to tidying up. When a terminally ill patient lives alone and is still ambulatory, close friends might band together to stage periodic "evenings with Jenny." On a set night of the week chosen by the patient and group, a different friend arrives with a full-course gourmet meal (easily available through takeout these days) and beverages, ready for an evening of camaraderie.

When a patient's mental abilities have declined severely, as they do with Alzheimer's and dementia, it is important to understand that mood swings, verbal or physical aggression, and combativeness are completely out of the patient's control. Instead of taking the behaviors personally, accept them as part of the disease and stay calm, patient, and flexible. Always acknowledge the patient's requests, and then act on them if you can. When helping with activities (eating, taking a walk, playing cards, and so forth), minimize distractions and focus on the patient's enjoyment, not how much she can or cannot achieve.

A QUESTION FOR PEGGY

Through a third party, I just learned that a friend of mine has cancer. She'll be at a luncheon I'm attending next week, and I'm not sure what to say to her. Or should I say nothing?

Because your friend will doubtless be working through the emotions of dealing with her illness, she may not be ready to discuss it with anyone just yet, so wait until she broaches the subject. If and when she does, say you're always ready to offer support and lend an ear. If her illness has become public and you know for sure that she's talking about it with others, you can take the initiative: "I just heard about your diagnosis from Linda. You know I'm here for you, so please let me know whenever I can help in any way."

Never let the tenderness you feel toward anyone with a debilitating disease lead you to treat her as a child. If the person is bedridden, give her notice of what you're going to do, whether it's turning or moving her, getting her out of bed, or getting her a drink of water. Avoid using more familiar names than you would normally. If you don't regularly call her "Honey," don't start using the term when she becomes ill.

Choose Your Words Well

Sometimes even the best-intentioned words can cause discomfort or be slightly offensive to a person who is ill. Things *not* to say include "I know how you feel" (no one knows exactly how a sick person feels), "You're going to be fine" (this is especially inappropriate for someone who knows he is terminally ill), and "It's not that bad" (often said to help the speaker himself feel more comfortable). It's not up to you to play psychologist and talk the sick person out of feeling morose.

It's far better to listen to what he has to say, accept and acknowledge the situation and his feelings about it, and make empathetic statements he can react to. Some appropriate responses: "It must be tough" or "You must be feeling pretty tied down." If his chances for recovery are slim, steer clear of remarks that sound either too optimistic or pessimistic and stick to the middle ground.

Professional Home Care

Professional nurses and hospice caregivers can be a godsend for a seriously ill person and her family. A skilled professional nurse will not only tend to the patient's needs but also bolster the strength of everyone concerned as they cope.

When nothing more can be done to save a patient in the last stages of cancer, Alzheimer's, AIDS, or other chronic disease, hospices and hospice care agencies provide emotional support, pain relief, and, if requested, spiritual guidance. The help these nurses offer allows families to find their own way (and at their own speed) as they struggle to come to terms with the terminal illness of a loved one.

In the end stage of a terminal illness, hospice caregivers often become temporary live-ins, providing twenty-four-hour care, making their interpersonal skills and bedside manner all the more important. A good hospice caregiver is pleasant and personable but also understands that he should let family members initiate and take the lead in conversations. He won't talk about his personal life unless asked; he doesn't stay in the living room to catch the end of a TV show when his time would be better spent with the patient; and he intuitively knows how much privacy to give family members, relatives, and friends when they gather at the patient's home.

If, after a day or two, the patient or family members have any doubts about a caregiver, they should request another. If there's ever a time when the right person is called for, this is it.

Caregivers usually develop close relationships with the people they care for, so when a patient dies, make certain you tell the caregiver how much his service meant to you. Inform him of all funeral arrangements (stories abound of families who didn't invite the caregiver to the funeral). If you think it appropriate, a small gift will underline your appreciation. If the caregiver's agency prohibits their employees from accepting gifts, a donation to the agency may be the alternative.

Visiting the Sick at Home

WHEN PLANNING TO VISIT SOMEONE who is ill at her home, always call first. *Never* arrive unannounced. Likewise, start a phone call by asking if it's a good time to talk; if the person isn't feeling well, she may not be up to it.

Unless you're visiting a close relative or friend who's indicated she would like you to linger, plan to stay no longer than forty-five minutes or so. While you're there, it's important to be in the sick person's "zone" and let her guide the conversation. People who are ill may show less enthusiasm for the things that usually interest them or become overexcited by a minor incident. But such reactions are usually temporary, and you can probably change the subject.

If the visit is to a fellow member of your house of worship or to anyone else who's receptive to praying together, saying prayers is appropriate and a nice way to show your support.

It's very important not to patronize or speak condescendingly. Just because the person is bedridden or using a wheelchair doesn't mean her mental faculties aren't sharp. Above all, when other people are present, don't talk about the sick person as if she weren't there.

Although running errands for sick friends and bringing food when you visit are welcome in most cases, you should always ask before doing any favors. Sick people may feel that friends and family members are going too far out of their way and could possibly resent the effort.

Visiting the Hospitalized

VISITING A PATIENT in the hospital brings more concerns, especially when the patient is seriously ill. The first is to be courteous toward nurses and other personnel and avoid asking for special attention from anyone who is obviously busy. (Your friend or loved one isn't the only patient on the floor.) Check with the nurse before you bring food, even if the patient has asked for it; certain foods may be restricted.

When you greet the patient, take his hand gently but don't hug. Some sick people don't like to be touched, especially if they've had surgery. If relatives are present, you'll want to shorten your visit to give them more privacy with their loved one. Introduce yourself, if necessary, leave your present if you've brought one, and wish the patient a quick recovery. Then, unless you're begged to stay, say, "It was so nice to meet all of you," and make your exit.

You should also leave sooner if other visitors arrive. Nothing is more exhausting to a person confined to bed than having to follow a conversation conducted by people seated on all sides of the room. When two or three people are present, either stand or put your chairs on the same side of the bed.

When you're engaged in a conversation with the patient, stay upbeat. The news that his son is failing math or the family car was involved in a fender-bender will hardly improve his mental outlook. Your job as a visitor is to cheer him up, not weigh him down with more worries.

When you've been asked to sit with the patient for a few hours, be sure to let him know that he needn't chat or entertain you. Take reading material along, attend to simple tasks as needed, sit where the patient can see you, and let him know that you're quite happy to have an hour or two in which to quietly enjoy your book or magazine if that is his preference.

Flowers and Other Gifts

Giving flowers to the sick sends the message that you care. Just be sure a floral arrangement is of manageable size and comes with its own container (vases or other suitable containers are very difficult to find in hospitals). Patients often prefer potted plants to cut flowers because they're easy to care for, last longer, and can be taken by a family member if the arrangements start to overcrowd the room.

When choosing a gift other than flowers or plants, be guided by the severity of the illness and the length of the hospital stay. Light reading matter (both in weight and content) and book audiotapes (which don't have to be held and can be listened to with eyes shut) will be welcomed by young and old alike. If the patient is to be hospitalized for some time, a new dressing gown or bed jacket can be a real day-brightener. As for food, make sure it's allowed on the patient's diet.

While touches from home (a favorite pillowcase, a vanity mirror) aren't gifts, they will be gratefully received. For some patients, news of friends and family may be the best gift of all; a lengthy hospital stay is an isolating experience.

∼ Four Don'ts for Hospital Visitors ∼

Here are four things you should remember *not* to do when paying a visit to a hospitalized person, whether she's an acquaintance or a member of your family:

Don't wear perfume or cologne. Scents can smell stronger, even nauseating, to people who are sick.

Don't sit on the edge of the bed. While you may think sitting on the bed shows personal concern, it may cramp or cause pain for the patient.

Don't forget who's listening. If doctors or other health professionals are in the room, don't talk to them as if the sick person weren't there.

Don't overstay your welcome. Visit briefly, cheerfully, and leave the patient rested and encouraged. In most cases, make up your mind before you arrive that you'll stay no more than fifteen or twenty minutes, then stick to it.

Semiprivate Rooms and Wards

If the hospital patient doesn't have a private room, be sure to consider the other people who will be affected by your visit. First and foremost, keep your voice low so you won't disturb others who may badly need their rest. In some instances, you might draw the curtains between the beds for privacy and quiet. On the other hand, if the person you're visiting and her roommate have become friendly, the roommate may enjoy being included in the conversation.

If you're going to the snack bar or vending machine for your friend, it's thoughtful to ask the other patient in the room if she'd like anything. If the person you're visiting is in a ward, you need make the offer only to someone with whom you've been talking or a patient who asks for a favor.

Don't turn on a television or radio in a semiprivate room without asking the patient's and roommate's permission. If both are fine with it, ask the patient's program choice and keep the volume low unless the roommate expresses a wish to watch or listen.

Courtesies for the Disabled

THE LARGEST MINORITY GROUP in the United States—some seventeen percent of the population—is made up of people with disabilities. But it's important to remember that the humanity of these fifty million individuals is in no way different from yours. Acknowledging this reality makes it easier to put aside any anxiety and be yourself when you interact with a person with disabilities. Some rules apply across the board:

➤ Never stare, no matter how inconspicuously.

➤ Never be overly solicitous. Take your cue from the person with special needs. If you want to help, *ask first,* since people who've mastered getting about in wheelchairs, on a crutch or a brace, or without the benefit of vision or hearing take great pride in their independence.

➤ Never ask personal questions of a person with an obvious disability. If he wants to talk about the condition, he will broach the subject.

➤ Never pity the person. As the saying goes, "Life is what you make it," and if the person doesn't see his life as tragic, then it isn't.

Sensitivity in Language

Sensitivity toward the disabled starts with your language. Put personhood first by speaking of a "person with a disability" rather than a "disabled person," "invalid," or "victim." Refer to a "person with cerebral palsy" or a "person with epilepsy" (not "a paralytic" or an "epileptic"). The words "deaf" and "blind" are fine to use, but "handicapped"—and especially "crippled"—should be avoided.

Watching your language doesn't mean banishing certain words and phrases. It's fine to ask a blind person, "Did you see that TV show last night?" (the blind use the word "see" as much as anyone else) and to invite someone in a wheelchair to "go for a walk."

Always refer to someone in a wheelchair as a "person who uses a wheelchair" instead of one who's "wheelchair bound" or "confined to a wheelchair," both of which contradict the liberation that the wheelchair provides. Also, many people who must communicate via sign language prefer the word "deaf" over the euphemistic "hearing impaired."

Those Who Are Hard of Hearing or Deaf

There is more than one degree of deafness, from partial loss of hearing in one ear to a complete lack of hearing. When you're with someone who is partially deaf, it may be necessary only to speak a little more distinctly or to repeat a remark. If you know that the hearing loss is in one ear, sit on the side of the good ear in movies, restaurants, or any other places where you may not be face-to-face.

If someone is completely deaf, you have more to consider when communicating:

➤ When the person isn't facing you and you need to attract his attention, a gentle tap on the arm or shoulder—not a shout—is appropriate.

➤ Maintain eye contact, keep your head up so that your lips are easily seen, and make sure that you aren't standing in front of a light source, which can impede the other person's vision.

➤ Speak slowly and clearly and don't shout. Also be ready to repeat your statement in words that are easier to understand.

➤ Don't exaggerate your lip movements; distorted lip motions can confuse even the best lip-reader.

➤ If speech alone isn't getting a message across, it's perfectly acceptable to use gestures or write notes.

➤ If you're speaking with a person who has an interpreter, direct your attention to the former, not the latter. You won't be excluding the interpreter, since she understands her role and won't expect to participate.

∼ Using a Text Telephone ∼

Pioneering devices in the mode of communication called text messaging, text telephones (also known as telecommunications devices for the deaf, or TDDs) allow two people to communicate by typing back and forth in a conversational manner over a phone line. Calls between a deaf person and a hearing person are made through a relay service, meaning the hearing caller speaks to a mediator who relays words to the recipient by teletyping them into a console; the words then appear in the display window of the recipient's device.

If conversing with a deaf or hard of hearing person over a TDD, you should address the person directly, as if the mediator weren't present. Don't say, "Tell him that . . ." or "Ask him to . . ." And, as with any other call, be sure to use your best telephone manners.

Those Who Are Blind or Have Low Vision

While people who are blind or visually impaired usually know how to get around—especially if they use a cane or a guide dog—there will be times when they need assistance. If, for instance, someone is trying to negotiate a broken sidewalk, ask if you can help. Instead of taking the person's arm, offer your own (people who are blind need their arms for balance). As you walk, tell him of any obstacles, stairs, or curbs. If he uses a guide dog, walk on the side opposite the animal.

Indoors, warn of anything protruding at head level (hanging lamps or plants), pulled-out drawers, or open cabinet doors. If you work or participate in group activities with a person who's blind, always identify yourself and introduce him to the group so that he doesn't feel excluded.

If you're eating with him, do the following:

➤ In a restaurant, read the menu aloud.

➤ Indicate where the condiments are on the table.

➤ Using clock terms, let the person know where everything is on the plate: "Your pasta is at six o'clock" (nearest to him); "Your spinach is at twelve o'clock" (farthest from him).

➤ When necessary—and only with his permission—cut his food into bite-sized pieces before either of you begin to eat.

When a person who's blind visits your home, lead him to a chair and simply place his hand on the arm or back; he's capable of seating himself. If he's staying with you for any length of time, indicate where the various pieces of furniture are and keep doors completely opened or closed—never halfway open, which can pose a hazard.

Here are more tips, from the American Foundation for the Blind (www.afb.org):

➤ Use a natural tone of voice. Don't speak loudly or slowly unless the person has a hearing impairment.

➤ Speak directly to the person—not through a companion or guide who may be accompanying him.

➤ Feel free to use words and expressions that refer to vision. It's fine to say, "Watch out for that step."

➤ When ending a conversation or leaving a room, make a point of saying goodbye so that the blind or visually impaired person knows you've left.

Those in Wheelchairs

When you meet a person in a wheelchair, offer a handshake just as you would to anyone else. The exception is when the person doesn't have the use of her right hand. In this case, shaking her left hand is fine, as is gently touching her arm or shoulder as a welcoming gesture.

Never lean over someone in a wheelchair to shake a third person's hand. And don't treat the chair as you would furniture (leaning on the wheelchair, for example, or setting your drink on the detachable desktop). A wheelchair is part of a person's personal space, and you should take care to treat it as such. When conversing with the person, either pull up a chair and sit at her level or stand far enough away so that she won't have to strain her neck to make eye contact.

Offer to push a wheelchair only when it appears the person needs help ("May I help you over this curb?"), and *wait for permission*. Then ask for instructions; otherwise, you could accidentally detach one of the parts by lifting the chair improperly. When pushing, watch the ground in front of you so that you don't run the chair over potholes, animal dung, broken concrete, large cables, or other hindrances.

Those Who Are Speech-Impaired

Speech problems range from stuttering to Tourette's syndrome to stroke-induced difficulties. If you listen patiently and carefully to someone with a speech problem, your understanding of his speech (or of any device he uses) will improve as he talks. Remain attentive to the conversation even if there are delays, and don't complete sentences unless the person asks for help. If you don't understand what he's saying, ask a question that will help him clarify the part you missed.

Those Who Are Mentally Disabled

Unlike mental illness, mental disabilities are congenital or result from traumatic head injury. While people with physical disabilities find it difficult to maneuver through space, those with mental disabilities more often have trouble with basic social and communication skills—listening, comprehending, and giving appropriate responses, whether verbally or nonverbally. As a result, they find themselves treated as "different" (especially by children), something to which they're very sensitive.

People with mental disabilities not only feel things just as deeply as anyone else but also often harbor a wealth of intelligence. Many with autism have shown extraordinary abilities on the computer, while others with a mental disability play the piano by ear, create intricate and beautiful artworks, or have other special talents.

When interacting with someone who is mentally disabled, do the following:

Get past the communication barrier. Give the person time to express himself. Being patient will often reveal that there's more to him than meets the eye.

Don't judge him by your own standards. A person who's disabled may be more childlike, so interact with him on his own terms.

Be understanding. Because a person with a mental disability may have struggled for his entire life, it's accepting of you to try to understand what he's feeling.

Don't ignore him. If you're in a group, make a point to include him in the conversation, then let him decide whether to participate.

It's a misconception that all service dogs are Seeing Eye, or guide, dogs. Specially trained dogs also devote their lives to aiding people who are deaf and those who are mentally disabled.

When you have the opportunity to interact with someone who has a service dog, don't ask the person what kind of disability she has; she'll tell you if she wants to. Be sure to speak in an adult tone, not a childlike voice. *Do* hold the door for the person if she's behind you.

While the person will welcome your comments on the good behavior and handsomeness of her dog, never pet, feed, or talk to the animal without first asking the person's permission. Attempting to gain the attention of the dog in any way will distract it from its important work.

Chapter Twelve

People Who Work
in Your Home

T HE RELATIONSHIP BETWEEN an employer and someone who works in the home is in many ways more complex than those in the traditional workplace. Sometimes the situation is strictly business; people employed by house-cleaning and maintenance services may rarely see the people in whose homes they labor. On the other hand, employer and employee may develop genuine friendships, and employees are valued like family members. Whatever the nature of the relationship, people tend to get to know a lot about one another when the workplace is a home.

No matter how friendly an employer and domestic worker may become, employment in the home is still a means to an end for both parties. Problems can arise when employers fail to respect their domestic employees as *individuals* with their own homes and families. Despite legal protections, home employees are often more subject to mistreatment than other workers. Obvious offenders are employers who still regard household employment as a kind of Victorian servitude or who take advantage of a worker's good nature to increase workloads without fair compensation.

A conscientious employer—at home just as in the executive suite—begins by respecting the people he or she employs. Consideration and open communication are the foundations of trust, loyalty, and *mutual* respect.

Your Responsibilities to Employees

TO ACHIEVE A PRODUCTIVE AND PLEASANT working relationship, an employer should think beyond the practical questions of an employee's duties and compensation. If this is your first hiring experience, ask yourself what you would expect of an employer. What is your management style? Are you willing to learn from an experienced worker? Are you patient enough to teach an inexperienced employee? If you've employed household workers before, analyze your past experience and consider what improvements you might make.

You are also expected to abide by all relevant state and federal laws and regulations, so it's wise to seek professional tax and/or legal advice to determine what your obligations are. Not following the legal requirements (including making accurate and timely payments) can have serious consequences for an employer.

The ABC's of Hiring

There are good employment agencies and recruitment firms that specialize in domestic hiring, or you may choose to conduct your own search. Finding and hiring the right worker requires the same professionalism, attention to details, and good manners as in business and industry. No matter how urgent your need for help may seem, try not to rush through the process.

Develop a comprehensive job description for the position. Think about the specific services you need, spell out an employee's duties in detail, and be honest about your expectations. (If you want a housekeeper to mind your children every day after school, don't write down "occasional babysitting.") Developing a complete job description helps you define your standards, aids an agency if you use one, and avoids confusion about duties after you hire someone.

Determine wages, benefits, and conditions, including hours of employment and time off. Since compensation varies regionally and locally, consult other employers as well as your state employment department to determine what is legal, fair, and reasonable in your area. If hiring a full-time employee, you might consider providing benefits such as contributions to the employee's medical insurance. Be sure to enumerate paid days off, including vacation, sick leave, and personal days.

Conduct the search ethically. Often the best way to find a good employee is to ask people you know for recommendations. But don't attempt to "steal away" a worker. If you want to compete for the worker, talk to the current employer first.

Be prepared for interviews. Prepare your questions in advance and try to anticipate questions that applicants will most likely ask. Interviews are most often conducted in the home, and you should treat interviewees as guests and give them your full attention. Schedule enough time for each interview, including a house or grounds tour if you want.

If it's obvious that an applicant won't be hired, you can hurry the interview along without being brusque. If the applicant's work qualifications are not adequate for your needs, it's fine to tell him or her ("I'm sorry, Ms. Bracewell. We want someone with at least five years' experience"). But don't raise personal issues or make comments that might be construed as biased.

Get permission for background searches. It's not unusual for employers to go beyond checking references (a must) and to conduct thorough background investigations of potential employees. An employment agency will provide basic information

When hiring an employee who is not a U.S. citizen, pay close attention to the person's immigration and work status. The laws can be very confusing. For example, it's illegal to knowingly hire an undocumented immigrant, but it is also illegal to avoid Social Security and other federal and state taxes for an undocumented worker in your employ. Unless you're prepared to wade through a mountain of federal immigration, Social Security, and labor laws and regulations, consult a specialist in immigration law before hiring a foreign national.

about applicants, but you should talk with an attorney before investigating further or doing anything that could violate an applicant's legal rights. If you want to see credit reports, criminal and driving records, and other personal history, you must inform applicants, usually during the interview, and get a signed release that authorizes others to provide information relevant to the job application. Also, be clear about requirements such as physical examinations and confidentiality agreements.

Follow up by contacting references. Even if an applicant has been referred to you by someone you know well, you should call other references, including past employers, before you make any final offer.

When making an offer, notify applicants and agencies as soon as possible. Contact the person you hope to hire immediately, though you may need to give him or her a day or two to consider your offer. If other people are waiting for your decision, notify them as quickly as you can after the position has been filled. Some applicants may ask why they weren't selected—information that can help them the next time they seek employment or bid for a contract. Give business reasons but avoid personal comments and any remarks that imply prejudice.

Trial Periods

You may wish to hire for a trial period to be sure that there's a good fit with a domestic worker. If so, determine the length of the trial period in advance and inform applicants of this requirement. At the end of the period, be scrupulous about sitting down with your employee and discussing his or her performance and future. (Don't leave a worker on tenterhooks waiting for a promised job review.) Make it a two-way conversation; this is an excellent time to evaluate any problems and possibly revise your own expectations as well as your employee's. Even if you don't have a trial period, most employees appreciate the occasional opportunity to talk about the job and their performance.

Clear Expectations and Open Communication

To start on the right foot, employers must be clear and open with new employees about their duties. Ideally, you'll be available in person during the first day or days to explain what you want done, how it should be done, and anything else that can affect the quality of your employee's work. If you can't be on hand, leave a number where you can be reached and don't be put out by calls during the initial settling-in period. (Once you and your employee are comfortable with the work arrangement, you can schedule regular times to check in, if you want.)

From the first day, you and your employee are building a relationship that will work well if it's grounded in respect and trust. Ongoing communication is essential, and the employer should set the standard. Many people who hire domestic workers are not used to being employers, and the most common mistake is being either too lax or too rigid. The goal should be a reasonable amount of flexibility on both sides. For example, if a daily worker agrees to stay late to assist with a party, a considerate employer would try to give him the next morning off.

One temptation of employing domestic workers is to increase their responsibilities without consulting them. This can happen unconsciously. An hour or two of watching the children each week turns into daily child-minding; an occasional early morning arrival becomes an expected starting time. But all alterations in job responsibilities should be discussed and agreed to by both parties. If new duties require more time or heavier labor, it's probably necessary to relieve the worker of other responsibilities or increase work hours and renegotiate salary or wages accordingly.

Considerate Treatment at All Times

Some relationships between employer and domestic employee are more complex than others, but the glitches that inevitably occur can be greatly eased with consideration and good manners.

"Please," "thank you," and more. An employer should always observe the common courtesies—greeting employees when they arrive, asking politely rather than commanding, expressing thanks for their work, leaving clearly written and polite notes of instruction, and honoring privacy.

Forms of address. It's often preferable for employers and employees to start a working relationship by addressing one another by courtesy title and last name until one or both request to be called by their first names. The employer might take the lead by saying, "Please call me Mrs. Jones [*or* Susan]," and ask the employee how he or she prefers to be addressed. Teaching children and adolescents to address an adult employee by courtesy title is a good way to instill respect, though they should abide by the wishes of an adult who wants to be called by first name. Young workers, especially babysitters, often choose first name for themselves and more formal forms of address for their employers.

Full-time, Part-time, Casual, and Contract Workers

As anyone who has ever employed someone in the home knows, domestic service has generated a confusion of tax and labor laws and definitions. The following explanations are general; you should consult an accountant or tax specialist before entering into any employment agreement.

Full-time domestic employees work exclusively or principally in your home. A full-time worker may receive hourly wages or a salary and is entitled to the same legal protections as any employee. An hourly employee who doesn't live in your home must be paid at least the minimum wage plus overtime for work done beyond the standard eight hours per day. Full-time, live-in workers must receive at least minimum wage for overtime.

Part-time employees may work only a few hours weekly or monthly for you and may have several employers. Since the livelihood of part-time workers depends on the income, you must pay minimum wages and overtime. Whether you're responsible for Social Security, FICA, and other federal and state payments depends on the amount you pay the worker during the year.

Casual workers are defined as those who work (1) twenty or fewer aggregated hours a week for all their employers or (2) more than twenty hours, but the work or the times when they work are not regular. A casual worker isn't dependent on his or her earnings to live and isn't subject to minimum wage and overtime requirements.

Contract workers work for a contracting business—pool maintenance company, babysitting service, caterer, and so on. You employ the company or service, and the business is responsible for its employees' wages or salaries, withholding taxes, workmen's compensation, and general liability insurance.

Independent contractors are self-employed, though they may hire others to work for them. In some instances, you may be expected to file a 1099 tax form reporting wages paid to an independent contractor.

Introductions. Introduce your employee by either courtesy title and last name or first and last names when you have visitors. Whether you offer any explanation of the employee's position will depend on the situation. Should you introduce employees who are serving when you entertain? Introductions may slow the service at a large gathering but would not be amiss at a luncheon or small dinner party. Common sense is your best guide.

Transportation. Usually employers are responsible for the transportation of domestic workers who don't have their own means of getting to and from work. If your employee takes the bus or subway, you might provide the fare or include a transportation allowance in his or her wages. Thoughtful employers offer to pick up and return employees to bus or train stops that aren't within easy walking distance and when the weather is bad. Taxis may be necessary—as when an employee stays late into the night or works on a holiday when public transportation is limited. You should pay for the cab or at least that portion of the fare above your employee's normal travel costs.

When an employee uses his or her vehicle as part of the job—shopping, picking up children, transporting garden supplies, and the like—you should pay for gas and maintenance. Be sure that use of personal vehicles is in the job description, and have your employee keep a mileage record so that you can figure the actual costs. Contract workers are not reimbursed for travel that's part of the job; these costs are borne by the contracting company.

Meals. Normally an employer provides a meal or meals for a domestic employee who works full days. You can prepare meals or have food available. Some workers prefer to bring their own food, but you should provide drinks. Give your employee time for a meal and a couple of snack breaks.

Part-time workers generally don't need a meal but appreciate a snack break if they work three or four hours a day. Contract workers manage their own meal breaks, but you should offer drinks, especially in very hot or cold weather and when the work is physically demanding.

Giving Effective Criticism

One of the marks of a good employer is the ability to give *constructive* criticism (see page 155: "Eight 'Good Boss' Behaviors"). Evaluate any problem carefully before talking with your employee. Did you give clear instructions? Did you expect your employee to handle a task that exceeded his or her authority or capability?

Discuss the problem calmly and privately, and give your employee the opportunity to explain. An employee with a proven record of honesty and good service is particularly deserving of your trust. Keep your discussion focused on the problem at hand—no personal attacks and no threats of firing unless you really mean it. Try to resolve the situation in a mutually satisfactory way. And don't hesitate to take responsibility for any role you played in creating the problem. (See also page 158: "Dismissing an Employee.")

Don't be hesitant to raise troublesome issues with a domestic worker. Little worries can build into big ones. An employer has the right to expect things done in his or her way, but an employee has an equal right to know exactly what is expected.

Tipping and Gifts

In general, domestic workers don't receive tips from employers. A raise or a bonus is the appropriate way to recognize outstanding work. (It's not a good idea to tip employees in someone else's home unless you've consulted the employer; tipping for routine service implies that an employee is not fairly compensated.)

My husband and I have two school-age children, and we both work full time, so I hired a part-time housecleaner. We pay her more than the average in our city, but she's been so helpful that I'd like to do more. She has children several years younger than ours, and I've thought about giving her some of my children's outgrown clothes and toys. But I'm afraid she might take my offer as an insult.

Used clothes and household items are not gifts in the traditional sense and generally aren't given by employers to employees. Whether you make the offer to your housecleaner depends on her sensitivities and your relationship. Think about how you interact. Do you have conversations beyond the usual employer–employee discussions? Have you talked about your children and families? If your relationship is strictly business, then the sudden offer of hand-me-downs may seem like charity, and she might be offended.

But if you're friendly, the offer will probably be taken in the spirit you intend. Present the idea in person. This way, you can judge her reaction by her nonverbal as well as verbal responses. You might want to offer just the toys first, which are less personal than clothing. If she seems pleased about the toys, ask if she would like to see the clothes. If the hand-me-downs aren't well received, think of other ways to show appreciation—a family Christmas gift, perhaps, or an end-of-year bonus in her check.

Gifts are usually limited to birthdays, holidays, and special occasions such as a retirement. You might give money or gift certificates, but items that reflect an employee's interests show that a gift was chosen specially. Use discretion and avoid gifts that are too personal, such as lingerie. When giving money, present it with a personally signed note or card in an envelope addressed to your employee. Be cautious about giving used clothing and household items; employees may be understandably sensitive to the notion that they need castoffs.

Gifts are rarely given to contract workers. Ask the contracting employer about any policies for tipping and gifts. You don't want to put a contract worker in the awkward position of having to refuse or return your gift.

Child-care Providers

WORKING PARENTS today aren't as likely as earlier generations to have ready-made child-care help—grandparents and other extended family—and must turn to professional providers. Luckily, there are many options for both in-home and out-of-home care. In-home child care has particular advantages for young children, most notably the level of individualized attention and the comfort of the home setting.

When choosing a child-care provider, look for someone whose child-rearing philosophy is very similar to yours. Talk with applicants about their approach to child care and discipline and be forthright about your goals for your child. Discuss lifestyle issues. Do you run your home on a well-defined schedule, or is your style more relaxed and spontaneous? Anticipate possible difficulties and define the caregiver's authority in your absence. Child-care experts recommend that you interview prospective caregivers at least twice before offering the position. Do take the time; children are most likely to benefit when parents and caregivers are consistent in their methods and messages.

Nannies

Today's nanny is likely to be a top-of-the-line specialist in the care of children, and a nanny's resume can be very impressive. Mary Poppins had magic, but a real-life nanny may have an academic degree in child development, psychology, or early education. Many nannies have special training in child care, and those without formal training often have extensive experience, which may include raising their own families or teaching at the elementary level.

A nanny's typical duties involve caring for a child or children's physical needs, including meal preparation, baths, dressing and laundry, and other child-specific housekeeping; organizing and supervising play and outings; and transportation, including drop-off and pickup at preschool and school. Nannies may be full-time or part-time employees. They normally work without supervision and are not expected to do housework that isn't child care–related. Whether or not a nanny lives with a family, she is a key part of the family structure. The nonprofit International Nanny Association (INA) provides in-depth information about all aspects of nanny employment at www.nanny.org.

Au Pairs

The French term *au pair* means "on equal terms." Au pairs are young people—usually women between ages eighteen and twenty-six but sometimes older—who travel to another country and live with host families for a specified time period. (The United States issues visas for twelve months' residence in the host home and an additional month of travel.) In the U.S., the primary goal is for the young person to experience American language and culture and attend college-level classes. The au pair receives a private room, board, and a stipend, or allowance, in exchange for assistance with household work that may include helping with the host family's children—responsibilities much like those of young adults living with their own families. An au pair is unlikely to have formal training; she may not be qualified to care for infants or young children beyond routine babysitting.

Families considering an au pair arrangement must understand that *au pairs are not employees*, even though their minimum income is determined by law. An au pair should be considered a working visitor or quasi-family member. There's been a regrettable trend among some host families to treat foreign au pairs as little better than cheap sources of child care. This attitude can lead to unfortunate, even tragic, outcomes for everyone. Families contemplating an au pair arrangement must think very seriously about their responsibilities. These include taking a semi-parental interest in their young visitors; accommodating language differences and acclimating the au pair to American customs; and seeing that an au pair is included in family activities and also has reasonable personal time for rest, recreation, and study.

Probably the best way to decide if an au pair is right for your family is to work with a reputable sponsoring organization. There are a number of au pair programs that operate according to the regulations of the U.S. Department of State. But there are also unsanctioned recruitment and placement programs, and you should investigate the service before making any commitments. To learn more about sponsoring organizations authorized by the U.S. government, contact the State Department in Washington, D.C. (www.state.gov).

The term *au pair* is sometimes applied to U.S. teens and young adults who live with and work for families in regions of the country distant from their homes—a college student, for example, who exchanges housework or babysitting for room and board during the school year. But these young Americans are more correctly defined as domestic workers employed as parent's helpers (see below).

Parent's Helpers

A parent's helper, or mother's helper, is a person who helps with housework and/or child care when a parent is present in the home. Some parent's helpers are as young as twelve or thirteen and are often gaining experience to become babysitters. Helpers under age sixteen are not subject to minimum wage laws but should be compensated. Adults may work part time or full time as parent's helpers and should be treated and paid as domestic employees. An adult parent's helper may be qualified to babysit for brief periods, but unless the helper has experience, she shouldn't be expected to care for children for long periods.

～ When Nanny Accompanies the ～ Family on a Vacation

If you take a nanny or other child-care provider along on the family vacation, don't expect her or him to work limitless hours minding the kids while you bask in the sun or hit the ski slopes. Child-care providers should have reasonable time to themselves, so work out a vacation schedule just as you do your home child-care schedule. The delights of travel are not just compensation for excessive overtime or duties beyond the provider's job description.

Babysitters

A babysitter's role is to care for children when a parent or parents are not present. In most cases, a babysitter doesn't do housework except as it relates to the children, such as serving their meals. Babysitters may work occasionally, part time, or full time. A babysitter who works in your home more than eight hours a week or who is paid more than $50 in a calendar quarter or whose vocation is babysitting must be paid at least minimum wage plus overtime. (People who babysit in their homes set their own rates.) A babysitter who works on a casual basis is not subject to minimum wage laws. Babysitters are typically paid by the hour, and rates can be substantially higher than minimum wage. Employers might consider other compensation such as contributing to the costs of CPR (cardiopulmonary resuscitation) classes and babysitter training programs that benefit both the sitter and the children in their charge.

Finding and Keeping Reliable Babysitters

Finding a dependable babysitter is no simple undertaking. If only for a few hours, the person you select will be responsible for your children, so conduct your search with the same rigor as if you were hiring a full-time child-care provider. It's usually best to begin your search close to home.

➤ Check with family, friends, and neighbors. Finding the right sitter is often done by networking with other parents.

➤ Contact the student employment offices of nearby universities and colleges, nursing schools, schools of education, and technical schools. Service organizations such as the YWCA, YMCA, Red Cross, and your local hospital may also be of assistance.

➤ Call babysitting services in your area. Before using a service, check it out with the local Better Business Bureau chapter and your state department of children's services.

➤ Place notices in *select* publications such as a church or club newsletter. It's wise to avoid advertising in large newspapers, over the Internet, or on bulletin boards in commercial businesses because screening applicants is so difficult.

To keep a good sitter, treat her or him very well. Be clear and specific about your house rules, including if and when a sitter may have a guest. Provide all food and drinks, diapers and clean clothing, appropriate reading materials and videos, and so forth for the children. Discuss use of the telephone, television, and audio equipment. Arrange transportation for the sitter to and from your home.

If a sitter is expected to drive your children, be certain she's licensed, has a good driving record, is well versed in the safety rules, and is comfortable with the arrangement. Always leave phone numbers where you can be reached and emergency numbers. For everyone's sake, don't expect an unqualified person to care for sick children or administer medication.

If possible, introduce your children to a sitter in advance and familiarize the sitter with your family routines, including bedtime rituals. This helps youngsters see that you trust the person who will be in charge of them. Remember to speak of babysitters respectfully in front of children; if you have complaints, talk with the sitter or service privately.

∼ Etiquette for Outside Day Care ∼

Out-of-home day-care options include full-time group centers, work-site day care, and home care, when the provider cares for a number of children in her own home. Part-time care is offered by parents'-day-out programs for young children; before- and after-school services for children of school age; and some commercial centers. Regardless of the care you select, the following considerations will help make your child's and your provider's lives easier:

➤ Be sure that you understand and accept all of the provider's policies and rules. Don't expect a provider to make exceptions for you and your child.

➤ Carefully observe the provider's drop-off and pickup times. Arrange backup— a grandparent, friend, or babysitter—who can pick up and mind your child whenever you may be late.

➤ Immediately notify providers of any change in your address or status (such as a divorce or marriage). Update phone numbers, including emergency contacts and your child's doctor. Also, give adequate advance notice when your child will be leaving under normal circumstances, like a family move or a shift from preschool to elementary school.

➤ Inform the provider if you suspect a problem such as an incompetent child-care worker or a danger in the physical environment. You may choose to keep your child at home until the problem is resolved. If nothing is done within a reasonable time, you can remove your child entirely and report the situation to the appropriate authorities. Reporting is an act of concern for other parents and children.

➤ Always keep a sick child at home. Inform the provider about your child's illness, and don't let him or her return until the possibility of contagion has passed. Tell the provider if your child has been exposed to illness, even though he or she may seem perfectly healthy. Your pediatrician can give you guidelines about infection periods.

➤ Follow the provider's policies for gift giving and tipping. Tipping, when allowed, may be appropriate if a provider's employee does something for you that falls outside normal duties. Parents often give nice (but not overly extravagant) holiday gifts to day-care providers.

Household Staff

BEFORE YOU SEEK household help, evaluate your needs, your time, and your budget. Full-time workers may sound like the perfect solution, but it's often best to err on the conservative side when you first hire domestic help; you can more easily increase than decrease the hours an employee works.

Except among the very wealthy, live-in employees are more likely to be nannies or companions caring for someone in the home, rather than cleaners or cooks. A live-in worker must have private quarters (at least a room and separate bath) and is provided with all meals when in residence. A live-in couple often has homelike quarters such as an attached apartment or guesthouse.

Full-time daily help—forty or more hours a week—is more common, especially in large homes and for families that frequently entertain. But part-time help is closer to the norm and is increasingly popular with young professionals who have little time to maintain their houses or apartments.

The Importance of House Rules for Live-in Help

House rules for live-in employees can vary significantly, depending on the maturity of the worker. A younger or inexperienced employee may need more limitations than an older or more experienced person. Still, you should discuss the following concerns with anyone who lives in your home and make your rules clear.

Privacy. Everyone must respect everyone else's privacy. (Be sure children are well schooled in the privacy rights of employees.) Live-in workers generally receive house keys and may have keys to their rooms.

Cleanliness. An employee's quarters are normally off-limits to others, but you can require basic standards of cleanliness and care of property.

Kitchen privileges. A live-in employee should, in most cases, have the same access to the kitchen as other family members. Provide some room for food storage in the kitchen or pantry. Some employers include a microwave oven and mini-refrigerator in the employee's room.

Smoking and candles. If you want a nonsmoker, say so in your initial employee search. If you allow smoking, be clear where it's permitted and insist on safe use. The same applies to burning candles and incense.

Guests. A live-in worker needs company, so determine places for visits other than his or her bedroom. You have the right to know who will be visiting and when, especially if they will use a room shared with your family.

Use of alcohol and drugs. Use of any controlled substances should be grounds for immediate dismissal. You can ban alcohol outright, especially if your employee is under age twenty-one; otherwise, discuss it with your employee and establish appropriate guidelines.

Noise levels. Both you and your employee should agree to lower the volume when requested.

Telephone. Discuss use of your phones and payment for any personal long-distance calls. Many employees have their own cell phones, which solves the problem of expenses (though you might need to limit use during work hours).

Transportation. If an employee has access to your car for personal use, be precise about scheduling and costs for gas and maintenance. If the employee keeps her own auto at your home, reimburse costs incurred when she drives for you.

Housekeepers and Butlers

Today's housekeeper and butler may prefer the title "house manager"—a relatively new term that encompasses the myriad duties involved in running a modern household. It's not unusual for house managers to handle budgeting and bill paying and to hire and supervise staff and outside contractors. Because of their responsibilities, housekeepers and butlers often command high salaries and excellent benefits, and competition for their services can be stiff. Finding the right person can be time-intensive, so using a reputable recruitment or employment agency may be your best bet.

Cooks, Cleaners, Chauffeurs, and Gardeners

These days, employer may have only one full-time or part-time domestic employee or may use services for cleaning and gardening. A person who cleans and cooks is a great find, but you should be clear about your priorities. (Don't expect a full day of heavy cleaning followed by a gourmet dinner.) Because demand for household workers exceeds supply in many areas of the United States, employers should be prepared to pay competitive wages.

A gardener's duties may involve only mowing and basic yard work or may extend to landscaping. Gardeners today are generally self-employed or work for contracting businesses. When you hire a gardener or gardening service, you should know exactly what equipment and supplies, if any, you are expected to provide. It's thoughtful to offer cold drinks and be sure that workers have access to drinking water.

A family chauffeur may be a reasonable choice for people who do not drive or whose driving is limited. When hiring a chauffeur, be certain the person is fully licensed—a regular driver's license and a chauffeur's license (also called a "hacker's license")—and meets your local community's age and experience requirements. Chauffeurs who work for contracting companies may have higher qualifications than the law requires.

~ Eight "Good Boss" Behaviors ~

Domestic workers who complain about their employers often have very good reasons. "Bad boss" behaviors are thoughtless, disrespectful, and selfish. The following "good bosses" will earn gold stars from people who work in their home:

Bosses who don't wait to clean up. No employee should have to confront several days' worth of food-encrusted dishes, dirty clothing scattered everywhere, or a yard full of litter from last week's party.

Bosses who don't let the garbage pile up. Employees shouldn't have to work in a house or apartment that reeks or plow through trash cans because the boss was too lazy to sort items for recycling.

Bosses who know that their employees can't read minds. No one can know where things belong or how chores are supposed to be done without clear instruction. When a boss wants the carrots diced, not sliced, she has to state her preference.

Bosses who provide supplies. A boss who wants a worker to provide cleaning products, mops, and brooms should be clear from the start. Otherwise, stock up on materials and provide money for any items that the employee must purchase.

Bosses who are civil. It takes very little effort to greet an employee courteously, speak in a civil tone of voice, and converse and discuss rather than bark orders.

Bosses who know how to criticize constructively. Some bosses blow up or drop snide or obscure hints; others never say a word when something isn't to their liking. None of these approaches are productive. Most employees respond to criticism when it's clear, calm, and leavened with some well-earned compliments.

Bosses who don't constantly expect overtime. If you expect too often that an employee stay till five when the workday ends at four, he or she may soon be looking for another employer. Workers should be *asked* in advance to work extra hours, and their decisions respected.

Bosses who pay on time. It's wrong to expect an employee to wait for wages because the boss "ran out" of checks or "forgot" to stop at the bank.

Clothing and Uniforms

A chauffeur in full livery or a maid in a frilled cap is a rare sight these days. Domestic employees normally choose their own work clothing. Comfort and appropriateness for the job are considered more important than style, though employers may want to set general dress standards (for example, jeans are fine, but no cutoffs). Be sure to inform prospective employees of any dress requirements. Provide employees a comfortable place to change and store their clothing and shoes.

The employer is responsible for furnishing uniforms. Whether you require uniforms, you should supply aprons and other cover-ups as necessary. If you want employees to wear anything that is beyond reasonable clothing costs—expecting a chauffeur to wear business suits, for instance—you should bear the expense.

Other Workers in Your Home

There are people who may work in your home but are not considered domestic workers. Many have special qualifications and are employed (or volunteer) to perform well-defined tasks and services. All should be respected for their skills.

Home health care providers. These can include registered nurses, practical nurses, nursing assistants, homemaker–health aides, therapists, and anyone else who provides medical or rehabilitative assistance to a homebound family member, including children. Whether you employ directly or use a service, the person is a professional whose duties are specific and limited. Be courteous and don't impose unnecessarily on the provider's time. A nurse, therapist, or health aide who works for a health care agency normally has several patients to see each day, so remember that he or she won't be able to socialize for long.

Paid companions. A frail or infirm person who doesn't require constant nursing may need care and company. One solution is to hire a person who serves, in effect, as a surrogate family member—helping with household chores, preparing meals, shopping, driving, accompanying the client on outings, and generally being available to assist with the routines of daily living. Whether part time or full time, companions should not be expected to do any nursing or physical labor (such as lifting or giving baths) unless they're qualified.

Volunteers. Volunteers who assist the homebound elderly and people with limited mobility are not employees. In fact, volunteers shouldn't be expected to do anything that you wouldn't ask of a guest. Meal service and hospice volunteers, church visitors and spiritual advisers, volunteer readers, Senior Companions, and other community volunteers give their time; even when they go the extra mile, they don't expect rewards. A gift from a grateful family may be appropriate, but be sure to check with the volunteer's agency first. You might make a contribution to the sponsoring organization, but do not tip a volunteer.

Secretaries. The duties of a secretary employed in the home may include managing an employer's social and civic engagements, correspondence, and travel arrangements or may be more typically business in nature. Full-time or part-time secretaries, business assistants, clerical workers, and temp workers are not domestic employees and shouldn't be asked to do household chores. Because of the home setting, the employer–employee relationship may be more casual than in a traditional office, but it should be based on professional respect and collegiality.

Maintenance and repair persons and contractors. People who come into your home occasionally or periodically to perform tasks that require special skills—appliance and car repair, pest control, telecommunications, security, house painting, construction, carpentry, plumbing, electrical work, pool service—work for themselves, contractors, or service companies. Thoroughly explain the work you want done and make periodic checks so any problems can be addressed quickly. Be considerate of workers' time by not engaging in excessive chitchat. Be as courteous to assistants and apprentices as you are to the senior person. Above all, be prepared to pay when the work is done and as arranged.

Dealing with a reputable contractor is your best protection against fraud, theft, and damage to your property. Before hiring a contractor, be sure that the company and its employees are fully licensed and bonded and ask to see a certificate of insurance. Call references, your local Better Business Bureau office, and your state consumer protection agency. Don't feel that you're showing lack of trust; a good contractor expects to be thoroughly checked out and will respect your caution.

When an Employee Leaves

EXCEPT WHEN A WORKER IS FIRED for serious misconduct, it's part of an employer's responsibility to make a departure—whether by resignation or dismissal—as pleasant as possible. Begin by reviewing and honoring all legal and contractual obligations, including severance payments if you let the employee go and transfer of any pension funds or insurance plans. Even if there was a conflict, be sensitive to other members of your family who may have good relations with the employee. Children often need help understanding why a person they like or depend on is going away.

∼ When Something Goes Wrong ∼

The washing machine that was repaired yesterday broke down again today. The basement is flooded because the new pump failed. Frustrating things happen, but getting angry often makes the problem worse. Step one is to calm down. Second, get in touch with the contractor or service company and explain the situation clearly. In a genuine emergency, be firm that you expect quick service. If you have a complaint about a contractor's employee, report the transgression to his or her employer or supervisor. You can do this in person, by phone, or in a business letter, but stick to facts.

Whatever the issue, if you call, ask to speak to a supervisor or someone in charge. It is both inconsiderate and pointless to expect the person who answers the phone to solve the problem or authorize restitution.

An instant dismissal should be for just cause. Otherwise, three weeks' notice is generally appropriate when a domestic worker resigns or an employer lets a worker go. Circumstances, however, may dictate an early departure. If an employee who resigns is determined to leave before three weeks, it's usually best to agree. Though an employer can try to enforce notice clauses in a legal contract, it's often better for everyone to simply move on.

Accepting a Resignation

When a valued employee resigns to take a higher-paying or more responsible position or to attend to family needs, you may want to make an alternate offer—a pay increase, continued service but fewer hours. Give the employee some time to consider. If he or she doesn't take your offer, accept the final decision without recriminations. If an employee gives "personal reasons" as the cause for a resignation, don't pry or subject him to a grilling.

No employer should connive to make a job so intolerable that an employee is forced to resign—a ploy sometimes used to avoid severance payments.

Dismissing an Employee

Theft, dishonesty, violation of confidentiality agreements, cruelty to children or others in an employee's care, serious negligence, drunkenness, and drug use are normally grounds for instant dismissal if an employee is caught in the act. But be very cautious about accusing a worker of illegal or immoral behavior based only on suspicions or circumstantial evidence. Be sure the facts support your action.

It's more likely that an employer will dismiss a household worker for poor job performance or general incompetence. Before being fired, an employee should in most cases receive a warning—a clear and rational presentation of your concerns—and have a chance to correct the problem. Good employers also review the job conditions and decide whether their own expectations are out of line. Since no one is perfect, you might want to put up with minor annoyances in order to keep an employee whom you and your family really like.

If the issue involves a clash of personalities or work philosophies, then it may be time to part ways. There are also situations when an employee is simply no longer needed (as when empty-nest parents "downsize" their lifestyle). Changes in an employer's finances may necessitate a dismissal. In such cases, honestly and tactfully explain the reason for the job termination, give adequate notice, and respect your contractual obligations.

Giving References . . . or Not

You would not give written references to anyone who has been fired for just cause. But if the employee resigned or the reason for terminating a position didn't relate to the employee's character or performance, you'll probably feel comfortable giving a reference and offering help with the worker's job search. Even if a job ends on a less than high note, you can provide a reference if you want. (Be fair: An honest employee whose work was up to par shouldn't be penalized for personal reasons.)

Letters of reference should focus on the positive and avoid negatives. The tone of the letter should convey feelings without the use of harsh words or excess praise.

Part Three

Children
and Teens

Chapter Thirteen

Teaching Everyday Manners

I T'S OFTEN SAID that the true test of a parent's teaching is how his child behaves when the parent is *not* around. When etiquette education begins early and is consistent throughout childhood and when the behavior of parents reflects their teaching, the result should be a young person whose everyday good manners are as natural as breathing. Not that every lesson will be learned quickly or easily. Children *accumulate* social skills—learning in fits and starts. Everyone will make mistakes along the way. But mistakes can be mended with love, respect, and sensitivity to a child's individual capabilities and limitations. Be patient; correct when necessary; be generous with your praise. And don't forget that as you teach your own child, you're also modeling everyday manners for other youngsters.

The "Magic Words"

"PLEASE" AND "THANK YOU" and "you're welcome" are called "magic words" because when they're said, other people tend to give us positive attention and comply with our requests (or turn us down graciously). In a sense, the "magic words" are the keys that unlock the whole treasure chest of respectful manners. From the cradle on, a child should hear these words and phrases used routinely in his home, and he will soon imitate.

Young children learn fairly quickly that "please" is usually more effective than a demanding "gimme." Saying "thank you" and "you're welcome" is a little harder because these courtesies do not, to a small child, produce tangible results. But by preschool age, children should know that "please" is the acceptable way to ask for what they want and to request permission to do things ("Please, may I be excused?"; "Please, may I go out to play now?"). They can be expected to say "thank you" whenever someone responds to a request, gives them something such as a birthday present, or does something for them ("Thank you for finding my cat, Mr. Rollins"). Children should also learn "you're welcome" (rather than "no problem" or similar phrases) as the appropriate response to a "thank you."

It's vital to teach children to say "no" politely and to accept "no" from others without begging, whining, or arguing. Older children eventually learn that accepting "no" with a polite reply ("Thank you for trying"; "Thanks for thinking about it") leaves a good impression and may bring better results the next time.

Parents should encourage use of the "magic words" among siblings and playmates. These courtesies help children make friends and promote sharing and cooperation. Once the basic courtesies become habits, you can expand your child's vocabulary by introducing words such as "grateful" and "appreciate." Variation in vocabulary enables a child to personalize his responses to others and underscores the true meaning of the "magic words."

The Importance of Apologies

Before they can make meaningful apologies, children must have some understanding of right and wrong, a degree of sensitivity to other people's feelings, and enough self-confidence to admit their own errors. Forcing very young children to say "I'm sorry" when they can't yet understand the reason may make them defensive and undermine lessons in truth telling. Older children learn that "I'm sorry" has multiple meanings: The expression can be an apology ("I'm sorry I broke your crayons") or a sympathetic statement ("I'm sorry your mom is sick"). Parents should set the example by making sincere apologies, whenever necessary, to children as well as adults.

Sincere apologies are delivered in a straightforward manner, without excuses.

A QUESTION FOR PEGGY

Help! My seven-year-old has suddenly forgotten all his good manners. He hardly ever says "please" and "thank you" anymore. He forgets to introduce his friends to me. At meals, he's always talking with his mouth full. He doesn't seem to be rude on purpose, but I'm at my wit's end.

Since your son isn't deliberately being rude, he's probably acting his age and responding to his changing world. Children experience stress as they deal with new routines, new ways of learning, and more time away from home. Their young minds are coping with so much change that forgetting their manners is understandable. Backsliding is normal, and your son may hit similar rough patches in middle and high school.

Continue making your expectations clear and prompting when necessary, but avoid correcting him excessively or criticizing him in front of others. Discuss the reasons for good manners. He's now thinking in concrete terms and can understand, for example, that talking with his mouth full is ugly for other people to see. It's also a good idea to back away from new rules for a while. As he grows out of this phase, your son's old good manners should reappear, and you can resume teaching new ones.

Role-playing can help children learn how to explain a situation without appearing to excuse themselves or blame others. It's possible to be *too* sorry, however, and people who constantly apologize for things they can't control may be regarded as insincere.

Greetings and Introductions

BY AGE ONE, most children wave "bye-bye" when prompted and often respond with smiles to a cheery "hi." With toddlers and preschoolers, parents should encourage greetings and model polite introductions at every opportunity. This includes introducing your child even though she's hanging back in shyness. (Let the person you are greeting know who is hiding behind you, but don't push your child to respond.) When children begin interacting regularly with their peers and later, as their activities expand to include hosting and being hosted by others, good greeting manners and introduction skills will facilitate all their social interactions.

Polite Greetings

By the time a child enters kindergarten or first grade, he should have these greeting manners pretty much down pat:

➤ Smile, stand tall, look the person being greeted or introduced in the eye, and say "hello" in a pleasant tone of voice.

➤ Say the person's name if it is known: "Hello, Mrs. Jacobs."

➤ Shake hands if the person extends a hand. All children need instruction in how to shake—neither too hard nor too limp.

➤ Listen to what the person says and answer any questions politely.

Some greetings are very casual, as when a youngster says "hi" to a neighbor. In places where a spoken greeting will disturb others, a wave is enough. Since adolescents are often self-conscious about attracting attention to themselves, parents may need to review meeting and greeting manners and remind older children that failing to acknowledge another person's presence is a sign of disrespect.

Shy Greeters

Some young children are temperamentally shy, and most are wary of adults who rush at them and try to touch, pat, kiss, or hug. Although shyness is no excuse to ignore courteous greeting manners, be sensitive to your toddler's or preschooler's normal instincts. Model the behavior you want your child to learn, and don't show embarrassment when she fails to speak or hangs back when introduced.

The best approach is to proceed normally when you meet other adults. Introduce your child or acknowledge her presence if she already knows the person. Your good manners and positive reactions will reassure your child that you trust the person. If your child is tugging at you or being disruptive, tell her to stop. You might want to cut a conversation short, but don't fail to leave graciously. Don't get angry or scold your child. As soon as you have some privacy, talk about the right ways to meet and greet others. Whenever she does manage a polite greeting, reinforce her good manners with some unqualified praise.

Making Introductions

Most preschoolers and all school-age children should be able to make basic introductions. Introductions among peers tend to be casual. ("Janie, this is Ben Rosen. He just moved next door.") New friends should always be introduced to parents, caregivers, and other family members; these introductions offer practice with more sophisticated language. ("Mom, I'd like you to meet Jeremy Bright. Jeremy, this is my mother, Mrs. Lincoln.")

Saying names clearly and accurately is important. When a youngster doesn't know a person's last name, he should ask, preferably before attempting introductions. If your child tends to mumble or slur names or speak too softly, some practice role-playing may help.

The Order of Introduction

Middle school is a good time to start learning some of the finer points of introductions. Since making the introduction is what really matters, young people needn't worry too much if they make a mistake in the order. They should simply proceed with the introduction, and work on the nuances later (see Chapter 2, page 7: "The Essentials of Greeting Others").

➤ Among peers, it matters little who is introduced first.

➤ A young person is introduced *to* an older person: "Mr. Roberts, I'd like you to meet my friend Ann Jeffords." (Teach your child to say the adult's name first, and the rest of the introduction should come easily.)

➤ When an adult holds a position of high rank or special significance, that person is named first: "Bishop McCarthy, I'd like you to meet my teacher, Mrs. Johnson. Mrs. Johnson, this is Bishop McCarthy."

Addressing Adults

Even in these casual times, children should be taught to call adults by their courtesy or professional titles and surnames (Mrs. Swenson, Dr. Singh, Rabbi Levine). Many adults expect children, especially youngsters they don't know well, to use titles and surnames. It's up to adults to say if they wish to be addressed by their first names. When an adult requests first-name use, children should be reassured that this exception is okay. But calling an adult by first name without being invited to do so may be judged as rude.

Unless a school or teacher has a first-name policy, children and teens should address all school personnel by title and surname—even if they are on first-name basis outside of school. Until an adult requests otherwise, this form also applies to coaches and other adult supervisors, employers and adult coworkers, clergy, and the like.

"Yes, Ma'am" and "No, Sir"

The use of "ma'am" and "sir" was once expected of all children when speaking to adults. Today, the teaching of these courtesies is largely a matter of parental preference and regional custom. While the general trend is away from the use of "ma'am" and "sir" by children, the custom has by no means disappeared.

Fond Farewells

As children begin to internalize greeting etiquette, they should learn about courteous partings. A short pleasantry ("See you at school tomorrow") or expression of gratitude ("Thanks for the help with those math problems") makes it easier to end an activity or get-together with friends. School-age children can learn to say, "It's been nice to see you" or "I'm glad to have met you," when leaving adults. In party settings, the ability to move away from groups with pleasant parting remarks is an important component of good manners for hosts and guests.

∽ Smart Teaching Tactics ∽

Parents spend a lot of time setting limits, making rules, and issuing orders. But for everyone's sake, it pays to lighten up when possible, so include the following tactics in your teaching toolbox:

Playing manners games. Simple stacking and sorting games teach valuable first lessons in taking turns and cooperating. Include etiquette in your young child's imaginary play: A game of "house" can include table setting, saying "please," passing pretend food, and asking to be excused. Play with dolls or stuffed animals offers many opportunities to practice good manners, from making introductions to sharing.

Signaling. Verbal prompting becomes problematic when it embarrasses a child. In front of others, try simple nonverbal signals—finger to lips for "quiet down" or "let someone else speak," tugging an ear for "watch your table manners," and so forth. Children often respond to nonverbal prompting when they've had a part in developing *secret* codes with their parents and other adult caregivers.

Role-playing. Acting out scenarios helps children learn the what's, when's, and how's of appropriate behavior. Role-playing encourages youngsters to anticipate problems and develop social confidence. By reversing roles, children learn to respect other people's points of view. Role-playing continues to be effective as adolescents face new challenges—job and college interviewing, for example—on their own.

More Everyday Courtesies

GOOD MANNERS are built from the ground up. Learning to take turns on the playground leads to cooperation in the schoolroom and eventually to the polished etiquette necessary for success in business and civic life. Habits of neatness and personal responsibility cultivated in childhood produce considerate adults who are welcome in virtually any social setting. A young person who is solidly grounded in the common courtesies will be well on his way to self-reliant and socially adroit adulthood.

Lending a Hand

Very young children are not naturally observant of other people, but they will take note of their parents' and caregivers' actions. At the grocery checkout, are you willing to let someone who has just a few items go ahead of you and your full cart? Do you take time to help people who ask for directions or information? By seeing thousands of such daily encounters, children learn to be aware of people in need. When they begin to respond to the needs of others, they will experience the personal satisfaction that comes from showing kindness.

Parents should also teach children to ask before stepping into situations where help may not be required. When a child dines at a friend's home, he should ask if and how he can help set or clear the table, no matter what the custom in his own family. He should say, "May I help you?" before aiding a person loaded down with packages. Parents can talk about circumstances that call for unsolicited assistance (holding a door, returning an item that someone has unknowingly dropped or forgotten) and those that require offers of help. Eventually, common sense will tell a young person when to ask before lending a hand.

Sharing and Taking Turns

Sharing is not instinctive; it takes years of patient teaching and prompting before children learn not to grab and push. Introduce sharing and turn taking in the toddler years by pointing out when you and other adults share; use everyday situations, like serving and passing food at the dinner table, to illustrate taking turns. When children begin to interact with their peers, it's time to teach sharing etiquette. Older preschoolers must learn to ask politely for what they want—"May I play with that doll, please?"—and wait for a response. Sharing is encouraged in preschool, and cooperation is a major element of elementary school education, but consistent reinforcement at home is vital.

Children also teach one another as they form friendships, play in groups, and participate in organized activities, and the schoolchild who is too self-centered may suffer rejection by his peers. Preteens and teens need guidance as more complicated questions arise—how to share expenses on dates, how to promote cooperation in student organizations, and so on.

Cleaning Up

Teaching children to pick up and clean up after themselves translates into consideration for others. First lessons often involve simple "putting away" rituals initiated in a child's first year. Young children like to imitate their caregivers, so you can encourage the neatness habit by allowing toddlers and preschoolers to help you clean and straighten at home and including cleanup as part of their playdate routine. By school age, they're ready for assigned, age-appropriate tasks, and you should discuss the importance of completing chores in a timely fashion. Household chores promote a child's self-reliance and sense of responsibility to his family. Consistent experience at home should translate into considerate behavior at school and in the homes of others.

Fair Trading and Borrowing

Trading and borrowing can be a problem before youngsters understand the relative value of possessions. Children lack the negotiation skills to make fair trades. They can mistake lending for giving away and often don't know that borrowing implies returning. Parents should carefully coach their children on the etiquette of lending, borrowing, and trading and make expectations clear by discussing the following principles:

➤ Before children have a good sense of the value of things, they should ask parents for permission to lend, borrow, or trade.

➤ The etiquette of borrowing involves taking something for a specified period, then returning it on time—with thanks—and in the same condition as when it was borrowed.

➤ If a borrowed item is damaged or lost, it must be repaired or replaced by the borrower. (Older children should be responsible for at least part of the cost.)

When teens lend and borrow, the items—clothing, jewelry, tapes and CDs, electronic and athletic equipment, and so on—are likely to be expensive. While you won't be so actively involved in the negotiations, do remind teens that the principles of fairness and integrity apply. Don't rush to replace money or items your teen has lost through lending; be clear that he is the one who's responsible for returning or replacing anything he borrows.

Giving and Accepting Compliments

Young children respond to praise, and most will try to win it. But they're not so quick to compliment others. Since children who receive compliments are more likely to give them, be generous with praise and pass on nice comments from other adults. Try to avoid attaching conditions to your kind words ("You look very nice in that outfit, but you'll look better if you change your shoes"). And don't overdo; children have excellent radar for false flattery.

With practice and prompting, children should learn to receive compliments with a smiling "thank you." It isn't necessary to repay a compliment with a compliment, and

A QUESTION FOR PEGGY

Our nine-year-old receives a weekly allowance to spend as she likes. We also let her earn money by doing special jobs at home. She's never complained before, but a new school friend gets a large allowance, and our daughter now wants the same. Are we being unfair not to give in?

You do not have to give an allowance you think is unreasonable. Allowances should be based on what a parent thinks is fair and sufficient as everyday "spending money." Your daughter's friend may receive more because she is expected to pay for necessities like school lunches and supplies. Some parents give large allowances but insist that a portion be saved. Your daughter can't learn about responsible money management if you increase her allowance just to match another child's. As long as the amount you are giving her is adequate, you're right to stick to your guns.

it is disrespectful to contradict a complimentary remark. If Janice is told that she looks pretty in her new dress, she shouldn't reply that she hates the dress, which implies that the person who admired her outfit is wrong.

Being on Time

Punctuality is another etiquette fundamental taught chiefly by example. Even though lateness is sometimes a symptom of disorganization, it is seen as a sign of disrespect for the people who are waiting. Habitual lateness teaches children that consideration for others is not important. Be sure children know that timeliness matters—whether showing up for an appointment, arriving at a party, or turning in a school assignment on schedule. Being late happens, but it should be a rare occurrence. Teach older children to call, if possible, when they must be late and to make polite explanations (not phony excuses) and apologies.

Standing Up for Adults

Within the limits of common sense, children should rise from their seats whenever an adult they haven't already greeted enters a room and acknowledge the older person with a direct look and a pleasant smile. A spoken greeting is courteous as long as it won't interrupt the adult.

There are times when a child need not pop out of her seat—if, for example, she has a plate of food on her lap or is holding a smaller child. It's generally unnecessary to rise in places like the movie theater or on planes. In a restaurant with chair seating, standing is polite if it doesn't inconvenience other diners or disrupt service. (Booth seating can make standing nearly impossible.) Most schools no longer require students to rise for teachers and other adults, but some do, and youngsters should follow the prevailing custom.

What is always rude is to ignore an adult or child who enters a room or gathering place. Youngsters should be attentive to what is going on, greet newcomers cheerfully, turn down TVs and music, and share the space (no sprawling on the couch). Even a teenager on the telephone can spare a smile and a wave for a new arrival.

Annoying Behaviors

SOME EVERYDAY BEHAVIORS AND HABITS are annoying and unattractive; some are dangerous to young people and others. Be on the lookout for any of the following:

Gum chewing. This habit ought to be confined to private times or the company of close friends—not during class, at work, or in worship services, and not when in conversation. Young people must understand that watching someone chew gum is, as older generations say, "like watching a cow chew its cud." Be discreet (mouth closed, no smacking or popping). Wrap used gum and dispose of it in a waste container. *Never* drop chewed gum or wrappers on the ground.

Playing loud music. In any setting where people may be disturbed, playing loud music is really intolerable. Music should never be so loud that it rattles others' nerves. If your child can't live without music, equip him with a portable player and earphones. Set firm rules about the use of booming car stereos.

Whispering, telling secrets, and giggling behind hands. These discourtesies usually peak in the middle school years. When you see it going on, tell the youngsters to stop. Make it clear that the behavior is extremely rude and immature and can be cruel to anyone left out of the whispering.

Spitting. When older children and teens spit, they're probably showing off or imitating popular sports stars. Spitting is disgusting and unsanitary. Stop the behavior when you see it, and be firm that, far from being "cool," spitting is childish and uncouth. (For your child's health, be alert for any sign of the highly dangerous habit of tobacco chewing.)

Smoking. Cigarette smoking attracts teens and some younger children. Many experiment, and a disturbing number will take up the habit. No one should encourage underage smoking, but teens who smoke must follow the rules: Do not smoke in anyone else's home or car (even if the owner smokes) or in designated nonsmoking areas; be sure cigarettes are extinguished and dispose of ashes and butts neatly (not on the ground or out the car window); never offer cigarettes to anyone who is underage. Finally, always ask permission before lighting up and don't argue if anyone says "no."

Grooming and Dressing

CHILDREN MAY SUDDENLY balk at soap and water. They may demand to wear the same shirt every day or get hysterical at the mention of washing their favorite sneakers. However, cleanliness is the first principle of good grooming, and parents must set standards. Hand washing is a must—especially before eating and after using the bathroom. Dirty faces should be cleaned before meals. By age five, most children can do their own washing, but you should continue to inspect hands and nails. Observant parents know when a child needs a bath or a shampoo, and they should insist.

Most young people become very conscious of personal hygiene when they reach puberty, but some may resist bathing, and parents have to use finesse. Instead of ordering a preteen to bathe, you'll probably be more successful if you and he can agree on basic standards. Try to accommodate his preferences for showers rather than tub baths, brands of soap and shampoo, sponges rather than washcloths, and the like. Because clean hair is essential, you might require regular washing and give more leeway on hairstyles. Parents may want to set limits, but negotiating is often the better approach with adolescents.

Clean and Neat

Some young children become attached to a particular hat or piece of clothing just as others cling to blankets or pacifiers. Children generally outgrow their comfort items by age four or five, so keep the items clean until then.

Clothing should at least begin each day clean and neat, even if you must wash your child's favorite shirt or athletic clothes every night or two. To weed out clothing that is too dirty or beyond mending, institute regular wardrobe inspections; a family clothing review doesn't leave a youngster feeling that he is being singled out.

What's in Style?

Today's parent may face the "but everyone's wearing it" battle fairly early in the elementary school years. Arguments over dressing choices often escalate during early adolescence, when youngsters are struggling to express their independence. Clothing is highly symbolic of how adolescents want to be perceived, and conforming to the style of their peer group is a way to separate themselves from older generations.

Since it's unlikely that a child will carry the fashions of adolescence into adulthood, parents can be tolerant of a youngster's style so long as it falls within acceptable guidelines of decency and respect for others. Negotiate the issues that really matter: cleanliness and fit of garments, fraying and holes, amount of bare skin that is acceptable, and so on. Treat your child's concerns seriously when you discuss appropriateness, propriety, and good taste. Because teens are very aware of how others react to them, avoid "I told you so" when they blunder; being left out of social occasions because of inappropriate dress or poor grooming is a lesson best learned without nagging. Older teens can benefit from the advice in Chapter 5, "Dress and Grooming."

Good Sportsmanship

LEARNING TO COMPETE in the spirit of sportsmanship is not easy for children and teens, in part because they see so many instances of poor winning and losing behavior in the popular media. But there are worthy role models among today's celebrity competitors, and parents should express approval of positive examples on and off the playing field.

You will lay the foundation through game playing with small children. Instruction in the concrete rules and courtesies of good sportsmanship usually begins when children join in organized sports and should be applied to all competitive activities, from the classroom spelling bee to the campaign for club president. Set out guidelines and let your child know that, win or lose, you expect thoughtful behavior.

Follow the rules. Be sure your child understands that the rules must be the same for everyone if winning is to have meaning.

Respect referees and judges. The role of officials is to enforce rules and make judgment calls. In some sports, they decide who wins or loses on the basis of performance. Since refs can make mistakes, youngsters should learn to protest respectfully. To challenge an official's call, groups should designate one teammate to speak. It's important to state the facts calmly and clearly, then give the official time to consider. Whatever the final verdict, accept it without complaint and go on with the game.

Be considerate of other team members. A considerate team player doesn't show off, claim personal credit for cooperative efforts, or berate other players for mistakes.

Win with grace. Parents and coaches must teach children to win without gloating, boasting, and grandstanding. Begin by encouraging youngsters always to thank the losing side. A gracious winner will observe the polite traditions of shaking hands after a competition and complimenting losers on some aspect of their play.

Lose without complaining. Losing is disappointing but not an excuse for sulking, pouting, or crying foul. Losers should always congratulate winners. It's very important that youngsters learn not to blame others—members of their own team, coaches, referees—for a loss, and adults must set the example.

Teasing and Bullying

Schoolchildren become skillful teasers long before they can control their emotions or understand the difference between playfulness and cruelty. Since the internal voice of conscience is not fully developed until adolescence, teasing often continues through middle school and into high school. Parents, teachers, coaches, and other adult supervisors must stop any hurtful taunting immediately and establish appropriate consequences for further incidents.

Nice parents can turn into monsters when their children compete. Blinded by winning-is-everything thinking, these parents don't realize how harmful their bad behavior can be. Aggressive sideline coaching will embarrass a child and can undermine his confidence and destroy the joy of competing. Yelling insults at coaches, referees, judges, and players is rude and crude and sets the worst possible example for young people.

When you encounter a tantrum-throwing parent, it's best to stay clear. If the parent is tossing objects or seems physically threatening, get the authorities immediately. Trying to intervene on your own can inflame the situation and may put you and others in danger.

If your child is being teased excessively by a playmate, you may want to halt playdates and get-togethers for a while. When discussing the problem with the parents, stay calm, focus on the specific behavior, and avoid criticizing the other adults' parenting. If teasing negatively affects your child's interest in school or extracurricular activities, solicit the help of teachers and coaches.

Repeated, abusive teasing focused on a particular victim crosses the line into bullying. Threats, sexual harassment, and physical aggression must be taken very seriously. Don't assume that "nice kids" don't bully, or that a young person's account of a bullying incident is exaggerated. Bullying is not normal behavior. Confronting a bully or his parents directly often causes more harm than good. Adults have the moral obligation to protect all children against abuse, and this often requires reporting bullies to school or legal authorities.

Out-and-about Etiquette

VISITING IS A WONDERFUL WAY to accustom children to new experiences and expand their circle of acquaintances. But until children have their visiting manners down pat, parents must be alert. By consistently following the guidelines below, parents show concern for the comfort and convenience of others while teaching their children the essentials of courteous guest behavior.

Call before visiting. Making a habit of stopping by without warning will soon earn you a reputation for being intrusive. Even intimate family members and close friends deserve consideration, so call ahead and be sensitive. If the other person seems hesitant, back off and suggest getting together at another time. Except in real emergencies, don't leave a child in someone else's care without a clear invitation.

Be prepared. Take everything you might need for a young child. Be sure older children are equipped for visits. Don't expect hosts to provide for your child's special needs or preferences. (If your youngster is a picky eater, for instance, take food for her or feed her before you leave home.)

Supervise your child. Allowing a youngster to run wild or get into a host's things is inconsiderate and can be dangerous in a home that isn't childproofed. Don't expect hosts or other guests to watch your child during a social gathering.

Keep the length of visits reasonable. The antics of an overstimulated, tired, or cranky child are anything but cute. At the first sign of trouble—grumbling, whining, whimpering, excess talking—pack up and politely take your leave. Departing early is not rude; forcing hosts and guests to put up with an unhappy, complaining child is.

Negotiate visiting with older children. In early adolescence, many children begin to turn away from family activities. Rather than forcing a resentful preteen or teen to attend every gathering, try to work out a reasonable compromise. For example, a youngster can go to the regular get-togethers with grandparents less frequently if he agrees to call them every week and have a good chat. Explain such changes to relatives to avoid hurt feelings.

Thank your hosts. Be sure to thank your hosts for their hospitality, and your children will soon follow your example.

In Public Places

Children need to experience the rich variety of people, places, and activities that make the world interesting and exciting. By going out in public, children begin to see, imitate, and eventually understand how people are expected to behave in myriad social situations and encounters. But it's up to parents and primary caregivers to determine appropriateness. The presence of children is not always wanted in public places. If you aren't sure whether children are welcome, check with someone who knows rather than risk inconveniencing others.

∼ When Children Are *Not* Invited ∼

When an invitation does not explicitly mention children, then children are not expected. It is not acceptable to show up at any social event with an uninvited infant or child. Nor is it permissible to call a hostess or host in advance and ask if your youngster can accompany you. (When caught off-guard by such requests, polite hosts will often agree, although the inclusion of a child will be inconvenient.) If you can't arrange child care or don't want to leave your child with someone else, then politely decline the invitation. If a sitter cancels at the last minute, call the host, explain, and express your regrets. Even if the host says to bring your youngster, it's best to pass unless you are positive that the host is sincere.

Children will misbehave in public. Sadly, many parents simply ignore their youngsters' public tantrums and mischief and, intentionally or not, expect bystanders to endure the chaos without complaint. The vast majority of people will tolerate normal childhood behavior, but not parents who fail to act responsibly.

Religious services. Before age four or five at least, children are generally not ready to sit through entire worship services and formal religious ceremonies, including weddings and funerals. If you must take a small child, sit where you can make a fast exit at the first hint of fussing and crying; a rear aisle seat is ideal. You might take a soft toy or a book to keep your child occupied, but be prepared to leave if he disturbs others. For less formal events such as church suppers and holiday programs, play it safe and check with the organizers before bringing a small child.

Performances. Use common sense when deciding whether to take children to movies, plays, concerts and musical performances, sporting events, and the like. Consider your child's interests, attention span, and endurance level. Many cultural and educational groups schedule child-friendly events so that parents can introduce their youngsters to live presentations.

Begin teaching good audience manners to preschoolers. By school age, a child should know to sit in his seat with a minimum of wiggling; whisper requests to go to the restroom; and clap only at appropriate times. He should not address performers unless audience participation is invited, and he must not push or run when entering and leaving an auditorium or theater.

Shopping. Since shopping trips can tire young children fairly quickly, it's a good idea to limit visits to stores and other places of business to an hour or so. At the supermarket, keep toddlers seated in the shopping cart the entire time. Teach preschoolers to stay close to you—always within your sight—and to hold your hand in crowded places. Even when older children are allowed more freedom in stores, be sure you know where they are at all times. Never ask a salesperson or store employee to watch a child. (See Chapter 44, page 767: "Taking Children to Work.")

Restaurants. Your child's age is a good guide to his readiness for dining out. Fast-food and family-style eateries cater to infants, young children, and their parents with speedy service and cheerful décor. Many mid-range restaurants welcome school-age children, but if you plan to take babies or toddlers, call ahead and ask if there are accommodations for little children. Older schoolchildren and preteens may be ready for more upscale dining, but check with the restaurant. (If the maitre d' sounds at all frosty when you phone for reservations, try another establishment.)

In general, be cautious when taking children to restaurants. Keep other patrons in mind; they should not have their meals ruined by unruly children and inconsiderate parents. In fact, ongoing at-home lessons in sitting still at the table and eating neatly are the best way to prepare your child for eating-out experiences that he and everyone else will enjoy. (See also Chapter 14, page 187: "In Restaurants"; "Avoiding Fine-dining Disasters.")

Today's adolescents must understand that hanging out at the mall or shopping center requires responsible, mannerly behavior, and it's up to parents to teach what is acceptable and unacceptable.

Alone or in groups, young people should pay attention and give others room on walkways and sidewalks, at store entrances and in shopping aisles, on escalators and elevators. No jostling or roughhousing. No screeching or shouting, no offensive language, and no roaring boom boxes. They should be careful with food and drinks, wipe up spills, and dispose of trash in waste containers. It's rude to paw through store merchandise or disturb displays. Making wisecracks to or about other shoppers and store personnel or causing delays in checkout and ticket lines is thoughtless and frustrating for others.

Parents may receive reports (often from acquaintances and sometimes from authorities) of their teen's poor mall manners. Treat the problem seriously and enforce appropriate consequences. Adolescents have to learn that in public places, their behavior affects many others, that it is being observed, and that disrespectful, inconsiderate acts will not be tolerated.

Public transport and planes. When a child acts up in a moving vehicle, there's no quick escape, so parents must manage to the best of their ability. Pack toys, books, or comfort items that can distract a child's attention. Bring snacks. If distractions don't work, at least hold your child so she doesn't disturb others. Stop annoying behavior such as kicking the backs of other passengers' seats. On a plane, you can ask for seating away from other passengers. On buses and subways, try for a seat near the door so you can leave with the least amount of hassle.

Going for a Ride

Good car manners, taught early and reinforced consistently, prepare your child to be a conscientious passenger no matter who is behind the wheel. Your actions will speak louder than your words, so model safe, considerate vehicle behavior as you teach the following passenger do's and don'ts:

Do exactly as the driver instructs. The driver controls the vehicle—including seating arrangements, buckling up, and touching the knobs on the dashboard.

Do stay seated and buckled up. On buses and in vans, children must have their seat belts fastened, remain in their seats until the vehicle has stopped, and keep their feet and possessions out of the aisle.

Don't play with window and door locks. Keep heads and hands inside.

I hate to go anywhere with my two-year-old because I never know when she's going to throw a fit. It always seems to start over nothing. She wants a piece of candy or a toy in a store. When I say no, she starts screaming and thrashing. Then everybody looks at us, and some people make ugly comments. I never know what to do.

First, be assured that tantrums are normal in early childhood and are most common during the "terrible twos"—a period that may begin around eighteen months and last for six months to a year or more. Toddlers have complicated thoughts and feelings, but they lack the verbal skills to express themselves. Their frustrations build, and the smallest trigger can set off an explosion. Child development experts say that toddlers cannot control their tantrums and that these angry displays are truly frightening for the child. It's hard on parents, but most children outgrow tantrums as they learn to communicate with words.

In the meantime, continue to take your child out, but plan short trips when she is rested and fed. Don't give in to her demands for toys and food, but look for other distractions when you see a tantrum brewing. Sometimes a short walk in a quiet area or a little window-shopping can be soothing.

People who stare and make comments may be ignorant of developmentally appropriate child behavior or simply rude, and you should ignore them. You don't need to apologize, but do protect bystanders from your daughter's thrashing. Forget your shopping, gently take your child outside, and let the tantrum play out. Some little ones are exhausted by tantrums; others quickly bounce back to their sunny selves, but they all need comfort and reassurance. Whatever your child's reaction, do not scold her. Just remind yourself that tantrums are normal behavior at her age and your daughter will outgrow them.

Don't throw toys, food, or other items. In car pools, children should hold books and other personal items securely on their laps.

Don't yell, argue, play loud music or video games, or create any noise that may distract the driver. When the driver asks for silence, passengers must comply instantly.

Don't eat or drink without permission of the driver. Eating in the car is not recommended for small children unless an adult other than the driver can supervise.

Don't litter. Put trash in a container (never out the window) and dispose of it at your destination. Tell the driver about any messy spills and offer to clean up.

Do offer to share expenses. This courtesy applies particularly to teens who frequently ride with their friends. A courteous passenger will chip in for gas and the occasional car wash.

Do thank the driver. Whether parents, friends, or professional bus, cab, or limousine drivers, the people who get a child safely to a destination deserve a courteous expression of gratitude.

Sleeping Over

Sleepovers with friends may start as soon as first grade and are often quite frequent by third and fourth grades, continuing through high school. Early sleepovers establish the pattern for future staying-over behavior and offer the perfect opportunity for youngsters to learn and practice their hosting and houseguest manners.

To make the experience relaxed for everyone, parents will be wise to consult before the event, whether or not you're already acquainted. Host parents should share plans such as eating out, attending religious services, or going to the movies. (Since parental standards often vary, be considerate of other parents' wishes.) Inquire about the young guest's likes and dislikes; you aren't prying to ask about a child's favorite foods or usual bedtime. You should also set drop-off and pickup times that are most convenient for everyone.

When your child is the guest, tell the host parent about concerns such as allergies and dietary restrictions, fear of pets, and the possibility of bed-wetting, sleepwalking,

∾ A Dozen Sleepover Courtesies for Guests ∾

Children who learn to observe these basic sleepover courtesies will become adult houseguests who are welcome wherever they stay.

➢ Pack everything that will be needed.

➢ Greet the host and his or her parents on arrival.

➢ Put away luggage and sleeping bag before playing.

➢ Follow all house rules without complaining.

➢ Keep bathrooms and family areas tidy.

➢ Ask permission to use the telephone.

➢ Wash hands and face and comb hair before meals.

➢ Dress for breakfast unless the host parents okay pajamas and robes.

➢ Make the bed or roll up sleeping bag in the morning.

➢ Pack up before going out to play.

➢ Be ready to leave at the scheduled time.

➢ Thank the host and parents before departing.

or nightmares. Always provide phone numbers where you can be reached in case of emergency. Be sure the host parents know who will be picking up your child after a sleepover. When your child is home again, check that he has all his belongings, and arrange to retrieve any forgotten items at the earliest convenient time.

Children must always thank their hosts, but thank-you notes are not necessary for most sleepovers. (For the etiquette of note writing, see Chapter 15, page 204: "Thank-you Notes.") The courteous response is to return the invitation and host a sleepover as soon as possible. You can talk to your child about the importance of reciprocating for sleepovers and other social activities.

Chapter Fourteen

Table and Party Manners

MEALTIME IS ONE OF A CHILD'S earliest social experiences. When a baby is put in her high chair and included in daily meals, she sees her parents and siblings enjoying their food and conversing with each other. Sooner or later, her parents begin teaching the manners that enable her to participate fully in the social side of eating. As she grows older and dines in new places, she learns to apply her manners to a variety of occasions and customs and to consider the sensibilities of others. Party manners are in many ways extensions of table manners, and a child who has a good start at the family table is better equipped to be a thoughtful host and a courteous guest.

The Manners of Eating and Dining

OVER THOUSANDS UPON THOUSANDS of meals, children build up their collection of table manners through an ongoing process of repetition. Under age six, they're introduced to the basics primarily at the family table. During the elementary school years, they master the fundamentals, including the correct use of utensils, and learn the etiquette of dining out. By age twelve or so, the essentials should be in place, and the teen years are a time to polish skills and learn what to do in more sophisticated dining situations.

Along the way, however, there will be countless mistakes and mishaps. Youngsters, when they're hungry, aren't always interested in the niceties of table behavior. Until they have the motor skills to manipulate utensils and pick up a glass with one hand, children literally can't be graceful eaters. At times of stress and change, forgetting their manners is common even among high schoolers.

The keys to teaching table manners are patience, repetition, and consistent modeling of gracious dining behavior. You will do endless prompting and reminding, but be conscious of your child's capabilities and avoid embarrassing him in front of others. When he makes mistakes, quietly tell him what to do. When dining out, nonverbal signals are a great way to prompt without calling attention to yourself and your child. Adults shouldn't laugh at a child's accidents or show amusement at deliberate displays of bad table manners.

The following guidelines indicate the *approximate* ages by which children should have routine control of their mealtime manners. When your child has mastered skills at the first level, then you can build on what she knows and begin teaching new manners, remembering that she will learn incrementally through lots of practice. If a child is a little late getting a skill, don't worry, but do continue to encourage her efforts and praise her successes.

By Age Six

Starting a Meal

Arrive at the table with clean hands and face.

Place napkin on lap.

Begin to eat when everyone else does or when given permission.

Sitting at the Table

Stay seated: no slouching, ducking under the table, or rocking of chairs.

Ask permission to get out of seat if necessary during the meal.

Keep elbows off the table while eating.

Eating

Use spoons and forks; begin learning to use a knife for cutting.

Eat bite-sized portions and chew with mouth closed.

Don't talk with food in mouth.

Ask for food—no reaching—and say "please" and "thank you."

Don't make negative comments about the food.

Talking and Noise

Join in mealtime conversation.

Don't interrupt when others are talking.

Don't make rude or disturbing noises (burping, snorting, singing, etc.).

Ending the Meal

Ask, "May I please be excused?" when finished eating.

Thank the person who prepared the meal.

Offer to help by removing own plate.

By Age Twelve

Starting a Meal

Unfold napkin roughly in half and place on lap: no shaking out napkin.

Leave plates and utensils alone until the meal begins.

Watch the host and follow meal-starting rituals without comment.

Children and Teens

Sitting at the Table

Sit with good posture and feet firmly on the floor throughout the meal.

Keep free hand in lap when not cutting food or passing items.

Eating

Hold and use spoons, forks, and knives correctly.

Cut bite-sized pieces—only an amount that can be chewed with the mouth closed.

Take reasonable portions of food; ask for seconds.

Try a bite of everything; leave uneaten food on the plate, not hidden in napkins.

Be observant and offer to pass food and table items to others.

Use knife blade or bits of crusty bread—not fingers—as "pushers."

Eat neatly; help to clean up any major spills.

If unsure how to eat something, ask a parent or host.

Talking and Noise

Initiate some pleasant mealtime conversation.

Don't whisper or talk to one person exclusively.

Drink quietly, holding glass with one hand.

Ending the Meal

Place knife and fork angled on plate, knife blade inward.

Place napkin (dirty parts hidden) to left of place or in center if plate has been removed.

Remain at the table until everyone is finished, unless excused early.

Offer to help clear the table when appropriate to the situation.

The Family Table

EVERYDAY MEALS are the best classroom, but what busy family has the time to sit down together, enjoy a leisurely meal, and talk about the day's doings? The answer isn't complicated. Parents who care about raising children who know how to behave in the company of others will *make* the time for seated family meals.

True, many families can't manage shared meals every day. But it should be possible to carve out a few hours for at least two or three family meals each week. The following suggestions will help make every family meal an opportunity for your child to learn and practice polite table manners.

Don't worry if the meal isn't elaborate. It can be takeout food that is warmed, served in real dishes, and eaten with real dinnerware. Introduce new foods when you can; a child used to variety at home is less inclined to be picky and fussy when eating out.

Clear and set the table. The basic family table setting introduces children to the correct placement and purposes of plates, bowls, and utensils. Starting with a clean, uncluttered table reinforces the special nature of any meal. Involve your child. Most toddlers can begin helping with simple tasks—a great way to introduce age-appropriate responsibility.

Use napkins to teach the fundamentals of neatness. Long before children give up bibs, they can be given napkins. Full-sized, cloth napkins stay on little laps well, though paper napkins are fine, too.

Establish meal-starting rituals. Children are more likely to settle down and use polite manners when a meal begins with some regular formality. A fundamental routine is to arrive at the table with clean hands and face. Many families say grace before meals. Others wait until everyone is served or until the head of household says to begin. Thanking the person who prepared the food is courteous.

Limit distractions and interruptions. Children can concentrate better on the meal, their manners, and others at the table if TV, radio, and loud music are turned off. Let the answering machine catch calls or designate one person to answer the phone and take messages. Ban handheld video games, portable tape/CD players, and cell phones.

The basic family place setting: napkin, fork, plate, knife, spoon, and glass or drinking cup. Soup bowls and salad plates can be added. For more on all table settings, see Chapter 23, page 379: "The Table."

Encourage conversation. Ask your children questions. Solicit their opinions. Try to avoid contentious issues that are better suited for discussion elsewhere. Promote conversational turn taking, especially among siblings.

Expect children to ask to be excused. Young children should be allowed to leave the table when they finish eating. Teach your child to ask, "May I please be excused?" when he has finished. Although adults and older children often linger at the end of a meal, it's unrealistic to expect young children to sit still without fidgeting.

Eating Out

LESSONS IN "EATING OUT" ETIQUETTE start well before a child can sit in a chair or hold a spoon. In the homes of family members and friends, babies and small children are exposed to different dining styles and see the pleasure adults take from sharing meals. Throughout the toddler and preschool years, dining-out experiences provide reinforcement for the table manners basics you're teaching at home.

Beginning in the elementary school years, children may dine out frequently, without parents or caregivers present. Since dining customs vary from family to family, children must learn to respect other people's rituals and go with the flow. If your child will be eating with a family whose customs are familiar to you, tell him what will be expected. If you can't coach him in advance, encourage him to watch the adult hosts and follow their lead.

A QUESTION FOR PEGGY

Our five-year-old still grips her spoon with her fist. I want her to use a fork, but she insists on a spoon. Can you suggest ways to teach the correct way to hold eating utensils?

Holding and maneuvering eating utensils requires manual dexterity, and your daughter may still be developing the necessary physical abilities. Observe how she usually holds pens and pencils; the hand position for holding utensils is very similar. Since children can be ravenous, it's often best to let them eat until nearly full before giving too many instructions. Limit the number of finger foods at meals, and serve snacks like flavored gelatin and yogurt that must be spooned. As your daughter makes progress holding a spoon, encourage use of a fork to spear foods like carrots, broccoli, and fruit chunks, but don't worry when she uses her spoon to scoop mashed potatoes and peas. There's a good chance she will have spoon and fork pretty well under control in another year, and you can begin teaching her to use a knife.

Parents should alert others in advance to any dietary concerns. If your child follows a restricted diet or is allergic to certain foods or food additives, you must inform anyone with whom he will be dining, including family members who may be unaware of the situation. Don't expect young children to explain, though teens can certainly give notice of special needs. Aside from genuine health, religious, or cultural issues, children must learn not to turn up their noses at any food or ask for something other than what is served.

At School

The customs of school dining often differ from the manners you expect at home. Supervision by adults may be only sporadic. When many children are fed in short shifts, eating is emphasized over conversation. Children eat different types of meals—purchased or brought from home. Parochial school meals will probably begin with a blessing, but in public and nonreligious private schools, children usually start eating as soon as they sit down and may leave the table without being excused.

Unless he's prepared, your child may be confused when he's expected to do something at school that seems to violate your teaching. Investigate school policies; then discuss these rules with your child. (Most parents do this when a child enters first grade, but a change of schools and a move to higher grades also require some attention.) Assure your child that you *want* him to follow the school's practices. Be clear that the fundamentals—chewing with mouth closed, sitting throughout meals, not making disruptive noises, and so on—apply wherever he is.

~ Eight "Mess Hall" Do's and Don'ts ~

Knowing these basics will guide young people through the courtesies of school and other cafeteria dining situations, including camp and retreats:

➤ *Do* follow instructions given by the adults in charge.

➤ *Don't* push, grab, or roughhouse in serving lines.

➤ *Do* hold food trays with two hands; don't touch another person's tray.

➤ *Don't* ask for someone else's food and drink.

➤ *Don't* make comments about other people's meals or eating styles.

➤ *Do* leave the table clean; dispose of trays, napkins, and drink containers as instructed.

➤ *Do* report any spills or messes to an adult.

➤ *Do* thank staff members and others who serve food, collect money, or assist in any way.

In Restaurants

Today's children quickly get used to fast-food counter service, but they need preparation for more traditional dining out. Before going to a nice restaurant, tell your child what will occur and what you expect: He will sit in his chair throughout the meal. He should whisper to you if he needs to go to the restroom. He will probably be given a menu; he can either tell you what he wants or respond directly to the server. He can ask an adult for recommendations or to explain menu items, but he is not to criticize the food. If he drops something or needs assistance, he should ask you to signal a server. He should stay seated until everyone has finished and then thank the host for inviting him.

You might take along games or toys to amuse younger children in restaurants, but be sure that play items are put away when the meal begins. By age nine or so, children should be able to sit and converse politely before the meal.

Avoiding Fine-dining Disasters

The simple truth is that very few children under nine or ten years of age are ready for deluxe dining. No matter how well behaved, a younger child has reasonable expectations—eating within a few minutes of sitting down, having different courses served with minimal delay, being excused as soon as he has finished—that will rarely be met in a fine restaurant. The results are predictable: a frustrated, bored child who acts out and disturbs everyone.

Parents who consider taking a young child to an upscale restaurant should think twice. Evaluate your child's readiness for an essentially adult occasion. While it might seem nice to give your child the experience, your first concern must be the comfort and convenience of other diners and restaurant staff. Ask yourself if you really want to have an expensive evening out interrupted or cut short. Are you really ready to sacrifice the pleasures of lingering over a meal and enjoying adult conversation?

If you must take a young child, plan ahead and be prepared to act responsibly. These tips should help make the experience more comfortable:

> ➤ Be sure your child is well rested before going out. You might give him a small snack before leaving home, but if he is too full, he may have more trouble settling down and sitting still at the restaurant.

> ➤ Prepare your child for what is expected (see "In Restaurants," above). It helps to gently remind youngsters of the etiquette basics before going out, but don't attempt a last-minute crash course in manners. Teaching table manners as an ongoing process is the best way to prepare children for new dining situations.

> ➤ At the restaurant, order something for your child right away. Fine restaurants prepare many menu items to order and some service may be slow, but you can consult with your server about an item that's ready and will appeal to your child.

> If your child begins to misbehave or disturb others, take him out of the dining area immediately. A short walk and some quiet conversation may be calming; then you can both return to your table. Don't let a child wander or run around in any space where food is being served.

> Plan to leave the restaurant as soon as the meal is ended. If there are others in your party, they will understand your early departure and appreciate your thoughtfulness.

It's a good idea to introduce youngsters to upscale dining by taking them to lunch or brunch occasionally at a nice restaurant or hotel. Midday meals require less time, and the daytime dining atmosphere tends to be less intimidating or overly stimulating for youngsters. Also, children who are allowed to participate, to some extent, when parents entertain formally in their home may be better prepared for dining out in the deluxe manner.

At Banquets

Older children and teens often get their first taste of banquet-style dining at school awards dinners, occasions hosted by social and academic clubs, weddings, and coming-of-age events. The primary differences between banquet dining and lunch at school are that the banquet menu is fixed and the food is usually brought to and removed from the table by servers. Diners should accommodate service (from either the left or right) by moving aside slightly and keeping hands in lap. Unless a server asks for help, diners shouldn't stack or pick up plates for removal.

Teach your child to accept what is put before him without complaint. It's all right to ask for drink refills or more bread but not for foods that aren't being served—no matter how much a child prefers a hamburger to the coq au vin. It is fine to quietly thank servers when they offer dishes or remove used dinnerware.

Depending on the occasion, diners might begin eating when they are served or wait for some signal from the hosts. At some events, guests may visit other tables between food courses, but teach young people not to leave anyone sitting alone at their own table.

∽ The Trouble With Braces ∽

Youngsters who wear dental braces are especially likely to get food lodged in the wires and bands. Since a sesame seed or stray piece of lettuce can be hard to remove with the tongue, young people should simply excuse themselves from the table, retreat to a bathroom, and fix the problem. There's no need for explanation. If a youngster sees that another child has something caught on her teeth, the considerate course of action is to whisper quickly, "You have spinach on your braces," and then drop the matter. No teasing and no open discussion.

Children need practical reasons *not* to do what comes naturally. Here are some common table misbehaviors and kid-clear reasons not to do them:

➤ Hand waving and wild gestures risk hitting other diners and causing spills.

➤ Taking very large portions from serving dishes might not leave enough food for others.

➤ Reaching for distant items may land an arm in someone else's plate.

➤ Slurping soup and bubbling drinks make ugly noises that spoil other people's appetites.

➤ Pushing food with fingers is messy and looks gross.

➤ Drinking soup from a bowl can lead to spills on the table and the other diners' clothing.

➤ Putting dirty utensils on the tablecloth or mat leaves stains and may ruin linens.

➤ Making rude comments about food hurts the person who prepared the meal.

The Party Whirl

NORMALLY AFTER AGE FOUR, a child's social life begins to gather steam. Birthday parties are the usual entry point, and the list will grow to include holiday parties, slumber parties, weekend get-togethers for pizza and music, school dances and after-game parties, summer picnics and pool parties, coming-of-age celebrations, and proms and other formal affairs. Your child will be host on occasion and often a guest, and he needs to learn the manners and responsibilities of both.

Issuing Invitations

Though invitations are often issued by phone or in person, send written invitations when you can. Involve your child so she can learn some basics of planning. Invitations should contain all the information that parents of guests need—full name of the young host or hostess, nature of the party (if it's a birthday, say so), location, day and date, and time. Be clear about ending as well as starting times so parents know exactly when to pick up their children.

Whether you add an RSVP, include your full name and phone number so parents can contact you if need be. Add any special requests such as wearing costumes for a Halloween party. When the party location isn't familiar to everyone, include directions or a map and a phone number for a site other than your home. If you plan to take the guests to another location during the party, add this information.

My son Ronnie, who's nine, just told me that he "hates" a classmate whom we've invited to his birthday party. Ronnie says the boy picks fights and is mean to everybody. Now I'm afraid the party will be a disaster. Is there a way to rescind our invitation to this troublemaker?

No. Once given, an invitation cannot be taken back, except when an event must be canceled. Whatever the reason for your son's animosity (children often swing through short-lived love–hate relationships with one another), you should meet the child before passing judgment. Constant adult supervision at the party will head off any possible problems, though you don't want to embarrass your guest by hovering over him. Before the party, talk to your son about his duties as host and encourage him to give the boy a fair chance. Who knows? The "troublemaker" may be a charming party guest.

Written invitations should be mailed. Don't hand out invitations at school or during extracurricular activities unless *all* the children in the class or group are invited. Leaving any child out in such a public way will cause embarrassment and hurt feelings. Also, clear the distribution in advance with teachers or adult supervisors. Children must learn not to make in-person invitations (for casual get-togethers and sleepovers as well as parties) in the presence of people who are not being invited.

Accepting and Regretting

An RSVP always requires an acceptance or regret. (For the details of written replies, see Chapter 18, page 250: "When and How to Reply to Invitations.") Even when an invitation doesn't include a reply request (RSVP or "Regrets only"), it's thoughtful to contact the host parents if your child cannot attend.

Since children's invitations tend to be casual, accepting or regretting is often oral. But children shouldn't accept until they check with parents or caregivers. Teach your child to thank the party-giver for the invitation and say that he needs to talk to you first. He should then reply as quickly as possible—usually within a day.

Accepting an invitation means making a commitment to attend. It is a *social obligation.* In a genuine emergency, it may be necessary to change a "yes" to a "no." Call the host parents, explain the situation, and express regrets. If you can't call before the event, get in touch as soon as you can and apologize. Teens should take on this responsibility unless there is a specific reason for a parent to make the apology.

The Polite Host or Hostess

Early hosting manners are simple. Three- and four-year-olds should be able to greet each guest, say "thank you" for presents, and say "good-bye" and "thank you for coming" when guests leave. As they approach elementary school age, children should learn to introduce guests to other children and to you, and to be sure that no one is left out of activities. They can greet guests at the door and take their coats, pass snacks and drinks, and escort departing guests to the door. Adolescents should be encouraged to participate in all aspects of party planning and understand that they are responsible for the comfort of their guests, not vice versa.

A young child naturally thinks that when it's *his* party, everyone must do what *he* wants. If no one else wants to play a certain game, a young host may demand to have his way or storm off in a show of temper. But a good host puts the needs of others first, accommodates guests, and adapts to circumstances. Parents must set the standard; your model is the most effective teacher of considerate hosting. Early attention to this fundamental will establish a lifelong pattern of thoughtfulness in all social and professional settings.

The Gracious Young Guest

A guest's first duty is to show up on time and greet the host and host parents courteously. That done, it's time to have fun, while observing the following guest manners:

Respect the host's home. No rough play. No peeking in drawers or handling valuable objects. No feet on furniture. No trespassing in off-limits places. By age six, children should know to leave bathrooms tidy, put trash in wastebaskets, and tell an adult about spills and help clean up.

~ JUST COMMON SENSE ~

The Etiquette of Receiving

Children must learn to say "thank you" with enthusiasm when they get a gift—any gift. Should a child receive an item she already has or doesn't want, she must express gratitude without negative comments. (For information about children's thank-you notes, see Chapter 15, page 204: "Thank-you Notes.") Teach by example, and never criticize a gift around your child. When you exchange a gift, explain that you need a different size or color, not that you want something "better." Most important, talk to your child about the true meaning of gifts—that the item is never as valuable as the spirit of generosity in which it was given.

Accept the food that is served. No asking for special things to eat or drink. If a child is offered a food she doesn't like, she should simply say, "No thank you." If offered a food she really can't eat, she can say something like "Thank you, but I'm allergic to peanut butter." If given a full plate, she can leave uneaten the food she doesn't want.

Cooperate and participate in activities. Be a good sport when playing competitive games. If a child can't take part in an activity, he should be an enthusiastic spectator. Complaining or sulking spoils the fun for others.

Offer to help. Older children and teens can offer to lend their host a hand with serving and cleaning up.

Thank the host and leave on time. Children should always thank the host and host parents when leaving. Until older children can go to parties on their own, parents must be responsible and pick them up at the scheduled departure time.

Choosing Appropriate Gifts

Gifts for children's birthdays and other occasions should obviously be selected on the basis of the child's age and interests. It's also important to consider the likely wishes of parents and the general norm among the child's peers. Excessively lavish and expensive gifts may be seen (rightly or wrongly) as an attempt to impress and outdo others.

Gifts of money may disappoint young children, who would rather get games and toys. But when given by adults, money and gift certificates can be just what an older child or teen wants. The practice of children giving money to other children is best avoided, no matter how convenient it may seem. Children need to see that choosing and giving the right gift takes time, thought, and care.

Planning Pointers for Parents

THE WATCHWORDS for successful children's parties are "simple" and "short." Simple food, simple decorations, inexpensive party favors, and a short guest list will add up to a special experience for a younger child. Youngsters are likely to be put off if their parents throw extravagant parties, especially parties that are out of sync with the norm among their friends. Older children's parties may be more elaborate and theme-oriented, but the suggestions that follow are easily adapted to any age. (For specifics of teen parties, see Chapter 16, page 213: "Coming-of-age Events"; page 216: "Proms and Graduations.")

Invite no more children than you and your child can manage. The recommended number is one guest for each year of a child's age plus one. (A three-year-old could invite four young guests.)

Set reasonable times and time limits. When deciding the party time, consider the napping and eating schedules of little children and the school and homework demands on older children. Toddlers and preschoolers can handle an hour or ninety minutes. Two hours is enough for younger schoolchildren, and three to four hours on the weekend (time for a movie and a meal) is the maximum for preteens. Teen parties should end in time for guests to get safely home before any legal curfews.

Avoid overplanning. Aim for a blend of organized activity and free play. Children under five or six cooperate better at games without winners and losers. Save competitive activities for older children. Keep your schedule of activities flexible, and remember that children will probably be more open to structured play at the start of a party, not the end when they are tired. Adolescents will do their own planning, but parents have the right to know what is scheduled.

Choose age-appropriate entertainment. Even children of six or seven may be frightened by boisterous clowns, flamboyant magicians, and live animal acts. Be conscious of film, video, and music choices; your child may be unfazed by M-rated (mature) movies and song lyrics, but stick with P (all ages) and PG (parental guidance) fare out of consideration for the standards of other families.

Supervise opening of presents. Until children are old enough to respect the property of others, it's unfair to put the host's or hostess's gifts up for grabs. You might provide an inexpensive group present or individual gifts for all guests to open while you whisk your child's things to a safe place. It's often best to open only those presents brought by guests during the party, saving the family gifts for a calmer time.

A QUESTION FOR PEGGY

Should parents be invited to children's parties? Who pays for the parents when the party is at a restaurant?

Because constant supervision of small children is essential, it's often a good idea to include parents for toddler and preschooler parties. You might invite a few parents you know well, or all parents. The host always pays, whether the party is at home or a restaurant. If a parent invites himself or sends an uninvited child along to the party—it happens—don't compound this rudeness by asking the parent to pay for the extra expenses. But before the next party, be clear that only the invited child is expected. A remark such as "It was nice to see you last year, but we're only having the children this time" is pointed but not impolite.

Stay alert. Older children and adolescents need supervision, but parents won't be as obviously present at their parties. Helping in the kitchen, serving food and drinks, and checking on the party every now and then signal to young guests that you haven't abandoned them. At party's end, parents should be sure that every guest has safely departed and be available to walk or drive any stragglers home. Be ready to take over immediately should your teen confront serious problems such as gate-crashers or guests who are drinking alcohol or using drugs.

Chapter Fifteen

Young Communicators

A MID ALL THE DAY-TO-DAY DEMANDS of child rearing, it's easy to forget that one of a parent's primary responsibilities is to teach his child to communicate. Fortunately, most early education comes naturally to parents and caregivers, and the higher skills of speaking and writing are then acquired cumulatively. Parents and primary caregivers are the first models, and your budding communicator will be strongly influenced by your attitudes as well as by your example.

The Conversational Basics

THE BEST WAY to raise a courteous conversationalist is to talk *with* your child as often as possible. Some parents feel awkward conversing with infants and toddlers, yet the more you do, the quicker your child will sense and imitate the basics of effective, polite interpersonal communication. It's important to be sensitive to a child's developmental capabilities and language skills, but just a few minutes of focused, daily conversation with a young child will lay the foundation.

As your child grows, you can talk about an ever-widening range of topics. Discuss your child's interests and activities, of course, but also seek other subjects—current events, books, sports, and popular entertainment. As abstract thinking emerges, preteens and teens often become concerned about social issues and questions of justice and ethics. Their ideas may not be sophisticated, but young people must practice in order to learn to express themselves cogently and with respect for the ideas of others.

From the outset, you'll want to guide your child, by your example as well as direct instruction, toward mastery of effective self-expression and genuine interest in what other people have to say.

Make eye contact. Encourage children to look directly at the person they are speaking with. Older children can understand that looking away shows lack of interest and that people who do not make eye contact may appear to be untrustworthy or disrespectful.

Speak clearly and correctly. Observe how others react to your child's speech. Do they often ask him to repeat or to speak up or slow down? Recognizing a problem will enable you to help your child. Beginning in the later preschool years, parents should gently correct pronunciation and grammar. Be sensitive about criticizing in front of others; a child or teen who becomes self-conscious about his speech may retreat into silence.

Take turns and don't interrupt. Taking turns isn't easy for children, but even the brightest little chatterbox must learn self-control. When your young child breaks in on you, stop and tell her firmly not to interrupt, and then return to your conversation. Older children and teens require subtler but no less consistent guidance as they learn how to participate without dominating a conversation.

Pay attention and respond appropriately. Competent conversationalists are *listeners* who are interested in other people. Good listening habits begin with parents and caregivers who listen attentively and respond to what children actually say.

Enter conversations politely. With practice, children can learn how to enter a conversation—approach quietly, smile, listen, and wait to be spoken to. When another person approaches a conversation in progress, speaker and listeners should acknowledge the newcomer with smiles and nods but wait until the speaker finishes to greet and make introductions.

End conversations pleasantly. This skill takes some time to master, but your example will be a powerful early teacher. Teach older children not to walk away from a conversation without some courteous remark. ("I have to go now, but I had a really good time talking with you.")

~ Baby Talk ~

"Baby talk"—the seemingly silly ways that adults communicate with infants—includes speaking in high-pitched voices and with broad gestures, using simple words and sentences, repeating the baby's nonsense sounds back to her, using more nouns than pronouns ("Mommy's changing Ginny's diaper"), rhyming, and singing. Baby talk introduces the sounds, rhythms, and forms of speech; teaches an infant to attach words to objects and actions; and encourages imitation. By six or seven months, most babies begin to show some understanding of language, and parents should cut back on baby talk. Around a child's first birthday, parents should completely stop their own use of baby talk.

Speaking Games

Most youngsters can't fully regulate their voices until they are well into the elementary school years. But games like the following will introduce young children to the basics of vocal moderation and conversation manners.

Volume control. Have a loud child pretend he's a mouse or other animal he perceives as quiet or ask a soft-spoken child to speak in his "elephant" or "lion" voice. Engage children in competitions: Who can talk softest and still be understood? Who can "whisper only" for the next five minutes? These simple games help young children distinguish between loud and soft speech.

Taking turns. Ask your child and his playmates a series of fun questions—What's your favorite toy? A food you don't like?—letting each child answer in turn. Then ask questions about the children's answers: What is Janie's favorite toy? What food does Barry hate? This game requires taking turns and exercises listening skills.

Listening. Children must learn to interpret not just words but also tone and inflection. Say a sentence in a variety of tones, emphasize different words, and have your child guess what each version really means: "We're going to the park *today*" (emphasis on time); "We're *going to the park* today" (emphasis on the activity). Repeat the sentence as a statement of fact, a question, and a command. Have your child say simple sentences in different moods—happy, sad, excited, frightened—and guess what feelings your young actor is expressing. This variation on role-playing relies on careful listening and promotes understanding of verbal and nonverbal cues.

The Right Times for Talk

Help your child learn when conversation is appropriate by clearly demonstrating when it *isn't.* School-age children respond to concrete reasoning, so when you can't talk to your child, take a few seconds to explain. ("This traffic is really bad. I have to concentrate on my driving.") If possible, give him an approximate time when you can listen. ("We'll be home in about twenty minutes. Then I want to hear all about your gymnastics class.") Follow through by having the promised conversation. Through countless repetitions of this scenario, children develop their sense of "right place, right time" for talk as well as the polite manners of asking others to be quiet.

Private matters. Even in our open society, there are some things the rest of the world doesn't want to hear. Encouraging toddlers to speak softly and directly to you when they want to go to the bathroom is a good start for lessons in private talk. Teach youngsters the correct terms for their body parts—no more baby words. In the preschool years, introduce the idea that some subjects are discussed privately out of consideration for other people. Private matters usually involve normal body functions, so frame your instructions in terms of thoughtfulness and good manners, not shame and guilt. And set the example in everything you say.

"Uh-huh," "like . . . ," "dunno," "whatever," "I mean"—the expressions favored by teenagers change from decade to decade. Verbal "fillers" like these are often used to fill in the silences between thoughts or when a speaker is trying to find the right words to express his ideas. This teen-speak is likely to fade away as a young person's language use becomes more sophisticated. But if a speech habit is excessive or particularly annoying, a parent can point out that verbal fillers interfere with effective communication. Be sensitive to your teen's feelings, keep your comments positive, and give your teen plenty of time to correct the problem in his own way.

Nonverbal Communication

Actions do speak louder than words, so it's important for children to understand the relationship between what they do and what they say. Posture, facial expressions, tone of voice, hand gestures, and a wealth of behaviors such as hair twisting, finger snapping, foot tapping, and noisemaking all convey messages. Children as young as three or four will often correct distracting habits when they become aware of them, so parents should tactfully alert their children to the behavior. Gentle prompting can help, but give children time to break the habit in their own way.

As their command of spoken language grows, youngsters tend to use fewer gestures, but nonverbal expressions often make a strong comeback in early adolescence. Preteens and young teens employ rude and disrespectful gestures to express frustration, assert their independence, or just show off. Parents are often subjected to displays designed to irritate rather than hurt, and ignoring the behavior may soon cure a young person's nonverbal attention seeking. But be firm that rudeness in any form is unacceptable. Immediately stop any behavior that is truly mean or obscene, and enforce consequences consistently.

Dealing With Slang

Using slang is one way children and teens bond with one another and show their independence from adults. Since slang is more annoying than offensive, there's no reason why children can't use the current jargon among themselves, but you can control it at home and around other adults. Tell your child that slang interferes with her ability to make herself understood. Ban any slang that is offensive, and be careful not to adopt faddish terms in your own speech; children may resent adults who use their special language.

Coping with Back Talk

Because schoolchildren and young teens often lack the verbal and social skills to express their feelings and thoughts gracefully, back talk and sassing are common at this age. You don't want to tolerate back talk, but you should also look for opportunities to teach the art of disagreeing without being disagreeable. When you negotiate privileges or sibling disputes, for example, model consideration by giving children time to make their points and listening carefully to their thinking, presenting your own ideas in a respectful manner, keeping the discussion focused on the primary issue, and ending the conversation pleasantly. If your child becomes angry or frustrated, you can always stop the discussion and return to it later, without recriminations for the child's earlier behavior.

Stopping Smutty Talk

The "potty talk" typical of young children can often be curtailed if you first tell the child to stop and then ignore further outbursts, depriving the child of attention. In the presence of others, stop the child immediately and be firm about the consequences of further outbursts.

Among school-age children, swearing and "dirty words" are attractive because the language shocks adults and is "cool" to peers. Firmly stop any use of bad language when you hear it, and make the consequences clear. Schoolchildren often don't understand this language, so try not to overreact. In age-appropriate terms, explain what the words mean and why they're offensive and disrespectful.

In the preteen and early teen years, rude language tends to become sex-related. Youngsters are extremely curious about sex, and despite their seeming sophistication, their comprehension is still limited. Be clear that crude language and dirty jokes aren't acceptable. At the same time, be open to your child's questions and concerns. Frank and nonjudgmental discussion of what sexual language really means and why it can hurt others can tweak an adolescent's conscience and, hopefully, avert serious problems, including sexual teasing and harassment of peers.

∼ The Spices of Speech ∼

Like pinches of salt and dashes of pepper, accents add flavor to ordinary speech. Despite the leveling influence of media-speak, our diverse land is still rich with distinctive regional and local accents passed on from parent to child. Although hearing ungrammatical speech can hinder a child's language development, accents should be respected and treasured as part of our cultural heritage. Children must learn never to tease or make stereotyped judgments based on accents; other speech differences, including multilingualism and English as a second language; and speech difficulties such as stuttering.

Telephone Fundamentals

THE SOUND OF A VOICE coming out of thin air has a kind of magic that appeals to some children and can frighten others. Until he understands that the disembodied voice heard through the receiver is a real person, a child can't grasp the etiquette of telephone conversations. But parents should begin teaching the basics as soon as their child is old enough to have the phone held to his ear. Early modeling is critical; a small child needs to see that the telephone is not a toy and that adults act courteously every time they are on the phone.

By their preschool years, children are ready for consistent instruction in phone manners. Be clear and firm about your expectations, and be ready for lots of prompting and reminding. Until they are six or seven years old, most children need adult supervision when they make and answer calls, but by school age, they should have a good head start on the following fundamentals.

Greetings. When placing a call, a child should say "hello" and her full name to the person who answers. However, children shouldn't give their names when they answer the phone unless they know who is calling (see page 202: "Exceptions to the Rules"). When a child takes the phone from someone or answers after being summoned, "Hello, this is Julie" is the polite greeting. "Yes," "Yep," "Who's this?" and other abrupt greetings are disrespectful.

Speaking in moderate tones. Begin by encouraging young children to use their "little voice" on the phone. Teach your child to hold the receiver so that his voice isn't muffled or distant. Don't hesitate to prompt if he becomes too loud or drops into mumbling and whispering; gently take over if he stops talking altogether. Role-playing and practice on extension lines can help children learn to moderate their voices and control the speed of their speech.

Time and length of calls. Establish your house limits, including times to call (usually no earlier than 8:00 or 9:00 in the morning and no later than 9:00 or 10:00 at night) and length of calls. It's fairly easy to control a child's phone use in the preschool and elementary years, though you will doubtless add limits such as no phone use during homework hours and at mealtime.

In middle school, youngsters tend to catch "phone fever," talking to their friends for hours and at all hours. Conflicts over phone use can escalate among siblings. It's a good idea to negotiate as many rules and limits as you can with preteens and teens. Adolescents may be more amenable to limits when expansion of phone privileges is linked to age and past record of responsible behavior.

Closing. Teach young children not to hang up until they have said "good-bye." Older children should learn to end calls with some pleasantry ("Thanks for calling, Aunt June"; "I'll see you at school tomorrow, Todd") before saying "good-bye." Youngsters should also learn to accept a "good-bye" and not prolong calls when the

The phone rings. You pick up. But before you can say "hello," your toddler is at your side, demanding your attention. Most young children don't like to share a parent with the phone and will do almost anything to regain the spotlight. These tips should help you manage little interrupters and show consideration for people on the other end of the line.

➢ Make long calls and business calls when toddlers and preschoolers are sleeping or are away on playdates or at preschool.

➢ Keep calls brief when little children are present. When you can, arrange to return the call at a quieter time.

➢ Use distractions if they work. (Sometimes just holding a child close as you talk will keep her still for a while.) Just don't subject the person on the phone to squabbling or the plaintive cries of a child in the background.

➢ Help others in the family by minding a child when someone else is on the phone.

➢ Before phoning, tell older children whom you will be calling and briefly explain the importance of the call. Giving advance notice rarely works with small children, but older preschoolers may be better behaved if they're entrusted with a "grown-up" responsibility.

other person is ready to finish. After a call, they should put the phone set back where it belongs.

Consideration for Others

Learning the following good manners helps youngsters consider the needs of family members and prepares children to be masters of phone etiquette for life:

No interrupting or eavesdropping. Though his reasons for interrupting change as a child grows up (the attention getting of a toddler becomes the personal convenience of a preteen), breaking in on others can continue into the high school years. Older children should learn to respect another person's phone conversations by not making noise and not hovering near someone on the phone.

Summoning others. When taking a call for another family member, a child should politely ask the caller to stay on the line and then go directly to the person being called. He should not yell for the person.

If you can't take a call, tell your child what to say—informing the caller that you will phone later or asking the person to call back at a specified time. Be sure your child understands that he's not to make up excuses for anyone. Never expect a child to deliver false excuses for you.

Taking messages for others. By second grade, most children can write down a caller's name and phone number. Older children can handle more complicated messages, learning to repeat name, phone number, and other details back to the caller and to correct any mistakes. Keeping pencils and paper near the phone and designating a place like a basket or bulletin board for messages encourages children to be responsible.

Leaving messages on answering machines and voice mail. Help your child work out and practice a basic message for electronic answering services—"This is Jeremy Herbert. Can Andy please call me at home tonight? My number is 555-1243. Thank you." Stress clear speech and polite manners.

Responding to a wrong number. The polite response is "You have the wrong number." Give the caller a moment to apologize (or not) and then hang up. Caution children not to give their names to or converse with anyone who dials a wrong number or asks for an unknown person—common tactics of obscene callers and others who use the phone to manipulate children.

Exceptions to the Rules

When safety is at issue, etiquette must sometimes be set aside. Parents and children should discuss the circumstances when interrupting and other "impolite" behaviors are necessary. Be clear that these situations are exceptional and also that your child won't be in trouble for putting safety first.

A QUESTION FOR PEGGY

My daughter is in seventh grade and dying to have her own cell phone. It seems to be the thing among her girlfriends, and Sarah is a responsible girl. But I've heard so many horror stories about children misusing cell phones and running up astronomical bills. Do you have an opinion?

At twelve, your daughter isn't likely to have a practical need for a cell phone, so you may want to wait until she's older. Should you decide to give her a phone, be absolutely clear about your expectations, including when and where the phone can be used, and spell out the consequences for violating your rules. (If you already have a cell phone, you could allow her restricted access for a trial period.) Discuss the costs and go over the etiquette of cell phone use thoroughly. It's also smart to restrict lending; young people often find it hard to turn down a friend's request to use their phones.

Interruptions. If a pot is boiling over or a playmate has been hurt, you need to know immediately. Talk with your child about the kinds of situations that require interrupting phone calls. He may use this loophole to interrupt for attention, but when he judges correctly, reinforce his good thinking with praise.

Hanging up. When a caller says anything that makes a child uncomfortable, he must hang up immediately. He should tell an older person what happened, and if the phone rings again, let an adult take the call. If a child receives a sales solicitation call, he can summon an adult or simply say, "No, thank you," and hang up.

Making excuses. A child or adolescent should never tell any caller that she is at home alone. If a caller asks for someone else in the family, she can say something like "Mom can't come to the phone right now" or "Daddy's busy right now" and ask to take a message. If anything in the caller's response sounds odd, the youngster should hang up. (Parents often set limits on calls to their workplaces, but children should know that you want to be called if they receive an obscene, scary, or strange call and there is no responsible adult at home.)

Personal identification and data. Though children learn to give their full names whenever they call anyone, they should not give their names, the names of others in the household, or any other personal information to unknown callers.

Off-limits Behaviors

Start teaching what is off-limits as soon as you begin instructing your child in the basics of phone use. The list of off-limits behaviors will grow as your child starts using the phone on her own, so try to anticipate problem areas and thoroughly discuss new rules with older children.

➤ Pressing keys, pulling cords, or touching a telephone when someone is using it can disrupt or cut off the call. Hands off is the best policy.

➤ Listening or talking into an extension when someone is on the phone is rude. When a child accidentally picks up, she should hang up quickly and quietly.

➤ Dropping, throwing, or banging receivers and yelling for someone else to come to the phone can be ear splitting for the person on the line. Lay the phone down gently and go get the person who is wanted.

➤ Respect the person on the other end of the line by not talking to someone in the room. If the conversation can't be delayed, a child should tell the person on the phone that she will call back, and then return the call as soon as she can.

➤ Children should ask before using other people's home or cell phones. A child should not make long-distance calls, including dialing 800 or 900 numbers, without the permission of a parent or another responsible adult.

➤ Young people should ask to use the phone in a place of business only in an emergency and limit calls on business phones to one or two minutes.

Saying It in Writing

WHATEVER ITS LENGTH AND CONTENTS, a personal note or letter has unique value. For the young person who writes it, the process itself promotes thinking and mental organization and encourages the child to find interesting, creative ways to say what's on his mind. For the recipient, a letter signifies that someone has gone the extra mile to communicate.

Handwriting notes and letters is the most personal choice. Typing is an option, particularly for long letters, but writing by hand should be emphasized. Commercial cards save time, but they are signed by hand and often include brief personal messages. (When choosing printed cards, parents should feel free to veto inappropriate messages and designs. A youngster's sense of humor is not always appreciated by others.)

A child's attitude about writing will reflect a parent's example. Talk about writing in positive terms, stressing that notes and letters are a way of showing care and respect for other people. Children who receive cards and letters can better appreciate the special pleasure of written correspondence, so drop your child a line now and then and ask grandparents and other close relatives and friends to write.

Thank-you Notes

CHILDREN WHO ARE FAMILIARIZED with thank-you notes early are less likely to regard this essential courtesy as a chore, and teaching should begin well before children can write. Include a toddler's scribbled drawings with your notes and letters to family and friends. Let your preschooler "sign" the notes you write for her, stamp and seal envelopes, and put notes in the mailbox.

As soon as your child can write, encourage her to create her own notes. Don't be too concerned about form and neatness at first. A first or second grader's notes can be a single sentence on a page of school paper decorated with crayoned pictures or stickers. The point is to make the process enjoyable. Her notes will become more sophisticated as her language and writing skills mature (see page 206: "Some Sample Thank-yous"), and you can introduce correct letter form and use of standard notepapers and ink pens.

Older children often worry about what to say—a common excuse for not writing—so help them out with ideas. Two characteristics distinguish a well-written note: personality and genuine interest in others. Encourage your child to think about the person she is writing and to express herself in her own way.

There are no hard-and-fast rules about the content of thank-you notes, but the following are the key ingredients:

My son received dozens of presents for his recent bar mitzvah, but he's so busy with school that he can't get his thank-you notes written. Since his father and I gave the party, would it be all right for me to write some of the notes?

You gave the party, but your son received the gifts. Writing thank-yous is his responsibility, and gift givers will rightly feel slighted to receive notes from anyone but him. If your son seems overwhelmed by the sheer number of notes, have him write just one or two every day, perhaps before he begins his homework. You might help by seeing that he has the necessary addresses, stationery, and stamps. Just don't let him fall back on thanking people by phone or e-mail. Appeal to his conscience: How would he feel if he devoted time and money to choosing just the right gift for a special occasion and never got a thank-you in return?

Express appreciation for the specific gift or kindness. "Thank you for the great new fishing rod"; "Thank you for the exciting day at the jungle park." A writer never indicates that she doesn't like, can't use, or wants to exchange a gift.

Refer to the intended use for money or gift certificates. "Thank you so much for the twenty-dollar check. I'm saving for a new computer program, and your gift will really help."

Show interest in the gift giver, not just the gift. "I hope I'll get to see you soon. I'd like to hear about your trip to Canada."

Add some personal information. A gift giver who doesn't see the writer regularly will enjoy hearing about a young person's interests and activities.

When to Write

Although it's almost never too late to send a thank-you note, encourage your child to write as soon as possible. Within a week is great; within a month is acceptable, although circumstances such as a child's illness can necessitate longer delays. Teach adolescents that notes to job or college interviewers should be sent no more than a day or two after a meeting.

In general, a thank-you is expected for any gift not opened in the giver's presence, but it's a good idea to have your child write notes for most presents, even if she thanked the givers in person. If a gift is sent by mail or delivery service, the child should call (or e-mail if appropriate) to tell the sender that the gift arrived, then follow up with a written note.

Thank-you notes aren't expected for playdates and sleepovers but should always be sent after an extended stay in someone else's home. (See Chapter 26, page 465: "Twelve Host Gift Ideas," for information about host and hostess gifts.) Notes of thanks are courteous for special acts of kindness—the friend who takes your child to the ice show, the teacher who stays late at school to tutor her. Although paid to perform services, people like the soccer coach at the community center or a favorite camp counselor will appreciate a note of thanks. Preteens and teenagers may also write notes to guest speakers and individuals or groups that sponsor school and club activities. Teens should certainly express gratitude in writing to anyone who agrees to provide employment references and college recommendations.

Thank-you Letters

A thank-you letter is an extended version of a note. Letters of thanks usually contain other news and are generally limited to family and close friends.

E-mail Notes

E-mail is quick and easy, and therefore doesn't always convey the personal effort that a handwritten note does. But e-mail might be okay if the recipient uses the medium regularly and won't be bothered by its casual nature. E-mail is not usually appropriate for expensive gifts and gifts for significant events such as religious ceremonies and graduations.

Some Sample Thank-yous

These examples include wording that is generally age-appropriate for children and preteens; teens can find further guidance in Chapter 17, page 231: "Thank-you Notes." Though brief, these letters are enlivened by genuine enthusiasm for the gift and the giver.

A basic note from a first- or second grader:

Dear Uncle Jeff,

Thank you for the book about dinosaurs. Tyrannosaurus is the best.

Love,
Barbara

A basic note from a third or fourth grader:

Dear Uncle Jeff,

The video game you sent for my birthday is great. It's hard but really fun. Will you play it with me the next time you visit? Thank you very much.

Love,
Barbara

A more sophisticated note from a seventh or eighth grader:

Dear Uncle Jeff,

Thank you so much for the telescope. It was one of my best birthday presents ever. I've set it up in my room, and last night I found Mars and Saturn. The instruction book is very helpful, especially the constellation guide.

I was hoping to enter the science fair at school this year, and now I can do a great project. I told my teacher about the telescope, and he said that I could track the phases of the moon for a month. Mom says that you were always interested in astronomy, so maybe you have some other ideas for my project.

Thank you again for remembering my birthday in such a terrific way.

Love,
Barbara

Closings for Notes and Letters

The complimentary closings used by adults—"Yours sincerely," "Respectfully yours," and the like—can sound a bit stuffy for schoolchildren. "Love" may strike a child as too mushy for his pals and adults other than family members. "Yours truly" is usually acceptable to children, and "Your friend" is a pleasant ending for youthful correspondence of all sorts. Teens should begin using the closings suggested in Chapter 17, page 242: "The Complimentary Close," particularly for their business and application letters.

Other Correspondence

THE GOOD MANNERS LEARNED though writing thank-you notes will carry over into other forms of correspondence. Whatever the purpose of a note or letter, the contents should be sincere and courteous. As they master the technical aspects of letter writing, young people should be encouraged to think about what they want to say, consider the interests of the person to whom they are writing, and then express themselves with personality.

Responding to Invitations

Though children reply to most party invitations in person or by phone, informal notes are simple to do. Response notes written by teens may be a bit more sophisticated in tone but need not be much longer than the following examples for younger children.

Dear Naomi,

I am really looking forward to your birthday party on May 21. Thank you very much for inviting me.

Yours truly,
Christie

Messages of regret do not require excuses for the absence, but a youngster may want to include a brief explanation:

Dear Larry,

I'm sorry I can't come to your skating party next Saturday. My family will be going to Dallas to visit my grandmother. I'll see you when we get back. Thanks for inviting me.

Your friend,
Jamal

The format for replies to formal invitations is the same for children as for adults. (See Chapter 18, page 264 "Replying to a Formal Invitation.")

Get-well Messages

Get-well notes are usually short and positive when the illness or injury is not serious. Commercial cards are fine as long as the message is appropriate and a personal note is added. Young people may feel uncomfortable writing to a person with a chronic or terminal illness, yet these messages mean a great deal to anyone who is seriously ill and may be confined to bed. The purpose is to express concern for the person, but the focus—especially when writing close family members—is often on what the young writer is doing in school and activities.

Expressing Condolences

Although parents generally include their children in messages of condolence, teens and occasionally preteens may need to write their own notes—when a friend loses a family member, for instance, or a teacher suffers a bereavement. Parents can often assist by talking to their child and helping him express his feelings before he tries to write a note.

When there's a death in his family, an adolescent should reply to all condolences addressed to him. (For more about condolence notes and replies, see Chapter 31, page 544: "Sympathy Notes and Letters.")

~ Just Nice Notes ~

Sometimes sending a note is just the right thing to do. A friend might make first-string, win a scholarship, or receive a special honor. Or a teen might find an article or old photo that would interest or amuse someone he knows. It's time for a note to say congratulations or simply "I'm thinking about you." Such notes are usually casual and short, from a line or two to a couple of paragraphs. A phone call or e-mail might do, but when it comes to expressing care, a handwritten note is top of the line.

Chapter Sixteen

Teen Dates and Special Occasions

*D*ATING. Just the word can strike fear in the hearts of many parents. Dating is a clear sign of a young person's growing independence and self-determination—a development that can rattle any parent. Some parents may be bewildered by today's relaxed attitudes and casual dating customs, and even those parents who welcome dating as part of their children's social lives may find their nerves on edge each time their teens go out.

Worries are inevitable, yet dating, whether in groups or one-on-one, has long-term benefits. Dating introduces young people to higher concepts of social interaction and the manners of close relationships outside the family. Through dating, adolescents expand and refine their understanding of friendship and cooperation; learn critical life lessons in the true meaning of intimacy, commitment, and personal responsibility; and build social self-confidence even in the face of rejection.

This chapter, which is intended for young people as well as parents, focuses on the specifics of thoughtful, polite behavior in a variety of casual and formal situations. Whatever the occasion, however, one lesson is consistent: The etiquette of modern dating is grounded in self-respect and respect for others—the twin principles that underlie all positive social interactions.

Boys and Girls Getting Together

IT USUALLY STARTS in the middle school years. Youngsters who could barely tolerate the opposite sex throughout grade school begin interacting more frequently across gender lines. Young adolescents get together in groups and even label themselves by their common interests and activities—the "jocks," "preps," "techies," and so on. Within their crowds, they get to know young people of both sexes, and group dating begins. Some will pair off inside the group, and a few may have their first one-on-one dates, but at this stage, the group is the key socialization unit.

This is the ideal time for parents and adolescents to begin talking about dating (see "The Etiquette of Dating," below). Parents will set rules—school-night versus week-end dating, date-night curfews, the age at which a teen can begin one-on-one dating, perhaps age limits on the people he or she can date—and determine consequences. But it's just as important to talk, and talk often, about the responsibilities that dating implies, *including good manners*.

The Etiquette of Dating

GROUP DATES AND PAIRING OFF within a group are likely to continue in high school, but casual one-on-one dating often becomes more frequent, and some high schoolers enter steady relationships. Whether teens date on a regular basis or occasionally, they should be well acquainted with the following dating manners and expectations.

Asking Someone Out

The timing depends on the nature of the occasion, but it's courteous to extend invitations as far in advance as possible. A day or two ahead is okay for casual dates, but be aware that last-minute invitations may be perceived as insults. For more formal occasions and sometimes for first dates, a week or several weeks is the norm. A month or even six weeks ahead is not too soon for invitations to special occasions, including proms and formal coming-of-age parties.

Pick the right moment to ask. Try to catch the person when you can speak in relative privacy. Don't interrupt a conversation or an activity to issue an invitation. Don't put the person on the spot by asking when others are present. Call at times when you know the person's family will not be inconvenienced. E-mail is a possibil-

---

∾ Who Pays for Dates? ∾

Today's customs can differ widely from community to community and group to group. The "boy pays" tradition is still observed in some places, particularly for first dates and major occasions. But "Dutch treat"—boys and girls paying for themselves—is now more popular, especially for casual group get-togethers. For many one-on-one dates, it has also become customary for the boy or girl who issues the invitation to pay the normal expenses (movie tickets, refreshments, cab fare or gas if he or she drives). Then if the couple decides, for example, to go to a more expensive restaurant than planned, the additional costs are shared.

Though teens are adept at working out their own financial arrangements, the normal costs of dating can stretch a young person's budget thin. Parents who inform themselves about current practices in their teen's crowd will be better able to determine when to pitch in with extra date money.

ity if you're sure the person will understand the casual nature of your invitation and you are aware that others may read your message.

Accepting a Date . . . or Not

The basic etiquette is to accept or turn down a date as quickly as possible. Most of the time, a teen will reply when she or he is asked. If a delay is necessary, explain the situation and then respond as soon as possible—preferably within twenty-four hours.

If you can't go but would like to, it's fine to suggest an alternative. ("I'm going out of town with my folks this weekend, but maybe we could get together next week.") You don't have to make specific plans; just let the person know that you'd like another opportunity to get together.

Turning down a date is no excuse for rudeness. Make your "no" clear and thank the person for the invitation. Don't manufacture an excuse; far from saving someone's feelings, social lies are disrespectful. If someone persists, you'll probably have to be very direct. ("You're so nice to think of me, but I just don't think I'm the person for you.") It's better to say "no" as honestly and gently as possible than to lead someone on indefinitely. Keep in mind that a date invitation is a compliment; to gossip about a person you've turned down is immature and cruel.

Keeping Your Word

By accepting a date, you're making a commitment, and honorable people honor their commitments. Genuine illness and family emergencies are legitimate reasons for breaking a date. Accepting a "better" offer or just having second thoughts is not. When you must cancel a date, inform the person as quickly as possible, and if you can, suggest another time to get together.

Good Manners for Good Times

No matter how casual, dating is more fun when everyone is on his and her best behavior. Mannerly behavior isn't stiff or forced. In fact, these respectful manners make it easier to get along with and enjoy other people.

Be clear about plans. When making a date, be clear about all details: time, place, activity, and transportation. Decide who will pay for what. When asking someone out for the first time, be considerate and don't expect him or her to finance an expensive evening.

Be on time. Arrive on time if you are picking up a date, and be ready to go if you are being picked up. Making a date hang around so you can stage a grand entrance is rude. If you're delayed, call your date, explain the situation, and revise the date time.

Pay attention to curfews, check the clock, and give yourself enough time to get your date home safely.

Show up in person. Go to the door and greet your date's parents. Answer their questions about plans and return time truthfully and politely. When meeting a date at work or a friend's home, make a personal appearance. If you must wait in the car or outside a place of business, don't embarrass yourself or disturb others by honking the horn, cranking up the stereo, or yelling for your date to come out.

Walking a date to the door at the end of the evening is an act of decency, respect, and safety that never goes out of style. Don't expect or demand a good-night kiss (or more).

Parents, while they're still chauffeuring for teens, should make sure that these courtesies are observed.

Steady Dating

Teens who become steadies often seem to live inside a charmed circle of two. But steady dating doesn't allow you to forget or ignore the feelings of others. Steadies have responsibilities, beginning with these demonstrations of respect for family, friends, and even strangers.

Be considerate of parents and family. Like it or not, a steady relationship also involves the people closest to you. To be trusted, you have to show trust and a fair degree of openness. For example, if your parents and family members don't know one another, you might see about getting them together.

Maintain your friendships. Most good friends understand that you won't be available as often as before. But when steadies are *too* exclusive, friends will feel rejected and may question your loyalty. Stay in contact. Be interested in your friends' lives if you expect them to be interested in yours. Remember that no friend enjoys being dumped.

Avoid excessive public displays of affection. Young love that is too physically expressive can be obnoxious. When around others, including family and friends, show your respect by exercising restraint. Public hand-holding and starry-eyed gazes are charming to most people; grabbing and groping are not.

Not Dating

Some teens just aren't interested in dating and often have good reasons for their decision. Dates may have lower priority than academics, jobs, sports, and the like. Teens may want to spend their time and energy on other pursuits. A teen might feel unready for one-on-one dating and prefer group interactions. Unless it's part of a pattern of isolation, not dating is probably not a problem.

Parents and friends shouldn't equate dating with sociability or popularity. They should avoid making negative remarks or trying to push teens into social situations that make them uncomfortable.

A good friend's cousin is coming to visit, and she wants me to go out with him. She's suggesting a double date—dinner and a movie. I'm seventeen, and I've never had a blind date before. I've heard they're always awful, so I probably won't go. But I don't want to hurt my friend's feelings.

Before you turn down the date, ask yourself some commonsense questions. Are your expectations realistic? Despite what you've heard, the goal of a blind date is simply to spend a few pleasant hours getting to know someone new—not to find Prince Charming. Do you want to miss a good time because of what others say but you've never experienced for yourself? Is it likely your friend would deliberately set you up with a bad date? It seems clear that by planning a double date, your friend probably enjoys her cousin's company and wants to make the evening comfortable for you and him.

Attitude is everything: Have an open mind, and you'll probably have a good time. Expect the date to be a disaster, and it probably will be—for everyone. If you really can't adjust your attitude and accept with pleasure, then you owe it to your friend and her cousin not to accept. Tell her as soon as possible, so she can make other plans.

Coming-of-age Events

THOUGH A TEEN'S SOCIAL LIFE tends to be freewheeling for the most part, there are a number of big events that mark the passage from childhood to young adulthood. To enjoy and appreciate these special occasions, teens need to be prepared for what will happen and what is expected of them. (Invitations for major events are discussed in Chapter 18, page 267: "An Invitation Potpourri.")

Confirmation

In the Catholic and Protestant traditions, young people are usually confirmed in their faith sometime between the ages of eleven and fourteen. Some Protestant confirmations also include baptism and/or first communion.

Protestant confirmation is normally part of Sunday services. In the Catholic Church, the confirmation ceremony is held separately from the regular mass and attended by family and close friends. In both traditions, services may be followed by church receptions attended by family, friends, and church officials and then luncheons at the home of the parents or relatives or at a restaurant. After-parties are usually restrained in tone. Gifts are often given by close relatives and friends and are generally of a religious nature: Bibles engraved with the young person's name, prayer books, gold crosses, or religious medallions. Written thank-yous are expected.

Bar Mitzvah and Bat Mitzvah

The bar mitzvah is celebrated for Jewish boys after they turn thirteen, although some Reform congregations have replaced the bar mitzvah with a confirmation service for both boys and girls. In some Conservative and Reform congregations, the bat mitzvah is celebrated for girls who have turned twelve or thirteen and is the modern counterpart of the bar mitzvah.

Bar mitzvah, bat mitzvah, and confirmation services are held as part of Saturday services, and the service is often followed by a reception at the synagogue, open to all members of the congregation. A luncheon, dinner, or reception for invited guests may be held later in the day. These invitation-only social events can be as simple or lavish as the family desires. Gifts, which may be religious or secular, are expected and can be sent or taken to the party. Thank-you notes for gifts are expected.

Quinceanera

A coming-of-age tradition that originated in Latin America, a quinceanera (or quince) commemorates a girl's fifteenth birthday. Depending on the practices of the family's Roman Catholic church, the event may comprise a religious ceremony followed by a party or a party only. The quinceanera party is often a formal dance (black or white tie) with the young honoree wearing an elaborate gown. A quinceanera may also be celebrated much less lavishly with a small group of family and friends. The invitation will indicate the level of formality. It's customary to take gifts to a quinceanera party, but presents are not opened at a formal ball. Written thank-you notes for gifts are expected.

∼ When to Take a Date to an Event ∼

Unless an oral or written invitation specifically indicates that you are to bring a guest or date, don't. And don't ask the host or hostess to include someone else. Religious occasions such as confirmations are normally for invited guests only. For some formal events and dances, the host or hostess may ask whom you would like to invite and then issue an invitation to that person. If an invitation is addressed to your name "and Guest," then you're expected to invite your own date. It's thoughtful to give your guest's name to the host when you reply to an RSVP.

My thirteen-year-old is invited to a friend's confirmation service and lunch- eon. I'm not familiar with the customs of the friend's religion. What should my child wear?

The easiest way to find out what is appropriate is to check with the friend's par- ents. Although customs can vary from congregation to congregation, the attire for confirmations and events that follow the service is generally "Sunday or Saturday best." This means neat dresses with sleeves or skirt-and-jacket outfits, hose, and party shoes for girls; suits or nice trousers and jackets, ties, and loafers or lace-up leather shoes for boys. (No open-necked sport shirts, tees, or athletic shoes.) It's a mark of respect not to wear religious jewelry of another faith. The friend's parents can tell you about correct headwear, or you can call the place of worship. If your child is invited to a more formal party such as a bar mitzvah celebration, the cor- rect choice is probably dressy party clothes for girls and suits and ties for boys. Be guided by the invitation, and ask if you are unsure.

Sixteenth Birthday Parties

Once upon a time, the sweet-sixteen party marked the end of childhood, especially for girls. Even now, turning sixteen has special significance, and some parents or rela- tives may want to host a party. The format can vary from a pizza party or picnic to an elegant dinner and dance. Surprise parties are a traditional form of sixteenth birthday celebration, as are slumber parties for girls. The invitation should be precise about the nature of the event. Birthday presents are expected, and thank-you notes should be sent to any guest whom the honoree hasn't thanked in person.

Formal Presentations

In a number of communities, formal presentation dances for high school students are held by school social clubs, sororities and fraternities, or adult social and charitable or- ganizations. (For details about presentations, see Chapter 18, page 263: "Presentation Balls"; Chapter 27, page 482: "At Debutante Balls"; Chapter 29, pages 499–513: "Cel- ebrating Life's Stages.") Since these events involve a good deal of preparation, dates should be invited well in advance. There is usually at least one practice session, which those who will be presented and their escorts or dates are expected to attend. Gener- ally, gifts are not expected—though parents and family members may want to give the presentee a special token of the occasion.

Special Occasion Gifts

When a teen is invited to an event at which presents are customary, he or she is expected to arrive with a gift. But what do you do when an invitation asks you to bring a date or guest?

If your date also received an invitation, then both of you bring presents. You and your date might give a joint present, but since this generally indicates a close relationship between the gift givers, you may want to stick to separate gifts or join with several more friends to purchase a group gift.

However, if your date did not receive an invitation, he or she is not expected to have a gift. The invited teen's present is assumed to be from both guests, but the gift card is signed by the person who received the invitation.

Proms and Graduations

SOME MILESTONES just have to be celebrated in a big way. Junior and senior proms—the chief social preludes to the end of high school—are often the first formal social events at which teens are the stars. Graduation parties are generally more casual than proms but just as exciting.

While each generation will party to its own themes, the formula for a happy event is timeless: equal parts of enthusiasm, good manners, and levelheaded regard for the safety and comfort of everyone. The guidelines that follow will almost guarantee an experience that will be remembered with pride and pleasure.

High School Proms

To be successful, prom nights require more planning and preparation than the usual social events a teen attends. In addition to all the dating basics discussed in this chapter, the courteous prom-goer will:

Ask early. Give your date plenty of advance notice—often six weeks or more. If you turn down a prom date, do so quickly and graciously. The person who invited you needs time to make other arrangements.

Think about the budget. Proms and the associated activities can be costly, even when dates share expenses. Be clear with each other about who will pay for what. Think creatively, and you and your date can cut corners but still have a special time. A corsage of fresh gardenias is lovely and less expensive than orchids. A rented tuxedo is an obvious choice. Dinner at a mid-range restaurant can be as much fun as dining at an expensive restaurant.

Arrange for rental vehicles well in advance. Study the details of the rental agreement and make reservations early because limousines and vans may be in short supply around prom time. (A parent may have to make the actual rental agreement.) Be re-

Age Issues

High school proms and graduation parties are, by definition, age-specific. In some cases, these events may be age-*inappropriate*. Unless you are in an established relationship, it's sensible to think carefully before inviting a much younger or much older date. Some schools have explicit rules about the ages of prom guests, so don't risk getting yourself or a date into an awkward situation. If your steady date is too young or too old for the party, you might take a mutual friend or go alone. Don't tempt a younger teen to break her or his curfew, and no matter what the age, never put a date in a situation—such as attending an unchaperoned after-prom party—that can cause embarrassment, result in punishment, or damage the person's reputation.

spectful of the limo driver and the vehicle, and be prepared to tip at the end of the big evening (see Chapter 46, page 805: "In Taxis, Private Cars, or Limousines").

Respect your date. Courtesy means a lot on a big night, so arrive on time or be ready when your date is at the door. Plan to spend a few extra minutes chatting with parents. At the party, be sure to dance with your date, and don't abandon her or him while you go off with friends. Introduce your date to anyone whom she or he doesn't know.

Thank everyone who helped with the prom. Creating a successful prom is no easy task, so express your appreciation to classmates, school officials, parents and chaperones, and others who made the evening memorable.

Plan after-party activities carefully. Although some schools plan after-prom events, teens often prefer to hold after-dance parties, especially all-nighters, at a classmate's home with parents and chaperones present. Prom night is not an excuse for alcohol or drug use, pranks, or vandalism—any behavior that can cause harm or damage reputations.

Make a commitment to be responsible and stick to it. You can have fun while keeping your behavior in check, and you may be able to influence others by your example. You can step in if someone who is intoxicated tries to drive or becomes aggressive, but do not engage in physical confrontation. Call on adults for help.

Graduation Invitations, Announcements, and Gifts

Graduation invitations are generally limited to the people who mean the most to the graduate—grandparents, close family, godparents, and supportive friends. Do not

∽ Corsages and Boutonnieres ∽

The tradition of giving corsages and boutonnieres to prom dates is still alive and well at many schools. Before ordering a corsage, it's a good idea for a boy to check with his date about the color of her dress and ask if she prefers a corsage or wristlet. With this information, a florist can recommend an attractive choice. When you present a corsage, your date will decide how to wear it and pin it on. The traditional corsage is attached at the shoulder (with the blooms facing upward), at the waist, or to an evening purse.

A boutonniere is a single flower—usually a rose or carnation—given (in some communities) by a girl to her date. The boutonniere is pinned to the lapel of his jacket where the buttonhole would be. The girl may pin it on or let her date handle this task.

invite school faculty or the parents of other students in the graduating class; these people are already included, so an invitation may seem like begging for a gift. (See also Chapter 18, page 270: "Graduations.")

Customarily, gifts are given by people who receive graduation invitations. But announcements are a different matter. Recipients of any kind of announcement are not expected to give gifts, though they may want to send a congratulatory note or card. If someone who received a graduation announcement does send a gift, the new graduate should acknowledge it with a gracious note of thanks.

There are no rules about what to select, but it's nice to choose a gift that reflects the significance of the graduation. Parents traditionally give something of special value and personal meaning. Other relatives and friends might choose gifts that say welcome to the adult world, such as monogrammed stationery and address books, fine pen-and-pencil sets, leather-bound books, picture frames, framed art or photography, and luggage. Gift certificates and money gifts are appropriate, especially if the giver isn't sure about the teen's tastes and interests.

Graduates should write personal thank-you notes for every gift and also send notes to anyone who entertains or does special favors for them.

Entertaining the Graduate

High school graduation represents the completion of many people's efforts, and proud parents, family, and friends often want to honor the graduate. Following morning or afternoon ceremonies, a brunch, luncheon, or supper party can be held at home or a local restaurant or club.

While there's no explicit time limit on when parties can be given, it's sensible to entertain within a few weeks of the graduation. However, it's not appropriate to hold a graduation party before the guest of honor has actually graduated.

Graduation-night Parties

Teens naturally want to celebrate their new diplomas with their friends, but the dangers of graduation night are well known. A smart option is to hold a party at a parent's home, provide plenty of good food, soft drinks, and entertainment, and let the grads party safely but in their own way.

Planning a graduation-night party requires that parents and teens work together so that everyone's expectations are crystal clear. Parents who host a party in their home should have other, responsible adult chaperones in attendance. Since the noise is likely to rise into the wee hours, tell neighbors about the party and ask for their indulgence. Inform local law enforcement, who are often out in force on graduation and prom nights, that there will be a party at your home. Host parents have a right to know who is invited, so they can be on the lookout for gate-crashers and pay close attention to young teens who may be brought as dates.

Do not serve alcohol (including beer), and watch for party guests who attempt to drink or use drugs. Never allow a teen who has been drinking or using drugs to drive. Some parents make the surrender of car keys a condition of attending an all-night graduation bash.

A number of local and national organizations, composed mostly of parents, now provide excellent ideas and advice for safe graduation night activities. Try an Internet search or check with your school principal's office for suggestions.

Part Four

Communication
and Protocol

Chapter Seventeen

Correspondence

I N A DAY WHEN PEOPLE COMMUNICATE globally in the blink of an eye, there's a misconception that they hardly ever put pen to paper anymore. But skeptics who entertain the notion that written correspondence can't withstand the juggernaut of e-mail need only look back a few years to the electronic book and the contention that "print is dead."

Yes, the multisheet letter is more likely to be computer generated today. But that doesn't mean handwritten correspondence isn't thriving. Smaller handwritten notes, meant for everything from thanking to offering condolences, are more popular than ever.

Another thing that hasn't gone out of fashion for correspondents is correct form and style. By structuring a letter or note in the traditional way, you stand a better chance of getting the reaction—and in the case of a business letter, the results—you want. Even e-mailed messages benefit from the adoption of a few timeless standards and practices (see Chapter 20, page 299: "Business E-mails").

The Stationery Drawer

THE ONCE-PRIM STATIONERY DRAWER is now stacked with new possibilities, including brightly colored papers and stationery intended for those who want fine paper but choose to design their own letterhead on the computer. What was once considered "proper" stationery is now but one of many choices, having given way to papers that reflect the writer's personality. It is a sign of the times that stationery with fanciful designs happily coexists with the calling card, an old staple now enjoying a revival, especially among the young.

Notepapers

Notepapers—meant for thank-you notes, acceptances and regrets, invitations, and other short correspondence—are available as fold-over notes, correspondence cards (one-sheet cards of stiffer paper), and informals (despite the name, the most formal of the lot). Because notes and cards come in countless styles, it's easy to find ones that suit your taste. After choosing the color and design you prefer, you can decide whether to add your initials or your name or to leave the paper blank (an advantage of blank cards is their usefulness to the whole family).

Correspondence cards and fold-over notes. Correspondence cards (usually 4¼ × 6½ inches) are the largest. The smaller fold-over notes must be large enough to meet the U.S. Postal Service's minimum requirement of 3½ × 5 inches. Both fold-over notes and correspondence cards are on the more casual side. If you decide to have your name printed or engraved on either, it's fine to substitute a nickname for your full name. On fold-over notes, the name is printed in the center of the first page; on correspondence cards, it is centered at the top. Titles (*Mr.*, *Mrs.*, *Ms.*, or others) are not used when printing a name on either. Of the two notepapers, correspondence cards tend to be more popular with men.

SUSIE SMITH

A correspondence card

Mrs. John Smith

An informal

At one time, almost all printed invitations, announcements, letterheads, and social cards were engraved. But modern technology offers a number of options. The following brief descriptions should help you choose the look that's right for your style and budget.

Engraving. The most costly method, engraving is done from a metal plate. The lettering can be felt as slightly raised on the top of the sheet, and the indentation, or "bruise," can be felt on the back of the paper. Many of today's print shops no longer do engraving.

Thermography. Less expensive than engraving, thermography uses heat to affix ink to the page. The lettering is raised above the paper and often has a shinier appearance than engraving. When well done, thermography can be similar in look to engraving.

Lithography. Sometimes less costly than thermography, lithography applies ink directly and flatly to the paper. Lithography can have a very crisp look as long as the paper doesn't absorb the ink and feather or blur the letters.

Laser. Whether done on a home printer or by a print shop, good laser printing looks similar to lithography. It's the least-expensive option, best suited for informal or casual invitations.

Embossing. Often used for monograms and symbols, embossing uses a plate into which the image is cut. When pressed onto paper, the image is raised above the surface, creating a three-dimensional look. In blind embossing, no ink is applied; in debossing, the image is depressed below the paper surface.

The quality of any printing is directly related to the quality of the paper, so it's smart to work with an experienced printer or stationery supplier when you need printed materials.

Informals. Informals ($3\frac{1}{2} \times 5$ inches) differ from regular fold-over notes in that they come only in white or ecru paper, sometimes with a plain raised frame. They are used for writing more formal short notes (despite their name "informal"), for issuing invitations, and as gift enclosures. Informals can either be plain or engraved on the front with a name (black ink only), though traditionally only the full social name (including *Mrs.* or *Ms.*) is used. Men traditionally use informals only as part of a couple: "Mr. and Mrs. Sanford St. John."

Stationery for Men

Traditionally, personal stationery for men differed slightly in size and color from that for women. A man's standard paper, a monarch sheet, measures $7\frac{1}{4} \times 10\frac{1}{2}$ inches. It comes in a variety of shades, with white, cream, or gray the most popular. This paper can be used for either typed or handwritten letters, and for all correspondence; it is neatly folded in thirds to fit into the envelope.

If marked on the sheet, the man's name appears in plain block or roman letters at the top center (no title—*Mr.* or *Dr.*, for example—is used on personal stationery). The full address can be shown beneath the name, but the personal telephone number, fax number, and e-mail address are optional.

Some men prefer using correspondence cards, described on page 224. These are in the more casual mode, and are handy for brief handwritten notes.

Stationery for Women

Personal stationery for women is traditionally smaller—approximately 6 × 8 inches. A correspondence sheet is a single page that is folded once from top to bottom to be placed in its envelope. A letter sheet, the most formal stationery for women, is a double sheet that is folded along the left side and opens like a book. The colors for formal correspondence are white, cream, light blue, or light gray; for personal letters, any pattern or combination of colors is appropriate.

At one time, monarch sheets—the papers that are 7¼ × 10½ inches and are used for long personal letters or business correspondence—were used mostly by men, but they are no longer associated with one gender or the other.

A QUESTION FOR PEGGY

Will stationery I create on my computer really look as good as the best I can buy from a high-end stationer? And just how hard is it to do?

Unless you want it to look engraved, you can indeed create eye-popping stationery as long as you choose the right typeface and paper. Letterheads for personal paper can be as creative as you like, while those for business should be appropriate for your line of work.

Type in your name and any other information you choose to include (address, e-mail, and so on), then experiment with different fonts and sizes until you find what you like best. (For business letterheads, you can also add a logo or a graphic using images from clip art.) You can even make your own business cards. But take care with letterheads and cards: An unusual font may be fun, but if it can't be easily read, it defeats your purpose. If you feel you aren't computer-savvy enough for the job, check out the software programs designed for creating personalized letterheads. For a true read, print out each sample design on the paper you intend to use rather than judging it by what you see on the screen.

Stationery for the Family

Stationery suitable for all the members of a family has the address—but not the name—engraved or printed in plain letters at the top. Children and teens may want something more their style and can choose from stationery designs appropriate for their age group.

Some families mark their stationery with a heraldic device, or coat of arms. Technically, this privilege is restricted to those directly descended through the male line from an ancestor who had the right to use a coat of arms as a personal, family, or clan mark. People who merely have the same surname—and are unrelated to the family with a proven right to use the device—are *not* entitled to use it in any manner.

In the United States, a woman is permitted to use the full coat of arms of her husband or father, whereas in the United Kingdom women are entitled to use only what is called, in the vocabulary of heraldry, a lozenge—a small diamond-shaped figure on which portions of the arms are displayed.

Where Does the Writing Go?

FOR LONGER LETTERS, there is no fixed rule about where the writing should go on a fold-over note. Still, two sequences have been traditionally followed:

Where to write on a blank fold-over, using all four pages

> Write on the first, second, third, fourth pages consecutively.

> Write on the first and fourth pages. Then, after opening the sheet, write across the two inside pages as if they were one.

On single-sheet stationery, it's fine to write on both sides. An exception is airmail-weight paper so thin that the writing shows through and makes the letter hard to read. If an initial, design, or name is printed on the top of the front page of a fold-over note, the writing can start on the front page. If the printing appears in the middle of the first page, start writing on the open center pages.

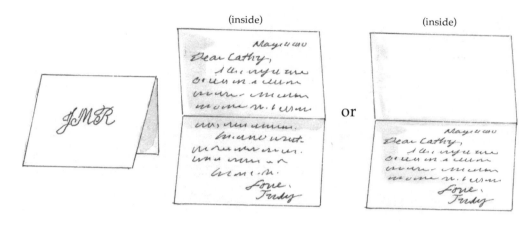

Where to write on a fold-over note with name or initial printed on front
(Note: The writing may continue to the fourth page, also correct.)

The Envelope

IS THERE A CORRECT WAY to address an envelope? Yes. Simply make sure the address and return address are not easily confused and that the writing is perfectly legible.

Addressing

It pays to double-check an address—especially when you're addressing one envelope after another, as when writing thank-you notes. It can take weeks for a misaddressed letter to be returned, and you can't necessarily count on the letter carrier to be familiar enough with the neighborhood to deliver it to the right house. Also make sure your handwriting is perfectly legible, even if that means writing in block letters.

The return address. While the U.S. Postal Service (USPS) has traditionally preferred that the return address (whether a printed label or written by hand) appear on the front of the envelope in the upper left-hand corner, today's printed envelopes for personal stationery may have the return address printed on the back flap. On plain envelopes, do your part and write your return address on the front.

The recipient's address. The placement of the USPS's ZIP codes and the post codes used in other countries differ. The ZIP code goes after the state name (use the USPS's designated abbreviations, such as *NY* and *TX*) in all cases. The same is true for addresses in other countries with states or provinces—Canada and Australia, for example.

Mr. and Mrs. Milton Reid
7100 Parsons Street
Columbia, MO 66208

Miss Rachel Rosenberg
1418 Old South Head Road
Sydney, NSW 2070
Australia

In countries where states or provinces are not used in the address, such as France and Germany, the post code goes after the city name:

Mr. Guy Sharpley
418 Boulevard Beaumarchais
Paris 75110
France

➤ *To a married woman.* Address an envelope to a married woman by using either her first name ("Mrs. Beatrice Monroe") or her husband's ("Mrs. David Monroe"). Time was when the proper address on a letter never used the woman's first name, unless she was a divorcée. Today, both forms of address are appropriate. For informal correspondence, the address can read simply "Beatrice Monroe."

➤ *To couples.* Formal correspondence to a married couple is addressed to "Mr. and Mrs. David Monroe." For informal notes, "Bea and David Monroe" is fine. When a married woman hasn't taken her husband's name, correspondence for both is addressed "Ms. [not "Mrs."] Beatrice Williams and Mr. David Monroe," on the same line. Correspondence to men and women who live together but aren't married is addressed with their names on separate lines, with the courtesy titles optional:

> Ms. Mira Patel
> Mr. James DeFranco

➤ *To a married woman doctor/two married doctors.* Even though a married woman doctor who uses her husband's last name may be known both professionally and socially in conversation as Dr. Sonia Harris, addressing social correspondence to the couple is a little trickier. If her husband isn't a doctor and the woman retains her title socially, address letters to "Dr. Sonia and Mr. Robert Harris." If her husband is also a doctor, the address is either "The Drs. Harris" or "Drs. Sonia and Robert Harris."

Correct Use of "Esquire"

Today, "Esquire" (abbreviated Esq.) is largely confined to business correspondence between lawyers and justices of the peace. Still, it pays to know how to use the designation correctly.

When Esquire or Esq. follows the name, *never* precede it with "Mr.," "Ms.," "Mrs.," or "Miss." Write "David Bowman, Esq." When writing to a lawyer and his or her spouse, this title is dropped altogether, with "Mr. and Mrs. David Bowman" the correct form. (See also, Chapter 22, page 325: "Sir," "Madam," and "Esquire.")

Personal and Other Notations

Add the notation "Personal" to a social letter only if it is being mailed to the recipient's business address. A letter to his home so marked would imply that you suspect another family member might open it.

For the most part, use "Confidential" only for business letters. Keep in mind that letters bearing this notation are sometimes opened by executive secretaries. Accordingly, it's often wiser to mark a confidential business letter as Personal.

If a letter addressed to someone else is delivered to you by mistake, write "Please Forward" and leave the letter in your mailbox for the letter carrier to pick up.

At times, you may accidentally open a letter addressed to someone else, especially a letter that is put in the wrong mailbox. Write "Please Forward; Opened by Mistake" and your initials on the face of the envelope, seal it with a piece of tape, and leave it in your box for the letter carrier.

Seals

Envelope seals are of two types: (1) decorative stamps that feature a charity or other nonprofit organization and help to raise money for the organizations that distribute them and (2) decorative seals, which include wax seals (once-functional seals that have made a comeback in recent years) or adhesive seals embossed with an initial or a design.

Organizational stamps or seals, which are affixed to the back of the envelope so that they overlap the flap, make it easy to support a worthy cause and encourage others to contribute. While seals may be used on any personal or business letters, they should not be used on notes of condolence or on formal invitations and replies.

Decorative seals add a nice finishing touch to the envelope, especially for events as special as charity balls and weddings.

∼ Folding Letters ∼

Which edge of a letter is inserted first into the envelope is hardly something worth worrying about, but those who stand by tradition will want to insert the open, or unfolded, edge first. The letter is placed so that when the recipient takes it from the envelope and opens it, the writing is right side up. The paper should be folded evenly and neatly—once for an envelope half as deep as the paper, twice for one-third as deep.

So Many Notes . . .

THE HANDWRITTEN NOTE—brief, informal, and a blessed alternative to the starkness of an e-mail read on the computer screen—has largely superceded the letter over the past few years. Thank-you notes account for the greater portion of such correspondence, but brief, warm messages are appropriate for virtually any other purpose, whether to congratulate someone or to apologize for a mix-up or mishap.

The sample notes on the following pages are for extending thanks or congratulations. Additional thank-you notes are covered in other chapters: Thank-you notes for wedding gifts (pages 674–679), thank-you notes for gifts in general (pages 523–525), children's thank-you notes (pages 204–207), and notes about letters of sympathy (page 545). (For information about greeting cards and appending notes to them, see page 237: "Greeting Cards.")

Thank-you Notes

THE TWO MOST IMPORTANT THINGS to strive for when writing thank-you notes are sincerity and promptness. Except for thank-yous written for dozens of gifts after a major occasion like a wedding, a note arriving more than a week after an event loses its fizz. You'll also want to use expressions that come naturally, writing as though you were conversing with the recipient.

Commercial thank-you cards with the words "Thank You" printed on the front are perfectly fine, although many people choose to use their everyday stationery. Cards that include a message written by the greeting-card company *always* require the addition of a personal note of your own. Though your added note can be brief, it must mention the gift or the occasion.

If you don't have a set of note cards and need to send one or two thank-you notes, blank commercial cards that feature an appealing design or a painting by a favorite artist are a good alternative to cards with preprinted messages. In fact, they're better, since the sentiments are entirely yours.

Whom to Address

When you've received a gift that comes from more than one person—a birthday present with a card signed "the Dubrowskis," for example—to whom do you write the thank-you? It's unwieldy to list every last member of the family in the address, so use "Mr. and Mrs. Fred Dubrowski." In the note itself, the salutation could read "Dear Fred and Dee," and the children could then be included in the text: "Please thank Diana and Sandy and Freddy for me, and tell them how pleased I am with the perfume."

For Dinner or Overnight Visits

A thank-you note for the host(s) of a dinner party is optional. However, when you've stayed overnight or longer at someone's house, you *must* write a note of thanks to your hosts—and promptly. Two forgivable exceptions are when the hosts are relatives who frequently spend the night at each other's homes or friends who are so close that you consider yourselves family. Even then, a note is in order if you don't expect to see your hosts for some time. (For a chart indicating when thank-you notes are obligatory or optional, see Chapter 30, page 525: "Note or Not?")

Following are a couple of examples—the first is for very close friends, the second for people you know less well:

> *Dear Roseanne,*
>
> *You and Clark are such wonderful hosts. Once again, Fran and I can tell you that there's no other house where we have such a good time and hate to leave so much. We especially enjoyed the party Saturday evening. Thank you so much for including us!*
>
> *Yours truly,*
> *Brian*

> *Dear Mrs. Silverman,*
>
> *Last weekend was the high point of my summer. Everything you planned was terrific, and I really loved the trip to the crafts fair on Sunday. I truly enjoyed every minute with your family, and I thank you again for inviting me.*
>
> *Very sincerely,*
> *Aida*

When New Acquaintances Have Entertained

When you've attended a dinner or party hosted by someone you were meeting for the first time—for example, when you visited relatives in another city and friends of theirs invited all of you over—a note will not only thank them but reaffirm your pleasure in the meeting.

> *Dear Vivian and Tony,*
>
> *It was such a pleasure to meet you, and so kind of you to invite Richard and me to your home. The meal was one to remember (paella worthy of a Spanish chef!), and the conversation was just as enjoyable.*
>
> *The evening was one of the high points of our trip to Seattle, and I hope we can return the favor if you're ever in Phoenix. In the meantime, thank you for your generous hospitality. Richard joins me in sending regards to you both.*
>
> *Very sincerely yours,*
> *Barbara Beckett*

When You've Been the Guest of Honor

Whether you've been welcomed to the neighborhood with a coffee, or a close friend has thrown your birthday party, a gift for the host—a thank-you arrangement of flowers or other token of your appreciation—is a good way to say thanks. It can be sent either the day before the party or the day after. Then follow up with a thank-you over the telephone or in a note.

Notes of Congratulations

YOUR NIECE HAS JUST GRADUATED from high school or a close friend calls to say he got the promotion he's been waiting for. Or perhaps a friend has given birth or a teenager you know has won a city-wide essay contest. A congratulatory note is a thoughtful way to express your happiness for them and to deliver a compliment.

∼ Your Natural Voice ∼

Have no fear: You don't have to excel at writing to compose a good note or letter. The best personal letters are conversational, reflecting both your personality and speech. A few simple steps will make the recipient feel as if the two of you were chatting:

➤ Don't replace phrases typical of your speech with more formal language. Someone who would say, "The buzz at work is . . . ," sounds stilted when he writes, "The topic giving rise to the most gossip . . ."

➤ Use contractions. Since you almost certainly choose "I don't know" over "I do not know" when speaking, go with the same words when writing.

➤ Occasionally insert the person's name to add a touch of familiarity and affection. "And, Beth, guess what we're going to do this summer?" makes Beth feel as though you're honestly thinking about her as you write.

➤ Use punctuation to enliven your writing. Underlining a word or using an exclamation point after a phrase or sentence gives emphasis where you want it. (Just don't overdo it—and no smiley face under the exclamation point, please.) You can set off phrases with a dash: "We went to a dance last night—what a party!" has more pizzazz than "We went to a dance last night, and it was great."

➤ Keep it as short as possible. The brief tale is always more interesting than the drawn-out one.

On the Birth of a Baby

You don't have to wait until you receive a birth announcement to send a congratulatory note to new parents. The sooner you mail it after hearing the news, the better. It's courteous, but not obligatory, for the recipient to acknowledge the congratulations with a brief note or phone call.

> *Dear Tamara,*
>
> *I was so delighted to hear the news of Jonathan, Jr.'s birth. Once you've had time to adjust to your new role (and what a terrific mom you'll be!), I'll give you a call to see when I can drop by to see you and Jon and meet the new family member.*
>
> *Much love,*
> *Helen*

> *Dear Helen,*
>
> *Jon, Jonathan, and I thank you for your note, and we're all looking forward to seeing you once things settle down. Jon and I very much want two of our favorite people to meet each other.*
>
> *Love,*
> *Tamara*

For Special Achievement

If someone or her close relative is honored for special achievement, wins an award, or has a smashing success in business, it's thoughtful to write a note like the following:

> *Dear Amanda,*
>
> *We were so happy to hear that David has been awarded a Fulbright scholarship. He well deserves it, and we're all so proud of him—and of you, too! The next time you see or write to David, please give him our love and congratulations.*
>
> *Sincerely,*
> *Millicent*

> *Dear Amanda,*
>
> *How thoughtful you were to write a note about David. I shared it with him when I spoke to him last night, and he asked me to extend his thanks along with ours for your good wishes and congratulations.*
>
> *Sincerely,*
> *Millicent*

On a Promotion or an Appointment

Congratulatory notes about promotions or appointments are usually reserved for close friends or friends with whom you once worked. If a newspaper article brought the promotion to your attention, you can clip it and enclose it with your note.

> *Dear Michael,*
>
> *Ginger and I were so happy to learn of your promotion to CFO. The business world needs men like you—if we had more men of your caliber, the economy would be in better shape. Our warmest congratulations!*
>
> *Best,*
> *Jim*

> *Dear Jim,*
>
> *Thanks so much for your note. Your good wishes mean a lot to me, and your unflagging support has carried me through some challenging times in the past. It will be great to know it's still there as I begin this new endeavor.*
>
> *Warmly,*
> *Michael*

For a Graduate

Even if you've given a gift to a young person on her graduation from high school or college, a note will personalize your congratulations all the more. A note (not a gift) is the usual response to a graduation announcement.

> *Dear Pia,*
>
> *Congratulations on having gotten through four years on campus without a scratch—and, from what I hear, for excelling in numerous ways. I want to wish you the best of luck as you step out into the world, and I know that you'll greet it with ability, courage, and confidence.*
>
> *Sincerely,*
> *Ingrid Burke*

> *Dear Mrs. Burke,*
>
> *The early map of Tennessee is something I'll treasure, and I can't thank you enough for your thoughtfulness. I also really appreciate your kind note. It's nice to know that someone besides my parents has confidence in me, because I know I've really got to get cracking! I look forward to seeing you the next time I visit Mom and Dad.*
>
> *Sincerely,*
> *Pia*

A friend just sent a nice note congratulating me for winning an award. Is there a proper way to let her know how much I appreciate her thoughtfulness?

Replying is always a considerate thing to do, and the choice of how to do it is yours. Either pick up the phone and thank the person for thinking of you or, if you see her often, leave the thanks for the next time the two of you get together. In either case, saying, "Thanks so much for your note! Your kind words mean a lot," is sufficient. It's also fine to respond in writing—a gesture that never goes out of style.

Notes of Apology

A NOTE OF APOLOGY may be called for when you've been responsible for something that adversely affects someone else. A phone call will suffice in most cases (and often can seem more sincere and contrite), but at other times you may want to follow a call with a note.

Dear Janice,

I do apologize for having to call you about Monday night. As I said on the phone, I accepted your invitation without remembering that Monday was a holiday— which meant that our houseguests from Rochester were actually staying till Tuesday.

Again, let me tell you how disappointed we were, and we hope it won't be too long before we can see you and Rolf again.

Affectionately,
Yvette

Occasionally, an unfortunate accident occurs. Although what happened may have been beyond your control, your note should offer to make amends:

Dear Mrs. Lee,

Your son has just informed me that our dog dug up your flower bed and ruined your beautiful zinnias. My husband will build the dog fence higher this evening so that Rover won't be able to escape again.

I will also replace the zinnias, although I'm afraid that new ones can't compensate for those you lost. If you would kindly call me with your variety preference, I will order seedlings from the nursery. In the meantime, I can only ask you to accept my apologies.

Sincerely yours,
Joy Cason

Greeting Cards

COMMERCIAL GREETING CARDS expressing good wishes for holidays, birthdays, anniversaries, and other occasions are typically sent by Americans, but they will mean much more if you add a short message of your own. No matter how delightful, a printed message can't beat a handwritten one. Many people prefer to use cards that are blank inside so that they can write sentiments that are theirs and theirs alone.

Signatures on Greeting Cards

When signatures are printed, there's no longer a rule for married couples about whose name goes first, but the last name is always used (unlike signed cards sent to close friends). Still, "Charles and Lisa Bell" makes sense because it follows the conventional "Mr. and Mrs." form.

When the signature is handwritten, the wife's name traditionally precedes the husband's—but, as with printed signatures, it's your call.

When children's names are included, the father's name always comes first: "Charles and Lisa Bell and Charles, Jr." Cards sent by a large family are more flexible, from "The Johnstons" (or "The Robert Johnstons") to "The Johnstons—Bob, Jean, Bobby, Zoe, and Jen" (listed in order of birth) to "The Johnstons—all five." In blended families with more than one surname in the mix, the simplest solution is to write "Chris and Peg Morita and all the family" or ". . . and all the children."

No social or professional titles are used for greeting card signatures.

Holiday Newsletters

Holiday cards are often used to share family news. Announcing an event as momentous as a birth in the family is perfectly appropriate, as are brief news notes or special thoughts to people whom you haven't seen for a long time. Then there's the printed history of the past year—the holiday newsletter.

Holiday newsletters are fine in themselves, but many people don't really care if the baby now has six teeth or Timmy is excelling at T-ball. With that in mind, enclose newsletters *only* in cards to those you think will be interested. An Emily Post Institute survey conducted in 2003 found respondents split on such newsletters' desirability: Fifty-three percent liked them and forty-seven percent did not.

The newsletter can keep those on your list up-to-date on your happenings, but share only news that's positive and not too personal. Keep your letter to one page or less and write a one- or two-sentence personal message in the card that accompanies the letter. Two other bits of advice:

➤ A handwritten salutation—"Dear Karen and Phil"—is warmer than the printed "Dear friends," and signing each letter individually personalizes it all the more.

➤ Don't turn your letter into a brag sheet. A passing mention that "Rick and I were lucky enough to visit Belize last September" is a humble and simple

I'm tempted to send electronic holiday greetings to my computer-savvy friends this year but wonder whether it's really appropriate. And what about sending a thank-you for a gift via e-mail?

E-mailing personal greetings or a holiday card downloaded from the Internet is perfectly fine, but with one caveat—it's appropriate only with people you e-mail regularly or with those who frequently check their e-mail (a December greeting read in January is not what you had in mind). Even then, you should remember a few do's and don'ts.

First, write your message as you would on a traditional card and refrain from using shortcuts such as acronyms, abbreviations, and lowercase letters only: The easier it is to read, the better the message. Second, be sure not to show other recipients' e-mail addresses in the address box; it's not your place to reveal them.

While an e-mailed thanks for a holiday gift may be all right if you and the giver e-mail each other frequently, it's still no substitute for a handwritten note. Thanking the person the old-fashioned way will stress how much the gift means to you.

report, while "Rick and I spent a week at the deluxe Playa Sedosa resort in Belize and had never felt so pampered" has overtones of "Don't you wish you were us?" Similarly, including your high schooler's near-perfect SAT score sounds more than a little boastful.

Social Cards

IN THE LAST FEW YEARS, social cards have begun to replace business cards for personal use. And it's about time: The days of scrawling your home phone number on a business card or matchbook cover can't fade away too soon. Although social cards (also known as calling cards, personal cards, and visiting cards) serve some of the same purposes they did in an earlier era, they are flexible enough in use and design to reflect your personality. (See Chapter 43, page 758: "Your Business Cards.")

You can have virtually anything printed on a social card, so long as it is in good taste. The cards are generally used in three ways:

As personal cards. Most social cards show only your name and phone number, but you can add your address if you want. Any practical information you think important can be printed under your name. For example, a mother actively involved in children's activities might add the helpful "Mother of Sam and Justine." Even someone who has a special interest can add it to his card, and with a touch of humor: A retiree who's an avid golfer might put "Golf Maniac" under his name.

As visiting cards. In an echo of Victorian times, social cards can be given out when you pay a visit to someone or left for her if she isn't at home. A brief message can be written on the face of the card or on the back.

As gift enclosures. Social cards come in handy when giving presents, especially if the gift is to someone you don't know well and a less personal message seems more appropriate. Just jot "Congratulations on your new job" or "With best wishes" above your name.

Your Address

Addresses are often left off of social cards so you can give your address only when you choose to, jotting it down on the spot. Depending on the circumstances, handing a stranger a nonbusiness card printed with your home address could seem a little too personal. At the same time, it's perfectly okay to have your address printed on the card if you wish.

~ Way Back When ~

Calling cards served a useful purpose before the invention of the telephone, but the rules for their appearance were as rigid as a Victorian corset. The proper paper for cards was white or cream white glazed or unglazed Bristol board. The size might vary within a narrow range, but women's cards were generally smaller than those for men, and plate markings (raised borders) were frowned upon for both. Titles like Mister and Doctor preceded the name, which was written out in its entirety—no abbreviations or initials were allowed. For Mister John Hunter Witherspoon Dunn to have his card printed as Mr. John H. W. Dunn would have sent more than a few society matrons scrambling for their smelling salts.

While we may look back with amusement at many nineteenth-century customs, calling cards were nothing to be laughed at. In fact, their use was grounded in graciousness. Rather than foisting yourself on someone at an inconvenient time of day, you stopped by his house and left a card. The card told the recipient you thought him worthy of your time and attention and placed in his hands the decision of whether to see you. A gentleman who called on a lady often attached his card to a tussy-mussy, a small bouquet of different blooms that transmitted a message in the Victorian language of flowers.

What About Titles?

Whether to use a title on your card is a matter of choice. Using a courtesy title—*Mr.*, *Mrs.*, *Ms.*, or *Miss*—may seem unnecessary and a little fussy to some people, while others prefer this slightly more formal touch. Professional titles, including Doctor, are also optional. Academic initials are better for identification purposes: "Dr. Harold Settle" and "Dr. Maria Vasquez" could both be mistaken for physicians, whereas "Harold Settle, D.D.S." and "Maria Vasquez, Ph.D." avoid such confusion. (Holders of honorary degrees should not use the title or initials on their cards.)

Military officers, members of the clergy, and government officials can use "Colonel Thomas Daye" (followed by "United States Army"), "The Reverend William Clarkson," "Judge Harriet Rowlands," "Senator James Wallace." In certain cases, a title goes under the name: "Mr. John Lewis" on the first line, with "Mayor of Chicago" below. "The Honorable," on the other hand, is never used on a social card. (See also Chapter 22, page 332: "Correct Use of 'the Honorable.' ")

Personal Letters

WHETHER HANDWRITTEN OR TYPED, written correspondence—as opposed to e-mail—reveals you as a person who takes time to communicate. Moreover, the ability to write a letter that the recipient will treasure is a gift.

To write a good letter, first try to think of what might interest the recipient. Second, write in a conversational, informal way: The language used in the golden age of letter writing may have been beautiful, but it was very much of its time. (See also page 233: "Your Natural Voice.")

One thing that hasn't changed is the standard letter format—a textbook case of "if it ain't broke, don't fix it." That's because simple logic dictates where the various elements of a letter are placed on the page.

Your Home Address and the Date

If your stationery isn't printed with your address, it's a good idea to add it for your correspondent's convenience, usually in the upper right-hand corner of the first page. (Placing it just below your signature is reserved for business correspondence.) The date follows the address.

> 31 Fieldstone Road
> Evergreen, Colorado 80439
> January 12, 2004

If your address is already printed on your stationery, the date is placed in the upper right-hand corner of the first page. Writing "January 12, 2004" is preferable to "1-12-04."

The Body of the Letter

THE BEST LETTERS will share news and information, mix good with bad news, respond to the questions asked by recipients in their letters, and ask about the recipient and comment on news she has shared. You should include only information you would be happy for others to see. This means no idle gossip, no defamatory or unattractive remarks about others, and nothing so personal that it would prove embarrassing to you or anyone else.

It's fine to mention people you both know, but don't go on at length about someone the recipient has never heard of and couldn't care less about—unless that someone will continue to play a significant part in your life. Writing about the Janet Sanders who won the city council seat is boring, while writing about the Janet Sanders who has become your closest friend is meaningful.

Letters Best Left Unwritten

The words you speak won't live forever, but those you put down on paper just might. Think twice about writing anything that could come back to haunt you.

The woe-is-me letter. A letter full of misfortune and unhappiness won't give your readers pleasure but will probably leave them irritated, worried, or depressed.

The tell-all letter. Remember that people change—and "people" includes you. There's nothing wrong with pouring your heart out in a letter, but providing too many intimate details of a love affair could eventually lead to embarrassment. It's wrong to reveal everything you know about someone's trials and tribulations when you've been sworn to secrecy—so check your impulse to tell all.

The angry letter. Bitter spoken words fade away in time, but written words stay on the page forever. Put a letter written in the heat of anger aside for twenty-four hours, then read it cold; you'll probably either soften the tone or leave the letter unsent.

Ending a Letter

End a letter with something positive, not by writing, "Well, I guess you've read enough of this" or "You must be bored to tears by now"—both of which strike a negative note. If you can, wind up the letter with something your correspondent can relate to. If you've reported on a trip, for example, "The mountains were so beautiful at sunset" is a simple declaration, while adding "They reminded me of when we were all in Colorado together" establishes a connection.

Signatures

The protocol for signatures is more complicated for women than for men, but it's not difficult to grasp.

If you're writing to someone whom you've never met face to face, sign with your first and last name. If you've spoken with the person on the phone—on a business call, for example—you could put your last name in parentheses. On letters to friends, you sign with your first name or the nickname the recipient knows you by.

When you write for yourself and your spouse (or sister or brother or anyone else), sign your own name only. It's not a sin to sign "Joyce and Paul," but Paul is not writing the letter and is better brought up in the text: "Paul and I had such a terrific time last weekend, and he asked me to tell you again how much he liked the golf course." Or "Paul joins me in sending thanks and love to everyone." On holiday cards and other greeting cards, however, joint signatures are fine.

A married woman or widow. Traditionally, a married woman or a widow signs both a business letter and a letter to a person she doesn't know with her full legal name—"Joyce Clark Rheingold" or "Joyce C. Rheingold." Her married name can be added as well unless it is printed on the stationery. In handwritten letters, her mar-

∽ The Complimentary Close ∽

In earlier days, the complimentary close of a letter—the word or phrase that precedes your signature—was long and flowery, but it has gradually been pruned. Even "Kindest regards" has almost disappeared, while "Sincerely yours," "Best wishes," and "Yours truly" are often shortened to "Sincerely," "Best," and "Yours." The standard complimentary closes for modern times depend on the type of note or letter:

➤ The preferred ending to a formal social note is "Sincerely," "Sincerely yours," "Very sincerely," or "Very sincerely yours."

➤ In friendly notes, the most frequently used closings are (from the least intimate to the most) are "Affectionately," "Cordially," "Fondly," and "Love."

➤ "Gratefully" is used only when a benefit has been received, as when a friend has gone out of her way to do you a favor.

➤ "As always" or "As ever" is useful in closing to a letter to someone with whom you may not be close, especially when you haven't seen him for some time.

➤ "Yours in haste" and "Hastily yours" are ill advised, possibly suggesting that you're writing only because you're obligated to do so.

➤ "Faithfully" and "Faithfully yours" are rarely used but are appropriate on very formal social correspondence—letters to a high member of the clergy, a member of the U.S. Cabinet, an ambassador, or anyone holding an equally important post. The same applies to "I have the honor to remain . . ." followed by "Respectfully yours."

ried name can be written in parentheses and placed underneath her signature: "(Mrs. Earl Rheingold)." In typed letters, the parentheses—though not the married name—are dropped.

If a woman would rather her marital status not be known, she can choose "Ms." In handwritten letters, a single woman, married woman, divorcée, or widow could use one of these signatures: "Miss [Mrs., Ms.] Margaret Brown." Or she could forgo titles altogether and simply sign as "Margaret Brown."

A business or professional woman's signature. When an unmarried woman starts her career using her maiden name, she may keep it throughout her professional life, preceding it with "Miss" or "Ms." if she chooses. If she marries, she could use "Ms." or "Mrs." when she signs with a courtesy title.

Other signatures. There are often occasions when the protocol of signing comes up, whether one's signature goes on a guest register or a business report:

➤ When husbands and wives sign most registers, including those at hotels and private clubs, "Mr. and Mrs. Matthew Harrison" is standard. When asked to sign a guest book, they usually sign "Judy and Matt Harrison" so that the wife's first name is on record.

➤ A man registers at a hotel simply as "Peter Norton." If he is accompanied by his wife, "Mr. and Mrs. Peter Norton" is the norm, as mentioned above. If their children have come, "Peter Norton and family" is a good choice.

➤ On lists of patrons or sponsors of a fund-raising party or other function, a man's or woman's name is listed with his or her title (Mr., Ms., Mrs., Dr., and so on). On professional or business listings, the name is signed without the title—"Richard Peterson," which is also the correct signature when the person signs reports, certificates, and the like.

Business Letters

BUSINESS CORRESPONDENCE is no small subject to tackle, consisting as it does of everything from letters of reference to letters of complaint. The letters are always typewritten and are best addressed to an individual, not to "Whom It May Concern."

Letters of Reference and Recommendation

When you're asked to write a recommendation or reference letter, assess your own feelings. Do you know this person well or only casually? Are you enthusiastic about his capabilities, or only lukewarm? Because your letter must be honest, it's kinder to politely refuse than to write a letter that, despite your best efforts, will likely betray your true feelings.

If you do write, include information about your relationship (employer, supervisor, client, teacher) to the person you're recommending and the length of your acquaintance. When possible, offer your evaluation of the person's qualifications. For a job applicant, you should cite examples of his workplace experience:

> *Bill Hatfield first demonstrated his organizational and leadership abilities when he orchestrated a major new client presentation during his first few months as my administrative assistant. In this and every project he has handled since, Bill has proved to be a natural self-starter, an imaginative planner, and a terrific team leader.*

Don't hesitate to be enthusiastic—but only if you're certain the person can live up to your glowing review. If you've agreed to give an oral reference, include a telephone number and times when you can be reached.

Letters of Commendation

It's sad but true that people are usually quick to complain and slow to commend. Often, someone performs an act of kindness or professionalism beyond anyone's expectation, and a letter commending the person(s) is important—especially when sent to his or her supervisor. Just be sure to include specifics:

> *Mr. Hal Walker*
> *Director, Public Relations*
> *Blue Sky Airways*
> *P.O. Box 7938*
> *St. Louis, MO 65902*
>
> *Dear Mr. Walker:*
>
> *As a business traveler, I fly frequently and have seen my share of problems—not only in airports but in the air. So when I see an opportunity to compliment airline personnel for their good service, I'm eager to do so.*
>
> *Such an opportunity presented itself on February 7 on Blue Skies flight 425 from Dallas to Chicago. The plane was full, with several demanding passengers, but the three flight attendants in coach—Sally Keene, based in Dallas, and Sarah McEvoy and Jenny Lou Fry, both based in Chicago—rose to the occasion without a hitch. They were not only efficient but so very calm and cheerful that it was a pleasure to be on the flight.*
>
> *I would appreciate it if you would see to it that my thanks are passed on to these three women.*
>
> *Yours sincerely,*
> *[Signature]*
> *Ralph D. Thomas*

Letters of Complaint

The difference between getting satisfaction from a complaint or being rebuffed often boils down to attitude. If fierce anger is expressed in a complaint letter, the chances of having the matter corrected may be lessened. Also, the person who receives the letter may very well be both innocent and ignorant of the problem. So write with a positive tone and avoid accusations, threats, and snide or derogatory comments.

➤ Address your complaint to the highest person up the chain of command, making sure to use the correct name and title.

➤ Demonstrate professionalism by sending a typewritten letter in the standard business letter format. It has been shown that a letter of this kind often gets much better results (whether an apology, a refund, coupons, or a voucher) than a casual note or a phone call.

➤ State your complaint clearly in the opening paragraph; then, give all the particulars necessary for the recipient to identify the source or cause of the problem. If, for example, the difficulty is with an order or invoice, give the identification number.

➤ Include all information that supports your complaint while avoiding negative or hurtful remarks. "The hotel desk clerk was unable to find any record of my reservation, credit card information, or confirmation . . ." is clear. "Your idiot desk clerk couldn't find a leaf on a tree, much less my room reservation . . ." manages to insult both the clerk and the reader.

➤ Propose a solution and make it reasonable. For example, when an order has gone astray, it is reasonable to ask for a repeat order to be sent by express courier, with the shipper covering the cost of the mailing. It's both unreasonable and greedy to expect a free order.

➤ Close on a positive note. You don't have to say "thank you," but you might remind the reader of your past experiences: "We have been dealing with Henson Hardware for more than a decade, and we have always appreciated your strong customer orientation." Or end with a brief statement of your expectations: "I would appreciate a response to this letter as quickly as possible."

Claim Letters

When a mistake is made in a business transaction—the exchange of a product or service doesn't go as expected—a claim letter from the customer is called for.

Claim letters typically request a refund, discount, or some other form of financial compensation. The style of the letter should be professional and the content thorough. To prove your case and demonstrate why your claim is legitimate, give all the details necessary for the recipient to understand your claim and make a fair and rational decision. Enclose photocopies (never originals) of all supporting materials—sales slips, invoices, bills of lading, shipping orders, postmarked envelopes, advertisements that made offers, warranties, guarantees, previous related correspondence, canceled checks, or credit card receipts or bills. As in complaint letters, avoid hostile language and threats, and maintain a courteous and businesslike attitude.

Request Letters

Letters that ask for something should be short and sweet. Request letters are rarely longer than one page, and often only a couple of paragraphs. Get to the point in the first sentence: "I am writing to request a price quotation for production of a four-color sales brochure to camera-ready stage." Then proceed to give all the information the reader needs to fulfill your request, whether you're ordering new office furniture, booking a plane flight, or confirming action on an insurance claim. Also include any special requirements (express delivery, for example) and note any enclosures.

Chapter Eighteen

Invitations and Announcements

AN INVITATION MIGHT BE COMPARED to the outfit you'd choose for a first date or an important job interview. The outfit creates a first impression of your style and sense of purpose. An invitation likewise reveals the style and purpose of an occasion. Is it for a laid-back afternoon of beer, pretzels, and football on TV? Or will it be a swank evening of gourmet dining and sparkling conversation?

Invitations can say a lot about you as a host, too. Were the invitations issued in plenty of time before the event? Are they neatly written or pleasantly spoken? Is all the information a guest needs to know included? Is the invitation wildly inventive, comfortably casual, or sleekly elegant?

When you receive an invitation in person or by phone, you'll need to tell the host whether you can attend. A printed or written invitation may include a request for your reply, and you have a social obligation to respond. But even when you can't attend, the invitation itself is a compliment. It says that you are important to the hosts and that they want you to be part of their special event. Be sure to thank them for inviting you whether or not you're able to attend.

The Basic Elements of Invitations

FROM A PHONE CALL inviting friends over for a bridge night to the most formal invitation to a gala ball, all invitations should include the following:

> The name or names of the hosts (usually first and last names; full names for formal printed or engraved invitations)

> The nature of the occasion

> The time and date of the event

> The location of the event

> On written or printed invitations, an RSVP or "Regrets only" notation if you want replies; phone number and e-mail address if you will take replies by these

means; and the name and/or mailing address for written responses if not the same as the return address on a written invitation

➤ Any special information such as directions and a map to the location, a notation about what to wear, or requests such as bringing a dish to a potluck supper (Requests that are specific to an individual are written in by hand on a printed invitation.)

Every guest should receive invitations in the same form. If you send written invitations, send them to everyone, even guests you have spoken with already. The point is to avoid having a guest think that she wasn't on your original list and is a last-minute fill-in. If you asked someone very far in advance, sending an invitation (or calling when you call other invitees) serves as a polite reminder.

Using e-mail is reserved for casual invitations when you know that invitees are regular Internet users and frequently check their e-mail.

When more than one person or couple is hosting, the name of the person at whose home the event will be held is normally listed first on a printed invitation. Aside from that, the order for multiple hosts' names is up to you. Alphabetical listing is easy. If the hosts are from the same family or represent several generations, the list might go from eldest to youngest. Sometimes names are listed in the most visually appealing style on a printed invitation—alternating shorter and longer names, for example.

Ending times are not included in most invitations, but there are exceptions. Invitations to children's parties usually include an end time, so parents know when to return for young guests. Invitations to parties that precede another event, such as a cocktail party before an opening night or a brunch before a business meeting, include an end time that allows guests to get to the next location. Both start and end times are included for open houses and other occasions when guests are free to come and go during the specified hours.

Dress instructions ("Black tie," "Business casual," etc.) can be added if the formality or informality of the occasion might not be clear to guests. (See Chapter 5, page 48: "Invitation Terms," for descriptions of attire notations.)

Requesting a Reply

Including an RSVP or "Regrets only" notation on a written or printed invitation tells invitees to let you know whether they can attend. An RSVP obligates all invitees to send their acceptances or regrets. "Regrets only" applies only to guests who must decline. Generally, an RSVP will give you a more accurate guest count. Also, when you haven't received a reply within a reasonable time, it may indicate that the invitation wasn't received; then you can call the person, explain your concern, and issue the invitation orally.

If you want only written replies, the RSVP or "Regrets only" is sufficient; you do not add other instructions unless responses are to be sent by a certain date or mailed to an address other than your return address (add the address for replies below the RSVP). If there are multiple hosts, the name and address of the person who is to receive the replies is included. The names and numbers of two or three hosts might be provided when you want phoned replies, making it easier for invitees to get in touch. Hours to call ("between 5:00 PM and 8:00 PM") can be included with a phone number when a host is difficult to reach at other times.

Sometimes reply cards are included in invitations. These cards are a convenience for guests and came into use as an effort by hosts to counter the problem of guests not replying on their own. Reply cards have traditionally been limited to large events (such as weddings and formal dances) and business occasions but are used more frequently today. (See page 266: "Reply Cards and Enclosures.")

Addressing Written and Printed Invitations

There is a basic, commonsense rule for addressing invitations: Include all the names of the people you're inviting. Generally, when inviting members of an extended family or unrelated adults who live in the same household, send a separate invitation to each adult or couple (plus their young children if they're included). Teenagers usually receive separate invitations, as does a child who doesn't live with his parent when you are inviting both.

A single invitation can be sent to unmarried couples who live together intimately, but the names are listed on separate lines. This same form is followed for same-sex couples in committed relationships.

An invitation to a couple and their children might be addressed to "Mr. and Mrs. Lawrence Rickman and Family" so long as this will not be misinterpreted as inviting other family members. A more precise form is:

Mr. and Mrs. Lawrence Rickman
Michael Rickman
Gloria Rickman
[or Michael and Gloria Rickman]

If you're inviting guests to bring dates or guests, this is noted on the invitation but not in the mailing address on the envelope. A casual or informal invitation might include a line such as "Please bring a date [or a guest]."

For information about addressing formal invitations, see page 263: "Addressing Formal Invitations."

Inviting in Person or by Phone

The most important concern when issuing oral invitations is to make your meaning immediately clear. Don't back into an invitation with questions like "What are you doing next Thursday night?" or "Have you and Elaine got any plans for Saturday afternoon?" The person has no idea why you're asking (though probably senses that you want something) and therefore has no idea how to respond. If he says, "I don't think we have any plans," then for all he knows, you might ask him over to help hang drywall in the room you've been renovating!

When you issue an invitation in person or by telephone, state your purpose up front: "Mike and I are planning a barbecue at our house Saturday afternoon, and we really hope that you can come. We'll fire up the grill at about four-thirty. Just neighborhood casual. Why don't you check with Elaine and call me later?"

Notice that this spoken invitation for a very casual get-together includes all the information the guest needs—nature of the event, day and time, location, and even a request for a reply. The person can accept on the spot or take a little time to consider. In either case, you've been a considerate host by leaving the decision to him.

When and How to Reply to Invitations

NO ONE IS OBLIGATED to accept an invitation or to explain the reasons for not accepting. However, *every invitee is obligated to respond promptly when an invitation includes a request for a reply.* An RSVP—the abbreviation of the French phrase *répondez s'il vous plaît*—asks you to notify the sender whether or not you will attend. It may be written as "Please reply" or "The favor of a reply is requested."

The notation "Regrets only" means that you are expected to reply *only* if you can't attend. Replies are made according to the following guidelines. (Formal written replies are discussed on page 264. See also Chapter 40, page 705: "Prompt Responses.")

Respond in a timely fashion. Usually, responses are made within several days of receiving a written invitation. If the RSVP or an enclosed card includes a request that you reply by a certain date, mail written replies so they will arrive no later than that date.

For in-person or phoned invitations, you can accept or regret when asked, but unless it is a last-minute invitation, it's acceptable to delay your response until you've checked your schedule or cleared the day with anyone else included in the invitation. (Always consult your spouse or live-in partner before replying to an invitation to you both.) Just tell the person that you will call as soon as possible, then follow up within a day or two.

Reply in the manner indicated on the invitation. If the RSVP appears on an invitation with no other notation and no reply card is included, then you're expected to send a handwritten response to the host at the return address on the envelope. When there are several hosts, the name and address of the person who is to receive replies should be written below the RSVP.

If the host or hosts prefer telephone replies, the phone number (and sometimes calling hours) will be included with the RSVP. Do your best to contact the person by phone, trying several times. If you can't get through, send a note with a brief message along the lines of "Yes, we will be there" or "We're so sorry, but we can't attend." (Leaving replies on an answering machine is risky; your message may be erased or not passed on to the person you called.)

An e-mail address may also be included with the RSVP; if so, you're free to accept or decline electronically.

Keep replies brief. Whether you write or phone, get to the point. You have no social obligation to offer excuses when you decline. You may want to explain, but there's no reason to go into great detail. The following two examples illustrate a polite written acceptance and an equally polite note of regret with a brief explanation:

Dear Denise,

Neil and I are delighted to accept your invitation for lunch on Saturday, April 10.

Yours truly,
Claire

Dear Mrs. Duvall,

I am so sorry that Richard and I must decline your invitation for March 21. We will be accompanying our daughter to the High School Debate Finals in Springfield that weekend.

Sincerely,
Alicia Barnes

Reply even if you have a potential conflict. There are times when you want to accept but there is a possible conflict with another commitment, such as a tentative business trip or an ongoing family matter. When the event is informal or casual, go ahead

∽ Accepting *and* Regretting ∽

When one invitation is sent to more than one person, it might happen that some people can accept and others must decline. Everyone on the invitation could contact the host, but it's often easier for one of the invitees to accept and decline for everyone. For example, an informal reply to an invitation sent to a couple and a live-in parent might be worded like this:

Dear Barbara,

Peter and I are really looking forward to attending your garden party on May 22. But my mother will be visiting a cousin in San Diego, and she is very sorry that she must decline your kind invitation.

For a formal, third-person reply (see also page 264: "Replying to a Formal Invitation"), the wording would be similar to this:

Mr. and Mrs. Peter Carlson
accept with pleasure
Mr. and Mrs. Bollinger's
kind invitation for
Saturday, May twenty-second
but regret that
Mrs. Edward Williams
will be unable to attend

and contact the host or hostess to explain the problem. ("I really want to come to the picnic, but there's a chance I may have to go to Portland for a client meeting. Can I let you know in a day or two?")

If the event is formal and your delay in replying might inconvenience the host, it's usually best to decline the invitation.

When Replies Aren't Requested

You are not expected to reply to an invitation that has no RSVP or "Regrets only" notation. However, it is always polite to notify the host when you can't attend; a phone call will usually suffice, though you might send a personal note or an e-mail.

The Obligations Created by an Invitation

MOST OF THE SOCIAL REQUIREMENTS created by an invitation fall to the hosts, but invitees, too, have some important obligations. Considerate guests will live up to the following expectations:

Reply promptly. Always respond in a timely fashion to invitations.

When you accept an invitation, you're obligated to attend. Never cancel just because you have a "better" offer; don't make up excuses or accept another invitation after canceling. A guest who backs out of a party because of a trumped-up "business trip" and then goes to another gathering may well be seen by mutual acquaintances, and reports will sooner or later reach the original host—causing hurt feelings as well as damage to the offender's reputation for honesty and thoughtfulness. It's never acceptable to accept an invitation and then fail to show up.

Do the right thing if you must change your answer. Changing a "yes" to a "no" is acceptable only when you have a very good reason: illness or injury, a death in the family, an unavoidable business or professional conflict. Call the host as soon as you can, explain, and apologize. If it's impossible to call before the event, as in a medical emergency, contact the host when you can and explain.

Changing a "no" to a "yes" is a slightly different matter. Circumstances change, and you may find yourself free to attend an event you've already declined. If your attendance is unlikely to cause problems (at a buffet, for example, there's usually plenty of food for a few more guests) and you know the host fairly well, then call immediately, explain the change in your situation, and you'll doubtless be welcomed. But if the occasion is formal and adding you in is likely to upset the host's plans or add extra expense, then it's best to let your regrets stand.

Respect the invitation and don't ask to bring an uninvited guest. An invitation is addressed to the people the hosts want to invite—and no one else. Some invitations will indicate that you can invite a guest or a date, and when you reply, you should indicate whether you will bring someone. Otherwise, an invited guest should never ask hosts to include another person. Parents shouldn't request to bring their children; if the hosts want youngsters at the event, the invitation will say so. (See also Chapter 13, page 175: "When Children Are *Not* Invited.")

If you will be entertaining a houseguest or a visitor at the time of the event, you can explain when you decline the invitation: "I'm sorry that I can't come to your party next week, but my roommate from college will be in town and she's staying with me." If the party is informal and numbers are flexible, the host might ask you to bring your friend. But an extra guest can seriously complicate the host's plans (a formal dinner with limited seating, for instance), so convey your regrets without hinting for special treatment.

Thank the host. Express your appreciation whether you're responding to the invitation, leaving the event, or thanking your host afterward.

Reciprocate the invitation. Some invitations—to weddings, balls, official functions, and those you pay to attend—do not carry any need for "payback." But invitations to social events in private homes or hosted by individuals as private occasions (parties at a restaurant or club, for example) do require some form of reciprocation.

You don't have to reciprocate in kind. The goal is to return the hospitality that you've enjoyed—not to replicate the event you attended. You might follow up an invitation to a formal dinner party by asking the hosts to a luncheon or to join you for dinner and a concert. Nor is it necessary to reciprocate immediately. Generally, you should try to entertain the host or hosts of an intimate, at-home gathering within a couple of months. When you attend a large gathering, you can include your hosts the next time you entertain in a similar way. (Note: Wedding invitations do not repay other social obligations.) If you rarely or never entertain on a large or formal scale, you can invite your hosts to a more casual event or take them out for a nice meal.

If the host can't accept your invitation the first time you ask, try again; you can ask the person about a convenient date in the future. (Should the hosts continue to refuse after you make repeated attempts and you sense discomfort or hesitation on their part, it may be wise to let the matter drop.)

When you decline an invitation, your obligation to the hosts is milder. But because their intention was to entertain you, a return invitation in the not-too-distant future is still in order.

A caveat: Be careful not to say anything that implies that a return invitation is *just* an obligation. It's fine to say that you had such a good time with the hosts that you want to get together again. But remarks along the lines of "It's time to return the favor" are hardly enticing.

A QUESTION FOR PEGGY

I'm a junior associate in a law firm, and last weekend, I attended a large, black-tie cocktail party hosted by one of the senior partners and her husband. (All the lawyers in the firm were invited.) My problem is that senior partners make it a rule not to accept social invitations from associates. How can I repay my hosts for their invitation?

Intraoffice socializing can be tricky, especially in businesses that maintain traditional lines of demarcation between senior, mid-level, and junior staff. Since it would be inappropriate for you to break your firm's unwritten rule, the best approach is to send your hostess a warm thank-you note. You might also send flowers or a gift—to her home address, not the office—if this would not be regarded as an attempt to curry favor. If you send a gift, it shouldn't be too personal or expensive. A book on a legal subject might be just the thing. Someday, when you are in a more senior position, you'll probably have opportunities to return your boss and her husband's kindness with an invitation of your own.

Casual Invitations

A PICNIC AND BALL GAME in the park, a backyard barbecue, an easygoing brunch with close friends—casual get-togethers are events where the mood is relaxed and most of the frills of formal entertaining are set aside (except good manners). "Casual" also describes most children's and teen parties.

Invitations for casual events are often issued by phone or in person; personal notes, commercial fill-in invitations, and e-mail (sent to regular users) are also popular. Casual invitations offer a lot of opportunity for creativity—attaching a packet of flower seeds to a handwritten invitation for lunch in your garden, for example.

Casual invitations might be made only a few days before the gathering, but they're usually issued one to two weeks in advance or even earlier for popular events like a Super Bowl party. But even off-the-cuff invitations, as when you see a neighbor in the street and ask him to dinner the next week, should include all the information your guests need (see page 247: "The Basic Elements of Invitations").

Spur-of-the-moment Events

Americans tend to be a gregarious people, needing little excuse to get together for a good time. But spur-of-the-moment invitations need to be complete, and hosts should clearly inform guests of the day, time, place, and nature of the party. Phoning is the obvious method, but you may not be able to reach everybody by telephone, and leaving messages on voice mail or answering machines is not always reliable. If someone is normally away from home during the day, you might write a note like the one below and drop it in the invitee's mailbox or attach it to his door where it is sure to be found. Or you can send an e-mail. You may need to leave written and phone messages in several locations.

The following is a handwritten note inviting a close friend to a last-minute event. In this example, the hostess signs only her first name. But whenever an invitee might know more than one person with the same name, hosts should use their full names.

June 23

Dear Justin,

Could you join us for a barbecue tomorrow night at 7:30? It's short notice, but Sam will be grilling the ribs you like so much, and we really hope you can make it. Please bring a date if you like. You can call me at 555-3215.

Diane [or *Diane Gleeson*]

Replying to a Casual Invitation

When a casual invitation includes an RSVP or "Regrets only," just follow the instructions on the invitation. Written invitations to a casual event are more likely to include a phone number and an e-mail address than are formal invitations, but the obligation to respond as soon as possible is the same. In case you don't receive a last-minute invitation until after the event, it's courteous to call the hosts, tell them what happened, and express your thanks for being invited.

~ Food and Beverage Notations ~

BYOB on an invitation means "bring your own bottle"; guests bring their beverages and the hosts supply glasses, ice, and maybe mixers. BYOF stands for "bring your own food" and indicates that guests should provide whatever they want to eat. For a "potluck" party, guests are requested to bring a dish that all the other guests can share. When an invitation says "chip in," guests contribute a specified amount of money to pay for food, drinks, or both.

Technically, events at which the guests bring or pay for food or drinks are *organized*, not hosted. BYOB, BYOF, and chip in are normally used for casual, often last-minute entertaining and allow friends to have a fun time while spreading the costs. Organizing a successful potluck party, however, requires careful advance planning and coordination so that guests will bring a varied menu to the table (see Chapter 25, page 458: "Potluck Suppers").

Informal Invitations

INFORMAL INVITATIONS CAN BE designed and printed for the occasion, or you might prefer printed, fill-in cards. Handwritten notes are also acceptable, though this approach can be time-consuming when the guest list is lengthy. It's also fine to issue informal invitations by phone, and you may want to follow up with a reminder card.

Some of the characteristics of informal invitations are:

➤ Informal printed invitations are not engraved. They may be produced by lithography, thermography, or laser printing. Colorful papers are commonly used, often with borders in complementary colors. Typefaces can be more modern than the traditional type styles of formal invitations. Commercial invitations with interesting graphics can also be used.

➤ Reply cards can be included and may be accompanied by a preaddressed envelope, but RSVP, "Please reply," or "Regrets only" is more generally used when the host wants replies.

➤ The wording of a printed invitation need not be in the third-person voice traditionally used in formal invitations. Hosts and guests can be referred to in the invitation by first names ("Denna and Craig DeMoss") or by courtesy titles ("Mr. and Mrs. Craig DeMoss").

➤ Abbreviations for months, states, and street addresses can be used. Numbers can be written numerically. Times are indicated as "7 o'clock." Use AM or PM if there might be any doubt about time of day.

This sample informal invitation would be printed for a special event:

Dr. and Mrs. Wilson Gray
invite you to join the Fine Arts faculty
at a cocktail reception
honoring
Emeritus Professor Amelia Carlisle
Friday, May 28
from 6 to 8 o'clock
The Crawford Art Gallery
2610 University Circle
RSVP
Ms. Melissa Antonio
212-555-6798
mantonio@finearts.stateu.edu

The details of the following printed, fill-in, informal invitation are written in by hand:

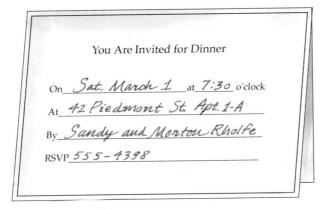

You Are Invited for Dinner

On _Sat. March 1_ at _7:30_ o'clock

At _42 Piedmont St. Apt. 1-A_

By _Sandy and Morton Rholfe_

RSVP _555-4398_

Using Your Informals for Invitations

You can use your own informal fold-over notes for informal invitations. If your notes are printed with your name(s), the invitation form would be similar to the following:

Brunch

Mr. and Mrs. Howard Brown

Saturday, September 18
12 noon

1444 Post Road   Regrets only
                      555-6655

When notes are plain or monogrammed, the invitation is handwritten and takes the form of personal correspondence. In the following example, the hostess signs her first and last names and includes her address, indicating the location of the event.

Dear Liz,

Howard and I hope that you, Ed, and the children can join us for brunch on Saturday, September 18, at noon. If you can't make it, please let me know by calling 555-6655.

Jean Brown
1444 Post Road

Replying to an Informal Invitation

When an informal invitation includes a reply request, respond by the method or methods indicated. Most informal invitations will have a telephone number, but you can also reply by personal note if you have trouble reaching the person. Use e-mail only if the RSVP or "Regrets only" notation includes an e-mail address.

Formal Invitations

DESPITE THE INFORMALITY of American entertaining these days, formal occasions still abound. Many couples choose to marry in formal style, and complete information for wedding invitations is found in Chapter 36, "Wedding Invitations and Announcements." Presentation and charity balls are popular; inaugural balls follow many federal, state, and even local elections. Official receptions and dinners are common in some parts of the country. Private affairs—dinners, dinner dances, teas, luncheons, cocktail receptions—offer numerous opportunities for formal entertaining, and in our casual times, people often look forward to a change of pace and the fun of dressing up.

The first notice that an event is formal is the invitation itself; both its look and wording immediately distinguish it from casual and informal invitations. The following list includes key points on the style and language of all formal invitations.

> ➤ Formal invitations are printed or engraved on cards of a good-quality paper stock. The paper is traditionally white or cream, but pastels are now options for all but the most formal events and official occasions. Papers may have a raised border or be edged in a color, such as silver for a twenty-fifth anniversary party. (Black borders are reserved for death announcements.) The standard proportions are three by four (3 units high by 4 units wide or vice versa); U.S. postal regulations require that all first-class mailing envelopes be at least 3½ inches high by 5 inches wide.

> ➤ Type style is a matter of choice, but plainer serif faces—classics such as Times Roman or Palatino—are easier to read. Work with your stationer or printer to select a single typeface; they can show you samples. (For an explanation of different printing methods, see Chapter 17, page 225: "A Printing Primer.")

➤ The invitation is phrased in the third person. "Request the pleasure of your company . . ." is the standard wording for formal social invitations. "Request the honour [or honor] of your presence . . ." is used for occasions held in a place of worship.

➤ Full names are used—not initials or nicknames—on invitations and for envelope addresses. If someone doesn't want to include his first or middle name, it can be left off the invitation.

➤ Courtesy titles (Mrs., Ms., Miss, Mr.) are abbreviated, as are "Dr." and "Sr." or "Jr." But religious and other professional or elected/appointed titles are written in full. Military ranks of commissioned officers are never abbreviated. For more on correct use of titles consult Chapter 22, pages 320–376: "Names, Titles, and Official Protocol," and Chapter 36, page 636: "Correct Usage of Civilian and Military Titles.")

➤ Punctuation is used only for words on the same line that require separation ("Saturday, the twenty-fourth of January") and for abbreviations ("Mr. and Mrs.").

➤ Numbers for dates and times are written out. Months and state names are written in full, as are addresses ("Center Street"; "Highland Crescent"). Street numbers are written numerically ("1042 Belgrave Boulevard") unless the street number is a single number ("Three Santa Fe Circle"). When addressing envelopes, the two-letter postal abbreviations for states can be used: "Lansing MI" with no comma between city and state.

➤ Times are written as "seven o'clock." Half hours are written as "half past seven o'clock" or the more conservative "half after seven o'clock."

➤ If the year is included—and this is optional—it appears below the date and is written out ("two thousand and four").

➤ Reply requests may be written as RSVP, R.S.V.P., R.s.v.p., R.s.v.p., or as "Please reply" ("Please reply by" when a date is included) or "The favour [or favor] of a reply is requested."

➤ The notations "Black tie" and "White tie" are traditionally excluded from invitations to weddings and private parties. But these days, hosts may include dress instructions to be clear that an event is formal. "Black tie" or "White tie" is conventionally printed in the lower right corner of invitations to proms, charity balls, formal dinners or dances, and any event for which clarification of dress standards may be necessary.

➤ When a single, divorced, or widowed person is invited to bring a date or companion, there are two options for addressing the envelope. If there's an inner envelope, it's addressed to "Ms. Halley and Guest," but the outer envelope is addressed only to "Miss Susan Halley" (no mention of "and Guest"). If there is only one envelope, it is addressed to "Miss Susan Halley and Guest." If the invitee's name is written on the invitation itself, it appears as "Miss Susan Halley and Guest." In this instance, there's no mention of "and Guest" on either the mailing or inner envelope.

The following example illustrates the language and style of traditional, printed formal invitations:

Dr. and Mrs. Joseph Edward Cooke
request the pleasure of your company
for dinner and dancing
on Friday, the thirteenth of August
at half past seven o'clock
Rivercrest Club

RSVP   Black tie
250 Garden Court
Louisville, Kentucky 40207

Fill-in Invitations

Printed or engraved fill-in cards are a convenience for anyone who frequently entertains in formal style. Guest names and information specific to the event are written in by hand, as in this example:

Mr. and Mrs. Albert Francis Campagna
request the pleasure of

Mr. and Mrs. James Walker-Klein's

company at

dinner
on Saturday, the fourth of December
at half after twelve o'clock

1020 Old Towne Road
Palo Alto, California 94303

RSVP

If there is a guest(s) of honor, a line is handwritten above the host's or hosts' names: "To meet Senator Gayden Lang and Mrs. Lang." If the invitee can bring a companion, then the guest's name line is written as "Mr. Harry Spencer and Guest."

Handwritten Formal Invitations

Formal invitations written by hand (never typed) follow the same form as an engraved or printed invitation:

Mrs. Edward Richardson
requests the pleasure of your company
at a luncheon
[or requests the pleasure of
Miss Eloise Leigh Hitchens's company at a luncheon]
on Wednesday, the fourteenth of July
at twelve o'clock
The Women's Club
223 Brighton Avenue

Please reply

Formal Invitations Sent by Groups

Today, very large, formal events are more likely to be hosted by groups and organizations than by individuals. The invitation format differs little from other formal occasions, although there is normally a reply card and envelope and possibly other enclosures. When additional information, such as a list of patrons or underwriters, is printed on the invitation, a single- or double-folded sheet of paper is used rather than a card.

The term "ball" is not so often applied to private formal dances these days, but it is often seen on invitations, like the following examples, to public and semipublic galas.

To a private benefit. When an event is held to benefit a charity, or the sale of tickets is expected to cover the costs of the event, a card including the amount of the subscription is enclosed with the invitation, as are a reply card and envelope. Lists of patrons, committee members, and debutantes (if the event includes a formal presentation) may be printed inside the invitation. The guest list is limited, usually to members or subscribers. Invitations are mailed four to six weeks prior to the event. Returning the subscription card and a check constitutes acceptance; regrets are not necessary.

The Board of Directors of the Cleveland Advertising Club
invites you to subscribe to
The Thirty-third Annual Diamond Ball
to be held at the Peacock Hotel
on the evening of Saturday, the eighteenth of September
two thousand and four
at half past six o'clock

Black tie

To a public occasion. Formal balls and banquets are often hosted by a charitable group, a club, or some other association. Invitations are sent to a large list of people who might be interested in attending. Guests pay set ticket prices. The prices are included on the invitation, and response cards (normally including a "Please reply by" date) and envelopes are enclosed. A list of patrons, committee members, and underwriters may also be enclosed. Invitations are usually sent four to six weeks before the event.

Returning the reply card and a check constitutes an acceptance; there's no need to send regrets.

The Hightsburg Good Neighbors Association
requests the pleasure of your company
at its Winter Ball
for the benefit of
The Pan-American Scholarship Program
Saturday, the thirty-first of January
two thousand and four
at seven o'clock
Hightsburg Convention Center

Single Ticket $75.00   Black tie
Couple $150.00
Table of ten $700.00

Presentation balls. Today, balls at which young women or young men are formally presented are frequently hosted by private organizations and cotillion clubs. These are usually large, elegant affairs, with invitations limited to members of the organization, the families and friends of the honorees, and special guests. Proceeds from ticket sales often benefit the sponsoring group.

The invitation might be printed or embossed with the logotype or symbol of the organization. Lists of committee members, sponsors, and the young people to be presented can be printed on the invitation or a separate sheet. Reply cards and envelopes and sometimes a separate card listing ticket prices are enclosed. Invitations are usually sent six weeks before the event—earlier if the ball is held in a busy social season.

The South Carolina Alumnae Association
of Delta Theta Delta Women's Fraternity
requests the pleasure of your company
at the Wisteria Cotillion
in benefit of the
Delta Theta Delta Children's Medical Research Foundation
on Saturday, the fifteenth of May
two thousand and four
at eight o'clock
Silverpoint Country Club
Columbia

Please reply by the first of May   *Black tie*

Note: When proceeds for an event are donated to charity or when a large number of invitations are sent for a public event, the enclosed reply envelopes usually are not stamped because the cost of stamps can be a considerable expense for the organizers.

Addressing Formal Invitations

Formal invitations are addressed like all correspondence, with these specific exceptions:

➤ Names of addressees and in the return address are written in full. Social titles (Miss, Ms., Mrs., Mr.), "Dr.," and "Sr./Jr." are abbreviated, but other professional and military titles are written out.

➤ Abbreviations are not used for street addresses and cities, but the two-letter postal code for states is acceptable. Street numbers are written numerically unless the number is a single number ("One Capitol Plaza").

The envelopes for formal invitations match the invitation in color and paper stock. The U.S. Postal Service requests that the return address be printed or written in the upper left corner on the face of the envelope. This is a help for postal sorting, but not a law, so some people print or emboss the return address on the envelope flap.

Replying to a Formal Invitation

Unless a formal invitation includes a telephone number or reply card, handwritten responses are expected to RSVP and "Regrets only" requests. Replies are sent to the host(s) at the return address on the envelope or the address that appears with the RSVP. If there are several hosts, one name and one address are usually included with the RSVP; you send your response to that person, though the names of all the hosts are included in a formal written reply.

There are two ways to reply to a formal invitation: (1) a formal note that follows the wording and style of the invitation and (2) a personal note. Personal notes might be sent when the invitee knows the hosts well and wishes to explain briefly why she or he must decline.

The formal note is much easier than people often think, because the wording is determined by conventional practice. Replies like the following are handwritten on plain or monogrammed notepaper, and lines are indented just as in the invitation. No punctuation is used except to separate words on the same line and for social titles.

Two versions of a formal acceptance:

Mr. and Mrs. Nicholas Stamos [or] *Mr. and Mrs. Nicholas Stamos*
accept with pleasure *accept with pleasure*
the kind invitation of *Mr. and Mrs. Fletcher's*
Mr. and Mrs. George Fletcher *kind invitation for dinner*
for dinner *on Friday, the ninth of July*
on Friday, the ninth of July *at half past eight o'clock*
at half past eight o'clock

Two versions of a formal regret:

Dr. and Mrs. Vincent Alvarado [or] *Dr. and Mrs. Vincent Alvarado*
regret that they are unable to accept *regret that they are unable to accept*
the kind invitation of *Mr. and Mrs. Doyle Ambrose's*
Mr. and Mrs. Doyle Ambrose *kind invitation*
for Friday, the sixth of August *for Friday, the sixth of August*

Notice that the time is included in the acceptance but not in the note of regret. This is done so hosts can be sure that guests have the correct time for the event.

Replying to multiple hosts. When there is more than one host, all the names appear on the reply, though the envelope is addressed to the host listed with the RSVP

~ Getting the Name Right ~

You might receive an invitation on which your name is spelled incorrectly or the title is wrong: Your name is Jon, but the invitation says "John," or the invitation is addressed to "Miss" and you prefer "Ms." Don't make an issue of a minor mistake. Just write a standard reply with the right spelling or title.

On the other hand, if the mistake could indicate that the invitation was sent to the wrong person, you should contact the host to clarify before you accept, regret, or ignore the whole thing.

---

or whose name appears with the return address on the invitation envelope. If there's no name indicated to receive replies, address your envelope to the first person or couple listed on the invitation. In your reply, list hosts in the order they appear on the invitation.

Formal reply to multiple hosts:

Ms. Juliana Vaden
accepts with pleasure [or regrets that she is unable to accept]
the kind invitation of
Mrs. Chambers and
Miss Underwood and
Mrs. Knight
for Wednesday, the thirteenth of October
at half past twelve o'clock
[Time is not included in a regret.]

Replying to a committee. When an invitation issued by a committee includes a long or complicated list of names, you can reply as follows:

Mr. and Mrs. Ken Ichida
accept with pleasure [or regret that they are unable to accept]
your kind invitation . . .

Replying to an organization. RSVP requests to an organization normally include a reply card or a name and address and/or phone number. The note of reply, however, includes only the name of the organization.

Mr. Herbert Wyatt
accepts with pleasure [or regrets that he is unable to accept]
the kind invitation of
the Tri-Cities Chapter
of the
American Association of Independent Businesses . . .

| 265 |

Invitations and Announcements

Reply Cards and Enclosures

More and more these days, reply cards are the best guarantee that hosts will receive responses to their invitations. Whatever the reasons, people are less likely to respond promptly on their own when a reply card is *not* enclosed, but it's hard to avoid replying when the host has supplied a simple card and an envelope that is already addressed and stamped.

A reply card is usually smaller than the invitation and printed in the same style. The card is placed, face up, on top of the invitation. When a reply envelope is provided, the card is placed under the envelope flap and, again, placed on top of the invitation so that the front of the card is visible.

The recipient need only fill in his name and those of any other people included in the invitation and indicate whether they will or won't attend. These two examples illustrate just how easy a reply card is to complete:

M*r. Warren Harris*	M*r. Warren Harris*
will *not* attend	✓ accepts
Friday, January second	____ regrets
	Friday, January second
	Columbus Country Club

The card on the right includes a printed *M*, which is completed as *M*rs., *M*r., and so forth. If you have another title, strike through the *M* and write in the appropriate word (Dr., Rev.). To save space, titles can be abbreviated on formal reply cards. If you're replying for several people, write their names under yours. People sometimes add a brief personal sentiment to a reply card ("Can't wait to see you!" or "I'm so sorry I can't be there"), but this isn't necessary or expected.

Recalling Invitations

WHEN AN EVENT IS CANCELED or delayed, it's essential to contact all invited guests as soon as possible. Informal and casual invitations can be recalled by phoning or sending a brief note. When there's time, formal invitations are recalled with a printed (not engraved) card, like the example below. However, telephoning or sending personal notes may be the most expedient method. In the case of a death or serious emergency in the family, friends can take over the responsibility for notifying guests.

A printed card canceling a social event:

Owing to an illness in the family
Mr. and Mrs. Theodore Marchetti
are obliged to recall their invitations
for Thursday, the ninth of December

When something like an unavoidable business trip requires canceling an event, the host may be able to reschedule and give guests a new date for the event. This could be done by phoning or in a personal note such as the following:

Dear Laurie and Jan,

I've just found out that I must be in Hong Kong for a conference on the sixteenth. I've rescheduled the dinner party for Friday, May 7, and really hope you can attend. I will be back on Wednesday, April 21, so please call and tell me if you can make it. I'm so sorry for the inconvenience.

Carl
915-555-5467

An Invitation Potpourri

LIFE IS MARKED BY MILESTONE events that we traditionally share with others. When the sharing takes the form of a party, invitations are needed. The following information and examples should provide guidance when you invite others to join in and celebrate these and other memorable occasions.

Baby Showers

Invitations can be casual or informal and are often very creative. Commercially designed fill-in cards are also popular. Invitations might be issued by phone or in person, especially for surprise showers and office showers given by coworkers, but handwritten and printed invitations are the norm.

Invitations can be sent from three to six weeks before the shower to give guests plenty of time to shop. Gifts are expected (except from those who can't attend), and the invitation can mention gift registry if the parents have registered—but not specific gift suggestions. It's okay to include a line such as "It's a boy!" or "The nursery is yellow and apple green" to guide guests. RSVPs are recommended. (See also Chapter 29, page 499: "Welcoming the New Baby.")

The mother is the traditional shower honoree, but fathers are often included, and today, men are also hosting. Though showers are usually given before the birth, they can be held after the baby arrives or before or after an adoption is finalized.

Typical wording for a printed or handwritten, informal shower invitation:

Molly Jenkins, Paula Kleeman, and Jennifer Wu
hope you'll join us
at a luncheon and baby shower honoring
Christy DieAngelo
Saturday, October 9
11:30 o'clock
305-B West 69th Street
Please reply to Jennifer, 202-555-0945

When the shower is for the parent(s) of an adopted child, it's a good idea to include the child's age (and perhaps clothing size) to help guests choose appropriate gifts. If the child is beyond infancy, be sure that shower invitations are not babyish.

Christenings and Birth Ceremonies

Invitations to religious ceremonies for infants—including Christian christenings and baptisms, the Jewish *brith milah* or *brit*, the Hindu "rice eating ceremony," and the Muslim *akikah*—are usually issued by phone, in person, or by personal note. (See also Chapter 29, page 502: "Baptisms and Christenings.")

First Communion and Confirmation Services

First communion for Catholic children and confirmation services in the Catholic and Protestant traditions may be followed by gatherings to celebrate these major events in a young person's life. The guest list is usually limited to family members and close friends, so invitations are commonly issued by phone, in person, or by a personal note from a parent. A printed informal invitation is an option for larger gatherings.

Bar Mitzvah and Bat Mitzvah

The Jewish bar mitzvah for boys at age thirteen and the bat mitzvah, a similar service for girls in some Conservative and Reform congregations, are deeply religious ceremonies. Members of the young person's congregation may be invited to a reception at the site immediately after the service, and the invitation is issued orally by the rabbi.

Traditionally, a by-invitation social reception and/or party follows later in the day, with the guest list including family, friends, and often the classmates of the honoree. Invitations to these parties, which may be quite elaborate, reflect the formality or informality of the occasion. Invitations by phone or personal note are fine for informal luncheons or dinners. Printed invitations are sent for a more formal occasion, and RSVP or reply cards are recommended. Invitations may be sent as early as a month to six weeks before the party.

A formal printed or engraved invitation to a bar mitzvah and reception:

Mr. and Mrs. Jacob Kenneth Rosen
joyfully invite you
to worship with them
at the Bar Mitzvah of their son
David Steven
Saturday, the seventeenth of July
two thousand and four
at ten o'clock in the morning
at Congregation Beth Israel
4205 Ocean Drive
and to celebrate with them
at a luncheon immediately following
Commodore Country Club

RSVP
1219 Willow Road
St. Petersburg, Florida 33733

Quinceanera

The quinceanera, which commemorates a girl's fifteenth birthday, may combine a religious service and a social event or consist only of a party. Quinceanera (or quince or quince años) parties may be informal gatherings of family members and friends, though very formal events similar to a debutante ball are traditional.

Invitations are issued by the honoree's parents or by the honoree and her parents. Invitations to informal quince parties can be issued by phone, personal note, or informal cards. Formal invitations may be printed or engraved and might include a "Black tie" or "White tie" notation. Gifts are expected but not mentioned on the invitation. RSVP or reply cards are recommended for formal invitations.

In the example below, a printed, formal invitation to the religious service would also include a card inviting guests to the quinceanera party afterward. Since the invitation itself is to a religious service, it does not include an RSVP.

Mr. and Mrs. Jorge Delgado
request the honour of your presence
at a Mass celebrating
the Fifteenth Birthday
of their daughter
Ana Theresa
on Saturday, the twenty-first of February
two thousand and four
at half past four o'clock
Saint Boniface Catholic Church

The reception card:

Please join us afterward
for the reception
The Pacific Club
902 Bayside Road

RSVP
11106 Nautilus Crescent
San Diego, CA 92138

Sweet-sixteen Parties

Today, sweet-sixteen birthday celebrations tend to be observed as the teen chooses and are more often casual parties with friends rather than gatherings that include adults. Invitations are casual or informal and are usually issued by the teen. When parents host (a supper party, for example, or a dinner dance), the invitation can be in their name. Whether casual or informal, the invitation should indicate whether guests are invited to bring dates. An RSVP with a phone number and e-mail address is most likely to generate replies from busy teens.

Graduations

Printed invitations to high school and college graduations are usually provided by the schools and are formal in appearance and wording. Since the invitation is issued in the name of the graduating class or the school, each student may be provided with social cards printed with his or her name. The student may substitute his own printed cards or write his name on plain social cards (available from stationers, paper suppliers, and printers). A card is included with each invitation so guests know who is inviting them. When the class is sizeable and space is limited, the number of guests may be restricted—sometimes to as few as four people or just members of the graduate's immediate family.

Families or friends may want to entertain for the graduate after the official ceremony—either on the day or sometime later—and invitations to graduation parties can be casual, informal, or formal depending on the occasion. The invitation should include the honoree's name and language that indicates the nature of the occasion, as in the following informal invitation to a dinner dance for several new graduates. Note that the hosts' names come after the main body of the invitation:

In honor of
Elizabeth Sinclair, Francine LaSalle, and Thomas Arnette
Vanderbilt University Class of 2004
you are invited for dinner and dancing
Thursday, June third
at seven o'clock
La Rive Gauche Restaurant
1631 Pennington Street
Corinth, Mississippi

Mr. and Mrs. William Sinclair
Mr. and Mrs. Oscar LaSalle
Mrs. Winifred Harris Arnette

RSVP
Mrs. William Sinclair
(662) 555-7770

Birthday Parties

Commercial fill-in cards are popular for children's birthday parties. Usually colorful and often reflecting the theme of the party, printed invitations are addressed to the child and should always be clear about the nature of the party, but no reference to gifts is made. Start and end times are included ("3:30 to 5:50"), so parents know when to pick up their children. An RSVP or "Regrets only" notation is helpful, especially when you need a guest count to plan games and other activities. Unless all children in the honoree's class or group are included, invitations should not be distributed at school or during extracurricular activities. (See also Chapter 14, page 189: "The Party Whirl.")

Invitations to birthday celebrations for teens and adults reflect the formality or informality of the party. An informal invitation might be worded like this one to a party given by adult children for their parent:

Louisa Penski Isaacs and Robert Penski
hope you will be with us
to celebrate the 60th birthday of our mother
Helen Tate Penski
at dinner
Wednesday, November 10
7 o'clock
742 Fernbank Terrace
Almaville

A note of caution: The example above includes the honoree's age, but hosts should always check before mentioning age. Though people today tend to be less sensitive about their years, it's still a personal issue; good manners dictate asking permission before revealing anyone's age.

Anniversaries

Parties for wedding anniversaries can range from casual get-togethers with close friends to elegant formal receptions and dinner parties. The form of the invitation depends on the nature of the event. The wedding and anniversary years are sometimes included at the top of the invitation. Formal invitations are often bordered in silver for twenty-fifth anniversaries, and in gold for fiftieth anniversaries. The following examples illustrate the wording for invitations when the event is hosted by the couple and when it is hosted by others.

A formal invitation issued by the couple:

1979–2004

Mr. and Mrs. Arthur Edward LaGrange

request the pleasure of your company

at a reception

honoring

their silver wedding anniversary

on Sunday, the tenth of October,

at four o'clock

The Century Club

RSVP

15 Prince Road

Wilmington, Delaware 19899

❧ "No Gifts, Please" ❧

Gifts are expected for birthday and anniversary parties, but when honorees really don't want presents, their wishes should be respected. In the past, any reference to gifts on invitations was considered in poor taste, because guests were assumed to know the occasions when gifts were obligatory, and even today, it's incorrect to mention gifts on wedding invitations. But in light of the current gifts-for-everything craze, it's a courtesy to inform guests when presents are not expected. The etiquette is to write "No gifts, please" at the bottom of the invitation—or to tell invitees when inviting them in person or by phone.

When you receive an invitation with a "No gifts, please" request, take it seriously. Showing up with a present when asked not to would embarrass the hosts, the honoree, and other guests who, correctly, didn't bring anything. If you want to give a special token of affection, do so at another time.

A formal invitation issued by the adult children of the honorees:

The children of
Anna and Gregory Hoffman
request the honor of your presence
at the
Fiftieth Anniversary
of the marriage of their parents . . .

[or]

Mr. and Mrs. Gregory Hoffman, Jr.
Mr. and Mrs. James Lee Daugherty
and
Ms. Christina Hoffman Reed
request the pleasure of your company
at a reception
honoring
the Fiftieth Anniversary
of the marriage of their parents
Mr. and Mrs. Gregory Hoffman . . .

Announcements

SOCIAL ANNOUNCEMENTS are sent to family members and friends to let them know about major events and achievements. The most common announcements, including birth and graduation announcements, are discussed here and in Chapter 36, "Wedding Invitations and Announcements." Formal announcements are printed or engraved cards, worded in the traditional third-person style. But today, announcements are often less formal in language and design.

A key point of etiquette for both senders and recipients: *Receiving an announcement does not obligate anyone to send a gift.* No response is required, but a note of congratulations is welcome when appropriate. When someone sends a gift, it's entirely his choice. Though unexpected, all gifts should be acknowledged with a thank-you note.

Handwritten Announcements

Handwritten announcements might be sent when there are a limited number to write. These can be written in formal style on plain or bordered cards, or the announcement might be made in a personal note reading something like this:

> *Dear Cousin Rudy,*
>
> *I wanted to let you know that Christopher received his B.S. in chemical engineering from the University of Missouri on June 1 and will begin working for his master's degree at MIT this fall. You can imagine how thrilled his father and I are. Chris sends his best and hopes to see you before he leaves for Cambridge.*
>
> *Love,*
> *Suzanne*

Newspaper Announcements

There's a good deal of misunderstanding about how announcements are placed in newspapers. There are two basic types of published announcements:

> ➤ Information submitted to the newspaper and published without charge, at the paper's discretion

> ➤ A notice published in space purchased by the person who supplies the information (as one purchases space for classified ads)

For announcements published at the paper's discretion, the information is given to the paper—often by filling in a form supplied by the paper or in a press release format—and newspaper staff write and edit the version that appears in print, including the headline. Though an unpaid announcement may appear just as you wish, it's more likely that it will be rewritten and perhaps shortened in accord with the publication's style and available space. Or it may not be published at all. You cannot dictate the contents of an unpaid announcement or the date when it will appear. Publication is a service of the newspaper, not an obligation.

A paid notice appears as you wrote it and usually on the date requested. However, newspapers may check the information for accuracy and suggest wording, and they can reject notices that include questionable language and facts. You pay for the space and placement in the appropriate section. For example, marriage, birth, and adoption notices might be printed in a paper's social or lifestyles section.

Whether you want a paid or unpaid announcement, contact the newspaper as far in advance as possible. Ask about deadlines and forms for submissions and about prices (usually a per-line rate with a minimum charge) for paid notices. Be aware that some newspapers now charge to run announcements that were once considered public service.

For announcements in newsletters and bulletins, contact the editor and ask what information is needed and when submissions are required. Publications of social and service groups, internal employee newsletters, the bulletins of religious congregations, and so forth, don't charge but will usually write and edit announcements to their style specifications.

Some Announcement Ideas

WANT TO SPREAD THE WORD about a new baby, a new graduate, or a new address? Here are some ideas for making announcements that convey your message in pleasing style. With the exception of sending birth and adoption announcements to shower guests, cards are not sent to people who attended a social event (such as a graduation party) that celebrated the event being announced.

Birth

Birth announcements can be sent to family and friends just as soon as the baby is named, but are rarely sent to business associates or casual acquaintances. Announcements include the parents' and baby's names, the baby's birthdate, some indication of the baby's sex if the name is not obviously male or female, and, if you want, the baby's birth weight and length. You might include a photo, and if you have a Web site devoted to the baby, you can add the Internet address to the announcement.

Birth—and adoption—announcements can be worded in formal, third-person style, but today's parents usually prefer more informal and personal language. One simple and attractive announcement that is sometimes used has a small card with the baby's name and birth date on it, tied by either a pink or a blue ribbon to the top of a larger plain card that gives the parents' names.

Expectant parents often purchase commercial announcement cards, or have cards printed, and address the envelopes. They can then fill in the important information after the baby arrives, such as in the following:

A New Member of our Family has Arrived

Jennifer Joy Brown
June 27, 2004
7 lbs., 3 ozs.
Jean and George Brown

If you have the talent and time, designing your own announcement makes a one-of-a-kind memory. Birth announcements can also be made by personal notes written by the father as well as the mother.

Mary Lou and Brendon O'Dwyer
[or Mr. and Mrs. Brendon O'Dwyer]
are happy to announce
the arrival of
Mary Katherine
September 28, 2004
7 pounds 8 ounces; 20 inches

A widowed, single, or divorced mother announces in her own name but does not include the father's name. A widow normally uses her married name ("Mrs. Thomas Garcia"). A single mother would use her name and title ("Ms./Miss Lucille Smith"). A divorced mother uses the name and social title she goes by. Parents who live together but aren't married can announce in both names and usually omit social titles ("Cynthia Lane and Clay Martin/are happy to announce . . .").

Birth announcements carry no obligation for gifts, so don't hesitate to send them for first babies and every new addition to the family. If someone sends a gift, be grateful and send a note of thanks.

Adoption

Adoption announcements are usually sent soon after the legal proceedings are completed, but they may be sent when a baby or child comes to live with his new family while the legal process is under way. Parents can have cards printed, design their own, or send handwritten notes to relatives and friends. Commercial card manufacturers now make cards specifically for adoptions. Commercial birth announcements can also be used; just be sure you can easily add "adoption" or "adopted" to the wording. When the child is older than an infant, the style of the announcement should suit his or her age; a card decorated with storks or baby bottles is inappropriate for a toddler or older child.

The wording includes the parents' and child's or children's names, the date of the adoption or when the child came to live with the family, and the child's age or birth date. When the child is adopted abroad, the country of origin may be included, as in the following example:

Mr. and Mrs. Daniel Shelton
joyfully announce
the adoption of
Daniel Ivan
born July 7, 2000, in Baku, Azerbaijan
and welcomed into our home on October 10, 2004

If the legal adoption is not yet completed, the announcement might be worded as follows:

Mr. and Mrs. Wallace Gunderson
are happy to announce
the arrival of
Patricia Gail
on March 22, 2004
age, eighteen months

Graduation

Given the limitations on invitations to high school and college graduations (see page 270: "Graduations"), families may want to send announcement cards informing relatives and friends of the new graduate's accomplishment. Graduation announcements are often printed in formal style, but more creative designs are just as acceptable.

Some schools provide printed announcements, and the graduate's social title and name is written in by hand. If the announcement doesn't specify the degree earned, the graduate's name can be followed by his or her degree ("Deborah Cushman, M.D."; "Joshua Beane, Ph.D."). Otherwise, social titles are used. When a woman is married but known to fellow students by her maiden name, she can include her maiden name in parentheses:

Mrs. Allen Harvey
(Angela Vargas)

Announcements carry no obligation to send gifts, but some people may want to give something special. If you don't want presents, you can add "No gifts, please" at the bottom of the card.

Printed announcements are not usually sent for middle school or eighth-grade graduations, though you can write personal notes to inform family and good friends.

Change of Address

Moving happens so often these days that it's hard to keep up with the addresses of even good friends. So it's considerate to send a change of address notice—either a printed card or a personal note—to people you want to stay in touch with. Be sure to include any new phone numbers. Another idea is to include a pre-addressed file card or social card with a brief note.

Special Achievements

You might want to blow your horn a bit when you or someone in your family does something very special—winning a prestigious fellowship, for instance, or earning a big promotion. Printed announcements are a possibility, but personal notes are probably more usual. If there was a published announcement, you might include photocopies with your notes.

Chapter Nineteen

The Good Conversationalist

MASTERING THE ART of everyday conversation means remembering that it's a two-way street, with thoughts and ideas shared in both directions. Expressing interest in another person and clearly conveying one's own thoughts and feelings is the primary goal of ordinary conversation among friends and acquaintances.

Must you be witty and eloquent? Not really. Few of us can continually pepper our speech with engaging stories and words of wisdom. The good conversationalist understands the need for simplicity, directness, tact, and attentiveness to what other people have to say—skills that can be learned and mastered.

The good conversationalist also knows that *how* we converse is vital. What we say and how we say it can make the difference between clarifying a point or confusing it, giving comfort or offense, and either showing ourselves as friendly, thoughtful people or as small-minded, long-winded boors.

The Basics

IF THERE ARE TWO THINGS for a good conversationalist to remember, they are "Think before you speak" and "Listen." Juggling both can be tricky, but if you're able to walk and chew gum at the same time, you can manage.

Thinking. Thinking—or, more precisely, being thoughtful—applies across the board, from the topic of conversation to the listener's reactions. If she really *thought*, would a computer programmer enthuse about a software program to a person who's never been near a computer? Or would a parent brag endlessly about his child's awards to someone who's never had children? Ask yourself if it's likely that someone will be interested in whatever you start to bring up.

Listening. It's only natural to be thinking of what you're about to say next in a conversation, whether to respond, affirm your conversation partner's point or take issue with it, relate a similar anecdote, or steer the talk to another subject. But many people try so desperately to think of what to say next that they barely hear a word the other person says. (This is especially true during introductions, when the other person's full name is usually given but just doesn't stick.) The result? You lose track of the conversation, an awkward silence hangs in the air, and you wish you'd paid more attention.

The fear of not knowing what to say is similar to that felt by someone learning to swim; it's not just the first stroke that intimidates but the thought of all the strokes that follow. The practical rule for conducting a conversation is the same as that for swimming: Take it one stroke (or word) at a time, and don't panic. Even then, your efforts will be wasted unless you really *listen*.

Empty other thoughts from your mind and concentrate on what the person is saying. Then show that you're not only listening but understanding by making eye contact, nodding occasionally, and intermittently saying, "I see" or "Really?" After you've picked up the rhythm of the other person's speech, you'll be able to inject longer confirmations without seeming to interrupt ("Oh, so you mean Kevin saved the day"). If you *don't* understand something, ask for an explanation, a habit that comes naturally to a good listener.

Interrupting. There's a fine line between the occasional interruption made to confirm a point and one that's made because you're bursting to throw in your two cents. The only time it's permissible to interrupt in the middle of a sentence is when you need to communicate something that honestly can't wait. Even then, precede what you say with "I'm sorry to interrupt" or a variation thereof.

When you're the one being interrupted—most often because that's simply the other person's style—listen politely for a few seconds before trying to finish your thought. Raising your hand in a nonthreatening "please wait" gesture can politely deflect an interruption, while a blunt "Stop interrupting!" merely answers one rudeness with another.

Personal space. A comfortable conversation involves more than just words; even a compliment can be offensive if delivered an inch from your face. The general rule of thumb is to stand no closer than about eighteen inches apart, although cultural and personal preferences should be taken into account. Personal space is less of an issue when you're seated, but you still may have to lean in a bit to catch the words of a soft-spoken person, then back away to speak.

Also be conscious of height differences. Stand far enough away so that the other person won't have to look up or down at you, which can quickly grow uncomfortable. Be considerate of people with physical disabilities—say, a person in a wheelchair or with a hearing impairment—and don't expect anyone on crutches, in casts, or with bad knees to stand and chat for any length of time.

Body language. While words and tone express the meaning of what's being said, a person's posture, facial expressions, and gestures send messages as well. Some of these messages are open to interpretation, but others come through loud and clear.

➤ **Posture when standing or sitting.** What a parent or teacher really meant when she told you, "Sit [stand] up straight!" was that slumping or slouching while speaking conveys laziness and disrespect. A slumper is likely to appear uninterested in the other person.

➤ **Facial expressions.** A smile denotes warmth, openness, and friendliness, but don't overdo it. False smiles make you look insincere, while never-ending smiles invite suspicion. Conversely, a frown or a furrowed brow suggests anger or worry, even though your words may be positive.

➤ **Eye contact.** Looking into the other person's eyes shows your interest in the conversation. Staring, however, can seem threatening, even strange. The desirable middle ground is reached by shifting your focus to other parts of the face from time to time.

➤ **Gesturing and fidgeting.** Go easy on the gestures. Using your hands to emphasize a point is fine, but gesturing nonstop is an unwelcome distraction. Some gestures and mannerisms to avoid are playing with your hair, tie, or jewelry; drumming your fingers; snapping the clip on a ballpoint pen; and jiggling the change or keys in your pocket.

➤ **Nodding.** Nodding doesn't necessarily mean you agree; it can indicate that you understand. But too much positive head-nodding can brand you as silly or too eager to please, especially in a business environment.

➤ **Pointing.** Because American culture historically regards pointing at others as negative or hostile, the gesture can be misconstrued, whatever the pointer's motive. (Are you merely pointing someone out or are you making some comment about him?) Pointing also attracts attention to a person who probably doesn't want to be the object of curious glances and stares.

A QUESTION FOR PEGGY

When I speak with someone and he keeps looking over my shoulder or to the side, I feel he's not hearing a word. I want to say so, but how?

The wandering eye will spoil a conversation virtually every time, and you have every right to do something about it. Stop talking in mid-sentence, then look at the other person as if you're curious about what he finds so fascinating. When he asks why you've paused, you can be frank so long as you speak in a non-accusing tone: "Because you looked away. Is something going on over there?" Then continue your conversation.

Voice and Vocabulary

VOICE VOLUME, TONE, AND RATE of speech are concerns for any good conversationalist. A too-loud voice can be unnerving. A too-soft voice puts listeners in the awkward position of having to ask you to repeat yourself. Inflections enliven your speech, but a monotone dulls it. Talking too fast makes you harder to understand, while talking too slowly may try the listener's patience.

Then there's the matter of enunciation and accent. Having good enunciation simply means pronouncing words clearly. Dropping letters (for example, the "g" in "-ing") and slurring words can not only make you appear a little too "rustic" but also bring your speech perilously close to mumbling. (At the other extreme, enunciating too perfectly risks making you sound affected.) On most occasions, drop letters from words only in informal chats.

You shouldn't be embarrassed by your accent, be it a regional drawl or a voice resonant with echoes of the country where you were born. When you notice another person's accent, don't dwell on it or make fun of it to the speaker or anyone else.

The Words You Use

A broad vocabulary is a plus for anyone, and expanding yours isn't as hard as you might think. Whenever you come across a new word or one that you can't quite grasp, look it up in the dictionary and then try it out in conversation. After you've used the word a few times, it should begin to come naturally. You might also want to consult the vocabulary-building aids found in assorted word books and magazines.

Having a good vocabulary doesn't mean using big words in place of small ones; it's the precision of the word's meaning, not its length, that matters. Saying "request" for "ask," or "prognosticate" for "predict," or "at this point in time" for "now" can sound unnatural and forced. Strive for a vocabulary that's wide-ranging yet simple and direct.

The way we use words can sabotage our speech without our realizing it. Head off these habits in particular:

> ➤ Peppering your speech with fillers—"y'know," "like," "um," "er," and similar meaningless interjections.

> ➤ Overusing adjectives like "absolutely," "cute," "interesting," "nice," "great," "super," and "awesome."

> ➤ Regularly mistaking one word for another—for example, "lay" when you mean "lie."

> ➤ Choosing words or phrases that sound pretentious or pompous—"retire" for "go to bed" or "comestibles" for "food."

More Things to Remember

A CONVERSATIONALIST WHO does the following will not only become well-spoken but will also please her listeners.

Know when to stop talking. People who talk too much are also usually the ones most likely to talk carelessly; those who talk too little can seem aloof. In conversation, the middle road is best. There are seldom regrets for what you've left unsaid. "Better to keep your mouth closed and be thought a fool than open it and remove all doubt," goes an old saying.

Keep abreast of the world outside. Reading a daily newspaper and a weekly news magazine will supply you with subject matter for small talk and show you as someone who is curious and informed. But never pretend to know more than you do. No person of real intelligence hesitates to say, "I don't know."

Don't horn in. When someone pauses to search for a word, don't jump to supply it. An exception is when the person asks for help: "Oh, what's the word I'm looking for?" Likewise, don't break in on whatever someone else is telling (for example, a description of a movie plot) and press your own "improved" version on listeners.

Avoid repetitions. The twice-told tale quickly becomes boring. If you think you might be repeating yourself, ask, "Did I tell you about Jack's week in Sicily?" If you're on the receiving end of a repeated story, politely let the speaker know: "Oh, yes, you told me about Lisa's party. It sounds like everyone had such a good time!"

Don't whisper. When you whisper or talk in low asides to one person alone, others may think that they're the subject or that an especially juicy tidbit is being kept secret.

A QUESTION FOR PEGGY

When I yawn, I automatically cover my mouth with my hand. But what do I say when, much to my embarrassment, I yawn in the middle of a conversation?

It happens to us all, and not necessarily because we're bored. If you yawn because you are tired, say so, stressing that it isn't the conversation that's at fault: "I got hardly any sleep last night, and I *promise* you're not boring me." If you yawn for no apparent reason, as sometimes happens, humor is an all-purpose deflector. "Oops, that was rude of me. Believe me, it's not the person or the hour . . . sometimes I just do that. Sorry!"

Do a friend a favor. When a friend is caught in one of those embarrassing moments of the spinach-in-the-teeth sort, step in. A man should discreetly indicate to another man that he has an open fly. A woman should quietly point out to another woman an unzipped skirt, popped-open button, or teeth covered with lipstick.

Keep jargon and euphemism to a minimum. Buzzwords ("twenty-four/seven") and vogue terms ("at the end of the day . . .") are inoffensive in themselves but can become tiresome when used repeatedly. And the regular use of euphemisms ("perspire" for "sweat," "expire" for "die") will sound a little too genteel to most ears.

Temper your slang. Slang is a part of everyday speech, but let your use of it depend on the situation and the person you're speaking with. "Gotta split!" is fine when saying good-bye to your best friend, but not so fine when addressing your doctor, client, or boss.

Use foreign phrases judiciously. To anyone but the most sophisticated, sprinkling your conversation with words and phrases from another language may seem pretentious. But there are exceptions: (1) when the word or phrase is from your native tongue; (2) when it is widely used and understood, like *smorgasbord* and *esprit de corps*.

Avoid playing "gotcha!" A thoughtful person corrects someone's grammar or pronunciation only when that person is her spouse, child, or extremely close friend or relative—and only in private, not in front of other people.

Words That Work

THE MOST ESSENTIAL WORDS IN the vocabulary of courtesy are nearly effortless to say but convey a wealth of meaning to others.

"Please"

To please can be defined as "giving pleasure," and there's no question that a request made with a "please" is much more pleasant than a curt command. Saying please expresses respect and consideration. It also improves efficiency because people are more inclined to comply with a polite request ("Please take your seats"; "Please answer the phone") than with something that sounds like an order.

"Thank You" and "You're Welcome"

Most people know to express their thanks for gifts, favors, awards, and the like. But we may fail to recognize and show appreciation for the everyday courtesies that come our way. A stranger makes room on the elevator for a new passenger or picks up and returns something that was dropped. A friend whispers that her companion has a dirt smudge on her face. A teen holds a door for a pregnant woman. Small kindnesses can go almost unnoticed if people are too busy or self-absorbed to care. Expressing thanks to everyone who provides a service or does a kindness is the hallmark of civility.

When someone says, "Thank you," the logical response is "You're welcome." Accepting thanks with grace is a way to encourage the habit, so think twice before brushing off an expression of gratitude with remarks such as "No problem," "There's no need to thank me," or "It really wasn't anything."

"Excuse Me"

Saying "excuse me" and "I beg your pardon" expresses a person's awareness that he has inconvenienced or might inconvenience someone else. Using these words can sometimes calm a situation and help achieve the desired results for both parties. These polite turns of phrase are called for whenever you do the following:

➤ Make a necessary interruption: "Excuse me for interrupting, but you have a phone call." (Not "You gotta call.")

➤ Make a request: "Excuse me, but this is the nonsmoking section. Would you mind not smoking here, please?" (Not "Hey, you, put out that cigarette *now*!")

➤ Acknowledge an error: "I beg your pardon. I didn't realize that you were already waiting in line." (Not "Don't get huffy. I'm moving.")

➤ Make a remark, usually whispered, that might seem embarrassing: "Pardon me, but your bra strap is showing." (Not "You need to pull up that bra strap.")

➤ Leave another person or a group: "Excuse me—I wish I could chat longer, but I have to get to the pharmacy before it closes." (Not "I've got to go. See you around!")

"I'm Sorry"

Making and accepting apologies gracefully are acts of courtesy and maturity. Saying "I'm sorry" is important for matters big and small. If you're in the habit of acknowledging minor incidents—accidentally bumping into someone, for instance—it's easier to fess up to larger mistakes. Sincere apologies can defuse volatile situations, since it's hard for most people to remain angry with someone who takes responsibility for his own actions.

"I'm sorry" is also one of the simplest and often kindest ways to express sympathy or regret. There's a natural tendency to dress up expressions of concern ("I'm so sorry you didn't get the promotion. Culpepper is a jerk for not seeing that you're better qualified than anybody else."), but such uncalled-for comments can often add insult to injury.

The Courteous "No"

HOW DO YOU POLITELY TURN down an offer or invitation? How can you say "no" to a request to do something you don't have time for? It's amazing how often people are hesitant to say no when they really want to. Yet one of the bedrock principles of good manners is honesty, and others deserve an honest answer to their requests. This point can be particularly important in interpersonal relationships (see Chapter 6, page 68: "Saying 'Yes' or 'No.'")

The simple "No, thank you" learned in childhood should be part of every adult's daily vocabulary. Obviously, "no" expresses a negative response, but the following guidelines should help you use the word considerately.

Accompany a "no" with a positive comment. Responses such as "No, but thanks for asking me" and "No, I don't need help right now, but you're very kind to offer" express appreciation for someone's effort on your behalf.

Avoid equivocating. A reasonable "no" is not a cause for guilt, so don't hem and haw. Responses such as "I don't think I can" or "I probably shouldn't" leave the other person with the impression that you would like to say "yes." Failing to be direct may prolong discussion, to everyone's discomfort.

Don't open the door to future requests unless you will welcome them. If, say, you won't be able to be a homeroom helper for your child's class either now or in the foreseeable future, respond clearly to the request: "No. With my work schedule, I'm sorry I can't help. I'll let you know if my situation changes." If you want to help in the future, say so. You can keep your name on the calling list by saying something like, "No, but I'd really like to help sometime. Please call me again next year."

Discussion Topics

WEATHER. SPORTS. FAMILY. WORK. NEWS. Movies. Sex. Politics. Religion. From the most mundane to the most volatile, your topic is conversation's main course, with vocabulary and other considerations serving as so many side dishes.

Some conversations flow naturally as one topic leads to another. Others bounce around from one topic to another with no rhyme or reason. But whatever course a discussion takes, the good conversationalist knows that certain subjects should be handled with care.

One topic to be wary of is *yourself*. This isn't to say that your opinions, your vacation plans, and even your cholesterol count aren't legitimate subjects for discussion. Only when they become the starting point for a lengthy monologue should topics focused wholly on you be avoided. (This is especially true of personal misfortunes, including sickness and surgery.) Good conversationalists understand the importance of not letting two very small pronouns—"I" and "me"—become the largest words in their vocabulary.

Agreeing to Disagree

Were it adhered to, the admonition to "never discuss religion or politics" would make for dull discourse indeed. That weathered piece of advice could do with an addition: "Never discuss religion or politics unless you know when to put on the brakes." Keeping a disagreement from escalating into a war of words is essential to civil conversation—and the trick is to "agree to disagree."

This doesn't mean being mealymouthed or weak-willed. Anyone who's watched or participated in formal debating knows just how passionate a good argument can be, even within very strict rules of conduct. Most arguments, however, don't have a referee, and people who disagree must regulate themselves. Win, lose, or draw, those who disagree with respect and courtesy are less likely to flaunt their victories or hold grudges when they lose than are people who regard arguing as a form of warfare.

Pick your battles with care. A spirited argument over a political issue can help open-minded people refine their positions, while wrangling over which flavor of ice cream is best is hardly worth the effort. Regardless of the topic, phrase your comments politely: "You're wrong!" is combative, while "I don't think I agree with you about that" is tactful. Substitute "It seems to me" for an abrasive like "That's not so!" which suggests you're calling your conversation partner's honesty or intelligence into question. At the end of an argument, try to clear the air with a comment like, "Well, we obviously don't agree on this one, but I can see your point of view."

Sometimes it's best to drop the discussion altogether. When voices are raised, you start talking over each other, or genuine anger starts to build on either side, it's time to switch to another subject. Cutting the argument short can be hard when you feel passionately about something, but you'll do yourself and the other person a favor by saying, "Let's agree to disagree."

Criticism and Gossip

It's the rare person who doesn't occasionally find himself drawn into a conversation designed to cut someone else into tiny little pieces. Criticism and gossip are everyday fodder for some people, and there's not much you can do about it except decline to join in. Remember that when your friend enthusiastically dissects another person's many shortcomings, you're possibly the next in line.

A good way to stop a criticizer or mean-spirited gossip in his tracks is to say, "But, Jim, Amanda says such nice things about you!" If he still rushes on, you can defend Amanda, try your best to change the subject, or decline to listen. Even when someone makes unkind remarks about a person you don't particularly care for, find something positive to say.

More objectionable than the garden-variety criticizer/gossip is the bigot—someone who makes joking or derogatory remarks about a religious, ethnic, or cultural

If, during a conversation, an opportunity to compliment another person arises, do so—but only if it's both warranted and sincere. Archbishop Fulton Sheen once remarked wryly that "a compliment is baloney sliced so thin that it is delectable. Flattery is baloney sliced so thick that it is indigestible," pointing out the risk of overdoing it. Like adjectives in writing, compliments have more impact when used sparingly, not when bunched together.

A typical compliment—"You did a fantastic job on the fund drive, Bill"—is even better when followed with a question: "What was the hardest part of organizing it?" This spares the receiver from having to fumble for a reply. The standard "Thank you" is always correct, though some compliment-receivers think it's insufficient (see "Responding to Compliments," below.)

Be careful with your wording, or else you might unintentionally end up giving a backhanded compliment—an insult disguised as praise. ("I'm so proud of you. I would've thought you were too timid to stand up to the boss!")

Responding to Compliments

Receiving compliments graciously is difficult for some people. Taught from childhood not to be show-offs, they have an impulse to negate praise by dismissing it. For instance, a typical response to "What a great job you did!" is "Oh, it was nothing." But this kind of modesty can ring hollow and even suggest that the complimenter doesn't know what he's talking about. A simple "Thank you" is the more suitable reply, especially when followed with, "I'm so glad you think so" or "Aren't you nice to say so?"

After you've received a compliment, you might respond in kind if you can do so sincerely: "Thank you. But look who's talking. That job you did for Mr. Powers couldn't have been better."

group. Again, discourage him by saying, "Let's get off that subject"; then introduce another. If that doesn't work, tell the person frankly that you find his remarks deplorable and would rather not listen. If he continues, say good-bye and walk away.

Every time anyone participates in hateful ethnic, racial, or other personal conversations—whether the comments are blatantly derogatory or couched in a joke—he's practicing a form of intolerance. Taking part is not just uncivil; it also implies that he is willing to accept bigotry and prejudice.

Your Personal Life

How far to venture into your personal life—whether sharing information about your family or your latest romance—is up to you, although there is something to be said for what the British traditionally call "reserve." Anyone but your closest confidants is likely to be put off by stories that reveal more than they need or want to hear.

Your family. The state of your relationship with your spouse and your children is generally a topic for close friends only. If your wife has joined the workforce after several years or your son has brought home the math medal, it's fine to let people know. How long you dwell on the subject should be determined by questions asked by the listener, not by your need to enumerate your wife's motivations or to boast about your son's brilliance. Serious family problems, on the other hand—an impending divorce or a teenager caught shoplifting—should be discussed only with close friends, usually when you're seeking advice or a friend has clearly offered a shoulder to cry on. (See also Chapter 7, page 82: "Informing Others.")

Your finances. For years, discussing money (both your own and the other person's) with anyone outside your family has generally been considered to be in poor taste. But there are a few exceptions. The rent one pays in an area where rates have gone through the roof is a regular topic of conversation among locals, and taxes and college tuition tend to be hot topics. Just avoid personalizing any discussion of finances; your salary or the cost of your jewelry and other personal possessions are off-limits.

Your love life. Discussing the details of your latest romantic entanglement, your lovers' spats, and even your sexual orientation can be perceived as far too personal, especially by people you don't know very well. You may feel compelled to unburden yourself to friends and even strangers, but your open confessions could become an infinite source of embarrassment. When you find a sympathetic ear in the form of a very close friend, don't bend it to the breaking point.

Your background. In general, family background should be a topic of conversation only when it naturally fits with the subject at hand or someone has asked you about it. Some people, however, use family background to aggrandize themselves. Those who announce to all and sundry that "my ancestors came over on the *Mayflower*" or "my brother is a well-known neurosurgeon" are likely to be seen as insecure or as social climbers.

Dealing With Nosy Questions

Some people, often total strangers, have no qualms about asking personal questions: "Why aren't you married?" "How much did you pay for that?" "Is this a planned pregnancy?" You can't politely answer, "None of your business," but you *can* say, "I'd rather not talk about that, if you don't mind." You can also change the subject.

Following are responses that should stop snoops, protecting your privacy whenever necessary and with the least amount of offense:

"How old are you?"
"Thirty-nine and holding."
"Old enough to know better."

"When are you going to have children?"
"Who knows?"
"That's a weighty decision I'd rather not talk about."

"Boor" is just another word for an ill-mannered person who frequently reveals his sad lack of social skills in conversation. The classic types here are known to everybody, but the responses are merely meant as suggestions on which you can build.

The Bore. The bore has been defined as "one who finds himself more interesting than he finds you." He drones on and on, never notices that no one cares what he's saying, and expects you to hear him out to the bitter end.

> **Suggested response:** If staying interested is a losing battle, try to change the subject. At a party, you might politely excuse yourself to talk with someone else: "I'd love to hear more, but Nancy is motioning for me to come over, and I think she and Jake are leaving soon."

The Name-dropper. Most name-droppers believe that you will be mightily impressed once you hear that they've met or had dealings with a VIP of any stripe. And you may be. Then again, you may see the dropping of names of the famous or powerful as compensation for the speaker's own insecurity—and you'll probably be right.

> **Suggested response:** Instead of taking the bait ("Wow! *Really*?") or asking how the name-dropper came to rub shoulders with the elite, say something on the order of "It's very nice that you know the vice president and that he shared his thoughts with you. But what do *you* think about tax cuts?"

The Balloon-buster. You say you found a great new dress shop and your friend counters with a better one. You say you're happy that your niece has handled her divorce so well, and your friend says, "Given her temperament, it's only a matter of time till she falls apart." Your friend is subtly telling you that she knows more than you and that you're fooling yourself if you think otherwise. She loves shattering people's illusions, taking the wind out of their sails, puncturing their balloons.

> **Suggested response:** Stand your ground. Don't get into an argument, but make it clear that you won't necessarily change your mind: "Thanks for the tip, but I know my taste—and I can't imagine a store that suits me better." To defend your niece, say, "I disagree. I'm close enough to Kathy to think that she's going to do just fine."

The Braggart. There's a big difference between sharing your accomplishments (or those of your loved ones) with close family members and extolling your (or their) virtues to anyone you happen to meet. Even when bursting with pride, the good conversationalist doesn't go on forever about what a wonderful job he did, how his talent for picking stocks made him a fortune, or how bright his child is.

> **Suggested response:** Comment politely about the braggart's remarks ("My, but Jeremy *does* sound smart!"), then redirect the conversation to another topic ("By the way, have you been in touch with Sue lately?"). If the person launches into yet another fabulous story about himself, the best you can do is excuse yourself at the first opportunity unless you've become interested in what he has to say.

The Condescender (aka The Patronizer). Talking down to a child or an adult ("I won't go into it because it's probably too complicated for you to understand") or over his head ("Of course, Nietzsche would have taken an entirely different tack, but I won't bother you with that") is the stock-in-trade of the conceited. A good communicator gears his conversation to the person or group listening without condescending or patronizing.

> **Suggested response:** If you feel you're being patronized, there's little you can do without appearing defensive. Just try to switch to another, preferably less lofty, topic. If, however, you're well informed on the subject being discussed, say something like "Mrs. Collins, I appreciate your trying to explain, but I happen to be well acquainted with Nietzsche's ideas."

The One-upper. We all know them—people who listen to news of your week at the island resort, your cousin's new job, or the college your daughter has applied to, then attempt to outshine you ("St. Bart's is nice, but we found Anguilla had better hotels"; "My cousin's an accountant, too, and she took only two years to become a CPA"; "I remember how ecstatic we were when our son got into Snobbington U., especially since they took only one in fifty applicants").

> **Suggested response:** When the one-upper has finished putting you in your place, smile and say, "Oh, really?" or "How nice." Then change the subject. The last thing you want to do is challenge her assertions, since she'll likely keep talking until she tops you.

> "Have you been sick?"
> *"Actually, I feel great."*
> *"Why? Do I look tired?"*

> "How much did you pay for that?"
> *"Only what it's worth."*
> *"Wouldn't you like to know!"*

Following are three all-purpose responses that can help deflect inappropriate questions, including "Did you mean to get pregnant?"; "Why aren't you married?"; and "Can't you have children?" After you respond, quickly switch to another topic.

> *"Why do you ask?"*
> *"What does that have to do with anything?"*
> *"Sorry, but I just don't discuss such things."*

The ability to make others smile and elicit laughter is a gift, but even the wittiest conversationalist should use humor with care. When you inject a joke into a conversation, make sure it is at no one's expense. Ethnic, racial, religious, or gender-based humor risks hurting someone else's feelings or making you look bad. Telling a "spastic" joke, for example, is insensitive and can cut like a knife when a listener has a relative or friend with a disability. Also remember that some people may not get your humor, especially inside jokes that are relevant only to a particular group. Until you get to know people very well, you're wise to leave jokes out of your conversations.

Humor and jokes are not the same thing. Some of our greatest humorists (think Bill Cosby and Garrison Keillor) made their mark through their wry observations on the human condition, understanding that—unlike hurtful jokes—humor works best when it's natural, healthy, and positive.

What to Say When

HEARING NEWS OF ONE KIND or another about someone's personal life is inevitable. In some cases you'll want to congratulate, in others, commiserate. If the person is a close friend, you'll probably have no trouble in coming up with something to say; for those you know less well, little more than a simple acknowledgment will usually do. Before venturing any comments, consider the following whenever . . .

Someone becomes engaged or marries. Genuinely wish the person well, with "What great news!"; "I'm so happy for you"; or "I know you're going to be so happy together." Show interest in his or her plans, but stop short of an inquisition and don't be too free with marriage advice or stories of marriages gone bad.

Someone is pregnant. Be happy for your friend or acquaintance, but don't pry. Avoid giving advice that may conflict with current medical opinion; future parents need to have confidence in their health care provider, and it's unfair to undermine that relationship. And don't share terrible labor and childbirth stories.

Someone miscarries. A reply of "Oh, I'm so sorry" is enough. Never offer up phrases like "It was for the best" or "It was God's will," and never imply that the miscarriage may have resulted from something the person did or didn't do.

Someone divorces. Because your response is dictated by individual circumstances and you can't always read someone's feelings (some may be happy, others sad), there is no all-purpose response. But "Thanks for telling me" or "I wish you the best" are safe ways to show your concern. If you know that the person regrets the divorce, a simple "I'm sorry" is enough.

Someone is ill. If a friend or friend's relative is seriously or terminally ill, your actions will speaker louder than words. Show sympathy by offering to help in any way you can—shopping for groceries, perhaps, or babysitting. (See also Chapter 11, page 134: "Choose Your Words Well.")

Someone dies. When a friend or acquaintance loses a loved one, simply give your condolences. You needn't worry about being eloquent. A simple "I'm so sorry" or "I'm thinking of you" will do. Never make comments such as "It was really a blessing" or "Be thankful his suffering is over." Offer practical assistance where you can. (See also Chapter 31, page 536: "What—and What Not—to Say.")

Someone is fired or downsized. A simple, sincere "I'm so sorry you've been laid off" is a good start. Be sympathetic but don't prolong the agony by going over the gory details. Find something positive and constructive to say: "There's no doubt your experience and talents are going to interest other companies." If you can give practical assistance, do—a recommendation, help with a resume update, information on other job openings. Even if you don't have specific leads, you can be a sounding board for a good friend and offer encouragement.

∽ Ten Conversational Blunders ∽

If you're sensitive to others' feelings when you speak—that is, you possess the admirable quality known as tact—you won't talk to your grandmother about how you dread getting old, to a wheelchair user about how much fun you have skiing, or to a country-dweller about how much better life is in the city. Indeed, the comments that count as off-limits could fill a hefty book.

The following are a mere sampling (for more, see page 290: "Dealing With Nosy Questions").

➤ "I can see I'll have to simplify this for you."

➤ "Are you tired? You look it."

➤ "As the President was telling me the other day . . ."

➤ "I just heard! Are you and that awful Chris really getting a divorce?"

➤ "Have you had cosmetic surgery? You look better somehow."

➤ "Why are you wearing that bandage [eye patch, neck brace]?"

➤ "What happened to Bobby's complexion since he went away to school?"

➤ "Isn't your baby a little small for his age?"

➤ "You live *there*? But it's such a dirty city!"

➤ "What made you choose that couch?"

Someone is depressed or addicted. What you say to a friend or acquaintance who has told you that she's depressed or addicted (most often, to drugs, painkillers, or alcohol) depends on your relationship and the seriousness of the problem. Give her the opportunity to confide in you: "Please know that I'm here for you if you want to talk." But be careful not to pry, especially if you're not close friends. If the person is in counseling, let her raise the subject. If a close friend seems seriously upset, volunteer to help her find professional help.

Chapter Twenty

E-mail Etcetera

ODERN MIRACLE, time-saver, sporadic source of frustration—e-mail is all of these and more. And then there's that virtual community known as the chat room. The trick is in how you handle both, and "handling" is interchangeable with "good manners." Etiquette had to strike out in new directions when cell phones came along, but it has plunged even deeper into unknown territory with the arrival of the Internet and e-mail.

The quest for an etiquette for Internet users, or netiquette, has reminded us that the more things change, the more they stay the same. Polite electronic communication requires that you treat others as you would have them treat you, even when interacting through the cold gray light of a computer screen. A recent Public Agenda survey found that some forty percent of respondents with Internet access had received "crude or nasty e-mail or chat room messages" over the past year.

Whether you're sending an e-mail, visiting a chat room, or posting on a bulletin board, three key considerations will help you communicate electronically, politely, and effectively:

Human contact still matters. Don't communicate electronically at the expense of personal interaction. There's a reason people often need to discuss things face-to-face, and there are times when no substitute will do—whether you're breaking up with your boyfriend or asking your boss for a raise.

Watch what you say—and how you say it. While the computer brings people together, its impersonal nature can lead to remarks that people wouldn't think of saying in person. Do whatever it takes to stay courteous, even if that means taping a note to your computer reminding you to be decent and polite.

Be careful when clicking Send. Whatever you say in cyberspace *cannot be taken back.* You have no control over where your message goes once you've hit Send; it can be saved and forwarded by any recipient who chooses to do so, and words have come back to hurt people, destroy friendships, and ruin careers.

I sent a friend an e-mail that included some pretty catty comments about a mutual friend named Diane. But for reasons I won't go into, I ended up accidentally sending the message to Diane at the same time. How do I make amends for this major goof?

You've just learned an e-mailing lesson the hard way: It's all too easy for messages to fall into the wrong hands. As difficult as it may be, you must apologize. Contact Diane immediately, meeting with her in person if possible. Admit your insensitivity and tell her how terrible you feel about hurting her (if that's how you truly feel). Ask for forgiveness, but don't expect the friendship to be patched up overnight; it might take months before she trusts you again. In the meantime, remind yourself of one of the edicts of e-mail culture: You can never be too careful.

The Exemplary E-mailer

IT'S ANYONE'S GUESS HOW MANY millions of e-mails are zapped into in-boxes around the globe every hour. The ever-growing volume of e-mail should come as no surprise, given that most messages are usually brief and informal, much like most phone calls.

There's a reason e-mail took off like a rocket—and it's not just because it is instantaneous. The ease of the medium has connected and reconnected people as never before, reviving friendships and promoting correspondence among family members (including children who otherwise wouldn't write to their grandparents). But whether you're using e-mail for personal correspondence or business matters, it's essential to remember a few do's and don'ts—from the moment you start an e-mail to the instant you click Send.

Address with care. Good manners are called for even as you fill in the address line. When sending an e-mail to a long list of recipients, don't put all the addresses in the To and CC lines. Most people don't want their e-mail addresses (often with full names included) displayed for all to see. It's better to send messages individually or use the blind-copy (BCC) feature, which allows you to show only one address.

What's your subject? Be sure to fill in the subject line, even in personal e-mail. Without some clue about the nature or urgency of your message, the recipients might ignore it for days or delete it if they don't recognize your address. What's more, a busy person who stops and opens a message labeled "no subject" will likely be frustrated if he finds a message that could have been read later in the day.

Keep it short and sweet. One of the benefits of e-mail is the ability it gives us to communicate concisely and quickly, so keep messages brief. Put longer communications in attachments or deliver them by snail mail or face-to-face. If you want to send an attachment, it's best to first ask the recipient if she minds.

No yelling, please. Avoid typing your message in capital letters because CAPS ARE THE EQUIVALENT OF SHOUTING. All-caps messages are also much harder to read. Capital letters also signify "flames"—messages that are highly emotional, angry, or insulting. Although flames are more likely to be seen in chat rooms and on message boards, they can appear in any e-mail message. (See also page 303: "Snuff That Flame?")

Watch those symbols. E-mail is singularly lacking in subtlety, and language that the sender finds funny or clever can easily be misunderstood by the recipient. Some senders use symbols, called emoticons, to indicate their emotional state. The symbols will hamper communication, however, if the recipient isn't sure what they mean. If used, emoticons (some examples of which are shown below) are better suited for casual messages between friends than for business e-mails.

:-)	smile, happy, laugh
:-(	frown, sad, unhappy
:-O	angry, yelling, shocked
{{***}}	hugs and kisses

Likewise, be careful when using on-line abbreviations, since they'll leave some recipients scratching their heads. Among the most common are these:

BTW	by the way
IMHO	in my humble opinion
IOW	in other words
LOL	laughing out loud
MorF?	male or female? [used in chat rooms]
OTF	on the floor [meaning laughing]
ROTFL	rolling on the floor laughing
WRT	with regard to

Many e-mail users have programs that don't allow for boldfacing, underlining, or italicizing words for emphasis. In this case, the usual way to add emphasis is to put asterisks on either side of the *words you want to emphasize.* An alternate method is to CAPITALIZE a few words, but not so many that your emphasis could be mistaken for shouting or flaming.

Check it over. Although e-mail tends to be informal in style, be sure messages are clearly organized and grammatically correct. Write in complete sentences and always check spelling and punctuation—especially in business e-mails. Even when sending a casual note, give it a good once-over.

In the workplace, your employer's e-mail system is meant for business messages—not office gossip, the latest jokes, or personal rants. Likewise, the Internet is a powerful research and communication tool for businesses, not a toy to amuse you at work. Save your Internet surfing, game playing, and chat room activities for your own time.

Beyond that bedrock advice, several concerns are worth paying attention to:

Brevity. Like memos on paper, business e-mails should be purposeful and to the point—so keep them brief.

Timeliness. Check your in-box first thing in the morning, in the middle of the day, and an hour or so before you leave—or more often to make sure you're not missing anything important. (Turning off the audible signal indicating you have e-mail will help you concentrate on your work.)

Attentiveness. Take special care not to use Reply All when you don't intend to. Once sent, e-mail can't be retrieved. Horror stories abound: The intern who criticized the way the company was run, the man who trashed the new boss, and much, much worse.

Caution. All electronic communications should be considered public documents. If you wouldn't write something in a memo and pin it to the bulletin board, don't e-mail it. Your employer has the right to read e-mail originating from or received on company office equipment.

Appropriateness. The more serious the message, the less appropriate e-mail becomes. Don't issue serious complaints or criticisms by e-mail, and never send an e-mail letter of resignation. Instead, arrange a personal meeting if possible or write a business complaint letter or confidential memo.

Discretion. Be careful about the messages you forward. If a former employee sends you an acerbic rant about his boss or department head, keep it to yourself. Broadcasting such e-mails to friends can backfire if they eventually reach management or Human Resources.

Emotionalism. Even though e-mail messages are familiar in tone, keep your emotions in check. Save "I'm so upset I could die!" for your closest friends, not business associates.

Efficiency. When an e-mail has numerous replies tacked onto the initial message, don't make all recipients wade through the whole message to find the part that applies to them. It's faster for you to delete unnecessary material than for recipients to read it.

Urgency. Flag messages as high priority only when they really are. Any recipient who rushes to read a message only to find it routine will be rightfully irritated.

Instant Messaging. If you don't get a response, stop until you know the recipient wants to IM.

Gossip. E-gossip about colleagues could have nasty repercussions, since you can't be sure it won't be forwarded. Save gossip for face-to-face talks—or better yet, keep it to yourself.

Confidentiality. Use snail mail or other traditional forms of transmission for private or sensitive materials—contracts, business plans, salary and sales information. Unless your system has an encryption program, e-mail isn't private, and messages can be accidentally or intentionally intercepted.

Patience. Be patient with technophobes. Many people still aren't up to speed on the newest technologies, don't trust e-mail, or simply abhor it. Communicate with an e-mail-averse colleague via phone or written notes. If you have the time and patience, you could offer your assistance.

Attachments. Don't send an attachment file unless you know the recipient can open it.

Porn. In many businesses, transferring pornography via e-mail is grounds for dismissal. If a subject heading or address suggests porn spam, ask a member of the tech support team to open the message. That way, the company knows it isn't your fault and may be able to block future e-mails from the source.

Vacations. Don't let e-mails that arrive while you're on vacation go unanswered. Most systems allow you to program an "out-of-office" response that tells the sender how long you'll be away and whom to contact if the message is urgent.

The End? If you're leaving your job, be sure your e-mail account is closed and incoming messages are forwarded to the appropriate person. Then let everyone know your new e-mail address.

About Those Forwards

Given the amount of clutter in e-mail in-boxes these days, it's not surprising how many people regard forwards as just more spam. Deciding what to send or forward to friends, relatives, and business associates deserves thought, so use common sense to judge whether a forward is going to be seen as just one more irritation.

Some people enjoy receiving jokes and chain letters, while others would rather be spared. If you're inclined to forward such iffy material, be sure your recipients are receptive. Check with them (via e-mail, naturally!) *before* you make it a habit. Be particularly wary of chain letters and virus warnings. Chain letters, which promise everything from easy money to petitions that implore you to "have your voice heard," are usually little more than time wasters. Virus warnings are legitimate about a tenth of the time, so check the validity of the warning first. An Internet search for "virus hoaxes" will lead to sites that instruct you how to distinguish a real warning from a hoax. The Internet can be a hotbed of misinformation. Unsubstantiated (and often irresponsible) rumors spread like wildfire on the Internet, so don't propagate them with forwards.

A recent e-mail etiquette survey conducted by Cidco Communications polled Internet users on which e-mail transgressions they found most offensive. Read the list and take heed.

1. Forwarding an off-color joke
2. Detailing a personal mishap
3. Writing a message in capital letters
4. Spreading gossip
5. Discussing personally sensitive issues
6. Criticizing another person
7. Complaining about work or one's boss
8. Using e-mail to dodge discussing difficult issues face-to-face
9. Going into detail about your own or another person's health problems
10. Arguing with family or friends

To stem the flow of forwards from friends and relatives, send an e-mail saying that you appreciate their thinking of you but that you have time to open only essential documents: "Unfortunately, it's impossible for me to read anything but business messages and a few personal ones, so I'd appreciate it if you would take my name off your jokes list. But I enjoy hearing from you, so please don't hesitate to write!"

E-mail Extras

E-mail systems have a number of extra features, and they, too, have their do's and don'ts. Here's a sampling:

Automatic signatures. Many e-mail programs automatically sign your message off with your name, address, e-mail address, and phone number—a letterhead of sorts. If your program doesn't have this feature, add the information yourself for anyone who might want to know other ways to reach you.

Attachments. Don't send attached files unless you know that the recipient has compatible software; it's frustrating to get an important file that can't be opened or translates into goobledegook. When you're on the receiving end, never open an attachment when you don't know who sent it or why. Once an attachment containing a virus is opened, it could send itself to everyone in your address book or crash your whole system.

Return receipts. Return receipts are the equivalent of certified snail mail—a notification that the recipient has opened your e-mail. Some people think the return receipt is insulting, suggesting that the recipient can't be bothered to read his e-mail or is clumsy enough to accidentally delete it. Others see it as a way of ensuring that an e-mail is received when the recipient's e-mail system is prone to problems. The bottom line? Use the feature for a good reason and be careful not to imply that the recipient isn't reliable.

Instant messaging. See page 304.

Responding to E-mails

Junk mail, commercial spam, and forwards can be ignored, but you should always respond to a real message, whether it's an invitation, a meeting notice, or a hello from a friend. (If you check your e-mail only once a week, let people know, lest they take offense at not receiving a timely response.) If you receive a lot of e-mails, your life will be easier if you set aside a few times during the day to read your messages and respond in an orderly fashion.

How fast should you respond? Within one to two days for personal messages and within twenty-four hours for business e-mails, depending on how pressing the matter is. Instead of including the entire contents of the message you received, leave just enough to make it obvious what you're responding to.

If you'll be away from your computer for a few days or longer, use the "vacation" or out-of-office feature, which tells the sender that you received the message but are unable to reply until a designated date. Once you return, respond promptly.

A QUESTION FOR PEGGY

During a lull in a staff meeting, I used my electronic planner to enter some appointments and check over my grocery list. A coworker later told me I'd been rude. Was she right?

Unless that lull was an official break, you shouldn't have flipped open your PDA (personal digital assistant). A tap on a handheld device is okay if it's related to what is being discussed, but taking care of personal business is unprofessional. Your associates might think that you're the kind of person who's more interested in your gadget than the business at hand.

Manners in Cyberspace

WHAT'S COME TO BE CALLED cyberspace is crammed with virtual communities— electronically connected individuals who regularly participate in everything from discussions of current events to critiques of poetry to tips for caring for cats. But no matter how specialized their interests, those communicating through a computer should follow a few guidelines.

Manners in cyberspace are situational, just as they are in real life. While speculation on, say, an actress's personal life may be acceptable fodder for a chat room whose subject is TV sitcoms, posting a nasty rumor about anyone on any site can quickly become gossip of the worst kind.

Chat Rooms and Message Boards

Chat rooms, discussion groups, and forums make it possible for e-mailers to post notes on a specific subject and trade opinions with others, as on message boards and bulletin boards. Before using such interactive sites for the first time, take a few minutes to look over the rules and regulations, then check out any FAQs (frequently asked questions)—a quick way to get a broad overview of the group. What's acceptable in one group may not be in another, so browse the messages or the archives for a while before plunging in. Such "lurking" (Internet lingo for initial browsing) will give you a feel for how to behave.

Try to fit in with the style and tone of the group, and phrase your messages politely. Also refrain from correcting other participants' mistakes—spelling, grammatical, or otherwise. Once you've learned the ropes, be patient with newcomers, whose errors may include posting very long messages or asking dumb questions.

The anonymity of cyberspace may make you more willing to participate, but it can also wreak havoc on good manners. A recent Public Agenda survey found that fifty-seven percent of respondents believed "it's much easier for people to be rude on the Internet because they can hide their identity." Anonymous you may be, but that's no excuse to start drawing on your worst instincts.

Snuff That Flame?

The flame (a no-holds-barred message expressing a strongly held opinion) becomes a real faux pas only when it's part of a larger flame war. A single emotional message can be entertaining—the reason flames are a traditional part of chat room exchanges. A flame war, on the other hand, is a series of heated messages that can seriously disrupt a discussion group. Such lengthy exchanges also monopolize bandwidth.

As illogical as it might seem, there is a polite way to flame. When you're itching to rant, signal your intention by writing FLAME ON. Once you've gotten things off your chest, write FLAME OFF and revert to your regular style.

When you share a computer with family members, roommates, or coworkers, there are some basic courtesies that everyone should observe:

➤ Let other users know when you need to use the computer. Think about priorities; your computer game can wait if someone else has real work to do. Parents need to help children negotiate computer time, especially when the computer is required for schoolwork, and to monitor its use carefully.

➤ If your computer uses a dial-up modem and you don't have a separate phone line for the computer, be conscious of times when others usually make phone calls and don't hog the line.

➤ If you're working on a time-consuming project, like a research paper, be considerate when someone needs to do, say, a quick Internet search and let the person have access.

➤ Never open another person's documents or files without permission; this is tantamount to reading someone else's mail. When trashing files, be careful not to dump something that isn't yours. If you need to close someone else's document, save it first.

➤ Don't look at e-mail that hasn't been sent or received by you, and don't use anyone else's screen names or passwords.

➤ If you have a home page or Web site, don't change the contents without the agreement of everyone included in the page or site.

➤ Keep the computer area tidy. Clear the work area before you leave it. If the mouse is sticky, clean it; if the printer cartridge needs replacing, do it. Tell the person who buys supplies when the paper is low, and report any problems to whoever maintains the computer.

➤ When computers are shared in the workplace, users are often on different shifts and may not see one another. If there's any problem with the computer or supplies, leave a note clearly explaining the difficulty in a place where the next person will find it easily.

Instant Messaging

INSTANT MESSAGING (IMING) HAS taken the e-world by storm. Kids and teens started the craze, then businesses followed when they saw the practicality of being able to send a message that could be viewed immediately or held for later. Instead of calling one another with questions or information—along with the attendant ringing and talking—IMers communicate not only immediately but silently. (See also Chapter 21, page 318: "Text Messaging.")

At work, instant messaging is the quickest way to receive and convey information. For example, during a phone call with a client you can IM another department to get the answer to a question. Such speed is one of the reasons IM has become an invaluable tool for businesspeople who regularly hold conference calls or do Web-based presentations. Be careful, though, not to fall into a trap of multitasking. When you're on the phone, it's not acceptable to send IMs that have nothing to do with the call. Your focus should stay on the person you're talking to.

IMs can come so thick and fast that they're intrusive. When you don't want a message, you can specify on your computer that you're unavailable but on-line or are not to be disturbed, and then hope that the senders take heed. If you prefer not to participate in instant messaging at all, just let your friends and coworkers know. The exception is when the IM feature is regularly used in your workplace, in which case you have little choice but to participate.

If you don't get a response to your IM, don't keep sending messages. The person at the other computer may not want to respond, could be busy with something else, or another person might be using his computer. Remember that each time you contact people, you're interrupting them (especially at work), so limit any frivolous or unnecessary instant messages.

Instant messaging tends to be ultracasual, but don't use words that are a little too colorful (or off-color). You never know who might see your IM at work and at home, since there's no guarantee that your IM is for the recipient's eyes only.

Chapter Twenty-one

Telephone Manners

ALEXANDER GRAHAM BELL'S miraculous invention of 1876 had the beauty of simplicity. Today the telephone can be a jack-of-all-trades that takes oral and written messages, identifies who's calling, signals when someone else is trying to reach you, and even doubles as a camera.

With an evolution so rapid comes the need for a new look at telephone manners, which sometimes seem in danger of disappearing altogether. Most telephone etiquette basics still apply, but grafted onto them are a multitude of do's and don'ts for conference calls, speakerphones, unwanted calls, and—most important—the piece of equipment that has excited the public in ways that Mr. Bell could never have imagined: the cell phone.

A simple phone call allows plenty of opportunities to put thoughtfulness into action and just as many for social blunders, whether you're answering and placing calls or using one of the newer telecommunication devices. And where do today's phone manners start? With your voice. While you'll do your phonemate a favor by speaking distinctly and clearly, the bigger issue is voice *volume.* With phoning no longer confined to home or office, keeping your voice low in the presence of others will be appreciated by the person you're talking to and everyone around you. Which brings us to that ubiquitous essential of modern life, the cell phone.

Using Your Cell Phone

WHILE THE PEOPLE of the late 1800s hailed the telephone as a miracle, their descendants see the cell phone as either an absolute necessity or a high-tech toy. No piece of equipment has made the growing pains of the Electronic Age more glaring. To the cell phone addict, this portable little tool is as necessary to communicating as utensils are to eating. To the peeved, phone conversations in public are the aural equivalent of secondhand smoke—noise that, if not dangerous, is a small assault on the senses. Can there ever be a truce?

The terms of a truce are grounded in consideration. Cell phone lovers will keep of-

Four Cell Phone Never-Evers

Talking too loudly into a cell phone ranks first on the annoyance scale, but four other habits aren't far behind. Unless you take pleasure in watching other people's blood pressure rise, remember these four cell phone never-evers.

Leaving the ringer on in quiet places. You're at the movies, the suspense has built to a climax and the audience is tensed with anticipation. Then it comes—not the dénouement, but the grating trill of a phone. If there's one way to infuriate people en masse, this is it. A ringing phone can cause even more consternation in a concert hall or house of worship. The vibrator mode will signal incoming calls without disturbing others—a boon for doctors, parents of young children, and others who must remain on call.

Ignoring those you're with. If you want your friends or relatives to think that your cell phone matters more than they do, then make or take calls when you're in the middle of a conversation. By doing so, you're making whomever you're with feel second best, left to wonder, "If I'm here, why is she on the phone instead of talking with me?" And making a "hang on a minute" signal makes phoning no less offensive.

Making repeated calls. Keep calls to a minimum on public transportation, in line at the bank or movie house, or in busy areas like airports. Your placing of one call after another (especially just to pass the time) eventually exasperates even the most understanding captive listener. Barring an emergency, limit your calls or move to a more private spot.

Using offensive language. Oblivious to those around them, some cell phone users (including otherwise well-spoken people) feel free to use obscenities and other socially unacceptable speech. The people nearby may try not to listen, but it's hard to ignore vulgarities and comments that are racist or sexist.

Telephone Manners

fensiveness to a minimum by remembering a few do's and don'ts, while cell phone haters can steel themselves and try their best to be tolerant.

The Good and the Bad

Cell phones are an obvious boon to communication. They give us the security of knowing we're able to get in touch with anyone on the spur of the moment, and that anyone can get in touch with us. They give us increased productivity and convenience. They allow us to call someone when we're caught in traffic or are otherwise delayed. And cell phones can be a lifesaver in an emergency.

The problem starts with having to listen to someone jabbering away in public—one more irritant in a stressful world. By invading everyone else's space, she shows herself unaware that the people around her exist—something of an insult in itself.

Cell phone etiquette is still evolving, and like most manners, it's situational. No matter where you make or take a call—in an airport waiting area, a theater, a meeting room, a train or bus, or a house of worship—virtually *all* situations call for you to avoid being intrusive, especially in public places.

> ➤ If you must make the call, speak as quietly as you can.
> ➤ Turn off the ringer. Switch to the vibrating mode and check your caller ID or capture your messages via voice mail.
> ➤ Keep calls as short as possible; the longer the call, the greater the irritation in those who have no choice but to listen.

Take-care Zones

The *where* of a cell phone conversation is an important consideration. Special care should be taken when having a chat on the street, in stores, in restaurants, in your car, and on public transportation and airplanes.

On the street. Don't shout into your phone while walking outdoors. (Talking loudly not only is intrusive but also can leave the impression that you're trying to show off.) Watch out for others when you're on a crowded sidewalk; don't get so involved in your call that you bump into passersby. Pay special attention when crossing streets.

If you wear a headset for safety reasons (the jury is still out on whether the waves from a cell phone held to the ear can do damage to the brain), be aware that suddenly breaking into a monologue can startle anyone who hasn't noticed your mike. This is especially true when you're standing on a corner with your hands in your pockets, waiting for the light to change. If after a long silence you suddenly exclaim to your phonemate, "You've got to be kidding!" the person standing next to you will naturally think you're addressing her.

In stores. When you're out shopping and must make a cell phone call, do it in private. It's annoying for others who have to listen to you discuss your shopping list while roaming the aisles. And no one should be slowed down in a cashier line because you're having second thoughts about the blouse you've chosen and need to phone a friend for advice.

In restaurants. The abuse of cell phones in restaurants has become so intrusive that some require the phones to be checked at the door. If cell phones aren't off-limits, turn yours off anyway and don't make calls at the table. If you must call, excuse yourself and go to the vestibule or outside.

In the car. Phoning from a moving vehicle is a serious safety concern. Carrying on a phone conversation affects the driver's concentration and diverts his attention from the road. In fact, recent studies have shown that people who are talking on car phones are at least four times more likely to be involved in an accident. Many municipalities have outlawed cell phone use while driving. Hands-free phones may lessen the risk somewhat, but the smartest choice is to pull into a parking area before making a call.

Calls from cell phones in the car usually require that the caller talk in a louder than normal voice—annoying to the person on the other end, so keep calls short. It's also a good idea to let your phonemate know if there are other people in the car who will overhear the conversation.

On airplanes. When flight crews instruct passengers to turn off all electronic devices before takeoff, they mean it. Some travelers drone on into their cell phones even as the plane taxis down the runway—behavior that's both irritating and dangerous.

On buses and trains. Buses and trains are especially conducive to cell phone blunders. The most common problem is volume, so keep conversations short and *soft*. If you can be heard two rows away, you're talking too loudly. Try to limit your calls to those that are really necessary; the people who are within earshot will be doubly annoyed if you're going on about something that obviously could wait. If you commute by train, you should phone from the train car's vestibule area or, better still, from the platform before you board.

Phone Manners in General

THERE ARE CERTAIN GUIDELINES for phone usage that apply across the board, from answering or placing calls to using special features such as call waiting. Answering machines and voice mail raise a whole different set of considerations.

A QUESTION FOR PEGGY

When I was at the movies recently, a cell phone rang and the owner proceeded to have a conversation as if he were in his own living room. Two people yelled, "Shut up!" which I thought was just as rude. When things like this happen, how can I politely let it be known that I'm upset?

What seems like the simplest, most reasonable solution—quietly asking the person to end the call or move to the lobby—may backfire by leading to a confrontation. Instead, find an usher or the manager and ask him to deal with the culprit. In this day of constant reminders about curbing cell phone usage, it's highly unlikely the offender isn't aware that his behavior is wrong—all the more reason to let someone official request that he put away his phone.

Answering the Phone

EXCEPT FOR BUSINESS CALLS, a straightforward "Hello" remains the greeting of choice when you answer the phone—particularly today, when you never know when a stranger is calling. A polite but less personal greeting is "Marshall residence," which is also used when you're answering the phone at another person's home.

It's just as important to know what *not* to do when answering the phone. Some things to avoid are these:

> ➤ Brusquely asking "Who is this?" when the caller is unknown or the call is for someone else. If the caller hasn't observed the common courtesy of stating her name (see page 312: "Placing Calls"), you can politely ask, "May I ask who's calling?" or "May I tell her who's calling, please?"

> ➤ Saying, "Wait a minute," and keeping the caller waiting while you vanish on an errand of your own. If the call comes at an inconvenient moment, it's okay to say, "I'll call you back in a few minutes," as long as you follow through on your promise.

> ➤ Letting a very young child answer. It can be difficult for a child under six to understand a message and relay it to the right person.

When It's for Someone Else

If an incoming call is for another person in the household, respond with "If you'll wait a moment, I'll get her." Immediately find the person and deliver the message. Don't shout, "Annie, it's for *yoo*-ou!" If you do have to call out to the person, be sure to cover the mouthpiece first.

If the person being called isn't available, offer to take a message, then *write it down*. Keeping a pad and pen within reach of the phone is an act of courtesy; it prevents wasting a caller's time while you search for something to write on. Be sure you get the name and number right by repeating them back to the caller. It's also helpful to note the day and hour of the call.

Wrong Numbers

When you're on the receiving end of a wrong number, "I'm sorry, you have the wrong number" is the direct and polite response. If the caller asks "Who is this?" you can answer, "What number are you calling?" or "Who are you calling?" (Give your number only if you feel comfortable doing so.) If the caller wants to argue (unlikely, but it happens), you might say, "Please understand: There is no Jason here," before hanging up. (See also page 312: "Dialing a Wrong Numbers"; page 319: "A Question for Peggy.")

"Is This Mr. Miller . . . er, Mueller?"

You're busy balancing your checkbook or just sitting down for dinner—and the phone rings. Guess who's calling? A solicitor, who often adds insult to injury by mangling your name.

Directing your anger at telephone solicitors is about as constructive as throwing the phone across the room. It's the organization that hires the solicitor that is to blame, not the individual who's trying to make a living. Common sense says that taking your frustration out on the solicitor is not going to keep such calls at bay.

You can, however, take steps to stop telephone solicitations. First, ask that your name be removed from the calling list, which the caller is bound to do by law. You're more likely to succeed if you're polite about it: "I know you're just doing your job, but I have a policy of not accepting telephone solicitations. Also, could you please see to it that I'm taken off your organization's list?" Another preventive measure is to sign up for the "do not call" registry in your state, if there is one; this will block most, but not all, unsolicited calls.

If a solicitor won't take no for an answer, be firm: "I'm sorry, but I'm not interested, and I must hang up now." Then do so. Just don't slam down the phone.

[311]

Caller ID

By revealing the name and number of a caller in advance, caller ID has screening as one of its purposes—a response to the rising flood of unwanted calls. On the positive side, caller ID allows you to decide whether it's worth interrupting what you're doing to take the time to talk. But answering your phone by saying, "Hi, Jim," may throw the caller off guard unless he's a close friend. Besides, the next time Jim calls and you don't answer, he might wonder if you're intentionally avoiding him.

Offensive Calls

The most unwelcome phone call of all is the obscene call. If your hello is answered with heavy breathing or worse, hang up at once; responding will only give the caller the satisfaction of hearing you become upset. If the call is repeated immediately, leave the receiver off the hook for a while.

Joke calls are innocent by comparison, but a nuisance nonetheless. Like the more upsetting callers, a youngster looking for a laugh will soon give up when he gets nothing but a busy signal. If obscene or joke calls keep coming, you should notify your telephone company or local law enforcement authorities and ask that the calls be traced. Caller ID or pressing the star button and then 69 (which will ring the caller's phone) can be effective weapons against offensive calls.

Still Using That Pager?

Manners guidelines for audible pagers are straightforward: Either turn them off when in the company of others or use the vibrator mode. Then excuse yourself to make a call in response. There is no need to explain the nature of the call to others, but if you must leave, it's courteous to explain why you were called away.

Placing Calls

WHEN YOU PLACE A CALL, the test of your manners starts even before the other person answers—with the number of rings. It's polite not to hang up before the phone has rung at least five or six times; little is more irritating than jumping out of the shower or running down the stairs only to find that the caller has given up.

Three other considerations to remember when calling:

Identify yourself. When the call is answered, state your name unless you're talking with a family member or close friend who knows your voice. If someone other than the person you're calling answers the phone, keep your conversation brief: "Hi, this is Louise Brown. May I please speak with Joan?"

Ask if it's a good time to talk. Once you reach the person you want (and you expect your call to last more than a minute or two), ask if you're interrupting. Saying, "Are you in the middle of something? I can call back," shows that you're considerate of the other person's time.

Keep any messages brief. If the person you want isn't there and you want to leave a message, keep it short. Unless the matter is urgent, it's thoughtless to expect whoever answers to write down a lengthy or complicated message.

Dialing a Wrong Number

Unless you are absolutely certain you know a phone number, double-check it before dialing. When you *do* dial a wrong number, simply say so and apologize. Don't demand, "What number is this?" Better to say, "I'm so sorry. I must have misdialed. I was trying 749-555-5903," which will keep you from sounding annoyed at somebody who simply answered his phone. Never just hang up without a word when you reach a wrong number; few telephone affronts are more glaring.

Timing Calls

As a general rule, place your calls between 9:00 AM and 9:00 PM unless you're certain a friend or relative doesn't mind being called earlier or later. Even those who don't go to bed at nine o'clock may consider their day "closed" after that hour.

If people you call frequently say or imply that they'd rather not be called at certain

When calling to extend an invitation to a friend, be direct from the start: "Hi, Marianne. We're having a few people over on Saturday night to play bridge. Can you and Hank come?" This approach leaves the person free to accept or to say, "Oh, I'm so sorry, but we're busy Saturday," if she'd rather not.

When responding to a telephone invitation, don't say, "I'll let you know" unless you explain immediately: "I'll have to ask Hank if he's made plans for that weekend" or "We have tickets for the high school play for that night, but I might be able to exchange them for two on Thursday." Otherwise, "I'll let you know" sounds as though you're waiting for a better invitation. In any case, respond to the invitation within a day or possibly two, calling back with an answer when you said you would.

times of day, then comply with the request. It's easy to tell yourself, "I know Scott reads between two and three, but I doubt if he'll mind if I call to invite him to my party." But resist the temptation; a call at the wrong time is no less disruptive because it comes from a friend.

When Calling on Someone Else's Phone

The advent of calling cards took much of worry out of making long-distance calls when traveling or visiting friends. If, however, you have no card and must place a long-distance call from someone else's phone, either call collect or give your host enough money to cover the call. If he refuses reimbursement, you might discreetly tuck the bills and a small piece of paper with a "Thank you!" under the phone when you leave, if you think this won't seem inappropriate.

Many phone companies charge set fees for local calls, small though the fees may be. Under these circumstances, keep local calls on a friend's phone to a minimum.

Calls in Progress

ONCE A CALL GETS GOING, try not to be long-winded. Most people are protective of their time these days, and someone who takes too long to get to the point can quickly become exasperating. Even friends who have plenty of leisure time will probably appreciate your brevity. Only when they volunteer something like "I'm enjoying catching up so much I could talk all day!" should you talk to your heart's content.

The guidelines for effective conversation (see Chapter 19, pages 280–295: "The Good Conversationalist") apply as much to a phone call as to a face-to-face talk. Speak clearly and be careful not to shout (many people unconsciously raise their voices while on the phone). Avoid focusing entirely on yourself; rather, ask your

My aunt travels to visit us at least once a year and stays for four or five days. Without fail, she makes several calls back home but never offers to pay. She's getting up in years and I'm concerned about upsetting or embarrassing her. How can I bring up the issue?

Let the matter drop unless your aunt's calls are putting a dent in your budget. She may think that because she's family, free long-distance calls are part of her guest privileges. However, if her calls increase your phone bill to the point of even slight financial strain, be frank but polite: "Aunt Judith, I wish I didn't have to bring this up, but I'm on a tight budget. Is it possible you could charge your calls home to your own phone?" If she's not wise in the ways of modern technology, introduce her to calling cards. Then, if she expresses interest, you could call together to sign her up.

phonemate what he's been doing or about the latest news of friends or relatives—anything that expresses interest in the person. As you listen, let him *know* you're listening. You can't show attention with a nod or a smile, so use verbal responses instead: "Yes, I understand," "Of course," "I see."

Using First Names

The question of using first names with someone you've never met can be an issue in a phone conversation. Assuming from the outset that a stranger wants to be on a first-name basis might be seen as overly familiar and impolite. Use your intuition to gauge your phonemate's expectations. If you're uncertain, use "Mr. Jones" until asked to do otherwise.

Whether your phonemate is a good friend or a stranger, don't overuse his first name. Beginning or ending every second statement with "Jack" can begin to sound either condescending or artificially friendly.

Call Waiting

The frustration quotient of being put on hold because of call waiting isn't as high as that of putting up with a cell phone shouter, but it comes close. If you feel insulted when your phonemate asks, "Do you mind if I see who this is?" your impulse might be to answer "Yes, I do mind!" But it's better to say, "Go ahead," then wait. But if more than ninety seconds pass, it's fine to hang up. When you're eventually reconnected with your phonemate, try not to betray your annoyance. Politely say that you were unable to hold and leave it at that, even though the person should have returned to you more quickly.

When your own call waiting feature signals, apologize to your phonemate and say you'll return immediately; put her on hold and quickly explain to the other caller that you'll have to call back. Try your best to keep a conversation from starting; *your responsibility is to the first caller*, who should never be left on hold for more than twenty seconds (thirty at the most).

There are some exceptions to the rule. If you're expecting an urgent or long-distance call (especially from overseas), tell your phonemate at the outset: "I'm waiting to hear from my mother in California. If she calls, I'll have to take the call and get back to you." When your mother's call comes in, arrange a time to call your phonemate back—then do so.

If you're expecting an important call and pick up your ringing phone to find someone else on the line, let the person know: "Hello, Kathy. I'd love to talk, but I may have to interrupt you—I'm waiting for a call from my doctor." Alerting an unexpected caller will keep her from feeling brushed off.

An alternative to call waiting is home voice mail, which enables you to keep talking while an incoming call is picked up as a message. When you hang up, you can retrieve the message by dialing a number provided by your telephone company. (See also page 320: "Voice Mail Systems.")

Other Interruptions

You're on the phone, the doorbell rings, and it's your neighbor. Naturally, you'll tell your phonemate that you must answer the door, just as you'll welcome your neighbor. If the call is important, explain to your neighbor that you have to finish it. Otherwise, don't continue the phone chat while the visitor tries to occupy herself. Say to your phonemate, "Joan just dropped by, so may I call you back in a little while?" Then be sure to return the call as soon as you can.

Another kind of interruption is the mechanical glitch. When a phone call in progress is disconnected, it is the caller's responsibility to call back. If you initiated the call, immediately redial the person you were talking with and apologize, even though the equipment was at fault: "I'm sorry; we somehow got disconnected. I think we left off with Jim's new car." If a bad connection or static on the line makes it difficult to hear, you can ask the other person to hang up so that you can try again. A second call often solves the problem.

If you're the one who was called and a mechanical glitch occurs, stay off the line. But don't hesitate to phone the person if he hasn't called back within a few minutes. Saying something like "I'm not sure why the phone went dead, but I just wanted to make sure we didn't have anything else to discuss" draws the call to a proper close.

Ending Calls

TRADITIONAL TELEPHONE ETIQUETTE SAYS THAT the person who originates the call is the one who terminates it. This "rule" isn't all that important, but it's helpful if a call seems to be dragging on. If you're the one who placed the call, say something

Telephone Manners

The following telephone errors are commonly made by people who otherwise mind their manners. In personal calls, these actions qualify as minor missteps; in business calls, they can make you look unprofessional.

Talking to someone else. Conversing with someone nearby while your phonemate is on the line is permissible only when a third party's participation is necessary or you say something like, "I hope you don't mind if I quickly ask John what he thinks about this."

Busying yourself with other things. Keyboarding, washing dishes, or shuffling papers while on the phone suggests that your attention is elsewhere.

Eating. Eating while on the phone is not only impolite but is seen by many as crude. A major blunder: using a hands-free phone to conduct a phone call while you eat lunch.

Chewing gum. Hearing the smacks of a gum chewer may not annoy most people, but many will take offense. To be on the safe side, save the gum for later.

Sneezing or coughing into the receiver. If you have to sneeze, cough, or blow your nose, either turn your head away or excuse yourself for a moment and put down the phone.

Laying down the receiver with a bang. If you have to leave for a moment, gently set the receiver on the desk so you won't startle your phonemate.

like, "I'll let you go now, Barbara. I'm glad I reached you, and we'll be looking forward to seeing you on the seventh. Good-bye."

If you're having difficulty ending a call with a long-winded phonemate, you may have no choice but to be firm. At the first pause in the conversation, say, "I'm sorry, but I simply must go now." Take this route whether you placed the call or received it, and only when really necessary.

Special Uses, Special Features

SPECIFIC ETIQUETTE GUIDELINES APPLY TO other kinds of telephone calls, including conference calls and calls using speakerphones (usually associated with the office, but also good for group discussions among family members who live apart), calls from public phones, and those using phone systems designed for the hearing impaired.

Conference Calls

Conduct a conference call in a quiet place. If you're having trouble understanding a phonemate who's ignored this obvious guideline (believe it or not, some people have been known to conduct conference calls from bars), diplomatically suggest to the group that you reconvene at another time. "I'm sorry, but it's difficult for me to hear with the noise in the background. Do you mind if we reschedule?"

When participants aren't acquainted with everyone, they should introduce themselves so that everyone else can link voices to names. To reinforce the link, participants should identify themselves the first few times they speak: "This is Cindy. I'm wondering . . ." If you aren't sure who's speaking, ask.

Speakerphones

You may be partial to speakerphones, but be careful when using one. Talking on a speakerphone gives your phonemate the impression that you're engaged in another activity at the same time. That may be okay if you're talking with a close friend, but others may think that you're not paying attention. Phonemates are also sometimes not as easy to hear on the other end, and speakerphone calls can seem less personal.

If the person with whom you're talking is using a speakerphone and it bothers you, politely ask, "Are you on a speakerphone?" If she doesn't offer to switch to a handheld phone, you could say something like, "I can't hear you well. Would you mind switching to the receiver?" If she fails to comply, ask if you can talk later, when she's able to use a regular phone.

Public Phones

Even in the cell phone age, public pay phones haven't gone the way of the horse and buggy. They can come in handy, especially if you have a calling card and your cell phone reception isn't all that great. The first rule of pay phone etiquette is to complete your call as quickly as possible, then hang up to free the phone for others. Some other considerations are these:

Be thoughtful. If you're in the midst of a call, ask someone who is waiting anxiously if her call is urgent. If you can, let her make her call; then call back and complete your own.

No hovering. When you're next in line for the phone, *don't hover.* Stand far enough away so that you're not within earshot of the conversation. If you're so close to the caller that you can hear what's being said, pretend that you can't and make an effort not to eavesdrop.

In case of emergency. If you have a minor emergency—say, you have only five minutes to change the time for meeting a friend—first look for a free phone. If one isn't available, try to determine if the person using the phone ahead of you is making a quick call or settling in for a long chat. If the latter, signal to him that you urgently need to use the phone; most people will agree to relinquish it. Give him a few minutes to end his call, then return the favor by finishing your call as quickly as possible.

Text Messaging

Text messaging, informally called texting, involves typing messages on a cell phone and zapping them to the recipient in an instant. Billions of text messages are sent each year, as more and more users are attracted to the medium's fast transmission, instant reception, and low cost.

Technically known as short messaging service (SMS), text messaging is more informal than e-mail and best used only for the briefest and most casual messages. If you have to notify someone of anything important or serious (a business matter, an urgent meeting, or sad news about a friend), text only as a prelude to a phone call. Here are some additional guidelines:

> Use common courtesy—a greeting to start the message and a thank-you or another courtesy to end it.

> Be mindful of your recipients' schedules rather than assuming they're always available to text you back.

> Keep your message short. Ask only questions that can be answered briefly.

> Be very careful when choosing a recipient from your directory; with a slip of the thumb text intended for a friend's eyes only could go astray.

> If you receive a text message by mistake, ignore it if you're certain it was missent. You aren't obligated to find the person the sender intended to text.

> When you text someone who doesn't have your number in his directory, start with a greeting like "Hi!"; then identify yourself and the company you represent, if any.

> Whenever possible, acknowledge text messages, either by texting back or with a voice call.

> Don't disturb others by scrolling through your phone's ring tones while in a public place.

For the use of text telephones for the deaf, see Chapter 11, page 138: "Using a Text Telephone."

Answering Machines and Voice Mail

WHETHER YOU USE AN ANSWERING machine or are connected to a voice mail system, certain practicalities and civilities should come into play.

Recording a Greeting

In a word, keep your greeting *short*. A musical overture, an avowal of how pleased you are someone has called, or a child's cute chatter will waste the caller's time—and pile up the cost if the call is long distance. There's also no need to say, "We can't come to the phone right now," which the caller has no doubt surmised. The simpler your message, the better: "This is Joe Garcia. Please leave a message and I'll call you back." If you prefer not to give your name, try "You've reached 719-555-4526. Please leave your name, number, and message and I'll get back to you as soon as possible."

Leaving a Message

A cardinal rule when leaving a message on someone's answering machine or voice mail is to state your name and number *first*. Then keep your message brief. Many people ramble on until they're about to be cut off, then give their number so quickly that it's lost in the shuffle. Most people have little tolerance for long messages, which may be passed over or deleted if the speaker doesn't get straight to the point.

Briefly state what you're calling about (especially important if the person doesn't know you), and close by repeating your number—a sign-off that allows the listener to jot it down without having to replay the message.

Returning Calls

The Golden Rule for returning calls left on your machine: Do it within twenty-four hours unless you're out of town or because of circumstances beyond your control. When away, you can check your messages via a remote message retrieval system. The alternative is to disconnect the machine until you return.

If you reach a machine when calling back, you can lessen the potential for telephone tag by stating where you can be reached, and when. If something comes up and you won't be available at that time, leave a second message explaining the circum-

---

A QUESTION FOR PEGGY

I came home to find a message on my machine that was obviously meant for someone else—a woman named Sally asked a Maureen to call her back. Am I obliged to call Sally and tell her of her mistake?

On the principle of "Do unto others . . ." you should call Sally back if she happened to leave her phone number. Consider it your good deed for the day. Letting someone know her message was not received is all the more essential if it sounded important in any way—the rescheduling of an appointment, for example.

stances and say when you plan to call again. And *do* it: Not calling back is the equivalent of standing someone up.

Voice Mail Systems

Voice mail systems are such a fixture of modern life that, by the beginning of the new century, Americans were met with a voice mail recording three out of every four times they called a business office—a not-so-welcome development for those who think of it as Voice Mail Hell. Two ways to ease the problem:

Take notes. When the seemingly endless menu of choices gets around to the option of connecting to a real person, jot down the number so you can bypass the menu next time. Also, ask a receptionist for the extension of someone you plan to call again.

Stay cool. Don't take out your frustrations on the person who eventually answers, who didn't create the system and can't change it. Voicing your dissatisfaction will begin your call on a hostile note.

When you reach the voice mailbox of the person you're calling, keep your message brief and to the point, saving longer conversations for the time that you actually speak. How long should you wait before calling someone back when your message goes unanswered? Your wait-time should be based on the urgency of what you have to say. You won't look pushy if you call back after one or two days and say, "I just want to make sure you got my message." (See also page 314: "Call Waiting.")

Chapter Twenty-two

Names, Titles, and Official Protocol

DESPITE THE CHANGES that have swept through American life, many traditions hold firm—among them, the protocol for addressing and corresponding with everyone from your closest friends and relatives to attorneys to dignitaries of every stripe. Yes, women have many more social titles to choose from these days, but the framework within which these and other titles are used essentially remains unchanged.

If you've ever been called *Mrs.* when you're a *Miss*, *Jack* instead of *Jake*, or *Pastor* when you should properly be addressed as *Father*, you know how important it is to get names and titles right. Not only has your identity been misconstrued, but the person responsible feels embarrassed when she learns of her error.

This chapter begins with a review of social and professional titles, then ventures into the rarified world of official protocol, with its emphasis on rank. Less personal (but no less important) protocol comes into play when displaying the American flag and playing the national anthem, and these guidelines are covered as well.

Men's Names and Titles

A MAN WITH THE SAME name as his father—say, John Griggs Davis—uses "Jr." after his name as long as his father is alive. He may either drop the suffix after his father's death or, if he prefers, retain it so that he won't be confused with his late father. Retaining it also helps to differentiate between his wife and his mother—especially if the latter is still living and doesn't wish to be known as Mrs. Davis, Sr.

When a man is named after his father who is a "Jr.," he is called "the third," once written with either the numeric *3rd* or the Roman number *III* but now confined almost exclusively to the latter. A man named after his grandfather, uncle, or cousin uses the suffix *II*. The wife of each of these men uses the same suffix after her name as her husband does—i.e., Mrs. John Griggs Davis III.

In writing, a comma is used to separate the surname and the suffixes *Jr.* and *Sr.*, though the trend is toward dropping the comma. *Junior* when spelled out, is written with a lower case *j*. When a name has a numeral suffix—as in Robert Conner III—no punctuation is used.

Affirming the Lineage

In some families, names are carried on through three or more generations—John (Sr.) is succeeded by John, Jr., and Johns III, IV, and V. But this presents something of a problem once John, Sr., has died. Does each man retain the title by which he has always been known, or does everyone "move up"?

The only "rule" in this regard is to use common sense. Moving up the suffixes is bound to cause confusion among acquaintances who used to know the new John, Jr., as John III—and then there are the changes that must be made on personal accounts and bank checks. While keeping a name through the generations reflects a proud family history, many people feel the complications outweigh the advantages. Indeed, it is probably wise for the succession to be discontinued after the third generation by giving the fourth-generation child a different middle name. He who might have been John Griggs Davis IV may be the first of a distinguished line of John Spencer Davises.

Women's Names and Titles

TRADITIONALLY, A WOMAN'S SOCIAL TITLE (also called a courtesy title) was tied to her marital status—a young girl or unmarried woman named Jane Johnson was known as Miss Johnson and became Mrs. Kelly when she married John Kelly. When she used her full name, she used Mrs. John Kelly socially and Jane Kelly (no *Mrs.*) informally.

By comparison, the woman of today has an abundance of choices for her name and social title—a decision based on personal preference and one that others should respect. *Ms.*, a title free of any reference to the woman's marital status, gained ground from the early 1970s on; it serves a useful purpose, particularly when there is uncertainty over whether a woman is single, married, or uses a professional name. The adoption of *Ms.*, however, doesn't mean that *Miss* has fallen by the wayside: Many unmarried women prefer to use the older title, and both titles are correct.

In recent years, more and more married women have chosen to keep their surnames rather than take their husband's. Others use both their own surname and their husband's, sometimes with a hyphen—although a double first name, such as Mary Beth or Betty Ann, doesn't easily lend itself to this choice. Still others insert the initial of their maiden name between the first name and surname.

A married woman may correctly choose to be addressed socially and in correspondence in any of the following ways:

> Mrs. John Kelly
> Ms. Jane Kelly
> Mrs. Jane Kelly (See "The *Mrs.* Question," below.)

Tradition held that a married woman should use the title *Mrs.* only in conjunction with her husband's name, not her own—"Mrs. Arthur Reynolds" rather than "Mrs. Susan Reynolds." The latter was acceptable only in the event of divorce. But societal changes gradually made this practice seem a relic from another time. Today it is acceptable for both married and divorced women to be referred to by their first names after the title *Mrs.*—as in "Mrs. Mary McGowan."

A married woman can choose to be addressed as either "Mrs. Mary McGowan" or "Mrs. John McGowan." In the case of a divorced woman, *Mrs.* [*or Ms.*] is correct only if she has retained her former husband's last name and she uses *her* first name, not his. (Many women retain their married name so that the surname won't differ from their children's.) Otherwise, she is referred to as *Ms.* or *Miss.*

The following are also correct, with the addition of either *Mrs.* or *Ms.*:

Jane Johnson Kelly
Jane Johnson-Kelly
Jane J. Kelly

Necessary Adaptations

A married woman who is widowed, divorced, or separated is faced with deciding how to adapt her name to fit the situation. Traditional rules were fairly rigid in this regard, but the women of today enjoy more flexibility.

A divorcée's name. Not so long ago, a divorced woman replaced her first name with her maiden name as her form of address: Sally Merritt DuPree was known as Mrs. Merritt DuPree. In today's world, including a divorcée's first name with her title and the last name she uses—Mrs. [or Ms.] Sally DuPree—has simply become the less confusing, more sensible thing to do.

➤ **Multiple divorces.** When a woman has been divorced from two or three husbands, she drops the previous husband's name and uses her first name (and, if she wishes, her maiden name) with the name of her last husband. For example, Beverly Griffin first married Douglas Turner and became Beverly Griffin Turner; she then married Thomas Reese, whom she has now divorced. She permanently omits the name Turner and calls herself Barbara Griffin Reese or Mrs. Beverly Reese, whichever she prefers. She also has the choice of dispensing with her husbands' surnames altogether and taking back her maiden name: Ms. Beverly Griffin.

➤ **Divorcées with children.** Because the children of a divorcée generally retain their mother's married name, the mother's resumption of her maiden name can confuse people who do not know the family well. If, however, a divorcée and her children have different surnames for any reason, she should inform the teaching staff at the children's school and her business associates—but for informational purposes only (no explanation is required).

➤ **A separated woman's name.** A woman who is separated but not divorced may continue to use her husband's name ("Mrs. Edward Nave"), but only if she prefers to. Her other choice is "Mrs. [or Ms.] Gwendolyn Nave."

A widow's name. Traditionally, a widow retained her husband's given name until she remarried—"Mrs. Rodolfo Alonzo." Widows may certainly continue to do so, but today using their own first name—"Mrs. Modesta Alonzo"—is an equally correct choice. (When you don't know how to introduce or address a widow, it's better to err on the side of tradition and use her husband's first name rather than her own. Better still, simply ask which of the two choices she prefers.)

When a widow remarries, she has the option of using her previous husband's surname as a middle name—becoming "Mrs. Modesta Alonzo McNeil" (the choice often made by women who were married for many years and had children)—or of dropping his name and using her maiden name in the middle: "Mrs. Modesta Cisneros McNeil."

An unmarried mother's name. Life will be far easier for an unmarried mother and her child if they both use the same last surname—the mother's own. Although it isn't necessary for an unmarried mother to use a title with her name, *Ms.* would be the appropriate choice.

Legal Name Changes

A PERSON WHO CHANGES THE NAME by which he or she has been known should immediately notify social and business associates of the change to avoid confusion and embarrassing situations. The quickest and simplest way of informing others is to send out formal announcements:

Mr. and Mrs. Joseph Diefendorf
Announce that by Permission of the Court
They and Their Children
Have Taken the Family Name of
Diefen

~ "Sir," "Madam," and "Esquire" ~

"Sir" and "Madam" (usually shortened to "Ma'am") are titles of respect and show deference on the part of the speaker. For this reason, they are never used between people of equal age and status. No matter how charming a gentleman may be, a woman of the same age does not address him as sir, nor does a man address a female contemporary as madam or ma'am.

On rare occasions, an older man may say sir to a male contemporary, especially if he doesn't know the other's name. Sir and ma'am are also used to address distinguished people, including when the terms serve to avoid too many repetitions of a formal name and title.

It is perfectly fine (and polite!) for a salesperson to call a customer sir or ma'am. The same goes for a pupil addressing a teacher. In short, the terms are used when there is an age difference or when one person is serving another in some way.

"Esquire," although used less frequently than in the past, identifies a man or a woman as an attorney. It is abbreviated and is written "James Dickerson, Esq." (See also Chapter 17, page 229: "Correct Use of 'Esquire.' ")

Professional Titles

SOCIALLY AS WELL AS PROFESSIONALLY, medical doctors, dentists, and other professionals are addressed by, and introduced with, their titles. A woman physician may or may not prefer to be known as "Dr." on an envelope addressed to her and her husband, but conversationally, "Dr." is always used.

People who have earned a Ph.D. or any other academic, nonmedical doctoral degree have the choice of whether to use "Dr." both professionally and socially. If, when meeting people with doctorates, you're unsure how to address them, "Dr." is always correct. If they'd rather the title be dropped, they will let you know.

Other Titles

EVERY DAY WE RUN INTO people who have an official title. The police officer at the desk is Sergeant Flynn; the head of the fire department is Chief Elmore; the club chef is Chef Palazzolo; the airline pilot is Captain Howe; and so forth.

When on the job, such people are always addressed by their titles, just as they are when the matter at hand is related to their work. Socially, many don't use their titles, though they may. Sometimes a title sticks: A local judge, for example, who's been called by his title for a number of years, is usually addressed as Judge even after his retirement. (See also page 331: "Official Titles.")

Official Protocol

IN ITS OFFICIAL SENSE, PROTOCOL is a system of universally accepted etiquette used when the representatives of different nations deal with one another. It also applies to official dealings on the national, state, and local levels. The word is aptly derived from the Greek *proto kollen*, or "first glue," and in its earliest English form referred to a sheet of paper glued to the front of a notarized document as verification of its authenticity. Today, protocol is the glue that holds official life together—the observance of precedence and rank in such aspects of official life as using proper forms of address, participating in ceremonies, and entertaining dignitaries.

Many of these "official" manners are observed by ordinary citizens on occasion. Protocol comes into play when you write a letter to a member of Congress, for example, or are introduced to a member of the clergy or the military. And as every schoolchild knows, there is also a protocol for displaying and handling the American flag and for behavior during the playing of the national anthem. (See page 370: "The Flag of the United States"; page 376: "The National Anthem.")

Precedence and Rank

THE TABLE OF PRECEDENCE, USED for ceremonies of state, is a list of the titles of U.S. government officials. It is unofficial, in that every new administration has the right to establish its own order of precedence. Traditionally, the following order has remained the same for years, with the significance of the rank of cabinet secretaries based on the date of the establishment of the department:

∼ To Learn More . . . ∼

Representatives at the Department of State's Office of Protocol (202-647-2663) are available to answer protocol questions over the telephone—queries as varied as where to seat the mayor at a bicentennial banquet and the order of the program for a high school graduation ceremony. They will also provide you with information about the American flag, the national anthem, and the respective ranks of U.S. government officials.

Address questions about state government protocol to the governor's office in your state capitol. You can find the necessary contact information at www.firstgov.gov. Questions on local government protocol can be answered by the mayor's office in your city or town. For answers to questions about military protocol, call a branch of the military in your city or state (see www.defenselink.mil/sites/a.html#armedforces).

Table of Precedence

The President of the United States
The Vice President of the United States
The Speaker of the House of Representatives
The Chief Justice of the United States
Former Presidents of the United States
The Secretary of State
The Secretary General of the United Nations
Ambassadors of Foreign Powers
Widows of Former Presidents of the United States
Associate Justices of the Supreme Court of the United States
Retired Chief Justice of the Supreme Court of the United States
Retired Associate Justice of the Supreme Court of the United States
The Cabinet
    The Secretary of the Treasury
    The Secretary of Defense
    The Attorney General
    The Secretary of the Interior
    The Secretary of Agriculture
    The Secretary of Commerce
    The Secretary of Labor
    The Secretary of Health and Human Services
    The Secretary of Housing and Urban Development
    The Secretary of Transportation
    The Secretary of Energy
    The Secretary of Education
    The Secretary of Veterans Affairs
    The Secretary of Homeland Security
Director, National Drug Control Policy
Director, Office of Management and Budget
President Pro Tempore of the Senate
Members of the Senate
Governors of States
Former Vice Presidents of the United States
Members of the House of Representatives
Assistants to the President
Charges d'Affaires of Foreign Powers
The Under Secretaries and the Deputy Secretaries of the Executive
    Departments
Administrator, Agency for International Development
Director, United States Arms Control and Disarmament Agency
Director, United States Information Agency
United States Ambassador at Large

Secretaries of the Army, the Navy, and the Air Force (ranked according to date of appointment)

Chairman, Board of Governors of the Federal Reserve System

Chairman, Council on Environmental Quality

Chairman, Joint Chiefs of Staff

Chiefs of Staff of the Army, the Navy, and the Air Force and the Commandant of the Coast Guard

(Five-Star) Generals of the Army and Fleet Admirals

The Secretary General, Organization of American States

Representatives to the Organization of American States

Director of Central Intelligence

Director, Office of Personnel Management

Administrator, National Aeronautics and Space Administration

Administrator, Federal Aviation Administration

Administrator, General Services Administration

Chairman, Merit Systems Protection Board

Administrator, Environmental Protection Agency

Deputy Assistants to the President

Deputy Under Secretaries of Executive Departments (see Cabinet for order)

Chief of Protocol

Assistant Secretaries of the Executive Departments

Special Assistants to the President

Members of the Council of Economic Advisers

Active or designated United States Ambassadors and Ministers (Career rank, when in the United States)

The Mayor of the District of Columbia

Under Secretaries of the Army, the Navy, and the Air Force (ranked according to date of appointment)

(Four-Star) Generals and Admirals

Assistant Secretaries of the Army, the Navy, and the Air Force (ranked according to date of appointment)

(Three-Star) Lieutenant Generals and Vice Admirals

Former United States Ambassadors and Ministers to Foreign Countries

Ministers of Foreign Powers (serving in embassies, not accredited)

Deputy Assistant Secretaries of the Executive Departments

Deputy Chief of Protocol

Counselors of Embassies or Legations of Foreign Powers

(Two-Star) Major Generals and Rear Admirals

(One-Star) Brigadier Generals and Commodores

Assistant Chiefs of Protocol

Seating at an Official Luncheon or Dinner

AT OFFICIAL LUNCHEONS AND DINNERS—i.e., those attended by such dignitaries as government or military officials and foreign diplomats—the host or hostess seats the guests according to rank. At the same time, the host sees to it that the seating does not slight any of the guests.

Traditionally, the host and hostess sit at the head and foot of the table. When they are friends with a number of the guests, they may choose instead to sit opposite each other at the middle of the table, where it will be easier for them to converse with more people.

When the event is attended by both men and women, seating is as follows:

➤ The highest-ranked male guest sits to the right of the hostess.

➤ The man next in rank sits to the left of the hostess.

➤ The wife of the man of highest rank sits to the left of the host. (If the man is unmarried, the woman of highest rank takes this seat.)

➤ Spouses in attendance who don't hold an official position are seated according to the rank of their husbands or wives.

What to do if the guest of honor is outranked by one or more people in attendance and therefore isn't entitled to the place of honor? If the host doesn't like the idea of seating the guests according to precedence because it places the guest of honor farther down the table, he can avoid the problem altogether by simply not inviting people of higher rank. Alternatively, the host could ask the highest-ranking guest to either act as a cohost or to decline the seat in favor of the guest of honor. The more practical solution is to divide the seating between two or more tables and appoint a cohost and cohostess for each one.

Guests who have no protocol ranking (as specified by the Table of Precedence) are seated according to the unspoken rank the host assigns to them. The host ranks the guests as he chooses, basing his decision on age, social prominence, personal accomplishment, and mutual interests shared by seatmates. Proficiency in a foreign language also comes into play when foreigners are among the guests.

Other considerations include these:

➤ When the guest of honor and second-ranking official have been placed, nonranking guests may be seated between those of official rank.

➤ At meals hosted by U.S. government personnel overseas, foreign guests have preference in seating over Americans of equal rank—except for the American ambassador to the country.

➤ Men and women should be alternated at the table insofar as possible.

Titles on Place Cards

At official functions, the correct use of place cards varies: Some cards carry only the title, while on others it is proper to display both title and surname.

On all formal occasions, the following appear without names:

The President
The Vice President
The Ambassador of . . .
The Minister of . . .
The Chief Justice
The Speaker
The Secretary of . . .
The Attorney General . . .

Title-only place cards at official functions also include "His Excellency, the Archbishop of New York," "Her Honor, the Mayor of Chicago," and so forth. Naturally, when more than one person holds the title, the surname is added: Senator Holmes, Governor Billings, Ambassador Martinez, Father Brusco, and the like.

Surnames may also be added at less formal affairs, except in the case of the President and Vice President. The names of guests without official titles appear as "Mr. Robineaux" and "Mrs. [or Miss or Ms.] Stockwell." Remember that the object of a place card is twofold: to show everyone where to sit and to give others at the table the correct form for addressing them.

A QUESTION FOR PEGGY

I was invited to a government reception and was soon introduced to a person who was obviously a VIP—possibly even a Cabinet member. But because the person who introduced us didn't use the person's title, I was at a loss for how to address him. What should I have done?

When the introducer leaves you high and dry, the safest tack is to simply say to the person to whom you've been introduced, "How do you do?" If the conversation continues and title remains unknown to you, you are on safe ground by addressing the person as simply either "Sir" or "Ma'am." In fact, when titles are used during a conversation, it's preferable to use these courtesy titles occasionally, since the constant repetition of "General Barcroft" can begin to sound a bit obsequious.

Official Titles

IN OFFICIAL CIRCLES, specific forms of address are used. The President and various other officials, including Cabinet members, are addressed by titles alone ("Mr. President," "Ms. Secretary.") Surnames are added when a position—Associate Justice of the Supreme Court, for example—is held by more than one person ("Justice Ward").

The following general rules are some that apply whenever you speak with certain officials at a public function. (See also page 336: "Official Forms of Address"; page 347: "Ambassadors of Foreign Nations.")

The President of the United States

The correct introduction of a man or a woman to the President is: "Mr. [Madam] President, I have the honor to present Mr. [Mrs.] Michaelson" (or "Mr. Michaelson of Denver, Colorado" if further identification is necessary). Both men and women respond in the same way: They bow slightly, and then let the President initiate a handshake.

Once out of office, the President becomes "Mr. [Mrs. or Ms.] Greene," although he is referred to—but not addressed directly—as "the Honorable."

United States Senators and Representatives

A senator is always "Senator Hawthorne," even when she is no longer in office. A member of the House of Representatives, on the other hand, should never be addressed as "Representative Carson" except when she is being introduced. Nor are the terms "Congressman" or "Congresswoman" used in conversation with—or in the introduction of—a member of the House.

Rank. When two or more senators or representatives are attending the same dinner, the highest ranking is given to those who have served the greatest number of consecutive years. (When several senators or representatives who were sworn in on the same day are present, their relative rank is determined alphabetically.) In all cases, a senator outranks a representative, regardless of his or her length of service.

Governors

Present and former governors are introduced and announced (but not addressed) as "the Honorable." On ceremonial occasions, one would present "the Honorable Henry Robertson, the former governor of the State of New York."

It is improper to call a governor "Mr." ["Mrs." or "Miss" or "Ms."]. In public, he is "the governor"; to his face, "Governor Robertson." Less formally, he may be addressed simply as "Governor."

Rank. Only the president and the vice president of the United States rank above a governor at an event held in the governor's own state. Outside his state, a governor ranks immediately below a member of the U.S. Senate.

When governors from several states are present, they are ranked according to the order of entry of their state to the union. Consulting an almanac or reference book would let the host know that the governor of Delaware would always rank first when present with other governors, while the governor of Hawaii would rank last.

Cabinet Members

Members of the Cabinet are usually addressed as "Mr. Secretary" or "Madam Secretary." However, when several are present and confusion could result, they are addressed as "Mr. Secretary of State" and "Madam Secretary of Commerce."

Rank. Cabinet members are ranked in the Table of Precedence (page 327) by how long their departments have been in existence, from the oldest on.

Justices of the United States

All associate justices are addressed with "Justice" and the surname: "Justice Thompson," not "Mr. Justice Thompson." The same rule applies to the chief justice. Present and former justices are both introduced as "the Honorable."

Rank. Although no official ranking exists for associate justices, length of service would be the determining factor if there were occasion for giving precedence.

∼ Correct Use of "the Honorable" ∼

The title "the Honorable" can cause confusion. Federal custom in the United States bestows the title "the Honorable," first when the person assumes office, and then by courtesy for life, on the following dignitaries: President and Vice President, U.S. senators, congressmen and congresswomen, Cabinet members, all federal judges, ministers plenipotentiary, ambassadors, and governors.

State senators and mayors are also referred to as "the Honorable," but only during their term in office; when they retire, so does the title.

The use of "the Honorable" is largely confined to introductions and to the announcement of the arrival of the person at a large public function: "the Honorable William Middleton." The title is not used to address the official directly, nor does the official use it when introducing himself. Likewise, the title is not printed on the official's letterhead and cards, nor does he use it when signing his name.

The Diplomatic Corps

In Washington, D.C., and other international capitals, the heads of foreign states and their staffs are known as the diplomatic corps.

An ambassador is a diplomatic agent who is the personal representative of the head of state of his or her country. Officially, ambassadors are called "Mr. Ambassador" or "Madame Ambassador" rather than "Ambassador Wainwright."

Rank. Ambassadors rank themselves according to their length of continuous service in Washington, with comparative rankings based on the date an ambassador presented his or her credentials to the president of the United States.

Church Dignitaries

The titles of Protestant clergymen and -women vary according to the denomination, although most are willing to be called "Pastor" or "Reverend," with or without the surname. If a Protestant member of the clergy holds the title of doctor, dean, or canon, his or her surname is always added to the proper title: "Dean Cavanaugh."

A Catholic priest is addressed as "Father" (with or without the surname), whatever his other titles may be.

When introductions are made to church dignitaries, the layperson is always the one presented. To a cardinal, say, "Your Eminence, may I present Mrs. Tarantino?" (the British use "Your Grace"). A non-Catholic bows slightly, but a Roman Catholic drops on the right knee, places the right hand (palm down) under the cardinal's extended hand, and kisses his ring.

When introduced to an archbishop, Mrs. Tarantino would correctly say, "How do you do, Your Excellency?"; to a monsignor, "How do you do, Monsignor Walton?"

Rabbis are called "Rabbi," with or without their last name: "Rabbi" or "Rabbi Rosen." (See also page 347: "Religious Officials of the Roman Catholic Church"; page 351: "Religious Officials of Protestant Denominations"; page 353: "Religious Officials of the Jewish Faith"; and Chapter 32, page 352: "Greetings for Clergy.")

Rank. In the Catholic Church, following the Pope in rank are cardinal, archbishop, bishop, monsignor, priest, and brother and nun. Some Protestant denominations have bishops, who rank above clergy. In the Jewish religion, rabbis rank above cantors.

Professional and Academic Titles

Physicians and judges are always introduced and addressed by their titles: "Dr. Morales" and "Judge Stone." When addressing a judge officially, use "Your Honor."

A Dr. title that indicates a man or a woman has received a doctorate in history, philosophy, literature, or another discipline is generally used professionally, though it is up to the individual whether to do so. The use of the title also depends on what is customary within the field. For example, though attorneys have doctorates, they do not use the title Dr.—but they often choose to place the initials "J.D." ("juris doctor") after their names.

If you're unsure how to address someone with a doctorate, follow this general rule of thumb: It's better to Dr. a person who would rather be referred to as Mr. (Mrs., Miss, or Ms.) than to do the reverse.

Military Titles

In the armed forces, the various grades of colonels, generals, and admirals are spoken to simply as Colonel, General, or Admiral; their surnames can be added, but during a prolonged conversation the title alone is the simpler option. (For the use of military titles in letters, see Chapter 17, page 240: "What About Titles?")

> ➤ In the Army and Air Force, noncommissioned officers are also addressed officially by their titles, although they may also use "Mr." or "Ms." socially. Warrant officers are called "Mr." or "Ms," both officially and socially.

> ➤ Naval officers who rank from lieutenant commander up are called "Commander." Officers below that rank are called "Mr." in conversation but are introduced and referred to by their titles.

> ➤ Chaplains in any branch of the service are called by their rank—"Colonel Smart"—although informally they are addressed as "Chaplain," "Father," or "Rabbi."

> ➤ Doctors in the service are generally called by their rank ("Major Hollingsworth"), although they may be called "Dr." socially when they are junior officers. Officially, they are addressed by their Army or Navy titles for as long as they remain in the service.

Members of the regular armed services retain their titles after retiring. However, it is poor taste for reserve officers who served for only a short time—or those who held temporary commissions during a war—to continue calling themselves "Captain," "Major," or "Colonel." They do, however, use the titles if they resume an active status in a reserve unit or the National Guard. In this case, the initials of their service always follow the name: "Colonel Victor Bacovich, U.S.A.R." (or "N.G.," "U.S.N.R.," or "U.S.M.C.R."). Reserve officers who remain in the service and retire with pay after twenty or more years are, like members of the regular service, entitled to use their military titles.

Rank. In the Armed Services, the Department of Defense is represented in the Cabinet by the Secretary of Defense, who ranks third among the Cabinet members. The heads of the military departments of the Department of Defense—the Secretary of the Army, the Secretary of the Navy, and the Secretary of the Air Force—do not have Cabinet rank.

The rank of deputies and assistants is as follows:

The social title of students attending any of the five United States military academies is "Mr." or "Miss" ["Ms."], since they are not permitted to be married. But the official title for both male and female students varies by branch of service.

All students at the U.S. Military Academy (West Point), the U.S. Air Force Academy, and the U.S. Coast Guard Academy are officially called "Cadet." Those at the U.S. Naval Academy and the U.S. Merchant Marine Academy are officially called "Midshipman."

➤ A Deputy Secretary of Defense is equal in rank to an Under Secretary of the Executive Departments, examples of which are the Departments of Commerce and Agriculture.

➤ Under Secretaries and Assistant Secretaries of the three military departments rank below the Under Secretaries and Assistant Secretaries of the Executive Departments.

➤ Assistant Secretaries of Defense rank third among Assistant Secretaries of the Executive Departments.

Chiefs of Staff. The Chairman of the Joint Chiefs of Staff takes precedence over all other officers of the Armed Services. The Chiefs of Staff of the Army and the Air Force, the Chief of Naval Operations, and the Commandant of the Marine Corps rank themselves according to the date of their respective appointments and are followed by the Commandant of the U.S. Coast Guard.

Representatives of Other Nations

Because customs vary greatly from country to country, no rules of official protocol apply across the board in the nations of the world, which number close to two hundred. However, help is at hand before you leave for foreign shores. The three main sources of information are the Washington, D.C., embassy for your country of destination, the consulate in the major city nearest you, and the mission to the United Nations in New York. All are able and willing to provide information to facilitate your communication and dealings with people in their homelands.

Here are a few guidelines for any American social or business travelers who have been invited to an official reception or ceremony and for hosts or hostesses who will be entertaining dignitaries overseas:

➤ Professionals from other countries are often given titles that, out of courtesy, should be used by the American traveler. In Italy, for example, a man who has completed university and earned a degree is called "*Dottore*" ("Doctor"), and a woman, "*Dottoressa*," out of respect for the person's academic achievement.

[335]

Likewise, a male German corporate president is called "*Herr Direktor*" out of respect for his position. On the other hand, a French lawyer would be addressed formally as "*Monsieur l'Avocat*," which literally means "Mr. Lawyer." It is only polite to respect the customary titles in other countries—certainly, at least, until bonds of friendship are formed and more personal forms of address may be used. (See also Chapter 45, page 794: "Adjusting Your Cultural Lens.")

➢ European heads of state, ambassadors, cabinet officers—and in some countries, high-ranking members of the clergy—may be referred to as "His Excellency"; they may be called "Your Excellency" in conversation. In correspondence, they would be addressed as "His Excellency, Giancarlo DiBeradino, Ambassador of the Republic of Italy," or "His Excellency, Ichiro Kawamura, Ambassador of Japan."

➢ A duke and duchess are called either "Duke" and "Duchess" or "Your Grace" in conversation—not, for example, "Duke Charles" or "Duchess of Kent."

➢ A prince or princess is called "Prince" and "Princess" in conversation.

➢ Countries that were formerly monarchies still refer to their royalty with the titles that were once held. A Russian princess, for example, although not recognized by her government as such, is still called "Princess" out of courtesy and respect.

➢ The king or queen of most Western European countries is addressed as "Your Majesty" and is referred to as "His [Her] Majesty."

➢ A prince consort to the queen is referred to as "His Royal Highness" and is addressed as "Your Royal Highness."

Official Forms of Address

AT ONE TIME OR ANOTHER, nearly every one of us either meets or has to write a letter to someone officially—a senator or a judge, or perhaps a clergyman or professor—and the last thing we want to do is address the person improperly. The pages that follow list the proper form of address in both business and social situations, in correspondence and on place cards, and in introductions and conversation. Should the occasion arise when you need to address an official overseas, a telephone call to that country's embassy or its mission to the United Nations will provide you with the correct information.

The President

Address

Business
The President
The White House
1600 Pennsylvania Avenue
Washington, D.C. 20500

Social
> The President and Mrs. [Mr.] Anderson
> The White House
> 1600 Pennsylvania Avenue
> Washington, D.C. 20500

Correspondence

Salutation
> Dear Mr. [Madam] President:

Complimentary close
> Most respectfully, *or* Very truly yours,

Introductions

Formal
> The President *or* The President of the United States

Social and in conversation
> Mr. [Madam] President *or, in a prolonged conversation,* Sir [Madam]★

Place Card
> The President

The Vice President

Address

Business
> The Vice President
> Old Executive Office Building
> Washington, D.C. 20510

Social
> The Vice President and Mrs. [Mr.] Adams
> [home address]

Correspondence

Salutation
> Dear Mr. [Madam] Vice President:

Complimentary close
> Very truly yours, *or* Respectfully yours,

Introductions

Formal
> The Vice President *or* The Vice President of the United States

---

★A woman does not use *sir* when speaking to a man, nor does a man use *madam* or *ma'am* when speaking to a woman. Where indicated, a man may use *sir* in place of the title or name when speaking with a male officeholder in any prolonged conversation.

Social and in conversation
Mr. [Madam] Vice President *or, in a prolonged conversation,* Sir [Madam]★

Place Card
The Vice President

The Chief Justice of the United States

Address
Business
The Chief Justice of the United States
The Supreme Court
One First Street, N.E.
Washington, D.C. 20543
Social
The Chief Justice and Mrs. [Mr.] Broadstreet
[home address]

Correspondence
Salutation
Dear Mr. [Madam] Chief Justice:
Complimentary close
Very truly yours, *or* Sincerely yours,

Introductions
Formal
The Chief Justice
Social and in conversation
Chief Justice *or* Sir [Madam]★

Place Card
The Chief Justice

Associate Justice, Supreme Court

Address
Business
Justice Smith
The Supreme Court
Washington, D.C. 20543

★A woman does not use *sir* when speaking to a man, nor does a man use *madam* or *ma'am* when speaking to a woman. Where indicated, a man may use *sir* in place of the title or name when speaking with a male officeholder in any prolonged conversation.

Social
  Justice Smith and Mrs. [Mr.] Smith
  [home address]

Correspondence

Salutation
  Dear Mr. [Madam] Justice: *or* Dear Justice Smith:
Complimentary close
  Sincerely yours,

Introductions

Formal
  Justice Smith
Social and in conversation
  Justice Smith *or* Sir [Madam]★

Cabinet Members

Address

Business
  The Honorable Jefferson Jones [Margaret Jones]
  The Secretary of State
  Washington, D.C. 20240
Social
  The Honorable Jefferson Jones [Margaret Jones]
  The Secretary of State and Mrs. [Mr.] Jones
  [home address]

Correspondence

Salutation
  Dear Mr. [Madam] Secretary:
Complimentary close
  Sincerely yours,

Introductions

Formal
  The Secretary of State *or* Mr. [Mrs. *or* Miss *or* Ms.] Jones
Social and in conversation
  Mr. [Madam] Secretary

Place Card

  The Secretary of State *or, if the only department secretary present,* The Secretary

★A woman does not use *sir* when speaking to a man, nor does a man use *madam* or *ma'am* when speaking to a woman. Where indicated, a man may use *sir* in place of the title or name when speaking with a male officeholder in any prolonged conversation.

The Attorney General

Address

Business

The Honorable Edwin [Edwina] Barnard
The Attorney General of the United States
The Department of Justice
Washington, D.C. 20503

Social

Man: The Honorable and Mrs. Edwin Barnard
[home address]
Woman: The Honorable Edwina Barnard and Mr. Samuel Barnard
[home address]

Correspondence

Salutation

Dear Mr. [Madam] Attorney General:

Complimentary close

Sincerely yours,

Introductions

Formal

The Attorney General, Edwin Barnard [Edwina Barnard]

Social and in conversation

Mr. [Madam] Attorney General *or* Sir [Ma'am]★

Place Card

The Attorney General

Former President

Address

Business

The Honorable Andrew Butler
[office address]

Social

The Honorable Andrew Butler and Mrs. Butler
[home address]

Correspondence

Salutation

Dear Mr. Butler:

★A woman does not use *sir* when speaking to a man, nor does a man use *madam* or *ma'am* when speaking to a woman. Where indicated, a man may use *sir* in place of the title or name when speaking with a male officeholder in any prolonged conversation.

Complimentary close
    Sincerely yours,

Introductions

Formal
    The Honorable Andrew Butler, former President of the United States *or*
        Former President Butler
Social and in conversation
    Mr. Butler *or* Sir

Place Card

    Mr. Butler

United States Senator

Address

Business
    The Honorable Stephen [Stephanie] Lazarus
    United States Senate, Washington, D.C. 20510
Social
    The Honorable Steven [Stephanie] Lazarus and Mrs. [Mr.] Lazarus
    [home address]

Correspondence

Salutation
    Dear Senator Lazarus:
Complimentary close
    Sincerely yours,

Introductions

Formal
    Senator Lazarus of [name of state represented]
Social and in conversation
    Senator *or* Senator Lazarus *or* Sir [Ma'am]★

Place Card

    Senator Lazarus

★A woman does not use *sir* when speaking to a man, nor does a man use *madam* or *ma'am* when speaking to a woman. Where indicated, a man may use *sir* in place of the title or name when speaking with a male officeholder in any prolonged conversation.

The Speaker of the House of Representatives

Address

Business
>The Honorable Phillip [Paula] Bronson
>The Speaker of the House of Representatives
>Washington, D.C. 20515

Social
>The Speaker and Mrs. [Mr.] Bronson
>[home address]

Correspondence

Salutation
>Dear Mr. [Madam] Speaker:

Complimentary close
>Sincerely yours,

Introductions

Formal
>The Speaker of the House of Representatives *or* Mr. [Ms.] Speaker

Social and in conversation
>Mr. [Madam] Speaker *or* Sir [Ma'am]★

Place Card

>The Speaker of the House of Representatives

Member of the House of Representatives

Address

Business
>The Honorable Ronald [Rhonda] Gilpin
>United States House of Representatives
>House Office Building
>Washington, D.C. 20515

Social
>*Man:*
>>The Honorable Ronald Gilpin and Mrs. Ronald Gilpin
>>[home address]

>*Woman:*
>>The Honorable Rhonda Gilpin and Mr. Ronald Gilpin
>>[home address]

★A woman does not use *sir* when speaking to a man, nor does a man use *madam* or *ma'am* when speaking to a woman. Where indicated, a man may use *sir* in place of the title or name when speaking with a male officeholder in any prolonged conversation.

Correspondence

Salutation

Dear Mr. [Mrs. *or* Miss *or* Ms.] Gilpin:

Complimentary close

Sincerely yours,

Introductions

Formal

Representative Gilpin of [state represented]

Social and in conversation

Mr. [Mrs. *or* Miss *or* Ms.] Gilpin *or* Sir [Ma'am]★

Place Card

Representative Gilpin

Ambassador of the United States

Address

Business

The Honorable Peter Franklin
The Ambassador of the United States
American Embassy
[foreign city, foreign nation]

Social

Man:

The Honorable Peter Franklin and Mrs. Franklin
[home address]

Woman:

The Honorable Jean Franklin and Mr. Peter Franklin
[home address]

Correspondence

Salutation

Dear Mr. [Madam] Ambassador:

Complimentary close

Sincerely yours,

Introductions

Formal

The American Ambassador *or* Our Ambassador to [foreign nation], Mr. [Mrs. *or* Miss *or* Ms.] Franklin

★A woman does not use *sir* when speaking to a man, nor does a man use *madam* or *ma'am* when speaking to a woman. Where indicated, a man may use *sir* in place of the title or name when speaking with a male officeholder in any prolonged conversation.

Social and in conversation

> Mr. [Madam] Ambassador *or* Mr. [or Mrs. *or* Miss or Ms.] Franklin *or* Sir [Ma'am]★

Place Card

> The Ambassador of the United States *or, if more than one ambassador is present,* the Ambassador of the United States to [foreign nation]

United States Ambassador to the United Nations

Address

Business

> The Honorable Sherwin [Sheila] Fryer
> United States Representative to the United Nations
> United Nations Plaza
> New York, NY 10017

Social

> *Man:*
>> The Honorable and Mrs. Sherwin Fryer
>> [home address]
>
> *Woman:*
>> The Honorable Sheila Fryer and Mr. Sherwin Fryer
>> [home address]

Correspondence

Salutation

> Dear Mr. [Madam] Ambassador:

Complimentary close

> Sincerely yours,

Introductions

Formal

> The United States Ambassador to the United Nations, Sherwin [Sheila] Fryer

Social and in conversation

> Mr. [Madam] Ambassador *or* Sir [Ma'am]★

Place Card

> Ambassador Fryer

★A woman does not use *sir* when speaking to a man, nor does a man use *madam* or *ma'am* when speaking to a woman. Where indicated, a man may use *sir* in place of the title or name when speaking with a male officeholder in any prolonged conversation.

Governor of a State

Address

Business
> The Honorable Christopher [Christine] Williams
> Governor of [state]
> [office address]

Social
> The Honorable Governor of [state] and Mrs. [Mr.] Williams
> [home address]

Correspondence

Salutation
> Dear Governor Williams:

Complimentary close
> Sincerely yours,

Introductions

Formal
> Governor Williams of [state]

Social and in conversation
> Governor Williams *or* Governor *or* Sir [Ma'am]★

Place Card
> Governor Williams

Mayor

Address

Business
> The Honorable Thomas [Marianne] Massengill
> Mayor of Springfield
> [office address]

Social
> *Man:*
>> The Honorable Mr. Massengill and Mrs. Massengill
>> [home address]
>
> *Woman:*
>> The Honorable Marianne Massengill and Mr. Thomas Massengill
>> [home address]

★A woman does not use *sir* when speaking to a man, nor does a man use *madam* or *ma'am* when speaking to a woman. Where indicated, a man may use *sir* in place of the title or name when speaking with a male officeholder in any prolonged conversation.

Correspondence

Salutation
Dear Mayor Massengill: *or* Dear Mr. [Madam] Mayor:
Complimentary close
Sincerely yours,

Introductions

Formal
Mayor Massengill *or* His [Her] Honor, the Mayor
Social and in conversation
Mr. [Madam] Mayor *or* Mayor Massengill *or* Sir [Madam]★

Place Card

Mayor Massengill

Federal Judge

Address

Business
The Honorable Eugene [Elinor] Hinkle
Justice of [name of court; if district court, give district]
[office address]
Social
  Man:
    The Honorable Eugene Hinkle and Mrs. Hinkle
    [home address]
  Woman:
    The Honorable Elinor and Mr. Eugene Hinkle
    [home address]

Correspondence

Salutation
Dear Judge Hinkle:
Complimentary close
Sincerely yours,

Introductions

Formal
Justice Hinkle *or* Justice Eugene [Elinor] Hinkle
Social and in conversation
Mr. [Madam] Justice *or* Judge Hinkle *or* Sir [Madam]★

★A woman does not use *sir* when speaking to a man, nor does a man use *madam* or *ma'am* when speaking to a woman. Where indicated, a man may use *sir* in place of the title or name when speaking with a male officeholder in any prolonged conversation.

Place Cards
   Mr. [Madam] Justice Hinkle

Ambassadors of Foreign Nations

Ambassador of a Foreign Nation

Address

Business
   His [Her] Excellency Marco [Marina] Franciosa
   The Ambassador of [foreign nation]
Social
   His [Her] Excellency the Ambassador of [foreign nation] and Mrs. [Mr.]
      Franciosa
   [home address]

Correspondence

Salutation
   Excellency *or* Dear Mr. [Madam] Ambassador:
Complimentary close
   Sincerely yours,

Introductions

Formal
   The Ambassador of [foreign nation]
Social and in conversation
   Mr. [Madam] Ambassador *or* Excellency *or* Sir [Madam]★

Place Card
   The Ambassador of [foreign nation]

Religious Officials of the Roman Catholic Church

The Pope

Address

Business
   His Holiness, Pope Pius X *or* His Holiness the Pope
   Vatican City
   00187 Rome, Italy

★A woman does not use *sir* when speaking to a man, nor does a man use *madam* or *Ma'am* when speaking to a woman. Where indicated, a man may use *sir* in place of the title or name when speaking with a male officeholder in any prolonged conversation.

Social
   [same as business]

Correspondence
Salutation
   Your Holiness: *or* Most Holy Father:
Complimentary close
   Your most humble servant, *or* Respectfully yours,

Introductions
Formal
   His Holiness the Pope
Social and in conversation
   Your Holiness *or* Most Holy Father

Place Card
   His Holiness, the Pope

Cardinal

Address
Business
   His Eminence, John, Cardinal Reilly, Archbishop of New York
   [office address]
Social
   [same as business]

Correspondence
Salutation
   Your Eminence: *or* Dear Cardinal Reilly:
Complimentary close
   Respectfully,

Introductions
Formal
   His Eminence, Cardinal Reilly
Social and in conversation
   Your Eminence *or* Cardinal Reilly

Place Card
   His Eminence, John, Cardinal Reilly

Archbishop and Bishop

Address

Business
> The Most Reverend Anthony Loren, D.D., Archbishop [Bishop] of Chicago
> [office address]

Social
> [same as business]

Correspondence

Salutation
> Your Excellency: *or* Most Reverend Sir: *or* Dear Archbishop [Bishop] Loren:

Complimentary close
> Your obedient servant, *or* Respectfully,

Introductions

Formal
> His Excellency, Archbishop [Bishop] Loren

Social and in conversation
> Your Excellency or Archbishop [Bishop] Loren

Place Card
> Archbishop [Bishop] Loren

Monsignor

Address

Business
> The Right Reverend Monsignor Carter
> [address of the church]

Social
> [same as business]

Correspondence

Salutation
> Right Reverend Monsignor: *or* Dear Monsignor Carter:

Complimentary close
> Yours faithfully, *or* Respectfully,

Introductions

Formal
> Monsignor Carter

Social and in conversation
> Monsignor *or* Monsignor Carter

Place Card
> The Right Reverend Monsignor Carter *or* Monsignor Carter

Priest

Address
Business
> The Reverend Evan Dowd [plus initials of his order]
> [church address]

Social
> [same as business]

Correspondence
Salutation
> Reverend Father: *or* Dear Father Dowd:

Complimentary close
> Yours faithfully, *or* Respectfully,

Introductions
Formal
> Father Dowd

Social and in conversation
> Father Dowd *or* Father

Place Card
> Father Dowd

Brother

Address
Business
> Brother David [plus initials of his order]
> [address]

Social
> [same as business]

Correspondence
Salutation
> Dear Brother: *or* Dear Brother David:

Complimentary close
> Faithfully, *or* Respectfully,

Introductions

Formal
  Brother David
Social and in conversation
  Brother David *or* Brother

Place Card

  Brother David

Nun

Address

Business
  Sister Mary *or* Sister Maeve Donohue [plus initials of her order]
  [address]
Social
  [same as business]

Correspondence

Salutation
  Dear Sister: *or* Dear Sister Maeve:
Complimentary close
  Faithfully yours,

Introductions

Formal
  Sister Maeve
Social and in conversation
  Sister Mary *or* Sister

Place Card

  Sister Maeve

Note: A bishop and priest in the **Eastern Orthodox** religion are addressed in the same manner as are a Roman Catholic bishop and priest.

Religious Officials of Protestant Denominations

Bishop

Address

Business
  The Right Reverend Theodore Norris, D.D., L.L.D., Bishop of Washington
    Office
  [office address]

Social

    The Right Reverend Dr. and Mrs. Theodore Norris
    [home address]

Correspondence

Salutation

    Dear Bishop Norris:

Complimentary close

    Respectfully yours, *or* Sincerely yours,

Introductions

Formal

    The Right Reverend Theodore Norris, the Bishop of [name of city, district,
        denomination]

Social and in conversation

    Bishop Norris

Place Card

    The Right Reverend Theodore Norris *or* Bishop Norris

Clergyman or Clergywoman

Address

Business

    The Reverend James Heifner (, D.D., L.L.D. [if held])
    [church address]
    The Reverend Joanne McLin (, D.D., L.L.D. [if held])
    [church address]

Social

    The Reverend Dr. and Mrs. James Heifner
    [home address]
    The Reverend Dr. Joanne McLin and Mr. Angus McLin
    [home address]

Correspondence

Salutation

    Dear Dr. Heifner: [*or* Dear Dr. McLin]: *or* Mr., Mrs., Ms., Pastor, Rector *if no
    doctorate held*

Complimentary close

    Very truly yours,

Introductions
Formal
> Dr. Heifner *or* The Reverend Dr. James Heifner [*if doctorate held; otherwise,* Mr., (Ms., Miss, Mrs.) *or* The Reverend . . .]

Social and in conversation
> Dr. [Mr., Mrs., Ms., Miss, Pastor, Reverend] Heifner

Place Cards
> Dr. Heifner *or* Dr. McLin [Mr., Mrs., Ms., Pastor, Reverend, *if no doctorate held*]

Religious Officials of the Jewish Faith

Rabbi

Address
Business
> Rabbi [*or, if he holds a doctorate,* Rabbi Michael Lichtenstein, D.D.]
> [address of synagogue or temple]

Social
> Rabbi [or Dr.] and Mrs. Michael Lichtenstein
> [home address]

Correspondence
Salutation
> Dear Rabbi [or Dr.] Lichtenstein: *or* Dear Rabbi:

Complimentary close
> Very truly yours, *or* Sincerely yours,

Introductions
Formal
> Rabbi [or Dr.] Michael Lichtenstein

Social and in conversation
> Rabbi [or Dr.] Lichtenstein *or* Rabbi

Place Card
> Rabbi Lichtenstein [*or, if he holds a doctorate,* Dr. Lichtenstein]

Cantor

Address
Business
> Cantor David Schwartz
> [address of synagogue]

Cantor Claire Liebowitz
[address of synagogue]
Social
Cantor and Mrs. David Schwartz
[home address]
Cantor Claire Liebowitz and Mr. Liebowitz
[home address]

Correspondence
Salutation
Dear Cantor Schwartz:
Complimentary close
Sincerely yours,

Introductions
Formal
Cantor Schwartz
Social and in conversation
Cantor Schwartz

Place Card
Cantor Schwartz

Other Professionals

Attorney

Address
Business
Joseph [Jessica] Gelineau, Esq. [*or* J.D., *if held*]
[office address]
Social
Man:
Mr. and Mrs. Joseph Gelineau
[home address]
Woman (assuming husband's last name):
Mr. and Mrs. Joseph Gelineau
[home address]
Woman (not assuming husband's last name):
Ms. Jessica Bennett and Mr. Joseph Gelineau
[home address]

Correspondence

Salutation
> Dear Mr. [Mrs. *or* Miss *or* Ms.] Gelineau:

Complimentary close
> Sincerely yours,

Introductions

Formal
> Mr. [Mrs. *or* Miss *or* Ms.] Joseph [Jessica] Gelineau

Social and in conversation
> Mr. [Mrs. *or* Miss *or* Ms.] Gelineau

Place Cards

> Mr. [Mrs. *or* Miss *or* Ms.] Gelineau

University Professor

Address

Business
> Professor *or* Mr. [Mrs. *or* Miss *or* Ms.] *or, if he or she holds a doctorate,* Dr. Alec [Aileen] Shannon
> [office address]

Social
> *Man:*
> > Professor *or* Mr. *or, if he holds a doctorate,* Dr. and Mrs. Alec Shannon
> > [home address]

> *Woman:*
> > Mr. and Mrs. Alec Shannon *or* Mr. Alec Shannon and Dr. Aileen Shannon *or* Mr. Alec and Professor Aileen Shannon [home address]

Correspondence

Salutation
> Dear Professor: *or* Mr. [Mrs. *or* Miss *or* Ms.] *or* Dr. Shannon:

Complimentary close
> Sincerely yours, *or* Sincerely,

Introductions

Formal
> Professor *or* Dr. Shannon

Social and in conversation
> Professor *or* Dr. Shannon [within the university] *or* Mr. [Mrs. *or* Miss *or* Ms.] Shannon [elsewhere, unless always known as Dr.]

Place Card

> Dr. [Mr. *or* Mrs. *or* Miss *or* Ms.] *or* Professor Shannon

Physician

Address

Business
Donald [Donna] Wasserstein, M.D.
[office address]

Social

Man:
Dr. and Mrs. Donald Wasserstein
[home address]

Woman:
Mr. and Mrs. Donald Wasserstein *or, if she keeps the title socially,* Mr. Donald
Wasserstein and Dr. Donna Wasserstein
[home address]

Correspondence

Salutation
Dear Dr. Wasserstein:

Complimentary close
Sincerely yours, *or* Sincerely,

Introductions

Formal
Dr. Wasserstein

Social and in conversation
Dr. Wasserstein

Place Card
Dr. Wasserstein

Dentist

Address

Business
Harry [Harriet] Steele, D.D.S.
[office address]

Social

Man:
Dr. and Mrs. Harry Steele
[home address]

Woman:
Mr. and Mrs. Harry Steele *or, if she keeps the title socially,* Mr. Harry Steele and
Dr. Harriet Steele
[home address]

Correspondence

Salutation
Dear Dr. Steele:
Complimentary close
Sincerely yours, *or* Sincerely,

Introductions

Formal
Dr. Steele
Social and in conversation
Dr. Steele

Place Card

Dr. Steele

Canadian Government Officials

The Governor General

Address

Business
His [Her] Excellency the Right Honourable Charles [Regine] Arnott
Government House
Ottawa, Ontario K1A 0A1
Social
Their Excellencies the Governor General and Mrs. [*or* Mr. *or* Dr.] Arnott

Correspondence

Business
  Salutation
    Sir [Madam]:
  Complimentary close
    Yours very truly,
Social
  Salutation
    Dear Governor General: *or* My Dear Governor General:
  Complimentary close
    Yours sincerely,

Introductions

Formal
The Governor General of Canada
Social and in conversation
Your Excellency

Place Card

The Governor General

The Prime Minister

Address

Business

The Right Honourable Laurence [Laura] McCarver, P.C., M.P.
Prime Minister of Canada
Prime Minister's Office
Ottawa, Ontario K1A 0A2

Social

Man:

The Prime Minister and Mrs. Laurence McCarver
[home address]

Woman:

The Prime Minister and Mr. Laurence McCarver
[home address]

Correspondence

Business

Salutation

Dear Sir [Madam]: *or* Dear Mr. [Madam] Prime Minister: *or* Dear Prime Minister:

Complimentary close

Yours very truly,

Social

Salutation

Dear Prime Minister: *or* My Dear Prime Minister:

Complimentary close

Yours sincerely,

Introductions

Formal

The Prime Minister *or* The Prime Minister of Canada

Social and in conversation

Mr. [Madam] Prime Minister *or* Sir [Madam]★

Place Cards

The Prime Minister

★A woman does not use *sir* when speaking to a man, nor does a man use *madam* or *ma'am* when speaking to a woman. Where indicated, a man may use *sir* in place of the title or name when speaking with a male officeholder in any prolonged conversation.

Members of the Cabinet

Address

Business

The Honourable Cyril [Sybille] Moore, P.C.,
Minister of [function]
House of Commons, Parliament Buildings
Ottawa, Ontario K1A 0A6

Social

Man:

The Honourable Cyril Moore and Mrs. Moore
[home address]

Woman:

The Honourable Sybille Moore and Mr. Cyril Moore
[home address]

Correspondence

Business

Salutation

Dear Sir [Madam]:

Complimentary close

Yours very truly,

Social

Salutation

Dear Mr. [Mrs. *or* Miss *or* Ms.] Moore:

Complimentary close

Yours sincerely,

Introductions

Formal

The Honourable Cyril [Sybille] Moore, Minister of [function]

Social and in conversation

Mr. [Madam] Minister *or* Mr. [Mrs. *or* Miss *or* Ms.] Moore *or* Sir [Madam]★

Place Card

The Minister of [function]

Senator

Address

Business

The Honourable Terence [Tania] Bell, Senator

★A woman does not use *sir* when speaking to a man, nor does a man use *madam* or *ma'am* when speaking to a woman. Where indicated, a man may use *sir* in place of the title or name when speaking with a male officeholder in any prolonged conversation.

The Senate
Parliament Buildings
Ottawa, Ontario K1A 0A4
In the case of a privy councillor:
Senator the Honourable Terence [Tania] Bell
Social
 Man:
  Senator Terence Bell and Mrs. Bell
  [home address]
 Woman:
  Senator Tania Bell and Mr. Terence Bell
  [home address]

Correspondence

Business
 Salutation
 Dear Sir [Madam]: *or* Senator: *or* My Dear Senator:
Complimentary close
 Yours very truly,
Social
 Salutation
 Dear Senator Bell:
Complimentary close
 Yours sincerely,

Introductions

Formal
 Senator Bell
Social and in conversation
 Senator *or* Senator Bell

Place Card
 Senator Bell

Chief Justice of Canada

Address

Business
 The Right Honourable Walter [Wendy] Hall, P.C.
 Chief Justice of Canada
 Supreme Court Building
 Ottawa, Ontario K1A 0J1

Social
> *Man:*
>> The Right Honourable Walter Hall and Mrs. Hall
>> [home address]
> *Woman:*
>> The Right Honourable Wendy Hall and Mr. Walter Hall
>> [home address]

Correspondence

Business
> *Salutation*
>> Sir [Madam]: *or* Dear Sir [Madam]: *or* Dear Mr. [Madam] Chief Justice:
> *Complimentary close*
>> Yours very truly,

Social
> *Salutation*
>> Dear Chief Justice Hall:
> *Complimentary close*
>> Yours sincerely,

Introductions

Formal
> The Chief Justice of Canada

Social and in conversation
> Mr. [Madam] Chief Justice *or* Sir [Madam]★

Place Card
> The Chief Justice

Canadian Ambassador (When Addressed by a Canadian Citizen)

Address

Business
> Mr. Raoul [Renée] Robineaux
> Canadian Ambassador to [name of country]
> [office address]

Social
> *Man:*
>> Ambassador and Mrs. Raoul Robineaux
>> [home address]

★A woman does not use *sir* when speaking to a man, nor does a man use *madam* or *ma'am* when speaking to a woman. Where indicated, a man may use *sir* in place of the title or name when speaking with a male officeholder in any prolonged conversation.

Woman:
> Ambassador Renée Robineaux and Mr. Raoul Robineaux
> [home address]

Correspondence

Business
> *Salutation*
>> Dear Sir [Madam]:
> *Complimentary close*
>> Yours very truly,

Social
> *Salutation*
>> Dear Mr. [Mrs. *or* Miss *or* Ms.] Robineaux:
> *Complimentary close*
>> Yours sincerely,

Introductions

Formal
> The Canadian Ambassador *or* Our Ambassador to [foreign nation], Mr. [Mrs. *or* Miss *or* Ms.] Robineaux

Social and in conversation
> Mr. [Madam] Ambassador *or* Mr. [Mrs. *or* Miss *or* Ms.] Robineaux *or* Sir [Madam]★

Place Card

> The Ambassador of Canada *or, if more than one ambassador present,* The Ambassador of Canada to [foreign nation]

Canadian Ambassador (When Addressed by a Non-Canadian Citizen)

Address

Business
> His [Her] Excellency
> [office address]

Social
> *Man:*
>> Ambassador and Mrs. Harrison Settle
>> [home address]
> *Woman:*
>> Ambassador Helene Settle and Mr. Harrison Settle
>> [home address]

★A woman does not use *sir* when speaking to a man, nor does a man use *madam* or *ma'am* when speaking to a woman. Where indicated, a man may use *sir* in place of the title or name when speaking with a male officeholder in any prolonged conversation.

Correspondence

Business

    Salutation

        Your Excellency: *or* Dear Mr. [Madam] Ambassador: *or* Dear Mr. [Mrs. *or* Miss *or* Ms.] Settle:

    Complimentary close

        Yours very truly,

Social

    Salutation

        Dear Mr. [Madam] Ambassador:

    Complimentary close

        Yours sincerely,

Introductions

Formal

    The Canadian Ambassador to [foreign nation], Mr. [Mrs. *or* Miss *or* Ms.] Settle

Social and in conversation

    Mr. [Madam] Ambassador *or* Mr. [Mrs. *or* Miss *or* Ms.] Settle *or* Sir [Madam]

Place Card

    The Ambassador of Canada *or, if more than one ambassador present,* The Ambassador of Canada to [foreign nation]

The Premier of a Province

Address

Business

    The Honourable Jacob [Judith] Alexander, M.N.A.*

        Premier† of the Province of [name]

    [office address]

Social

    Man:

        Premier and Mrs. Jacob Alexander

        [home address]

    Woman:

        Premier Judith Alexander and Mr. Jacob Alexander

        [home address]

*For Ontario, use *M.P.P.*; for Quebec, use *M.N.A.*

†For Quebec, use *Prime Minister.*

Correspondence

Business
  Salutation
    Dear Sir [Madam]: *or* My Dear Premier: *or* Dear Mr. [Mrs. *or* Miss *or* Ms.]
      Alexander:
  Complimentary close
    Yours very truly,
Social
  Salutation
    Dear Mr. [Mrs. *or* Miss *or* Ms.] Alexander:
  Complimentary close
    Yours sincerely,

Introductions

Formal
  The Premier★ of the Province of [name],★ Mr. [Mrs. *or* Miss *or* Ms.] Alexander
Social and in conversation
  Mr. [Madam] Premier *or* Mr. [Mrs. *or* Miss *or* Ms.] Alexander *or* Sir [Madam]

Place Card

  The Premier of the Province of [name]

Members of Canadian Provincial Governments—Executive Council

Address

Business
  The Honourable Ryan [Rita] Cowlishaw, M.N.A.†
  [office address]
Social
  Mr. and Mrs. Ryan Cowlishaw
  [home address]

Correspondence

Business
  Salutation
    Dear Sir [Madam]:
  Complimentary close
    Yours very truly,

★For Quebec, use *Prime Minister.*
†For Ontario, use *M.P.P.*; for Quebec, use *M.N.A.*

Social
> *Salutation*
>> Dear Mr. [Mrs. *or* Miss *or* Ms.] Cowlishaw:
>
> *Complimentary close*
>> Yours sincerely,

Introductions
Formal
> The Minister of [function]

Social and in conversation
> Mr. [Mrs. *or* Miss *or* Ms.] Cowlishaw

Place Card
> The Minister of [function]

Mayor

Address
Business
> His [Her] Worship Charles [Christine] Durrell, Mayor of [City Hall, city, province]
> [office address]

Social
> His [Her] Worship Mayor Charles [Christine] Durrell
> [home address]

Correspondence
Business
> *Salutation*
>> Dear Sir [Madam]: *or* Dear Mr. [Madam] Mayor:
>
> *Complimentary close*
>> Yours very truly,

Social
> *Salutation*
>> Dear Mayor Durrell:
>
> *Complimentary close*
>> Yours sincerely,

Introductions
Formal
> Mayor Durrell, or His [Her] Worship, the Mayor of [city]

Social and in conversation
> Mr. [Madam] Mayor *or* Mayor

Place Card
> The Mayor of [city]

White House Etiquette

ALTHOUGH CUSTOMS VARY somewhat during different administrations, the following details represent the conventional pattern from which each administration adapts its own procedure.

A Formal Invitation to the White House

An invitation to lunch or dinner at the White House is somewhat of a command and automatically cancels almost any other engagement that is not of the utmost importance. The reply must be written by hand within a day of the invitation's arrival. If the recipient is not near Washington, his reply should be sent by express mail or overnight delivery service to ensure prompt arrival.

There are very few acceptable excuses for refusing an invitation to the White House, and the reason must be stated in the note of regret. Unavoidable absence from Washington—because of illness or the recent death of a close relative—was once the only possible excuse, but today "a wedding in the family" or "an unavoidable business trip" reflects a less rigid attitude in society as a whole.

These are the correct forms for replies:

Mr. and Mrs. Virgil Harris
accept with pleasure
the kind invitation of
The President and Mrs. [surname]
for dinner on Thursday, the fifth of February
at eight o'clock

Mr. and Mrs. John Hemphill
regret extremely
that owing to Mr. Hemphill's illness
they will be unable to accept
the kind invitation of
The President and Mrs. [surname]
for dinner on Friday, the third of September

An engraved invitation to an evening at the White House should be taken to mean black tie attire unless white tie is specified on the card. Women wear conservative evening dresses, not pants; to a white tie dinner, they wear long gloves.

All the names of guests expected at the White House are posted with the guards at the gate. You give your name to the guard, present your invitation or admittance card, and wait a few seconds until you are recognized and escorted to the appropriate room.

After the guests arrive, the President and the First Lady enter and speak to each guest and shake hands. Guests, of course, remain standing.

At a formal dinner, the President goes into the dining room first with the highest-ranking woman guest. The First Lady follows with the highest-ranking man.

An Informal Invitation to the White House

Informal invitations to dinner or luncheon at the White House are now issued more frequently than formal invitations. They are sent by letter or may be extended by telephone by the President's or First Lady's secretary. The replies should be sent, in the same form, to whoever issued the invitations. Written acceptances (or regrets, when the reason is valid) are sent on personal stationery, either engraved or plain.

A typical invitation might be worded something like this:

Dear Mrs. Ihms,

Mrs. [surname of President and First Lady] has asked me to invite you to have lunch with her at the White House on Thursday, the thirteenth of May. Luncheon will be at one o'clock.

Yours truly,
Helen Walter
Secretary to Mrs. [surname]

The reply might read:

Dear Ms. Walter,

Will you please thank Mrs. [surname] for her kind invitation and tell her that I shall be delighted to lunch with her at the White House on Thursday, the thirteenth of May. Thank you very much.

Sincerely,
Gay N. Ihms

Meeting the President and First Lady

When you are invited to the White House, you must arrive several minutes before the hour specified, at the very least. It is an unpardonable breach of etiquette not to be standing in the drawing room when the President makes his entry.

The President, followed by the First Lady, enters at the hour set. If the group present is small, the President and First Lady make a tour of the room, shaking hands with each guest. If the occasion is a large reception, they stand in one place; the guests then form a line and pass by in turn to be greeted. Men precede their wives unless the wife is the more prominent one; an aide serves as announcer. Guests are greeted first by the President and then by the First Lady.

If a woman is wearing gloves, she removes the right one before shaking hands with the President. If the President speaks with you, you address him as "Mr. President." In a long conversation, it is proper to occasionally alternate "Mr. President" with "Sir."

Call the wife of the President "Mrs. [surname]" and interact with her as you would with any formal hostess (see Chapter 27, page 481: "Receiving Lines"). After you have left the line, you should not sit down while either the President or the First Lady remains in line.

Business Meetings

Requests to see the President on a business matter are made through one of the presidential aides (the one whose area of responsibility includes the subject you wish to discuss) or through your state senator or representative. Your reason should be a valid one, you should be sure that no one else can solve your problem, and your letter should be stated in such a way that, if possible, the matter can be settled without a personal interview.

If you have a business appointment with the President, it is extremely important to arrive several minutes ahead of the appointed time. You will have been told, no doubt, how much time you are allowed for your meeting, but take less time than that allotted if possible.

If a buzzer should ring when you are in a corridor of the White House, an attendant will ask you to step behind a closed door. The buzzer means that the President or members of his family are leaving or entering; it is a precaution for their safety and privacy.

You will undoubtedly receive a list of instructions for your visit. An example of a custom a man should follow: removing his hat as soon as he reaches the White House portico.

An Audience with the Pope

AN AMERICAN TOURIST VISITING ROME can indeed be granted a group audience with the Pope. Moreover, although there are often hundreds of people in a day who wish an audience, no one with a proper introduction is denied. At the same time, very few people can be granted one of the three types of audiences that are considered to be personal, so group or collective audiences are arranged for the great majority.

Requests by Americans for group and personal audiences alike are cleared by the Pontifica North American College, then sent to the Office of the Master of the Chamber (*l'Uffizio del Maestro di Camera di Sua Santi*), in the Vatican. Mail your request well ahead of your departure date so that you will have your acknowledgment in hand before you go.

On your arrival in Rome, either present your request and the approval you received or mail it to the monsignor in charge, whose name and address can be obtained from the concierge of your hotel (the concierge will also probably be able to give you any other information you may need about the procedure).

Each applicant must fill out a form requesting the kind of audience desired and, at the same time, show his or her credentials; for a Roman Catholic, this may simply be a letter of introduction from his parish priest or a prominent layman. (Non-Catholics as well as Catholics are granted audiences, but their requests must be arranged through prominent Catholic laymen or members of the Catholic clergy.) Also include on the form the length of your stay in Rome, along with your address and telephone number, so that you can be notified of the day and hour of the audience.

The reply—and the invitation, if the answer is favorable—will be sent to you within a few days. Most people receive a general admission ticket, meaning no reserved seat. Others, who are considered important in some respect, often receive a reserved seat in a special section.

The General Audience

General audiences are held at 11:00 AM on Wednesdays at St. Peter's Basilica. During the summer months, they take place at 10:00 AM. People without reserved seats should arrive very early if they want a location with a good view. Choice places are often filled early in the morning.

Everyone rises as the Pope appears, seated on a portable throne called the *Sedia Gestatoria* and carried by eight Swiss Guards. At the end of the aisle, he leaves the portable throne for a fixed one; when he sits down, the people may then be seated. He delivers a short address, and then everyone kneels as he gives his benediction to all those present as well as any articles they have brought to be blessed.

The group rises, and if the Pope has time, he greets each person in the special area. The audience is over when he mounts his portable throne and is carried out.

For general audiences, it is required only that everyone be dressed in a sober and suitable manner. Women must have their hair covered and must wear black or dark everyday dresses with necklines that are not too low and skirts that are not too short. They may not have bare arms or legs, so they should avoid sleeveless blouses and should wear stockings under a skirt. Dress pants are permitted. Men in the general audience wear business suits and shirts and ties. In the reserved section, some men will be seen in formal daytime wear, and women in long-sleeved black dresses and mantillas, but this is no longer obligatory.

Other Audiences

The "private" audience is reserved for cardinals, heads of state, ambassadors, or others in important positions. Another type, the "special" audience, is granted to people of slightly lower rank or to those who have an important subject to present to the Pope. The third type, the *baciomano*, is the only special audience to which laypeople are invited.

At the *baciomano* each visitor comes into the personal presence of the Pope, kisses his ring, and exchanges a few words with him, addressing him as "Your Holiness." Visitors stand in a single row around the room until the Pope enters. They then kneel and do not stand again until he leaves the audience chamber or makes a sign for them to rise. The Pope passes from one visitor to another, extending his hand so that all may kiss his ring. He also may ask a question and exchange a few words with each. As in the general audience, visitors customarily take with them one or more rosaries or other small religious objects, which are also considered to be blessed when the visitor receives the papal blessing.

The rules of dress are not so strict as they once were, but even now many men wear evening dress with tails or a morning coat for a private or special audience, and women wear long-sleeved, high-necked black dresses and veils or mantillas over their hair. Male visitors can also be admitted if they wear very dark blue or gray business suits. No one may wear any but the most functional jewelry—wedding rings and watches.

Non-Catholics at Audiences

At a general audience, every person present—including non-Catholics—must kneel, rise, and sit at the prescribed time. Non-Catholics, if they do not ordinarily do so, need not make the sign of the cross.

At the *baciomano*, non-Catholics are told on their arrival the proper manner of kneeling and kissing the Pope's ring. If they object to these requirements on the grounds of their own religion, there may be some slight modification. But since the procedures are strictly followed, these guests would be wiser to forgo *baciomano* than to make an issue.

The Flag of the United States

THE PREMIER SYMBOL OF AMERICAN patriotism, the flag of the United States has become even more revered in the last four years, and the rules and customs governing the flag's handling and display are something that all citizens of the United States can easily learn.

Displaying the Flag

American flags are out in force on holidays—especially the Fourth of July, Flag Day (June 14), and Memorial Day (see below)—but it is perfectly fine to fly the flag every day of the year. Indeed, there has been a passionate renewal of national spirit in the United States, and with it a greater interest in the flag.

The traditional time for flying the flag is between sunrise and sunset, but it may also be flown at night as part of a patriotic display. The flag is not customarily flown in inclement weather unless its display is required on a special occasion.

Following are basic rules for displaying the flag:

On Memorial Day. The flag is displayed at half-staff until noon and at full staff thereafter until sunset.

On an angled staff. When the flag is displayed from a staff projecting horizontally or at an angle from a windowsill, balcony, or the front of a building, the union (the name for the blue field of stars) should go all the way to the peak of the staff. The exception to this rule is when the flag is flown at half-mast.

U.S. flag on an angled staff *U.S. flag suspended over a street*

Over a street. When displayed over the middle of a street, the flag is suspended vertically with the union to the north on an east–west street; on a north–south street, the union is to the east.

Over a sidewalk. When the flag is suspended over a sidewalk from a rope extending from house to a pole at the edge of the sidewalk, the flag is hoisted union first. (See also page 374: "Raising and Lowering the Flag.")

In a house of worship. When the flag is used on the chancel or platform in a church, synagogue, or mosque, it should be placed on a staff on the clergyperson's right (any other flags are on the left). When displayed in the seating area in the place of worship, the flag should be on the congregation's right as they face the front.

On caskets. When used to cover a casket, the flag is placed so that the union is at the head and over the left shoulder. The flag should not be lowered into the grave or allowed to touch the ground.

On cars and boats. On a car, the flag is flown on a small staff affixed to the end of the front bumper, on the right looking forward and within the line of the fender. The staff should be tall enough so that the flag clears the car hood. Note: *A flag that has become soiled or tattered should be promptly removed and replaced.*

➤ On a powerboat, the flag is flown from 8:00 AM until sunset. It flies from a staff at the stern when the boat is anchored. If the boat has a gaff, the flag may be flown from the gaff when the boat is plying the waters.

➤ On a sailboat, the flag is flown from the stern in the harbor or under power. It is permissible for the flag to be flown while the boat is under sail.

When mounted. When the flag is displayed but not flown from a staff, it should be flat (not tucked or draped), whether indoors or out.

➤ When displayed horizontally or vertically and mounted flat against a clear-glass window, the union should be to the left of the observer in the street.

➤ When displayed vertically or horizontally against a wall, the union should be uppermost and to the observer's left.

Displaying the U.S. flag across a wall

In Displays With Other Flags

The American flag is often grouped with other flags in various ways, and rules apply in these cases as well.

Crossed staffs. When displayed with another flag from crossed staffs, the American flag should be on the left when viewed from the front, and its staff should be in front of the staff of the other flag.

Displaying flags crossed

On a flagpole with other flags. When flags of states or cities or pennants of societies are flown on the same flagpole with the flag of the United States, the latter should always be at the peak.

Next to other staffs. When flown on a staff adjacent to staffs flying other flags, the national flag should be hoisted first and lowered last. (See also page 374: "Raising and Lowering the Flag.")

In a procession. When carried in a procession or parade with another flag or flags, the American flag should either be on the marching right, or when there is a line of other flags, in front of the center of that line.

∼ How Not to Use the Flag ∼

There are certain clear-cut situations in which the flag itself (not a smaller reproduction, such as a pin) should never be used—as an article of clothing, as a portion of a costume, or in any way that is disrespectful. Designs using the flag's blue union and red and white stripes are exempt.

➢ Do not use the flag as a covering for a statue or monument that is to be unveiled.

➢ A federal statute decrees that a trademark cannot claim protection in "the flag . . . coat of arms, or other insignia of the United States or any symbol of the United States."

➢ The flag should never be hung upside down except as a signal of distress.

In a large grouping. When a number of flags of U.S. states or cities are grouped and displayed from staffs, the American flag should be at the center and at the highest point of the group.

If the flags of two or more nations are displayed, they should be flown from separate staffs of the same height, and the flags should be of approximately equal size. International usage forbids the display of the flag of one nation above that of another nation in times of peace.

Displaying a number of flags grouped together

Raising and Lowering the Flag

The flag should be raised briskly and lowered slowly and solemnly. When flown at half-mast, the flag should be hoisted to the peak for a moment and then lowered to the half-mast position; the flag should again be raised to the peak before being lowered for the day. (See also page 371: "Over a sidewalk," and page 373: "Next to other staffs.")

Care of the Flag

The U.S. flag should be carefully protected in storage and in use so that it will not be damaged. Every precaution should be taken to prevent it from becoming soiled, tattered, or torn. It should also not be permitted to touch the ground or water or a floor.

- When handling the flag, do not let it brush against other objects.
- If the flag gets wet, it should be smoothed and hung until dry—never rolled or folded while still damp.
- Flags should be dry-cleaned, not washed.

Saluting the Flag

Whenever the flag passes by, as in a parade, men and women pay it their respects:

- Women stand quietly with hands at their sides, or they may place their right hands over their hearts if they wish.
- Men remove their hats and hold them, in their right hands, over their hearts. This rule also applies to women wearing sport caps.
- Men and women in the armed forces give the military salute as the flag passes.
- When the Pledge of Allegiance to the flag is spoken at a public dinner or in a house of worship, men and women both stand quietly at attention while they either repeat it or listen to the person giving the pledge.

∽ Guidelines for People of Other Nationalities ∽

When certain patriotic customs are observed in the United States, people who are not citizens should join in to an extent:

- When "The Star-Spangled Banner" is played, foreigners as well as U.S. citizens stand. It is then up to them whether to sing.
- When the Pledge of Allegiance to the flag is said, foreigners stand, but they do not repeat the words.
- When the anthem of a foreign country is played officially—as, for instance, in honor of a visiting team of athletes—everyone present rises and stands at attention. Men remove their hats (and women their sport caps), but they do not salute.
- Foreigners residing in the United States may display the flag of their own country on its national holidays. Out of courtesy, they should display the U.S. flag also.
- On U.S. national holidays, foreigners should display the U.S. flag or none—not their own.
- When foreigners attend a parade or other patriotic event, they stand respectfully while the flag passes by, but they need not salute in any way or recite the Pledge of Allegiance.

The National Anthem

EVERYONE, EVEN VERY YOUNG CHILDREN, should rise and remain standing during the playing of "The Star-Spangled Banner." The anthem is not easy to sing, and you needn't do so if you don't have the necessary range or ear. But you must stand quietly until "O'er the land of the free, and the home of the brave" has rung out and the music ends.

If you're on the way to your seat at a sports event or any other public place and the first strains of the anthem are heard, stop where you are and stand at attention until the end. Do not talk, chew gum loudly, eat, or smoke during the singing of the anthem.

Naturally, when you're at home and the anthem is played on television or radio, it isn't necessary to rise. But if at a large private party the orchestra plays the anthem at the start of the dancing, the guests do rise and show their respect.

The anthem is never played as dance music, nor are improvisations permissible.

Part Five

Dining
and
Entertaining

Chapter Twenty-three

Table Manners

S OME PEOPLE ARE SO PROFICIENT at wielding eating utensils that they could teach a course in table manners. Many more are fairly comfortable with their table manners but feel they need to brush up on the finer points. Then there are those who feel uncomfortable to the point of dreading what could be seen as a mistake at a fine restaurant or a dinner party. Are the nervous overreacting? That depends. The world's not going to end because you don't know which fork to use or have no idea what to do with an artichoke. Then again, there are times when good table manners become vitally important. One instance is when you are taken to lunch by a potential employer who, for all you know, may be looking to gauge your overall finesse. (Legions of job applicants have missed being hired simply because they chewed with their mouths open or held the fork like a shovel.)

That's why it's a good idea to practice good table manners on a daily basis at the family dinner table or even when eating alone. When used routinely, table manners become second nature, lessening the chances of any missteps whether you're dining inside or outside your home. There are plenty of bonuses in not having to worry about concentrating on *how* you're eating—one being the opportunity to focus on the people with whom you're sharing a meal.

The Table

IT'S EASY TO MAKE SENSE of a traditional place setting—especially an informal one, which calls for only a few utensils. The basic rule: Utensils are *placed in the order of use*—that is, from the outside in. A second rule, although with a few exceptions: Forks go to the left of the plate, knives and spoons to the right.

The Informal Place Setting

When an informal three-course dinner is served, the typical place setting includes these utensils and dishes:

Dinner plate. This is the "hub of the wheel" and usually the first thing to be set on the table.

Two forks. The forks are placed to the left of plate. The dinner fork (the larger of the two) is used for the main course, the smaller fork for a salad or appetizer. Because at an informal meal the salad is usually served first, the small fork is placed on the outside at the far left.

Napkin. The napkin is folded or put in a napkin ring and placed either to the left of the forks or in the center of the dinner plate. (A folded napkin is also sometimes placed under the forks, though this makes diners go to the trouble of removing the forks before opening their napkins.)

Knife. The dinner knife is set immediately to the right of the plate, cutting edge facing inward. (If the main course is meat, a steak knife can take the place of a dinner knife.) The dinner knife could also be used for a first-course dish.

Spoons. Spoons go to the right of the knife. A soupspoon (used first) goes farthest to the right, and a teaspoon (and sometimes a dessertspoon) between the soupspoon and knife.

Glasses. Drinking glasses of any kind—wine, water, juice, iced tea—are placed at the top right of the dinner plate.

Other dishes and utensils are optional, depending on what is being served:

An informal place setting

Salad plate. This is placed to the left of the forks. If the salad is to be eaten with the meal rather than before or after, you can forgo this plate and serve salad directly on the dinner plate. However, if the entrée contains gravy or other runny ingredients, a separate plate for the salad will keep things neater.

Bread plate with butter knife. If used, the bread plate goes above the forks, with the butter knife resting on the edge.

Dessert spoon and fork. These can be placed either horizontally above the dinner plate (the spoon at the top and its handle to the right; the fork below and its handle to the left) or beside the plate. If placed beside the plate, the fork goes on the left-hand side, closest to the plate; the spoon goes on the right-hand side of the plate, to the left of the soupspoon.

Coffee cup and saucer. If coffee is to be served during the meal, the cup and saucer go just above and slightly to the right of the knife and spoons. If it is served after dinner, the cups and saucers are brought to the table and placed in the same spot.

The Formal Place Setting

The one rule for a formal table is for everything to be geometrically spaced: the centerpiece in the exact center, the place settings at equal distances, and the utensils balanced. Beyond these placements, you can vary other flower arrangements and decorations as you like. A formal place setting usually consists of the following:

Service plate. This large plate, also called a charger, serves as an underplate for the plate holding the first course, which will be brought to the table. When the first course is cleared, the service plate remains until the plate holding the entrée is served, at which point the two plates are exchanged.

Butter plate. The small butter plate is placed above the forks at the left of the place setting.

Salad fork. Unless the salad is to be served first, the small salad fork is placed at the left and closest to the plate.

Dinner fork. The largest of the forks, also called the place fork, is placed to the left of the salad fork and is used to eat the entrée and side dishes.

Fish fork. If there is a fish course, this small fork is placed farthest to the left because it is the first fork used.

A formal place setting

Dinner knife. This is placed to the right of the dinner plate.

Fish knife. The specially shaped fish knife goes to the right of the dinner knife.

Butter knife. This small spreader is placed diagonally on top of the butter plate.

Salad knife. This knife, *if* provided, would be set between the dinner plate and the dinner knife. (Note: There is *no* salad knife in the above illustration.)

Soupspoon or fruit spoon. If soup or fruit is being served as a first course, the accompanying spoon goes to the right of the knives.

Oyster fork. If shellfish is to be served, the oyster fork is set to the right of the spoons; it is the only fork ever placed on the right.

Glasses. These number four and are placed so that the smaller ones are in front. The water goblet is placed directly above the knives; just to the right goes a champagne flute; in front of these are placed a red- or white-wine glass and a sherry glass.

Knife blades are always placed with the cutting edge toward the plate.

No more than three of any implement is ever placed on the table (except when an oyster fork is used, in which case there are four forks). If more than three courses are served before dessert, the utensil for the fourth course is brought in with the food; likewise, the salad fork and knife may be brought in when salad is served.

Dessert spoons and forks are brought in on the dessert plate just before dessert is served.

Handling Utensils

DECIDING WHICH KNIFE, FORK, or spoon to use is made easier by the "outside-in" rule—using utensils on the outside first and working your way inward. If you find yourself confused (a utensil seems out of place, which could simply mean the salad is being served later), just wait to see what is served before choosing a utensil. Or watch the others at the table and follow suit.

How to Hold?

It's surprising how many people make a fist to hold their utensils, especially when the more comfortable alternative is the correct one: The fork or spoon rests on the middle finger of your hand, with your forefinger and thumb gripping the handle.

With that most obvious of guidelines established, be aware that there are two different holding styles from which to choose: the American style (usually with fork tines up) and the Continental (or European) style (with fork tines down).

Is one style more proper than the other? Not at all. In fact, there's no reason not to use both during a meal: You might want to eat the meat Continental style and the other dishes American style. Either way is correct, so use whichever is more comfortable for you.

The method for cutting food is the same for both techniques. Hold the knife in the right hand (or reversed, if you're left-handed) with your index finger pressed just below where the handle meets the blade. Hold the fork, tines down, in your left hand and spear the food to steady it, pressing the base of the handle with your index finger. As you cut food, keep your elbows just slightly above table level—not raised high and out.

Then come the differences in the two styles:

American (or zigzag) style. After the food is cut, the American method calls for placing (not propping) the knife on the edge of the plate, then switching the fork to your right hand before raising it, tines up, to your mouth.

American style of eating

Continental style. Once the food is cut, the knife is kept in your hand or laid across the plate as the other hand lifts the fork to your mouth. The fork is held tines down with the index finger touching the neck of the handle. The fork remains in the left hand.

Continental style of eating

Resting Utensils

Knowing where to rest utensils during and after the meal is important as well. First, never place a knife, fork, or spoon you've been using directly on the table; instead, place it diagonally on the edge of your plate.

When you pause to take a sip of your beverage or to speak with someone, place your knife and fork on your plate near the center, slightly angled in an inverted V and with the tips of the knife and fork pointing toward each other. (Don't worry about tines up or tines down, though it makes sense that the tines will face down if you're eating Continental style.) You may also rest your utensils in the American style, with your knife slightly diagonal on the top right rim of your plate and your fork laid nearby with tines up. These two resting positions, recognized by trained waitstaff, signal that you're not ready to have your plate removed.

or

Two resting positions for utensils during a meal

At most restaurants, used utensils are replaced with clean ones for the next course. If, however, a waiter asks you to keep your dirty utensils for the next course (a practice apparently meant to cut costs), it's okay to ask for clean ones.

If soup or dessert is served in a deep bowl, cup, or stemmed bowl set on another plate, place your utensil(s) on this underplate when you finish. If the bowl is what is called a soup plate (shallow and wide), leave the spoon in the bowl.

At the end of the course, lay your knife and fork side by side diagonally on your plate (if your plate were a clock face, they would lie at four o'clock); the knife blade faces inward, but the fork tines can be either up or down. This position not only serves as a signal to the server that you're finished but also decreases the chance that the utensils could fall to the floor when the plates are cleared.

Utensils indicating that the course is finished

Using Your Napkin

Be it cloth or paper, your napkin goes into your lap as soon as you sit down. The tradition has been for diners to wait until the hostess puts her napkin in her lap, but nowadays this custom is observed only at more formal meals. The significant word is "lap." Don't tuck a napkin into your collar, between the buttons of your shirt or blouse, or in your belt. (An exception can be made for the elderly or infirm; if someone is prone to spilling food, she has every right to protect her clothing.) Partially unfold the napkin (in other words, keep it folded in half), and don't snap it open with a showy jerk of the wrist.

Use your napkin frequently during the meal to blot or pat, not wipe, your lips. It's also a good idea to blot your lips before taking a drink of your beverage—especially if you're a woman wearing lipstick.

Put your napkin to the left side of your plate when the meal ends or whenever you excuse yourself from the table. Instead of folding or crumpling the napkin, just leave it in loose folds that keep any soiled parts out of sight. At the end of the meal, leave your napkin to the left or, if your plate has been removed, in the center of the place setting.

The Particulars of Serving

HOW A MEAL IS SERVED depends on its style. At a formal dinner, the food is brought to each diner at the table; the server presents the platter or bowl on the diner's left, at which point the food is either accepted or refused. (Alternatively, plates are prepared in the kitchen and then brought to the table and set before the diners.) At a more casual meal, such as an informal seated dinner party, either the host dishes the food onto guests' plates for them to pass around the table or the diners help themselves to the food and pass it to others as necessary.

Which way is food passed around the table when it is first served? Tradition says to pass counterclockwise (to the right)—but the point is for the food to be moving in only one direction. One diner either holds the dish as the next diner takes some food, or he hands it to the person, who then serves herself. Any heavy or awkward dishes are put on the table with each pass. Cream pitchers and other dishes with handles should be passed with the handle toward the person receiving them.

Serving Yourself

Your first concern when helping yourself to food is to pay attention to what you're doing and avoid spills. Then keep the following in mind:

➤ Gravy should be spooned directly from the gravy boat onto the meat, potatoes, or rice on your plate, whereas condiments, pickles, and jelly are put alongside the foods they're meant to accompany.

➤ Olives, nuts, radishes, or celery are placed on the bread plate. If no bread plate has been provided, put these items on the edge of your dinner plate.

➤ If the meal has started and something that would ordinarily be on the table is missing—salt and pepper, for example, or butter for the bread—mention it to the host only if you're certain it's an oversight: "Anne, is there any butter for the rolls?" Asking for anything else can be awkward and seem rude, especially at a dinner party. For one thing, the host might not have any steak sauce or pickle relish on hand; for another, requesting something additional suggests you think the food isn't up to par.

Refusing a Dish

When you're among friends, it's fine to refuse a dish you don't care for with a polite "No, thank you." At a dinner party where the host has gone to a great deal of trouble, it's good manners to take at least a little of every dish being offered.

If you're allergic to a food or on a restricted diet and your host urges you to help yourself to food you shouldn't eat, explain to her (not to the table at large) why you have no choice but to decline: "Sarah, shellfish is off-limits for me, but I'm sure all the other delicious dishes will more than make up for it."

During the Meal

YOUR FIRST CONCERN once the meal is served is when to start eating. Do you wait until everyone else's plate is full even as your food grows cold? Unless the meal consists of cold courses, your fellow diners (including the host, if any) will usually urge you to go ahead and start. If the group is large, begin eating once at least three of you have been given your food.

At a small table of only two to four people, it's better to wait until everyone else has been served before starting to eat. At a formal or business meal, you should either wait until everyone is served to start or begin when the host asks you to.

The other mealtime guidelines that follow are easy to digest. They're based on doing everything unobtrusively—the reason you shouldn't eat noisily, wave your fork in the air while talking, or snap a cloth napkin open instead of unfolding it.

Posture, Fidgeting . . . and Those Elbows

You needn't sit stiff as a rail at the dinner table, but hunching your shoulders over the plate (a posture often associated with using a fork like a shovel) is a definite "do not." Likewise, slouching back in your chair (which makes it look as if you're not interested in the meal) is not appropriate when eating with others.

As for not putting your elbows on the table, this drummed-into-us taboo applies only when you are actually eating. It's a different story when no utensils are being used; in fact, putting your elbows on the table while leaning forward a bit during a mealtime conversation shows that you're listening intently.

When waiting for the food to arrive or after the meal, you may want to keep your hands in your lap, if only to resist the temptation of fiddling with the utensils or other items. Refrain from drumming your fingers, jiggling your knee, or other fidgety habits, and always keep your hands away from your hair.

Cutting, Seasoning, and So On

As you begin and continue the meal, there are certain things you'll want to remember to do and others you'll want to avoid.

Cutting food. Cut your food into only one or two bite-sized pieces at a time. Doing this makes sense, since a plateful of cut-up food is not only unattractive but cools and dries out more quickly than food that is mostly intact. (The exception to the rule is when you help a young child cut his food.)

Seasoning food. When at a dinner party or restaurant, always taste your food before seasoning it. Hastily covering a dish with salt or drowning it in ketchup implies that you think the cook's creation needs improving on.

Chewing food. Once you start to eat, don't literally bite off more than you can chew: Take a manageable bite, chew it well, and swallow it before taking another. Also remember that smacking, slurping, and collecting food in a ball in one cheek are major faux pas. When you have a mouthful of food, avoid two more things: taking a drink and talking. If you have more than a few words to say, swallow your food, rest your fork on your plate, and speak before you resume eating.

Reaching. Just how close does something on the table have to be before you reach out and get it yourself? That's simple: within easy reach of your arm when you're leaning only slightly forward. Don't lean past the person sitting next to you or lunge to perform what's known as the boardinghouse reach. A request to "please pass the [item]" is required for everything beyond that invisible boundary, as is a thank-you to whoever does the passing.

Using a finger bowl. If you encounter a finger bowl (used either after eating a hands-on meal such as lobster or at a more formal meal when dessert is served), dip your fingers into the water and then dry them with your napkin. (See also Chapter 25, page 455: "Finger Bowl Finesse.")

Assorted Table Tips

➤ Remember to make good use of your napkin, wiping your fingers as necessary. Also use a small area of the napkin to blot your lips fairly often.

➤ If a piece of food keeps eluding your fork, don't push it onto the tines with your finger. Instead, use a piece of bread or your knife as a pusher.

➤ Sop up extra gravy or sauce only with a piece of bread on the end of a fork; the soaked bread is then brought to the mouth with the fork.

➤ When you've finished eating, don't push your plate away from you. Nor should you loudly announce "I'm finished" or "I'm stuffed."

When Things Go Wrong

DEALING WITH UNEXPECTED DIFFICULTIES at the dinner table—from food that tastes off to a coughing fit to spotting a tiny critter inching along a salad green—is a concern for the polite diner. Such challenges can be managed with aplomb just by staying calm and keeping your sense of humor.

Spills. If you spill food on the table while taking it from a serving dish, neatly pick up as much as you can with a clean spoon or the blade of your knife; then wet a corner of your napkin in the water glass and dab the spot. If you knock over a drink, quickly set the glass upright and apologize to your tablemates: "Oh, I'm sorry. How clumsy of me! I hope none of it got on you." Get a cloth or sponge and mop up the liquid right away. In a restaurant, discreetly signal the server, who will put a napkin over any stains. In someone's home, immediately tell your host and help with the cleanup. (See also Chapter 24, page 422: "What Do I Do When . . .")

Food that's too hot or spoiled. If a bite of food is too hot, quickly take a swallow of water or another cold drink. If that's impossible or doesn't help, discreetly spit the scalding food onto your fork (preferably not into your fingers and definitely not into your napkin), and put it on the edge of the plate. The same goes for a bad oyster, clam, or any other food that tastes spoiled. Remove it from your mouth as quickly and unobtrusively as you can.

A QUESTION FOR PEGGY

I was a guest at a small dinner party last week, and I found a hair in a helping of potatoes au gratin. I didn't want to embarrass the hostess, but I couldn't bring myself to eat even a bite of the dish. No one said anything, but the hostess must surely have noticed my untouched potatoes. Should I have told her the reason once we were in private?

You get a gold star for not bringing it up, since finding a hair, that proverbial fly in the soup, or any other foreign object should either remain unmentioned until the time is right or not discussed at all. At a private dinner, you don't want to call the attention of the hostess or anyone else to the problem. You did your best in an awkward situation, and in the process saved the hostess any embarrassment.

  If a foreign object isn't detected until you have it in your mouth, spit it quietly onto your fork or spoon and put it on the side of your plate. It's then up to you whether to continue eating the food or let it be.

Wayward food. Occasionally running your tongue over your teeth may let you know if you have a bit of food caught between your teeth. If the food stays put, excuse yourself from the table and remove it in the restroom.

If you notice food stuck in a fellow diner's teeth or on her face or clothes, you're doing a favor by telling her. If only the two of you are at the table, just say, "Millie, you seem to have a little something on your chin"; if you're in a group, it's better to silently signal Millie by catching her eye and lightly tapping your chin with your forefinger.

Coughing and sneezing. When you feel a sneeze or a cough coming on, cover your mouth and nose with a handkerchief or tissue—or your napkin, if that's the only thing within reach. (In an emergency, your hand is better than nothing at all.) If a coughing or sneezing bout is prolonged, excuse yourself until it passes.

Coughing and sneezing often lead to nose blowing. If you need to, excuse yourself and blow your nose in the restroom, being sure to wash your hands afterward.

Choking. If you choke on a bit of food and a sip of water doesn't take care of the problem, cover your mouth (if you can, though that would hardly be the time to worry about manners!) and dislodge the food with a good cough. Then remove it in the most practical way you can. If you have to cough more than once or twice, excuse yourself and leave the table.

Serious choking is another matter. If you find yourself unable to cough or speak, do whatever is necessary to get fellow diners to come to your aid. Thankfully, many people (and most restaurant personnel) are trained to perform the life-saving Heimlich Maneuver—a technique anyone will benefit from learning.

Food-by-food Etiquette

FACING UNFAMILIAR OR HARD-TO-EAT foods or wondering whether the way you eat a particular food at home is "not done" in public is something that happens to most of us at one time or another. What you do depends on the situation. With friends, don't be embarrassed to say, "I've never eaten escargots before. Please show me how." If you're at a formal function or among strangers, just delay eating until you can take a cue from the other diners. Reviewing the guidelines below will help keep you from wondering what to do.

Apples and Pears

When served as part of a meal, an apple or pear is eaten with the fingers but is cut in quarters first (a paring knife is often set out for the purpose). Cut the core away from each quarter, then peel if desired.

Apricots, Cherries, and Plums

Eat an apricot, cherry, or plum with your fingers. To expel the pit, cup your hand over your mouth and push the pit forward with your tongue into your fingers. Then deposit the pit on your plate.

Artichokes

Artichoke leaves are always eaten with the fingers. Pluck off a leaf on the outside, dip its meaty base into the melted butter or sauce provided, then place it between your front teeth and pull forward. Continue leaf by leaf, placing discarded leaves on the edge of your plate (or on a plate provided for the purpose), until you've reached the artichoke's thistlelike choke or when the leaves are too small or meatless. Use your knife to slice off the remaining leaves and the choke, exposing the artichoke heart. Then cut the heart into bite-sized pieces and eat it with a fork, dipping each forkful into the melted butter or sauce.

Asian Dishes

The Asian cuisines most often encountered by Americans are those of China, India, Japan, and Southeast Asia (including Thailand, Vietnam, Korea, Malaysia, and Indonesia). Though there's no real need to follow the eating traditions from each country, it doesn't hurt to know a bit about them. For instance, at a Chinese or Japanese meal it's fine to hold the rice bowl close to your mouth; in Korean custom the bowl is left on the table. And then there are chopsticks, the use of which makes Chinese and Japanese food "just taste better" to many people.

It's also nice to follow the Asian custom of serving tea to your fellow diners before you fill your own teacup. (Traditionally, milk or sugar is added only to Japanese green tea, but there's no harm in doctoring any Asian tea to your liking.)

A meal at a Chinese restaurant is usually communal, with dishes being shared. All diners should have a say in what to order and then take equitable portions from the platters—even of the foods they like most. Near the end of the meal, don't take the last food left on a platter without offering it to the other diners first.

Sushi and sashimi. In Japan, the assorted raw fish dishes called sushi are eaten with chopsticks or the fingers. Whichever method you choose, there's a correct way to dip a piece of sushi into the accompanying soy sauce. So that the sticky rice won't break up, only the fish side is dipped into sauce; the piece is then brought to the mouth and eaten in one bite. If you forgo tradition altogether and use a fork, cut any pieces that are too large to eat in a single bite with your knife and fork.

A typical Japanese meal begins with sashimi—thinly sliced, raw, boneless fish served without rice. Before eating sashimi, diners mix a dollop of the green horseradish mustard called wasabi into the dish of soy sauce that is provided. The fish is then dipped into the sauce with chopsticks or a fork.

Chopsticks are used to eat Chinese, Japanese, Korean, and a few other Asian foods. The secret to mastering these ancient utensils will hardly come as a surprise: patience and practice.

The first thing you should know is which end of the sticks to use. The food you're eating is picked up with the narrow end, while the broader end is used to pick up food from a communal serving plate. Once used, the small end of chopsticks should never touch any bowl or platter used by others.

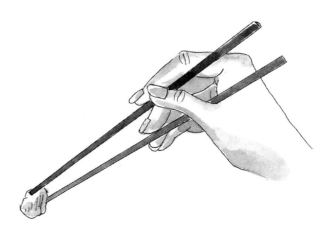

Using Chopsticks. Rest the lower chopstick on your ring finger, supporting it in the V of the thumb and forefinger. Hold the upper chopstick like a pencil, between the middle and index fingers and anchored with your thumb. Make sure the tips of the chopsticks are even. When you are picking up food, the lower chopstick remains still as the upper chopstick pivots, with your thumb as the axis.

A few more chopstick do's and don'ts . . .

Do decide which piece of food you want before you start in on an appetizer platter with your chopsticks. Poking the food as you decide what you want is a no-no, and once your chopsticks have touched a piece of food, you must take it.

Do bite in half any dumplings and other small items that are a little too large to eat, holding the piece firmly in your chopsticks as you carefully bite.

Do raise your rice bowl to a point just under your chin when eating rice (unless you happen to be dining in Korea, where all dishes remain on the table).

Do rest your used chopsticks on your plate or a chopstick rest, not directly on the table.

Don't pour any sauce over the food. Instead, use your chopsticks to dip a piece of food in the sauce (usually in your own small bowl) before raising it to your mouth.

Don't tap chopsticks on a dish to attract the attention of the server.

Don't grip the edge of a dish with chopsticks to pull it toward you.

Don't stick chopsticks upright in your rice bowl, rest them on the rice bowl, or transfer food to another diner's chopsticks. (These gestures are practiced only at Japanese funerals.)

Asparagus

When asparagus stalks are firm and aren't sauced, it's fine to pick them up with your fingers, one stalk at a time. (Asparagus is traditionally a finger food, and the English and many other nationalities still see it as such.) Think twice, however, about using your fingers for unsauced, firm spears if your fellow diners use a knife and fork or if you're a guest at a formal meal. When in doubt, use utensils.

Avocados

Avocado slices are cut and eaten with a fork. When an avocado is served halved, hold the shell to steady it and scoop out each bite with a spoon. When tuna salad or any other mixture is served in an avocado half, it's fine to hold the shell steady while eating the contents—this time using a fork.

Bacon

Eat fried bacon as a finger food when it is dry, crisp, and served whole. If the bacon is broken into bits, served in thick slices (as with Canadian bacon), or limp, eat it with knife and fork as you would any other meat.

Baked Potatoes (White and Sweet)

Baked white potatoes and sweet potatoes can be eaten in more than one way. The most common is to slit the top lengthwise with a knife, push on each end of the potato to open it wide, and mash some of the flesh with a fork. An alternative is to slice the potato clean through and lay the halves skin-down side by side.

Add butter, salt, and pepper (plus extras like sour cream, cheese, or bacon bits, if desired) and use your fork to mash the additions lightly into the flesh before taking a forkful from the shell.

Another method is to slice the potato in half lengthwise and use your fork to scoop the flesh of both halves onto your plate. Neatly stack the skins together on the edge of your plate and mix butter and any other condiments into the flesh with your fork.

If you like to eat the skin as well as the flesh, cut the potato into two halves and use your knife and fork to cut the potato and skin into bite-sized pieces, one or two at a time.

Bananas and Plantains

At an informal dinner, it's fine to peel a banana and eat it out of hand; just peel it gradually, not all at once. At a more formal dinner, follow your fellow diners' lead on whether to use fingers or fork. When a banana is eaten with a fork, the banana is peeled completely (the skin goes onto the edge of the plate) and cut into slices, a few at a time.

Raw plantains are eaten in the same way, although these fruits are usually served fried and eaten with a fork.

Berries

Berries are usually hulled or stemmed before the meal, served with cream and sugar, and eaten with a spoon. Sometimes berries are served as or with dessert, or perhaps as part of breakfast. If strawberries are served unhulled, you can hold the berry by the hull to eat it; the hull and leaves then go onto the side of your plate.

Beverages

Beverages drunk at the table and at parties have a set of manners all their own, and some guidelines apply across the board: (1) Take a drink only when you have no food in your mouth; (2) sip instead of gulping; (3) if you're a woman, don't wear so much lipstick that your drinking glass will become smudged.

Water and ice. Avoid the urge to gulp water at the table, no matter how thirsty you are. When drinking a beverage that contains ice cubes or crushed ice, don't crunch the ice in your mouth.

Beer and soft drinks. When served at a meal, beer and soft drinks should be served in a mug or glass. Drink them straight from the bottle or can only at a picnic, barbecue, or other very casual occasion. (Good beers are often served in the bottle with an empty glass, which lets the drinker control how much he pours and the head on the beer.)

Coffee and tea. Four quick don'ts: (1) Don't leave your spoon in the coffee cup or teacup or mug; place it on the saucer or a plate. (2) Don't take ice from your water to cool a hot drink. (3) Don't dunk doughnuts, biscotti, or anything else in your coffee unless you're at an ultracasual place where dunking is the norm. (4) Don't crook your pinkie when drinking from a cup—an affectation that went out with the Victorians.

When serving tea, note that a pot of freshly brewed loose tea tastes best; a second pot of hot water is used to dilute oversteeped tea and is poured directly into the cup. If using tea bags, put two or three bags in a pot of hot water and pour the tea when it has steeped. When putting a tea bag directly into a teacup or mug for steeping, allow it to drip briefly into the cup as you remove it (no squeezing it with your fingers or the string). Then place the bag on a saucer or plate.

What to do with empty packets of sugar and individual containers of cream? Crumple them and place them on the edge of your saucer or butter plate.

Cocktails. When you drink a cocktail, the only nonedible item you should leave in your glass is a straw; swizzle sticks and tiny paper umbrellas go onto the table or your bread plate. At parties, hold such accoutrements in a napkin until you find a waste receptacle.

If you want to eat cocktail garnishes like olives, cherries, or onions, by all means do. Garnishes on cocktail picks are easy to retrieve at any time, while those in the bottom of the glass should be fished out with the fingers only when you've finished the drink. (Think twice about eating an orange slice, since chewing the pulp off the rind is messy.)

Wine. See Chapter 24, page 419: "Ordering Wine"; Chapter 25, page 442: "Choosing and Serving Wines."

Bouillabaisse

To be enjoyed to the fullest, this seafood stew from Marseilles—made with varying combinations of white fish, clams, mussels, shrimp, scallops, and crab legs—requires using not only a soupspoon but also a seafood fork, knife, and sometimes a shellfish cracker. A large bowl should be placed on the table for shells. If no receptacle is provided, place empty shells on the plate under your soup bowl.

Bread

Before eating bread, use your fingers to break it into moderate-sized (not bite-sized) pieces. Then butter the bread one piece at a time, holding it against your plate, not in your hand. Hot biscuit halves and toast can be buttered all over at once because they taste best when the butter is melted. (See also "Butter," below.)

Fried or flat bread. The breads nan, papadam, poori (from India), and pita (from the Middle East) are brought whole to the table on plates or in flat baskets. Break or tear off a fairly sizable piece with your fingers and transfer it to your plate, then tear off smaller pieces to eat.

Round loaf on cutting board. If a restaurant serves an entire round loaf of bread on a cutting board, use the accompanying bread knife to cut it in slices rather than wedges. Start at one side by cutting a thin slice of crust, then slice toward the center.

Burritos

See page 409: "Sandwiches."

Butter

There are various ways to serve butter at the table: Place a stick on a butter dish with a butter knife; slice a stick of butter and serve the pats on a small plate with a small fork (or on individual plates with little butter knives); or spoon whipped butter from a tub onto a small plate and provide a butter knife. When diners need to transfer the butter to their own plates and no communal utensil is provided, they use their own clean knives or forks. (See also page 405: "Olive Oil.")

When individually wrapped squares or small plastic tubs of butter are served in a restaurant, leave the empty wrappings or tubs on your bread plate (or, if no bread plate is provided, tucked under the edge of your dinner plate), not on the table.

Cantaloupes and Other Melons

Use a spoon to eat unpeeled cantaloupes and other melons that have been cut into quarters or halves. When melons are peeled and sliced, eat the pieces with a fork.

Caviar

Caviar is traditionally served in a crystal bowl on a bed of cracked ice. Use the accompanying spoon to place the caviar on your plate. With your own knife or spoon, place small amounts of caviar on toast triangles or blini. If chopped egg, minced onions, or sour cream is served, spoon the topping sparingly onto the caviar.

Cheese

When served as an hors d'oeuvre, cheese is cut or spread on a cracker with a knife. Provide a separate knife for each cheese so that the individual flavors won't mingle.

When cheese is served with fruit for dessert, it is sliced and placed on the plate with the fruit. Like the fruit, it is eaten with a knife and fork, not with the fingers.

When an after-dinner cheese course is ordered at a restaurant, the cheese will come arranged on plates centered with bread or crackers, a piece or fruit, or perhaps a small fruitcake of some sort. Cheeses served on bread or crackers are eaten with the fingers, but a knife and fork are used for everything on a plate holding cheeses and fruit or fruitcake (the cheeses are eaten separately so that the full flavor comes through). Start with the milder cheeses and progress to the strongest.

Cherries

See page 391: "Apricots, Cherries, and Plums."

Cherry Tomatoes

Except when served as part of a salad or other dish, whole cherry tomatoes are eaten with the fingers. But be careful: They're notorious squirters! It's best to pop the whole tomato into your mouth. If the tomato is too large to eat in one bite (as some varieties are), pierce the skin with your tooth or a knife before biting the fruit it in half. When served whole in a salad or other dish, cherry tomatoes are eaten with a knife and fork after being cut with care.

Clams

See page 405: "Oysters and Clams."

Condiments

The perker-uppers we add to dishes—from salt and pepper to bottled sauces to relishes—have their own etiquette guidelines.

Salt and pepper. Don't salt or pepper your food before tasting it, because assuming that the dish is well seasoned to begin with is an implicit compliment to whoever prepared it.

When someone asks for the salt or pepper, pass both. These items travel together, so think of them as joined at the hip. (Even a saltcellar is passed with the pepper.) If the shakers are opaque and you can't tell one from the other, the pepper shaker is the one with the larger holes.

At formal dinners, a saltcellar—a tiny bowl and spoon—sometimes takes the place of a shaker. You can use the spoon to sprinkle salt over your food as needed or you can fall back on the old tradition of placing a small mound of salt on the edge of your plate and then dipping each forkful of food into the salt. If no spoon comes with the cellar, use the tip of a clean knife; if the cellar is for your use only, it's fine to take a pinch with your fingers.

Ketchup and such. At all but the most informal meals, serve ketchup, mustard, mayonnaise, and any other bottled sauces in small dishes. At picnics and barbecues, these condiments can come straight from the bottle.

Pouring steak sauce or ketchup over your food is fine if you're with family and friends or at a chain restaurant. But even the most avid bottled-sauce lover will probably have to do without at more formal dinners and tonier restaurants.

Other condiments. Now that international cuisines are part of the American culinary scene, you're more likely to encounter several separate condiment dishes on the table. Spoon a small portion of the sauce or chopped-vegetable condiment onto the edge of your dinner plate or butter plate, replenishing it as needed. Never dip food directly into a communal condiment dish, and don't take anything from the condiment bowl directly to your mouth; it goes onto your plate first.

Corn on the Cob

Perhaps the only rule to follow when enjoying this handheld treat is to eat it as neatly as possible—no noisy nonstop chomping up and down the rows. To butter the corn, put pats or a scoop of butter on your dinner plate, then butter and season only a few rows of the corn at a time.

If no prongs for holding the cob are supplied, butter in a way that will keep your fingers from becoming greasy. Corn served at a formal dinner party should always be cut off the cob in the kitchen and buttered or creamed before serving.

Crab

When tackling a hardshell crab, start with the crab legs. Twist one off, then suck the meat from the shell; repeat with the second leg. Put the legs on the edge of your plate. To eat meat from the body of the crab, use a fork to pick the meat from the underside.

A softshell crab is eaten shell and all, whether it's served in a sandwich or on a plate. In the latter case, cut the crab with a knife and fork down the middle and then into bite-sized sections. You can either eat the legs shell and all or pull them off and suck out the crabmeat inside; place any inedible parts on the side of your plate.

Cranberry Sauce

See page 397: "Condiments."

Cream Puffs

See "Desserts," below.

Crudités

See page 401: "Garnishes"; page 402: "Hors d'Oeuvres."

Desserts

What do you do with a dessert fork and spoon when you find them in your place setting? Depending on what you're eating, these utensils are often interchangeable.

In general, eat custards and other very soft desserts with a spoon, using the fork for berries or any other garnishes. Cake, pie, or crepes being served à la mode—i.e., with ice cream—may be eaten with either or both of the utensils. For firmer desserts such as dense cakes or poached pears, switch the utensils—the fork for eating, the spoon for pushing and cutting.

When you're served layer cake with the slice upright, turn it on its side with a dessert fork and spoon or any other utensil that remains at your place. If all of the other utensils have been cleared, then do your best with your fork and the fingers of the other hand. (See also page 402: "Ice Cream"; page 407: "Pastries.")

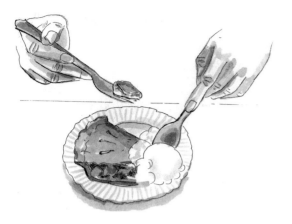

Pie or Cake à la Mode. Use a dessert fork and spoon: the spoon is used to cut and place a bite of pie or cake, plus a little ice cream, onto the fork. The dessert is eaten with the fork, with the spoon mainly being used as an aid.

Empanadas

See page 409: "Quesadillas and Empanadas."

Escargots

Escargots (French for "snails") are baked or broiled and can be eaten in a number of ways. Shelled snails served on toast are eaten with a knife and fork. Escargots in a snail plate (ovenproof plates with indentations that keep unshelled snails in place while they are cooked in garlic butter and are being eaten) are usually grasped with snail tongs. Squeeze the handles to open the tongs, which will snap around the shell as you release the pressure. The snail is removed with a pick, an oyster fork, or a two-pronged snail fork held in your other hand. The garlic butter that remains in the shells can be poured into the snail plate and sopped up with small pieces of bread on the end of a fork.

Using snail tongs

Fajitas

Fajitas (flour tortillas with a choice of fillings) are filled and rolled by the diner, then eaten with the fingers. To keep things neat, spread any soft fillings (usually refried beans, guacamole, sour cream, or melted cheese) onto the tortilla first, then add the strips of beef, chicken, or seafood and top with any garnishes. Roll up the tortilla and eat it from one end. Your fork is used only to eat any filling that falls to the plate.

Figs

Whole figs can be eaten with your fingers at an informal dinner. If they are halved or are accompanied by prosciutto or a crumbly cheese, use your knife and fork.

Fettuccini

See page 406: "Spaghetti and other long noodles."

Fish

Fish as an entrée is often served as a fillet and eaten with a knife and fork. More daunting is a whole fish that you must fillet for yourself; it will most likely come with a fish knife and fish fork, tools designed for the job.

The first step is to anchor the fish with your fork and remove the head (placing it on a plate for discards). Then use the tip of your knife to cut a line down the center of the fish from gill to tail, just above the middle of the body. You can either (1) remove the skeleton at this point, lift the top half of the flesh with the knife and fork, and put it on the plate or (2) eat the flesh directly from the fish.

If you detect a fish bone in your mouth, work it to your lips unobtrusively; then discreetly push the bone onto your fork with your tongue and deposit the bone on the side of your plate.

Fondue

Eating fondue means sharing a bowl with others, so don't even think of "double dipping." When you spear a piece of French bread and dip it into the pot of melted cheese, hold the fondue fork still for a moment to let the excess drip off. Use your dinner fork to slide the cheese-covered bread onto your plate, then to eat it. The fondue fork is rested on your plate between dips. The same method applies to melted chocolate, a dessert fondue into which strawberries or cake squares are dipped.

Meat fondues require a few extra moves. When the bowl of cubed raw meat is passed, spoon several pieces onto your dinner plate. Spoon small pools of the sauces being served onto your plate. Firmly spear a piece of meat with your fondue fork and place it in the pot with the other diners' forks. When the meat is cooked, remove it and slide it onto your plate with your dinner fork. When it has cooled, cut it into smaller pieces to eat.

French Fries

When French-fried potatoes accompany finger foods like hamburgers, hot dogs, or other sandwiches, eat them with your fingers. At other times, cut them into bite-sized lengths and eat with a fork. Don't drown French fries in ketchup or other sauces. Instead, pour a small pool next to the fries and dip them in one by one, replenishing the sauce as needed.

Frog's Legs

Frog's legs can be eaten with either the fingers or a knife and fork. In the latter case, also use your knife and fork to move the inedible portions to the side of the plate.

Game Birds

See page 409: "Poultry."

Garnishes

Most garnishes aren't just for show. That sprig of parsley or watercress at the edge of the plate not only looks good but is tasty and nutritious. In all but the most informal situations, eat lemon slices or other citrus garnishes only if they are peeled and can be eaten with a fork. (See also page 394: "Cocktails,"; page 411: "Other garnishes.")

Grapefruit

Grapefruit should be served with the seeds removed and with each section loosened from the rind with a grapefruit knife. The rind, plus any seeds encountered, should be left on the plate.

Grapes

When pulling grapes off a bunch, don't pull them one at a time. Instead, break off a branch bearing several grapes from the main stem. If the grapes have seeds, eat them in one of two ways: (1) Lay a grape on its side, pierce the center with the point of a knife, and lift and remove the seeds. (2) Put a grape in your mouth whole, deposit the seeds into your thumb and first two fingers, and place the seeds on your plate.

Gravies and Sauces

Can you properly sop up gravy or sauce left on your plate with bread? Yes, but only with a fork. Put a bite-sized piece of bread into the gravy or sauce, sop, and then eat it using your fork Continental style (see page 384: "Continental Style").

Hors d'Oeuvres

At parties, you may be choosing hors d'oeuvres from platters set on a table or taking them from a passed tray. When taking more than two or three, use one of the small plates provided; anything less is held on a napkin. A napkin also goes under any plate you're holding so that you'll be able to blot your lips.

Take small portions from tables and trays and avoid returning for plateful after plateful of food, which could make it look as if gobbling food is more important to you than socializing. Also remember not to eat, talk, and drink concurrently—one action at a time, please.

There is usually a small receptacle on the table or tray for used food skewers and toothpicks. If not, hold any items (including remnants such as shrimp tails and the swizzle stick for your cocktail) in your napkin until you find a wastebasket. Don't place used items on the buffet table unless there's a receptacle for the purpose.

When crudités (raw vegetables) or chips and dip are offered, spoon some of the dip on your plate. When a communal bowl is used don't double dip—that is, never dip again with the same vegetable or chip once you've taken a bite of it. (See also Chapter 25, page 452: "A Dozen Dinner Guest Do's and Don'ts.")

Ice Cream

When you eat ice cream from a bowl, about the only misstep is to give into temptation and drink the meltage. Ice cream in a cone should be wrapped in a napkin to catch the inevitable drips.

You might want to take a cue from the old country when eating Italian ice cream, which is of two types: dairy ice creams (*le crème*) and fruit ices with no cream (*le frutte*). A serving typically consists of two or three scoops of different flavors, but Italians do not mix dairy and fruit types because the textures and flavors aren't complementary. (See also page 398: "Desserts.")

Kiwis

Use a sharp paring knife to peel away the fuzzy, inedible outer skin of a kiwi; then slice the fruit crosswise as you would a tomato. There's no need to remove the seeds, which are edible. Cut a slice into bite-sized pieces with your fork.

Lemons

Lemons are generally used as an accompaniment or garnish to other dishes. Cut a lemon into wedges, slices, quarters or halves, depending on what it's being used for, removing the visible seeds. (See also page 401: "Garnishes.")

When squeezing a lemon section over a dish or into tea, shield other diners from squirts by holding a spoon or your cupped hand in front of the lemon as you squeeze. (Some restaurants fit lemons with a cheesecloth covering to prevent the problem.)

The lemon is then placed on the edge of the plate (or saucer) or, in the case of iced tea, dropped into the glass if you choose.

Linguini

See page 406: "Spaghetti and other long noodles."

Lobster

A large paper napkin or plastic bib is provided for the lobster eater. Be sure to wear it, since handling this crustacean usually results in more than a few squirts and splashes. Holding the lobster steady with one hand, twist off the claws and place them on the side of your plate. Using the cracking tool (a shellfish cracker or nutcracker) that is typically provided, crack each claw (slowly, to reduce squirting) and pull out the meat with a fork or small lobster pick. You'll need to remove the meat from the tail (often already cut into two solid pieces) and cut it into bite-sized pieces.

Spear each piece of meat with your fork and dip it into the accompanying drawn butter or sauce before eating. (True lobster-lovers get additional morsels out of the legs by breaking them off one at a time, putting them into the mouth broken end first, and squeezing the meat out with the teeth).

A large bowl or platter should be provided for the empty shells. Finger bowls with hot water and lemon slices are often put at each place as soon as the meal is finished (see Chapter 25, page 455: "Finger Bowl Finesse").

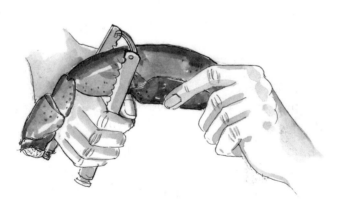

Cracking a lobster claw

Mango

Most varieties of mango are too large to be served individually. The fruit is usually divided so that the clingstone in the center can be removed. Because the skin is too tough to eat, the flesh is cut from it and eaten with a knife and fork.

Meats

A sizzling cut of meat can bring out the cave dweller in even the most well-behaved diner, but it's not always uncivilized to eat certain kinds of meat with the fingers.

Chops. At a dinner party or relatively formal restaurant, pork, lamb, and veal chops are eaten with a knife and fork. The center, or eye, of the chop is cut off the bone, then cut into two or three pieces. If the chop has a frilled paper skirt around the end of the bone, you can hold the bone in your hand and cut the tasty meat from the side of it. If there's no skirt, do the best you can with your knife and fork.

Among friends or at home, you can hold the chop and bite off the last juicy morsels of pork, lamb, veal. But if a chop is too big to be eaten with only one hand, it should stay put on the plate.

Grilled meats. At an informal barbecue, hamburgers, hot dogs, ribs, and pieces of chicken are most enjoyed when eaten with the fingers. But sausages without buns are eaten with a knife and fork, as are fish, steak, and other meats served in large portions.

Steak. Don't smother steak with steak sauce, especially when dining in a good restaurant. If you use a sauce, pour a small pool next to the steak and dip each forkful of meat before eating.

Melon

See page 396: "Cantaloupes and Other Melons."

Mints and Other Small Treats

When dinner mints, candy, petits fours, or candied fruits are offered in pleated paper wrappers or cups, lift them from the serving dish in the paper, transferring them to your plate before eating. Then leave the paper on your own plate, not the serving plate.

Muffins

At the table, cut regular muffins in half either vertically or horizontally and butter the halves one at a time. (As with all breads, hold the bread on the plate—not in the air—as you butter it.) English muffins are split in half, and each side is spread with butter, jelly, honey, or marmalade.

Mussels

When eating *moules marinières* (mussels served in their shells in the broth in which they were steamed), remove a mussel from its shell with a fork, dip into the sauce, and eat it in one bite. Anywhere but a formal dinner, it's fine to pick up the shell and a little of the juice, then suck the mussel and juice directly off the shell. The juice or broth remaining in your bowl can be either eaten with a spoon or sopped up with pieces of roll or bread speared on your fork. Empty mussel shells are placed in a bowl or plate that has been put on the table for the purpose.

Olive Oil

When bread is served, a small, shallow bowl or plate of olive oil is sometimes set on the table instead of (or alongside) the butter. Either spoon a small pool of olive oil onto your bread plate or dip a bite-sized piece of the bread into a communal bowl of oil. Be sure not to double dip.

Olives

The olives on an antipasti platter are eaten with the fingers; you also use your fingers to remove the pit from your mouth while cupping your hand as a screen.

    When olives come in a salad, eat them with your fork. If they are unpitted, remove a pit from your mouth by pushing it with your tongue onto the fork tip; then deposit the pit on the edge of your dinner plate.

Oranges and Tangerines

Eat these citrus fruits by slicing the two ends of the rind off first, then cutting the peel off in vertical strips. If the peel is thick and loose, pull it off with the fingers. Tangerines can be pulled apart into small sections before eating, while some varieties of oranges are more easily cut with a knife.

    Seeds should be removed with the tip of the knife, and sections are eaten with the fingers. The membrane around the peeled sections can also be removed with the fingers.

Oysters and Clams

Both of these bivalves are usually opened, served on cracked ice, and arranged around a container of cocktail sauce. Hold the shell with the fingers of one hand and a shellfish fork (or smallest fork provided) with the other hand. Spear the oyster or clam with the fork, dip it into the sauce, and eat it in one bite. Alternatively, take a bit of sauce on your fork and then drop it onto the oyster. If a part of the oyster or clam sticks to the shell, use your fork to separate it from the shell.

    If oyster crackers are served and you'd like to mix them with your individual serving of sauce, crumble them with your fingers before mixing. Horseradish, too, can be mixed in, or a drop can go directly onto the shellfish if you like the hot taste.

    When you order raw oysters or clams at an oyster or clam bar or eat them at a picnic, it's fine to pick up the shell with the fingers and suck the meat and juice right off the shell.

    Steamed clams. Don't eat any steamed clams that haven't opened at least halfway; they may be spoiled. Open the shell of a good clam fully, holding it with one hand. If the setting is casual, pull out the clam with your fingers or a seafood fork. If the clam is a true steamer, slip the skin off the neck with your fingers and put it aside. Then, holding the clam in your fingers, dip it into the broth or melted butter (or both) and eat it in one bite.

If no bowl is provided for empty shells, deposit them around the edge of your plate. In a more casual setting, it's okay to drink the broth after you've finished eating the clams. In a more formal setting, follow the host's lead.

Papayas

These tropical fruits are served halved or quartered, with the seeds scooped out and discarded. The pieces can be either peeled and sliced—in which case they are eaten with a fork—or eaten from the shell with a spoon.

Pasta

Pasta comes in almost every shape under the sun, so it's not surprising that different forms are eaten in different ways.

Spaghetti and other long noodles. The traditional method for eating spaghetti, linguine, tagliatelle, and the like is to place the fork vertically into the pasta until the tines touch the plate, then twirl it until the strands form a fairly neat clump. When the fork is taken to the mouth, neatly bite off dangling strands so that they will fall back onto the fork.

Using a fork and spoon to twirl spaghetti

The alternative is to hold the fork in one hand and a large spoon in the other. Take a few strands of the pasta on the fork and place the tines against the bowl of the spoon, twirling the fork to neatly wrap the strands.

For those who haven't mastered the art of twirling pasta strands, there's the simple cutting method. Just be sure not to cut the whole plateful at one time; instead, use your knife and fork to cut small portions.

Lasagna and other layered pastas. With layered pasta dishes such as ziti and lasagna, a string of melted cheese can stretch from plate to fork to mouth with every bite. Cutting portions through with a sharp knife should prevent the problem.

Penne and other tubular pastas. Clumps of small-sized tubular pastas can be speared with a fork, while rigatoni and other larger tubular pastas should be cut into bite-sized pieces.

Ravioli. Small ravioli can be eaten in one bite, but standard squares (about 2 × 2 inches), should be cut in half with your fork. If you eat Continental style, push the bites onto the fork with your knife.

Pastries

Traditionally, a dessertspoon and dessert fork are used when eating such pastries as cream puffs and éclairs; the pastry is held in place with the spoon and cut and eaten with the fork. Bite-sized pastries such as rugalach are eaten with the fingers. The general rule? If you can't eat a pastry without getting it all over your fingers, switch to your utensils.

Breakfast pastries. Croissants are eaten with the fingers. When adding jelly, preserves, or the like, carefully tear off small pieces and spoon on the topping.

- ➤ Danish pastries are cut in half or in quarters and eaten either with fingers or fork.
- ➤ Popovers are opened and buttered before being eaten (in small pieces) with the fingers.
- ➤ Sticky buns should be cut in half or in quarters with a knife and eaten with the fingers. If a bun is too sticky, use a knife and fork.

Éclairs. These cream-filled puff pastries are always eaten with a knife and fork. Just cut into them gently so that the filling doesn't squirt out. (See also page 398: "Desserts"; page 404: "Muffins.")

Peaches and Nectarines

Peaches are cut to the pit, then broken in half and eaten. If you don't like the fuzzy skin, peel the peach after halving it. When eating a nectarine (peeled or unpeeled, as desired), halve the fruit, remove the pit, and cut each half into two pieces.

Peas

To capture runaway peas, use your knife as a pusher to pile them onto your fork (held tines-up by necessity). Alternatively, use the tines of the fork to spear a few peas at a time. Never mash peas on the plate to make them easier to eat.

Pie

A slice of pie is cut and eaten with the fork, with the help of the dessertspoon if the crust is difficult to cut with the fork alone. When a slice of cheese is served with apple pie, it can be lifted with the fork and spoon, placed on top of the pie, and cut and eaten with each bite.

Pineapple

This rough and prickly tropical fruit is peeled, then sliced into round pieces and served on a plate. Use a dessertspoon and fork—the spoon for pushing the pieces, the fork for cutting and eating.

Pita Bread

See page 395: "Fried or flat bread."

Pizza

Take your pick: (1) Fold a pizza slice vertically at the center (to keep the toppings intact) and eat it with your fingers; (2) leave the slice on the plate and cut a bite-sized piece with a knife and fork. Deep-dish or Sicilian pizza, on the other hand, is normally eaten with utensils.

Plantains

See page 393: "Bananas and Plantains."

Plums

See page 391: "Apricots, Cherries, and Plums."

Popovers

See page 407: "Pastries."

Pork Chops

See page 404: "Meats."

Potatoes

See page 393: "Baked Potatoes (White and Sweet)"; page 401: French Fries.

Poultry

At a formal dinner, no part of a bird—be it chicken, turkey, game hen, quail, or squab—is picked up with the fingers. The exception is when a host encourages his guest to use fingers for eating the joints of small game birds served without gravy or sauce.

The no-fingers rule doesn't always apply when you're dining at home or in a family-style or informal restaurant. It's fine to eat fried chicken with your fingers and to do the same with the wings, joints, and drumsticks of other poultry. When eating a turkey drumstick, however, start with a knife and fork to eat the easily cut pieces of meat before you pick the drumstick up and eat the rest.

With the exception of a meal of fried chicken, there are certain situations in which utensils are always used. When eating the breast of a bird, use your utensils to cut off as much meat as you can, then leave the rest on the plate. Also use utensils when boneless poultry pieces are covered with sauce or gravy or are baked, broiled, or sautéed.

Quesadillas and Empanadas

When served as an appetizer, a quesadilla—a flour tortilla topped with a mixture of cheese, refried beans, or other ingredients and then folded and grilled or baked—is cut into wedges and eaten with the fingers. When served whole as a main course, it is eaten with a fork and knife.

Empanadas, which range in size from very small to quite large, are Mexican or Spanish turnovers filled with meat and vegetables. Small empanadas served as appetizers are finger food, while larger ones are eaten with a knife and fork.

Salad

When salad is served with a main course rather than before or after, it is best placed on a separate salad plate so that the salad dressing doesn't mix with any gravy or sauce.

Main-course salads—usually complete with pieces of chicken, shellfish, or cheeses and cold cuts—are put in the center of the place setting, just as any other entrée would be.

What about cutting up salad leaves? Large pieces of lettuce or other salad greens can be cut with a fork—or, if they're particularly springy, with a knife and fork. Just don't cut salad into smaller pieces all at one time.

Sandwiches

Sandwiches more than an inch thick should be cut into halves or quarters before being picked up and held in the fingers of both hands—although a sandwich of any size can be eaten with a knife and fork. A knife and fork are always used for a hot open-faced sandwich covered in gravy or sauce.

Wraps. Burritos, gyros, and other sandwiches in which the filling is wrapped in thin, flat bread (usually tortillas or pita bread) are most easily eaten with the hands. Any filling that falls to the plate is eaten with a fork.

Sashimi

See page 391: "Sushi and sashimi," under "Asian Dishes."

Seafood

See page 391: "Sushi and Sashimi"; page 39: "Bouillabaisse"; page 398: "Crab"; page 400: "Fish"; page 403: "Lobster"; page 404: "Mussels"; page 405: "Oysters and Clams"; "Shrimp," below.

Shish Kebab

Shish kebab (chunks of meat and vegetables threaded onto skewers and then broiled or grilled) are eaten directly from the skewer only when they are served as an hors d'oeuvre. When eating shish kebab as a main course, lift the skewer and use your fork to push and slide the chunks off the skewer and onto your plate. Place the emptied skewer on the edge of your plate and use your knife and fork to cut the meat and vegetables into manageable pieces, one bite at a time.

Shrimp

Shrimp can be easy to eat or take a little work, depending on how they are served. The shrimp in a shrimp cocktail should be served peeled and are usually small enough to be eaten in one bite. The traditional utensil is an oyster fork, although any small fork will do. If the shrimp are bigger than one bite's worth, just spear each shrimp with your fork and cut it on the plate on which it's served.

Shrimp served as a main course are eaten with a knife and fork. When squeezing lemon over the shrimp, use your cupped hand or a spoon to shield other diners from squirts. If sauce is served in a separate bowl, dip your shrimp into it only if the bowl is yours alone; if the dish is communal, either spoon a small pool of sauce onto your dinner plate for dipping or spoon it over your shrimp. In some shrimp dishes, including garlic prawns, the shrimp are served unpeeled. Pick up a shrimp, insert a thumbnail under the shell at the top end to loosen it, then work the shell free. An extra plate should be provided to hold the discarded shells.

Shrimp served as hors d'oeuvres are eaten with the fingers. Hold a shrimp by the tail and dip it into cocktail sauce, if you prefer; just be sure not to double dip.

Snails

See page 399: "Escargots."

Soups

When serving soup, place the soup plates or bowls on an underplate—or on a saucer if cups are used. When the soup is finished or the spoon is laid down, the spoon is left in the soup plate, not on the dish underneath. If the soup is served in a cup, the spoon is left on the saucer.

How to eat soup. Hold the soupspoon by resting the end of the handle on your middle finger, with your thumb on top. Dip the spoon sideways into the soup at the near edge of the bowl, then skim from the front of the bowl to the back. Sip from the side of the spoon, being careful not to slurp. To retrieve the last spoonful of soup, slightly tip the bowl away from you and spoon in the way that works best.

If you want a bite of bread while eating your soup, don't hold the bread in one hand and your soupspoon in the other. Instead, place the spoon on the underplate, then use the same hand to take the bread to your mouth.

French onion soup. This tricky-to-eat soup warrants its own guidelines. That's because it is topped with melted cheese (notorious for stretching from bowl to mouth in an unbroken strand) with a slice of French bread underneath. To break through to the soup, take a small amount of cheese onto your spoon and twirl it until the strand forms a small clump. Then cut the strand off neatly by pressing the spoon edge against the edge of the bowl; you could also use a knife or fork for cutting. Eat the clump of cheese and then enjoy the soup. If any strands of cheese trail to your mouth, bite them off cleanly so that they fall into the bowl of the spoon.

Crackers or croutons. If oyster crackers come with the soup, place them on the underplate and add a few at a time to your soup with your fingers. Saltines and other larger crackers are kept on the bread plate and eaten with the fingers. They can also be crumbled over the soup and dropped in, two or three crackers at a time. Croutons are passed in a dish with a small serving spoon so that each person can scatter a spoonful or more over his soup directly from the serving dish.

Other garnishes. Garnish soups with such optional toppings as croutons, chopped onions, or chopped peppers before you begin eating. With your clean soupspoon, spoon a portion from the serving dish and sprinkle it directly into the soup; you needn't place garnishes on your salad plate or bread plate unless you think you'll be wanting more. Put the serving spoon back on the garnish's underplate.

Spaghetti

See page 406: "Spaghetti and other long noodles."

Squab

See page 409: "Poultry."

➤ Chewing with your mouth open or talking with food in your mouth

➤ Slurping, smacking, blowing your nose, or making any other unpleasant noises

➤ Holding a utensil like a shovel

➤ Picking your teeth at the table—or, even worse, flossing

➤ Failing to place your napkin on your lap or not using it at all

➤ Taking a sip of a drink while still chewing food (unless you're choking)

➤ Cutting up all your food at once

➤ Slouching over your place setting or leaning on your elbows while eating

➤ Executing the boardinghouse reach rather than asking someone to pass you something that's far away

➤ Leaving the table without saying "excuse me"

Steak

See page 404: "Meats."

Strawberries

See page 394: "Berries."

Sweet Potatoes

See page 393: "Baked Potatoes (white and sweet)."

Tacos

Crisp tacos are eaten with the fingers, since cutting the crisp shell with a knife and fork will leave it cracked and crumbled. Do use a fork, however, for any filling that falls to the plate. Soft tacos, topped with a sauce, are eaten with a knife and fork; unsauced soft tacos can be eaten with the fingers.

Tangerines

See page 405: "Oranges and Tangerines."

Veal Chops

See page 404: "Chops."

Watermelon

Serve no more than a quarter of a small watermelon at one time. At picnics and other informal affairs, you can hold the slice in your hands and eat it bite by bite. When using a fork, carefully flick the seeds away with the tines and push them to the side of your plate; then use the edge of the fork to cut bite-sized pieces.

Wraps

See page 409: "Sandwiches."

Ziti

See page 407: "Penne and other tubular pastas."

Chapter Twenty-four

Eating Out

PART OF THE FUN OF EATING out is the sheer variety of restaurants to pick from. We can tuck into barbecue with the kids at Jim Bob's Rib Shack or—when we can afford it—dine in the lap of luxury at the four-star Café Beaucoup D'Argent. Even those of us who live in the smallest cities are usually able to choose between a diner's meat-and-two-veggies menu and a sampling of ethnic cuisines. And as we enjoy ourselves, we won't have much more than basic table manners to worry about.

Right?

Not exactly. Understanding the place setting and not holding your fork like a shovel are only the starting points. How you interact with the waitstaff and other patrons—from hemming and hawing over the menu as the server waits patiently to letting your kids run free—can have a ripple effect that affects service for everyone. Of course, the more formal the restaurant, the more you'll have to watch your p's and q's. But most rules of good eating-out behavior apply as much at a coffee shop as they do at a white tablecloth-and-candles establishment.

Reservations or Not?

UNLESS YOU'RE THE KIND OF PERSON who loves to hang out at the bar while you wait for a table, reserving a table beforehand almost guarantees that you'll be spared frustration. It also enables you to specify any special seating preferences you might have beyond smoking or nonsmoking areas—a table in the garden, perhaps, or one in a quiet corner. If you're unfamiliar with the restaurant, there's another advantage: When you call to reserve a table, you can ask about any dress rules and which credit cards are accepted.

Some restaurants ask that you call to reconfirm your reservation a day or two ahead—and with good reason, given the number of thoughtless people who don't bother to cancel when their plans change. Not only is it an abuse of good faith to make a reservation and then fail to show up, but it could cost you money. Many restaurants, especially those in urban areas, ask for a credit card number when you reserve. If you don't cancel, you might be surprised to find a penalty charge appearing on your next bill.

If you're inviting one or more people as your guests, consider a few things before deciding where to reserve. First, find out if a guest especially likes or dislikes certain ethnic foods (simply ask when extending the invitation). You could also give the guest a choice of two or three restaurants. If you're hosting a group, pick a restaurant with a wide range of foods so that everyone present will find something to his taste.

Choosing a restaurant you know will help stave off problems. You may be eager to try the hottest new spot in town, but don't risk it unless you've been assured that it has quality food, good service, and the kind of atmosphere you seek.

On Arriving

IF YOU DECIDE TO USE VALET PARKING, you're about to have your first restaurant "etiquette encounter"—saying "thank you" to the attendant as she takes charge of your car. (Coming full circle, you'll reward a parking attendant with a tip when your car is returned.)

On entering the restaurant, your next encounter is with the person(s) standing behind the podium in the entryway: the maitre d', host, or hostess. Your behavior at this stage calls for little more than common sense: (1) Don't block traffic as you patiently await your turn, and (2) once you're face-to-face with the maitre d', smile and say "hello." If you've reserved a table, say, "We have a reservation in the name of Mullins"; if not, "We'd like a table for four in nonsmoking, please"—not "Table for four! And nonsmoking!" (Note: "Maitre d'," the term more often heard in upscale restaurants, is used in this chapter to avoid confusion with a restaurant patron who hosts others.)

If the restaurant has a coat check room, tradition says a man always checks his topcoat, while a woman has the choice of taking hers to the table. Packages, briefcases, umbrellas, and other items are usually checked; exceptions are folders of papers (often needed at a business meal), notebooks, or other small items. Rather than check their handbags, women normally take them to the table, where they're kept in the lap or at the feet—never on the tabletop.

What if your fellow diners arrive at different times? Here are some guidelines:

> ➤ The first arrival should wait for the second instead of being seated—unless, that is, arrangements to the contrary were made beforehand or the restaurant is quickly filling up (another reason for reserving a table in advance).

> ➤ When two of group arrive together, they should ask to be seated—either because they are crowding the entry or they need to hold the reservation until the others arrive. They should also tell the maitre d' that others are coming and ask him to direct them to the table. If the restaurant's policy is to seat a group only when all members are present, the early arrivals should wait in the designated area or stand where they won't impede the flow of traffic.

Being Seated

When the maitre d' leads you to a table, is there any protocol involved? Only if you want to stand on tradition. If a man and a woman are dining together, the "rule" is for the woman to walk directly behind the maitre d', with the man following her; in a mixed group, all the women precede the men.

Don't feel insulted if you're seated in a heavily trafficked area, near an air-conditioner vent, directly under a loudspeaker, or close by the kitchen, restrooms, or door. At the same time, don't hesitate to ask for another table when yours is less desirable. Just stay calm and polite: "Could we be seated a little farther from the door, please?" or "We'd prefer a table with a banquette if one is free." If you can't be accommodated, just grin and bear it if you made a reservation; if you didn't, you can say "thanks anyway" and try for a better table at another restaurant.

> If a group meal has an official host, it's the host's choice whether to direct guests to chairs. If he chooses not to, guests ask where they should sit.

> The better seats are those that look out on the restaurant or out a window onto scenery, not at a wall—something to keep in mind when you're hosting a meal or simply wish to give a fellow diner the better view.

> At a table with a banquette, women are traditionally seated on the banquette, the men on chairs opposite them.

> The host and hostess customarily sit opposite each other, and time was when couples were split up so that they would have a chance to chat with people other than their spouses. Today, seating choices depend more on the preferences of the group.

> A male guest of honor—say, a relative whose birthday or retirement is being celebrated—is traditionally seated at the hostess's right; a female guest of honor, at the host's right.

See also page 424: "Tips for Restaurant Hosts and Guests."

The Table Setting

At most of the more formal restaurants, only a service plate and a bread plate are on the table from the start. Small first-course and salad plates are brought out by the waiter as needed, then set on the service plate. (The service plate will be replaced by your plate of food when the waiter brings the main courses.)

Today even the most formal restaurants rarely set tables with every utensil under the sun. Flatware is usually kept to a minimum, with additional utensils brought out whenever ordered dishes require them. The most traditional place setting is the "out-side-in," meaning that you start with the outermost utensils and work your way toward the plate. (See Chapter 23, page 379: "The Table.")

The usual glasses on a pre-set table are the water goblet and two wineglasses—the larger one for red wine, the smaller for white. At more formal restaurants, there may be additional glasses: the cylindrical champagne flute, which is better at keeping the

Much of the success of your meal hinges on your interaction with your waiter or waitress. For better or worse, servers are quick to introduce themselves today—but even if they don't, a polite diner will treat them with respect. "Respect" doesn't mean thanking a waiter or waitress for every little task performed, but the occasional expression of gratitude is definitely in order. Treating a server as a robot is unforgivably rude, and an imperious or condescending manner shows you not as superior but small. In brief, do the following:

➤ Respond with a "hello" when the server first greets you, not a demand ("We need water!").

➤ Answer her questions with actual words, not grunts.

➤ Add "please" to your requests.

➤ Look at her as she recites the specials, and don't grimace if she describes something you don't like.

➤ Before you order, make sure everyone else at the table is ready to order.

➤ When you want your plate to be cleared, signal by placing your knife and fork in the "I'm finished" position—beside each other diagonally on the plate. (See also Chapter 23, page 384: "Resting Utensils.")

Call the server by catching his eye and giving him an expectant look. If he's some distance away, you can raise your hand to chin level, index finger pointing up. If he's looking elsewhere and isn't taking orders at another table, you can also softly call out "Waiter?" Snapping your fingers, waving your hand furiously, or addressing him by anything other than his name or "waiter" (or, in the case of a woman, "Mary," "waitress," "Miss," or "Ma'am") is less than polite. "Boy" and "honey" are permissible only if the waiter is your son and the waitress your wife. (See also page 429: "Paying the Bill.")

wine bubbly than the saucer-shaped champagne glass of old; and a sherry glass, also cylindrical but smaller.

The Finer Points of Ordering

EXPERIENCED RESTAURANT-GOERS know that more than a little thought goes into ordering, from choosing pre-dinner cocktails to picking the meal courses to selecting the wines served during the meal. They also know how important it is to have made up their minds by the time they let the server know he can take their orders.

If you aren't ready, simply tell your server that you need more time. Holding him there as you keep changing your mind has repercussions: New arrivals at his other tables become impatient, some patrons have to wait longer to order, and the food your server is responsible for delivering to someone else must wait in the kitchen or under a heat lamp.

Two other important points:

> The signal that says you're ready to order is a *closed menu*. If you keep browsing the menu after you've decided what you want, how is the server to know?

> If those in your group want separate checks, make the request of your server at the start, even before you order a drink or appetizer. Asking for individual checks at the end of the meal slows down service for everyone in the restaurant because the server will have to spend time preparing them. Keep in mind that there's always the chance that a restaurant won't allow separate checks. If you plan to request them, find out if it's permissible by calling in advance or asking when you arrive. (See Chapter 6, page 69: "The 'Who Pays?' Dilemma.")

Ordering Pre-dinner Drinks

It's fine to order beverages the first time the waiter asks, even if every guest at your table hasn't been seated; latecomers can order when the server returns with the first round. If there is a host, he can take charge and ask the guests what they would like. (See page 424: "Tips for Restaurant Hosts and Guests.")

Ordering Meals

Is it necessary to order the same number of courses everyone else does? Not really, especially when you're going Dutch. If you're the only one who orders an appetizer, you needn't ask the server to bring it with everyone else's main course—unless that's the extent of your meal; your companions have drinks, the bread basket, and conversation to occupy them until their dishes arrive. At a hosted meal, you should order an appetizer or first course or dessert when no one else does only at the host's urging.

Once you've narrowed down your choices, it's fine to ask your server which dish she recommends. When she recites a list of daily specials, it's smart to ask the cost of the dishes that interest you (specials are generally on the expensive side). If you're the guest at a meal, however, it's best to leave questions of cost to the host. (For menus without prices, see page 424: "Tips for Restaurant Hosts and Guests.")

It's fine to tell the server that you'd like to share an appetizer or dessert—and possibly even a main course if you know the servings to be huge. Just be sure to compensate the server with a more generous tip unless an "extra plate" fee is charged. She would have received a larger tip for two full meals, so you might want keep that in mind when calculating how much to leave.

If you aim to have a leisurely conversation during the meal, order foods that can be eaten with ease. Lobster or crab in the shell, unboned fish, and pastas that may be messy or difficult to eat could make more demands on your time and concentration than you'd like. Also think twice about ordering a food that is unfamiliar to you. Unless you know how to eat an artichoke or tackle the crab claw in a bouillabaisse, stick with a dish that poses no unexpected challenges. (See also Chapter 23, page 390: "Food-by-food Etiquette.")

Ordering Wine

Dinner wine is really a condiment for food, so it's best ordered after the menu choices have been made. The orderer (preferably the most qualified person at the table) can either choose a wine that goes best with the greater number of dishes or ask the advice of the server—or, in tonier restaurants, the wine steward (also called the *sommelier* or, if a woman, *sommelière*). Given the wide range in character of both red and white wines, the old rule that the former should be served with meat and the latter with seafood is a little musty. An easy alternative to a shared bottle is wine ordered by the glass, which allows the diners to match the wine with their meals.

When the server brings the unopened bottle to the table, he shows it to the orderer. If this is you, confirm the choice with a nod. The server then uncorks the bottle and pours a small amount of wine into your glass, which you sniff before taking a sip; a simple "That's fine" will let him know that the wine neither smells nor tastes off. (Briefly swirling the wine in the glass before sniffing releases its aromas—but making a show of the tasting procedure is best left to connoisseurs.) If you recognize the smell of a tainted, or "corked," wine, sniff the cork if the waiter hands it to you. Otherwise, put the cork directly on the service plate or on the table.

The server pours the wine, serving the host or orderer last. (A diner who doesn't care to drink wine should either momentarily place her fingers over the glass when her turn comes or simply say, "No thanks"; turning the glass upside down is never the signal to use.) From that point on, it's up to the orderer to refill the guests' glasses if the waiter doesn't return to pour. White-wine glasses are traditionally filled three-quarters full; red-wine glasses, which are larger, are filled halfway.

A QUESTION FOR PEGGY

I know next to nothing about wine, but at a recent dinner for six the host insisted that I choose the wines. What should I have done?

When you're put on the spot in this way, be honest: "I'd love to, but I know so little about wine, I think I should leave it up to you." What you should *never* do is fake it; otherwise, you could end up with a wine that doesn't fit well with the food. Don't be embarrassed about asking for help, since even alleged wine experts often know little about pairing wines with food. You could ask the server or the other guests for suggestions as you look over the list: "Which red do you think will go best with the dishes we're having?" Another tip: Don't think you have to order wine priced at the high end of the scale to get one of good quality.

Start-to-finish Guidelines

IN ALL BUT THE MOST informal restaurants, good manners require that you observe a number of civilities and procedures, from the proper use of your napkin and buttering your bread to enjoying your coffee and dessert.

Using Your Napkin

Put your napkin in your lap shortly after you sit down. As you use it, blotting or patting your lips is preferable to a washcloth-style wipe—and remember that this square cloth should never do double duty as a handkerchief. (For more on using napkins, see Chapter 23, page 386: "Using Your Napkin.")

When the meal is finished, traditional etiquette says you shouldn't place your napkin on the table until the host or hostess has done so, signaling the meal's end. The practice is largely obsolete, but remembering it may come in handy if you're in a group that leans toward formality. In any event, leave the napkin to the left of the place setting in loose folds, positioned so that any dirty part is out of sight.

Bread and Butter

If you want a piece of bread and the bread basket is close to your place setting, it's perfectly fine to pick up the basket and ask, "Bread, anyone?" After everyone has been served, pick out a piece and put it on your bread plate, along with a pat or two of butter. If the butter comes in a dish, use your butter knife to scoop out a portion to deposit on the edge of the bread plate. (The bread plate is also the place to put jam or jelly, as well as any finger foods served on a communal platter.)

Once you've taken a piece of bread from the basket, it's yours: Don't tear off a portion of a slice and then put the rest back in the basket. Put your bread on the bread plate. Each time you want some, break off one or two bites' worth, butter it while holding it on the plate (not in the air), and eat. Don't hold your bread in one hand and a drink in the other (the polite diner uses only one hand at a time), and don't take the last piece of bread without first offering it to others.

When an uncut loaf (with cutting board and knife) is placed on the table, the host—or whoever is closest to the basket—cuts three or four slices, leaving them on the board. If manageable, the board is then passed when diners want to cut their own.

First Courses

Appetizers are eaten with the small fork to the left of the dinner fork. If you're having soup, the server will probably bring the soupspoon with the soup; if it is already part of the place setting, it is to the right of the knife or knives.

If a platter for sharing has been ordered—say, of antipasti or stuffed mushrooms—it is passed around the table, with each diner holding it as the person next to him serves himself, using only the serving utensils provided.

Beverages

Before taking a sip of water, wine, or any other beverage, blot your lips with your napkin to keep the glass from becoming soiled. And remember that the water goblet is not a substitute for a finger bowl. If you want to clean your fingers, use your napkin—or, if a dish has been messy to eat, excuse yourself to clean your hands in the restroom if no finger bowl or hot towel has been provided. (See Chapter 25, page 455: "Finger Bowl Finesse.")

Main Courses

The period spent eating the main course is meant to be enjoyable, but sometimes uncertainties or difficulties will creep in. Following are some of the problems that might crop up and tips for how to deal with them:

The food arrives at different times. If a significant time elapses between the arrival of the respective diners' hot dishes, the host (or if there is none, the other diners) should urge the first who have been served to go ahead and eat. If everyone is having cold dishes, follow the rule of waiting until everyone is served.

You want to send food back. As a rule, send a dish back only if it isn't what you ordered; it isn't cooked to order (a supposedly medium-well fillet arrives bleeding, for instance); it tastes spoiled; or you discover a hair or a pest. Just speak calmly and quietly to the server when making the request. (See also page 424: "Tips for Restaurant Hosts and Guests.")

Your side dishes come separately. When vegetables are served in individual small dishes, it's perfectly proper to eat them directly from the dish. Or, if you choose to transfer the food to your dinner plate, use a fork or spoon to carefully slide them onto the plate. You could also ask your server to transfer the side dish to your plate when he brings it. If necessary, ask for the empty dishes to be removed so that the table isn't overcrowded.

You want to taste one another's food. Accepting another person's offer to taste a morsel of his dish—or offering a bite of yours—is fine as long as it's handled unobtrusively. Either pass your bread plate to the person so he can put a spoonful on it or (if he's sitting close by) hold your plate toward him so that he can put the morsel on the edge. Do not hold a forkful of food to another diner's mouth, and don't ever spear something off the plate of anyone else.

You're faced with unfamiliar foods. If a food you're not sure how to eat comes on a platter of appetizers—a type of sushi, perhaps, or crab in the shell—you, as a polite diner, have three choices of how to proceed: (1) Wait until someone else starts to eat and follow suit. (2) Ask how the food should be eaten (fingers or fork, for example). (3) Avoid the food altogether. Only the ill-mannered diner cries, "*Ewww* . . . what's that?"

You're not sure how to rest your utensils. During the meal, never place a fork or spoon you've been using directly on the table. Instead, place the utensil diagonally on the edge of your plate, not propped against it like an oar. In fact, how you place your utensils on your plate is a code to the waiter, letting him know whether you have finished a course. (For resting utensils during and at the end of the meal, see Chapter 23, page 384: "Resting Utensils.")

Leftover Food

When you have food left over that you don't want to go to waste, it's usually acceptable to ask for a doggy bag—today, often a lidded container slipped into a small paper bag. When not to request one? First, at most business meals. (If you're dining with a business associate who's a close friend, it's fine to request a bag if you're going Dutch—but if she's the host, leave leftover food behind.) Second, at a wedding reception or other special function.

"What Do I Do When . . ."

It's the rare restaurant meal during which at least one spill or other perplexing glitch doesn't occur. These pointers will help you cope more easily.

I've dropped something? Don't pick up a dropped utensil and put it back on the table. Tell your server, who will retrieve it and bring a replacement. The exception is when you drop utensils that might be stepped on or impede traffic around your table; in that case, act fast and pick it up yourself.

Likewise, if a napkin falls from your lap, ask your waiter for a replacement instead of fumbling around at your feet to retrieve it. Also inform the waiter if you've dropped food. If, say, a spoonful of ice cream falls to the floor, quietly tell the waiter at the end of the meal so that it can be cleaned up before the next diners are seated.

My fork or glass is unclean? Don't use your napkin to try to rub smudges off a utensil or glass. Also don't announce the problem to everyone—especially the host, if there is one. The next time a server stops by, discreetly ask for a replacement.

I spot a hair or bug? If there is a speck floating in your water or a pest or hair in your food, simply refrain from drinking or put down your fork until you catch the attention of the waiter. While it's probably impossible to keep the rest of the table from knowing something is amiss, try your best to avoid a fuss. If you want a replacement, you'll probably be served one fairly quickly. Regardless of how long your new dish takes to arrive, insist that your tablemates continue eating.

Someone at the table has food on his face? If you notice a speck of food on someone's face (or on a man's moustache or beard), subtly call the person's attention to it— a favor he will appreciate. Either say, "Oops, there's something on your cheek," or signal silently by using your index finger to lightly tap your chin or whatever part of the face is affected. As prevention for yourself, occasionally dab your chin and upper lip with your napkin to remove any wayward bits of food.

I have spinach in my teeth? Running your tongue over your teeth may let you know if you have a bit of food caught between your teeth, or one of your dining companions might discreetly let you know. If you can execute a quick wipe of your teeth with your napkin without attracting attention, do so. If the food won't budge, resist the temptation to dislodge it at the table with your finger or utensil; excuse yourself instead.

I knock over my drink? If you spill your beverage, immediately set the glass upright and apologize to all present: "Oh, I'm so sorry. That was so clumsy of me!" Don't feel as if you have to crawl under a chair; accidents happen to everyone. If the spill is wine (especially red), discreetly signal the waiter or a busboy, who will put a cloth over the stain.

The waiter tries to whisk my plate away? If a server tries to take your plate before you've finished (maybe you've paused for a bit before taking that last bite of steak), don't hesitate to say, "Oh, I'm not finished," even if he's already on his way to the kitchen. If you *have* finished but don't want those who haven't to feel rushed, simply raise your hand slightly and say, "If you don't mind, please wait until everyone's finished before you clear the plates."

Condiments

Condiments range from salt and pepper to the individual small dishes that accompany Chinese, Indian, and other ethnic foods. For ways to handle these and other condiments, see Chapter 23, page 397: "Condiments."

A QUESTION FOR PEGGY

There seem to be so many things to dispose of during a meal—the paper on a straw, the little containers for butter, sweeteners, and jelly. Where am I supposed to put them?

It's simple. Just place the containers for butter and jelly on the edge of the bread plate. Crumple any paper tightly and put it under the rim or on the edge of your bread plate or coffee saucer. The aim is to keep the table looking litter-free.

In our more relaxed world, people who dine together think in terms of "hosts" and "guests" less often than they used to. But if you extend the invitation and it is understood that you're paying (as at many business meals), you're the host, like it or not. Today's hosts wear the mantle more lightly, but there are still a few things for them to consider—as there are for guests.

When You're the Host . . .

➢ Give careful thought to your choice of restaurant. Do the guests like exotic food or down-home cooking? Are they vegetarians or unrepentant carnivores? If you're hosting a group, choose a restaurant with enough menu choices to please everyone. (See also page 414: "Reservations or Not?")

➢ Reserve a table in advance. You may not mind sitting at the bar waiting for a table, but others of your party may rather do anything but.

➢ Arrive a few minutes before your guests to relieve them of the worry of whether they should proceed to the table. If you wait at the table, give the maitre d' the names of the guests and ask her to direct them to you.

➢ If you wait in the foyer for several guests and some are more than ten minutes late, it's all right to go ahead and be seated, asking the maitre d' to show tardy guests to the table.

➢ As the host, you traditionally walk behind the guests if the maitre d' leads the way to the table. If she doesn't take the lead, you lead the guests. (See also page 416: "Being Seated.")

➢ If you're a woman, make clear to the maitre d' on your arrival that the check is to be presented to you and you alone—not to one of the men in a mixed group. Some women prefer to make advance arrangements for receiving the check (and sometimes for paying the bill).

➢ If a latecomer arrives after you're seated, stand as you extend your greeting.

➢ Whether you order a pre-meal drink or not, make it clear that your guests may order drinks, and of any sort.

➢ When ordering food, tell guests to feel free to order anything on the menu. Or get the point across by either recommending a dish at the middle or high end of the price range or telling them what you're having (again, a dish that is mid- to high-priced). Saying that a certain appetizer "looks delicious" lets guests know that you expect everyone to have a first course.

➢ If there's a lapse in the service and meals arrive at different times, urge those who've already been served to go ahead and start eating, especially if they are having hot food.

➢ If a mistake occurs—the wrong dish is brought to a guest, for example—tell the guest affected that you'll inform the waiter, then do so politely.

➢ When paying the check, don't display or disclose the total. Even a joking "Well, it's a darn good thing we enjoyed our food" could make guests feel they've ordered too extravagantly.

When You're a Guest . . .

➤ If you've arrived before the host and have taken a seat at the reserved table, it's best not to order anything other than water, especially if you're a guest at a business meal. When waiting for a close friend or family member, you might feel comfortable ordering a drink—but that's all.

➤ Never criticize the choice of table to the maitre d', no matter how much you dislike the location. The host alone should request a switch.

➤ When ordering a drink, try to stay somewhat in line with what everyone else orders. In a free-spirited group, tequila shots may not raise an eyebrow. But such choices are usually a bad idea if everyone else is having iced tea, fruit juice, and club soda.

➤ When your host orders a drink at a meal with a time limit (a business lunch or a pre-theater dinner, for example), order at least *some* kind of beverage so he won't think you're worried about pre-meal drinks slowing things down.

➤ As a general rule, don't choose the most expensive dishes on the menu, even if your host says, "Please don't hesitate to order anything you want." Try to order in the same general price range as the other guests. At the same time, don't feel you have to order the cheapest items on the menu, which could imply that you think that's all the host can afford.

➤ If there are no prices on the menu, keep from going overboard by remembering that some foods (pork, chicken, pasta, and rice-based dishes) are generally less expensive than others (beef, fish, shellfish, caviar, and anything that's served with truffles).

➤ If you need to send food back, do it only if there is really something wrong with it, not because you've decided you don't like it.

➤ Never complain about the food or service. Sounding dissatisfied could make it appear that you question the host's taste in restaurants.

➤ Even if the host has tipped the coat check person because he, not you, collected all the tickets on arrival, it's a nice gesture to try to reimburse him: "Jack, won't you please let me take care of this?"—but also know when to take no for an answer.

Fruit and Cheese

It's possible that a fruit course may be served at some point during the meal—either with the salad, after the main course (in that case, often with cheese), or as dessert. The days of peeling your own fruit are largely past, but a whole fruit should be quartered, cut up, and eaten with a knife and fork.

Cheese, seen on the menu in many upscale restaurants, is served before the dessert course. The server (a *fromager* [froh-mah-ZHAY] if male, *fromagère* [froh-mah-ZHEHRE] if female) will either bring a tray of cheeses or wheel out a cart, suggesting the most suitable choices. Slices of different types are then arranged on a separate plate (often centered with a piece of fruit, a wedge of fig, or plum cake) for each diner. While the cheese can be eaten on bread, the full flavor comes through if you eat it with a knife and fork. Start with the milder cheeses and progress to the strongest.

Dessert

In some place settings, a dessertspoon and fork are placed horizontally above the dinner plate. Use the fork for eating and the spoon as a pusher—or vice versa, depending on the softness of the dessert. (See also Chapter 23, page 398: "Desserts.")

Coffee and Tea

If a waiter places a pot of coffee or tea on the table but doesn't pour, the person nearest the pot should offer to do the honors, filling her own cup last. Two other points:

> ➤ Do not take ice from your water glass to cool a hot drink. Just be patient.
> ➤ Do not dunk doughnuts, biscotti, or anything else into your coffee.

For steeping and drinking tea, see Chapter 23, page 394: "Coffee and tea.")

Using Hot Towels

In some upscale restaurants, steamed hand towels are brought to diners at the end of the meal. Use the towel to wipe your hands and, if necessary, the area around your mouth. (Wiping the back of your neck or behind your ears is best not done in a restaurant.) Most waiters will take the towel away as soon as you've finished. If not, leave the towel at the left of your plate, on top of your loosely folded napkin.

Watch Your Step!

THERE ARE SOME BEHAVIORS that a restaurant patron should avoid as a matter of course. A few have to do with table manners and overall finesse, others with being considerate of everyone else. Even a smooth sophisticate who knows her place settings to a tee can come off as a boor to her companions and other patrons—not to mention the unlucky waitstaff—if she thinks only of herself. (For more on behavior while dining, see the chapter "Table Manners," page 379.)

Assorted No-no's

The first consideration is your posture. To show that you're alert and engaged, don't slouch. Sit up straight and don't stoop to eat your food. Also don't fidget with your tie or jewelry, drum your fingers, or jiggle your knee. A few other things to avoid:

Smacking and crunching. Eating as quietly as possible is essential to good table manners. For many, other people's smacking noises are as cringe-making as on a blackboard.

Chewing sloppily. Keep bites reasonably small and chew with your mouth closed. Don't form food into a ball in one cheek or take a sip of anything while chewing.

Talking while eating. Make sure not to talk with even a little bit of food in your mouth; it doesn't take that long to swallow.

Reaching. Avoid the boardinghouse reach. Reach for something only within the invisible boundary that separates your personal space from the other diners'.

Sopping and plate-pushing. Using a piece of bread to sop up the sauce left over from a dish is fine—but only when the bread is speared by the tines of your fork. When you finish the meal, leave your plate exactly where it is: Pushing it away, even slightly, is a faux pas akin to the boardinghouse reach.

Picking your teeth. Toothpicks should be used in private, not as you walk out of the restaurant or, worse still, at the table. Also refrain from noisily cleaning your teeth with your tongue at meal's end—an equally unattractive habit.

Dinner Conversation

Rule number one for socializing at the table: Don't talk so loudly that other diners become annoyed. The same goes for laughter, which escalates in proportion to the amount of alcohol being consumed. The occasional burst of laughter in a crowded restaurant is one thing, but repeated outbursts amount to disturbing the peace.

As you talk, sit up straight and don't fidget. And choose your subjects with care. While politics, religion, and other potentially volatile topics aren't really off-limits, discussing them could risk nettling your dinner companions and putting a damper on the meal. Also avoid talking about anything bleak or unappetizing, including illness or surgery—two topics that are especially off-putting while people are eating.

The no-elbows-on-the-table rule applies only when you are actually eating, not conversing. Whenever your utensils aren't in hand, putting your elbows on the table and leaning slightly forward shows you're listening intently to what is being said—not to mention making it easier to hear in a noisy restaurant.

Another major concern: Turn off your cell phone from the moment you walk into a restaurant to the moment you leave. Indeed, more and more restaurants are requiring diners to either turn off their cell phones or switch them to vibrator mode. (See also page 430: "How Do You Spell 'Obnoxious'?"; Chapter 21, page 308: "In restaurants.")

Restaurants that cater to children have become part of the American landscape, with birthday parties and children's entertainment the stock-in-trade of some national chains. At the other end of the spectrum are the high-end restaurants with quiet, formal settings, many of which don't allow children under age twelve. A good rule of thumb for parents is *not* to take young children to fancy restaurants; save that for when they're eight or nine and able to sit quietly at the table and practice good table manners.

Even in the most kid-friendly places, children should be taught to speak softly and to be on their best behavior when eating out. With some clear reminders and careful attention, eating out can be a good learning experience for children of all ages. (See also Chapter 14, page 187: "In Restaurants"; Chapter 14, page 185: "Eating Out.")

➤ Before going, remind your child of what's in store. She'll be given a menu, the waiter will take her order, and everyone will stay at the table until the meal ends.

➤ Since a young child probably isn't accustomed to waiting for meals, take a small drawing pad and colored pens (or other quiet playthings) to keep her occupied. Just be sure to put them away before the food arrives. For very small children, bring something they can eat while they wait for their order to arrive: single packs of applesauce, crackers, individual servings of yogurt, and so on.

➤ Place your order as promptly as possible. For efficiency's sake, order for any child who's five or under. Be positive she knows what she wants before the waiter comes to take the orders. It disrupts service for the waiter to have to stand there while the child repeatedly changes her mind.

➤ If a toddler gets restless or noisy and you can't stop the disturbance, escort her from the dining area and stay with her until she calms down.

➤ Keep children seated in their chairs. If they run near servers who are carrying heavy, scalding-hot dishes, they risk harming themselves and others.

➤ If your child spills something or makes another mess, do whatever you can to clean it up. The less you occupy the busboy and waiter, the less you delay service for other diners. Because cleanup for your party will be larger than for those without children, be generous to the waitstaff with both your appreciation and your tip.

➤ If your child starts irritating other diners—say, by peering over the back of a booth or jumping—don't wait to put a stop to the behavior. (As obvious as that seems, it's amazing the number of parents who are willing to let mischief slide.) If the diner beats you to the punch (preferably with a polite "Excuse me. You probably don't realize it, but your daughter's jumping is shaking our booth. . . . Would you mind asking her to stop? Thanks"), apologize and say that it won't happen again. Then take pains to see that it doesn't.

➤ Know when to leave. Children find it hard to sit still for long periods, and it's unrealistic to expect them to. Unless dessert and coffee are served right away, you'll be wise to forgo them.

Excusing Yourself

When you need to get up to go to the restroom, it isn't necessary to say where you're going—a simple "Excuse me, please; I'll be right back" is sufficient. At other times, a brief explanation is in order: "Please excuse me while I check with the babysitter." Leaving without a word is rude.

When You Run Into Friends

If you happen to cross paths with friends at a restaurant, is it necessary to introduce them to your dining companions? If a friend or acquaintance drops by the table, the answer is generally no. If you want to talk briefly with the person, step aside before doing so. If, on the other hand, your intuition tells you that introductions all around are expected, by all means make them.

Unless they're sitting in a booth or on a banquette, where rising would be difficult, it's polite for both men and women to rise when someone is being introduced or has stopped by to talk; when the group is large, however, only those closest to the visitor rise. Traditionally, women did not rise for either sex, even if the visitor was elderly. Things are different now—especially at business meals, where anyone should stand briefly for introductions.

If you run into friends while being seated, don't conduct a lengthy conversation with them while the rest of your party sits down and begins to peruse the menus. You don't have to sit immediately, but do tell your tablemates that you'll "be there in a minute"—and then keep your word. Likewise, don't say you're leaving the table for "just a minute" to visit someone else and then stay away so long that the people at your table feel shunned.

Grooming at the Table

In most circumstances, it is more polite to excuse yourself and put on lipstick in the ladies' room than to do it at the table. The exception is when the restaurant has an informal atmosphere and you're among friends, in which case you can apply the lipstick quickly. What you *should* avoid is a primping routine—no compact, no powder. And then there's that never-to-be-broken rule: Whether you're a man or a woman, don't use a comb at a restaurant table, nor should you rearrange your hair or put your hands to it wherever food is served. Using dental floss at the table is a major never-ever. Believe it or not, some people have no qualms about doing something so private in public.

Paying the Bill

IF YOU'RE HOSTING A MEAL, it's a good idea to let the maitre d' or waiter know in advance that the check should be given to you, lest an eager guest try to pay it himself. (Note to guests: Don't take the edge off the host's hospitality by trying to grab the check. Your turn will probably come.)

Less-than-desirable behavior is magnified in a restaurant because paying patrons have rightful expectations of a relatively tranquil meal. Here are some acts to avoid at all costs.

Holding court on a cell phone. Even though you'd think that the diner who gabs away on his cell phone would be an extinct species by now, he's still hanging on. As pitiful as he is (trying to transmit the message "I'm on the go, I'm a deal-maker, I'm *connected*" while appearing just the opposite), he's responsible for a serious disruption. To everyone's misfortune, he's never heard of the rule that says there's a time and a place for everything.

Bribing the maitre d'. People who charge to the front of the line in a busy restaurant and flash a large bill at the maitre d' insult not only the restaurant management but whomever they've just pushed past. A tip for a maitre d' who has given you a good table and attentive service is acceptable (it's usually given on leaving), but trying to buy a good table is inexcusable.

Flaunting your wealth. A noisy table of big-spending revelers flaunting their riches by ordering bottle after bottle of exorbitantly priced wines (not to mention puffing away on cigars) is one of the worst kinds of showing off. There's no excuse for such behavior, no matter how large one's bank account.

Getting soused. The table in the corner that periodically explodes with laughter, whoops, and hollers that almost startle other diners out of their chairs is either listening to the funniest person on earth or drinking too much. In a calm setting, few things irritate restaurant patrons more than the tipsy table that erupts in a rafter-rattling roar.

Taking over. Groups celebrating a special occasion sometimes seem to think they've rented a private room. They tie balloons to chairs, stand on chairs to make speeches, and toast whomever in full cry—to the chagrin of everyone present.

Overdoing displays of affection. A romantic candlelit dinner for two is undoubtedly the time for a bit of cooing and moony gazing, but couples who paw each other or kiss passionately are hard to ignore. The prohibition on this sort of behavior falls under the umbrella of respecting the right of other patrons not to be distracted from their own pleasurable dining experience.

When the check comes, keep it out of view as you look it over. It's not a guest's business to know what the cost of the meal came to—nor your obligation to disclose it. When you're ready to pay, signal the waiter by putting the check holder to the edge of the table, with the bills or the credit card sticking out a bit.

Going Dutch is another matter. Splitting the bill can be approached in two ways. First, you each pay only for what you ordered; second, you split the bill in equal shares even though the cost of the food isn't even-steven. The latter is preferred by many because it's simpler, and friends don't usually mind if some pay a little less than their share. There may be times, however, when you feel like you're subsidizing the others (they shared two bottles of wine and you had none; they had steak and you had a dinner salad). If you feel you're overpaying more often than you should, don't be afraid to say you'd like separate checks; just make sure to ask before ordering, for both your fellow diners' and the server's sake: "Hope nobody minds, but I'm going to have to ask for a separate bill tonight." Putting the shoe on the other foot, it is incumbent on those whose orders were disproportionately large to insist that they put more into the kitty.

If you're paying cash and want the server to keep the change, tell her so directly. Saying "Keep the change, thanks" will prevent the server from standing in line at the cashier for no reason.

∾ Complaints . . . and Appreciation ∾

Restaurateurs can tell you that keeping diners happy is one big job. They also point out that people are much more likely to voice their complaints than their appreciation. That's not to say that you shouldn't let it be known when the service is slow, a server is rude or careless, or the food comes badly prepared. The restaurant depends on its customers' approval for its livelihood, and its faults can't be corrected unless they're brought to the management's attention.

Make a complaint quietly, without attracting the attention of other diners. Speak first to whoever committed the error. If he makes no effort to correct the situation, take your complaint to the manager or captain.

Rudeness and laziness might be reported, but don't confuse them with the inability to serve too many people. Often, a server works as hard and fast as possible but still can't keep up with patrons' requests. If this is the case, you could still complain to the management, but be careful not to put the blame on the server, who's undoubtedly no happier about the situation than you are.

If after making a legitimate complaint you receive no satisfaction at all, you might reduce the tip (or, in the most extreme cases of bad service, leave none) and avoid that restaurant in the future.

On the other side of the coin, appreciative comments and a generous tip are more than welcome when you're pleased with the service. While tips are expected, comments like "The food couldn't have been better" or "The service was especially good" are a pleasant surprise and mean a great deal to someone who is trying to do her best. The management will also appreciate hearing from a customer who is satisfied and doesn't hesitate to say so.

Buffet Restaurants, Diners, Etcetera

THE ADVANTAGE OF A BUFFET restaurant is that you can sample as many foods as you like. It is also slightly more economical because your tips to the staff are smaller.

Because you're permitted to make as many trips to the buffet as you wish, there's no reason to overload your plate. Also, leave your first plate and utensils on the table for the waiter or busboy to remove. Health codes in many states don't allow dirty dishes to be taken back to the serving stations, since soiled utensils and plates could spread germs . . . and besides, clean plates look more appetizing.

Cafeterias

When a cafeteria is crowded and there are no empty tables, it's fine to take an empty chair at a table already occupied—but only if you ask, "Is this seat taken?" or "Do you mind if I sit here?" Diners who join a stranger are under no obligation to talk, but it's all right to start a casual conversation if the other person seems receptive.

Diners, Coffee Shops, and Delicatessens

Most diners and coffee shops have both booths and tables served by waitstaff, while delicatessens often have tables for customers but no table service. At diners and coffee shops, all the guidelines for dining at a regular restaurant apply.

At a deli, you usually place your order and then either pick it up or wait until a counter person delivers it. The customer clears the table and disposes of paper plates and plastic utensils on leaving. No tips are expected in this case.

Fast-Food Establishments

The etiquette you should observe in these most casual of restaurants boils down to treating those who serve you with respect. That means not directing your attention solely to your companion(s) or your cell phone conversation as you order and pay (especially at a drive-through) and handing your bills and change to the server instead of putting the money on the counter. And a "please" and "thank you" are essential.

Two other tips: Save time for everyone in line by deciding what you want to drink before you order, especially when a drink comes with a meal package. And when ordering at a drive-through window, be sure to drive your car close enough so that the server won't have to strain his back when he hands over your food.

Chapter Twenty-five

The Dinner Party

INTERESTING PEOPLE, GOOD FOOD, and a pleasant setting are the ingredients. What brings them together to make a great dinner party? Not champagne and caviar, not fine china and silver—though these are certainly gracious embellishments. The indispensable elements are the hosts and the spirit they bring to the occasion.

Many years ago, Emily Post wrote, ". . . if the enthusiasm of your [the hostess and host's] welcome springs from innate friendliness—from joy in furthering the delight of good-fellowship beneath your own roof—you need have little doubt that those who have accepted your hospitality once will eagerly look forward to doing it again and again." Her advice is as fresh today as it was in 1922, just as her prediction that "perhaps in time the term formal dinner may come to mean nothing more exacting than company at dinner" has proved correct.

The very formal dinner party, though still a staple for ceremonial and certain business events, has given pride of place to informality. The etiquette of today's dinner party owes much to the casual style of family meals. Rigid rules have been replaced by flexibility, and today's successful hosts are more concerned with the needs of their guests than the perfection of their table settings. Whether a seated meal with candlelight and professional servers or a grab-a-plate-and-serve-yourself cookout, a great party is always grounded in enthusiasm and friendliness.

But you can't throw a party on good intentions alone. Even the most casual get-together requires careful organization, thoughtful execution, and courteous manners. Although primarily devoted to the etiquette and intricacies of hosting a dinner party, this chapter is also intended to guide dinner party *guests* and maximize everyone's enjoyment of the occasion.

The First Steps to a Successful Party

FUN AS IT MAY BE to dream up a scrumptious menu and think about whom you will invite, first things must come first—when you will hold the party, how many guests you'll include, and how much money and time you're prepared to spend. These businesslike basics will largely determine all other decisions.

Date and Time

The time of your party is up to you, but be conscious of local customs and work schedules, particularly if the party will be on a weeknight. Consider time changes; a party might begin a little later during daylight savings time, a little earlier during the darker months.

Consult your own calendar and be attuned to what is going on among your likely guests. A conflict with religious services, a major sport or cultural event, or parents' night at the neighborhood school can cause problems. Check with a guest of honor before setting a date (or with a family member if the party will be a surprise). If you plan to hire help, keep in mind that experienced cooks, servers, and caterers are usually booked well in advance for holidays as well as graduation and wedding season.

The Guest List

All sorts of things might go awry during the evening, yet your party can be a rousing success—with the right guest list. The key is to invite people whom you like and have every reason to believe will be interested in each other, whether they already know one another or are strangers.

The mix of guests will largely determine the *personality* of your event—peaceful, relaxed, intense, spirited. If you want a tranquil evening, don't include guests who are likely to bicker. You can ask your ardent Republican friend to this dinner and your equally vehement Democratic friend to your next gathering. But if you and your other guests enjoy lively political discussions, invite both.

Sometimes, the occasion itself will dictate all or part of your guest list—dinner for business associates and their spouses, members of a club or an organization, a guest of honor (in which case the guest is often asked to suggest people whom he or she would like to include), or family members. When entertaining people you don't know well, especially at a large party, it's a good idea to include a sociable friend or two who will be willing to help you keep the evening running smoothly.

There's no foolproof formula for the guest list. And few hosts have escaped the classic party poopers—the nice guy who becomes a buffoon after one cocktail, the quiet type who decides to flirt outrageously, the egotist who has to have the spotlight, the sloppy eater. Managing difficult guests is, for most people, a matter of learning through experience, and experience comes through doing. Don't be discouraged if an occasional gathering doesn't go according to plan; every party is a chance to learn and hone your hosting skills.

How Many Hosts?

Co-hosting is an excellent way to throw a large dinner, which may be too expensive for an individual or couple. Bonding together with friends is also a good way to host events honoring others—graduation, engagement, wedding, anniversary, birthday, promotion, and retirement dinners.

Co-hosts should get together at the outset; discuss dates, guest list, budget; and de-

Themed dinner parties can be loads of fun. But if too obscure, too cute, or too difficult, the theme can fall flat. An obscure theme is one that guests simply don't get or don't care about. Decorating in the colors of your alma mater may delight guests at an alumni reunion but can bewilder or go unnoticed by those who have no reason to make the connection. "Too cute" includes themes that are childish, inappropriate to the guest list, or overdone. For example, it's traditional to serve green beer at a St. Patrick's Day dinner, but coloring food green can put guests off their meals. A theme is too difficult when its execution consumes too much of the hosts' time, energy, and often their budget. Whether as subtle as decorating with seasonal flowers or as elaborate as a Halloween party with everyone in full costume, a good theme is one that all guests will appreciate and enjoy.

cide who will do what. Duties should be divided as fairly as possible, taking advantage of each person's skills and interests. If one of the hostesses has a great eye for color but can't boil water, she's the obvious choice to do the centerpiece—not the crown rib roast. Co-hosts also share hosting responsibilities, including greetings and introductions, kitchen duty, and serving or supervision of hired servers.

The host at whose home the party will be held has the greatest responsibility, and others should offer to assist with cleaning in advance of the event as well as post-party cleanup. Supplementing the "home host's" tableware and kitchen equipment is another way to pitch in. Sometimes a co-host can't physically help (often the case with an elderly or infirm person or someone who lives out of town). But able-bodied people who are too busy to contribute their time should think twice before co-hosting.

How Many Guests?

Most people can handle intimate dinners for four to six people; entertaining larger numbers depends on your ability to accommodate everyone comfortably. Take an objective look at your house or apartment and picture it with your guests present. Where will they sit? Is there plenty of room for people to move about freely and eat in comfort? If your dinner table is designed for eight, then inviting twelve for a seated meal will mean cramming. Pity the people who will be stuck at the corners of the table, and invite fewer guests or opt for a buffet.

Do you have plenty of comfy seating for before and after the meal? What about bathrooms? Too many guests and too few facilities can cause lines. Do you have enough plates, glasses, utensils, and table linens for the number of people you want to invite, or are you prepared to purchase, borrow, or rent the necessary items?

Experienced hosts take everything into account, including the weather. Thirty people may be optimal for a buffet in the warm months, when guests can overflow onto the porch or terrace. But the same number may be too many to confine inside in the dead of winter.

Budgeting Money and Time

A successful dinner party is one that seems almost effortless but has been planned with military precision. One of a host's first steps is budgeting, so decide how much you can spend on the evening; account for everything, down to the last swizzle stick. It's better to trim your supply list at the beginning than to overspend on decorations and then be forced to nickel-and-dime on food and beverages.

Wise hosts and hostesses budget their time as carefully as their money. One person or a couple can manage a small casual dinner, but assistance of one kind or another is usually needed for eight or more at a seated dinner and for larger groups at a buffet. Do you have family members or friends who can help with cooking and service? Would it be a good idea to hire one or several servers, kitchen assistants, or bartenders for the evening? Or is professional soup-to-nuts catering the best way to go? (See page 437: "The Catered Affair.")

Cooking and serving are only part of a host's responsibilities. If you're stuck in the kitchen or preoccupied with getting the meal on the table, who will greet your guests, make introductions and keep conversation going, and spot little problems before they become big ones? Hosting a dinner party is a good example of multi-tasking, so decide which tasks you can handle and which require help.

Advance Preparations

WITH THE DAY AND TIME, guest list, and budget decided, you're ready to plan exactly how to organize the evening. For many hosts, this is the best part of preparation—calling for equal parts of creativity and common sense.

∾ Alternatives to Dining at Home ∾

Hosting at a restaurant or club is often the only way that very busy people can entertain. It enables them to give parties in distant locations, making arrangements by phone and e-mail, or to entertain on a larger scale than is possible in small apartments and condos. It's also a great way to reciprocate those who have hosted you when you don't have the capacity for at-home dinner parties. If you worry about cost, consider all the expenses of an at-home party, plus your time; your actual expenditure for dining out may be the same or even less.

The first steps of planning are the same as for an at-home affair: deciding on the date, the guest list, and how much you want to spend. Then scout for a place if you don't have one in mind; consult with proprietors; settle on menu, seating arrangements (you may want to book a private room or terrace seating), and type of food service (seated or buffet, with or without bar service); and organize the method of payment, including gratuities. Unless you're familiar with a restaurant or club, sample the cuisine before making a final commitment.

The Dining Format

No matter how formal or casual, there are two basic formats for dinner parties—the seated meal and the buffet—but each allows for a good deal of variation.

Seated dinner with food served at the table. Guests are seated at the dining table. The food is brought to them, or serving dishes and platters are placed on the table and passed. The meal is served in courses, and plates are changed between courses. The number of courses can range from two to six, and the level of formality is entirely up to the hosts. (See page 453: "The Formal Dinner Party.")

Semi-buffet, or seated dinner with buffet service. The meal is eaten at the dining table and perhaps smaller tables set for dining, but the food and plates are put out on a separate buffet table or tables, and guests serve themselves. Drinks, dessert, and sometimes the salad course may be brought to the guests at their tables. Semi-buffets adapt beautifully for outdoor parties with seating at patio or picnic tables.

Buffet with casual seating. This is the true buffet. Guests serve themselves at the buffet and then sit where they please in the party area—living and dining rooms, family room, patio. A buffet requires adequate seating and table space (coffee table, side tables, and tray tables), so diners will have a place for glasses and cups and saucers. Casual buffets include barbecues, pool parties, and box suppers.

Cocktail buffet. A cocktail buffet is basically a cocktail party (see Chapter 27, page 472: "The Return of the Cocktail Party") at which the food is sufficient to constitute a meal. The menu is more extensive and heartier than hors d'oeuvres, and food can be eaten with the fingers only or with no more than a plate and fork. Food is put out buffet-style on one or more tables, and guests take items at their leisure. A cocktail buffet often begins later than a conventional cocktail party—6:30 or 7:00 PM—and lasts two to three hours. A *cocktail reception* is the most formal type; the party is usually in honor of a person or event, and the dress is often black tie for men and fancy cocktail or evening dresses for women.

The Catered Affair

Caterers can be lifesavers for busy hosts, and catered meals are often less expensive than people imagine. But finding and hiring just the right caterer requires a considerable investment of time. If you've never hired a caterer, ask family and friends for recommendations, or check out local business listings. Search carefully, meet personally with prospective caterers, and check every detail before signing a contract.

A caterer who comes to your home offers *off-premises* services. *On-premises* catering is done at the caterer's location—hotel, club, restaurant. Some caterers do both, so you might ask your favorite restaurant if they also cater off-premises or can suggest someone.

➤ Before calling caterers, establish your budget; the date, time, location, and format of the party; and the approximate number of guests. Think about what you want the caterer to do—full meal and bar preparation and serving, food preparation only, all food or just part of the meal. Do you want the caterer to supply plates, dinnerware, and glasses? Some caterers also offer furniture rental, table linens, and decorations and flowers.

➤ If you don't have a specific caterer in mind, meet with several and get more than one estimate. Caterers usually give average per-person estimates, but you can ask for an itemized list that breaks out food, serving personnel, and equipment costs. Does the estimate include tax and gratuities? How is payment to be made? Discuss the menu in detail and inquire about your options. Consider the labor involved in food preparation and serving. Paying careful attention to specifics can save you from unpleasant surprises when the final bill is submitted.

➤ Some caterers will come to your home for an interview. If not, you should be clear about your facilities and possible limitations such as a small kitchen or difficult access for catering vehicles. If the dinner will be at a clubhouse, on a boat, or at some other site away from your residence, describe the place and its location clearly.

➤ Check references. Be certain the caterer is properly licensed and has a valid catering permit. Check the caterer's insurance (general liability and liquor liability) and workers' compensation coverage. Your state or local health department has information about licensing requirements in your area.

➤ Visit the caterer's kitchen. Most caterers offer samples of their cooking, so taste the cuisine. You can ask to see photos of catered meals to get a sense of the caterer's presentation style.

➤ Determine whether the caterer is able to be flexible—for instance, if meals can be provided for any guests whom you know have special requirements, such as kosher or vegetarian meals.

➤ Finally, you should have a comfortable professional relationship with the catering service you hire. The caterer and his or her helpers will be working in your home, and even if they handle everything, you should oversee the work so that it's done to your satisfaction.

Inviting Your Guests

Although casual dinners may be arranged at the last minute, invitations to a dinner party are normally issued a week or two before the event—three to six weeks if the occasion is formal or the social calendar is crowded. In general, the more formal a dinner, the earlier invitations are mailed, since guests need time to prepare for an elegant evening.

The formality of the event usually dictates the nature of the invitation. For very formal dinners and cocktail receptions, invitations are printed, engraved, or handwritten. Invitations to less formal dinners can be printed to order, pre-printed cards with information filled in by hand, handwritten notes, or issued by phone or in person. E-mail is a possibility as long as the invitees are regular e-mail users.

Phoned or in-person invitations are often a must for events like a potluck supper when guests are expected to contribute food and other items, though you might follow up with an attractive invitation.

Invitations to seated dinners and small buffets usually include an RSVP because the host needs to know exactly how many people to plan for. A notation of "Regrets only" or no request for a reply may be fine for a large buffet-style dinner; as long as you have an approximate number, there's usually plenty of food for a few extra people. But an RSVP will give you the most accurate guest count. (See also Chapter 18, page 248: "Requesting a Reply.")

In addition to date, time, place, names of the hosts, and RSVP, an invitation should indicate the nature of the party (for the wording and meanings of dress notations, see Chapter 5, page 48: "Invitation Terms") and any other pertinent information, including directions to the party location if needed.

Determining the Menu

YOUR MENU WILL DEPEND on the formality or informality of your party, whether food is served at the table or buffet, who will be doing the cooking, the tastes of your guests, and your budget. Also consider the size of your kitchen and how it is equipped and ventilated. If you have one oven, for instance, you won't be able to bake or roast everything, so include dishes that can be cooked or warmed on your cooktop as well. You also need adequate cold storage and freezer space for items prepared in advance.

A good dinner menu is a balance of richness and simplicity. For example, a first course of a heavy soup or shellfish in a cream sauce might be balanced by an entrée of roast beef au jus or chicken baked in fresh herbs. A sauced entrée might be accompanied by crisp, lightly seasoned vegetables. Everything should complement everything else; flavors should enhance flavors. Too many sauces or "sweet" items can be overwhelming. Consider food textures, colors, and aromas. Envision the full plate you will set before your guests. Will it appeal to the eye and nose as well as the taste buds? For inspiration, today's cookbooks, cookery magazines, and their Internet versions often include sample menus as well as recipes.

If you're the chef, ask yourself what you do well. A basic rule of cooking for a group is to avoid experimenting. You'll feel more confident preparing foods that you are familiar with, and it's usually easier to adapt recipes you know than to try something totally new.

Many people think that a dinner party menu has to include more courses than a family meal, but that isn't necessarily the case. A formal dinner menu traditionally comprises five or six courses, but most at-home dinner parties consist of three or four, and in some cuisines (Asian and Indian, for instance), a main course and dessert are more than adequate.

An elaborate formal dinner menu can include as many as six courses:

1. Soup, fruit cup or melon, or shellfish
2. Fish or sweetbreads (often omitted if shellfish is served first)
3. Entrée, or main course (usually roast meat or fowl with vegetables)
4. Salad
5. Dessert
6. Coffee and cordials (with fresh fruits and/or cheeses served after dessert as an option)

Note that salad is served *after* the entrée, contrary to the U.S. restaurant practice of serving salad first. The reason is that fresh greens and salad vegetables in vinegar-based dressings are served to cleanse the palate between the meat course and the dessert and dessert wine. Traditionally, wine is not served with the salad course because the vinegar in the dressing will interfere with the taste of a good wine.

If a light sorbet is served between courses, it is also intended to clean the palate. The serving is small, and diners may have a taste or eat it all.

An at-home dinner party menu is often limited to a starter course (soup, fruit, a vegetable or shellfish dish, pasta), entrée, and dessert, with coffee after. Salad can be served as a starter or accompany the entrée.

A buffet dinner menu may eliminate the starter course, though the host will often provide more than one entrée and a greater variety of side dishes. Buffet-style dessert

∾ Resources for the Cook ∾

Thanks to the wealth of resources available today, preparing party meals is easier than ever, and even inexperienced cooks can put together wonderful dinners for groups. Supermarkets and sometimes the corner grocery offer prepared foods, from deli fare to whole roast turkeys and baked hams. Check out the produce department for washed salad greens, and the freezer section for cooked entrées. The average mall includes gourmet stores, ethnic markets, and specialty food and beverage shops. Even small towns probably have a bakery and perhaps an independent butcher who will cut meats to order (a great find for kitchen novices who pale at cookbook instructions like "butterfly" and "fillet paper-thin"). If you don't mind the shipping costs, you can put together an entire party meal with food catalogs, a credit card, and a telephone.

Many dishes can be completely or partially prepared in advance and refrigerated or frozen. The time saved on party day is a blessing, and some dishes actually improve after a day or two. Recipes today often include information about advance preparation and proper storage as well as nutritional content.

sometimes includes more than one sweet plus fresh fruit for diners who prefer a lighter end to the meal. You might set a separate table featuring several desserts or a single, spectacular creation such as a tiered cake. Dessert plates, forks, and spoons are put on the dessert table.

A cocktail buffet menu may include hors d'oeuvres or just a hearty spread of foods that can be eaten while guests stand. Napkins are essential, since finger food is often eaten directly after being taken from trays or containers. Toothpicks and skewers are provided for fruit wedges, meatballs, chicken wings, and other foods that are sticky or greasy. (Put out an empty plate or bowl, so guests can dispose of used skewers and bones.) Crackers, toast points, and flat breads serve as bases for meats, pâté, and flavorful spreads. If plates and utensils are needed, usually dessert plates and forks are sufficient.

Dietary Considerations

If you know that a guest follows a special diet but aren't sure of the specific restrictions, don't hesitate to call and ask. It's especially wise to inquire if the guest is the only one (or one of a few) whom you're inviting. There are also some precautions a host or cook can take without consulting guests. One is to avoid cooking with peanuts, peanut oil, and additives such as monosodium glutamate (MSG) that commonly cause allergic reactions. Another is to steer clear of very hot or heavily spiced dishes unless you know your guests enjoy them. If you serve a highly spiced dish, also provide a blander alternative for guests who can't take the heat.

In general, a guest with dietary restrictions should *not* alert his host ahead of time—except when he's the only guest or one of a few. When the restrictions are due to allergies, other medical conditions, or religious sanctions, it's especially important to inform the host. A vegetarian may also say something if he's the only guest. He can offer specifics. For example, does he exclude red meats only or all meat, fish, and fowl? Are eggs and dairy products, including cheese, off the list? Whatever the dietary restriction, the thoughtful guest should offer to bring his own food to a small gathering or when visiting overnight with a relative or good friend.

At a large gathering, a guest with food restrictions should eat what he can, though it's imperative that he ask the host if he has questions about any off-limits ingredients. When asking, he should take the host aside so that others won't think there might be something wrong with the food. Some people with allergies and other food restrictions simply eat something before attending a dinner party to ensure that they won't be hungry if there isn't much served that they can eat.

When a dietary "restriction" is simply a matter of taste, the guest makes his preferences known only if his host asks ("Do you eat meat?" or "Do you like Brussels sprouts?"). It's rude for a guest to inquire about a party menu just to see if he'll like what's being served.

Choosing and Serving Wines

For those who aren't wine connoisseurs, purchasing and serving wine may seem like crossing a minefield. But people have been making, drinking, and enjoying wines for millennia, without the wine snobbery that sometimes crops up today.

Trust your taste buds. If you think a wine tastes good with a certain food, your guests will probably agree. Try to find a wine shop with knowledgeable staff who can make recommendations based on your menu and your budget. (Very good wines need not be expensive or rare; purchasing by the case can save money.) Food and wine publications offer useful suggestions, but try to sample a wine you don't know, preferably with the food you plan to serve. Keep a record of wines and brands you particularly like for future reference.

You don't have to serve a different wine with every course, but even with the most casual dinner, it's nice to have a white (perhaps for cocktails and first course) and a red, as long as the wines go with the food.

The following fundamentals should help with wine selection and service—and eliminate some misconceptions.

Red and white. Traditionally, white wines are served before red, and dry ("sec") wines before sweet. But the food more often determines the choice of wine. For instance, a somewhat sweet wine may be particularly suited for a rich, sweetish entrée such as lobster.

Red wine with red meat and white wine with fowl and fish remains a serviceable guideline, but the specific food is a better way of deciding which wine to serve. In general, wines should be comparable to the food in "body" or "weight" (relative strength), so that one doesn't overpower the other: robust wines with hearty dishes, lighter wines with more delicate fare. The variety of wines today is so great that color is no longer a predictor of strength.

Uncorking. Wine is usually uncorked about a half hour before being served in order to aerate, or "breathe." Wine is generally opened, tasted, and allowed to air—and corks are sniffed for vinegary or "off" smells—in the kitchen. Champagne is often opened, with care, at the table and served as soon as the cork is popped.

Temperature. Generally, white and pink wines are chilled before serving; red wines are not. But the old rule of serving reds at room temperature was made back when room temperatures tended to be colder than in modern housing, so a red wine may benefit from slight chilling. Any wine that is too cold or too warm loses its distinctive flavor. Your wine dealer can provide temperature guides, but again, trust your instincts and your taste.

Between pourings, a chilled wine can be returned to the fridge or kept in an ice bucket on a side table. For serving, the bottle is usually wrapped in a large dinner napkin or white towel to hold the chill and prevent dripping from condensation.

Decanting. Aged red wines and port wine develop sediments, so they are decanted—poured into a glass container or carafe—to separate the clear wine from the sediment. The bottle is stored upright for twenty-four hours; then the wine is carefully poured into the decanter until the sediment reaches the top of the bottle. To catch stray bits, you can pour through cheesecloth. Other wines can be poured into carafes simply because it is an attractive way to serve.

Pouring. At the table, wine is poured before each food course if there's a new wine for that course. This gives the diner a chance to smell and taste the wine on its own. Traditionally the host pours for women and older guests first, then the men, and fills his or her glass last. At a buffet, however, wine is offered when a guest is seated or set out on the drink table for guests to serve themselves.

> Wineglasses are filled approximately halfway, though sparkling wines are often poured to the two-thirds level so the drinker can enjoy the bubbles. Filling a wineglass near the rim makes it difficult to savor the aroma, and a full glass is easier to spill.

> Still wines are poured into the center of the glass, but sparkling wines are poured against the inside of the glass (tilt the glass slightly) to preserve the natural carbonation. To prevent drips, give the bottle a *slight* twist to end pouring.

Holding the glass. Since white wines are normally chilled, a white-wine or champagne glass is held by the stem to prevent the transfer of heat from the hand. Red-wine glasses, which are sometimes larger and a bit heavier, may be held by the bowl. The bowl of a cognac glass is cupped in the hand because cognac benefits from warming. This also explains why cognac and brandy glasses are not made of cut crystal, which interferes with the warming.

Alsace   Bordeaux   Burgundy   Sherry Flute   Coupe   Flute   White wine

The shapes of standard wine and liqueur glasses have evolved to enhance enjoyment of the aroma, or "bouquet," and to maintain the correct temperature. Whether plain or crystal, transparent glasses give a clear view of the color and body of the drink.

I have a number of friends who rarely or never drink alcohol (several are recovering alcoholics) and others who, like me, enjoy mixed drinks and wine with dinner. I always find myself worrying about how to make everyone happy when I entertain.

First, be sure to stock your bar with a variety of nonalcoholic beverages: soft drinks, still waters, flavored waters, soda water and tonic, fruit juices, iced tea. Then serve nonalcoholic drinks just as you do wines and spirits, in bar glasses or wineglasses with appropriate garnishes like lemon and lime slices. Offer alternatives with meals. Most people who don't drink wine will choose water, but some may enjoy coffee or hot or cold tea. If you serve champagne, you can also chill a bottle of sparkling grape juice.

The goal is not to call special attention to guests who don't drink alcohol. Serving all drinks in the same way, for instance, can avoid rude questions about why a guest is not having a cocktail. Also be attentive to seating arrangements. A friend in recovery should not have to spend the evening next to a wine aficionado extolling the virtues of every wine served.

444

Setting the Scene

ANOTHER KEY INGREDIENT for a successful dinner party is ambience—the mood set by the surroundings. As you prepare, think about how you can best organize your home to make your guests comfortable and complement the meal. Consider your own convenience. As host and perhaps chef and server, you have a lot to do, and your physical surroundings should facilitate your every movement.

The House

A clean and tidy home is the obvious place to start. Even though the party is at night, the exterior should be neat, drives and walkways should be swept and well lighted, and anything that might cause falls, including ice and slush, should be removed. If you live in an apartment, check your hallway for clutter. In inclement weather, think about convenient storage for wet coats, umbrellas, boots, and overshoes that are sure to arrive with guests.

Adequate seating is a must. At very casual dinners, some guests may sit on the floor, but not everyone is comfortable that way, so provide as much seating, including floor pillows, as you can. If you don't have enough chairs, either borrow or rent some or use items like sturdy trunks, low stools, and ottomans that can do double duty as seating and tray tables.

A few more suggestions for setting the scene follow:

Rearrange furniture and other items if necessary to facilitate conversation and freedom of movement. Arrange seats in clusters so that your guests can easily visit. Large pieces of furniture might be shifted if they block easy access to the party areas. Protect valuable items by putting them where they can't be accidentally broken or damaged.

Put out plenty of drink coasters. Cocktails and other pre-dinner drinks are served with a paper or cloth napkin, but these won't prevent water rings on furniture. If smoking is allowed, be sure to put out ashtrays.

Set drink and buffet tables apart from main gathering points and doorways. If you use multiple dining tables, be sure there's plenty of passage room for guests to get to their seats and sit without bumping into the person behind them.

Be conscious of fragrances. Flowers with strong scents, aromatic candles, pungent potpourri, room fresheners, and the like can become stifling in enclosed spaces, set off allergies, and ruin the flavors of the foods you serve.

Adjust room temperatures and lighting. A large group of people will affect the climate of a room, so it's often wise to adjust thermostats before a party (slightly lower than normal heat settings and higher settings for air-conditioned spaces). Adjust as needed during the evening. Lighting should be bright enough for people to see, but not glaring. Table lamps tend to be softer and more flattering than overhead lights,

A QUESTION FOR PEGGY

I'm having a buffet supper for twenty, and some of my guests have never been to my condo. My sister says I should be prepared to show off my house, but I'm doing the party by myself, and I just don't have time to clean the upstairs. I'd like to confine the party to my downstairs and backyard.

Except for a housewarming, hosts have no obligation to give house tours, though they may if they want. A host should make it obvious where guests are and are not to go. Before anyone arrives, you can turn off your upstairs hall lights and shut doors to upstairs rooms. Courteous guests know not to open closed doors or enter unlighted areas. If asked for a tour, you (or perhaps your sister) might take a guest on a quick walk through your downstairs. If you see someone wandering into an area where he isn't wanted, divert his attention with some polite chat and gently usher him back to the party area.

and dimmer switches allow for easy adjustments. Candles provide a warm glow but are inadequate after sundown.

A lighted house always seems to say, "Welcome," so open the curtains or blinds before your guests arrive. You can close them once the party is under way.

Subdue the music. Recorded classical or contemporary middle-of-the-road instrumental music is usually a safe bet. Be certain the music is just loud enough to be distinct; when turned too low, it becomes an uncomfortable and distracting buzz.

The Dinner Table

Table setting is discussed in detail in Chapter 23, page 379: "The Table." The following ideas apply particularly when you entertain at dinner.

Table linens. Keep tablecloths and place mats uncomplicated. Very frilly or lacy mats, napkins, and table runners and crocheted tablecloths can snag utensils, glass bases, even guests' bracelets and watchbands, causing spills. Plastic tablecloths and mats are fine for casual outdoor dining, but they can detract from the overall appearance of a more formal table. (See also page 453: "The Formal Dinner Party.")

Cloths for dining tables should fall no more than fifteen to eighteen inches below the edge of the table. Cloths for buffet and serving tables may touch the floor. A floor-length cloth on a bar table is a good way to keep bottles, ice chests, and other supplies out of sight. Be sure to equip bar and food stations with plenty of cocktail-sized napkins, paper, or cloth.

Table decorations. Flowers and other decorations should be centered on the table and arranged in low containers, so they don't block the view from one side of the table to the other. For the same reason, candelabra are placed with their broad sides facing the ends of the table, and clusters of candlesticks are avoided if they will interfere with guests' line of sight. Candles should be new, unscented, dripless, and burn higher or lower than the eye level of seated diners. Light candles before guests enter the dining area.

Everything on the table should serve the cause of dining, so don't clutter place settings with decorative extras. Guests shouldn't have to forage through table favors, oversized place cards, exotic napkin holders, and other knickknacks to find their plates and utensils. Individual menus are provided only for the most formal dinners.

Flowers are pretty on buffet tables, if there's room. Arranging buffet food at different height levels, while intended to showcase the food, can actually impede self-service and sometimes put a dish literally beyond a guest's reach.

Buffet tables. The placement of dinner plates indicates the starting point of a buffet table. On a large or round table, putting plates in the center gives no clear place to begin and also forces guests to reach over the food. Although silverware and napkins may be arranged next to the plates, placing utensils at the end of the buffet frees guests from carrying too many items as they serve themselves. You can also provide dinner trays—set with utensils and napkins—at the end of the serving table. For a seated semi-buffet, dining tables are set with everything except plates.

The arrangement of the food on a buffet is up to you, though gravies and sauces are placed beside the dishes they accompany and breads are often available at the end of the line. (If bread and rolls are placed on the plate first, they can become soggy with sauces, meat juices, and dressings.)

When serving drinks buffet-style, it's usually more convenient to use a separate table. Guests can take their filled plates to the table or wherever they are sitting and then return to the drink table. Expecting guests to juggle a full plate, utensils, and napkin while pouring a beverage is an open invitation to accidents.

Traffic pattern around a buffet table: A table against a wall.

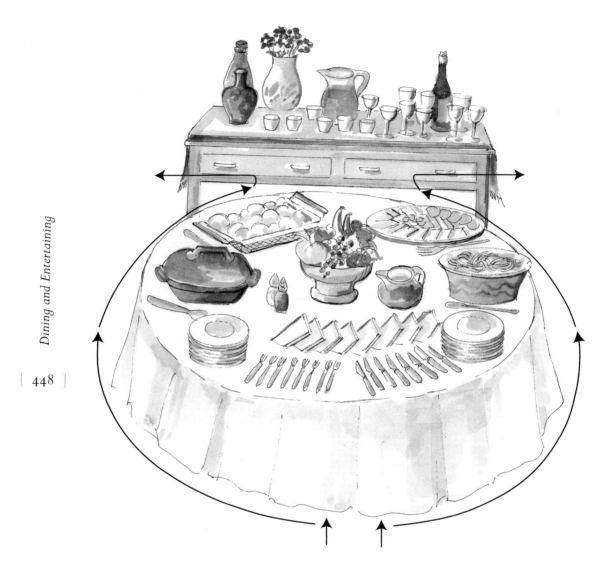

Traffic pattern around a buffet table: A table in the center of a room.

Let the Party Begin

A HOST OR HOSTS SHOULD be ready on the dot to answer the door, greet guests, and take coats. After a gracious greeting, you'll want to offer each new arrival something to drink. But don't abandon a guest at the door in order to get him a cocktail. Usher guests to the party area, make introductions as necessary, and then get the drink or direct the guest to the drink table.

If separate groups of guests arrive at the same time, welcome everyone inside first,

The Etiquette of Cocktail Glasses and Wineglasses

If you're holding a partly consumed cocktail when dinner is announced, you can take it to the table and finish it before the meal begins. Or you can leave your glass on a side table, atop a coaster or glass-topped surface. Just don't take an empty drink glass to the table. Do the same with a wineglass. A host should not expect guests to use the same glasses for pre-dinner and dinner wines.

Specialty beers are increasingly popular as an aperitif and are usually served in a tumbler or Pilsner glass. Sometimes a bottle and empty glass are provided so the guest can pour for himself, but beer and soda are served in cans or bottles only at the most casual affairs.

At the dinner table, don't turn wineglasses upside down to indicate you don't want wine. Instead, you should simply say, "No, thank you," when wine is offered. Or put your hand over the glass (above, not on, the rim) to signal a server to pass you by. An experienced server will then remove the glass.

then make introductions. (When you're a guest, don't stop to chat at the door, especially if there are other guests behind you.) A single host may have to do some fancy footwork when guests come in rapid-fire order, so it's pragmatic to ask one or two good friends to help with introductions and beverages. Couples and co-hosts can share greeting responsibilities.

Once everyone has arrived, a host should mix and mingle while attending to these essential courtesies:

Encourage conversation. When introducing guests for the first time, bring up subjects they may have in common. If you see someone on his own or trapped in a conversation, politely go to the rescue.

Pass hors d'oeuvres and offer to replenish drinks. Refill bowls of munchies before the last olive or pretzel disappears.

Pick up empty, abandoned drink glasses. Dump out and wipe ashtrays. In other words, police the party area, but don't be obsessive.

Check periodically on bar supplies and napkins. Refill ice buckets as needed.

Take quick peeks in bath and powder rooms to see that everything is in order. Replace soiled or wet hand towels.

Dinner Is Served

When the group is small, the host simply announces that dinner is served. With larger numbers, the host or hosts approach conversation groups and invite them into the dining area. Try to spot a few good friends who will begin the movement; most people will follow. Ringing a bell or sounding a gong is an antiquated custom but might be fun if it fits with the theme of the evening, such as a Victorian dinner.

Seating shouldn't be a problem if you've planned in advance. Place cards are easiest with a larger group—eight or more at the table—and when multiple tables are used. Otherwise, guests will look to the host for guidance.

Convivial seating. Man-woman-man-woman seating is no longer a rule. Gender-specific seating really doesn't fit an age when men and women frequently attend events by themselves or with same-sex partners. Aim instead to seat guests between people with whom they're likely to be congenial. It's still a good idea to separate married couples and close friends simply because they are likely to converse too much with each other or discuss domestic subjects that others cannot join in. Think about your guests' personalities. If you seat a shy person next to a very talkative one, the shy guest may spend the entire meal in enforced silence.

Honored guests. A female guest of honor sits to the immediate right of the host, a male honor guest to the immediate right of the hostess. If there is one host or hostess, the honor guest may be seated next to the host/hostess or at the opposite end of the table. But these guidelines are flexible.

∾ Clearing the Table ∾

Places are cleared between courses, including the utensils used for that course and empty wineglasses if you will be serving another wine. Even at casual dinners, plates shouldn't be stacked or scraped at the table. Remove one or two plates at a time. Don't ask people to pass plates, utensils, or glasses to you unless the items are beyond your reach.

Bread plates and butter knives are left on the table until the dessert course. Salad plates are not taken away until the diner is finished. If someone has used the wrong knife or fork for a course, don't ask her to hold on to it. Replace the utensil (which may necessitate a quick wash and dry in the kitchen).

The process of clearing may sound time-consuming, but actually it goes quickly and is a lot easier and safer than balancing stacks of china and handfuls of silverware. It goes even faster if two people are clearing, so when you don't have servers, arrange in advance for a friend to help. You'll be too busy serving the next course to wash dishes or load the dishwasher, so plan for a place in the kitchen where dirty plates and dinnerware can be placed.

A special consideration. If you can, seat left-handed guests at the left end of each side of the table, where they are less likely to bump elbows with right-handed neighbors.

When to start eating. Hosts traditionally take the first bite of food to signal guests to begin eating. Some hosts observe rituals such as saying a blessing. But when you're serving, you may want to tell your guests to begin eating before you, so their food won't go cold; it's fine for guests to start eating before the host does if he encourages them to do so. At a buffet, guests normally begin eating when they sit down.

Hosts should be conscious of the dinner conversation, guiding it if necessary. Don't be panicked by natural lulls; people tend to stop talking when a course is served and they begin to eat. Then the chatter picks up. Be alert to uncomfortable situations. When one person is dominating the table talk, you can direct questions to those who aren't holding sway. If an issue is raised that you know is troubling for some guests, bring up an entirely new subject. A considerate host is always gracious . . . and sometimes a little firm.

After Dessert

Coffee and cordials are served either at the table or in the living room. Though coffee traditionally follows a meal, it's fine to serve coffee with dessert if your guests prefer. A host is not obligated to offer after-dinner drinks, and today's hosts might pass up this finishing touch if guests are driving home.

Fresh fruit and/or cheese might be served after dessert, and hosts may put out after-dinner mints and nuts. (At a formal dinner, bowls of mints and nuts can be placed on the table as decorative items, then offered at the end of the dinner.) However, when the meal is over, hosts aren't expected to continue providing food. Assuming that the meal has been sufficient, the after-dinner hour is your reward—a time to relax with your guests and enjoy the pleasant afterglow of your hard work.

Conversation is the most popular after-dinner activity, but guests may enjoy listening to music, dancing, or playing games such as Trivial Pursuit, Pictionary, and charades. Which activity to choose depends on the mood of the evening, and no one should be goaded into participating.

Saying Farewell

All good things must end, and well-mannered guests will know when to depart. Hosts should be on hand to say farewell and show their guests to the door.

Don't begin cleaning up or washing dishes until your guests have gone (unless someone has seriously overstayed his welcome and more subtle hints have failed). In general, if a guest offers to help you clean up, respond with a pleasantly firm, "Oh, this is your night out. We're not doing dishes now. Thanks for offering, though." The exception is if guests are close friends or family members and it's customary that you all pitch in when dining at each other's homes. If guests brought food, you may want to return their serving dishes washed and dried. If you borrowed items for the party, it's probably best to return them the next day or within a few days.

Good guest manners begin the moment you receive a dinner invitation and continue beyond the end of the evening.

Do respond to an RSVP as quickly as possible. If the invitation includes "and Guest," tell the host whether you plan to bring someone—even when you don't yet know whom. Call the host with the name of your guest as soon as you can.

Don't bring a guest unless invited to do so. Regardless of the circumstances, don't ask a host if you can bring a guest. Parents must remember that if children are not included in the invitation, they aren't invited.

Do arrive on time. Five or ten minutes after the start time is okay. No guest should show up early. If the invitation says "around six," this means between six o'clock and six-fifteen. If you're going to be more than fifteen minutes late, call, explain quickly, and give the host an estimated arrival time. A host should not be expected to delay a meal longer than fifteen minutes for a latecomer.

Do bring a gift if appropriate. It's nice to present a host or hostess with a token of appreciation—a bottle of wine (but don't expect it to be served), candy, or gift soaps. If you send flowers, call the host in advance to check on the party color scheme, or, better yet, send an arrangement on the day after the party, with a nice note. If you take flowers to the party, be sure they're in a vase. (A busy host doesn't have time to search for a container and arrange your flowers.) Don't bring food unless specifically requested. People who dine frequently with one another are not expected to bring gifts on every occasion.

Don't gather in the kitchen unless the host asks you to. Some people love to cook with an audience; others really can't concentrate. You can offer to help a host who is cooking, but don't insist if she or he turns you down.

Don't change place cards or ask to sit in a special place at a seated dinner. Hosts put a good deal of thought into seating arrangements, and a polite guest doesn't try to out-think them. It's rude to manipulate seating in any way.

Do compliment the food graciously. Just be realistic. (The soufflé may be marvelous, but don't say that it's the best you ever tasted unless you mean it.) You're commenting on the food, so avoid backhanded compliments like "I never guessed you could cook this well." If you know the host didn't cook, don't mention it unless he or she does. The host will convey your compliments to a cook or caterer.

Don't be a double dipper. One chip, cracker, shrimp, veggie, or fruit tidbit is for one dip, and only one, in the bowl. Double dipping is unsanitary and inconsiderate of the hosts, who will have to toss out a dip when they catch a double dipper.

Do be on your best behavior. Unless asked by the host, don't open closed doors, cabinets, drawers, and medicine chests. Tidy the bathroom after use. (Hang guest towels neatly on the rack, but don't refold them.) If you don't see ashtrays, go outside to smoke if you must. Don't inquire about the cost of anything.

Don't let your cell phone interrupt. Turn ringers and beepers off. If you must call, go to a secluded spot. If you need to use your host's phone, ask for permission. If you expect to receive a call during the party, ask the hosts before giving their number to anyone. Don't answer a host's phone unless he or she requests you to.

Don't be the last to leave. Unless a host specifically asks you to stay, it's best to make your departure when other guests begin to leave. In general, guests are expected to stay for at least an hour after dinner. If you must leave early, inform the host before the party or when you arrive.

Do thank your hosts—all of them—when you leave. You may want to follow up with a thank-you note, but personal notes are expected only for formal dinner parties. Otherwise, call the host within a day or two or send an e-mail if that's the best way to reach the person. If there were multiple hosts, you might call everyone or just the one or two you know best.

Above all, never abuse a host's trust. When a guest accepts an invitation, he or she enters into a kind of unwritten social contract to act responsibly. Excessive drinking, drug use, aggressive behavior, crude language—these behaviors violate the fundamentals of decency. Hosts commit themselves to make the occasion pleasant and safe. Guests should do no less.

If you've hired servers or caterers, you must see that they are dismissed with your thanks (and payment if that is the arrangement). A good host doesn't delay an employee's departure beyond an agreed-on time. If you want a worker or workers to stay throughout the party, be sure that this is clear when you contract for services.

A host's last duty is to see that guests depart safely and soberly. Do not under any circumstances allow an inebriated guest to drive. Another guest might take the person home. You might call for a cab; pay for it if you must. In the worst case, you may have to put your guest to bed for the night. Don't worry about embarrassing a guest who has overindulged. What matters is that the person is alive the next day to regret his or her behavior.

The Formal Dinner Party

THERE'S FORMAL, and then there's FORMAL. At the highest end of the formality scale are official dinners hosted by or for high-ranking public officials and diplomats. These events are governed by strict protocol, and guests are informed of (and often instructed in) the rules by protocol officers. (See Chapter 22, page 326: "Official Protocol.")

For most people, a formal dinner is one at which they are seated at a dining table and the entire meal is served by someone other than themselves. A very formal evening for more than six or eight is difficult for a host who handles cooking and service.

If you don't have household employees, then hiring servers for the night will enable you to prepare a delicious meal and then enjoy it with your guests.

People today tend to regard at-home formal dining as an opportunity to dress up, set a beautiful table, use their very best manners, and enjoy lively conversation over an excellent meal. There are, however, some fine points of etiquette for very formal meals, and many of these manners apply equally well to more casual dining.

➤ A housekeeper, butler, other domestic employee, or a willing family member may open the door to guests, take their coats, and show them to the party area where they are immediately greeted by the hosts. The hosts should be present to greet and mingle during the traditional pre-dinner "cocktail hour," which may be shorter than an hour but rarely longer.

➤ If place cards are used, the host or hostess enters the dining room after all the guests. Otherwise, the host or hostess leads the way and indicates where guests are to sit.

➤ Women sit down as soon as they find their places; men stand at their places until the hostess is seated or the host signals them to be seated. In the traditional man-woman-man-woman order, each man customarily holds the chair of the woman on his right, but women today often seat themselves if they wish. Guests of honor sit to the right of the hostess and host; otherwise, hosts determine the seating order.

➤ The formal table is laid with a *white* cloth of damask, linen, or lace, which falls no more than eighteen inches below the edge of the table. Matching white napkins are a generous size: approximately twenty-four inches square. Damask cloths are laid over a felt pad or white blanket folded to fit the table; linen and lace cloths are placed directly on the table surface. To be truly formal, candles in the dining room are white.

➤ Plates are served from the diner's left side but removed from the right. No serving dishes or platters are put on the table, and meat is not carved at the table. Plates (warmed for hot courses) are filled in the kitchen or at a side table and placed before each diner. Salt and pepper containers are placed on the table, but vegetables, breads, and condiments are passed by the server; diners take adequate portions, and the serving dishes are returned to the kitchen or sideboard. (When there is more than one server, one will normally set the plates with the main item before each diner, and another server will follow, offering vegetables, bread, etc.) All plates are removed between courses, as are the utensils used for that course—but only when *all* diners have finished with the course.

A *charger*, or service plate, is a large plate (usually twelve inches in diameter) that is put on the table with the place setting and not removed until the main course is served. (See Chapter 23, page 381: "Service plate.")

➤ Wine is served from the right before each course and replenished as needed. The wineglasses at each place indicate the number of different wines to be

Finger bowls are for cleaning fingers and reducing stains on napkins (not for drinking or rinsing food or utensils). And quite useful amenities they are, especially if you have something greasy or sticky on your digits. There's really nothing mysterious about finger bowls.

Most often seen at a formal dinner, a finger bowl is a smallish glass bowl containing cool or lukewarm water and sometimes a small fresh flower. The bowl is usually brought in on the dessert plate just before dessert arrives. You dip only your fingers—one hand at a time—into the water, rub or swish gently, shake off excess water with equal caution, and then use your dinner napkin to dry your fingers. The whole thing is done in a matter of seconds. When finished, you lift the finger bowl and the little doily it was placed on and move them to the upper left of your place setting.

You might also encounter a finger bowl with a thin slice of lemon instead of a flower after a more informal, hands-on meal, such as one with lobster. The lemon helps to cut the grease. After you've dipped your fingers, as above, either a server will remove the bowl or you can move it to the side of your place setting.

---

served. Water glasses are refilled throughout the evening. Coffee cups and saucers are usually not included in the original place setting, but they may be if a guest prefers coffee or tea with his meal.

➤ The salad course generally follows the main course, but if salad accompanies the entrée, it is served on a separate plate. The salad is usually dressed, either in the kitchen or at a side table, just before it is served.

➤ Dessert forks and spoons may be set on the table with the original place setting (positioned horizontally above the plate) or brought to the table with the dessert course.

➤ The server may sweep the table between courses, using a tightly folded napkin to brush crumbs into a plate or a silent butler held just below the table edge. This is done unobtrusively so that conversation isn't interrupted. The server will add or replace knives, forks, and spoons as needed.

➤ Coffee and tea may be served at the table or when the guests retire to the living room. The host or hostess may pour, or the hot coffee can be brought to each guest from the kitchen or a serving table. Since tastes vary, put sugar bowls and creamers (plus a bowl of sugar substitute packets) on the table or on a tray passed to guests. Coffee spoons are placed on the saucer. After-dinner cordials and fortified wines like port are served with the coffee course.

Lunch, Brunch, and Other Dining Occasions

THOUGH CONSIDERABLY REFINED ACROSS 30,000 years of civilization, the impulse to share one's table with friends and strangers alike seems basic to all cultures. The evening dinner party is particularly suited to today's busy schedules, but whatever the time of day and degree of informality, entertaining good company at a meal is hospitality at its best.

Luncheons

When convenient, the lunch hour can be the perfect time to gather friends and colleagues and perhaps conduct a little business. Though luncheons are often held at restaurants and clubs, an at-home lunch is a very nice way to host a club or committee meeting, entertain business associates, and honor out-of-town visitors and special guests. Traditional lunch parties, including bridge and bridal luncheons, remain popular but are often scheduled on weekends so that guests won't have to worry about getting back to work.

Luncheon food is normally lighter than dinner fare: a starter or salad course and an entrée, a salad or soup and sandwich, or a bountiful luncheon salad—plus dessert and coffee. Because many people prefer not to drink alcohol in the middle of the day, it has become less common to offer cocktails, but guests might enjoy a glass of sherry or a nonalcoholic drink. Wine may accompany the meal, but water, iced tea, and fruit drinks are the mainstays of luncheon beverages.

Whether a lunch is seated or buffet, the etiquette varies little from the basics of dinner parties. The main difference is that food and service are often streamlined. During business hours, lunch may last for no more than an hour, so the meal begins soon after guests arrive and serving tends to be informal. With careful planning, the occasion will not seem rushed. Hosts have to be attentive to the time constraints of their guests, just as guests should not be tempted to linger when the host must return to his or her job.

Breakfast

A breakfast party is a more elaborate version of the everyday morning meal. Breakfasts can begin as early as 8:30 or as late as 10:00 AM and often precede an occasion such as a graduation ceremony, a morning wedding, a noontime sports event, or a business meeting. (Traditionally, breakfast buffets are served after midnight at balls and formal dances, but these are catered at the event site.)

The menu is based on the classic eggs-bacon-toast formula. Dishes such as eggs Benedict, omelets, ham and biscuits, French toast, Belgian waffles, and sweet pastries are typical, though hosts should also provide alternatives like fresh and stewed fruits and low-cholesterol quick breads for health-conscious guests. A variety of juices as well as coffee and tea are served; alcoholic drinks are not. Breakfast is usually a buffet and can be served in the kitchen if you have a large enough space.

Brunch

Brunch, combining the virtues of a late breakfast and an early lunch, seems made for leisurely weekend get-togethers. Brunches might also be associated with other social activities—a gathering for out-of-town guests on the day after a wedding or graduation, for example.

Typically, brunches begin around 11:00 AM or noon. A brunch can be a seated affair, but informal buffets are more popular, and even relatively formal brunches have a casual mood. Menus typically blend traditional breakfast and lunch fare: creamed chicken on waffles, sausage or ham rolls, mushroom quiches, frittata, seafood casserole, fruit compote, green salads. Foods tend to be light and often feature fresh fruits and vegetables in season.

Bloody Marys, with or without alcohol, and mimosas (champagne and orange juice) are often served, as are lighter white and blush wines. But have plenty of non-alcoholic beverages available. Alcohol-free fruit punches go well with brunch food and add a colorful touch to the buffet.

Late Suppers

When people don't have the time or appetite for a meal before a night at the theater, a concert, or a sports event, a late supper is a good way to draw the evening to its end. When you host an intimate group of friends, the atmosphere is relaxed and convivial. The supper menu is lighter and less extensive than a full dinner. Choose foods you can prepare in advance and assemble quickly or whip up at the last minute, like omelets. If you include dessert, serve something refreshing—a fruit ice, for example. (Quality chocolates and mints or cookies served with coffee can easily substitute for a dessert course.) Light wine is a pleasant accompaniment, depending on the lateness of the hour, but guests may prefer water, coffee, or another nonalcoholic beverage. Service tends to be informal—from a buffet or on dinner trays—no matter how simple or elegant the meal.

∾ A Tidy Ending for Outside Occasions ∾

At picnics, tailgate parties, and other events at outside locations, cleanup is an absolute. Use waste containers available at the site or bring your own. Don't leave any food behind; your leftovers will attract animals. Pick up and dispose of every bit of litter, including cigarette butts, drink cans, and pull-tabs. Outdoor cooking—if allowed—is a fire hazard, so take a fire extinguisher. Be sure that all fires, including those in grills, are completely out before leaving the site; douse coals with water and rake ashes for any smoldering embers. Someone must clean up the mess, and the ultimate responsibility falls on the host. Even if you miss the kick-off or first inning, do the right thing and leave the area clean and safe for the people who use it next.

Picnics and Barbecues

Day or night, picnics and barbecues seem to exemplify the American style of home entertaining. The informal nature of the typical backyard gathering makes it a popular last-minute activity. But even the most casual event needs organization, so plan ahead when you can. By issuing invitations a few days to a week before the party, you have a better chance of assuring that people can attend.

Picnic and barbecue menus are virtually limitless. If others bring food, you'll want to coordinate so that you don't wind up with too much of the same thing. (See "Potluck Suppers," below.) Be very conscious of food safety: Keep foods at the correct temperatures and don't leave foods out for longer than an hour—a half hour in warm weather. (For information about food storage and handling, with links to other sources, search at www.foodsafety.gov, a service of the U.S. government.)

BYOB, or "bring your own bottle," on an invitation indicates that guests are expected to supply their beverages. Usually, this means alcoholic drinks, and the hosts provide basics—sodas, bottled water, and perhaps tea and fruit juice—as well as ice and drink glasses.

An etiquette note: Consider neighbors when grilling or barbecuing—especially if you live in close quarters. If outdoor cooking is permitted, be sure the cooking area is well ventilated so that smoke and odors don't collect in hallways or blow into a neighbor's windows. (See Chapter 10, page 127: "Smoke and Odors.")

Potluck Suppers

Potluck suppers are a fun way for family and friends to share their bounty in a casual and inexpensive way. Basically, a potluck (or covered dish) supper is organized by one or several people or a group, and everyone who comes contributes something to the meal. Be clear when issuing a potluck invitation. "Potluck" means that all guests share the food. The notation BYOF literally means "bring *your own* food," and guests will show up with food for themselves, not dishes to be shared.

Organization is important so that the potluck menu will be varied. Participants might be given a choice of foods within categories (salads, vegetables, breads, casseroles, desserts). To assure a balanced spread, the organizers should know what participants plan to bring. Participants are also informed how many people will attend so they can prepare adequate quantities.

Sometimes organizers provide an entrée such as fried chicken or burgers and hot dogs or a dessert like homemade ice cream. Those who don't cook can bring packaged items like buns and chips or paper plates and napkins, coolers and ice, or bags of charcoal. The organizers may provide drinks, but if alcoholic beverages are included, participants often bring their own.

Progressive Dinners

The progressive dinner, a popular nineteenth-century entertainment that has undergone a revival with the growth of cooking and gourmet clubs, is similar to a potluck in that several participants provide the food. The difference is that each course is prepared by a different cook. Traditionally, guests go from house to house, and the number of homes visited depends on the number of courses served. Today's progressive party might be held at one location, though different cooks prepare and serve each course.

The dinner might be organized by the hosts or by a group such as a food or wine club or it might be held to celebrate a holiday. Menus are carefully planned and coordinated, and the people who aren't cooking are considered guests for the occasion, though they may assist with serving. Progressive dinners can range from very casual to very formal. When held at several homes, each host usually decides the format (seated, buffet, semi-buffet) for his or her course.

Groups that regularly hold progressive dinners may not be too concerned about costs because expenses tend to even out as group members rotate cooking assignments. But hosts of a one-time progressive dinner should address food and beverage costs as a first step, so one host doesn't bear an unreasonable share.

Wine-tasting Dinners

Friends who share an interest in wines get together for a multi-course dinner (or sometimes lunch) in order to enjoy different wine varieties served with appropriate foods. Wine-tasting dinners might have a single host but are often staged by groups of wine lovers on a fairly regular basis. One person usually selects the wines to be served. A sparkling wine is often tasted first, followed by a selection of whites and reds during dinner and a sweet dessert wine to finish.

Before each wine is tasted, the person who chose it will talk a little about the wine and the reasons for his or her choice. A guest shouldn't take a sip before the spiel is finished. Nor should anyone ask for a wine that isn't being served.

Chapter Twenty-six

Hosts and Houseguests

Perhaps you've invited your sister and brother-in-law, who live in another town, to be your guests over Labor Day weekend. Or you opened an e-mail from a friend to find he will be passing through your city and wonders if you know of any good hotels—and you reply that he's welcome to stay in your guest room. Whether by design or accident, you've taken on the role of host and all its attendant duties.

Having friends or relatives stay overnight or for the weekend gives you the opportunity to relax, have more time to talk, plan activities you all enjoy, and share several meals together. But hosts and guests alike have a rather delicate balancing act to perform. The former's most important task is making his guests feel at home. The latter's duty is to behave differently than he would at his own. That means refraining from keeping to his own schedule, helping himself to food in the fridge without permission, taking control of the remote, and so forth. Also, behaviors that might not be noticed over the course of an evening can begin to grate after two or three days—exactly the opposite of what everyone wants.

This chapter begins with the responsibilities of hosts, with guidelines for everything from preparing for your houseguests to welcoming them and bidding them adieu, then switches to pointers for the guests.

First Moves

HOSTING CAN INVOLVE inviting a person for one night or a group for a long weekend (an occasion still referred to as a house party in some parts of the United States), or any variation thereof. Begin by laying out the particulars as clearly as possible: When will the guests arrive? When will they be leaving? A phone call followed with a note or e-mail will prevent confusion over dates and times. Also let guests know whether you have anything planned for their stay, and on which days—a dinner at a high-end restaurant (which means dressing up a bit) or any other event for which they may have to bring something.

If your guests are coming by car, make sure they know the way—and that means not limiting your directions to a phone call. To ensure that guests understand and have a take-along copy, write the directions down and send or e-mail them in advance. If guests will be arriving by train or plane, discuss the options for getting to your house—being picked up by you or a car service, for example, or taking a taxi or public transportation.

Welcoming Houseguests

Once your guests arrive, show them to their room or sleeping area and the bath they will use. Then give them a chance to tidy up and unpack. If they're unfamiliar with your home, conduct a quick tour whenever they're ready: the bathroom, cabinets for towels and other items, light switches, the telephone, and kitchen appliances. Show them how to adjust the air conditioner or heater, if necessary. Then tell them to help themselves to snacks or beverages from the fridge during their stay, noting any foods that are off-limits: "Please help yourself to anything you see except the blueberries—they're for the pancakes tomorrow morning."

No Guest Room?

If you live in a one-bedroom apartment or a house with no guest room, don't think you can't play host. A sofa bed, futon, or air bed can be set up in the living room or den, or children could be doubled up to vacate a room if the visit isn't lengthy. (In the latter case, arrange the toys neatly, remove some clothes from the closet, clear enough drawer space for the guest's needs, and make sure the room is sparkling clean.)

The important thing is to give your guests advance warning that they won't have a separate room or that they'll have to share a room. While some guests may be perfectly fine having to sleep on a sofa or air bed in the den, others may choose not to come if they have to make do with makeshift or shared quarters. Even then, it's not a good idea to move out of your own room so you can give it to your guests, since they would almost certainly feel they were imposing.

Checklist for Hosts

HERE'S A CHECKLIST of the items and comforts you should attend to, plus a few optional ones that will add a nice touch.

In the guest room or sleeping area . . .
➢ Bed, sofa bed, futon, or air bed made up with clean sheets and pillowcases
➢ Extra blanket at the foot of the bed
➢ A good reading light at each bed
➢ Clock radio
➢ Box of tissues on the nightstand
➢ Wastebasket

- ➤ Coat hangers in the closet
- ➤ Luggage rack, if you own one

In the bathroom . . .
- ➤ Fresh bath towels, face towels, washcloths, bath mat
- ➤ Fresh cakes of soap
- ➤ Glasses for drinking and brushing teeth
- ➤ New roll of toilet paper in the dispenser and an unopened one in the cabinet
- ➤ Box of tissues

Nice touches . . .
- ➤ Vase of flowers
- ➤ Calendar
- ➤ Reading matter (magazines, short books)
- ➤ Two pillows for each guest—one medium-firm and one soft
- ➤ Wooden coat hangers with bars or pressure clips for trousers; plastic hangers for dresses
- ➤ Clothes brush, lint roller, and pincushion stuck with both safety pins and straight pins
- ➤ Shampoo, bath oil, bath powder, and hand lotion on the washstand
- ➤ New toothbrush, just in case the guest has forgotten her own
- ➤ Headache and stomachache medicines in the guest bathroom medicine cabinet

Schedules and Routines

Share your routines with the guests: "Sunday is our morning to sleep in—if you get up first, the bread and English muffins are in the bread drawer and the coffeemaker will be all ready to go—just push the start button." Also give them a heads-up on any absences you foresee: "I have to go to a meeting Monday morning, so I'm leaving you on your own. I should be back around eleven o'clock."

If your guests are visiting during weekdays, it's important that you share your normal schedule with them so that they can plan their time accordingly. ("Mom and Dad, the girls leave for school at seven-thirty, so we're up and running at about six forty-five. I wanted to warn you because that's when they take over the bathroom.") This is a gentle way to familiarize your visitors with the way things are done in your household and help them to fit right in. If they know that after arriving home from work you need a ten-minute break and a clothes change, your guests will be less likely to greet you at the door expecting to chat about what everyone's been doing.

This doesn't mean expecting your visitors to do everything your way; they're your guests, and their happiness and comfort are as important as yours. Yes, your routine will be disrupted, but the more forthcoming you can be about what happens when—and why—the more pleasurable the visit will be for everyone.

My son and his girlfriend are students at a nearby college, and we've invited them to spend their Thanksgiving break with us. The problem is, they've been living together for six months, an arrangement that we're not happy about. How should we handle the situation?

Parents have a right to insist that their standards be observed in their own home, and you should make that clear to your son. If he says, "Well, then we won't be able to come," you have to decide whether your relationship and continued communication with him is more important than upholding your standards. (This is an individual matter of conscience, not one of etiquette.) Still, you can stand your ground. If you and your son understand each other and have a good relationship to begin with, he's more likely to accept the rules you establish than to put you in a difficult position. Just be sure to let your feelings be known from the very beginning—not when he and his girlfriend are carrying their bags up the stairs.

Easing Your Way

You can save yourself a lot of trouble by preparing whatever you can in advance—mainly meals. Any number of cookbooks feature make-ahead dishes of every sort, and one with exceptionally good recipes can become a host's best friend. Even if you can't prepare all the meals ahead of time, plan your menus and stock your kitchen with whatever ingredients you'll need; otherwise, you'll have to spend time shopping after your guests have arrived.

The one meal that you can't easily organize in advance is breakfast. Because one of the joys of a weekend away from home is being able to sleep late, a good host doesn't awaken guests unless they've asked to be. Unless you've told your guests to help themselves to breakfast, make coffee and put out eggs, fruit, cereals, or other breakfast foods before they rise. It's okay to go ahead and eat—but if you do, be there to help guests as they arrive.

When good friends are visiting, don't be afraid to ask them to pitch in: "Belinda, would you mind reading the children a bedtime story while I get dinner ready?" Or "Tom, would you please watch the grill for a few minutes?" And don't refuse their offers. Most guests sincerely want to help and might feel uncomfortable if they're consistently rebuffed.

When the Kids Come

The children of houseguests may either utterly charm everyone present or run around like little hellions. But if the host has children of roughly the same age, the battle is half won: The kids can often be left to themselves and can also play with neighborhood children. Even if the host has no children, she might arrange a playdate for her visitors and other kids in her neighborhood.

Treating any child who is present with tolerance and respect—not as a pint-sized interloper who should be seen but not heard—will make everyone's stay that much easier. Parents obviously shouldn't shirk their duties, no matter how much they're looking forward to a relaxing visit. It's their responsibility—and theirs alone—to keep their children in line, clean up after them, and get them to bed at their regular hour.

(For children's sleepovers, see Chapter 13, page 179: "Sleeping Over.")

When Guests Depart

Under normal circumstances, do what you can to make your guests' departure as easy as possible—enlisting your teenager to carry their bags to the car or asking them whether they double-checked to make sure they left nothing behind. Even if guests must get up at 4:00 AM to catch a plane and you choose to stay in bed, you can help with their departure plans ahead of time—say, arranging for a taxi.

Naturally, you'll tell guests how much you enjoyed their stay and that you hope they'll come again. A polite host not only sees his guests to the door but also stands on the porch until they're out of sight, waving the occasional good-bye. Were he to disappear from view, he could leave the impression he's eager to get back to his routine. (He probably is, but in the spirit of good manners he would never admit it.)

∽ The Guest Who Stays Too Long ∽

The problem of guests overstaying their welcome is so universal that it has given rise to proverbs for centuries. Most of us know of the one that equates houseguests with fish: Both "start to stink in three days." But a Portuguese proverb says it more subtly: "Visits always give pleasure—if not the coming, then the going."

So what is a good host to do? Not much besides dropping a few hints, and then remembering the houseguest's thoughtlessness before deciding whether to invite her again.

➢ Let her know you've enjoyed her visit but that it's important that you return to your regular schedule.

➢ Don't feel obligated to keep entertaining her.

➢ If applicable, mention a specific time and event: "Dan is coming home on Friday, so I'm afraid we're going to need his room back."

Note: If the guest has to stay longer because of airline cancellations or other unavoidable problems, be as helpful as you can. The situation is probably as difficult for her as it is for you.

Recording Visits

A tradition that abides is a guest book for guests to sign, often with a comment on their stay: "Great company, great conversation, great food! Thanks for a weekend we'll always remember." Good stationery stores sell books for the purpose, so you can find one that fits your style, from ultracasual to formal.

Keeping a second record is purely practical. In a notebook, the host can list foods that were served so that she doesn't offer the same dishes when the guests return; any foods that guests particularly liked or disliked or are allergic to; and the activities and events that occurred. For example, if the Braders last visited you two years ago and were taken to the old mill and the town museum, a note to this effect is a reminder to make other plans the next time around.

∼ Twelve Host Gift Ideas ∼

Houseguests are expected to give a gift to the host(s). For an overnight stay, something on the order of a bottle of good wine is sufficient. A longer stay requires an item that's a little more expensive. If the hosts have young children, it's also nice to present a small token gift to each one.

You can take a gift with you and present it as soon as you arrive or could buy one during your stay. (You might get a good idea of what the host wants or needs after a day or two.) A third option is to send a gift as soon as possible after you leave.

An important consideration: Decorative items with simple designs and neutral colors are safer choices than those with bright colors and busy patterns. Everyone will appreciate an unadorned silver-plate picture frame, while a frame adorned with birds, hearts, or stars may not be to the recipient's taste.

Other gift ideas:

➢ New best-selling book you know will interest the host
➢ Hand towels for the powder room or beach towels for sunning
➢ Packages of cocktail napkins, perhaps with the host's monogram
➢ Desk calendar for the coming year (appropriate in late fall or winter)
➢ Bottle of liqueur or cognac you know the host is fond of
➢ Sturdy canvas tote bag (preferably without a logo)
➢ For a keen cook, two or three unusual kitchen utensils, such as a pasta lifter or egg separator
➢ For a golfer, a dozen golf balls
➢ Set of nicely packaged herbs and spices or a selection of peppercorns (black, white, red, green)
➢ Picture frame, with a picture taken during your visit sent later
➢ Candles and informal candlesticks
➢ Houseplant in a permanent, simple-yet-decorative pot

There's more to being a good houseguest than just being nice and doing your part to help out. Here are some important things to consider when you plan to stay over at someone's home:

Do bring your own toiletries. Don't count on your host having stocked the guest bathroom cabinet with everything you might need.

Do offer to help. Any time you see a chance to help the host, do offer—but be specific. "I'll peel the carrots"; "It's my turn to clear the table"; or "Let me take those packages in." At the same time, don't overdo it. Prowling about the kitchen just waiting for an opportunity to pitch in can be distracting to the cook.

Do be adaptable. Be ready for anything—or for nothing. If your host has planned a swim in the lake and you're not a swimmer, be enthusiastic nonetheless: "I can't swim, but I'll love sitting on the bank and watching." Conversely, if your host has nothing planned and you're at a loss for what to do, settle in with a good book or take walks, now and then letting the host know what a nice, relaxing time you're having.

Do tidy up after yourself. Unless the host has household help and instructs you not to, straighten up your room and make the bed (see page 468: "How to Leave the Bed"). Keep your bathroom immaculate, especially if you're sharing it with other people. Don't leave a ring in the tub, a rim of shaving cream in the basin, hair on any object or surface, or dirt on the soap. If no sponge is handy, either ask for one or use a paper towel or tissues to wipe up.

Do appear to enjoy yourself. Even if you aren't having the best time, act as if you couldn't be more pleased. In this case, pretending isn't really deceitful: It's courteous, considering that your host's knowledge of your unhappiness could ruin the weekend.

Do ensure your host has some time alone. Usually, both guest and host need some "breathing room" away from each other, and it's often easier for the guest to suggest a way to make it happen. "Ed, I've taken up walking for an hour every day and thought I'd do it now unless there's something you've got scheduled." This gives him the opportunity to say, "Now's a fine time. I have some paperwork to do, so I'll tackle it while you're out."

Do host your hosts. If your stay is for three days or more, tell your hosts before you arrive that you would like to take them out to dinner one evening. Then also handle the reservations and pick up all expenses—not only the meal but also tips, cab fares, and so forth. A dinner isn't the only way to express your gratitude, of course; one alternative is to take your hosts to a movie and out for drinks or supper afterward.

Do have a supply of portable snacks if you've brought your children. Granola bars, bottled juices, and the like will stave off the kids' hunger pangs until mealtime. It's probable that the host will offer to forage around for food to keep the little ones happy, but a parent can also prepare a snack from the food in the refrigerator if the host has given blanket permission to "help yourselves."

Do treat any household help courteously. If during your visit any household employees come on duty, greet them as you would anyone else and thank them if they aid you in any way. Don't tip an employee unless she volunteers to run an errand or perform any other special service—and even then, check with the host first to make sure a gratuity is appropriate. (See also Chapter 46, page 813: "Houseguests and tipping.")

Don't make other plans without letting your host know. An example: If your host lives in the same town as another friend whom you'd like to visit, you must tell your host before you arrive: "Madeline, I'm hoping to have time for a short visit with Sandra Dowd. Is that okay, or would it disrupt your plans?" If she says that's fine, ask her which day and time would be the best for seeing your friend.

Don't ask to bring your pet. This admonition applies only for a host you don't know very well, whom you will put in a difficult position if she's unenthusiastic. With friends, go ahead and ask. If they say, "No problem," assure them that your pet's behavior will be exemplary—but only if it's true. If your pet is prone to chewing things or jumping onto furniture or into laps, arrange for it to be cared for while you're away.

Don't delay returning a borrowed item. Return it as soon as you no longer need it—and in as good shape, or even better than as when it was lent to you. Take care not to crease or stain the pages of a book, clean a clothes brush of lint, and switch any small appliances back to their original settings.

Don't accept an invitation before checking with your host. If you run into other friends in the area and they invite you (and perhaps your host as well) over for drinks or dinner, never accept the invitation before discussing the matter with those with whom you are staying.

Don't answer your hosts' telephone without asking. This rule applies even if you're right next to the phone. At the start of your stay, ask, "Jenny, do you want me to answer the phone when it rings, or should I let the answering machine pick up?" You should also ask your host whether she wants to be told of any calls that come in while you're using the phone.

Don't use more than your share of hot water. In weekend houses with small hot water heaters—or in any house where you know a number of people will be bathing—keep your showers short. Other bathroom no-no's: Don't use any towels or washcloths other than those specified as your own, don't leave the bathmat in a wrinkled heap on the floor, and don't leave the toilet seat up.

Don't make the first move to go to bed. When to end the evening is the host's prerogative. You can hint that you're tired, but the custom is to wait for the host to give the signal. The exception is when your hosts are family or close friends who won't mind if you retire early or stay up late. Just conform to the host's habits as much as possible.

Don't leave without making sure you have all your belongings. The reading glasses hidden behind the lamp on the nightstand, the shoes left under the bed—wrapping up and mailing forgotten items is a chore for your host. Do a thorough check of your room or sleeping area, no matter how sure you are that you've packed everything.

Guidelines for Guests

JUST AS THE GOOD HOST SHOULD be clear when issuing an invitation, house-guests should be prompt with their replies and precise about their arrival times. Promptness is all the more important if the invitation is for a longer visit and you'll be one among several guests.

Replying to Invitations

Handwritten or e-mail replies should be sent right away, regardless of the nature of your visit (even your scatterbrained ex-college roommate probably books her appointments and social activities in advance). Include the time of your arrival and your means of transportation: "Dear Rhonda, what an exciting invitation! We plan to drive up by car and should arrive about 7 o'clock on Friday the 12th. Can't wait to see you and Bill. . . ."

If you receive a phoned invitation for a weekend party for several guests, don't say something like, "I'll have to find out about a job interview I've been waiting for. I'll let you know next week." If you can't give a definite answer within a day or two, it's better to refuse so that the host can fill your place with someone else.

Guests who are coming and going by plane or train should always confirm their return reservations. No matter how successful the weekend party, it should end when the host expects it to (with the final day made clear in her invitation). Likewise, no guest should risk being put in the position of overstaying because he suddenly finds there are no seats left on the Sunday-night plane.

How to Leave the Bed

On the morning of the day you're going to leave, ask your hostess what she would like you to do with your bed linen, then follow her wishes. If you're uncertain what to do, standard practice is to remove the sheets, fold them, place them at the foot of the bed, and pull the blanket and spread up neatly so that the bed will look made. If you make it up with your sheets in place, it is all too easy for a busy hostess to forget, turning down the bedspread for the next guest only to find used sheets.

Should you make the bed with fresh sheets? That depends. If the two of you are only casual friends, your hostess may feel uncomfortable because she thinks such a task the duty of the host. But if you're close friends and you visit frequently, go ahead and ask for fresh sheets and save your host the trouble.

Saying "Thank You"

Overnight visits require handwritten thank-you notes—with the emphasis on "handwritten"—within a day or two of your return home. (The only exception is when your hosts are relatives or close friends who often visit you in return. Even then, a call the next day to say, "We're still talking about how fun the weekend was!" is appreciated.) E-mailing your thanks to anyone but your relatives and closest friends is inappropriate because it reduces the host's considerable effort on your behalf to the level of a casual lunch or a lift to work.

Extended Visits

EXTENDED VISITS ARE almost entirely restricted to family members who come to stay for a week or more, often over a holiday. The following are a few guidelines for dealing with problems that may crop up over the course of a longish stay.

Tips for Hosts

> When, say, your mother is staying with you and you're invited somewhere, should you ask if you may bring her? In general, don't. For an invitation to dinner or any other occasion that requires the host to have an exact guest head-count, you can say, "I'm afraid we can't come—Mother is staying with us." This leaves it up to the host whether to suggest that you bring your mother. When the invitation is to an open house, a cocktail party, or a church or club festivity, one more guest wouldn't cause any difficulty, so feel free to ask if you may bring someone else along.

> When an invitation to an event doesn't include your houseguest, it's up to you and your guest whether you should go, though in most cases it's better not to. If your guest is a close relative who's visiting for more than a few days, you might agree that it's fine for you to go alone. Just be sure he has something to do and to eat while you're away.

> Plan together how you and your guest will handle your routines (work, school, shopping, and so forth) and any special activities—together or separately?

> Arrange for use of a car if your guest needs one, or help with transportation plans.

> Offer your guest the use of your computer for e-mail and Internet access.

> Give your guests permission to use your washer and dryer whenever they like.

Tips for Guests

> Thoughtful guests make a point of immediately saying that no one needs to entertain them—then proving the point by finding things to do.

> It's disruptive when the guest follows the host from room to room or chats nonstop with a child who is trying to complete his homework.

> A thoughtful guest doesn't sit in on every conversation, but rather goes on a walk or to another room in the house so that the host family can have some private time together.

➤ A guest who has to stay longer than expected for business reasons, interviews, or other scheduled events should share his schedule with the host.

➤ Helping with routine activities (shopping, preparing a meal, or assisting the children with homework) helps keep the host's daily life from being unduly disrupted by the guest's extended stay.

Chapter Twenty-seven

Parties Galore

PARTIES CAN BE AS DIFFERENT as night and day. At one extreme is the informal gathering of shorts-wearing friends and neighbors at a backyard barbecue; at the other, the formal ball, with all its intricate planning and adherence to tradition. The requirements for a successful party of any kind, however, are precisely the same: Hosts do all they can to make their guests comfortable, and guests mind their manners by being both flexible and appreciative of their hosts' efforts.

Even the most carefree parties demand guests and hosts alike to meet certain expectations. The host must have planned sufficiently, and then look after the assembled partygoers to varying degrees. Guests should fit their behavior to the occasion, with the Party Animal calming down at a reserved affair, the Show-Off yielding the spotlight, and the Shrinking Violet making an effort to blossom.

Cocktail parties open this chapter, which then moves on to parties as varied as open houses, ultracasual parties, reunions, cooking parties, parties on the water, and formal balls. (See also Chapter 26, page 433: "The Dinner Party.")

A "Congenial Stew" of Guests

TODAY'S BEST HOSTS AND HOSTESSES (for the sake of simplicity, hereafter referred to in this chapter as hosts) agree that the right mix of guests—a "congenial stew"—can make all the difference when holding a party. You might enjoy mixing and matching people who don't know one another but who you suspect will get on famously. Your primary goal is to invite guests who are likely to be interesting to one another and whom you can count on to be sensitive, thoughtful, and entertaining.

How to Invite

Party invitations range from a spontaneous, same-day phone call or e-mail ("My cousin Francesca is in town unexpectedly and we'd love it if you and Lawrence could join us for a barbecue tonight") to a formal engraved invitation to a charity ball sent well in advance.

When to Send?

Whether you're mailing printed invitations or inviting guests by phone, timing is key. Send an invitation too late and the guest may already be booked; send it too early and it can be misplaced or forgotten.

The following guidelines aren't set in stone but will give you an idea of how to time invitations for different kinds of parties:

Anniversary party	3 to 6 weeks
Bar or bat mitzvah	1 month
Bon voyage party	Last minute to 3 weeks
Charity ball	6 weeks to 3 months
Christmas party	1 month
Cocktail party	1 to 4 weeks
Debutante ball	6 weeks to 3 months
Formal dinner	3 to 6 weeks
Graduation party	3 weeks
Housewarming party	Few days to 3 weeks
Informal dinner	Few days to 3 weeks
Lunch or tea	Few days to 2 weeks
Thanksgiving dinner	2 weeks to 2 months
Ultracasual party	Same day to 2 weeks

See "Invitations and Announcements," page 247, for advice about sending party invitations and for sample invitations.

The Return of the Cocktail Party

THE NEW INTEREST IN COCKTAILS (both classic and new) is only one reason cocktail parties have enjoyed a recent resurgence. Another is that they're the answer to a busy person's prayer, offering a simple solution to the rule that all invitations must be repaid. Cocktail parties also require less preparation than a dinner party, can be less expensive, have set time limits, and make it possible to entertain a lot of people in a small setting. On the minus side, guests don't have the "favored few" status they do at a dinner party, and the hosts' attention will be spread thin.

Please Come For . . .

Cocktail parties can be large or small and as simple or elaborate as you wish. For a small or last-minute party, it's fine to invite by phone. For a larger party, invitations on fill-in cards are the better choice.

A cocktail party invitation typically specifies a set time: "Cocktails from 5:00 to 7:00." If you're planning a cocktail buffet—a cross between a cocktail party and a buffet dinner—your invitation need only state the arrival time: "Cocktail buffet at 6:30."

"Cocktail buffet" in the invitation tells guests that more than snacks will be provided. Although you needn't set out a soup-to-nuts buffet, guests should have enough food so that they won't need to make dinner plans for later.

Some hosts choose to leave RSVP off the invitation, especially if the party is a big one. For one thing, they could be inundated with phone calls (the usual way to respond to parties of this kind); for another, cocktail buffets don't need the exact guest count normally required for dinner parties. Whether to add an RSVP notation is your decision.

Advice for the Host

When hosting a cocktail party, stock your liquor cabinet with the basics: Scotch, bourbon, a blended whiskey, gin, vodka, rum, white and red wine, and beer. If you know several guests are partial to martinis or Bloody Marys, stock up accordingly.

≈ Six Ways to Be a Good Host ≈

No matter the kind of party you're throwing, there are some things a host should remember, even before the party starts.

Invite clearly. Include necessary information for your guests in the invitation. Is the party a casual get-together or more formal? What about the attire? Maybe a guest would benefit by knowing ahead of time who else will be there, which you might mention when they RSVP.

Plan well. Preparing your guest list carefully is key to a successful party. Then do as much as you can ahead of time. (Lower the stress level by serving food and refreshments you know will work.) Get everything ready well before your guests arrive, so you'll feel relaxed from the very beginning.

Remain calm. Giving a party can be enjoyable, especially if you approach it with simplicity. Get help if necessary, and don't let your guests think you're huffing and puffing. They'll feel far more comfortable if they don't have to wonder whether they're causing you any trouble.

Keep guests feeling welcome. Make sure guests are warmly greeted, then made to feel welcome throughout the party. Look after each guest as much as you can. If you notice that a guest has an empty glass or if there's one person standing alone, remedy the situation as quickly and cheerfully as possible.

Be flexible and gracious. Your soufflé falls. Or one friend arrives with an unexpected guest. The ruined dessert? Have a fallback. The uninvited guest? As discourteous as it is for someone to spring a surprise on you, be gracious. No polite host would ever send an uninvited guest packing.

Be appreciative. Thank people for coming as you bid them good-bye. And don't forget to thank anyone who brought you a gift.

Also make sure nondrinkers have a range of juices, soft drinks, and bottled waters to choose from. A smart host will have enough supplies (especially ice) on hand, mix drinks correctly but moderately, and set out plenty of coasters and napkins.

Hors d'oeuvres are the only food served unless you're hosting a cocktail buffet (see Chapter 25, page 437: "Cocktail buffet"). Virtually any finger food will do as long as it tastes good, looks tempting, and can be eaten with little fuss. The hors d'oeuvres are usually served on a buffet table (and sometimes passed on trays), but it's also a good idea to have bowls of snacks placed around the room—nuts, chips, pretzels, olives, and the like.

If you and your spouse or partner are acting not only as hosts but as bartenders and servers as well, follow your greeting to a guest with an offer to get him a drink. If the choice of beverages is limited, save embarrassment all around by asking, "Will you have a martini, wine, beer, or juice?"—not "What would you like?"

You can also invite your guests to refill their own glasses if they want another drink. Just be sure to have the beverages, a jigger, and a bucket of ice in clear view. A self-serve bar will help free up your time to visit and perform other duties.

At a large cocktail party, guests expect to stand for long periods, but you still should provide enough chairs for those who need to rest. When the guest list is small (say, six to ten), people are more likely to gravitate to chairs and couches, so make sure there are enough seats for everyone present.

Need Hired Help?

When you're planning a cocktail party for more than twenty people, it's wise to hire a bartender for the evening, if possible. If the guest list is in the forty-to-fifty range, two bartenders would be needed, with their tables set up in two different places to prevent a crush at the bar.

Be sure that you instruct the bartender how you want the drinks mixed and tell her to rely on a jigger or other measure. If you let her pour by eye, you may find your liquor supply running out long before you'd planned. (You might also have some unexpectedly boisterous guests on your hands!) Ask your bartender to wrap a napkin around each glass, whether a fresh drink or a refill. Napkins prevent drips and make holding a wet, icy glass more comfortable.

The Art of Mingling

If as a guest you find yourself on the sidelines, don't be embarrassed to introduce yourself to someone. When the person is alone, the introduction is easy (see Chapter 2, page 16: "Self-introductions"). More difficult is joining a group conversation. To smooth the way, walk past to see what is being discussed. (Not that you want to eavesdrop, but this is a party, where mixing is desirable.) If the subject is sports, computers, a current news story, or any other impersonal topic, you've found a conversation open to all. Smile and make eye contact with one or two people, and wait for someone to acknowledge your presence. Then listen patiently and wait for a lull before joining in. If, on the other hand, the subject is personal or about people you don't know, move on.

Juggling Acts

How on earth do you juggle your drink and your plate and shake hands at the same time? Only with great difficulty, so try to find a place to set one of the items down.

Standing close to a table could solve the problem. Just make sure the table isn't set or decorated in such a way that even the temporary addition of a wineglass spoils the effect or your dish could be confused with whatever is being served. Another option: Some people are poised enough to joke about their dilemma, asking someone to hold their glass while they extend their hand. The important thing is to make the effort to greet another person in a pleasant way.

What to do with toothpicks after you've eaten an hors d'oeuvre? There's usually a small receptacle on or near the food platter for used ones. If not, hold any items (including drink stirrers) in your napkin until you find a wastebasket. Don't place used items on the buffet table unless a waste receptacle is available.

The Tipsy Guest

The guest who drinks too much at a party used to be laughed off later as "the guy who put a lampshade on his head" or "swung from the chandeliers"—but when anyone who's inebriated plans to drive home, overindulgence no longer raises even a smile.

When it becomes obvious that one of the guests has had too much, the host or the person tending bar should not serve him more liquor. The guest may be insulted and become abusive, but that is preferable to having him become more intoxicated.

As the host, you are responsible for seeing that a drunken guest is taken safely home. You may ask a good friend to take him; you can go yourself if the inebriated person's home is close by; or you can arrange for a cab. The person's car keys should be taken away if he is not willing to go with someone else. If he has reached the stage of almost passing out, two or three of the other guests should help him to a bed to sleep it off overnight. If the offender has a spouse or a date present, the host and hostess should offer this person accommodations or see that he or she gets safely home.

"Would You Please Leave Your Shoes at the Door?"

While removing your shoes when entering someone else's home isn't typically a part of U.S. culture, as it is in Japan and elsewhere, politely asking family, friends, and party guests to do so is fine—especially in locales with long seasons of inclement weather. Just make sure you have a stash of comfortable slippers, flip-flops, or nonskid slippers or socks for visitors to wear. That way, guests won't feel so uncomfortable about exposing their bare or stocking feet. Be careful, though. If you're throwing a more formal party or you don't know your guests all that well, asking them to remove their shoes could be awkward.

The Ultracasual Party

SOME GATHERINGS ARE SO CASUAL they hardly qualify as parties: the after-work get-together at a coworker's apartment, the impromptu invitation for a few neighbors to "drop by this evening," the occasional gatherings with a group of close friends. Many of these parties are potlucks, with each guest bringing a dish or a sweet.

While most of the rules for a "real" party can be suspended—the only written invitation would be one delivered via e-mail, and "anything goes" attire is fine as long as it's not sloppy or too revealing—there are still a few hosting duties to perform. First, make sure the party area, kitchen, and bathroom are clean, and close off any messy rooms. Unless the party is both a potluck and BYOB, estimate how much food and alcohol to buy, and stock the fridge with soft drinks and sparkling water to accommodate nondrinkers. Vary the choice of food (whether hors d'oeuvres or a buffet) so that all the guests will find something to their taste.

Paper napkins are the sensible choice for very casual parties, with large colored ones more festive than plain white. If no buffet is being served, a stack of smaller cocktail or luncheon-sized napkins will be sufficient.

Sturdy paper or plastic plates, plastic utensils, and disposable cups are not only in keeping with the spirit of the affair but also make cleanup easier. If you're using your own dinnerware and utensils, there's no need to match styles and patterns.

Party Time

When guests arrive, it's fine to have someone else open the door for them if you're occupied, but do make a point to greet them as soon as possible. If it's coat season and you don't have a coat closet, either direct guests to a bed where coats, jackets, and handbags are being piled or take the items to the bedroom yourself. Make sure clothing doesn't end up in a crumpled heap and won't be covered with pet hair.

As guests arrive, ask what they'd like to drink. As you hand them their drinks, tell them that they're welcome to help themselves from the countertop, refrigerator, or ice chest—or, if the party is large, perhaps from the ice-filled "cooler" that is your bathtub—for the rest of the party.

Have plenty of large garbage bags handy so you can periodically collect empty cans or used paper plates and stash them out of sight. Wash glasses and other dishes as needed, or let guests take on the task if they volunteer.

When guests leave, show them to the door and tell them how much you enjoyed their company—one nicety that should never be ignored.

Open-house Parties

MOST OPEN HOUSES—PARTIES WHERE guests can arrive anytime between the hours specified in the invitation—are usually held after the host has moved into a new home or to celebrate a holiday. Depending on the degree of informality (open houses

Even at the most casual parties, there are some things a polite guest should do:

Tell your host whether you're attending. And do it immediately. If you delay your reply, you could hinder the host's planning and also make it seem as if you're waiting for something better to come along. Even if no RSVP has been requested, it's thoughtful to let your host know if you won't be able to be there.

Be on time. Punctuality means different things to people in different locales, but in general guests should arrive at or shortly after (usually only fifteen minutes) the time stated on the invitation. Do *not*, however, arrive early.

Be a willing participant. When your host says that it's time for dinner, go straight to the table. If you happen to be asked to participate in a party game or view Susie's graduation pictures, accept graciously and enthusiastically no matter how you really feel.

Offer to help when you can. If you're visiting with the host in the kitchen as he prepares the food, be specific when you offer to help: "I'd be happy to work on the salad or fill the water glasses." Even if your offer is refused, your gesture will be appreciated. When the party's end draws nigh, you could also offer to help with the cleanup.

Don't overindulge. Attacking finger foods as if you haven't eaten in a week will not only attract the wrong kind of attention, it will also leave less food for other guests. Also be sure to keep any consumption of alcoholic beverages on the moderate to low side.

Thank the host twice. In some parts of the United States, a second thank-you by phone is customary the day after the party (the first having been delivered on leaving the party)—a gesture that's gracious anywhere. If the party was formal, written thanks are in order. In fact, a written note is always appreciated—even after very casual parties.

can be quite casual), you may send written invitations or commercial cards or invite people by phone. Some hosts include an RSVP or "Regrets only," while others are willing to guess about the final number of guests.

Refreshments range from the simple—dips, sandwiches, bowls of nuts or olives, and punch—to elaborate buffets of country hams, hot biscuits, cheese puffs, and bowls of shrimp. Guests generally stay no longer than an hour or hour and a half so that the crowd won't balloon to unmanageable proportions.

Housewarmings

IF YOU'VE RECENTLY MOVED to a new house, you might choose to host a housewarming, typically a cocktail party or buffet. Depending on the casualness of the party, you can send written invitations, phone your friends, or e-mail them.

Expect to give tours unless you're comfortable letting guests wander through the house on their own. Just make sure someone is always there to open the front door and welcome guests as you play tour guide.

Gifts are often brought to a housewarming party. If the group is small enough and every guest has brought a gift, opening the presents can be a part of the festivities. If the party is more of an open house, with guests coming and going, either open each gift and thank the guest as it's given or wait until after the party—in which case a thank-you note is a must. Even if someone has been directly thanked for a gift at the party, a thank-you note is a good idea—and always appreciated.

Typical gifts are guest towels, place mats, houseplants, drinking glasses, nice dishcloths or napkins, and (for the host who gardens) spring bulbs and seeds. Other ideas include a guest book intended as a keepsake of the party; a picture frame (take a photo in front of their new home to add later); and tickets or discount coupons to local movie theaters, restaurants, or shops.

A QUESTION FOR PEGGY

My wife and I threw a party last weekend, and to our surprise one couple stayed after everyone else had left. I tried dropping a hint by saying we had to get our six-year-old to a bus for a field trip at the crack of dawn, but it went right over their heads. How should I have handled the situation?

Be glad that your party was such fun that guests wanted to linger. Still, it's okay to let guests know it's time to go. Just be honest, saying how much you've enjoyed their visit but that you have to get up early for work (or whatever the case may be).

To stave off the problem in the future, send a signal as the party draws to a close. One way is to ask, "Would anyone like a nightcap? Some coffee?" Then, once the drinks and any last refreshments have been served, start tidying up a little. If most people soon begin to leave, you could ask someone who stays firmly planted in his chair, "Dan, shall I bring your coat?" Or you could be pleasantly blunt: "Dan, I'm going to have to kick you out in fifteen minutes, since I have a six o'clock flight tomorrow morning"—an explanation that asks for Dan's understanding, gives him a chance to finish a drink or a conversation, and then depart as though it were his idea in the first place.

Common Interest Parties

FRIENDS WHO SHARE a common interest often set up regular gatherings to discuss books, cook, quilt or knit, or even watch a favorite show or sports event on TV. Hosting is usually rotated among the members, and refreshments are served—either during the activity or afterward, as common sense demands.

If such gatherings have any etiquette guidelines in common, they are to pay attention to the subject at hand, avoid getting into arguments, and respect the opinions of others. (See also Chapter 48, page 845: "Cards and Other Games.")

Book Groups

Friends and acquaintances who form a book club draw up a reading list and discuss a book after everyone has read it, usually meeting once a month. The behavior guidelines are straightforward: Listen when others are talking and take care not to interrupt. Respect the viewpoints of others, and don't leave the impression that your interpretation of the author's work is the correct one and somebody else's is wrong.

Cooking Groups

Serious cooks who meet regularly get the chance to try out new gourmet dishes, taste a variety of wines, and have a great time in the bargain. A certain cuisine—say, Italian, Mexican, or Thai—is often chosen, and club members, who usually number six to twelve—are assigned certain dishes to prepare. The party is held at a different member's home each time the group meets, and the host is usually responsible for sodas, coffee, tea, mixers, condiments, and the table setting. Depending on the space in the host's kitchen, dishes can either be made ahead or prepared on site, with various members offering to pitch in as others look on while relaxing and sipping wine.

Constructive criticism of the dishes is part of the point of such parties, but criticizing a cook's skills is out of bounds. Be sure to help with the cleanup, and thank the host just as you would after any party.

Craft Groups

Friends who enjoy quilting, needlework, leatherwork, or any other craft have fun working on their individual projects together, but their parties could also have a purpose—making items for a hospital, nursery, or other organization. Members of the group take turns hosting and should have some extra project supplies on hand in case they're needed. During the session, criticism of another person's work should be constructive, of course, and everyone should pitch in to clean up at the party's end.

Formal Parties

THOSE OPULENT BALLS familiar to us from the movies—men in tails swirling elegantly gowned women around the floor to the strains of a Strauss waltz—may have gone the way of the dance card, but they are echoed in today's formal dances, be they club dances, school formals, corporate events of one kind or another, or charity or debutante balls.

Unlike the grand parties of old, large formal parties are usually hosted by a committee. Special duties are allotted to each member of the committee, with one taking charge of invitations, one of decorations, another of the food, and so forth. (See also Chapter 18, page 258: "Formal Invitations.")

The Party Begins

Once you've arrived, you'll most likely begin the evening with pre-dinner drinks and hors d'oeuvres served from a bar, buffet tables, trays carried by waiters who circulate through the room, or a combination thereof. A guest's concerns at this phase:

The bar. If there is no true bar on the premises, bartenders will serve from a table, mixing drinks or pouring wine or beer. Before ordering, be certain it's your turn; if in doubt, a gracious "You go first" will be well received.

Waiters may be serving wine, passing through the room with trays. Don't make a beeline to a waiter; either wait patiently until the waiter comes your way or go stand in line at the drinks table or bar. Take a napkin and keep it wrapped around the base of your glass. Remember to keep the drink in your left hand so that your right one is ready for handshakes. When your glass is empty, look for a sideboard or table where used glasses and plates are deposited; if you can't find one, ask a waiter or the bartender what to do with your glass.

Don't tip the bartender unless there's a cash bar, in which case you will pay for your drinks—an arrangement unlikely at most formal affairs, but a possibility. Gratuities are built into the waitstaff's fees, so leaving money on the table or tray puts bartenders and waiters in an awkward position.

Passed-tray service. When taking food from a passed tray, try not to bring the food directly to your mouth; instead, put it on your plate or napkin before picking it up to eat. Also remember not to eat, talk, and drink at the same time.

A buffet table. When hors d'oeuvres are set on a buffet table, guests pick up plates and help themselves to both finger foods and dishes that require a fork. Take small portions, and don't return for plateful after plateful; the food at this stage of the party should take a backseat to the people around you.

Food stations. Food stations are smaller tables set in strategic locations around the room, each holding a different kind of food—ethnic specialties, perhaps, or all vegetarian

"Shall We Dance?"

These days, women don't have to be asked to dance but instead can take the initiative and ask men. If in doubt about the appropriateness, just remember that the more formal the party, the more you should stick to tradition. Speaking of formal, tradition says that every man at a private ball should dance with the hostess and the women he sits between at dinner, but he dances the first dance of the evening with his wife or date.

Today's dancing etiquette is otherwise based on common sense:

➤ Don't come to the party wearing too much perfume or cologne.

➤ If the dance floor is crowded, dance in compact steps and keep your arms in.

➤ If you bump someone, say, "So sorry!"

➤ Don't correct or criticize your partner on the dance floor.

➤ Execute any drops, flips, lifts, or turns only when you have plenty of space (yes, swing is back).

Time was when a man could cut in on a couple by tapping the man's shoulder and then taking over as the woman's dance partner. Today, this custom is largely confined to avid dancers of a certain age and to young teens thrilling to their first dance parties.

dishes. Try not to frequent only one; other guests may be just as fond of Mexican food as you are, and you don't want to be responsible for the sudden dearth of empanadas.

Dress for a Ball

"Black tie" (tuxedo) is accepted at most balls, even if the invitation says "formal"; only if the invitation specifies "white tie" must a man wear white tie and tails.

For women, dresses are usually long. A ball is also the time to wear your finest jewelry. Pants on women are acceptable only if they are very full and styled to look like a ball gown. With sleeveless or strapless gowns, women may wear long gloves, which they leave on through the beginning of the ball but remove when they begin dancing or eating. (See also Chapter 5, page 58: "Gloves.")

Receiving Lines

The members of a receiving line include the host and hostess at a private ball, the committee heads at a public ball, and honored guests (a debutante, for example) and their escorts. At a large function, this may be the only time a guest is able to say hello to the hosts and thank them for the party.

It's fine for a guest to hold a drink while waiting to be received, but the glass and any food should be disposed of before he or she goes through the line. When the moment arrives, the guest shakes hands and briefly exchanges a few pleasant words with each member of the line.

Midnight Supper or Breakfast

Since most balls begin well after the dinner hour, a late buffet supper (or "breakfast") is often served; it begins after midnight and continues for an hour or more. Food might consist of a variety of sandwiches, platters of cold meats and assorted vegetables, or eggs with bacon or ham. There may be hot drinks, bowls of iced fruit punch, or champagne.

People may serve themselves whenever they feel like it, and small tables are usually provided. Guests can sit where they please—in any vacant chairs or with a group making up a table.

When you're ready to leave a formal ball (usually after the supper, though older people often leave before midnight), find the host and hostess and thank them, just as you would at a smaller party. If there's a guest of honor, you should say good-bye to him or her as well.

At Debutante Balls

The phrase "presenting a debutante to society" has seen its day. Today a debutante ball is a celebration of a young woman's "coming of age" (somewhere between her eighteenth and twenty-third birthday) at a formal ball or party. Celebratory customs vary around the country, with the age of the debutante and the rituals of the ball or party differing from place to place.

The most elaborate party is a private ball. Somewhat less elaborate is a small dance; less elaborate still is a tea dance. Often, a dance is given for, or by, the families of several debutantes. Or the dance could be given by an organization that invites a group of girls to participate. Many balls or cotillions of this kind are benefits, handled by a committee representing the sponsoring charity. Thus these balls serve a double purpose, since the parents of the girls invited to participate are sometimes expected to give a substantial donation to the charity in return for the privilege of having their daughters presented.

Whether the party is a ball or dance, the debutante's mother—or grandmother or whoever is giving the party and "presenting" the debutante—stands near the entrance. The debutantes stand next to them, each debutante paired with her mother or other presenter. The debutantes and their mothers (or other presenters) are the only people who formally "receive." On entering, the guests approach the hostesses, who introduce the debutantes to those who don't know the young women being presented.

Each debutante receives guests for about an hour, after which she's free to enjoy the dancing. She usually dances the first dance with her father and the next with the man (or men) she's asked to be her escort(s) for the evening. The debutante then goes to supper with her escort(s). She will have decided in advance who will join her at the table reserved for her group.

∼ Party Ahoy! ∼

A harbor, lake, river, or coastline provides the opportunity for another party locale: a boat. A boat owner might enjoy entertaining friends on a day cruise or an evening sunset sail. Other hosts might want to book a party boat that plies local waters. Still others may prefer a historic vessel moored at a jetty—the kind that a number of river towns and harborside cities have turned into party boats outfitted with dining rooms and reception rooms. (Old paddle steamers are popular in the South.)

An invitation to an on-the-water party should make clear whether it is on a moored boat or one that will cruise. Dinner cruises are popular, especially in cities where the skyline forms a glittering backdrop. But a party boat that sets sail brings a new set of concerns. Because people are unable to leave when they choose, the cruise should be kept to two hours or less; this way, the partygoers won't start feeling trapped or end up drinking more than they should. In any case, it's wise to stock up on nonalcoholic drinks. Seasickness medicine should also be available on board should the waters turn choppy.

If you're hosting a party on your own boat, be sure to follow boating safety rules (including having the correct number of life vests on board), and don't forget to orient your guests to the layout of the boat, pointing out the location of the galley and the head.

The debutante's dress. The debutante traditionally wears a white gown. While a pastel color or a color in the trim of the gown is acceptable, scarlet, bright blue, and black are inappropriate. When the ball is an assembly or cotillion, the committee determines the color of the debutantes' gowns, a decision that must be followed. Although they must wear the same color, the young women may choose their own styles. Long white gloves are worn during the presentation.

Parents' and guests' attire. The mothers of the debutantes wear evening dresses in any color except white or black, while female guests wear evening dresses in any color other than white. Traditionally, long gloves are worn, unless a woman's dress is long-sleeved. Male guests' attire is black tie, but the escorts and the fathers of the debutantes usually wear white tie.

Flowers and gifts. It's customary for family members and very close friends to send flowers (whether bouquets or baskets) to the home of the debutante at the time of her coming-out party. The debutante's escort(s) may also send flowers and give her a corsage if one will be worn—but they should ask before doing so. Young women often don't wear flowers on their gowns but instead pin them to a purse or wear them on the wrist.

Relatives and very close friends of the debutante or her family can also send gifts, though this isn't required. Members of the organizing committee and guests of the family can also send gifts if they wish.

Reunions are parties with a built-in plus—the opportunity to catch up with old friends or to reunite with family members who live far away. Reunions can be held by anyone, from former workmates to military buddies, and class reunions are a long-standing custom. Each has its own unofficial code of conduct.

Class reunions. High school and college reunions hold a special place in the American psyche. To many people, they're the time to proudly show who they've become (the unpopular boy who became a business tycoon, the gangly girl who's now a model). To others, they're a chance to revisit old times and revive friendships. In any event, keep the following advice in mind:

➤ **Invite** *everyone*. Unless close friends who keep in touch want to plan their own mini-reunion, the planners of a class reunion should invite every member of the class. If someone can't be tracked down through mailings, phone calls, and Internet searches, that's that. But no planner should fail to invite someone because "she wouldn't want to come anyway"—or for any other reason.

➤ **Don't just stick with your old crowd.** Make a point to greet and chat with as many classmates as possible. After all, that's the point of the party!

➤ **Forgo the bragging.** The need to impress can backfire. If you go on and on about your accomplishments, your great job, or your brilliant and beautiful children, your boasting will overshadow your successes. Counter the urge to brag by expressing interest in others.

➤ **Make others feel included.** If a classmate seems to be hanging back or spends too much time alone, walk over and strike up a conversation. If you feel someone has been left out of the conviviality, ask him or her to dance when the opportunity arises.

➤ **Don't be scornful.** Don't scorn the city or town where someone lives or what they do for a living. People want different things out of life, and your attitude should be one of approval of the road they've taken.

➤ **Don't embarrass classmates.** Don't bring up incidents they would probably rather forget, no matter how funny they may be. What's a fond memory for some may be anything but for others.

➤ **Thank the planners of the event.** They volunteered their valuable time, and their reward is their classmates' appreciation and the satisfaction that a good time was had by all.

Family Reunions. In some U.S. families, what was often a one-day picnic to bring together relatives from far and wide often ballons into a weekend gathering with scheduled events and entertainment. The etiquette guidelines for family reunions apply no matter how long or elaborate the gathering. (See also Chapter 9, page 105: "Gathering the Family Together.")

Dining and Entertaining

- ➤ **Provide a range of activities.** Just because people are related doesn't mean they share the same interests. Everybody might enjoy a sack race or a game of tug-of-war, but others will appreciate having a golf, bowling, or softball game scheduled as well. Sightseeing trips and shopping excursions can be scheduled as alternatives.

- ➤ **Watch your manners.** You should never suspend the social graces just because you're with family. Use the same good manners you would with a group of friends or total strangers, whether dining, socializing, or competing in a congenial game.

- ➤ **Respect the organizer.** Don't complain about the way the reunion was organized, which does nothing more than make you look petty. Perhaps you would have done things differently, but accept the party for what it is and thank the organizers for their hard work.

- ➤ **Don't get into one-upmanship.** Competing with relatives over whose children are the more outstanding or whose job outshines whose introduces a sour note to the festivities. You can mention your child's or your own latest accomplishments, but take care not to brag. Always ask about the other person's children or work, show interest, and give praise where praise is due.

- ➤ **Zip your lip.** Don't spread gossip about any family member(s), and keep any personal or family secrets to yourself. A confessional to a relative can either wait until another time or be suspended altogether.

- ➤ **Don't be disapproving of other people's children.** Criticizing the behavior of a relative's child is as bad an idea at a reunion as commenting on the behavior of a stranger's child in a supermarket. Mothers and fathers won't be any less sensitive about criticism of their parenting abilities just because it comes from a relative.

- ➤ **Spread a little sunshine.** Let your relatives know when you particularly like something about them. Don't fawn over anyone, but give compliments where compliments are due and tell people how much it means to you to get to know them better.

Chapter Twenty-eight

Toasts and Toasting

TOASTS RANGE FROM THE MOST ROUTINE ("To us!" spoken while clinking glasses) to the most touching—a five-minute homage from the father of the bride that could make grown men cry. In one form or another, toasting to love, friendship, health, wealth, and happiness has been practiced by almost every culture from the beginning of recorded history. The Greeks and the Romans, the potentates of Africa and Asia, and the indigenous peoples of South America and the Pacific Islands all drank to their gods, as did the Europeans—notably, the Vikings, who used the skulls (*skalle*) of their vanquished foes as goblets. That singular custom gave rise to the standard Scandinavian toast: *Skål*.

Who Toasts—and When

IN YEARS PAST, it was the prerogative of the host or hostess to offer the first toast, whether at a small dinner party or a soirée. Nowadays, the more informal the occasion, the less this "rule" applies: Around a dinner table with friends, a guest can propose the first toast (and often does), usually as a way of thanking the host for bringing everyone together. The only real guideline is to make sure that all the glasses are filled before toasting. The glasses don't have to hold champagne or wine or any other alcoholic beverage; it's perfectly fine for nondrinkers to toast with water, juice, or a soft drink. Even an empty glass is better than nothing. It's the gesture and warm wishes, not the alcohol, that really matter.

The "host toasts first" mandate *does* still apply at receptions and other large functions (though the best man usually leads the toasting at a wedding reception). It is also the responsibility of the host to attract the crowd's attention when the time comes, which he does by standing and raising his glass—not by banging on a glass with a utensil. No matter how large and noisy the crowd, repeating "May I have your attention" as often as necessary is the more courteous option.

When it comes to sitting or standing, do what comes naturally. If toasts are made over pre-dinner drinks in the living room, the toaster may want to stand. At the dinner table, the toaster may remain seated if the group is fairly small. A table of a dozen or more usually requires the toaster to stand so that people will be able to hear.

Although the host often stands as he delivers his toast, everyone else—including the person or persons being toasted—remains seated. The exception is when the toaster asks everyone assembled to "rise and drink to the happy couple" or "stand and raise your glasses to our esteemed leader." The guests respond by taking a sip of their drinks, not by draining the glass; the idea is to save enough of the beverage for any toasts that follow. On ceremonial occasions, a toastmaster or the chairman of the committee often takes charge, sandwiching the necessary toasts between the end of the meal and before any speeches. Toasters are usually expected to stand on such formal occasions.

When to Toast

If a toast is to be offered at a meal, the first usually comes at the very beginning. Traditionally, the first toast is offered by the host as a welcome to guests. Toasts offered by others start during the dessert course.

Toasting isn't confined to a meal or special event. Spontaneous toasts are in order whenever they seem appropriate, as when someone raises his glass and offers good wishes or congratulations to his companions.

∼ The Origins of "Toast" ∼

Ironically, the cheerful clinking of a friend's glass before drinking evolved from one of the darker practices of the distant past. The custom dates back to the Middle Ages, when people were so distrustful of one another that they weren't above poisoning anyone they perceived as an enemy. As a safeguard, drinkers first poured a bit of wine into each other's glass, acting as mutual "tasters." Trustworthy friends, however, soon dispensed with the tastings and merely clinked their glasses instead. This custom is said by some to explain why "to your health" is the most common toast worldwide. Some other historians hold that clinking glasses provided the noise that would keep evil spirits at bay.

And the word "toast"? In the ale houses of Elizabethan England, a bit of spiced toast was usually put in the bottom of a cup of ale or wine to flavor it, and possibly to soak up the dregs. In time, any male or female whose qualities or accomplishments were frequently honored with a group drink came to be called "toasts" (hence the phrase "toast of the town"). One story—attributed, in a 1706 edition of *The Tatler*, to "many Wits of the last Age"—claimed that "toast" was first used in this manner during the reign of Charles II (1660–1684). That label, it was said, was bestowed on a well-known belle from the town of Bath. As the beauty luxuriated in the healthful waters of the public baths, an admiring gentleman scooped a little bath water into a cup, added the customary piece of toast, and raised the cupful of water to her before drinking it.

The word "toast" as used today—"a sentiment expressed just before drinking to someone"—did not begin to gain currency until the early 1700s.

Replying to a Toast

When toasted, the "toastee" does not stand, nor does she drink to herself. All the recipient need do is sit and smile appreciatively. Once the toast is finished, she simply acknowledges the toast with a "thank you." She may then stand and raise her own glass to propose a toast to the host or anyone else she wants to honor. The same procedure is followed by a group of people who have just been toasted.

Prepared Toasts

Anyone who wants to deliver more than the simplest toast should prepare beforehand, if only to rehearse mentally so as not to fumble the words. Keep whatever you say short and to the point—you want the spotlight to be on the toastee, not you. If, however, your toast has been designated as the principal one of the event, think of it as a small speech that should be prepared and rehearsed. When you deliver the toast, a glance at your notes is acceptable, but you still want to seem fairly spontaneous.

Including a few personal remarks—a reminiscence, praise, or a relevant story or joke—is all to the good, but they should be in keeping with the occasion. Toasts at a wedding should tend toward the sentimental, those in honor of a retiring employee toward nostalgia, and so forth. And a touch of humor is rarely out of place.

Spur-of-the-moment Toasts

Joining in a group toast is blessedly easy, with glasses raised and shouts of "Cheers!" "To your health!" or "To Stan!" ringing out. Similarly, a spontaneous toast is relatively effortless in that it can be both brief and generic: "To Stan—God bless him!"

Should you draw a blank when you're suddenly asked to offer a toast, just remind yourself that a few sincere and complimentary words are all you need: "To Stan, a terrific guy and a friend to us all!" It's easier still when you can tie the toast to the occasion (what a good toaster should do in any event), whether you're at a dinner party or barbecue, an office party or a gathering of your high school classmates. In a pinch, try toasts along the lines of these:

> "To Suzanne—a great hostess and a fabulous cook."
> "To Dan—Cincinnati's best . . . and soon to be most famous? . . . barbecuer."
> "To Paul—the host with the most!"
> "To Gretchen—a great boss and a wonderful friend."
> "To the class of '72—the smartest and best-looking by far!"

A Toast Sampler

THE FOLLOWING TOASTS are intended to give you a few ideas for various occasions, from weddings to holidays to housewarmings. Use the samples as a framework on which you build toasts that fit the toastee(s) and express your own feelings. Be sincere.

You don't need to make it long; some of the most memorable toasts are brief. In some cases, you might choose to insert an appropriate proverb or saying, so a few of these are provided here as well.

Wedding Toasts

Weddings and the events surrounding them elicit so many toasts from well-wishers that whole books are devoted to the subject. But there's no reason to feel intimidated. As with all toasts, it's more important for the sentiments to be heartfelt than eloquent.

Engagement party toasts. In days past, a party was often held to announce an engagement. Today, engagement parties are usually a way for friends of the bride and groom to meet the couple's respective families a few months before the big event.

Parent(s) to couple

➤ "I [*or* we] propose that we all drink to the health and happiness of Keiran and the woman that he, to our great joy, is adding permanently to our family: Candace Roe."

➤ "Candace's mother and I have always looked forward to meeting the man she would choose to marry. I have to say we couldn't be happier with her choice—wonderful Keiran Matthews. Please join me in wishing them a long and happy marriage."

Bride and groom to future in-laws

➤ "Bill and Daphne [*or* Mr. and Mrs. Matthews], I'm so happy you're finally able to lay eyes on the friends I've been telling you about. It also gives *them* the chance to get to know *you*—a couple for whom I have the greatest respect and whose family I will be proud to join. Everyone, please join me in toasting Bill and Daphne Matthews!"

➤ "I remember the first time Candace took me to meet her parents. They quickly bowled me over with their hospitality, good cheer, and great sense of humor. Please join me in toasting two people whom I not only look forward to having as in-laws but as lifelong friends. To Ken and Fiona [*or* Mr. and Mrs. Roe]!"

Rehearsal dinner toasts. The rehearsal dinner—usually held after the wedding-eve rehearsal for the bride and groom, their families, attendants, and selected friends—allows any guest present the opportunity to toast the happy couple and others.

Parents to parents

➤ "I'd like to ask you to join me in toasting two wonderful people without whom this wedding could never have been possible: the mother and father of our soon-to-be daughter-in-law, Lynne—Mr. and Mrs. Brown."

Parents to couple

➤ "I don't need to tell you what a terrific person Lynne is, but I do want to tell you how happy Brett's mother and I are to welcome her as our new daughter-in-law. Here's to Lynne and Brett!"

Best man to groom

➤ "Brett and I have been friends for what seems like a lifetime now, and I've always noticed what a lucky guy he is. Tonight, all of you can see just what I mean as you look at Lynne. Please join me in a toast to both of them. May their lucky numbers keep coming up for the rest of their lives."

Wedding reception toasts. Traditionally, the best man offers the first toast. Friends should keep their toasts to three or four minutes at the most, which will give family members and other attendants more time to propose their own.

Best man or maid of honor to couple

➤ After a brief speech, the head attendant could propose the toast by saying, "To Rosemary and John—extraordinary individuals in their own right. May they enjoy happiness and prosperity their whole lives long," or "To Rosemary and John—may they always be as happy as they are today."

Groom to bride; bride to groom

➤ "All my life I've wondered what the woman I'd marry would be like. In my wildest dreams, I never could've imagined she would be as fantastic as Keisha. Please join me in drinking this first toast to my beautiful bride."

➤ "I'd like you all to join me in a toast to the man who's just made me the happiest woman in the world. To Michael!"

Parents to couple

➤ "We're thrilled you're now a part of our family, and we know that Matt's [or Sherry's] life will be blessed and enriched by having you as his [her] wife [husband]. Matt and Sherry, we wish you health, wealth, and lifelong happiness as you set off on your greatest adventure."

➤ "As long as I've known Sherry, she's kept the perfect man in her mind's eye. And the first time I met Matt, I knew immediately that she had found him. Kids, you were no doubt meant for each other, and I want to wish you a long and happy life together."

➤ "Love does not consist in gazing at each other, but in looking outward in the same direction." (Antoine de Saint-Exupéry)

Anniversary Toasts

Whether part of a large anniversary party or made over an informal family dinner, toasts add to the gaiety of the occasion.

Friends to couple

➤ "Many of us can well remember that day twenty-five years ago when we drank a toast to the future happiness of Ann and Roger. It's more than obvious that our good wishes have served them well, so I'd like to ask that all of you—old friends and new—stand and raise your glasses to another twenty-five years of the same."

Children to couple

➤ "Mom and Dad, how can we ever thank you? You not only built a home full of life and love but you also equipped Edith and me with everything we needed to make our way in the world. Now it's time to rest on your laurels. On your fiftieth wedding anniversary, we wish you continued good health and good fortune—and many more years to enjoy them. To Mom and Dad, with love and eternal gratitude!"

Family Toasts

Family members often have occasion to toast one another—birthdays, anniversaries, the receipt of awards or medals, or successes of any other sort.

Child to mother

➤ "We all love our moms, but I defy anyone to find a better one than mine. Mother, you've put up with me through thick and thin, and for that you have my lifelong gratitude. Even more, I thank you for just being the wonderful, intelligent, loving person you are. To Ellen Hawthorne, my beloved mother!"

➤ "The hand that rocks the cradle/Is the hand that rocks the world." (William Ross Wallace)

Child to father

➤ "Here's to my loving father. If before I die I can become just half the person he is, I will have achieved a life well lived."

➤ "Blessed indeed is the man who hears many gentle voices call him father." (Lydia M. Child)

Wife to husband

➤ "Lorenzo swept me off my feet twenty years ago, and he's still pretty cute today. More important, he's the same outstanding, caring person he's always been, as his loving wife and children can confirm! Please join me in a toast to my dear husband."

Husband to wife

➤ "Even if we had lived a century ago, my wife would never have been satisfied with the role of 'the little woman.' On top of a successful nursing career, she's always fought the good fight to make the world a better place. And she did it all while being the best wife a man could ever wish for. To Amy!"

Sibling to sibling

➤ "Sally, if there were an award for best big sister, you'd win hands down. Anyone who could have put up with the likes of me deserves a medal. Thanks for a lifetime of love, warmth, fun, and understanding. To Sally!"

➤ "How good and pleasant it is when brothers dwell in unity!" (Psalm 133:1)

Parents to child

➤ "Life changed forever when you came into the world, Scott, and only for the better. We love you, admire you, and couldn't be more proud of you. To our son, Scott!"

Birthday Toasts

Birthday toasts have plenty of room for humor, so long as you're sure your digs about being "over the hill" won't be taken seriously.

➤ "Yes, Roger, you're forty-five, but I have it on good authority that middle age doesn't start till fifty. And ten years from now, I'll make sure to find the expert who's bumped it up another five years. In any case, we all know there's plenty of life left in the old boy yet. To Roger!"

➤ "Another candle on your cake?/Well, that's no cause to pout./Be glad that you have strength enough/To blow the darn things out." (partydirectory.com)

Holiday Toasts

During the winter holidays, you'll more than likely be taking part in a toast even if no alcohol is consumed.

Christmas

➤ "With all the presents opened and the table cleared, let's remind ourselves of what we're celebrating: the birth of the man who shone a light on the world that will never be extinguished. Please join me in toasting the real spirit of Christmas."

➤ "Here's to all of us . . . God bless us everyone!" (Tiny Tim, in Charles Dickens's *A Christmas Carol*)

New Year's Eve or Day

➤ "Be at war with your vices/At peace with your neighbors/And let every new year find you a new man [woman]." (Benjamin Franklin)

➤ "May you have warm words on a cold evening/A full moon on a dark night/ And the road downhill all the way to your door." (Irish toast)

St. Patrick's Day

➤ "May leprechauns be near you to spread luck along your way/And Irish angels smile upon you on this St. Patrick's Day." (Irish toast)

Fourth of July, Memorial Day, Veteran's Day

➤ "To the wisdom of our Founding Fathers and to every last serviceman and servicewoman who upheld and defended their legacy: freedom for one and all. God bless America!"

Thanksgiving

➤ "May it be God's will that our blessings continue to crowd out our misfortunes and rewards exceed our losses." (Anonymous)

➤ "As we express our gratitude, we must never forget that the highest appreciation is not to utter words, but to live by them." (John F. Kennedy)

Business Toasts

In the business world, the most common times to toast are parties thrown for someone's retirement or the sealing of a business deal and at corporate events that call for full banquets, some of which may be formal enough to require a toastmaster.

To your boss

➤ "Nobody can accuse me of being a kiss-up for what I'm about to say about Ben, because everybody knows it's true. Ben, we appreciate that you have strong opinions but that you still ask for ours. We appreciate your ethics in a time when many bosses are giving big business a bad name. And we wholeheartedly admire your unparalleled managerial skills. Everyone, please join me in toasting a boss we're all blessed to have."

To a retiring employee or a member of the firm

➤ "It's often said that nobody is indispensable, and that may sometimes be the case. But I speak for all of us at Smith and Robbins when I say that there will never be anyone who can replace Jim. Although we'll miss him greatly, we know how much he's looking forward to his retirement—or should I say, 'to life on the golf course'? Jim, we wish you all the happiness you so richly deserve in the years to come."

Reasons for toasting in a foreign language may rarely come your way, but you never know when an international toast may come in handy. For example, you might have good friends whose ties to the old country are strong, and you could surprise them with a toast in their native tongue. Or when traveling abroad, you might find yourself at a dinner or reception where you're expected to make a toast. Following is a sampling of international toasts, with their pronunciations shown in informal phonetics; capital letters indicate the syllable(s) to stress.

Language	Toast	Pronunciation
Arabic	*Besalamati*	beh-suh-la-MAH-tee
Chinese*	*Gan bei*	kahn-BAY
Czech	*Na zdraví*	nahz-DRAHV-ee
Dutch	*Proost*	PROHST
Finnish	*Kippis*	KIP-pis
French	*À vôtre santé*	ah votruh sahn-TAY
German	*Prosit*	PROHST, with guttural R
Greek	*Stin ygia sou*	steen ee-YAH soo
Hebrew	*L'chayim* or *mazel tov*	luh-CHI-um, with guttural CH; MATZ-uhl tohf
Hungarian	*Egészségere*	eh-geh-sheh-GEH-ruh
Italian	*Salute* or *cin cin*	sah-LOO-tay; chin-CHIN
Japanese	*Banzai* or *kampai*	BAHN-ZYE; KAHM-PYE
Korean	*Chukbae*	shook-BAY
Malaysian	*Slamat minim*	she-lah-maht MEE-noom
Polish	*Na zdrowie*	nahz-DROH-vee-eh
Portuguese	*A sua saúde*	ah suah SOW-deh
Russian	*Na zdrovye*	nahz-doh-ROH-vee-eh
Scandinavian†	*Skål*	SKOAL
Spanish	*Salud*	sah-LOOD
Turkish	*Serefe*	sheh-REH-feh
Thai	*Choc-tee*	chock-DEE

*Cantonese, Mandarin.

†Danish, Swedish, Norwegian.

To a guest of honor at a banquet

➤ "We're gathered here tonight to honor a man who has given unselfishly of his time and effort to make this fundraising campaign so successful. Without the enthusiasm and leadership that Bob Wells has shown all through these past months, we could never have reached our goal. Please join me in drinking a toast to the man who more than anyone else is responsible for making it possible to see our dream of a new hospital wing finally come true."

➤ "Ladies and gentlemen, you've already heard of the magnificent work our guest of honor has accomplished during her past two years in Washington. Right now we would like to tell her that no matter how proud we are of her success in her chosen career, we're even more pleased to have her home with us again. It's great to have you back, Sharon!"

Toasts for Awards and Accomplishments

Special achievements in sports, academics, or any other field deserve to be acknowledged by toasts from friends, family members, and coworkers.

For a trophy or medal

➤ "We all know the medal Kevin won for the two-hundred-meter butterfly resulted from more than just his ability as a swimmer. It was a testament to his great discipline and resolve, and for that we congratulate him."

For special achievement

➤ "Henry, your fellowship to study overseas will not only expand your horizons but should be your springboard toward achieving even more. We always knew you had it in you, and we wish you a productive and exciting year."

Graduation Toasts

Graduating from high school or college may be one of life's landmarks, but toasts can range from the inspiring to the humorous:

➤ "Here's to Jennifer—whom I've always thought was in a class by herself!"

➤ "Twenty years from now you will be more disappointed by the things you didn't do than by the ones you did do. So throw off the bowlines. Sail away from the harbor. Catch the tradewind in your sails. Explore. Dream. Discover." (Mark Twain)

➤ "Learning is a treasure that will follow its owner everywhere." (Chinese proverb)

Housewarming Toasts

Housewarmings would seem incomplete without the guests expressing their wishes for the hosts' happiness in their new home.

Guests to hosts

➤ "Here's to Dan and Brittany, whose beautiful new house is sure to be filled with warmth, laughter, and love."

Hosts to guests

➤ "May our house always be too small for all of our friends." (Irish toast)

Bon Voyage Toasts

Friends who are about to set off on an extended vacation can be toasted over a dinner with friends or any time a toast seems appropriate.

➤ "May the weather be perfect, the exchange rate in your favor, and the places you visit enrich you with memories forevermore."

➤ "Not traveling is like living in the Library of Congress but never taking out more than one or two books." (Marilyn vos Savant)

Part Six

Celebrations
and
Ceremonies

Chapter Twenty-nine

Celebrating Life's Stages

MARKING THE IMPORTANT STEPS along life's long and winding road is a meaningful and steadfast tradition. This chapter spans the incredible journey, starting at the very beginning with baby showers for parents-to-be and ceremonies for newborns. Later come such landmark events as birthdays, coming-of-age celebrations, and wedding anniversaries.

Celebrating these milestones raises myriad questions—how to plan special events, ways to invite, what to wear. Then there are the perennial concerns about gift giving and thank-yous. This chapter offers the answers, plus some insights into dealing with changes in long-standing traditions.

Welcoming the New Baby

IT'S HARD NOT TO MAKE a fuss over a new baby, even before the little bundle of joy is born. That is why we "shower" parents-to-be with presents. Not only do these gifts make their lives easier and provide for the new member of the household but they also help family and friends feel connected to the big event.

Timing and Inviting

In an effort to beat the clock, showers are usually given four to six weeks before the baby's due date. Parents who receive gifts in advance of the birth have the advantage of knowing what they'll need to buy or borrow. However, showers can also wait until a few weeks after the birth. In fact, some expectant couples prefer to defer receiving gifts until after the baby's arrival.

Invitations are sent out three weeks before the shower. Invitations with personal flair are easy to come by, given the range of designs and the ability of personal computers to create something original. But however creative your invitation, don't forget the essentials: the mother's (or parents') name(s), the shower's date and time, and a request to RSVP. Some shower hosts include gift ideas in their invitations, an acceptable option these days. Others prefer to omit information about gifts but prepare themselves to suggest ideas for the new parents and baby if guests ask. Either way is fine. (See also Chapter 18, page 267: "Baby Showers.")

Hosts and Honorees

Traditionally, close friends, cousins, aunts, sisters-in-law, or coworkers of the mother-to-be hosted baby showers. Because gifts are central to showers, hosting by a member of the honoree's (or husband's) immediate family appeared self-serving. But times have changed, and today it is appropriate for anyone to host a baby shower as long as there's a legitimate reason. For example, some parents-to-be live far from their home-towns, and their mothers and siblings may want to host a shower so that longtime friends can attend.

Honorees can vary as well:

Adoptive mothers. Showers for an adopted baby—whether an infant, an older baby, or a toddler—differ in that they're held after the baby has been brought into the home. Notations giving the child's age and perhaps the correct size for clothes are helpful additions on the invitation.

Single mothers. A shower for an expectant or new single mother is a good way for her family and friends to show their love and support.

Grandmothers. When friends learn that one of their group is about to become a grandmother, they could stage a "grandmother shower" during (or at the end of) a regular get-together like a bridge game or coffee klatsch. Gifts are opened on the spot, whether they are intended for the mother-to-be or for the grandmother. Gifts for the grandmother include articles she can use when caring for the new baby at her own home—toys and stuffed animals, storybooks, bibs, and so on.

Encore Showers

Is it all right to give showers the second, or even third, time a couple has a baby? Yes, but only when the guest list is limited to close relatives and very close friends and guests who didn't attend a shower for the first baby. Showers for the next baby are also more appropriate if several years have passed since the last baby was born, since the parents will have fewer hand-me-downs for the new arrival. Location is also a fac-tor. When a growing family has moved to another city, it makes sense for their new friends to throw a shower, regardless of how many children the parents have.

If parents already have a good share of baby clothes and equipment, the hosts could consider a theme shower designed to make the parents' lives easier. One idea is a "stock the cupboard" shower. Or have a "fun for Mom and Dad" shower, with gifts the parents themselves will enjoy: a promise for a set number of babysitting sessions, tickets to a play (timed well before the baby's due date), or videos of their favorite movies or television series.

Baby clothes and crib linens are the most common shower presents, and they're often the most welcome. Close relatives might consider a silver fork and spoon or perhaps a first piggy bank. A more imaginative idea is to personalize a scrapbook with the baby's birth date and fill the first few pages with photos of the parents, grandparents, and baby's first home. A good add-on gift is a newspaper from the day the baby was born (put the paper in a protective sleeve of clear plastic and tie it with ribbon); years hence, it will provide fascinating reading for the child and parents alike.

When the new baby has a big brother or sister, it's thoughtful to take or send a very small present for him or her as well. It's hard for young children to learn to share Mommy or Daddy, much less watch as piles of presents are given to the new arrival. On the card, write how lucky the new baby is to have such a wonderful big brother or sister.

Male Guests

It is not uncommon for men to be included on baby shower guest lists these days—and some lucky guys even become shower honorees. (An Emily Post Institute survey showed that over a third of respondents had attended showers where the guest list was mixed.) Still, when you plan a shower, you should check with the expectant parents to see whether they prefer a women-only party or a mixed one.

Thank-yous

Thank-you notes should be written for shower gifts, and the wise expectant mother or father writes them as soon as possible. Even when the giver has been enthusiastically thanked in person and has told the new parent not to bother with a note (and when close friends and relatives have said the same as a thoughtful gesture), a note is always appreciated, if not a must.

It is not acceptable for the hostess to hand out blank envelopes to shower guests so that they can write in their own names and addresses. While this dispersal of envelopes is intended to be helpful, it suggests that the honoree sees thanking the givers as something of a chore.

Gifts

If the person who's hosting the shower scribbled "Remember, Joan needs practical baby clothes," there's no reason to take offense; nor do you have to take her advice. Some people are stumped about what to give at a baby shower and are grateful for any guidance. But guests should always feel free to choose whatever gifts they think best.

While registering for shower gifts at a store or on-line is practical and time-saving for the parents-to-be and guests alike, many people feel that registering robs a shower of its charm. If the host and honoree decide to go the gift registry route, they should never include registry information on the invitation (though enclosing it on a separate sheet of paper is fine, given the purpose of a shower). Nor should the host insist that guests use the registry. In any case, the choice of a gift is always up to the giver. Also, half the fun of giving and receiving presents is the element of surprise. (See also Chapter 30, "Giving and Receiving Gifts," pages 514–528.)

Christian Ceremonies for Infants and Young Children

AS A CHILD GROWS and matures, a few special occasions commemorate his religious and academic achievements or simply celebrate a landmark age. Although parties are not obligatory for these, some kind of celebration is customary. If a ceremony is conducted in a faith other than your own, you're not expected to do anything contrary to your own religion. At the same time, you'll want to follow along and participate in all other aspects of the service, such as standing with the congregation.

Baptisms and Christenings

Different Christian denominations have different ceremonies for baptisms and christenings. (The words are used interchangeably here, but there is a difference. Both of these Christian sacraments use water in the ritual, but a baptism admits the individual into Christian life, whereas a christening is a baptism in which the person is named.) Most churches mandate sprinkling the child's forehead (affusion) or pouring on water (aspersion); Baptist and Eastern Orthodox churches practice total immersion.

The first step for parents comes during pregnancy, when they should ask the church about what needs to be planned in advance. Scheduling the event is one concern, since many churches restrict baptisms to certain dates. Some churches also provide a preparation class, which can usually be attended before the birth of the child. Another possible step for new parents is to select godparents for their child, a custom in many Christian denominations and a requirement in some (see page 503: "About Godparents.")

The child's clothes. Traditionally, christening gowns were worn by both males and females, with white being the usual color. The baby's gown—often one that was worn by the baby's mother, father, or one of his grandparents—is provided by the parents, not the godparents—a former tradition that has gone by the board. It isn't necessary to go to the expense of buying a traditional christening dress if you don't have a family heirloom; any plain white dress or outfit will do.

Older children who are being baptized dress nicely but do not wear white or other special clothing. The exception is when church custom calls for white robes, most often when the baptism is by total immersion.

The church ceremony. In most Protestant churches, baptisms are held during the regular church service or directly afterward. In many Catholic churches, a special baptism ceremony is arranged, either for one baby or several. The minister or priest explains to parents how the ceremony will be conducted.

No fee is ever required for baptism, a church sacrament. However, a donation commensurate with the elaborateness of the christening is sometimes given to the officiant after a private ceremony (put the money or check in an envelope). When the officiant is a close friend of the family, a personal gift is often given as thanks—a desk set, an article of clothing, or other appropriate item.

The christening party. Receptions, which vary in elaborateness depending on the religion and ethnic group, aren't really necessary but are often held. An at-home gathering for close friends and family enables the parents to relax and enjoy their guests as the baby naps in her crib. Often, christening cake—an elaborately iced white cake—and champagne or punch are served. Eating the cake symbolizes partaking of the baby's hospitality, and toasts are made to her health and prosperity.

∽ About Godparents ∽

Godparents should be either family members or very close friends. Because the obligation of godparents is traditionally a spiritual one (at one time, their role was to see that the child was given religious training and confirmed at the proper time), godparents are usually of the same faith as the parents. Although only one godparent is actually required, a female and male are usually chosen, though not necessarily from the same couple. The godparents of a Catholic child must be Catholic, but other denominations have no such restrictions.

Asking someone to be a godparent is usually done when the birth is announced or even before. While a handwritten note is always nice, it's perfectly fine to ask in person, by phone, or even via e-mail with an oral follow-up: "It's a boy! We'd be delighted if you would be his godfather. We'll call you soon." (If the person replies that he's unable to shoulder such a serious responsibility, the parents should graciously accept his decision and assume he has the child's best interest in mind.)

Beyond spiritual obligations, a godparent is expected to take a special interest in the child, much as a relative would. He remembers his godchild with a gift on birthdays and at Christmas until the child is grown—or perhaps longer if they remain close. However, if the godparents have lost contact with the child and his or her parents, they need not continue to give presents. Nor are godparents obligated to adopt or give financial help to godchildren who lose their parent, contrary to what some people think.

A godparent always gives a christening gift to his godchild—as nice a present as can be afforded. The typical gift is an engraved silver cup, mug, or bowl with an inscription: "Beau Burns/March 29, 2003/From his godfather/Don Newberry." Other popular presents are a silver fork and spoon, a government bond, or a small trust fund to which the godparent makes yearly payments until the child reaches the age of eighteen.

Gifts. If the christening follows within a few weeks of the child's birth, relatives and close friends who've already welcomed the baby with a gift aren't obligated to bring a second gift to the party. When gifts *are* given, they usually have religious overtones, although any age-appropriate gift is fine. Typical christening gifts include a keepsake Bible, an angel figurine or porcelain crib ornament, or a pearl baby bracelet with a cross.

Jewish Ceremonies for Infants

RITUALS FOR JEWISH INFANTS INCLUDE the circumcision of boys, naming ceremonies (usually for girls), and, in the more traditional congregations, redemption of the firstborn.

Brith Milah

A healthy male child is initiated into the Jewish community on the eighth day after birth through the covenant of circumcision, known as *brith milah* (covenant of circumcision) in Hebrew and *bris* (covenant) in Yiddish. If the parents choose to have the bris performed before the child comes home from the hospital, they should check the hospital's facilities and policies regarding the use of a room for the bris, whether or not refreshments may be served, and the number of guests permitted.

Relatives and close friends are invited to the bris by telephone, since the time between birth and the ceremony is short. When the bris is held in a synagogue, family members and guests dress as they would for a service; tradition requires that all men wear *yarmulkes* or hats, but the specific rules of the synagogue, be it Orthodox, Conservative, or Reform, determine whether women should wear head coverings. (Non-Jewish female guests might check with a member of the baby's family or telephone the synagogue to find out if head coverings are required.) If the bris is held at home, men wear hats. Custom determines whether women will be present for the ceremony; if they are, they are sometimes asked to wear a head covering.

Gifts. In general, guests are expected to take a gift for the baby. Either cash or a lasting memento of the occasion (an engraved silver picture frame, a comb and brush, or a fork and spoon) is often given.

Naming Ceremonies

Girls are named in the synagogue on the first Sabbath that falls closest to thirty days after birth, when the father is called up to the Torah. The naming ceremony is the *brit bat* (the covenant of the daughter) or the *brit hayyim* (the covenant of life). The mother may be present with the child. In some Reform congregations, boys are also named in the synagogue (in addition to being named at the bris); both parents are present, and a special blessing is pronounced by the rabbi. Friends and relatives may be invited to attend the religious service during which the baby is named. There may be a reception following the service.

Gifts. Invited guests usually give a small gift to the child—not with religious overtones, necessarily, but simply any item that's appropriate for a baby.

Redemption of the Firstborn

The Orthodox and Conservative Jewish ceremony of redemption of the firstborn, the *pidyon haben*, takes place only if the firstborn is a boy and may be performed when the baby is thirty-one days old (unless that day is the Sabbath or a holiday). The occasion consists of a brief ceremony and a celebration, generally held in the home. Informal notes of invitation to a redemption ceremony are sent about ten days beforehand to close friends and relatives.

Gifts. Because the *pidyon haben* ceremony occurs so soon after the bris, it is not necessary to bring a gift.

Coming-of-age Celebrations

THOSE WHO HAVE FRIENDS FROM other cultures and of other faiths should never hesitate to ask them about the best ways to celebrate their new baby's or child's milestones. What's important is that friends are able to attend or participate in the occasions.

First Communion

For a Catholic child, first communion takes place when the youngster is six or seven. It is the first occasion on which she actually receives communion—an important event in the child's religious life. The child attends a course of instruction to learn both the meaning and the ritual of communion, and class members sometimes receive their first communion together. Although some families celebrate the occasion with elaborate festivities, most take into account the youth of the participants and restrict the party to relatives and perhaps a few close friends.

For Protestant children, first communion takes place at an older age, usually between eleven and fourteen, depending on the denomination. In many Protestant churches, the children take part in communion along with their families without any ceremony or fanfare. Often, the ceremony is held during a regular church service, with the entire congregation participating.

Clothes. Catholic girls may wear white dresses (some with elaborate veils and headpieces) and boys may wear dark suits with white shirts and ties, but there is no hard-and-fast rule for clothing.

In Protestant churches, girls wear nice dresses and boys wear shirts and slacks with or without a jacket and tie.

Gifts. In Catholic congregations, immediate family members give meaningful gifts of a lasting nature—a Bible or a personalized book, for example, or a religious medal or cross. In Protestant churches, celebrations are at the discretion of the parents, and gifts are given only by immediate family members, if at all. Guests who are invited to either a Catholic or a Protestant communion party should take gifts of the same sort.

Confirmation

Confirmation—the moment when the young person receives power and grace from the Holy Spirit—is a religious occasion, not a social one. Because it is a thoughtful and serious event, it is celebrated with a measure of restraint.

Catholic children are generally confirmed between the ages of eight and fifteen, or sometimes when a little older. Protestant children are usually confirmed at age twelve or thirteen. If no childhood confirmation occurs, a person can be confirmed at any age; there is also a special confirmation for those who change their faith. The service (in the Catholic church, separate from the regular mass; in the Protestant church, part of a regular Sunday service) is usually attended by family members and close friends of the young person.

Some churches hold an informal reception after the ceremony, giving the child, parents, and friends the chance to visit with one another and with the officiating clergy. Afterward, the family and a few friends usually gather at the parents' home or a restaurant for lunch.

Catholic girls and boys often wear red robes to signify the fire of the Holy Spirit; the most common alternatives are white dresses for girls and jackets and ties for boys. Some Protestant ministers request that girls wear white, but most only ask that they wear simple, modest clothes in quiet colors. Protestant boys wear dark blue or dark gray suits or jackets and ties with slacks.

Gifts. While gifts are not obligatory, those given are usually of a religious nature—a Bible engraved with the child's name, a prayer book, a gold cross, or a religious medal.

Bar Mitzvah

The coming-of-age ceremony for male Jewish adolescents is the bar mitzvah (son of the commandment), which celebrates his acceptance as an adult member of his congregation. In the Orthodox and Conservative branches and some Reform congregations, it takes place on the first Sabbath (Saturday) after the boy becomes thirteen and he has undergone a period of religious instruction. Other Reform congregations have replaced the bar mitzvah with a "confirmation" service at which both boys and girls are confirmed, sometimes at an older age than the traditional thirteen. (See also Chapter 16, page 213: "Coming-of-age Events.")

The celebration. The bar mitzvah is one of the most important events in a Jewish boy's life, and families generally make it as memorable an occasion as they can. The religious ceremony, which takes place on Saturday morning, may be followed immediately by a gathering in the social rooms of the synagogue. This is open to any member of the congregation who wishes to offer congratulations.

The luncheon, dinner, or reception that follows later in the day usually includes all the close friends of the parents as well as friends and classmates of the boy. Only those who receive invitations may attend.

The reception itself is just like any other. Dinners and luncheons may be sit-down or buffet, and the party may be held at home, a club, hotel, or restaurant. There may or may not be a band and dancing after the meal is over.

Dress. For the ceremony, guests wear clothes that they ordinarily choose for a religious service. If the party is a luncheon, they go there directly without changing. If the celebration is later in the day, they change into clothes more appropriate for an evening party. If the affair is "black tie," this should be specified on the invitation. Otherwise, women wear cocktail dresses or long skirts, and men wear dark suits.

Gifts. Everyone invited to a bar mitzvah is expected to either send or take a gift. Any of the following gifts is acceptable: prayer book, religious charm or pendant, a gift of money, jewelry, or a pen-and-pencil set. Select the gift based on your closeness to the youngster. Gift certificates to music, clothing, and video stores, and fitness centers, and sports equipment are also appropriate, depending on the age of the recipient.

Bat Mitzvah

In some Conservative and Reform congregations, a bat mitzvah, a ceremony corresponding to a bar mitzvah, is held for girls of twelve or thirteen. The bat mitzvah (daughter of the commandment) tradition began in the twentieth century. Girls read from the Torah, lead parts of the service, and usually deliver a speech to the congregation on the importance of attaining religious adulthood. Like a bar mitzvah, a bat mitzvah is part of a larger service and is almost always on a Saturday.

Guests. Guests should follow the practice of the synagogue during the service, with men wearing a *yarmulke* (or *kippah*) at all services except those of some Reform congregations. *Yarmulkes* are available outside the sanctuary. Some Conservative synagogues also require that women wear a hat or other head covering. When a *tallith*, or prayer shawl, is available at the entrance to the sanctuary, it is only for Jewish people. Non-Jewish people should neither pick up a *tallith* nor wear religious symbols of other faiths.

Reception. The reception may be as simple or as elaborate as the parents wish. Invited guests are expected to give a gift, even if they decline the invitation. Those who attend the bat mitzvah either send a gift to the girl's home or take one to the reception. Gifts should not be taken to the religious ceremony but are presented at another time.

(See gift suggestions for bar mitzvahs, page 507.) The bat mitzvah girl must write thank-you notes for all gifts.

Islamic Birth Ceremony

Some Moslems hold an *akikah*, or a birth ceremony. The form of the ceremony varies greatly but always is a welcome to a newborn infant. Men and women usually sit in different parts of the room.

Clothes. While men generally dress in a shirt and slacks, women should wear a dress or a skirt and blouse. Arms should be covered, and hems should reach below the knees. The head should be covered with a scarf. Neither men nor women should wear crosses, Stars of David, or jewelry that depicts signs of the zodiac or the faces or heads of people or animals.

Gifts. Guests take gifts to the ceremony, which is generally held in the home of the parents or in a general-purpose room in the mosque.

Happy Birthday!

BIRTHDAY PARTIES BRING OUT THE kid in us all, regardless of our age. Apart from the dyed-in-the-wool curmudgeon, who could ever get tired of listening to even an off-key "Happy Birthday to You," blowing out the candles on the cake, and opening presents? Beyond these three traditions, a birthday party is conducted like any other celebratory gathering, whether it takes the form of a backyard barbecue or a dinner dance.

Depending on the formality of the party, invitations may be printed, fill-in, or phoned. Unless "No gifts, please" is specified (a request invitees should heed), guests should arrive with presents.

Gifts. Almost anything is suitable as a birthday present so long as it's not too personal or too expensive. Anything you've made yourself is all the more special because you spent time sewing, baking, or constructing it.

Gag gifts have their place, but it's wise to give them only in conjunction with a "real" birthday present. That cheap aluminum walking cane for a friend having his fiftieth birthday won't be quite so funny if every other present he opens is not only more expensive but also genuinely useful.

➤ **For children** See Chapter 14, page 192: "Choosing Appropriate Gifts."

➤ **For teenagers** Clothing, sports equipment, and CDs or tapes of a favorite group are usually a good choice for teenage boys and girls. Other ideas include wall posters, a video game, computer software, a watch, or a gift certificate to a local fitness center or movie theater.

➤ **For sweet-sixteen parties** Birthday gifts for these coming-of-age celebrations for girls include a charm bracelet with one charm; a pair of earrings, perhaps set with

You can personalize a gift of jewelry by choosing items that feature the recipient's birthstones. These are the traditional stones for each month:

January Garnet
February Amethyst
March Aquamarine, bloodstone, or jasper
April Diamond
May Emerald
June Pearl

July Ruby
August Sardonyx, peridot, or carnelian
September Sapphire
October Opal
November Topaz
December Turquoise or lapis lazuli

the girl's birthstone; any book on her special interest or hobby; personalized stationery; perfume; or a scarf, belt, or other fashion accessory.

➤ **For quinceanera parties** For quinceanera—a girl's fifteenth-birthday celebration in Latin cultures—religious items such as rosaries or crosses are appropriate. Monetary gifts and personal items for teenage girls are also popular gifts. (See also Chapter 16, page 214: "Quinceanera.")

➤ **For a husband or wife** The ideal choice is any present the spouse knows the partner wants but has avoided buying because he or she thought it too extravagant.

➤ **For friends** The better you know someone—and therefore his or her special interests—the easier it is to zero in on an appropriate gift. Just be careful not to give something so expensive that your friend will probably feel obliged to reciprocate in kind.

➤ **For an older couple** Welcome gifts include a newspaper or magazine subscription, a gift certificate, an easy-care houseplant, or any book of interest to the couple. A thoughtful group gift from family members is travel tickets for a special vacation.

Anniversary Parties

PARTIES ARE USUALLY HELD only for milestone anniversaries: the first, tenth, fifteenth, twenty-fifth, fiftieth, and seventy-fifth. In other years, the couple usually prefers a romantic dinner for two, a weekend vacation at a fine local hotel, or a small, informal party at home for friends and family. (A note for modern times: Couples who divorce but subsequently remarry each other celebrate the anniversary of their first marriage, not of the remarriage.)

Who hosts an anniversary party? The couple's children and their families often want to take on the role, but it's also perfectly correct for the couple to throw the party themselves. If the couple has no children, close friends sometimes become the hosts and take care of all the arrangements.

If the celebration will be large, it's important to get an early start on planning—especially if the party will be held outside the home. Depending on local demand for party space and the size of the guest list, the hosts may decide to rent a party space as much as a year in advance. To guard against anything going awry as the date nears, it's wise to finalize decorating and menu ideas a few months before the party.

A cocktail party, buffet, dinner dance, or most any other kind of party is appropriate, but some elements are standard—or at least should be considered:

Décor. This can be as simple as vases of flowers or bunches of balloons. Pictures of the couple, whether displayed in frames on side tables or blown up as posters, have become an almost essential addition to the décor, documenting the couple's life together and bringing back memories for family and friends. Sometimes the decorations reflect the traditional colors of the anniversary: silver and white for the twenty-fifth anniversary, gold for the fiftieth.

Music. Background music, including tunes from the era when the couple was married, can be provided by a piano player, a DJ, or a family member who's responsible for manning a CD player.

Guest book. A guest register that allows space for comments makes a nice keepsake for the couple. On the same table where the guest book is placed, a family photo album or scrapbook could be made available for browsing.

The Gifts Question

Gifts are almost always given to a couple celebrating a first anniversary, since they may need some new household items. But when a couple has been married twenty-five years or more, their hope chests are probably fully stocked. Many choose to include the notation "No gifts, please" on the invitation, which is perfectly fine. A guest who wishes to give a gift regardless does so at another time, not at the party; showing up with a gift risks embarrassing both the couple and empty-handed guests.

When gifts *are* given, they need not necessarily be of silver, gold, or the other traditional materials allotted to each anniversary. Gifts may be totally different from the traditional suggestions or they may be something similar but not identical—for example, a stainless-steel or pewter platter instead of a silver one is acceptable on a twenty-fifth anniversary. Other gifts you might consider include a photo album to be filled later with pictures taken at the party, or any book related to the couple's hobbies or interests.

Following is a list of traditional materials, with a few additions and gift suggestions:

1st anniversary: Paper or plastics—books, notepaper, magazine or newspaper subscriptions

2nd anniversary: Calico or cotton—cotton napkins and place mats, cotton throw, tapestries

Small parties celebrating a birthday, anniversary, or graduation are often held at a restaurant, and for good reason. A sit-down dinner at a favorite dining spot frees the hosts of preparation and cleanup, while the guests can pick and choose from a menu.

Who pays the bill depends on whether the dinner is being hosted by a member of the honoree's immediate family or organized by a friend or group.

➤ A wife hosting a birthday dinner for her husband, children hosting an anniversary dinner for their parents, or a sibling feting another sibling is obligated to pay for everyone present. Just as you don't charge your guests for a party in your own home, you wouldn't when you host a party elsewhere.

➤ If a friend decides to plan a restaurant dinner for someone, she generally acts only as an organizer/coordinator, *not* as host. When making plans, she lets it be known that there's a get-together in honor of so-and-so and she hopes the invitee can join them. Whether by phone or a note enclosed with the invitation, she says something like, "Several of us are getting together at the Copper Kettle to celebrate Alfred's birthday. Hope you can join us." The organizer should also make it clear that everyone is chipping in for the honoree and, if possible, give the estimated cost of the restaurant meal.

➤ At work, if coworkers organize a celebratory dinner for someone and the tab isn't being picked up by the company, the organizers should state up front what the probable tab will be per person. Otherwise, some invitees may be so surprised by the cost of the evening that they might have decided not to attend had they known.

3rd anniversary: Leather or simulated leather—photo album, leather bag or suitcase

4th anniversary: Silk or synthetic material—silk flowers, silk handkerchiefs or scarf

5th anniversary: Wood—picture frames, hand-painted wooden trays, wicker baskets

6th anniversary: Iron—fireplace tool set, wind chimes

7th anniversary: Copper or wool—copper bowls, pots, or kettle; wool afghan

8th anniversary: Electrical appliances—hand mixer, blender, waffle maker, espresso maker

9th anniversary: Pottery—ceramic vase, platter, picture, bowl, set of mugs

10th anniversary: Tin or aluminum—pretty cookie or biscuit tins, mailbox, rustic birdhouse

11th anniversary: Steel—stainless-steel kitchen utensils or bowls

12th anniversary: Linen—damask tablecloth

13th anniversary: Lace—tablecloth, napkins

14th anniversary: Ivory (now endangered), antique jewelry

15th anniversary: Crystal or glass—Christmas ornaments, carafe
20th anniversary: China—hand-painted bowl, platter
25th anniversary: Silver—ice bucket, wine bucket, engraved goblet
30th anniversary: Pearls—pearl-handled steak knives
35th anniversary: Coral (now endangered)—brooches, figurines
40th anniversary: Ruby—jewelry
45th anniversary: Sapphire—jewelry
50th anniversary: Gold—jewelry, gold-leaf stationery
55th anniversary: Emerald—jewelry
60th, 70th, and 75th: Diamond—jewelry

Reaffirming Marriage Vows

YEARS AGO, a couple wishing to reaffirm their wedding vows waited until their tenth or twenty-fifth anniversary. But now the happy pair can ceremoniously vouch for their commitment to each other any time they please. Couples might want to celebrate in conjunction with a fortieth or fiftieth birthday party or other occasion. Or they could be marking the end of a difficult time in their lives. Still others might have gotten married on a shoestring and now want a larger wedding, or have had a civil ceremony and want to add a spiritual component to their vows.

Today's ceremonies are often personalized with vows written by the couple and, if the reaffirmation is a religious one, perhaps a blessing of the couple's children by the officiant. Sentimental objects and souvenirs also play a role; many couples send invitations featuring an old wedding photo.

The couple can host the ceremony themselves, or their children could be hosts.

A QUESTION FOR PEGGY

My husband and I want to celebrate our tenth wedding anniversary by inviting several people to have dinner at our favorite restaurant. How do we let them know that we don't want any presents but would appreciate it if they would cover the cost of the meal?

You can't be hosts *and* ask guests to pay. You'll therefore have to decide whether you want to actually host an anniversary celebration (in which case you should pay for your guests' meals) or just organize a gathering of friends, with everyone paying their share of the bill.

The question of gifts is a separate issue. If you host an anniversary party and don't want gifts, write "No gifts, please" on the invitations; otherwise, your guests are sure to bring them on what's normally a gift-giving occasion.

The site can be anywhere the couple desires—their house of worship, at home, in a park, on the beach, or even on a cruise. Unlike a wedding, a reaffirmation of vows isn't legally binding, so virtually anyone can officiate: a member of the clergy, a judge, a close friend (often, the best man or maid of honor at the actual wedding), or one of the couple's children. Some couples choose to have no officiant and simply recite their vows on their own.

The guest list can be confined to close friends or family, or so large that even long-lost friends and new acquaintances are invited. As with other anniversary parties, the couple may have "No gifts, please" printed on the invitations, if they choose.

The Ceremony

Couples reaffirming their vows often invite members of the original wedding party to the ceremony. But couples who choose to walk down the aisle together rarely have any attendants. Couples who *do* want others to stand with them during the ceremony often enlist their children or ask attendants (maid of honor and best man) from their wedding. At a large celebration, the couple may want to duplicate some features of their wedding, including the music, the vows, and the exchange of rings (new ones, perhaps). Other couples may choose to keep the ceremony simple, reciting new vows that draw on the memories of their life together.

The reception can take any form, from a quiet family dinner to a gala affair with a re-creation of the couple's original wedding cake (with the lighthearted ritual of the first slice), a round of toasts, and dancing.

Celebrating a Retirement

WHEN A RETIREMENT PARTY is thrown by a company or an organization, the event can range from a group lunch at a nice restaurant to a lavish party with speeches, skits, or even a good-natured roast. The nature of the party has to do with the rank of the retiree and the style of the company. In either case, it's always nice to include the retiree's spouse and any adult children who can attend.

As fun as company parties can be, a party given by family and friends can be all the jollier. It's generally a good idea to invite a few workmates the retiree is close to; all share a work history, and they'll be able to speak of specific accomplishments in any speeches and toasts. (See also Chapter 28, page 493: "Business Toasts.")

For someone whose work has spanned many years and different organizations, a large celebration complete with many of the retiree's current and former associates can be especially meaningful. Plans can be as grand as the organizers envision. In a typical scenario, a group of the retiree's colleagues determine the guest list, choose the site for the party, and arrange for catering if necessary. Guests who toast or speak about the honoree do so during a specified period, and at a company-sponsored party the employer presents the honoree with a gift. Individual gifts are rarely given, but guests bring cards, whether singly or collectively.

Chapter Thirty

Giving and Receiving Gifts

ONE OF LIFE'S PLEASURES is choosing a gift for those we care about and watching it be enthusiastically received. But to many, gift giving isn't quite so simple as it sounds, considering the thousands of items to choose from and the differences in personal taste. (That effusive "Thanks so very much!" may be coming from the lips while the brain is processing "What on earth was she thinking?") Both the character and cost of the gift should be tailored to the person and the occasion; giving an engraved sterling silver urn to a teenager who won the high school science fair is about as appropriate as wearing an evening gown to the office.

The aim of this chapter is to cover the nuts and bolts of gift giving—presentation, response, and acknowledgment. (For more information, see "Gifts" subentries in the index under "Anniversaries," "Birthdays," "Business," "Celebrations," "Ceremonies," "Graduations," "Houseguests," "Parties," "International Travel," and "Weddings.")

First Considerations

DECIDING WHAT TO GIVE is made easier if you equate the perishability of the gift with the importance of the occasion. Flowers or a box of candy will be enjoyed for the short term, whereas a hardcover book or objet d'art will last a lifetime. The amount you spend has little to do with permanence; the cost of a bunch of peonies may be twice that of a book, but the flowers will fade and die within a week.

Temporary gifts. Falling into the temporary, or perishable, category are flowers, candy and other foodstuffs, beverages, and tickets to everything from operas to baseball games. While temporary gifts are always appropriate, they're especially advisable under certain circumstances—for instance, when a permanent gift could become a lasting reminder of the illness or death of a family member.

Enduring gifts. A gift that lasts can serve as a lifelong reminder of an event or a special milestone. The nature of the occasion will help you make your choice. When giving a gift to a retiree, for example, remember that he's probably looking forward to

Perishable they are, but gifts of food, beverages, and flowers will always rank among the most popular.

Food. Before giving food, check with a family member to find out if the recipient favors any particular food or needs to avoid any. If time permits, expand your options by scanning catalogs and magazines for mail order firms, which offer everything from prime steaks to specialty cakes. You can add a special touch by preparing the present yourself and packaging it attractively—baking your prized brownies, perhaps, or a putting together a basket of exotic fruits.

Wine and spirits. Before sending a gift of wine or spirits, the obvious first step is to find out whether and what the recipient drinks. Then shop accordingly. Don't buy liqueurs, many of which are an acquired taste, unless you're sure the person is fond of a certain type. If you give champagne, go for high quality. If you can't afford good champagne, you're better off giving a bottle or two of good-quality still wine.

Flowers. Thanks to credit cards, teleflorists, and the Internet, you can send flowers to anyone at any time. You can also pair an arrangement with another gift (a vase or a small picture frame, perhaps) or attach theater tickets or a gift certificate. But don't send flowers without thinking; while a mixed arrangement is always appropriate, long-stemmed roses may imply romantic sentiments to the wrong person. This advice applies twice over when sending flowers overseas; in foreign countries, certain flowers may have connotations, and an experienced florist should be able to keep you from making a mistake. (See also Chapter 11, page 136: "Flowers and Other Gifts"; Chapter 25, page 452: "A Dozen Dinner Guest Do's and Don'ts"; Chapter 31, page 534: "Flowers and Contributions.")

newfound relaxation and freedom. Choose a gift that "keeps on giving"—say, a high-quality putter (or, if it's a group gift, a set of golf clubs), a nice set of books, or membership in a travel club.

Group Gifts

A group gift is appropriate on many occasions. Some examples: when friends invited to an anniversary party pool funds for one big present, when coworkers pitch in for a gift to a workmate or boss, or when weekend guests band together to give their host something nicer than they could afford individually.

On the other hand, it can be the *recipients* of a gift who constitute the "group." For example, rather than giving a present to every child in a family, you could give a game or play equipment to be used by all. A caveat: Group gifts of this kind aren't always the best idea. If a godparent gives a gift meant for all the children in the family, for example, her godchild may think of it as less special.

Personalizing Gifts

GIFTS MARKED WITH A MONOGRAM or anything else specific to the recipient(s) are all the more appreciated. Beyond the traditional engraved silver or monogrammed towels or handkerchiefs is a grab bag full of new possibilities: an original ode to the person written in calligraphy and framed, a coffee mug bearing a picture of a child or family member, a T-shirt with the recipient's favorite saying or any other suitable inscription. (Note: Traditionally, when monogrammed handkerchiefs or other articles are marked with a single letter, the initial of a woman's first name is used; when the gift is for a man, the initial is that of his last name.)

Because a personalized gift can never be returned, make sure that it is something the recipient wants and is of the right size, color, and style. Unless the person has expressed a desire for something in particular, talk to a family member who can help you decide what to buy.

It's possible for the recipient to have the gift marked later. (If free engraving is offered with the purchase, it will be honored at a later time.) If there is a charge, make clear to the recipient that the bill should be sent to you, no matter how much time has passed since the gift was received.

Gifts of silver are still given on twenty-fifth anniversaries and other important events and are often engraved to commemorate the occasion. Once in a while, the hosts present mementos of the party to all guests. For an anniversary party, paper matchboxes or coasters could be marked "Robert and Lavinia Miles/July 18/ 1975–2000" or monogrammed "RGM and LHM."

Wrapping and Opening Presents

THE ELEMENT OF SURPRISE IS half the fun of gift giving—hence the wrapping that keeps the recipient in suspense. Wrapping paper can even be said to hold a special place in our hearts: A child eagerly ripping the paper off a Christmas present provides a classic Norman Rockwell moment. Then again, some wrapping paper may be so beautiful that the recipient removes it meticulously because it's too nice to destroy.

When using thin tissue for wrapping, make sure you use enough layers to keep any words printed on the gift box from showing through. Tissue is also used in decorative gift bags, to hide their contents. Gift bags' popularity probably has something to do with their practicality, since they can be reused; they're more environmentally correct, since reuse saves paper. By the same token, brown paper bags and newspaper can be creatively recycled as wrapping paper, and they look smart when tied with some colorful yarn.

Any box will do for gifts so long as it doesn't carry the name of a store other than the one where the present was bought. (You could mark a line through the store name on an old box, but you'll take the elegance of your presentation down a notch.) You don't want the recipient attempting to exchange the gift at the wrong store. Another tip: Don't forget to remove or obliterate the price tag.

Unwrapped Gifts

While suspense is part of the fun with birthday and holiday presents, hostess gifts and house gifts are usually presented unwrapped. But you might add a little something extra. Wine for the host of a dinner party requires nothing more than removal of the price tag and a quick polishing of the bottle, but a ribbon knotted around the neck adds a nice touch. A fruit-and-cheese basket can be dressed up with colored cellophane or ribbons. And homemade cookies or other treats packed in a lidded tin (decorative or plain vanilla) is a dual gift of sorts, since the recipient will be able to reuse the container.

When Giving to . . .

YOUR GIFT CHOICES ARE AFFECTED by who you're giving them to and the nature of your relationship—so consider the following guidelines and suggestions.

Family members. You'd think that family members should be the easiest to buy for, but often it's just the opposite. Thanks to doting relatives and your own penchant for supplying your toddlers with everything they want and need, the youngsters may have everything under the sun. Likewise, your elderly grandmother may have been through so many birthdays, anniversaries, Christmases, and Mother's Days that you long ago gave up on choosing a gift that was "fresh."

One solution to the difficulty of choosing is to browse specialty stores and catalogs for something different. You could also get your computer into the act: Kids will love a collage of their favorite professional athletes or cartoon characters scanned in with photos of the children themselves.

Close friends. Whatever the occasion, first try racking your brain to remember if a good friend mentioned something she really would like, whether a night at a touring

---

A QUESTION FOR PEGGY

I started exchanging Christmas gifts with a few friends and relatives several years ago, but some of us seem unable to break the habit even though we're no longer all that close. It's an expense I'd rather not have to bear, so is there a graceful way to bow out?

Yes, and it's not as hard as you think. Be frank. Months before Christmas, either write or say to the person, "I've loved your gifts, but what with the economy like it is [or the new baby, or redecorating the house, or whatever seems a good reason], why don't we just send cards this year? Simply write us with family news, which will be the best present of all."

Traditional monograms for married people consist of three initials or the last-name initial only. The husband's initials don't change unless the couple uses a hyphenated last name; the wife generally uses her maiden name as her middle name. But today, with some couples using both last names and some wives keeping their maiden names, monograms can be a bit more complicated.

Initials in a couple's monogram generally include first names. However, a middle-name initial can be substituted if that is the name a person uses. The initial of a nickname is not normally included in a monogram.

The following chart should help individuals, couples, and gift givers choose the type of monogram that best suits items. The order of initials depends on whether the letters are of the same size or the initial of the last name is larger, in which case it is centered. The monograms illustrated below are for a couple named Jane Anne Bowen and Thomas Ryan Noel.

	When initials are the same size	When center initial is larger	Single initial
Single woman (used for personal items and stationery before marriage)	First, middle, last: *JAB*	First, last, middle: *JBA*	Last: *B*
Single man (used for personal items and stationery before and after marriage)	First, middle, last: *TRN*	First, last, middle: *TNR*	Last: *N*
Married couple		Wife's first name, married/last name, husband's first name: *JNT*	Married/ last name: *N*
Married woman (for personal items and stationery)*	First, maiden name, married/last name: *JBN*	First, married/last name, maiden name: *JNB*	Married/ last name: *N*
Married couple with hyphenated last name		Wife's first name, hyphenated married name, husband's first name: *JB-NT*	Hyphenated last name: *B-N*
Married woman with hyphenated married/last name (married men use the same form)	First, middle, hyphenated last name: *JAB-N* **or** First, hyphenated last name: *JB-N*	First, hyphenated last name, middle: *JB-NA*	Hyphenated last name: *B-N*
Married couple when wife keeps her maiden name	Wife's maiden-name and husband's last-name initials separated by a dot, diamond shape, or other design: *B · N*		

Married couple when wife keeps her maiden name and both wife and husband come to the marriage with hyphenated last names	Same as above; for Lynn Carter-James and John Lyle-Wiesner: *C-J · L-W*	
Individual or married couple when the last name includes a capitalized article (Von, Van, Du, etc.)	For Anna Smith Von Haegel: *ASVH*	For Anna and Carl Von Haegel: *AVHC* *VH*

*NOTE: A woman who remarries does not use initials from her previous marriage or marriages in monograms. She should follow the forms above, using her maiden-name and new-married-name initials.

When having a wedding gift monogrammed, givers should be guided by the way a couple plans to write their name(s). If you aren't sure of the correct monogram, you might check with the couple's parents or a bridal attendant.

Here are some tips for monogramming of specific items:

Stationery. Any of the above forms is appropriate. When husbands and wives share stationery, the married/last-name initial, hyphenated initial, or double last-name initials (when the wife retains her maiden name) are used.

Linens. Many people today prefer the single last-name initial, or hyphenated initials for couples with a hyphenated last name. The other forms are also appropriate.

Towels are marked at the center of one end. Rectangular tablecloths are monogrammed at the center of each long side, and square cloths, at one corner. Dinner napkins are marked diagonally at one corner or centered. Top sheets are monogrammed so that when the sheet is folded down, the letters can be read by someone standing at the foot of the bed. Pillowcase monograms are centered approximately two inches above the hem.

Flatware. The choice of monogram is usually determined by the shape of the flatware handle. The last initial or hyphenated last initials are often used. In some cases, a couple's initials are stacked in an inverted triangle shape, with the couple's first-name initials on top and the last initial below:

$$\begin{matrix} \text{JT} \\ \text{N} \end{matrix}$$

Clothing and other personal items. Choose the individual's personal monogram or the married/last-name initial (single or hyphenated).

musical, a particular book, or a kitchen appliance that would make her life easier. If the cost fits the occasion, try to grant her wish. Whatever gift you eventually choose, either enclose the "blind" exchange receipt or save the actual one so your friend can exchange the gift for another style or model if she likes.

Friends who are traveling or moving. Bon voyage gifts are generally given a few days before the travelers strike out on their journey. And a good thing, too—a bulky item given when a departure is imminent can be a nuisance, no matter how laudable your intentions. Anything other than a box of film or a passport case (if you're sure the recipient doesn't have one) should be given in advance. Typical gifts include a currency exchange guide, a set of electric converter plugs, and a travel kit of small cleaning and laundry products. In addition to film, give the travelers a prepaid processing mailer that will allow them to see their photos as soon as they get home. For friends going on a cruise, you might arrange to have champagne or wine served as a surprise as their dreamboat plies the seas.

When friends are moving away, a choice farewell gift is something that will serve as a memento: a picture of their friends, candids of the going-away party, a subscription to the local newspaper, or a gift certificate for a store in their new city or town. Another good idea is stationery printed with the family's new address.

Friends' children. It's easy to fall into the trap of taking a small gift to a child each time you visit—whether a relative or the child of a close friend—but it's a bad idea for everyone concerned. If you show up regularly with presents, you'll be doing the child a disservice by reinforcing expectations that are both unrealistic and inappropriate.

If a child asks you for a gift, it is his parents' job, not yours, to teach him that it's bad manners to ask people to bring him things. Since you don't know if they've spoken to him about his behavior, you would be out of line if you mention it. The next time you see the child, simply say, "It's so great to see you! I hope you know how much I enjoy visiting you, even though I can't bring you something every time I come." That leaves the door open for the parents to take the matter further with the child if they choose.

Coworkers and business associates. For exchanging business gifts, see Chapter 44, page 770: "Exchanging Gifts."

Doctors, lawyers, and other professionals. While professionals aren't given gifts for services rendered, there are occasions when a patient or client wants to express special thanks for extraordinary consideration—for example, a doctor who worked overtime and made house calls to care for a sick child. In such cases, any of the following gifts are appropriate: a food specialty, such as homemade cheesecake or a deluxe box of cookies; an accessory to a favorite sport (such as golf or tennis balls); a bottle of wine or spirits; or a gift certificate for two to a nice area restaurant.

Nurses. Gifts of money should never be offered to hospital nurses, but cookies, candy, or fruit that can be shared by everyone at the nurses' station is always welcome. Because hospitals usually have three shifts, it's a good idea to give three of the gift items, clearly marked "first shift," "second shift," and "third shift." (See also Chapter 46, page 811. "Health Care Providers.")

The same applies to private nurses (food, not money, as a gift), but personal gifts, such as articles of clothing or accessories, may be given to a private-duty nurse who has served over a period of time.

Buying a gift certificate instead of picking out a gift can set you on the horns of a dilemma. One school of thought says, "The easy way out!"—no mulling over the choices, no effort to personalize. The opposing school begs to differ, saying that nothing could be more thoughtful than giving the recipient the freedom to choose exactly what she wants and needs. For many, a gift certificate is the answer to presenting to people gifts they can need and really use.

Money, too, is sometimes seen as an easy way to avoid the trouble of choosing a regular gift. But an elderly person with a limited income might love the chance to shop for some long-desired object, and there are few teenagers who don't relish a little extra cash. Many of today's brides and grooms also prefer gifts of cash. The answer to whether to give money lies in how well you know the recipient. (See also Chapter 38, page 669: "Cash and Checks.")

Other financial gifts, such as bonds, are often given to young people as coming-of-age gifts. Long-term bonds usually mature just when the recipient is launching his own life—a wise and thoughtful gift that's worth the wait.

Teachers. Christmas, Hanukkah, and end-of-year gifts are probably the most common times for giving gifts to teachers. A box of your lemon squares and a card created by your child can be enjoyed every bit as much as costly, store-bought gifts. Still, gift shops offer a wider selection of teacher-oriented items, or you may want to consider a couple of other options:

> ➤ A donation to a worthy cause in the teacher's name. Your child's teacher may favor a particular cause, or you can contribute in his or her name to any established (and noncontroversial and nonpolitical) group.

> ➤ Gifts of supplies and materials to the classroom. Too many teachers have to pay for classroom supplies out of their own pockets. You can ask the teacher what items will be most helpful—packs of notebook paper, a quantity of pencils, art supplies, or packets of juice drinks and paper cups—hardly glamorous, but needed. (See also Chapter 46, page 816: "Holiday Tips and Gifts Guide.")

Clergy. It is appropriate to give a gift to a member of the clergy over the holidays or when he or she is feted for an ordination or a birthday or leaves for another post or retires. Any of the following items would make suitable presents: a leather diary or address book, pen-and-pencil set, magazine subscription, wristwatch, wallet or briefcase, or a gift certificate to a local department store.

Household help. Holiday gifts are given to housekeepers and other household help, usually as an accompaniment to a cash gift equivalent to a week's or month's salary, depending on the hiring arrangements. (A once-a-week cleaning service employee would receive an extra day's pay, while a live-in housekeeper might receive a bonus of a month's pay.)

Typical gifts include articles of clothing, soaps, perfume, items related to a special interest they may have, or (if they live in) items for their rooms. A nanny or au pair would receive a present from the children in addition to a cash gift from the parents. (See also Chapter 46, page 816: "Holiday Tips and Gifts Guide.")

All-Purpose Gift Registries

TIME WAS WHEN PEOPLE REGISTERED only for wedding gifts, but the use of general registries has exploded over the last few years. Internet sites now include wish lists, where the gifts an individual would like to receive are on worldwide display. But there's a fine line between letting your family and closest friends know what you'd like and maintaining a standing "buy me this" roster, which seems little more than an aggressive plea for loot.

Having a personal registry is appropriate *only* as an aid for close friends and family members with whom you ordinarily exchange gifts. Your nearest and dearest don't have to make use of it, but when they're at a loss for what to give, your registry will provide an answer. Yes, general gift registries are a natural outgrowth of the Internet's ability to make life a little easier in an increasingly hectic world, but their use should be *confined to adults*. Kid's registries could teach children to focus on gifts more than relationships with family and friends—in effect, a lesson in greed.

If anyone outside the tight-knit circle privy to your registry asks what you'd like for a certain occasion, say "Whatever you pick" or "Whatever you choose will be wonderful"—not "Oh, just check out what's on my registry at [Web site address]." To re-

∼ Peggy's Top Five Guidelines for ∼ Stress-Free Gift Giving

If you take the following advice, gift giving should rarely be a hassle:

➤ Ask recipients for hints or a wish list, gathering ideas throughout the year and keeping a list. Be on the lookout for the items when shopping, and when browsing catalogs and Web sites as well.

➤ Trust your judgment. Forget about being afraid the gift isn't perfect. If you think the person will like it, chances are you're right.

➤ Stick to your budget. Spending more than you should takes the fun out of gift giving.

➤ Buy it when you see it. If you're shopping in July and see a sweater that your mother would love, buy it; it may not be there when you look in December.

➤ Have some gifts stashed away in the closet—but make sure they're nice ones.

fer to a personal registry is easily perceived as calculating, putting emphasis on "what's in it for me" instead of the friendship.

Including registry addresses on an invitation to a housewarming party (plus salting the list with big-ticket items) is an example of the misuse of these registries. Drawing such pointed attention to gifts is likely to make guests suspect that the party is being held just so you can rake in the goodies.

Receiving and Acknowledging Gifts

RULE NUMBER ONE WHEN YOU'RE opening a gift in the presence of the donor: Thank the person enthusiastically. Even if the present is the last thing you wanted, thank the giver for his thoughtfulness, drawing on the actor in you to mask your disappointment. Be pleasant but noncommittal: "It's so nice of you to think of me in this way!" or "What an imaginative choice!"

Broken or Damaged Gifts

The crystal vase mailed to you by a friend looks beautiful, but it's broken into three pieces. What to do? Take or send it, along with its packaging, to the shop where it was purchased. If it came from another city or a mail-order catalog, mail it back with a letter describing the problem; any good store will replace merchandise on reasonable evidence that it was damaged. Don't let the donor know unless you insured the package—in which case you are obligated to inform her so that she can recover her costs and replace the gift.

Many people send fruit baskets as gifts, and sometimes the fruit arrives spoiled. Just call the fruit company and ask for a replacement, which they'll most likely provide. If the givers are good friends, tell them of the problem when you write or call to thank them, but in a positive context: "We really appreciate the gift, but in case you're thinking of using this company again, we thought you'd want to know that a few pieces were spoiled. New fruit arrived, though, and it's delicious." If the givers are acquaintances or business associates, it's better to keep the matter to yourself.

Acknowledging Gifts

All gifts must be acknowledged. Furthermore, thanks of any kind should be prompt—particularly when a gift hasn't been hand-delivered by the donor and she is left wondering whether it has arrived.

Gifts of money. When given money, the recipient should indicate how it will be used when thanking the donor—it will help furnish your apartment, perhaps, or build up your savings. If you can be more specific about the use, do so: "Your check for $50.00 is going into our 'new camcorder fund,' and we can't tell you how pleased we were to receive it." It's fine to mention the amount, just as you would specify a nonmonetary gift when thanking.

Holiday and birthday gifts. You should write thank-you notes for holiday and birthday gifts as soon as possible, preferably within two or three days of receipt. (A good rule of thumb is to acknowledge Christmas or Hanukkah gifts before New Year's Day.) Even though a warm "Thank you!" in person is technically all that's required, a handwritten note is always appreciated—and a *must* when you haven't been able to thank someone directly.

When it comes to acknowledging children's gifts, a child who is old enough to write is old enough to handle her own thank-you notes. Even a preschooler can draw a picture and "sign" her name on a note you've written for her. It's never too early to begin teaching the habit. (See also Chapter 15, page 204: "Thank-you notes.")

Shower gifts. Thank-you notes are necessary for presents that have been given in person at a shower. If a sincere thank-you was expressed in person when the gift was received, and the gift-giver insists on no thank-you note, a note is not required (though always appreciated nonetheless).

Thank-you gifts. Do thank-yous need to be written for thank-you gifts? Yes. Gifts sent as a "thank you for . . ." require a note of appreciation in return. These gifts, as with any others, mean that someone put effort in selecting something for the recipient. It's necessary to let the sender know the present arrived and is appreciated.

Acknowledgment cards. Printed acknowledgment cards expressing appreciation for sending something can be used in three instances:

➤ After the death of a prominent person when scores of sympathy notes, gifts of flowers, or donations to charities are received

A QUESTION FOR PEGGY

As I was leaving a recent baby shower, the honoree handed me a scroll tied with ribbon. When I unrolled it, I found a photocopied thank-you note. At another baby shower, I received a one-size-fits-all thank-you letter printed out on the computer. I should mention that neither person thanked me personally at the shower. Have these letters become acceptable?

In a word, no. While it might be said that these efforts to be prompt with thank-yous is a step in the right direction, any thank-you is much more meaningful when it is personalized. You and the other shower guests surely felt slighted and saw the honorees as lazy. Both people should have mailed handwritten notes after thanking guests individually at the party. One of the keys to a sincere thank-you is a mention of the specific present ("I can't wait to see the baby in the new jumpsuit!"), which you can hardly do in a note meant for all.

- When a public official is elected and receives a landslide of congratulatory messages
- When a bride and groom have such a large wedding that they simply cannot write personal thank-you notes immediately; the printed acknowledgment states that a personal note will come later. (See also Chapter 38, page 674: "The Importance of 'Thank You.' ")

~ Note or Not? ~

The occasions listed below will tell you at a glance when a thank-you note for a gift is obligatory, optional, or unnecessary.

Occasion: Birthday, anniversary, holiday, and other gifts

Obligatory: Always, unless you've thanked the giver in person. For a very close friend or relative, a phone call is sufficient.

Optional: Optional, but only if you've given thanks in person. Even if you've said, "Thank you," a follow-up note is always appreciated.

Occasion: Shower gifts

Obligatory: Note to each person who has given a shower gift, even if thanks have been expressed in person.

Optional: Optional only if someone insists on no thank-you note.

Occasion: Gifts to a sick person

Obligatory: Notes to out-of-towners and calls or notes to close friends are obligatory as soon as the patient feels well enough to do them.

Optional: A close friend or relative of the ill person could write the notes on his or her behalf, if desired.

Occasion: Congratulatory cards or gifts

Obligatory: All personal messages or presents must be acknowledged.

Optional: Optional for preprinted greeting cards with no personal message. Form letters from firms need not be acknowledged.

Occasion: Wedding gifts

Obligatory: Even if spoken thanks have been given, all wedding gifts must be acknowledged within three months of receipt, but preferably as the gifts arrive.

Occasion: Host/hostess gift received after visitors have left

Obligatory: Even though the gift itself is a thank-you, the host must thank his or her visitors (especially if the gift has arrived by mail).

A neighbor unexpectedly drops off a Christmas gift, and you have nothing to offer in return. On your thirtieth birthday, your uncle gives you a yogurt maker—the exact model that's already gathering dust in your kitchen cabinet. You unwrap a present to find a ceramic figurine so ugly that you have to stifle a yelp. In these and other cases, you appreciate the gesture, but you find yourself in a bind.

The right thing to do? Issue a warm thank-you—although you'll be mentally crossing your fingers behind your back in a couple of cases.

Unexpected gifts. You find yourself on the spot when someone offers you a holiday gift but you are empty-handed. When it happens, there's little more you can do than say, "Oh, you shouldn't have! But thank you!" (though if it's still early in the season, you could present the person with a gift later). To stave off a repeat in the future, you could buy a few token items to have on hand to give in return—unique tree ornaments or tins of candy or nuts—if you want to. Or you might send a card well before the holidays and hope the person understands that you expect only a card in return.

Awful gifts. So how do you react to that jaw-dropper someone saw fit to give you—that raccoon kitchen clock, the Uncle Sam table lamp, or the collector's plate picturing Yosemite Falls? It's all very well to say, "It's the thought that counts," but sometimes we have to secretly wonder what the giver was thinking.

The last thing you want to do in a case like this is hurt the person's feelings. While your thank-you should be gracious, you don't want to lie. Noncommittal comments such as "The bowl is so unique" or "You really do have the most original ideas!" may pass as praise for some people, but others may be onto your game. A better tack may be to avoid describing the gift in any way, stressing your appreciation instead: "This is so thoughtful! The generosity of friends like you is something I really appreciate."

Duplicate gifts. If someone gives you something you already have or you are given the same two gifts at a party (say, a small kitchen appliance), you must handle the situation with care. If you already have the item and can easily exchange the duplicate, it's all right to do so without the giver's knowledge. Just don't lie if she asks how you liked your new hand blender: "I love those blenders so much I already owned one, and I didn't think you'd mind if I exchanged it for the food mill I've always wanted. Thanks for making my life in the kitchen easier!"

If you receive the same two items, it's important not offend either giver. Putting the duplicate away (assuming you'll eventually use it), is a safe way to go. Or, if one of the givers is a close friend who you're positive will be understanding, tell her directly: "We were given two hand blenders, and would love to exchange one for a coffeemaker. Would you mind terribly if we exchanged yours?" (See also page 527: "Regifting.")

High-maintenance gifts. Presents that need constant care—birds, animals, bonsais, or potted plants that only the greenest of thumbs could keep alive—are dealing the recipients a hand they may not choose to play. A plant can be left to fade away and die, but giving a puppy to a young child without first consulting his parents may cause the friendship itself to wither.

Too-expensive gifts. If someone gives you something so expensive that you could never afford to reciprocate at the same price level, how you react depends on whether the gift is a personal gift or a business one. If it's personal, say something on the order of "Sally, this is stunning, but you really shouldn't have! I'll love wearing cashmere, but please remember that I would be just as happy with *anything* coming from a friend as close as you." You've managed to thank her while gracefully dropping a hint.

If a super-expensive present comes from a business associate, it is inappropriate because it could smell like a bribe. Tell him that as much as you appreciate his thoughtfulness, you (or your company) have a policy only to accept small gifts from those with whom you do business. Some businesses issue written statements that are mailed to clients and other associates, stipulating that gifts over a certain monetary value can't be accepted. Including a copy of the statement in a "thanks, but . . ." note to the giver could defuse an awkward situation. (See also Chapter 44, page 772: "Where to Draw the Line?")

A newspaper "card of thanks." In some small towns and rural areas, it is not only permissible but expected that recipients of a large number of gifts or contributions—after a birthday, anniversary, retirement party, funeral, or even a political campaign, for example—put a public "thanks" in the newspaper. The notice is typically headed "card of thanks" and is followed by a brief message such as this: "We wish to express our thanks to all those wonderful people and organizations from whom we received cards and gifts on the occasion of our fiftieth wedding anniversary. Sincerely, Mr. and Mrs. Samuel Briggs."

When a card of thanks is published, personal notes have to be written only to people who went out of their way to give something very special or to assist or participate in the celebration.

Regifting

A NEW WORD HAS BUZZED its way into the language in recent years—"regifting," or passing a gift you've received along to someone else. Is this just another indication that something that was once unacceptable is now standard practice? Not really. It's a symptom of the surplus of "stuff" many people find themselves with, and their desire to be practical and give away things they know they will never use. Still, gifts should be recycled only rarely, and only when the following criteria are met:

➤ You're certain that the gift is something the recipient would really like to receive.

➤ The gift is brand new (no cast-offs allowed) and comes with its original box and instructions.

➤ The gift isn't one that the original giver took great care to select or make.

Simply put, you have to *make sure you don't hurt feelings*—neither the original giver's nor the recipient's. Would the person who gave you the gift mind that you passed it along? Do he and the recipient of your gift know each other, and would it be awkward if they realized that you've recycled a gift from one to the other? Following are two scenarios where recycling a gift would be appropriate:

➤ Your sister's coffeemaker just stopped working, and her birthday is days away. You, who are on a budget, have been given a coffeemaker that's a duplicate of the one you already have. Your sister has always liked yours. Instead of stashing the extra coffeemaker in your closet, you wrap it in its original box and present it to her. She's delighted.

➤ You've been given two copies of the same book. Your best friend, with whom you exchange Christmas gifts each year, is a fan of the author. You decide to give her the book—not as a holiday gift, but as a surprise: "Edith, I received two copies of this book and want you to have one." An "unofficial" gift of this sort is not wrapped.

Only you can decide whether to pass along a gift, and if so how to do it appropriately. Think through each situation carefully and then, if in doubt, don't do it.

When You Want to Exchange a Gift

IN MOST CASES, you needn't feel guilty about exchanging a gift; the giver's aim was to please, not to give you a sweater that will forever hang in the back of your closet. If the item was the wrong size, there's no reason not to report the exchange to the giver and tell her how much you enjoy the new item. It's trickier if you just don't like the gift and would like to trade it for something else. In this case, not letting your friend know demonstrates tact—the quality defined as "the ability to appreciate the delicacy of a situation and to do or say the kindest thing." (See also page 526: "Thanks, But . . .") The time *not* to exchange is when you've received something so unique—like a one-of-a-kind painting—that the gift giver would undoubtedly be hurt if you traded it in for something else. You'll know when extra thought has gone into the gift selection.

Many stores make exchange easier and less awkward by enclosing a ticket in the gift box that doesn't show the price. However, if the recipient wants to exchange a shirt for a sweater, the price differential will make the price of the original gift obvious.

Chapter Thirty-one

Grieving and Condolences

A S THEY HAVE IN EVERY CULTURE from the beginning of time, the rituals observed after the death of a loved one or friend salve our grief. All religions hold that the soul or spirit is sacred and that the embodiment of that spirit deserves respectful and ceremonious treatment. Yet things change with time, and the trend in recent years has been to both mourn the deceased and celebrate his life. The result is services that are customized to reflect the person's personality, interests, and accomplishments.

More and more of today's families are deciding what the nature of a funeral or memorial service should be, then taking an active part in planning it. It only makes sense, after all, that the choices everyone will find the most comforting—from the music to the burial clothing to the tone of the service itself—are more important than following a preordained script.

Funeral directors and clergy are willing to see that the family's wishes are fulfilled. Personalization can range from a display of photographs near the coffin to an all-out tribute. A career military man or woman, for example, might request an Army crest affixed to the casket; a red, white, and blue guest book; and a display of photographs taken during his or her service years. He or she also would almost certainly want to be buried in uniform. (See also page 539: "Memorial Services.")

If some things about funerals and mourning have changed, others have stayed the same: the ways to go about notifying others of the death and the particulars of the funeral, enlisting the participants, and offering and accepting condolences.

Notifying Others

AS DIFFICULT AS IT MAY be, informing others of the death is the first duty of the bereaved. It starts with telling family members, then proceeds to the practical—notifying the funeral home, the clergy, and the newspaper.

Notifying other family members is a job for someone who can keep her composure and break the news to immediate family members by telephone as soon as possible and in the gentlest way. An alternative is to start a chain of calls, with the original caller asking the first person she tells to call another family member, and so on down the line. If the funeral or memorial service arrangements have been made, share this information as well.

Others must also be notified, including:

The funeral director and clergy. The family member charged with handling the details discusses with the funeral director or member of the clergy such matters as the date, time, and place for the service; burial versus cremation; clothing for the deceased; whether the casket, if there is one, will be open or closed during the service; eulogies and music; and how traditional or personalized the relatives wish the funeral to be. (The National Funeral Directors Association provides information and answers questions and can be contacted at 800-228-6332 or www.nfda.org.)

If the family has no affiliation with a place of worship, the funeral director should be able to recommend someone to officiate. In many funeral homes, staff members are able to preside.

Newspapers. An obituary is written by a newspaper staff member, whereas a paid death notice is submitted either by the funeral home staff or a member of the family. Obituaries and notices alike include the name of the deceased, date of death, and the names of immediate family and various relatives. Unlike an obituary, a notice—which is usually written by a family member—includes the location where friends may call on the family and specifies where any memorial contributions are to be sent.

Almost all newspapers require that a funeral director confirm the death, but the form and submission for death notices differ from paper to paper—so use the format of those in your local paper as your guide. Regardless, some aspects of notices and obituaries are traditionally ordered or phrased in certain ways:

➤ Because the deceased's date of birth is normally given, some papers don't note his age. However, if the deceased is a young child, his age is usually placed after his name.

➤ For identification purposes, a woman's notice or obituary always includes her given and maiden names. The same is true when married daughters and sisters are mentioned.

➤ Daughters of the deceased are listed before sons, and by married names.

➤ The word "suddenly" is sometimes inserted immediately after the words "died" or "passed away" to indicate that there had not been a long illness or that the death was accidental.

Charities or organizations. Many families find comfort in naming a charity or an organization (perhaps the deceased's alma mater, a scholarship fund, or a medical research facility) to receive donations memorializing the deceased. Call the organization of choice to set the process in motion.

Making Arrangements

SHORTLY AFTER THE DEATH, the immediate family will usually make arrangements for the service with a funeral director, who will assist them in putting all the pieces together to create the service they have in mind. As hard as it may be for a family to make decisions on the heels of a loved one's death, planning the service may actually help them deal with their loss once all of the other arrangements have been made.

A major decision for many these days is whether to have a memorial service rather than a funeral. Memorial services (by definition, a service without the body present) are most often held following a cremation, when a funeral has taken place far from the home community, when the deceased died overseas, or when there are no remains. A notice of the service is put in the obituary column of the paper, just as a funeral notice would be.

Other decisions include whom to choose as pallbearers (if any), and what should be engraved on the monument if the words haven't previously been chosen.

Clothing for Burial

While burial clothing once was expected to be of subdued solid colors and in a conservative style, the decision now rests on what the deceased would have wanted. A uniform, a favorite brightly colored dress, sport clothes, and even a well-worn gardening outfit are some of the choices made today.

Pallbearers

If the coffin will be carried during the funeral, the family of the deceased asks close friends, relatives, and sometimes coworkers or business associates to be pallbearers. The elderly or frail may have trouble carrying the casket, so this should be taken into account when choosing. Professional pallbearers provided by the funeral home could also perform the duty.

Today, honorary pallbearers participate in funerals almost as a matter of course. Their role is to escort (not carry) the coffin, though in some cases they push it during the processional and recessional.

The family of the deceased appoints the honorary pallbearers (usually no more than eight) from those the deceased was close to, whether friends, fellow club members, schoolmates, colleagues, grandchildren, or hospital or hospice staff who were especially caring. A phone call is the logical and appropriate way to request that someone act as honorary pallbearer.

Ushers

The family also chooses the men and women who will serve as ushers. Although funeral homes will supply personnel, it's preferable to enlist members of the extended family or close friends, who will be more likely to recognize those who attend. The guests can then be seated according to the closeness of their relationship to the family.

Bulletins

The cover of a bulletin used for a funeral or memorial service is imprinted with the name of the deceased and often his birth and death dates; a photograph of the person in his prime is also a nice addition. Inside is listed the order of service and information. The bulletin for a memorial service includes additional information, such as "Interment took place in Oaklawn Cemetery on June 14."

Reproducing the obituary on the back cover of the bulletin is a good idea because some of the attendees may have missed seeing it in the paper. Bulletins can also include an invitation: "Following the service, all are invited to join the family for lunch at 142 Northwood Boulevard, Colorado Springs."

Some bulletins include a separate sheet for remembrances, which might read, "If you have any memories of James you wish to share with the family, please write them below and place in the basket at the rear of the church. They will be most welcome."

Eulogies

If the family chooses, family members or friends can be asked to deliver a eulogy. Because an officiant or two will be speaking, the number of eulogists should usually be kept to two or three. (See also page 540: "When You're Asked to Give a Eulogy.")

Honorariums

A contribution is sometimes given to the officiant who presides at a funeral service. Because customs differ from place to place, rely on your funeral director to suggest the proper honorarium, if any—especially because anything from $100 (for a very small funeral or memorial service) to $300 or more (for an elaborate service) could be appropriate. The check is presented after the funeral, either by you or the funeral director. Accompanying the check with a personal note of thanks will express your appreciation all the more.

The organist who plays at the funeral service could also be due an honorarium. Consult whoever is planning the service for the appropriate amount.

The Monument

Because the engraved monument chosen for a loved one is usually the only memorial that is permanent (the word "monument" is gradually supplanting "tombstone"), it should be chosen with great care. Something simple and straightforward is often preferable to an ornate stone with sentimental carvings and a flowery inscription. For example, in the emotion of the moment, the urge may be to write something about the deceased being "the only love" of the spouse—a sentiment that could eventually

The protocol for a survivor who was divorced from the deceased is fairly straightforward:

➤ If cordial relations have been maintained with the family, the former wife or husband attends the funeral but does not sit with the family.

➤ If there was ill feeling between the ex-spouse and the deceased, the ex should not attend the funeral; instead, he or she sends flowers and a sympathy note.

➤ If the ex-spouse and the deceased had children who were in custody of the deceased, the ex-spouse should ask them whether his or her presence would be comforting or disruptive, and then do as they wish.

In an age when more and more families are "blended," funeral directors and clergy members are equipped to answer the kinds of questions that crop up, so don't hesitate to ask them to help you with any problems you might have keeping the family-tree branches untangled.

---

cause distress. "Beloved husband of Jessica" expresses true devotion without excluding other members of the present or future family.

As a rule, titles—Dr. or Mayor, for example—are not used on monuments. Exceptions are made for people of high military rank or who were in active military service at the time of death.

Memorials On-line

In recent years, the Internet has played a growing role in bereavement, enabling people from far and wide to share their memories of the deceased and offer tributes and condolences. Web sites, including www.legacy.com, www.mem.com, and www.memorialsonline.com, make it possible to celebrate a loved one's unique life story with photographs, souvenirs, or keepsakes (a postcard written by the deceased, for example, or one of her straight-A report cards), awards (merit badges, certificates of achievement), or anything else that captures the person's essence. Two other advantages of this electronic archive are the ability of anyone to visit it from anywhere in the world and the ease with which the family can update it.

Your Role as a Friend

DON'T FEEL THAT GETTING in touch with someone who's just lost a loved one is an intrusion. It's the support of friends and acquaintances that helps ease the pain of the bereaved. Give them your condolences and offer specific ways in which you might help, such as assisting with meals, child care, or notifications.

With their beauty, color, and scent, flowers serve as graceful notes during the mourning period, whether at the visitation, the funeral service, the graveside, or the home of the bereaved. While roses, lilies, carnations, and other traditional choices have never gone out of style, arrangements that are more personalized and dramatic are increasingly common.

The etiquette of sending flowers largely involves who sends what:

Floral baskets and living plants. These are the standard offerings. Virtually any type of plant is suitable and can be chosen to reflect the personality of the deceased (a brightly colored display for someone who was always the life of the party, pastels for someone known for her gentleness). Flowers can be sent to the bereaved's home or workplace or to the funeral home.

Floral wreaths, crosses, and sprays. These more elaborate displays are often sent by a group. They are also a good choice for companies or associations that want to honor the deceased.

Floral tributes. Sent most often by good friends or family members, tributes are personalized designs based on the deceased's occupation, clubs, hobbies, or even personality. A standing wreath, for example, could be centered with a photograph of the person, a club or association emblem, or a crossed pair of miniature skis or hockey sticks.

Casket arrangements. These are traditionally supplied by family members—siblings, children, or grandchildren of the deceased. Lid sprays, often of roses or calla lilies, cover the unopened section of the casket at an open-coffin funeral and the entire casket once it is closed. Smaller arrangements, usually provided by the family, can be placed inside the casket by the funeral director.

No real rules apply for timing the delivery of flowers, but it's good to get them to the bereaved as soon as possible—either at home or to the funeral home in time for the visitation or funeral. But flowers are also appreciated after the funeral: Some close friends send flowers to the home over the course of a few months as a lasting reminder of their love and concern.

When a group of people pool their resources for a more costly arrangement, the flowers can have greater impact. If the list of names on the enclosure card is long, the senders can be identified as a group: "The Murchison Family," "The Sixth Street Book Club," or "The Copyediting Department, Sun-Light Publishing." Later, a card can be signed by the individuals who chipped in and then be sent to the bereaved.

It is necessary to record the receipt of flowers so that the givers can be thanked. The funeral home usually makes a record of any flowers sent there, while a family member or close friend should keep track of flowers sent to the home of the bereaved or elsewhere.

"In Lieu of Flowers"

When the notations "in lieu of flowers" or "family and friends are making contributions to . . ." appear in a death notice or obituary, you can send both flowers and a charitable contribution. If you wish to send only one expression of sympathy, however, follow the family's wishes and choose the contribution.

➤ Try to give at least what you would have paid for a flower arrangement.

➤ When you send a check to a charity specified by the family, include a note saying whom the donation memorializes: "I am enclosing a donation in loving memory of Rowan McGuire"; on the notation line of the check itself, add "In memory of Rowan McGuire." Include your address in the note so the organization will know where to send an acknowledgment, which also serves as your tax receipt. It's a good idea to confirm with the charity that they will notify the deceased's family of your donation.

➤ If you do as the notice advises and send a contribution to "your favorite charity," choose one that might mean something to the bereaved family as well. You'll also need to include the address of the deceased's family so that the charity will know where to send an acknowledgment.

➤ Ordinarily, cash is not sent to the family in place of flowers or a charitable contribution, but exceptions can be made. For example, if the bereaved person is having financial difficulties, a group (fellow employees, club or lodge members, neighbors) could take up a collection.

➤ If you want to be sure that the bereaved knows of your contribution, it is all right to mention it in person or in your sympathy note: "We've remembered dear Maria with a contribution to the Benevolent Society."

If you are a very close friend of the deceased or someone in his family, you could pay a visit. Just be sure to ask permission beforehand, since some people prefer to be only with family members in the first days after the death.

E-mailing Condolences

If you're certain that a bereaved friend uses e-mail fairly frequently, you can precede a phone call or written condolence with an e-mail—an immediate and nonintrusive way to show her that you are thinking of her in the initial days after her loved one's death. But an e-mailed message should be followed by a handwritten note and, whenever possible, attendance at the funeral or visitation. (See also page 544: "Sympathy Notes and Letters.")

Visits Versus Visitations

Visiting customs vary from region to region. In some, visitation is allowed only during the hours noted in the newspaper. In others, visitors pay their respects at any time during the funeral home's visiting hours. The visit needn't last more than a few minutes, but it's important to sign the guest register so that the family will know you were present.

An official visitation (also called a wake or, in some locales, calling hours) is when family members receive visitors to accept expressions of sympathy. The hours—often 6:00 to 8:00 in the evening—should be included in the death notice in the newspaper.

If the casket is to be open at the funeral, it will be open at the funeral home as well. Generally, visitors pass by the coffin before making their way to the family members and offering sympathy. If a kneeling bench is placed beside the coffin, the visitor may kneel and say a prayer, although he could simply stand in front of it for a moment instead. Any friend who feels uncomfortable viewing the body may bypass the coffin and go directly to the family.

How you express your sympathy depends on your closeness to the bereaved. While acquaintances and casual friends needn't say any more than "I'm so sorry" or "He was a wonderful person," closer friends can confide, "We're going to miss Victor so much, too," and offer to help in some way. Refrain from asking about the illness or death. If, however, a family member brings the subject up, offer as much comfort as you can as you discuss the deceased's last days.

Although you should follow the religious customs of the bereaved family during your visit, you're not expected to do anything contrary to your own faith. For example, if a crucifix hangs above the coffin of a Catholic, a Jew can properly refrain from kneeling and a Protestant from crossing herself. Instead, simply show reverence and respect by standing and bowing your head.

As soon as you've expressed your sympathy to each member of the family and spoken for a moment or two with those you know well, the choice is yours on how much longer to stay.

∼ What—and What Not—to Say ∼

Tension often accompanies a conversation with the bereaved because you're not sure what to say. This chart will help ease your mind.

Don't Say . . .	Say Instead . . .
"He's in a better place."	"I'm so sorry about your loss."
"Did he have life insurance?"	"He was a man who took care of business."
"Call me if there's anything I can do."	"Can I bring you dinner tomorrow night?"
"It's God's will."	"She was an extraordinary person."
"I know how you feel."	"Please know that I am thinking of you."
"Now you're the man of the house."	"Your father was an example for us all."

Signing the Guest Register

The guest register at the funeral home, usually placed by the door of the viewing room of the deceased, tells the family who stopped by to pay their respects. Visitors should use a formal signature, including any title: "Dr. and Mrs. Michael Grizzafi" or "Ms. Deborah Hall," not "Mike and Julie Grizzafi" or "Debbie Hall"; full names and titles are a favor to anyone who might write a note acknowleging the visit. If no family member is present and you haven't been able to express your sympathy in person, your visit alone can properly take the place of a sympathy note; still, a note is always welcome.

During the Service

IF EVER THERE WERE A place for decorum to be maintained, it is at a funeral service. A processional accompanied by a Dixieland band may be a time to joyfully celebrate the life of the deceased, but the service itself requires a solemn and respectful demeanor.

The "rules" are simple: Sit quietly and don't get up during the service. The exception is when you have a cough that won't stop or you have to quiet a crying or unruly child; in both cases, you should quickly go to the vestibule.

If a eulogy or tribute to the deceased is sprinkled with humor, as many are, it's fine to laugh, though not too raucously. What is *not* fine is doing anything that distracts others: fidgeting, squirming in your seat, twirling a strand of your hair, or chewing gum (particularly out of place at a funeral).

Clothing

Because the nature of funerals and memorial services varies so widely today, it is no longer necessary to wear black or dark gray. (The exception is when you've been asked to be one of the pallbearers or honorary pallbearers.) Remember, though, that your choice of clothes reflects the seriousness you assign to the occasion.

Funeral-goers are advised to forgo casual clothes and wear those that were once considered required attire for a religious service—jacket and tie for men, a suit or nice dress for women. The funeral home or someone from the family of the deceased can also give you guidance on what to wear.

Arriving

When attending a service, be on time and enter the house of worship as quietly as possible. If there are no ushers, remember that the seats closer to the altar or front should be taken by very close friends, with acquaintances seating themselves in the middle or toward the rear.

If you arrive at the service late, enter a pew or row of seats from a side aisle, not the center aisle. If a processional has begun, wait outside instead of trying to squeeze past those who are a part of the cortege and are waiting to walk down the aisle (see "Processionals," page 538).

Children

Children should be encouraged to take part in the ceremonies surrounding a death to whatever degree they find comfortable. Those exposed to the rituals learn that death is a natural part of life and that rites are observed when someone dies.

Always consider a child's age before taking her to a funeral, memorial service, or prolonged visitation. Because very small children are prone to restlessness and may have trouble staying quiet, think twice about including them.

Older children should sit with their family, closest to whoever can give them the most comfort. As for the youngsters' attire, it should be as respectable as that worn by adults, though it's customary in most religions that children do not wear black.

Processionals

At some funerals, the coffin is brought into the services as part of a processional. The officiant and the choir (if any) enter the building from the rear, preceding the funeral cortege. Directly after clergy and choir come the honorary pallbearers, two by two; the coffin; and, unless they have chosen to be seated beforehand, the family—the chief mourner first, walking with whomever he or she chooses. The rest of the funeral cortege then follows.

The family and pallbearers occupy the front pews or seats, with others in the cortege filling vacant places on either side. The service is read when everyone is seated. At the end of the service, the recessional (with all the processional participants except the choir) moves out in the same order the processional came in.

A QUESTION FOR PEGGY

At a funeral I recently attended, I was startled to see several women wearing brightly colored dresses. The styles weren't inappropriate, but I've always thought you were supposed to wear black or another somber color to funerals. Were the women out of line?

While you'll never go wrong with black or subdued colors, bright colors are considered appropriate today as long as the clothing is in good taste—no wild outfits, please. This change is in line with thinking of the funeral as a celebration of the deceased's life. (I know of a woman who wore a red dress to her best friend's funeral because red was the friend's favorite color.) It simply boils down to being respectful. Which colors to choose depends on the expectations of the bereaved, your own feelings, and the location of the event. When in doubt, dress conservatively and use color only as an accent.

At the Service's End

A recessional ends the service, whether a processional took place or not. As a rule, the officiant leads the honorary pallbearers, followed by the coffin (carried or guided by the pallbearers) and then by members of the immediate family. It is common practice for one or more of the relatives to stop at the rear of the building to briefly thank those who have attended the service, with perhaps a special word to close friends.

If the deceased is to be buried, the site of the interment will be announced. Unless the grave site is on the place of worship's grounds, a processional of cars will form to drive to the cemetery. Everyone attending is welcome to follow the family to the graveside service unless the burial is private—that is, attended by immediate family only—but no one is obliged to attend. As the casket is lifted into the hearse, the family enters limousines waiting immediately behind. (Note: The after-service protocol for a cremation or mausoleum interment is the same as that for a burial.)

The coffin is normally placed graveside at the cemetery, with flowers that were sent to the funeral home or house of worship placed around it. The religious leader says the prayers common to the rite of burial, and a eulogy may be given as well. At the end of the service, no cortege is formed, so guests leave as they wish.

Memorial Services

A MEMORIAL SERVICE—A SERVICE without the presence of the body—is designed by the family and usually consists of verses, prayers, hymns, and a eulogy delivered by a member of the clergy and sometimes by one or a few family members or close friends. As at a funeral, ushers escort guests to seats and a guest register is set out for signing.

Also like a funeral, a memorial service can be as unique as the life it commemorates, and most funeral directors and officiants will do all they can to make it so. Underlying the move toward personalization may be the therapeutic value of the planning process for the bereaved. A personalized service can also benefit friends because it gives them something to talk about with the bereaved, when they might otherwise have to search for the right words.

In a personalized service, an arrangement of items is usually set up where the service is held. The tableau for an avid sportsman might include his fishing gear, a favorite team pennant, or a letter sweater; for a gardener, her tools and pots of her favorite plants. Whatever the theme, photographs of the person at every stage of his or her life are placed around the room where the service or a reception afterward is held.

Even cremation urns can be personalized. An engraving of a military emblem, the insignia of a fraternal organization, a symbol of a favorite activity or hobby, or anything else that reflects the deceased's interests and personality is appropriate.

Services for Cremations

The service preceding or after a cremation differs in some ways from that for a funeral. Whether the family accompanies the body to the crematorium before or after the service is a matter of choice. If they do, a very short service is held there as well.

Many officiants incorporate the burial prayers into the memorial service, thus eliminating the need for a service at the crematorium. The ashes, in an urn, are later delivered to the family to be kept or scattered in accordance with the wishes of the deceased. An alternative is for the urn to be placed in a memorial building or a special section of the cemetery. Another option is to have the ashes at the service and have them interred or scattered immediately afterward.

After the Funeral or Memorial Service

A luncheon or reception—usually in a reception room at the house of worship or at the home of the deceased or a relative—is often held after the service. If it is held at the home of the immediate family, other relatives and friends provide the food.

The spirit of these gatherings ranges from solemn to exuberant and celebratory. After-service wakes, with toasting and testimonials to the deceased, are the function of choice in various regions and among some ethnic groups. It is up to the family to decide the tone for the event; whatever would most please their loved one and give the family the most comfort are the determining factors.

∽ When You're Asked to Give a Eulogy ∽

Friends are often asked to give one of the eulogies at a service, and whether to accept is a personal decision. If you decline because you are too upset, be honest with the family and explain that you don't want to risk detracting from the important things that need to be heard about the life of the deceased. If you accept, approach the task with great sensitivity. While the officiant(s) will review the person's life and accomplishments, you should speak of the attributes that exemplify his or her humanity.

When writing the eulogy, don't be afraid to ask others to share their memories of the deceased. You might also want to ask the family if there is anything about the person that they feel should be mentioned—or not mentioned. It's wise to have a friend read over your eulogy before you finalize it, and you'll also probably want to practice reciting your words a few times.

Relate stories that show the deceased in a positive light, and handle any humor with care. If you like, include a poem, passage, or anything else you feel reflects the life of the deceased.

Remember that the subject of your eulogy is the person's best qualities, not your feelings. And the more eulogies that are to be delivered, the shorter yours should be—no less than two minutes but usually no longer than eight or ten.

Religious Customs

DIFFERENT RELIGIONS TAKE DIFFERENT APPROACHES to funeral services, and customs vary not only from denomination to denomination but from region to region. Anyone who is attending a funeral for someone of another faith—be it Islamic or Buddhist, Unitarian or Baha'i—should ask knowledgeable friends or the funeral director to provide a general idea of what to expect.

Christian Funerals

While the funeral services of each Christian denomination and even each church may be unique, virtually all are based on scriptures from the Bible and prayers. The services can last from fifteen minutes to over an hour, depending on the particular service and the denomination.

Except in some parts of the South, Catholic funerals are always held at a church, not at a funeral home. Protestant funeral services, on the other hand, can be held at a church, a funeral home, at the grave site, or at another location.

While a Catholic funeral can be customized to some degree through the personalization of the wake or other elements, the service itself is highly ritualized in most churches. The same is true of Eastern Orthodox and Episcopal funeral services.

In many Protestant services, friends and relatives are sometimes asked to share memories of the deceased by giving eulogies.

Jewish Funerals

Jewish funerals generally take place early in the day in the chapel of a funeral home, rarely in a synagogue. They also are held as close to the death as possible (ideally within twenty-four hours), since embalming the body is forbidden and prompt burial is considered a mark of respect.

At an Orthodox service and at some Conservative services, no flowers are placed on the casket or in the chapel. Instead of ordering flowers, friends and relatives make a donation to a charity in the name of the deceased. Reform congregations, however, do permit flowers. (If you're unsure whether flowers are permitted and the newspaper notice doesn't specify, call the officiating rabbi or the funeral home for guidance.)

The coffin at an Orthodox and Conservative Jewish funeral is left closed so there is never a viewing of the body. The Reform ritual sometimes permits viewing.

In all congregations, the service includes a reading of Psalms by the rabbi, a eulogy by the rabbi or a close friend or relative, and the recitation of the memorial prayer. After this prayer, the family leaves the chapel first, directly behind the coffin as it is carried to the hearse for the burial service. Usually, only close friends go with the family to the cemetery.

At the grave site, the first memorial prayer, or Kaddish, is recited. Male mourners drop a handful of earth into the grave, followed by all other men who wish to participate. It is customary to stay at the site until the coffin is covered.

For seven days following a Jewish burial, mourners follow the custom of sitting *shivah* (Hebrew for "seven"). The period begins the moment the family returns home from the cemetery. Only close relatives sit *shivah* for the first three days, with friends making condolence calls in the days thereafter, except on the Sabbath. Visits usually last for a half hour or so. Most people pay calls in the afternoon or evening or on the Sunday of the week of the death, although regular meal hours should be avoided. Mourners usually sit on a low stool, but friends paying a condolence call are not expected to do so.

Usually, religious services that last from ten to twenty minutes are held twice a day (morning and evening) and might occur when friends are visiting. Non-Jewish visitors should stand when others stand during the service.

When calling on an Orthodox household, one should knock and enter, not ring the doorbell. The door is usually left unlocked so that no one needs to attend it. In many households, mirrors are covered with sheets as a sign of mourning.

Islamic Funerals

Although the funeral and burial practices of American Muslims vary from culture to culture, locale to locale, and even mosque to mosque, some Islamic traditions hold fast. First, Islamic funerals must take place within twenty-four hours of the death if at all possible. Second, in preparation for the funeral, the body is ritually washed and enshrouded by an *imam*, relative, or close friend. Although in Muslim countries the body is always prepared at home or at a mosque, in the United States the preparation must take place at a hospital, funeral home, or some other location that meets health department codes.

The funeral is held at a mosque and takes place after the noonday prayer; if no mosque is available, the service can be held at a funeral home. The service is conducted by an *imam*, a relative, or a close friend. In some cultures and mosques, the service is attended by men only.

Muslims are never cremated. In the United States, cemetery codes require the body to be placed in a coffin. (Because Muslims have distaste for ostentation of any kind, a plain pine casket is preferred.) The coffin bearing the deceased is driven to the cemetery, after which mourners take turns reverently carrying it to the grave site. After the coffin has been lowered (with the face of the deceased turned to the right, facing Mecca), members of the family shovel earth into the grave; they then recite a verse from the Qur'an (Koran).

Non-Muslim friends of the deceased are welcome to attend the funeral but should dress conservatively, stand perfectly still when the funeral prayers and verses from the Qur'an are being recited, and keep their emotions under control.

Sending flowers to the bereaved is not a part of Muslim tradition, but they will be respectfully received. However, most Muslims would prefer that a donation be made to a humanitarian cause.

The Days and Weeks After

HOW LONG should close relatives of the deceased wait before resuming an active social life? The answer is up to the individual. Some survivors may deal with grief by plunging into their regular activities, while others may want to spend time with close friends but otherwise keep to themselves as they adjust to the loss of a loved one.

Widowers or widows may start to date when they feel up to it but should consider the feelings of in-laws, their children, and others close to them. Evenings at home with friends or some other inconspicuous activities might be wiser choices than more public activities. One year is generally considered the appropriate "waiting period" before remarrying, but if close family members have no qualms about a shorter time, then there is no reason not to wed sooner.

Religious Jews restrict work, social, and recreational activities after the burial of a close relative—most assiduously during the first seven (or, for many Reform Jews, three) days of the month-long mourning period. During this time, they generally remain at home and receive condolence calls. The restrictions are significantly relaxed during the next twenty-three days, but some remain in effect even then—and a few until a year after burial. If you want to extend a social invitation to a Jewish mourner or express your sympathy in person, it's best to ask for guidance from her relative or close friend or, after the first week of bereavement, the mourner herself.

Children

Many people are uncertain about whether children who have lost a parent should participate in their usual school activities and after-school entertainment. The answer is yes. Older children, however, may not wish to go to a purely social party for two or three weeks, or even longer, after the death of a parent.

Offering Condolences as Time Goes By

Be understanding of the changes a friend is going through in the weeks and months after the loss of a loved one. Don't take it personally if she seems moody or doesn't return phone calls right away. And when you are in her presence, be careful of what you do and say. Find the middle ground between sympathy and encouragement: You don't want to pity her, but you also shouldn't harp on how strong she is or tell her to "get beyond it." Most important of all, stay in touch. Many are the widows and widowers who lament, "I lost not only my spouse but also my friends."

Friends and relatives of the deceased often wonder whether they should make a gesture to one or more of the survivors on the first anniversary of the death. It's never wrong to show that you care about someone who has suffered a loss, but each person grieves differently. Let the person's state of mind and personality be your guide, judging whether a condolence would comfort or only serve as a sad reminder. In most cases, a card or handwritten note, a home-cooked meal, an offer to spend some time together, or a telephone call would be very much appreciated.

Sympathy Notes and Letters

BECAUSE NOTES AND LETTERS OF CONDOLENCE are too personal to follow a set form, one simple rule should guide you: Say what you truly feel. A single sincere line expressing the genuine feeling you had for the deceased is worth more than an eloquently written treatise.

As you write, don't dwell on the details of an illness or the manner of death. Nor should you suggest that the loss is a "blessing in disguise." Also remember that those with an aching heart shouldn't have to wade through condolences that go on and on. Do, however, ask if there is something you can do to help.

Following are two examples of short but appropriate sympathy notes:

Dear Vanessa,

We were so very sad to hear of Robert's death. If Ken or I can help by shopping, running errands, or doing anything else for you, I honestly hope that you'll call on us. In the meantime, you are in our thoughts and prayers.

With deepest sympathy,
Carolyn

Dear Mr. Logan,

I know how little words written on a page can mean to you at such a time, but I still want to let you know that you are in my thoughts. I would also like to help you in any way I can, so please don't hesitate to call on me.

Your mother held a special place in our hearts for as long as we knew her. The countless hours she spent with our son Carey will always be remembered, and we will miss the nurturing presence of Dorothy Logan very much.

With deepest sympathy,
Edward O'Neill

Whom to Address

When you feel you should send condolences in writing, it's sometimes hard to know to whom you should address your note. Some guidelines:

➤ If you knew the deceased well but not the family, address the note to the closest relative—usually the widow, the widower, or the oldest child. You can also add "and family" if you wish.

➤ If you didn't know the deceased but do know one of the relatives, write to that person rather than to the spouse or other family member.

➤ When sending a condolence note to a friend whose parent has died, the note is usually addressed to the friend, not the surviving parent.

Under most circumstances, a note or letter of condolence should be sent within a week or so after learning of the death. But that doesn't mean you're prohibited from writing weeks later—or even after a few months, for that matter.

If you put off the note because you felt you couldn't find the right words (often the case for many people), your sentiments will be welcome regardless of their time of arrival. In a note written entirely by hand, just say you've held the family in your thoughts and prayers and will continue to think of them.

➤ Letters to children who have lost a parent are addressed with their names on separate lines: Miss Renée Wynn (the daughter), with Mr. Charles Wynn (the son) underneath. The salutation reads: "Dear Renée and Charles."

➤ If a friend's ex-spouse dies and the couple maintained a close relationship, write a sympathy note to your friend (and also to any children the couple had) if you wish.

Acknowledging Expressions of Sympathy

Handwritten notes of condolence should always be acknowledged (by the recipient, if possible), as should flowers, mass cards, contributions to charities, and acts of kindness. The exception is when the writer asks that her note not be acknowledged—a thoughtful thing to do when writing a close friend or when someone you know well will receive a great number of condolences. A pre-printed card with no personal message added does not require a written thank-you note.

If the list of thank-yous is so long that the recipient isn't up to the task, a family member or a close friend may write for him or her: "Mother asks me to thank you for your beautiful flowers and kind message of sympathy."

Following are two sample responses:

Dear Paige and Will:

On behalf of my family, I want to thank you for your expression of sympathy after the death of my sister Louise. The beautiful floral wreath meant all the more to us because it came from lifelong friends.

Sincerely yours,
Fred

Dear Ms. Huffman:

My family and I were touched by your tender expression of sympathy. Your words spoke beautifully of Darren, his spirit, and the joy he brought to us all. Please know how much we appreciate your kindness and concern.

Very sincerely,
Jason Floyd

Letters are customarily also written to pallbearers, honorary pallbearers, and ushers. You do not need to acknowledge visits to the funeral home in writing.

A personal message on a fold-over card is preferable to any printed card, and it takes only a moment to write "Thank you for your beautiful flowers" or "Thank you for being so kind."

As for the printed acknowledgments given to you by the funeral director, you should use them only if you add your personal message to the printed "Thank You."

Chapter Thirty-two

Attending Religious Services

BECAUSE BEING ON OUR best behavior is simply part of the package when we attend religious services, what is there to say about etiquette? Enough to make a discussion of it worthwhile. After all, much has changed, from what one wears to the nature of services themselves. In some evangelical churches, for example, traditional services have given way to spirited participatory ones in which hymns and organs have been replaced by rock music and electric guitars. And still more considerations come into play when you attend a service for a religion other than your own, as discussed within this chapter, starting on page 549.

For further information regarding ceremonies tied to religious services, including weddings, birthing and coming-of-age celebrations, funerals, and memorial services, you might want to consult a spiritual advisor.

A Few Basics

THE MOST IMPORTANT THING to remember at a religious service is also the most obvious: Be quiet and sit still when quiet is expected, especially during prayers and when listening to a sermon. Talking and fidgeting are simply annoying at a performance or movie, but in a house of worship they intrude on the meditation of others. No one should get up in the middle of a sermon to go to the restroom or to attend to any other personal business. If you become ill or for any other reason have no choice but to leave, simply follow the rules of common courtesy and slip out at a time when your departure is least likely to be noticed.

Punctuality. If you arrive after the service has started, enter as unobtrusively as possible and wait for an appropriate moment to take a seat—preferably one near the rear. It's all right to enter a pew during a prayer, but only if you don't have to move past anyone to take a seat. Otherwise, remain standing until the prayer is finished.

Seating. When you are seated at the end of an aisle, it's helpful to move toward the center of the row when someone else wants to take a seat (*always* move in when the person is elderly infirm or is a parent with young children in tow). At a wedding, however, people who arrived and were seated first are not expected to move; instead, they rise and let others move past.

Strangers to a church should avoid taking a place in the front seats unless they have been invited to do so or an usher escorts them there. This is in line with what visitors should do in any case: Follow the congregants' lead when unsure of the elements of the service.

If you ever expect to leave before the end of the service, choose a seat near the back so that your departure will be less noticeable.

Singing. The congregation acts as one during a service, but joining in the singing of a hymn is a matter of choice (do stand with the congregation for the hymn, unless you're too frail to do so). You needn't keep from singing just because you're notoriously bad at it and want to spare the other congregants' ears. You're singing a song of praise, not performing.

Clothing. If you wear a topcoat to worship in cold weather, either hang it in the coatroom or on a coat rack or fold the coat and take it with you to your seat. Then keep it beside you or in your lap instead of draping it over the back of a seat; the same goes for a sweater or scarf. (See also "A Question for Peggy," below.)

Photographs. Picture-taking is usually not allowed in a house of worship without permission from the officiating clergyperson before the service begins. Some houses forbid taking pictures for religious reasons, and even those that allow picture-taking want to keep the service as free of distractions as possible.

A QUESTION FOR PEGGY

Whatever happened to dressing for church? I recently attended a service in a large city as the guest of a friend, and I was surprised by how many people in the congregation dressed casually. In my small-town church, people still wear their "Sunday best."

For better or worse, the casualness that has swept through American life has reached even into houses of worship. It once was a given that men would wear a jacket and tie and women wore a dress or suit. But no more. The degree to which dress standards have changed over the past few decades can be illustrated by how even shorts will fail to raise eyebrows in some congregations.

Today's advice is to follow the lead of the congregation you're visiting. In most places, that means your clothing should at least be presentable: clean, pressed, relatively subdued, and—for women—not too revealing. In other congregations, dressing down may be frowned on. When in doubt, simply call the church office and ask how the church members typically dress.

Attending Services of Other Faiths

VISITORS TO HOUSES OF WORSHIP other than their own are usually attending weddings, funerals, or memorial services. But when you attend a regularly scheduled service—whether at the invitation of a friend or because you want to learn more about the faith—it's natural to feel a little nervous about unfamiliar rituals. Unless you're with a friend who prefers to sit in the front, you'll feel more comfortable if you take a seat near the back.

You'll obviously want to watch and see what others do and then follow suit—rise when the congregation rises, sit when they sit. But you needn't participate in reciting a creed or doing anything else contrary to your own religious practices, nor are you expected to. Make a donation if an offering plate is passed, as a way of showing that you respect a religion that is not your own.

Following are nutshell overviews of what to expect when attending services of the major religions.

Roman Catholic Churches

Roman Catholic masses are held at intervals on Sunday but can also be held on Saturday evening, when the Sabbath is said to begin.

On entering the church, Catholics have the choice of whether to genuflect—as do visitors. Another tradition is dipping the fingers into the font of holy water (located at the church entrance) and making the sign of the cross. Non-Catholics are welcome to do this, though most do not.

The Catholic mass requires extensive participation on the part of the congregation in reciting prayers and in song. A non-Catholic listens silently, although if he knows the words, he may participate. He also follows the congregation's lead for standing and sitting but is not expected to kneel during the service, though he may, if he wishes.

At the most solemn part of the mass, holy communion (during which the congregation kneels), the priest prays aloud and elevates the host and the chalice of wine, which are believed at this point to become the body and blood of Christ. In most churches, only Catholics can receive communion.

Votive candles (or often, electric candles) sometimes line the side aisles of Catholic churches, with receptacles for contributions nearby. Catholics will light a candle and offer a prayer to the saint before whom the candles are placed, and guests are welcome to follow suit.

For Catholics and non-Catholics alike, no head covering is required—neither for men nor for women. Men sometimes wear jackets and ties, but shirts and slacks are the more usual choice. Women may wear skirts, dresses, or slacks.

Protestant Churches

Protestant services, held on Sunday mornings with the exception of services for Seventh-Day Adventists, are somewhat similar to one another in form. Some denominations, including Pentecostal and other evangelical faiths, assign music an important part in the service. The congregants of others, including some Episcopal churches, occasionally kneel at certain times. Usually, a printed bulletin provides the order of service, guiding the congregation to specific pages in the worship book being used and making it easy to follow along.

Dress standards sometimes vary among Protestant denominations. Mormons, for example, see shirts and slacks for men as fine but draw the line at jeans and shorts. Some Baptist and Pentecostal churches in or near beach communities even welcome members wearing T-shirts and shorts.

In most Protestant churches, a baptized Christian is welcome to receive holy communion. There are several different practices in the way communion is administered, including drinking from the common cup, electing to use individual cups, and intinction (dipping the bread or wafer into the wine). If a visitor doesn't wish to receive communion, she need only stay seated when others go forward or pass the communion tray along.

Note: Although Protestants do not genuflect when entering the sanctuary of a Protestant church and most don't make the sign of the cross, Catholic visitors should feel comfortable doing either.

Orthodox Christian Churches

The names of the two branches of the family of Orthodox Christian Churches, all of which are self-governing, are *Eastern Orthodox* (so named because in the first millennium the influence of the Church was concentrated in the Eastern part of the Christian world) and *Greek Orthodox* (Greek was the first language of the ancient Christian church through which the faith was transmitted). Individual churches use national titles—Russian Orthodox, Serbian Orthodox, Romanian Orthodox, and so on. Because of theological, jurisdictional, cultural, and political differences, the Orthodox Church broke with the Roman Catholic Church in the Great Schism of AD 1054. Its teachings are based on the foundations laid by the Apostles.

Visitors are welcome to attend Orthodox services but are not expected to take part in any element of the liturgy. As the priest makes his processionals through the sanctuary, everyone stands and faces him as he circles through; while worshipers make the sign of the cross as he passes, visitors may merely bow their heads. Visitors do not take communion, nor do they follow the worshipers' lead and venerate (kiss) the prominently displayed holy icons—pictorial representations of the Holy Trinity.

Traditionally, Eastern Orthodox churches were not furnished with pews. Nowadays many have pews; others have chairs placed to the side of the sanctuary. Sit erect; looking too relaxed (and even crossing your legs) is considered disrespectful. Visitors should stand when the congregation stands and may kneel when it kneels if they choose. When greeting the priest before or after the service, the congregants kiss his hand; visitors offer a standard handshake.

Jewish Synagogues or Temples

Services in Reform, Reconstructionist, Conservative, and Orthodox synagogues or temples differ widely in practice. Services are usually held on Friday evenings, when the Sabbath begins, and Saturday mornings. The amount of Hebrew spoken during the service again varies, with the least usually used in Reform services and the most in Orthodox services. During many Orthodox services, some portions of the service are read individually and out loud, a practice that may sound confusing to the visitor who is unfamiliar with this practice. Visitors can hold prayer books and can read along with the congregation when the prayer is in English.

Guests may be seated where they wish but should respect the separation of men and women in Orthodox synagogues. Visitors are expected to stand with the congregation but need not read prayers aloud or sing if this would be contrary to their own beliefs. Some congregants kneel in Orthodox services, but non-Jews do not.

A jacket and tie is appropriate for a man to wear, and women usually wear dresses or skirts; pantsuits for women are not worn to Orthodox and most Conservative services. In Orthodox congregations, women should wear clothing that covers their arms, hems should be below the knees, and heads should be covered with a hat or veil. Women should not carry a handbag to an Orthodox service because this is a form of labor (carrying an object in public), which is prohibited on the Sabbath. Women are also expected to wear a hat or other head covering in some Conservative synagogues, as well. Men are expected to wear a *yarmulke* (*kippah*), or skull cap, on their heads in most synagogues or temples. These are usually available for visitors outside the door of the main sanctuary.

Many times, a *tallith*, or prayer shawl, is worn by congregants. Non-Jews do not wear the *tallith*, although there is no prohibition against doing so.

In many congregations, the rabbi or other leader will make announcements, periodically, about the service. In others, it is assumed that those present are familiar with the order of service and there are no announcements.

Islamic Mosques

Muslims are required to pray five times a day, either in a mosque or wherever individuals happen to be at prayer time. Prayer is preceded by washing with water (or even a symbolic washing with soil) to cleanse the body and spirit. Worshipers face Mecca, prostrate themselves or bow, and recite fixed prayers.

Like the worshipers, non-Muslim guests remove their shoes when entering a mosque. Guests then have the freedom to sit on the floor or in a chair and also to come and go. In most mosques, non-Muslim visitors (including women) do not have to cover their heads as long as they are dressed conservatively.

At a Muslim worship service, men form the prayer lines in the front, with children behind and women in the back. Some mosques have a separate worship area for women. In the first part of the service, an *imam* leads the prayers voiced by the Muslim congregants in unison; in the second part, the congregants pray individually as they wish, bowing or prostrating themselves as the *imam* delivers the sermon.

Buddhist Temples

Services, which can last one to two hours, take different forms. Some are services of silent meditation while others include a sermon by a priest. Usually, there is chanting, silent meditation, and a sermon, with an incense offering by the priest or a monk. Some temples have pews, while others have meditation floor cushions instead.

Neither men nor women are required to wear a head covering. Clothing should be comfortable for worship in those temples where seating is on floor cushions.

Other Religions

From Hinduism to Shintoism, a number of other religions are practiced in the United States. If you're not attending a service with a friend who can guide you, the simplest way to get answers to any questions about behavior is to call the organization's office beforehand and ask. Most, if not all, will welcome you with open arms and see to it that you feel comfortable.

Greetings for Clergy

ONE OF THE MOST CONFUSING aspects of greeting officiating clergy is knowing what to call them. Since it is polite to use someone's title, use the following as a guide. Keep in mind that while these titles are correct, it is not uncommon for someone usually called by one title to refer to himself by another—a pastor who introduces herself as Reverend So-and-So, for example. You might also find that some clergy ask to be called by their title and first name, such as "Pastor John." Some Episcopal clergy prefer being addressed by first name and "father," as in "Father Andrew," while a female priest might ask to be called "Mother Anne." Your best choice is to ask about the individual preference, and then use that desired greeting.

Religion	*Title to Use When Greeting*
Baptist	Reverend *or* Pastor
Buddhism (Tibetan, Mongolian)	Lama
Buddhism (Zen)	Roshi
Catholic bishop	Your Excellency
Catholic cardinal	Your Eminence
Catholic nun	Sister
Catholic priest	Father
Christian Science	(No clergy)
Churches of Christ	(No special title for clergy)

Eastern Orthodox bishop	Your Grace
Eastern Orthodox nun	Sister
Eastern Orthodox priest	Father
Episcopal	Dean, Canon, Reverend, Father/Mother *or* Dr./Mr./Mrs./Ms.
Hindu	Swamiji
Islam	(No clergy); prayer leader/advisor: *Imam*
Jewish	Rabbi
Lutheran	Pastor
Methodist	Reverend *or* Pastor
Mormon	Bishop (counselors are called Brother)
Presbyterian	Reverend *or* Pastor
Quaker	(No ordained clergy)
Seventh-Day Adventist	Elder *or* Pastor
Unitarian	Reverend
United Church of Christ	Pastor, Mr., *or* Ms.

(See also Chapter 22, page 347: "Religious Officials of the Roman Catholic Church"; page 351: "Religious Officials of Protestant Denominations"; page 353: "Religious Officials of the Jewish Faith.")

∽ When You're a Sightseer ∽

The world's great cathedrals, temples, and mosques are not only houses of worship but tourist attractions as well. Millions of visitors a year are drawn to these international treasures—usually not to worship but to soak up the history, architecture, and art. But what if a service is being held when you arrive?

Show respect. That means not walking around to take in the sights, even if you tiptoe and stay silent. Either stand still until the service is over, sit in a pew, or leave. (The exception is when a private ceremony is being held at the main altar or in a side chapel, in which case you may sightsee as long as you keep your distance and avoid intruding.) Remember that even if no service is in progress, you are obligated to conduct yourself reverently and quietly. It is also customary for a sightseer to leave a donation in the offering box.

Many religious institutions with world-renowned choirs also draw tourists (the Mormon Tabernacle Choir, for example, or the rousing gospel singers in churches in New York's Harlem). Because tourists are expected to sit through the whole service, dress becomes an important issue. To show up at a church dressed in the standard tourist uniform of Bermuda shorts and a short-sleeved shirt would be an insult to congregants who have donned their Sunday best. Either dress as the worshipers do or buy a recording of their music that you can enjoy at home.

In an increasingly multicultural society, it is respectful to know what people of other religions are celebrating during holidays and whether there is a traditional holiday greeting. (Saying to a workmate, "Hope you have a blast on your day off!" is hardly appropriate for either Good Friday or Yom Kippur, both days of serious reflection.) In the list that follows, most holy days have no traditional greetings; those that do show the appropriate greeting.

Christian Holy Days

Advent. The four weeks of preparation before Christmas

Christmas. The celebration of the birth of Christ

Greeting: Merry Christmas; Happy Christmas in the United Kingdom and British Commonwealth

Ash Wednesday. First day of Lent, the season of preparation and penitence before Easter

Maundy (or Holy) Thursday. The day commemorating the institution of the Eucharist; observed four days before Easter

Good Friday. The day commemorating the crucifixion, death, and burial of Jesus; observed three days before Easter

Easter. The celebration of the resurrection of Jesus

Greeting: Happy Easter

Pascha. Eastern Orthodox version of Easter, lasting for forty days—the time from the exodus from Egypt to the Pentecost

Greeting: Christ is risen

Response: Truly He is risen

Jewish Holy Days

Rosh Hashanah. The religious New Year

Greeting: Happy New Year (Shana Tovah in Hebrew)

Yom Kippur. The Day of Atonement

No traditional greeting, but *Have an easy fast* is appropriate.

Sukkot. The Feast of Booths, an eight-day harvest holiday

Greeting: Happy holiday

Hanukkah. The Festival of Lights

Greeting: Happy Hanukkah

Celebrations and Ceremonies

Purim. A celebration of deliverance from destruction

Greeting: Happy holiday or Happy Purim

Passover. The celebration of the Jewish people's freedom from slavery in Egypt

Greeting: Happy Passover

Islamic Holy Days

Ramadan. A monthlong time for reflection and spiritual discipline, including fasting between dawn and dusk

Greeting: Ramadan Mubarak ("May God give you a blessed month")

Laylat al-Qadr. The last ten days of Ramadan, during which special prayers are offered

'Eid al-Fitr. The Feast of the Breaking of the Fast, celebrated at the end of Ramadan

Greeting: Id Mubarak ("May God make it a blessed feast")

'Eid al-Adha. Commemorating Abraham's obedience to God

Greeting: Mubarak (see " 'Eid al-Fitr," above)

Isar an Mi'raj. A day commemorating the Night Journey and the Ascension, the night when the Prophet Muhammad is believed to have ultimately traveled to the heavens, where God commanded him to initiate prayers five times a day

Buddhist Holy Days

Nirvana Day. The commemoration of the death of the Buddha

Hanamatsuri Day. The commemoration of the birth of Buddha

Bodhi Day. The day on which Siddhartha Gautama said he would meditate under the Bodhi Tree until attaining enlightenment

Hindu Holy Days

Duhsehra/Durga Puja. Celebrating the triumph of good over evil

Rama Navami. Worship of Rama, regarded as God incarnate along with the god Krishna

Krishna Janmashtami. The birthday celebration of Krishna

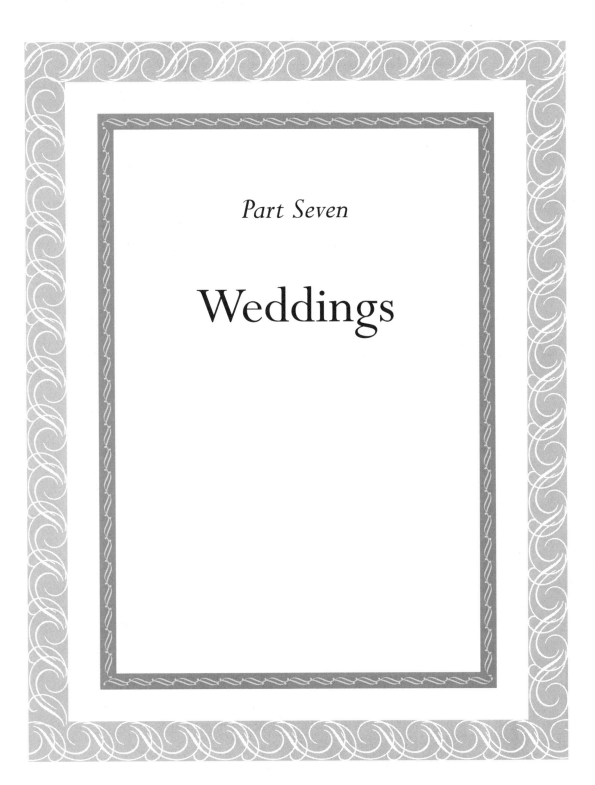

Part Seven

Weddings

Chapter Thirty-three

The Engagement

Perhaps one of you popped the question in the most romantic or surprising way imaginable. Or the decision just sort of evolved. However it happened, you've decided to get married, and between that decision and your wedding day lies the period of engagement.

Couples often ask how long an engagement should be. The simplest answer is, as long as it takes. You might want to marry at a specific time of year or on a certain date, such as your parents' anniversary. If you have a very special location in mind, you may need to reserve wedding and reception sites as much as a year to eighteen months in advance. Religious requirements can be a factor in the equation. And sometimes an engagement is shortened or prolonged by events beyond a couple's control, such as military service or a business relocation.

An engagement may last only a few days or weeks or extend over a number of years. The average period is about fourteen months, but however long, an engagement is an exciting, sometimes dizzying time.

Hopefully, it will also be a time for contemplation and mutual consideration of the monumental step you're preparing to take. You are two individuals who have pledged to become a couple, and during the engagement, you will begin to sort out what it means to act in tandem. Parties, presents, and pretty clothes may come to mind first, but they're only symbols. The real essence lies in ideals of commitment, mutual respect, fidelity, compromise, ongoing communication, and enduring love.

This chapter and the next provide guidelines for the activities associated with an engagement and the first steps of wedding planning. Yes, you will often be in the spotlight during this busy time, but life will go on around you. One of your primary responsibilities will be to remain attentive to the needs and feelings of others and to nurture your relationships with *all* the important people in your life. You may sometimes feel as if your feet barely touch the ground, but be sure that while you're floating on air, your head is still firmly attached.

Making It "Official"

THE TERM "OFFICIAL ENGAGEMENT" IS a misnomer. There is no official validation for an engagement—no tests to take, papers to sign, or fees to pay—although some religions and sects have specific requirements (posting of the banns, pre-wedding religious instruction or counseling) for an engagement to be solemnized in the faith. What is generally considered an official engagement is one that has been announced to family, friends, and, if the couple wishes, in a public forum such as the newspaper.

Telling Family and Friends

You may want to shout it from the rooftops or write it in the sky, but before informing the world of your engagement, consider the people closest to you. Usually, people know when romance is in the air and marriage is a possibility, but family and good friends deserve your special attention, and there is an order to the telling.

Children. If one or both of the engaged couple have children, they must be told before anyone else. This is critically important for young children and teens whose lives will be dramatically changed by the addition of a stepparent and perhaps stepsiblings. (See Chapter 7, page 81: "Telling the Children First"; Chapter 41, page 721: "The Engagement.") They may be thrilled, but they are just as likely to be doubtful, reluctant, and even frightened or resentful. It takes love, honesty, and infinite patience to transform individuals into a family, so respect every child's need to question your decision and seek your reassurance.

It's just as important to inform adult children before publicly announcing an engagement. No matter how far away they may live or how independent they are, children of any age should be uppermost in the couple's concerns.

Parents. After children, parents deserve priority. Couples can inform their own parents or speak as a couple with both sets of parents. If your parents don't know your fiancée or fiancé, it's your responsibility to arrange a meeting. If parents live at a distance, you can make introductions by phone, but also plan to visit as soon as you can. Nothing is better than getting together in person.

When parents are separated or divorced, the news is conveyed to each—in person, if possible, or by the most convenient means. Even if a parent and child are somewhat estranged, a parent really should not hear the news of his or her child's marriage plans from outsiders.

In the event that the announcement will be a total surprise, each of the couple should be considerate of his or her own parents and talk privately with them first. This allows parents to ask questions that they may be hesitant to ask with their future son- or daughter-in-law present. (Couples who are mature enough for marriage should understand that parents have perfectly normal worries and should be allowed to express their concerns. Openness at this stage may prevent difficulties later.)

The old custom was for a suitor to speak first with the father of the young woman;

a gentleman declared his intentions and got the father's consent before proposing to the daughter. Although this tradition is obsolete, it's still a sign of respect for a prospective groom to meet with his future in-laws and discuss his career and life plans. This conversation might take place before the engagement, when the couple tells parents of their engagement, or soon thereafter—whenever seems most appropriate.

Close family and friends. Depending on your family structure, there are probably some relatives—siblings, grandparents, close aunts, uncles, and cousins—and good friends whom you will want to inform soon after you tell your parents. When and how you spread the word is up to you, so long as you're sensitive to people's feelings and thoughtful of what is going on in their lives.

One mistake is making promises before you have planned your wedding. For example, some couples find themselves with a much larger wedding party than they want, or can afford, because in the euphoria of becoming engaged, they ask too many people to be bridesmaids and groomsmen. Or they risk hurting the feelings of people they care about by having to rescind such invitations.

If you become engaged during a time of difficulty—when a family member or close friend is seriously ill or recently deceased, for example—you can certainly share your good news, but keep it low-key and don't expect everyone to react as they would under happier circumstances. Depending on the situation, a couple may have to delay parties and newspaper announcements.

Colleagues and coworkers. The easiest way to spread the news among the people you work with is to tell one or two people and ask them to tell others. A newly engaged employee may want to inform a boss or supervisor first as a matter or courtesy. At some point, you should discuss your impending change in status with the person in charge of employee compensation and make necessary alterations in benefit, insurance, and pension plans.

Getting Families Together

When the families of engaged couples don't know one another or are only slightly acquainted, the couple has an obligation to arrange a get-together of some sort. Organizing the first meeting is traditionally the responsibility of the groom's parents, but the diversity of today's family structure, not to mention hectic work and travel schedules, often make it difficult to follow custom. The bride- and groom-to-be are best positioned to know when a meeting will be convenient for everyone and what kind of gathering is most likely to put everyone at ease.

Who actually hosts the occasion is a matter of preference more than tradition. (If the bride's mother is a homemaker who loves to entertain and the groom's is a busy professional with little time to plan social events, why stand on custom?) A casual event, such as a barbecue or weeknight supper, is often most comfortable. But if one set of parents has a more formal lifestyle than the other, a good compromise might be a dinner or weekend brunch at a nice, mid-range restaurant.

When parents are divorced and when there are stepfamilies to consider, a couple

Who Contacts Whom?

The parents of a newly engaged couple may live too far apart for a face-to-face meeting. The conventional etiquette calls for the parents of the future groom to contact the bride's family. But nowadays, it matters very little who makes the first move, though a bride's parents might want to wait a bit to give the groom's side a chance to honor custom. A phone call is the easiest route; if the couple live near one set of parents, they might all get together for a conference call to distant relatives. Handwritten notes are always nice. E-mail is possible, and some people may find its casual tone an easier way to introduce themselves and express their pleasure at the engagement.

will often have to organize several get-togethers. Engaged couples should think carefully about their family structures and have realistic expectations. In the best of all worlds, everyone will receive the news of an engagement with joy, but it is too much to hope that your engagement and marriage will heal old wounds caused by divorces, remarriages, and other complicated family arrangements.

The Engagement Ring

A new sparkler on a woman's left hand can be the only clue that people need to realize a wedding is in the offing. An engagement ring, however, is not essential for you to be "officially" engaged, and many couples choose to put the money toward other purposes. Others wait and purchase an engagement ring later in the marriage when they can afford it (a romantic way to celebrate a special wedding anniversary). Some women simply don't like to wear rings, and another type of jewelry might be substituted.

Engagement rings can be new or antique, bought from the showcase or custom-designed. Rings may be passed down in a family, and heirloom stones might be reset in a more contemporary style. Traditionally, the man selects and purchases the ring on his own, but today's couples often make this decision together and may share the cost. The following recommendations should help you find the right ring and get a fair deal.

Cost. The old wisdom was that the cost of an engagement ring should equal two months of the groom's salary. Today's wisdom is to spend what you can afford without getting into too much debt. Couples should discuss their options before taking on an expense that might be a burden. Negotiating the price of a ring with a jeweler—just as you might bargain over the price of an automobile—is an acceptable practice.

Size. If the ring is to be a surprise, sizing may be a problem. The man could consult the parents or good friend of his intended bride, as long as they can keep a secret. Just be sure that resizing is included in the purchase agreement.

Stones and styles. Though the diamond solitaire is regarded as the traditional engagement ring, the choice of stones, cuts, metals, and styles is purely individual. Issues to consider include personal taste, the look of the ring on the hand, and how the ring will be worn. If you plan to wear your engagement ring with your wedding ring, consider how well they will fit together.

Jewelers. If you select a precious gem, the wisest course is to work with a reputable and knowledgeable jeweler. Look for certification by the American Gem Society. If possible, do some comparison shopping. Since few people have the ability to judge the quality of gems or the value of antique jewelry, you might also consult an independent appraiser.

Cautions. Be sure the dealer provides written certification with a diamond or other precious gem. Check the dealer's repair and return policy; they should have one. Then insure the ring immediately.

Newspaper Announcements

If you want to announce your engagement in print, the first step is to contact the appropriate department of the newspaper(s) in which you would like the announcement to appear. Usually an individual in a paper's social, living, or style section handles announcements, and you can call the paper's main number and ask for the person who takes engagement news. Most newspapers provide information forms for couples to complete. If you submit your own announcement, the newspaper will check with you personally to ensure that the information is accurate. Before contacting a paper, study its engagement section, especially if you want the announcement in a paper that you aren't familiar with. This will tell you what kinds of details the paper normally reports and whether they use photographs.

∼ Wearing the Ring ∼

Most American women follow the centuries-old European style of wearing engagement and wedding rings on the third finger (next to the pinky) of the left hand. According to the ancient Greeks, the third finger—fourth if you count the thumb—contained the "love vein," which ran directly to the heart. Since cultural and religious practices vary, however, there's no single correct way to wear a betrothal ring.

Although a bride-to-be usually begins wearing her ring as soon as she receives it, the ring should not be worn until she and the future bridegroom are free to marry. If either or both are still married, the ring is not displayed until divorces are finalized. This is an issue of respect not just for former spouses but for the institution of marriage itself. Some women in this situation wear the ring on a longish chain around their necks, so it cannot be seen.

Generally, an engagement announcement appears two to three months before the wedding date, though this isn't a hard-and-fast rule. Information is submitted several weeks in advance. Couples often haven't set the wedding date when an announcement appears. If you delay contacting the publication until the last minute, however, the paper may not be able to accommodate you.

Most announcements are brief and follow a format similar to the one below. But some papers use an informal style, include more information, and may ask to interview couples about details of their courtship and engagement.

Traditionally, the parents of the bride-to-be make the announcement. The basic wording includes full names with courtesy or professional titles, city and state of residence if not the same as the hometown of the newspaper, highest level of education of the couple, and their current employment.

Mr. and Mrs. Allen Perry of Fairview, Maryland, announce the engagement of their daughter, Jane Ellen Perry, to William Paul Kruger, Jr., son of Dr. and Mrs. William Paul Kruger of Newcastle, Missouri. A September wedding is planned.

Miss Perry, a graduate of Richmond Nursing College, is a physical therapist with Bonaventure Hospital in Baltimore, Maryland. Mr. Kruger was graduated from Monroe University and is employed as loan manager with First Bank of Baltimore.

Engagement and wedding announcements are a public service of the newspaper—though many papers now charge fees—and you cannot dictate or edit the contents. Using or dropping courtesy titles, for example, is determined by a publication's overall style, not the preference of people whose names appear in the paper. Larger newspapers tend to have a more concise announcement style than suburban and rural publications, and virtually all publications give some precedence to prominent community members.

The following samples indicate how a number of different family situations may be treated in print.

When parents are divorced . . .

Divorced parents are listed as individuals, by their current legal names and residence, and never as a couple. If the bride's parents are divorced, the mother usually makes the announcement, though the father may do so if he was the custodial parent.

Ms. Martine Cousins of Hartsville, Colorado, announces the engagement of her daughter, Sarah Louise Baker, to . . . Miss Baker is also the daughter of Mr. Albert Baker of Boulder.

When the groom's parents are divorced, the announcement follows this pattern:

Mr. and Mrs. Lamar Hughes announce the engagement of their daughter, Caroline Hughes, to Justin Marc DuBois, son of Mrs. Thomas Shelton of Centerville, Ohio, and Mr. Jean Marc DuBois of Brighton, Michigan.

When the parents of both the bride and the groom are divorced, the usual form is as follows:

Mrs. Walter Murray of Gladstone, Washington, announces the engagement of her daughter, Elizabeth Leigh Considine, to John Carter Lowndes, son of Mrs. Harriett Lowndes of Seattle and Mr. Houston Lowndes of Palmetto, California. Miss Considine is also the daughter of Mr. Horace Considine of Melbourne, Australia.

A stepparent is not usually included in a formal announcement unless he or she is an adoptive parent or the other parent is not a part of the bride or groom's life, but stepparents might be mentioned in a lengthier or more informal announcement.

When divorced parents make a joint announcement . . .

Divorced parents of the bride-to-be may want to make the announcement together. Both are listed by their names (whether or not they have married again) and places of residence.

Mrs. Walter Murray of Gladstone, Washington, and Mr. Horace Considine of Melbourne, Australia, announce the engagement of their daughter, Elizabeth Leigh Considine, to . . .

When a parent is deceased . . .

The surviving parent of the bride makes the announcement.

Mr. Gerald MacKenzie Brown announces the engagement of his daughter, Leslie Brown, to . . . Miss Brown is also the daughter of the late Marie Compton Brown.

When a parent of the groom is deceased, this form is generally followed:

Mr. and Mrs. Gerald MacKenzie Brown announce the engagement of their daughter, Leslie Brown, to Peter Carelli, son of Mrs. Benjamin Carelli and the late Mr. Carelli [or, when the mother is deceased: Mr. Benjamin Carelli and the late Mrs. Carelli or the late Katherine Boyd Carelli].

If both the bride's parents are deceased, a close family member (or members) may make the announcement.

Mr. and Mrs. Seth Sheridan announce the engagement of their granddaughter, Cynthia Sheridan, to . . . Miss Sheridan is the daughter of the late Mr. and Mrs. Frederick Sheridan [or the late Frederick and Margaret James Sheridan].

When the bride is a divorcée . . .

When the bride is a young divorcée, it's still traditional for her parents to announce her engagement, using the name she has adopted since the divorce. (See Chapter 7, page 84, "Names and courtesy titles.")

Mr. and Mrs. Joseph Crane announce the engagement of their daughter, Portia Crane Bowman, to . . .

An older woman or one who is independent of her family might want to announce her own engagement, following the basic format for couples, below. When the groom-to-be is divorced, there's usually no indication of his status in an announcement. However, some papers now mention previous marriages and the children of engaged couples in informal announcement stories.

When the couple makes the announcement . . .

It's not uncommon for older couples and those who do not have close family to make their own announcement.

Ms. Gayle Ann Parker and Mr. James Newsom [or Gayle Ann Parker and James Newsom] are pleased to announce their engagement. [This may be followed by information about their parents or simply about the couple and their planned wedding date.]

When the groom's parents announce . . .

In some situations, the bride's parents cannot make the announcement—as when her family lives overseas or when she doesn't have family and prefers not to make her own announcement—and the groom's parents place the notice in their local newspaper. The wording will be similar to the following:

The engagement of Anna Livmann, daughter of Professor and Mrs. Ernst Livmann of Stockholm, Sweden, to Edward Dodd, son of Mr. and Mrs. Seymour Dodd, is announced.

The Engagement Party

AN ENGAGEMENT IS DEFINITELY SOMETHING to celebrate, and a party may be the perfect way for family and friends to toast the future bride and groom. Modern engagement parties may be as formal or informal as you like—and are by no means mandatory.

The hosts. Although the bride-to-be's parents usually host the engagement party, any family member or friend may do so. When families live in different parts of the country, the parents of the bride and groom each might host parties in their hometowns—an alternative to the more traditional post-honeymoon party given by the groom's family to honor their new daughter-in-law.

What kind of party? Cocktail parties and dinners are popular, but there is no standard party format. Sometimes, engagements are announced at surprise parties. From a casual brunch to a formal reception, there are many possibilities. Whatever suits the couple and the guests is just fine.

The guests. Generally the guest list is limited to the couple's relatives and good friends. It can be as short or lengthy as you want—and can comfortably accommodate. However, it's poor taste to invite anyone to an engagement party who will not be on the wedding guest list.

Invitations. Written or printed invitations are normally sent, but for an intimate gathering, phoned invitations are acceptable.

~ If Parents Disapprove ~

It's hardly surprising that parents will be anxious to some degree when their children become engaged, whether they express their concerns or not. Usually, the anxiety disappears as parents grow accustomed to the engagement and become involved in the wedding plans. But when a couple senses tension or a parent makes his or her objection clear, it's usually best to address it openly. First and foremost, *stay calm* and approach any discussion adult to adult. Second, be willing to listen to parental concerns and to take them seriously. (For instance, parents may worry that marriage will adversely affect education or career plans, so explain your long-range goals.) Third, try to remember how important your happiness is to your parents and don't let minor disagreements get out of hand. Do you really want to draw lines in the sand over the choice of a florist or caterer?

When parents are on board, most other family members will follow. Yet it may be impossible to overcome objections, and you will have to proceed on your own. But don't sever family ties. Be sure that your parents—or any other family members who disapprove—know how much you want them at your wedding. When you act from goodwill, there's a very good chance that the doubting Thomases will put their misgivings aside and attend.

The announcement. Whether the news will be a surprise or is already known among the guests, the host, usually the bride's father, traditionally makes the announcement and toasts the couple. At a very large party with guests who already know about the engagement, the couple and their parents might compose an informal receiving line to welcome guests and make introductions.

Gifts and thanks. Traditionally, gifts for the couple are not brought to the engagement party. However, sometimes close relatives and friends do bring gifts, and in various locales it has become customary that most (even all) guests want to and do give the couple something. If there are gifts, they are usually not opened at the party, since it's most typical that not all guests have brought them. Even if the couple opens a gift and thanks the person directly at the party, a thank-you note for each gift is expected—and is obligatory. Handwritten thank-you notes are also a must for all gifts that are opened later, received after an announcement appears in the newspaper, or sent after word reaches the grapevine.

When It Doesn't Work Out

ONE OF THE UNDERLYING PURPOSES of a period of engagement is to give a couple time to test their commitment, and not every engagement ends in marriage. When an engagement is broken, it can be a time of great sadness, confusion, and all too often, ill will. But whatever the feelings of the people involved, they shouldn't be embarrassed about taking a difficult step that prevents future and even greater unhappiness.

There are important do's and don'ts associated with a breakup—some grounded in respect and consideration for others and a few practical matters, too.

Do tell close family as soon and as tactfully as possible. Your children and your parents should be the first to know. When children are involved, particularly if they have developed a good relationship with the person you were engaged to, they often feel an intense loss. Explain the breakup as best you can without demeaning the other person.

Don't expect family and friends to choose sides. A broken engagement should not be a declaration of war by either party. Some people will instantly rally around you, but many do not want to be drawn into your very personal decision, no matter how sympathetic they feel.

Do inform everyone involved in the wedding as soon as you can. A family member or friend may be able to help you out by getting in touch with people who have been contracted for services (caterers and the like), but you should personally speak with the

A QUESTION FOR PEGGY

I've reached the age when everybody I know seems to be getting engaged. I've attended a number of engagement parties, and I still can't figure out the etiquette of gifts. Some people bring presents, others don't. Is there any rule about engagement gifts?

Generally, engagement gifts are not obligatory and are not expected—especially not from casual friends and acquaintances. But whether to give something to good friends is often a matter of local custom. For instance, when an invitation states that the event is an engagement party, the implication may be that gifts are expected if that's the tradition in your area or among your circle of friends. When the announcement is to be a surprise, some people who already know about the engagement may bring gifts, but this is their choice. If the reason for the party is not mentioned in the invitation, there's no specific reason to take a gift. Although gift instructions are usually not included on invitations, some couples are very conscious of taxing their friends' budgets, and they will often tell guests (through the hosts) not to bring presents. If you really aren't sure what to do, call the host and ask.

An engagement gift is really a good-hearted gesture of affection, and it need not be expensive or elaborate. Or you might prefer to save your money for the main wedding gift. Trust your common sense, ask the hosts or others invited to the party for advice if you need it, and do what you think is right for the occasion.

When my fiancé and I broke off our engagement, our decision was mutual, so I hope we can be friends again someday. But what should I do with my engagement ring? He hasn't asked for it, and my friends say I should keep it.

Most U.S. states consider an engagement ring to be like any gift—the property of the person who receives it—so you probably have no legal obligation to return it. But ethics trump law in this situation. Do you really want to keep a ring that was given to symbolize a pledge that you have both agreed not to honor? Since your decision was mutual, what is more important to you now, the ring or keeping some kind of positive relationship with your ex-fiancé? The decision is yours, and your conscience is a much better guide than the opinions of friends.

The unique circumstances of a broken engagement often determine what is done. When the man purchases the ring, he traditionally relinquishes it if he alone breaks the engagement, though the woman may choose to return it. If the woman cancels the engagement, it is correct for her to give back the ring—especially when it's an heirloom of the man's family—and any other jewelry she received from her ex-fiancé. But when a couple shared the cost, then the one who keeps the ring ought to refund the other person's money, regardless of who precipitated the breakup. Or they might sell the ring and divide the return based on the proportion each person originally contributed.

officiant, attendants, and others who agreed to participate in the planned wedding. Remember to contact anyone who has planned a social event in your honor.

Do return all engagement, wedding, and shower gifts, including money gifts. This is generally the woman's responsibility, since gifts are traditionally sent to the bride-to-be. But there's no reason why the man cannot return gifts given to him and his former fiancée as a couple or by his personal friends. Accompany returned gifts with a brief note such as the following:

Dear Claudia,

I am sorry to have to tell you that Roberto and I have broken our engagement. I'm returning the beautiful crystal bowl that you were so thoughtful to send.

Love,
Ashley

Do inform invited guests, but don't run a newspaper ad. Placing an ad was often done to announce a wedding cancellation in the days before telephones. But today, when an engagement is broken after invitations have been mailed and there is sufficient time, you can send a printed card like the following:

Mr. and Mrs. Nathan Morris
announce that the marriage of
their daughter
Rebecca

to

Mr. Oliver Sandburg
will not take place.

If there isn't time for printing and delivery of notices, call the people on the guest list. While it's preferable to talk personally with guests, you can leave messages and resort to e-mail if that's the most efficient way to reach someone.

Chapter Thirty-four

Planning the Big Event

A BEAUTIFUL BRIDE, A BEAMING GROOM, elegant attendants, and a happy complement of family and friends . . . to make the dream come true requires time, effort,
and major doses of the three C's of wedding planning—*consideration, communication,* and
compromise.

Marriage is a legal and, for many couples, religious commitment. A wedding and its
associated activities are the celebration of that commitment in the presence of family
and friends. The success of the marriage, of course, depends on the two of you. But
the success of the wedding often depends on how willing you are to adjust to outside
circumstances, to include other people in the planning, and to consider their needs as
well as your own.

In earlier eras, brides-to-be (and their mothers) generally took charge of wedding
planning and preparation, but today, the decisions and tasks are far more likely to be
shared. Grooms now tend to be closely involved and their wishes are given equal
weight. A contemporary engaged couple is regarded as a team, and the way they work
together to create their wedding can be a foretaste of how they will deal with other
major events and decisions in their life together. Couples who consider the feelings of
their partners, communicate openly and honestly about matters large and small, and
are willing to make compromises with one another usually find that the normal
stresses of planning (and conflicts with others) can be kept to a minimum.

The Major Decisions

ONCE YOU BECOME ENGAGED, you may feel as if someone has shot a starting gun
and you are now in the race of your life. So many decisions to make, so many hurdles
to jump, and so little time to get everything done. If you lack a clear-cut strategy and
organization, it's easy to become entangled in small details and find yourself stuck in
wedding planning gridlock.

There's a well-worn truism: "First things first." With those three words in mind,
couples and their families can begin by making the key decisions and then work their
way down the list toward the finishing touches. Taking things in the most logical or-

der will help you to gauge what you can accomplish in the time you have, what you can do on your own, how much help you will need from others, and what extras you may want to simplify or eliminate entirely.

This chapter focuses on the major decisions (guest list, budget, time, location, officiant, and wedding style) and also the initial steps of planning. As you move through the process, be kind to yourselves and your loved ones and honor the basic values—consideration, communication, and compromise. Guard your health and nurture your relationships. Remember that a wedding is not a competition but the joyous celebration of one of life's most meaningful milestones. And have fun!

The Guest List

Beginning with the guest list may seem a little odd. Isn't budget more important? Frankly, no, because your budget priorities and other major decisions will frequently depend on the number of people you want with you when you exchange your vows. In the long run, it's easier to modify spending or the style of a wedding than to leave out people who really matter to you. Also, by starting with a *preliminary* guest list, you will be better able to pare it down if you have to cut costs.

Traditionally, the guest list was divided equally between the bride's and groom's families and friends, but this is no longer considered necessary. Everyone must keep in mind whose wedding it is. Certainly the bride and groom will seek input from their families, but it's up to the couple to make the final choices. If everyone is willing to be tactful and accommodating, the process should proceed without too much fuss.

A preliminary guest list often starts with four separate lists—the bride's, the groom's, her parents', and his parents'—which are drawn up with these priorities in mind:

The VIPs. The indispensable core of a list includes close family and good friends without whom the wedding day would be incomplete. If a couple both have very large families, this group may constitute nearly the entire guest list. In addition, there are some guests who are always included, regardless of their relationship to the couple.

- ➤ The person or people who perform the ceremony and their spouses or partners
- ➤ The spouse, fiancé/fiancée, or domestic partner of each invited guest
- ➤ The parents of children in the wedding party
- ➤ Everyone who gives or is invited to the engagement party, showers, and other prenuptial parties (An exception: Coworkers who throw a workplace shower are not necessarily invited to the wedding.)

While it isn't a must to include the parents of the bridesmaids, groomsmen, and ushers, it's extremely nice to do so.

Other family and friends. There are relatives and friends who may not be so close but are important to you (the aunt you haven't seen in years but who always remembers your birthday; the high school or college mentor who meant so much to you, though you now get together infrequently). This group also includes relatives and friends who are important to the bride's and groom's parents, though the couple may not know them well or at all.

Acquaintances and friends of the family. Another group might include business associates and coworkers, professional colleagues, other friends of parents, and sometimes the in-laws of in-laws (a brother's wife's parents, for instance).

Guests of guests and children of guests. The spouses, fiancés/fiancées, and live-in partners of guests *must* be included, even if you don't know them. But you have to decide if you want single, unattached guests to bring dates and parents to bring their children.

Once you've combined the original lists, done some more prioritizing, and made some cuts, you'll probably wind up with two lists: (A) must invite and (B) maybe invite. Though you'll probably add or trim names before the invitations go out, you now have a preliminary estimate of the number of guests. It's time to discuss costs and begin your preparations.

The Budget

The days when the bride's parents were expected to bear all the expenses of the wedding and reception are over. It's now more common for engaged couples, especially those who are established wage earners, to pay all or most of the costs or at least to share some of the expense with their parents. The groom's family may also make a substantial contribution.

As soon as possible, everyone needs to determine how much they can afford and to discuss finances. In the early days of planning, people have a tendency to overestimate their financial capabilities (and underestimate actual costs), so the first rule of budgeting is to be realistic. The second is to be considerate. A parent may be willing to take a second mortgage or deplete retirement savings in order to finance an elaborate wedding, but is this the kind of sacrifice you want? If you're paying for the wedding, you may have to borrow some funds, so how much debt are you both comfortable taking on?

∼ Keep It to Yourself ∼

Your A and B guest lists are for your eyes only. The B list may serve as a standby—people you will gladly invite if and when invitees on your priority list send their regrets. But other than you and intimate family who are involved in developing the guest list, no one should ever be told who is on your lists or how your decisions were made. No notations or codes, such as letters or numbers, are included on invitations or place cards, although tables at a seated dinner reception are usually numbered for a seating chart. Even hinting that someone was on a second or B list can cause hurt feelings, destroy friendships, and damage your reputation as a thoughtful and gracious person.

With your preliminary guest list and overall budget amount, you'll be able to establish *per-person* spending limits. If, for example, you have a list of a hundred people (don't forget to include yourselves, the wedding party, and immediate family) and a total budget of $15,000, then your per-person limit is $150. Should the caterer give you an estimate of $100 per person for food, drink, and service for the reception, then you would have $50 per person (or $5,000) to spend on everything else—from the wedding dress and flowers to your license and rings. Can you do it, or is it time to adjust your plans?

The costs of some items are fixed—wedding license and any required medical tests, officiant's fee, postage, and so on—and other costs afford little room for squeezing—wedding rings, gifts for attendants, accommodations for out-of-town attendants. Start your budgeting with these items and anything else that you consider an absolute, such as the fees for your place of worship and reception site. As you get estimates for other expenses, be sure they include all applicable taxes as well as tips or gratuities. Before signing any contracts, read them carefully and look for hidden costs.

Don't think that you have to sacrifice quality to cut costs. With creative thinking and smart planning, you can have your dream wedding without breaking the bank. The chart "Budget Categories," below, will give you guidelines to help you determine which elements are essential for you.

BUDGET CATEGORIES

This chart of the basic budgeting categories should help you determine the items that are essential to your wedding and begin the process of investigating costs and getting estimates. Traditionally, different items and services were paid for by the bride's and groom's families, but because today's wedding costs are most often shared, items are not broken out here as specific to bride or groom.

Items	Mandatory or Optional	Actual or Estimated Costs
Attendants		
Accommodations		
Bridesmaids' luncheon		
Bachelor dinner		
Ceremony		
Officiant's fee		
Fee for house of worship or secular location		
Fees for musicians and/or singers		
Decorations (other than flowers)		
Flowers		
Ceremony		
Reception		
Rehearsal dinner, if there is one		

Items	Mandatory or Optional	Actual or Estimated Costs
Flowers		
Bridal bouquet		
Bridal attendants' flowers		
Corsages		
Boutonnieres		
Gifts		
Bride's gifts for attendants		
Groom's gifts for attendants		
Bride's gift for groom		
Groom's gift for bride		
Honeymoon costs		
Transportation		
Accommodations		
Passports if traveling abroad		
Legalities		
Marriage license		
Health/physical/blood test fees		
Music for the reception		
Musicians		
DJ		
Audio and lighting equipment, if necessary		
Photography		
Engagement photo		
Bridal portrait		
Wedding photographer		
Wedding videographer		
Reception		
Location		
Food and beverage costs		
Decorations (other than flowers)		
Favors		
Wedding cake		

Items	Mandatory or Optional	Actual or Estimated Costs
Rehearsal dinner		
Location		
Food and beverage costs		
Decorations (other than flowers)		
Stationery		
Invitations/enclosures		
Announcements		
Printing and envelopes		
Calligraphy		
Postage		
Ceremony program		
Thank-you notes		
Transportation and parking		
Limousines for the bridal party		
Traffic officials at the ceremony, reception		
Valet parking		
Travel and lodging costs for officiant, if necessary		
Trips necessary for wedding planning		
Wedding attire		
Bridal gown		
Bridal accessories		
Groom's outfit		
Bride's ring		
Groom's ring		
Beauty costs (hair, nails, makeup)		
Wedding consultant fees		
Hourly or per-day service		
Full service		
Miscellaneous		
Telephone bills related to planning		
Wardrobe costs for wedding-related events		
Rental of awnings, tents, chairs, tables		
Tips (if not included in above costs)		
Taxes (if not included in above costs)		

∽ The Wedding Consultant ∽

A wedding consultant or coordinator is hired to manage some or nearly all aspects of wedding planning and preparation. It isn't necessary to use a consultant, but their services can be a godsend for couples who are employed full-time or are staging large or complicated weddings.

A full-fledged *bridal consultant* can do anything you need. A *wedding day coordinator* steps in on the big day to assure that everything goes according to schedule. The following are typical of a consultant's services.

➢ Helps locate and reserve wedding and reception sites

➢ Helps with decisions about suppliers and vendors (Most consultants can advise about suppliers' and vendors' past performance and negotiate contracts.)

➢ Coordinates among suppliers/vendors and wedding and reception sites so that schedules are met and items or services are provided exactly as agreed

➢ Assists with budgeting, shopping, and wedding etiquette and might assist with travel arrangements, accommodations for guests, and honeymoon planning

➢ Coordinates the rehearsal with the officiant

➢ Supervises last-minute details, which may include transportation, on the wedding day

When selecting a wedding consultant, these are some key qualities you should look for.

Professionalism and experience. You want someone who understands the *business* of weddings. Certification and/or membership in a consultants' association may indicate professional commitment. Be sure to check references; talk frankly with some of the consultant's previous clients.

Congeniality. A congenial consultant isn't dictatorial and won't pressure you into decisions you aren't comfortable making.

Good manners. A consultant will be your wedding etiquette expert. He or she will also serve as your intermediary with officiants, site managers, suppliers, vendors, and even members of the wedding party. You want him or her to represent you well.

In general, a full-service consultant is paid approximately ten to fifteen percent of the total wedding costs. To avoid unscrupulous planners, look for someone who provides wedding packages at fixed rates or charges a flat fee based on the services you request.

You might need only planning advice and referrals, and planners usually charge an hourly rate for consultations. Or you might hire a consultant at a daily rate for help with specific events.

When you first speak with consultants, inform them of your wedding date, approximate number of guests, and overall budget.

Date and Time

Setting the date tends to make the wedding real for many couples. Suddenly it's no longer an eventuality but an actual event to mark on the calendar and work toward. You may have a specific day in mind, but there are issues to consider before you carve it in stone.

Time of year. The most popular wedding months are, in order, June, September, August, May, October, and July, but the busy months may vary depending on the climate where you live. In peak months, rates are usually highest and wedding and reception sites can be difficult to secure without booking many months ahead. You can probably save on costs by considering the less busy months.

Religious practices will affect planning if you have a religious service. There may be restrictions on the use of religious sites during high holy days such as Passover and Lent. Check with a clergy member or spiritual leader before setting a precise date.

If you expect members of the wedding party and guests to travel from distant places, you should factor in holidays and traditional vacation times when transportation and accommodation costs are highest. A destination wedding during peak season (see page 581: "Faraway Places") may be particularly expensive for everyone.

Think about your honeymoon. September may be your ideal wedding month, but it might not be the best time of year for an island trip, unless you enjoy heat, humidity, and tropical storms. If you want to travel to an exotic locale in the Southern Hemisphere, remember that the seasons there are reversed.

Day of the week. Most weddings are held on Fridays, Saturdays, or Sundays—scheduled around regular religious services and other holy day observances—but a weekday wedding is always an option. A Thursday-afternoon wedding might be just the thing, for example, when guests are not expected to travel long distances and when Friday is a light workday (as it often is in the summer months). The advantages of weekday weddings often include greater availability of wedding and reception sites and lower costs from vendors and suppliers. For a secular service such as a wedding in a judge's chambers, you will probably be limited to a working day when public buildings are open.

Time of day. Time can affect costs and availability. The later in the day a wedding is held, the more formal—and more expensive—it's likely to be. When the ceremony is scheduled at midday or anytime between 4:00 and 8:00 PM, guests will expect either a seated meal or a substantial buffet at the reception. Also, wedding and reception sites may be more difficult to reserve at popular times during the busiest wedding months. Even if you plan a home wedding and reception, be conscious of what else is scheduled, especially at the height of the wedding season when guests may have conflicts with other weddings at the same time.

Locations

If you want to be married in a *house of worship*, consult with the appropriate authorities as soon as you have an approximate wedding date and time. It may be possible to make tentative reservations for several dates and then confirm the day and time when you have reserved your reception site. Check on food and beverage policies if you want the reception at the ceremony site; alcohol is often prohibited, and kitchen capacity may be limited.

If you choose a *secular location*, you have a number of options: home, a hotel or wedding hall, a restaurant or club, city hall, historic and cultural sites that provide wedding and reception services. Whatever you select, be certain there's adequate space for your guests, including parking areas.

The Officiant

The person or people who perform the marriage service may be either religious or secular officials. If it's important that a specific person officiate, then his or her availability will be a factor in your choice of day and time. If you want an officiant from another congregation—when a relative is a clergyperson, for example, or when you're marrying in a house of worship other than your own but wish your clergyperson to officiate—you should consult with the spiritual leader of the wedding location as soon as possible.

Policies regarding guest clergy vary among religions and sects. Couples from different religious traditions may want officiants from both traditions but should inquire about restrictions or prohibitions on interfaith services.

You are responsible for transportation, accommodations, and meals for an officiant who must travel to the ceremony, so don't forget these expenses as you budget.

If you choose an officiant whom you don't know, be sure that the person is legally qualified. Contrary to popular belief, ship captains are not universally authorized to perform legally sanctioned ceremonies; public servants such as city clerks may or may not be qualified. An out-of-state officiant, whether clergy or secular, may be required to have a certificate of authorization from your state.

Your Wedding Style

Wedding style is largely a matter of personal preference, but the degree of formality will be heavily influenced by your budget and the location and time of the wedding. A formal evening celebration is generally the most costly, while an informal, afternoon wedding with a simple buffet reception is often the least expensive.

There are three traditional levels of formality. Today's weddings, however, may overlap styles to reflect the interests and creativity of the couple and their guests. The following descriptions are guidelines, not absolutes:

Formal

> **Ceremony:** The ceremony usually takes place in a house of worship or a large home or garden.
> **Attendants:** The bride and groom usually have between four and ten attendants each.
> **Attire:** The bride and her attendants wear long gowns in formal fabrics. The groom and his attendants wear cutaways or tailcoats. White tie is the most formal attire.
> **Reception:** The wedding meal is usually a sit-down dinner or semi-buffet. Decorations may be elaborate. If there's dancing, the music is provided by an orchestra or full band. Limousines are often hired for the wedding party.

Semiformal

> **Ceremony:** The ceremony can take place at a house of worship, chapel, civic site for civil ceremonies, hotel, club, home, or garden.
> **Attendants:** The couple might each have from two to six attendants.
> **Attire:** The bride and her attendants usually wear long, ankle-length, or midcalf-length gowns in simpler fabrics than for formal wedding gowns. For daytime, the groom and his attendants wear gray or black strollers with striped trousers or formal suits; for an evening wedding, dinner jackets with black trousers or formal suits.
> **Reception:** A buffet is usually served, perhaps a cocktail buffet for late afternoon receptions. Music is provided by a small band or DJ.

Informal

> **Ceremony:** The ceremony can be held at a house of worship, chapel, rectory, civic site, home, or garden.
> **Attendants:** The bride and groom each usually have one to three attendants.
> **Attire:** The bride and her attendants usually wear simple floor-length gowns or ankle-length, midcalf-length, or street-length dresses. The groom and attendants wear suits or sport jackets and slacks.
> **Reception:** The reception can be held at a restaurant, club, fellowship hall, or at home. Morning weddings are often followed by a breakfast, brunch, or lunch. Afternoon receptions might include a buffet or simply hors d'oeuvres and wedding cake. A small ensemble, a single musician, or a DJ can provide music.

Family Matters

If your family or families are complicated by divorce, remarriage, step relationships, or family feuding, you are strongly advised to give serious thought to these issues as early in the planning process as possible. Your marriage is highly unlikely to heal rifts

Exchanging vows as the sun sets over the ocean. Marrying against the backdrop of a majestic mountain lodge or an ancient European castle. A romantic destination wedding can be realized with thoughtful planning.

Begin with an assessment of your guests' ability to finance what is usually a three- or four-day vacation trip. Guests at a destination wedding are expected to pay for their transportation and accommodations, and there are often extra expenses such as acquiring the correct attire for the location as well as the wedding. You should understand that because of the costs and scheduling, some people you want at your wedding probably can't attend; as a result, destination weddings are generally small.

Unless you can commute back and forth to the location, you'll need someone on-site to manage the preparations, and you might work with a wedding consultant in your area who can coordinate with a planner in the wedding location. Hotels in popular travel sites may have a wedding planner on staff. There are also travel agents who specialize in destination weddings and can advise on the best times to travel as well as bargain rates for fares and lodging. With expert help, couples can sometimes achieve savings over a traditional at-home wedding—for themselves and their guests.

It's very important to inform guests of your plans as far in advance as possible—well before the traditional mailing of wedding invitations. Also, have a Plan B up your sleeve in case anything happens to prevent that planned wedding. If the site is struck by a hurricane or snowed in, for example, do you want to reschedule at another time or go ahead with your wedding in another location?

If your destination is outside the country, you and your guests will probably need passports and perhaps special visas. There may be recommended medical precautions and inoculations. Consult with both the U.S. Department of State and the embassy of the country, and provide all necessary information to your guests. Also check on any legal requirements, such as a period of residency or a published announcement of intent to marry.

Remember, too, that the perfect destination may be closer than you think. There may be locations in your own state or region that meet all your requirements for romance, adventure, and convenience.

among family members, but with forethought and tact, you can prepare yourself to head off serious difficulties.

Unfortunately, divorced parents are not always friendly. Although well-mannered adults will lay their differences aside for a wedding, you should avoid putting them in awkward and uncomfortable situations. Seating divorced parents together at the ceremony or reception isn't necessary (see Chapter 39, page 688: "Seating the Families and Special Guests"). Asking divorced parents and their spouses to the same social events can be stressful for everyone, including other guests. Most parents will do everything in their power to make your wedding special, but you have responsibilities to them as well, and this may mean adjusting what you want to what others *need*.

The traditional wedding vows include the words "for better, for worse." Couples would be wise to apply these words to their families. Will your plans make difficult family relationships better or at least keep them on an even keel? Or will having everything your way cause pain and lingering resentment? When you look back on your wedding in ten or fifteen years, will you be proud of everything you did and remember a day that was happy for everyone?

More Decisions

WITH THE BIG DECISIONS MADE, you're ready to tackle the details. The size and style of your wedding will determine your exact to-do list, but this will give you a general idea of what you need to accomplish. (For specifics, see Chapter 35, "The Nuts and Bolts of Preparation," and following chapters.)

> Check with city or county officials about requirements for the marriage license; talk with spiritual leaders about any restrictions on or requirements for religious ceremonies.
> Ask attendants (see "Choosing the Wedding Party," below) and confirm their participation.
> Shop for the wedding dress if you plan to purchase it or find someone who can make the necessary alterations to a family or borrowed gown.
> Choose wedding clothing and accessories for the bride, groom, and attendants.
> Shop for wedding rings.
> Interview and contract with a wedding consultant if that's your choice.
> Plan the reception menu and interview caterers.
> Discuss music for the ceremony and reception; interview musicians and DJs.
> Interview florists.
> Investigate sources of rentals for necessary equipment such as tents, awnings, chairs, tables, and outdoor lighting.
> Interview photographers and videographers and review their portfolios.
> Order invitations, enclosures, announcements, and other printed material.
> Consider gift registry.
> Discuss your honeymoon trip and consult with travel agents as necessary.

Your Wedding Theme

Wedding themes can be as simple as a unified color scheme or extremely elaborate. The point is for couples to agree on their themes as soon as they can; the theme will affect other decisions—from invitations and flowers to the types of music and musicians you select.

The more extravagant the theme, however, the more likely that costs will rise. Be aware that themes can get out of hand and place unfair burdens on others. Using Renaissance or Victorian colors for flowers and table decorations can be enchanting, but expecting wedding attendants to purchase expensive, custom-made period attire is probably going overboard for most people. A good theme complements the ceremony and adds interest to the celebration; it should neither break the budget nor detract from the fundamental sanctity of the occasion.

Choosing the Wedding Party

FOR MANY COUPLES, the choice of attendants is easy—sisters, brothers, and dearest friends. But if you have a large family or a wide circle of good friends, the decision can be quite hard. You aren't required to ask siblings, though it certainly promotes family unity. You can choose one best friend over another to be maid of honor or best man, but you may risk causing a break that is difficult to mend.

Fortunately, etiquette has kept up with the times, and today's couples have many options for organizing their wedding parties and choosing their attendants:

> ➤ There is no required number of attendants. The average is four to six bridesmaids and at least as many groomsmen and ushers, but you can include as many or as few as you like. Some couples have a large number of attendants, but even a formal wedding with just one or two attendants on each side is perfectly acceptable. Since ushers have the practical responsibility of seating guests at the ceremony, the general rule is one usher for every fifty guests, though you may have more.

> ➤ It's no longer considered necessary to have an equal number of bridesmaids and groomsmen or ushers, so you don't have to worry about pairing up. You can have more bridesmaids than groomsmen or vice versa. (One groomsman can easily escort two bridesmaids in the recessional, or bridesmaids can walk alone or in pairs.)

> ➤ You can have two maids of honor, a maid and a matron of honor, or two best men. Though not so common, two chief attendants may be the right solution when you don't want to choose between siblings or very close friends. The attendants can share duties—for example, one maid of honor holds the groom's ring while the other takes the bridal bouquet. This arrangement can also be advantageous when for some reason, one of the honor attendants can't participate in events leading up to the wedding.

> ➤ You can toss a coin or pull straws to decide who will be maid of honor or best man. When good friends are amenable to luck-of-the-draw decisions, leaving the choice up to fate eliminates any hint of preference or favoritism.

> ➤ You can have pregnant bridesmaids. Unless there's a religious restriction, today's brides can certainly invite a friend who is expecting. Just be considerate

of her needs and capabilities. For instance, you can see that a chair is placed near the altar area so that the mother-to-be can sit during a lengthy service, and excuse her from a formal receiving line.

Whom to Ask

Participating in someone else's wedding is at once a pleasure and a responsibility. When you consider whom to include, you'll want to think about your expectations and how much you are likely to depend on your attendants—not just at the wedding but throughout your planning and preparation. You might consider these fundamental traits:

Reliability. An attendant should be a person you can count on to stay in touch in the weeks and months preceding the wedding, to listen to instructions, to follow up on requests without being reminded, and to show up on time and ready for all events.

Consideration. Considerate attendants may offer suggestions but will understand that they aren't in charge. They will look for opportunities to be helpful but won't add to the bridal couple's worries with special demands or needless criticism.

Courtesy. In a sense, attendants are like ambassadors for the bridal couple and their families. At pre-wedding events and during the wedding reception, they will mix and mingle with guests, make introductions, look out for people with special needs, and behave appropriately at all times.

When to Ask

Once you've decided whom you want in your wedding, give them as much advance notice as possible. Three to six months before the wedding date is fairly standard. This gives attendants time to organize their calendars, purchase clothing and have necessary alterations made, arrange transportation, and plan and host any parties they may wish to hold. If your schedule is very tight, you can probably find ways to cut a few corners (off-the-rack bridesmaid dresses rather than custom-ordered, a bridesmaids' luncheon and bachelor party but no shower or vice versa) to relieve the strain on you and your wedding party.

It's always nice to ask in person, but don't delay contacting someone who lives at a distance. Call, write, or e-mail your invitation—whatever is the easiest way to get in touch. Supply the wedding date even if you aren't sure of the time, the location if travel will be required, and some sense of the formality of the event. The person may accept immediately, but don't push for an instant reply. Even the closest friend may need a day or two to consider.

It's a great honor to be asked to be in a wedding, but people have other obligations and accepting may not be possible. Don't be offended or expect a detailed explanation if someone turns down your invitation. A refusal is often based on important family, job, or financial concerns, so be sensitive. Express your disappointment without any hint of disapproval. Rather than jeopardize a relationship, assume that the person has made a conscientious decision and is doing what he or she thinks is best for everyone.

Attendants' Responsibilities

ALTHOUGH ATTENDANTS' DUTIES WILL VARY based on the size and style of the event, there are some expectations common to most weddings. The list below comprises the basic responsibilities of all adult attendants. It is followed by specifics for each category of attendant, including children.

- ➤ Pay for their wedding attire and accessories (excluding flowers)
- ➤ Arrange and pay for their own transportation, unless provided by the wedding couple
- ➤ Attend prenuptial events (Timely regrets are essential when it's not possible to attend, but attendants should definitely be on hand for the rehearsal and rehearsal dinner.)
- ➤ Contribute to attendants' group gifts to the bride and groom (and usually, give an individual gift as well)
- ➤ Understand specific duties and follow instructions
- ➤ Arrive at specified times for all wedding-related events
- ➤ Assist the bride and groom and be attentive to other guests at the wedding and reception

Hosting or co-hosting a pre-wedding party or shower is nice but by no means mandatory.

Attendants have a special duty to see that the wedding and the reception run smoothly. They are expected to be gracious and visit with guests, assist the elderly and anyone else who needs help, be attentive to young children in the wedding party, be

~ JUST COMMON SENSE ~

Keeping Everybody Up to Speed

From the time your attendants accept your invitation, it's your responsibility to keep them informed. Communication is essential to a well-planned wedding, and all the members of your wedding party need updates—especially about any changes that will affect them. Don't overload family and friends with details, but do maintain regular contact and be particularly attentive to wedding party members who live elsewhere. Write, phone, e-mail. No matter how casual your communication, it will be appreciated for the information you provide and as a sign of how much you care about others.

available for picture taking, and generally help out whenever needed. If there's a formal receiving line, all bridesmaids may be asked to participate or only the maid/matron of honor and perhaps the best man.

Maid or matron of honor

➤ Helps the bride select bridesmaids' attire

➤ Helps address invitations and place cards

➤ Organizes bridesmaids' gift to the bride and often organizes the bridesmaids' luncheon if there is one

➤ Holds the groom's wedding ring and the bride's bouquet during the ceremony

➤ Witnesses the signing of the marriage certificate

➤ Helps the bride during the reception (gathering guests for cake cutting, dancing, bouquet toss, etc.)

➤ Helps the bride change into her going-away clothes and takes care of the bride's wedding dress and accessories after the reception

Bridesmaids

➤ Attend rehearsal, rehearsal dinner, and bridesmaids' luncheon if there is one

➤ Supervise children in the wedding party if asked

➤ Assist the bride at the reception as requested

➤ Participate in activities such as a receiving line and the bouquet toss

➤ Contribute to bridesmaids' gift to bride (and usually give individual gifts to the couple)

Junior bridesmaid. A junior bridesmaid is a girl between eight and twelve years of age who serves as a bridesmaid but has fewer responsibilities than adult attendants. Parents pay for her dress and accessories (excluding flowers). Junior bridesmaids attend the rehearsal and, depending on the girl's age and maturity, the rehearsal dinner. They may be invited to the bridesmaids' luncheon. They don't give bridal showers, though they can attend pre-wedding social events when invited. Other than participating in the ceremony, junior bridesmaids have no further obligations, but if asked, they should be in the receiving line. A junior bridesmaid may give a separate gift to the couple or be included in her parents' gift.

Best man

➤ Organizes bachelor party for the groom, if there is one

➤ Coordinates the groomsmen and ushers' gift to the groom

➤ Makes sure that groom's wedding-related payments are prepared; delivers prearranged payments to officiants, assistants, and musicians and singers at the ceremony

Last month, I was a bridesmaid for a college friend. I was thrilled to be asked, but as soon as I said yes, my friend began to make demands. I work and also attend school at night, but the bride was constantly calling me for favors like getting her shoes dyed for a party and picking up her dry cleaning. She did this to all her bridesmaids and never asked us if it was convenient. It went on for months, and now I wonder if I should have just backed out of the wedding.

Your friend obviously didn't understand that an attendant is not a paid servant. The chores you mention might be appropriate in the days just before the wedding, when attendants should be ready to run errands and handle some last-minute tasks. But to demand such favors throughout her engagement was selfish and inexcusable.

It's sad that some brides, and grooms as well, get so wrapped up in *their day* that they forget about others. An attendant is expected to be supportive and to provide reasonable assistance, but not to be at a couple's beck and call.

Under the circumstances, you could have backed out, but a better course would have been to talk with the bride when it was clear that her requests were excessive. Perhaps an attendant who was especially close to her could have had this conversation. Or all the bridesmaids could have addressed the problem together, so long as you didn't give the impression of ganging up on her. Sometimes a reality check is a real kindness, especially when a bride or groom is alienating friends who, in the long run, are immeasurably more important than dyed shoes.

[587]

Planning the Big Event

- ➢ Sees that groomsmen and ushers arrive on time and are properly attired
- ➢ Instructs ushers in correct seating of guests (if there is no head usher)
- ➢ Keeps the bride's wedding ring during the ceremony
- ➢ Witnesses signing of the marriage certificate
- ➢ Drives bride and groom to the reception if there's no hired driver; has car ready for couple to leave after the reception and may drive them to their next destination
- ➢ Offers first toast to bride and groom at the reception; dances with the bride, mothers, maid of honor, and other single female guests
- ➢ Gathers and takes care of groom's wedding clothes (returning rental items on the next business day)

Groomsmen and ushers. Groomsmen stand with the bridegroom during the ceremony. They are usually close relatives and friends, and often, but not always, the number of groomsmen is equal to the number of bridesmaids.

Ushers help prepare the wedding site for the ceremony and escort guests to their seats before the ceremony.

Groomsmen may also serve as ushers, and this is fairly common at small to medium-sized weddings. But when the guest company is large or when the bridegroom has only a best man and perhaps one other attendant, additional ushers are often needed. An older friend or family member might be asked to serve as *head usher*; his duties include supervising the ushers, seeing that all pre- and post-ceremony tasks are completed, and managing late arrivals. (For specific duties of the head usher, see Chapter 39, page 686: "Who's in Charge?") The head usher or best man will instruct the ushers in seating guests and the correct order for seating family members before the processional.

The duties of groomsmen/ushers are to:

➤ Attend rehearsal, rehearsal dinner, and bachelor party if there is one

➤ Contribute to ushers' gift to the groom (and usually give an individual gift)

➤ Know the seating order; review special seating arrangements prior to the ceremony

➤ Greet guests and escort them to their seats

➤ Hand each guest a program, if programs are provided

➤ Lay the aisle runner, if one is used, before the processional

➤ After the ceremony, remove pew ribbons, close windows, retrieve any programs or articles left behind

➤ Help guests who need directions to the reception site

➤ Coordinate return of rental clothing with the head usher or best man

Children as Attendants

You have to decide if you wish to have children in the wedding party. There are good arguments on both sides. When well behaved, children add a special charm, and being included in the wedding can be very meaningful for youngsters whose parent is marrying for a second time. But young children are unpredictable, and their charms can wear thin when they cry, whine, chatter, or freeze up during the service. No matter how often they've rehearsed, children under age nine or so need constant monitoring; you'll have to arrange for a parent, babysitter, or one of your attendants to supervise each child at all times before, during, and after the ceremony.

If you're prepared to manage potential problems and disturbances, then by all means invite a child or children to participate. But you have no obligation to do so, and you shouldn't yield to pressure if you want to limit your attendants to adults.

In general, couples who want young attendants are advised to include as few as possible and to aim at the older end of the age range; children of school age are better able to follow instructions than preschoolers are. Young attendants aren't normally invited to prenuptial events unless their parents are included and other children will be attending.

Flower girl. Flower girls are usually between the ages of three and seven. Their role is to precede the bride down the aisle, carrying flowers or flower baskets. They stand with the bridesmaids during the service, though young children may sit with the bride's family or their parents. A flower girl's parents pay for her dress and accessories (excluding flowers). She attends the rehearsal but usually not the rehearsal dinner. There may be more than one flower girl, and this can be a nice way to include girls too young to be junior bridesmaids.

Ring bearer. The ring bearer is a three- to seven-year-old boy who walks down the aisle and carries the wedding rings (or a reasonable facsimile) on a small cushion. He stands with the groomsmen or may sit with the groom's family or his parents during the service. His outfit is provided by his family. He is expected to attend the rehearsal but generally not the rehearsal dinner.

During the ceremony, the ring bearer traditionally enters after the maid or matron of honor. He is followed by the flower girl. But a very young boy and girl may enter together. The children exit together immediately after the bride and groom, but if a child has fallen asleep, wandered back to his parents, or is in any way disagreeable, the recessional walk can be dispensed with.

Train bearers and pages. These are young attendants who hold and carry the bride's train and may assist with arranging the train when the bride reaches the altar. They are rarely included except in the most elaborate formal or state weddings.

Other helpers. In some parts of the country, it's customary for family members and friends who have a special relationship with the couple to assist at the wedding and the reception. Though not strictly members of the wedding party, these gracious helpers are usually presented with corsages and boutonnieres in the wedding colors. They are included in some wedding photographs, and their names and responsibilities are often listed in lengthier newspaper accounts of the wedding.

At a home or church reception, their duties, or "honor roles," might include serving cake, pouring tea and coffee, and greeting guests. They can hand out ceremony programs, be in charge of the guest book, or participate in the wedding service as readers, soloists, cantors, or altar assistants. It is appropriate to thank helpers with a gift, such as a framed wedding photo, and a note of appreciation.

Social Events Given in Your Honor

AS SOON AS YOUR ENGAGEMENT is announced, friends and family may begin asking how they can entertain for you, and even events like the rehearsal dinner, held very close to your wedding day, require advance planning. The occasions discussed below are considered customary, though none is obligatory. Nor is it essential to have showers and other parties that include gift giving. It is perfectly acceptable for the bride and groom to suggest a "non-gift" occasion when others ask about entertaining in their honor.

The recent trend of naming honorary attendants, or honorary bridesmaids—guests who have no role in the wedding but are given special status—probably derives from the custom of asking certain friends and relatives, usually older women, to perform tasks such as keeping the guest register. Honorary attendants typically have no duties but are invited to the rehearsal dinner, seated near the family at the wedding service, and presented corsages.

This practice might be appropriate when a dear friend cannot be in the wedding. But when there's a full cast of literal attendants, "honorary" may seem more like a euphemism for "second-tier friend" than a true honor. Reasonable people understand that every friend and relative can't be in a wedding and will feel honored to be included among the guests.

Weddings

Whatever the event, the couple should express their appreciation with a thank-you note or notes sent to the hosts within a day or two of the party. Thank-you gifts are usually in order as well; flowers are always nice, but you might want to send something that will be longer lasting. (See also Chapter 38, page 675: "Whom to Thank.")

[590]

Showers

A shower is an intimate gathering of friends, given to extend good wishes to the bride, the couple, or occasionally only the groom and to present the honoree(s) with gifts. The custom goes back to ancient traditions of "showering" newlyweds with grains of wheat or sweet cakes as symbolic wishes for fertility and prosperity.

A shower may have a theme that indicates the type of gifts expected. Opening the presents is usually the high point of the party, but the real purpose is to bring good friends together to celebrate the upcoming marriage. Gifts are great, but secondary to conversation, conviviality, and gracious manners.

Showers can be held in any form the hostess or host chooses—a brunch or supper, a traditional afternoon tea, an evening get-together—and are more often casual than formal these days. The ideal timing is from two months to two weeks before the wedding—after the couple has firmed up their wedding plans. Post-wedding showers are also acceptable, especially when the wedding was arranged on short notice. Unless the shower is a surprise, the honoree is consulted about the date, time, theme, and guest list, but party planning is up to the hostess or host.

Shower gifts and thank-yous are discussed in Chapter 38, page 674: "The Importance of 'Thank You.'"

Who should host a shower? The traditional hosts are friends of the bride, the couple, or their parents. Wedding attendants may throw a shower, but this is *not* an obligation, and bridesmaids often substitute an attendants' party (see below) for a shower. Workplace showers hosted by coworkers are popular, as are showers for the couple hosted by mutual friends and attended by men as well as women. Showers for the groom are a recent phenomenon. A couple never hosts a shower for themselves.

Can a family member host the party? It has long been considered a breach of etiquette for family members to host showers, because doing so gives the appearance of being self-serving. But it's becoming increasingly correct for family to host in certain situations, as when the bride is visiting her future in-laws and the groom's mother or sister invites hometown friends to meet her. Also, more mothers or sisters of the bride are giving showers. Today, people should be guided by individual circumstances when deciding if family members will host.

Who is invited? Normally, anyone invited to a shower should be invited to the wedding. The one exception is a workplace shower to which a large number of coworkers contribute. (If an office shower involves only a few coworkers, thoughtful couples will include these colleagues in the wedding guest list.) Parents, close family members, and wedding attendants are included but not expected to bring presents. Showers are *intimate* gatherings for people you know very well—not excuses to haul in more gifts.

How are invitations issued? Usually, the host or hosts send pre-printed invitations with the party details filled in or handwritten notes. Invitations may also be issued in person or by phone—a convenient method for workplace or surprise showers. Invitations should include the theme of the shower and any pertinent information such as the couple's color preferences for kitchen, bath, and linen showers. It's okay for the hostess to include gift registry sources, but never specific gift requests or suggestions.

How many showers can be given? Some couples prefer no shower at all, while others want as many as possible. But one of the basic principles of all good manners is consideration for others, and it is patently inconsiderate to put too much strain on wedding guests. Inviting the same people to the wedding and multiple showers and expecting them to bring gifts every time is inconsiderate. As a general rule, *two showers is the limit*, with different guests invited to each.

At a shower, ask someone to make a list of gifts and givers as the presents are opened. Gift tags often fall off, and no one's memory is perfect, so put it down on paper. *Do not* ask guests to fill out envelopes with their addresses. This is sometimes done as a convenience for the bride when she writes thank-you notes, but it implies laziness and lack of basic courtesy.

The bride and/or groom is expected to write thank-you notes for *all* shower gifts, even when guests were thanked in person at the shower.

Attendants' Parties

It's traditional for attendants to entertain the bridal couple. The guest list for the attendants' parties discussed below is generally limited to the members of the wedding party and perhaps the couple's parents, siblings, and other close family members. Parties can range from a formal seated dinner to a casual picnic. Attendants might prefer to entertain in other ways (showers, luncheons, dinner parties, cocktail parties, etc.) and to co-host with people who are not in the wedding party. In fact, attendants' parties are entirely optional and may simply be impossible to arrange when attendants live in different or distant locations.

Bridesmaids' party. Usually held a day or two before the wedding or on the morning of the wedding, this event is hosted by the bride's attendants and usually organized by the maid or matron of honor. In some communities, the bride and her mother host the party as a thank-you to the bridesmaids. A luncheon, brunch, or afternoon tea is traditional, but it can easily be a dinner or cocktail party. Bridesmaids often give their gift(s) to the bride at this event, and the bride may also present her attendants' gifts.

Groom's dinner. The purpose is for the best man, groomsmen, and ushers to honor the groom, and the event is usually organized by the best man. Dinner is often the most convenient time, but a lunch or brunch is also an option. The gathering can be as formal or casual as the hosts like, but because guests may be coming directly from work, the mood and attire are often business casual. The groomsmen usually present their gift(s) to the groom, and vice versa.

Bachelor and Bachelorette Parties

The basic idea for these events is to treat the groom or bride to one last night out as a single person. The guests are good friends, the atmosphere is relaxed, and there's no reason not to have a great time—so long as everyone is willing to exercise self-control. Bachelor and the more recent bachelorette parties have earned bad reputations because of the immature behaviors they seem to encourage and the consequences they engender—from titanic hangovers to serious accidental injuries.

Use common sense. Friends really shouldn't throw a bachelor or bachelorette party if they know or sense that either of the couple is against the idea. No real friend would do anything that could cause dissension between future husband and wife.

Anticipate problems. Appoint designated drivers or arrange for taxi or limo service if alcohol is served. Be clear that drug use is banned. Whatever entertainment is planned, it should not embarrass, humiliate, or endanger the honoree or any of the guests. It's wise to hold a bachelor or bachelorette party a week or more before the wedding, so everyone can rest after what will probably be a late night. If gifts are given, they're usually inexpensive and often humorous, and guests should be able to find items that are both funny and in reasonably good taste.

Rehearsal Party

Traditionally, the dinner following the wedding rehearsal was hosted by the groom's parents, but today, just about anybody may host. The party need not be a seated dinner; you could follow a daytime rehearsal with a brunch or an afternoon rehearsal with a cocktail buffet. A post-rehearsal party is not obligatory, but it's an excellent way to entertain attendants and family members. The party can be held at a home, restaurant, or club, though usually not at the bride's or the couple's home if it is to be the site of the wedding.

The guest list normally includes all members of the wedding party and their spouses or partners; the close families of the couple; and special guests such as the officiant and his or her spouse. Is the host obligated to invite out-of-town guests? Though a nice thing to do, this is entirely optional. If children are in the wedding, they may be invited unless you and the hosts want to limit the affair to adults. When children are included, their parents are also invited.

Chapter Thirty-five

The Nuts and Bolts
of Preparation

YOU'VE SET THE DATE, settled on the hour and location, and decided who will be there when you take your vows. The time has come to turn your dreams into reality, and whatever the style and size of your wedding, there's a lot to be done.

This chapter and the three that follow ("Wedding Invitations and Announcements," "Wedding Attire," and "Wedding Gifts") address the essentials of preparing for a wedding in the American tradition. Etiquette will play a central role in most of the decisions you will make; not only the etiquette of wording invitations or seating guests at the reception but also the core values of respect and consideration for everyone involved—yourselves, your families and friends, and the professionals who will help you create the wedding you want.

For many couples, their wedding is their first experience organizing a major social event from start to finish. Unless your wedding is very small or very casual, you will need assistance. Before calling on others, however, evaluate your own time and limitations. Be honest with yourselves, and try not to overestimate your capabilities.

Knowing what you can reasonably do, you can better allocate your resources and delegate responsibilities to others. A few people are natural delegators, but most have to draw deeply on their empathy. Whether you're working with hired professionals or family and friends who volunteer their time, you will have to trust them to do what you ask to the best of their abilities. Successful delegation also requires sensitivity to other people's lives and schedules and gratitude for their efforts on your behalf.

Even with the best of help, there may be times when all the details of preparation seem overwhelming. Be kind to yourselves. Take a break and remind yourselves of the ultimate goal of your hard work. Think about the three C's of wedding planning—*consideration, communication,* and *compromise.* A healthy dose of each can revive your spirits and put the inevitable glitches of wedding preparation into perspective.

Contracting for Services

CHANCES ARE, you'll be working with suppliers and vendors, either directly or through your wedding consultant. (See also Chapter 12, page 157: "Maintenance and repair persons and contractors.") Whether you're buying supplies or hiring services, be clear about what you want but also be open to suggestions. Experienced wedding suppliers can often help you avoid common problems and pitfalls.

Review contracts so that there are no misunderstandings about responsibilities. When you make agreements well in advance of the wedding, call back closer to the day and confirm times, delivery schedules, directions, site access, and other critical details. You'll have to coordinate some services—for instance, if you will have a live band followed by a DJ at your reception, both need to know exactly when the switch will be made so they can plan a smooth transition.

Photographers, musicians, disc jockeys, event coordinators, and other professionals hired for a wedding, reception, and any other event that requires working through the lunch or dinner hour should be fed. Arrange meals through your caterer or site manager, and coordinate meal breaks with your service providers. (Caterers generally arrange meals for their employees, but check to be sure.)

If you don't have a wedding coordinator, it's smart to have a "point person" on your wedding day—someone whom suppliers can go to with problems and questions. This might be a parent, an honor attendant, or a good friend or family member who is thoroughly acquainted with your plans.

~ JUST COMMON SENSE ~

Write It Down

It can be a special book just for weddings or a plain spiral notebook, but a planner is a must. Whether your wedding is large or small, you have a lot to keep track of, and pen and paper are more trustworthy than memory. A planner doesn't have to be neat and pretty. *Accurate* and *thorough* are what matters. Today's couples often keep separate planners and compare notes every day or two.

You might back up your written planner with a computer record, but a planning book that you can take to meetings and use to jot down ideas and questions whenever they occur to you is really the best tool. Devote a few minutes each day to reviewing your notes and organizing information into general categories (locations, food, flowers, registry ideas, etc.). Include details from discussions with vendors and suppliers. Think ahead. You may get a recommendation for a supplier early in your engagement but forget the name by the time you actually need it. Record names, addresses, phone numbers, and e-mail addresses of anyone you might need to get in touch with. And don't lose your book!

Don't Overlook the Obvious

Talented family members and friends may be delighted to help with the preparations—saving you money in the bargain—so be open to offers of assistance. Don't assume that someone who is hired will necessarily do a better job than a reliable relative or friend.

Should you pay? You have to use good judgment. If someone takes on a major task such as catering the reception or doing the bouquets, then it's appropriate to bring up payment. If the person refuses, don't pressure, but do discuss your financial responsibility for materials and supplies. If helpers are obviously going to personal expense—for example, driving a great deal on errands for you—you should reimburse their costs. If they won't accept reimbursement, give a nice gift along with your note of thanks.

When someone offers to help and you don't want to accept, be gracious when you decline and avoid implying that the person is not capable. You might ask the person to do something else. ("Thank you so much, Aunt Daisy, but we've already paid the caterer to do the hors d'oeuvres. I could use your help with the place cards. You have such beautiful handwriting.")

Repaying With Courtesy

In the excitement and stress of preparing for the wedding, brides- and grooms-to-be can sometimes forget that their wedding day is not the high point of everyone's life. Remember the Golden Rule, and keep these fundamental courtesies in mind.

Always say "thank you" for favors large and small. You don't have to write thank-you notes for every favor, but when you do your thank-yous for wedding gifts, you should write extra warmly to everyone who voluntarily lent you a hand. While a present to someone who's helped you is nice, no gift can make up for the failure to say "thank you."

Keep requests reasonable. Don't expect people to do more than they're capable of. If your local baker can't duplicate the complicated wedding cake you saw in a magazine, accept his assessment and be open to alternatives. If your maid of honor can't leave her job to help you shop for your wedding dress, don't imply that she's letting you down.

Treat suppliers, vendors, and their employees with respect. Your dealings with the companies or individuals you hire should be both professional and courteous. Don't expect more than you contract for or demand last-minute changes for frivolous reasons. Take problems or complaints to a senior person. Don't berate a contractor's employees (such as caterer's assistants or delivery people) or ask them to do anything that their employer hasn't approved.

Take responsibility for your own mistakes. Before blaming others, review the situation and determine where the error was really made. Were your expectations realistic? Did you give clear instructions? Did you make required payments and live up to other terms of your agreement? Hold your temper, and when you are even partially at fault, apologize. Then move on and solve the problem.

Ceremony and Reception Locations

IT's IMPORTANT TO FIRM UP all the details associated with the wedding and reception location or locations as quickly as possible. For a home wedding and/or reception, you have more leeway. Still, you should consult with your officiant about any special requirements.

Ceremony Site

Once you've decided on the location, make an appointment to meet with the officiant or his or her representative or the site manager. Presumably, you've had a preliminary conversation, so at this meeting, you'll confirm your wedding date and time and discuss the following issues:

Length and format of the ceremony. Civil ceremonies are usually relatively short, but the duration of religious services can vary. Do you wish to personalize the ceremony with specific readings and music? Is it okay to have others read or perform music? Do you prefer traditional vows? Can you prepare your own vows? Will communion be offered?

Number of guests and seating arrangements. You should have your guest list almost completed by now. You might find that you'll need to accommodate a different number than you had originally told the officiant or site manager. (You won't have a nearly exact count until you receive the replies for the reception.) At a site other than a house of worship, you will need to work with the manager on seating arrangements, platforms or altars for the officiant, and the general organization of the room or outdoor setting.

∼ No Pestering ∼

Pre-wedding jitters can make people do strange things—like calling their caterer or florist incessantly in the months before the wedding. Checking in is smart when there's a long lag time between engaging a vendor and using his or her services, or a change that the vendor needs to know about. Nagging and pestering are something else. Vendors and suppliers are businesspeople—not your best friends or personal counselors.

On the other hand, don't let yourself be pushed into decisions that you're uncomfortable with. It's your wedding, and what's important to you matters—not the latest fad or "hot" wedding item.

Site facilities. Inquire about dressing areas and any restrictions on flowers and decorations, music, photography and videotaping. Ask about guest parking and vendors' access. If you're planning a religious ceremony at a site other than a place of worship, are there items for the service—altar, altar cloth, kneeling cushions, *chuppah*, aisle runner—that you're expected to provide?

The names you want used in the ceremony. How do you want the officiant to address you during the ceremony? Full names? Nicknames? Will the bride take the groom's name? Will the couple take a double name? Also, do you want the officiant to introduce you to the guest company at the end of the ceremony?

The rehearsal. Reserve the site and set the time for your rehearsal. If the site is heavily booked, you may have to adjust your plans. Rehearsals are usually held on the day or evening before the wedding but can be earlier if this will be convenient for your wedding party. Reserve a few extra minutes in case the rehearsal runs overtime.

Any requirements you must fulfill. Different religions and sects have different traditions, so be sure to clarify. If premarital counseling or instruction is required, make your appointments now. Ask about any documents you must provide, such as baptismal certificates. If you want an officiant from another congregation to participate in or perform the service or you will marry in a house of worship other than your own, ask about any special requirements or permissions. If you plan an interfaith service somewhere other than a house of worship, be sure the officiants can perform the service at the location. Clarify all requirements for the ceremony itself.

Fees. Discuss amounts and methods of paying the site fee, officiant's fee, and fees for other participants (organist, other musicians, sexton, altar boys, choir director, and so forth) provided through the place of worship.

Schedule enough time with the officiant or site manager to address all your concerns. Larger congregations and many secular sites have planning staff who will be available to answer further questions and coordinate with your suppliers and vendors.

Reception Site

You'll go through much the same process with the manager or representative of your reception site (or the officiant if your reception will be held in the house of worship). Make an appointment to confirm the day and time of the reception; discuss your plans, including space needs; finalize your rental contract; and make the required deposit payment. Rented facilities often charge substantial cancellation fees, so read the contract thoroughly and ask about anything you don't understand.

Unless you plan a home reception, there are three basic types of reception sites:

Hotels, private clubs, and reception halls. Food, beverages, and service are generally provided by the site. The location may offer complete wedding packages, so ask about all the possibilities.

Sites that offer only space. The reception areas of most houses of worship, private meeting halls, civic sites, public parks, historic sites, galleries, museums—a wide variety of places—offer physical space, but you must provide everything else and also arrange access for your suppliers and vendors.

Restaurants. A restaurant wedding reception is a kind of hybrid. Some restaurants offer a full array of services, but most provide only the space, food and beverages, wait service, and cleanup. It may be possible to rent the entire restaurant or a private party room.

Whatever site you select, you should have at least one guided tour before signing an agreement. Look at the place from a practical point of view. Is the space large enough or possibly too large for your number of guests and the style of the reception? Are there storage spaces, a coatroom, and convenient restrooms? Are there private rooms if you plan to change clothes before you leave the reception? Check the lighting, electrical supply, and food preparation areas. If there's no kitchen, is there adequate water and cold storage? What kind of access is there for catering and delivery trucks? No detail is too small.

The site manager can probably provide much of the logistical information you need, including room measurements, but you should see for yourself. You may have attended other weddings and social events at the location, but to get a real sense of the place, see it in its everyday state.

The Military Advantage

When one or both members of an engaged couple are on active duty, they may have access to base facilities, including chapels and officers' clubs, for their ceremony and/or reception. The principal advantages are price (often lower than comparable off-base locations), convenience for guests who are also in the service, and flexibility. Base clubs will generally accommodate scheduling changes when a groom or bride is re-posted—without charging extra.

Retired service members and reservists also have access to military facilities, but children and other relatives of veterans do not. (For more about military traditions, see Chapter 36, page 636: "Military Titles"; Chapter 39, page 689: "Military seating protocol"; page 697: "A Military Wedding"; Chapter 40, page 716: "The Arch of Steel.")

Outdoor Ceremonies and Receptions

An outdoor service and/or reception might be held at home; a club, restaurant, reception hall, or place of worship with outdoor facilities; a favorite natural spot like a park or beach; or a historic site that is available for entertaining.

Be weather-conscious. Whatever the general climate, the weather on your wedding day is the great unpredictable. But you can check with meteorological sources in

Some couples wish to keep the wedding ceremony intimate and limit the guests to close family and friends. It is entirely correct to do so, and then follow a private wedding service with a larger reception if you like. (See Chapter 36, page 626: "Invitations to the Reception," for invitation formats.)

But the reverse—large wedding ceremony and small reception—is not acceptable, even though it will reduce costs. Those not invited to the reception will feel left out, as if they're not important enough to be included in the later celebration. Everyone invited to the wedding should be included in the reception, with the following exception:

Sometimes, a couple will invite all members of their religious congregation to the ceremony and a punch-and-wedding-cake reception immediately afterward, and wedding gifts are entirely optional. The ceremony and reception at the place of worship fulfill the etiquette fundamentals, so it's fine to host a separate, more elaborate reception later, with a guest list of family and good friends.

your area about historical weather trends such as periods of high wind or frequent thunderstorms.

Have a Plan B. You might feel as if you're planning two weddings, but you must have a fall-back plan. This will include an alternate indoor site and a plan to notify guests. (You can prepare "just in case" phone lists and provide these to attendants and family members.) Be ready to make a quick decision as early as possible if the weather doesn't cooperate.

Check on fees and permits. For a public site, there may be fees and you may need special permits, so talk with the appropriate authorities. Ask about any restrictions, such as bans on alcohol or campfires.

Think about access to the site. That remote sandy cove or field of wildflowers may be beautifully romantic but nearly impossible to get to. Consider your suppliers and your guests. Caterers, florists, and so on need access for their vehicles. Where will guests park? If walking to the site is difficult, you'll have to provide some form of transportation. Also plan ways for your guests, particularly the disabled or elderly, to get around easily. If the site has uneven walking surfaces, installing temporary level walkways may be necessary.

Provide directions. If the site is off the beaten track, include maps and detailed directions in your wedding invitations.

Planning the Wedding Feast

YOU'RE PROBABLY THINKING A LOT about the foods and drinks to serve at your reception, but before you decide on the menu, you need to consider logistics. The time and location of the reception, who will prepare the feast, the type of food service (discussed below), and your budget will be major factors in determining the final menu.

Passed-tray Service

Passed-tray service is ideal for afternoon and cocktail receptions when a full meal isn't provided. Waiters or helpers circulate among the guests and offer hors d'oeuvres from trays. Finger foods are the general rule, and cocktail napkins are provided. Sometimes the food trays are supplemented with crudités, cheeses, and fruit served from a buffet table or tables. If sauced or dipping foods are served, small plates, napkins, forks, skewers, and other utensils can be placed on these tables.

Determining costs for a passed-tray reception requires a reasonable estimate of quantities, and it's better to have too much than too little. Caterers and reception sites usually charge a per-person fee for hors d'oeuvres and can provide guidelines (say, six or seven servings per guest), but you may want to increase quantities if you expect a hungry crowd. Hiring servers or using a caterer's serving staff will add to the cost.

Passing hors d'oeuvres may precede a full buffet or seated dinner that includes a cocktail hour. In this case, fewer servings are probably needed.

Buffets

Buffet service adapts to any wedding style and is particularly well suited for brunch and luncheon receptions. Whether a buffet is more or less expensive than a seated meal depends on the costs of the foods served, the number of service staff required, and the amount of food likely to be consumed. Though a buffet doesn't involve separate food courses, guests are welcome to return to the buffet for second helpings, so people tend to eat more.

Guests select what they want from a single, long service table or several food stations devoted to different types of food. Serve-yourself is one option, but you may want waiters to serve at the buffet table, especially if the menu includes items such as large roasts that are carved on the spot or sauced dishes that can easily be spilled or dripped.

Guests sit at dining tables, which may or may not have assigned places. These tables can be large or small, though very large, circular tables tend to impede cross-table conversation. Normally, places are set with tableware, glasses, and napkins, but guests might pick up their own utensils and napkins at a casual buffet. Drinks can be served from a separate service table(s) or at the dining tables by waitstaff.

When guests return to the buffet, they leave their used plates on their tables and receive a clean plate at the buffet. (Waiters remove the used plate.) At a small or very casual reception (such as an outdoor barbecue or clambake), guests usually take their plates back to the buffet for another helping.

Seated Meals

At a traditional sit-down dinner or luncheon, guests are usually assigned places at dining tables and are served by waitstaff. Place cards can either be set on the tables or laid out alphabetically (complete with instructions regarding assigned tables) on a separate table where guests pick them up early in the reception. At a large reception, tables are often numbered, and the individual place cards indicate which table a guest is to go to. (See page 604: "Assigned Seating.")

Generally, a wedding meal comprises three courses—soup, salad, or appetizer; entrée (or entrée choices) with vegetables; and dessert—but can be more lavish. Whether you offer a choice of entrées, the food items are predetermined, so it's easier to estimate quantities than for a buffet. Per-person cost may actually be less than for a buffet, but the primary deciding factors will be the food itself (lobster will be more expensive than chicken) and the number of waitstaff required.

There are several variations on the method of service.

Plated service. The food is already arranged on the plates when they are set before the guests at the table.

Russian service. Empty plates are on the tables, and the waitstaff serve each course from platters. There may be more than one waiter; one serves the meats, another the vegetables, and a third might serve salad.

French service. One waiter holds the serving platter while another serves the plates. French service can be very efficient when guests are offered a choice of entrées.

You can also mix these styles—perhaps having plated salad and dessert courses and Russian or French service for the main course.

Do You Need a Caterer?

You may not need professional catering if the reception will be small and you have family and friends to help. But if the reception is not held at home, be sure there are adequate kitchen and preparation facilities, plus refrigeration, at the reception site.

In general, *hiring a caterer is recommended for receptions of more than thirty people.* Food preparation and service is a major undertaking and can be exhausting. It can also distract you and your families from seeing to the comfort of your reception guests and enjoying yourselves. Using a professional caterer can relieve the stress and allow you to be a guest at your own party.

The information on selecting, hiring, and working with caterers in Chapter 25, page 437: "The Catered Affair," should be helpful. Whether you use an on-premises or off-premises caterer, it's important to meet early and discuss all your options. Be ready with the information the caterer needs—the number of people to be served (guests, wedding party, plus musicians, photographers, etc.); the date, time, and style of the reception; location details, including the size of the space and its kitchen facilities; your general food preferences; and your budget. You should also talk about beverage and bar service (see "What to Drink?" below). Schedule a food tasting before you finalize the deal; pay attention to the quality of the service as well as the food you sample.

If you've never employed a caterer before, you should know that many caterers offer several levels of service, ranging from food preparation and delivery only to complete reception management. It's smart to talk to more than one caterer and learn as much as you can about their capabilities. You may find a company that can supply everything you need, including waitstaff, dinnerware and glasses, tables, chairs, and linens. Some large caterers provide (from their own inventory or through reliable suppliers) tents, dance floors, sound systems, floral and other decorations, plus post-party cleanup service.

Before you enter an agreement, check the caterer's references. Friends are a good source for recommendations, but it's essential to talk with people who have actually hired the caterer you're considering. Also, be sure you understand all costs. Is breakage insurance included or extra? Are gratuities and taxes included in the caterer's estimate? How will you be charged for any overtime?

What to Drink?

You will provide beverages, but you don't have to serve alcohol if you don't want to or you have religious or moral reasons not to. Some couples and their families don't drink alcohol themselves but do provide alcoholic drinks for their guests. Others restrict alcohol to wine, wine and beer, or just champagne for toasting. Budget is always a consideration, but these days, people are also limiting or eliminating liquor for health and safety reasons.

If you serve liquor, carefully estimate the amount of alcoholic drinks likely to be served. If you plan a seated dinner, your needs will include drinks for the cocktail hour and also with the meal. The two basic ways a caterer or a reception site can charge are:

Open bar. The hosts pay a flat fee for drinks served during a specific time period—either during the cocktail hour or for the entire event.

Consumption bar. Drinks are charged at a per-drink rate, and a running tab is kept for the time the bar is open. The hosts are charged for what is actually served.

The word "bar" doesn't have to be taken literally. Whether you offer liquor or not, beverage service may mean that drinks are passed on trays or served at drink stations (tables set up at convenient locations in the room) or from the buffet table. At a seated dinner and often at a buffet, wine is poured at the dining tables. For a very casual outdoor reception, drinks might be kept in ice coolers so guests can serve themselves.

You have many nonalcoholic beverage options. Juice-based punches are traditional, but not everybody wants sugary drinks, so it's a good idea to provide several choices. Diet colas, natural juices, water and tea (plain and flavored), coffee—just think about your guests' tastes. Any beverage can be substituted for champagne.

We're working on a very tight budget for our wedding and reception. Lately we've heard of couples who finance their receptions with a cash bar or by asking guests to pay for their dinners. Is this okay?

Just imagine being invited to a dinner party at which the host or hostess handed guests a bill. You'd be shocked. A wedding is no different; the couple and their families are hosts, not restaurateurs. You might cut costs by serving simple hors d'oeuvres, wedding cake, and nonalcoholic punch at an afternoon reception; planning a home reception to eliminate the expense of a rented hall or hotel; or limiting the number of guests you invite. You don't have to have a bar; if you want champagne, you could limit it to one or two glasses per guest for toasting. There are many ways to stage a beautiful wedding on a tight budget, but charging guests isn't one of them.

Assigned Seating

For sit-down dinners and formal buffets, the couple usually determines the seating arrangements. Deciding who sits with whom requires tact, consideration, and a sense of fun, so it's wise to begin thinking it over early—though you won't be able to complete your plan until you've received most of the guest replies. Be sure to get an exact diagram of table placement from your reception site manager.

Place cards are recommended for seated dinners and formal buffets with more than twenty guests. For small receptions with only a few tables, you can put a card at each guest's place. At larger receptions, tables are usually numbered. The number of each guest's table is then written on his or her card. On entering the reception area or after going through the receiving line, guests pick up their cards at a small table near the reception entrance; the cards are arranged alphabetically by last name. Sometimes, particularly at informal and casual receptions, couples use place cards only at the bridal party and parents' tables, and other guests seat themselves as they wish.

Parents' tables. Customarily, each set of parents has their own table, complete with some family members, close friends, or both. If the numbers of people involved are small, the bride's and the groom's families can be seated together. However, it's probably best to seat divorced parents and their families at different tables. The divorced parents may be amicable, but their separate entourages of family and friends are often too large for a single table.

The bridal party table. The bridal table is generally a rectangular or U-shaped table set at one end of the room. The newlyweds sit at the center, facing all the guests, and no one is placed opposite them. The bride sits to the groom's right. The best man sits next to the bride, and the maid or matron of honor is seated next to the groom. Bridesmaids and groomsmen then alternate places. If there's enough room, spouses and partners of wedding party members can be included. The children or siblings of the couple can also sit at the table. (Including the children of an encore couple is a thoughtful way to emphasize family unity.) When young children in the wedding are seated with the bridal party, their parents are also included.

If the bridal party is large, two round tables might be used. The bride, groom, best man, maid of honor, and some other attendants, plus spouses and partners, are seated at one table; the rest of the attendants and their spouses or partners are at the other.

Informal bridal party seating. Some couples prefer not to have a formal bridal table, choosing instead to move about the room and visit with guests during dinner. Still, a table should be reserved for their attendants, even though they may not all eat at the same time. At a buffet, the couple can go to the buffet table with their guests or a waiter can bring filled plates to them wherever they're seated. Though the members of the wedding party may not sit with the couple for the meal, they should all gather for toasts and the cutting of the wedding cake.

Other guest tables. Deciding where to seat other guests is up to you. Your basic objective is to make each table as congenial as possible. Couples usually try to mix and match—considering guests' interests and personalities. The following practical guidelines will help you devise a successful seating plan:

➤ Married, engaged, and steady couples can sit at the same table, but to keep conversation flowing, it's usually best not to put spouses and other committed couples next to each other.

➤ Seating one stranger at a table where the rest of the guests are close friends can leave the person feeling like the odd man (or woman) out.

➤ Dining and conversing with people of other generations can be interesting for everyone, so try to vary ages if possible.

➤ Younger children are usually seated with their parents. But older children and teens often enjoy *not* being with their parents. Take your cues from what you know about a young person's preferences.

➤ Infirm or disabled guests need special consideration. A person who has difficulty walking may need a table near the entrance or restrooms. A person with impaired sight or hearing might enjoy a place near the bridal table or the band. People in wheelchairs should have easy access to tables.

You can ask some people if they have seating preferences (a guest with a physical disability, for example), but don't make it a general practice. Taking requests will just confuse your seating chart. Trust your instincts and common sense.

The Wedding Cake

AMONG THE OLDEST WEDDING TRADITIONS is the cake—probably because wheat and other grains, seeds, and nuts are universal symbols of fertility. The ancient Greeks served sesame seed pies. Small wheat cakes were shared at Roman weddings. Wheat biscuits were broken over the bride's head at early Anglo-Saxon weddings.

In the 1800s, wedding cakes reached their literal high point in Europe and the United States. The cake for the 1871 marriage of Queen Victoria's daughter Princess Louise stood five feet high and weighed almost 225 pounds. (The 1947 wedding of Princess Elizabeth and the Duke of Edinburgh featured a four-tiered cake—nine feet high, 500 pounds, and decorated with, among other things, sugar replicas of Buckingham Palace and Windsor and Balmoral Castles!)

Wedding cakes have, in the main, come back to earth, but are still the visual focal point of many receptions. (For information on placement, cutting, and serving see Chapter 39, page 703: "Cutting the Cake.") The traditional cake is round or square, multi-tiered, and frosted in white or pale pastels. But there's no real limit on the size, shape, color, and style. Cakes often reflect the color scheme or general theme of the wedding.

You might want a sheet cake rather than tiers. Some couples skip the cake cutting and serve individual iced cakes to their guests. Another option is to display a frosted cardboard or foam-core *faux* cake, with slices of real cake plated in and served from the kitchen.

Costs and Cake Bakers

The cost of the cake will depend on the quantity required, the cake size, the relative simplicity or elaborateness of the decoration, and who does the baking. A custom-designed, professionally baked cake can cost thousands of dollars. If you have a caterer or your reception site is catering, they may be your best source. Or you can use a bakery or grocery bakery department. You may have a favorite restaurant that includes a bakery or a master baker who does wedding cakes. Fortunate indeed is the couple with a relative or friend who is a skilled baker and offers to make the cake.

Orders are usually placed at least six to eight weeks in advance of the reception—earlier if you want a popular baker during the busiest wedding months. If you're marrying on very short notice, a professional bakery or grocery store bakery can usually supply a quality cake and often add the decorative touches you want.

If your cake is prepared by someone other than your caterer or the reception-site baker, you need to coordinate delivery and final preparation of the cake. (Tiered cakes are usually assembled at the reception site.) Provide your caterer and baker with each other's names and phone numbers. Your baker may also need contact information for your florist and reception site manager.

A custom that is experiencing a revival, the groom's cake is smaller (one or two tiers) than the wedding cake and usually of a different flavor. A rich, fruit-and-nut-filled cake is traditional, but today's choice is more likely to be an iced chocolate, carrot, or rum cake—sometimes baked in a novelty shape, like a football, or decorated in a manner that reflects a special interest of the groom. The groom's cake can be served at the reception and is usually placed on a separate table from the wedding cake. Or wrapped slices can be presented to guests. (See page 612: "Favors for Your Guests.")

Flowers and Decorations

WHATEVER THE SEASON, flowers add beauty and romance to any wedding. The kinds and amounts of flowers are your choice, but the following guidelines can help you plan your floral scheme. (Bouquets and flowers for the wedding party are discussed in Chapter 37, page 663: "Flowers for the Wedding Party.")

➤ In general, the more formal the wedding, the more formal the floral arrangements and bouquets. White is the traditional color for very formal weddings.

➤ White and brightly hued flowers tend to stand out when the wedding is held in the twilight and evening hours, when the lighting is soft, or when the ceremony is in candlelight.

➤ Flowers can provide a unifying visual theme. You might work with a limited color palette (reds and pinks, for instance) for both the ceremony and the reception. You can choose flowers and arrangement forms that reflect the overall theme and formality of the wedding—straw baskets of wildflowers, for example, for an informal summer wedding.

➤ Locally grown seasonal flowers are usually fresher, last longer, and are less expensive than flowers shipped from distant suppliers.

➤ Choose flowers and greenery with the architecture and décor of the wedding and reception sites in mind. A high or vaulted ceiling calls for taller arrangements and plants. A lush outdoor site may need few or no extra adornments. If the reception is under a tent, however, flowers can soften the space and add romance.

➤ Scents should be subtle. Strongly scented flowers in a small or enclosed space can be stifling, but intense fragrances will dissipate in an outdoor setting. If you or your attendants are allergic to certain flowers, use silk flowers for bouquets and boutonnieres or mix silk and real. Scentless candles are also recommended.

There are many ways to have dreamy flowers and still save money. It might be possible to share ceremony floral arrangements (and costs) with another couple marrying in the same location on the same day. You might buy flowers in bulk or pick them from your garden, and you and a helpful friend could do the arrangements. Be creative. Adding a few stemmed flowers to potted houseplants can make elegant table decorations. Instead of an expensive floral arrangement on the buffet table, you might use sprays of seasonal blossoms and ivy tucked around serving dishes or topiaries of an herb like rosemary (symbolic of wisdom and faithfulness).

Even if your budget is small, you may want to work with a florist. A florist can advise you about what seasonal flowers are available and may be able to get lower prices on fresh flowers purchased in bulk. He or she may also have rental services for live or artificial greenery and silk flower arrangements for the altar. Some florists and floral designers offer fee-based consultation service, and it may be worth the expense to get expert guidance and referrals to suppliers even if you or a helper will do the flowers.

Employing a Florist

If you don't have a florist in mind, get recommendations from friends, caterers, the managers of your ceremony and reception sites, even local nurseries. Interview possible choices, but always call for an appointment. In your initial calls, it's courteous to tell florists that you are speaking with several people and aren't yet ready to sign a contract. Tell them the date and time of the wedding; if a florist is booked solid for your wedding day, you needn't waste his and your time.

The three most important criteria for choosing a florist are professional competence, experience with weddings, and a collaborative approach. A good florist will listen to your plans and be respectful of your taste and budget. You, in turn, need to be open to new ideas and willing to consider alternatives.

During interviews, look at each florist's portfolio. This will give you a feeling for their design capabilities and problem-solving skills. For example, if you want imaginative designs and a florist's album contains only photos of very traditional arrangements, you need to be very clear about your objectives. Some florists welcome the opportunity to be unconventional; others are less flexible.

After making your choice, discuss these specific issues with the florist:

Your budget for flowers. Everything from choice of flowers to numbers and types of arrangements will depend on how much you want to spend. Be prepared to discuss your priorities: The bridal bouquets? The reception table centerpieces? An experienced florist can stretch the budget if he knows what matters most to you.

Before signing a contract, discuss financial arrangements, including initial deposits and other payment deadlines. Be sure there are no hidden costs, such as taxes, delivery charges, and gratuities. You may want an itemized bill to ensure you receive what you paid for. (Itemizing also protects the florist when a client adds extras that aren't part of the original estimate.)

~ Helping the Florist ~

A florist shouldn't have to guess about your taste in flowers and floral designs. But it isn't always easy to describe what you like in words. So why not say it with pictures? You can clip photos from wedding, gardening, and home decorating magazines. If you don't know the correct names of flowers and plants, you might get a seed catalog or even seed packets at a local garden supply store. Do some research at the library. Then tell your florist what attracts you to certain flowers and arrangements—colors, shapes, perhaps associations with special places.

The overall theme of the wedding and details of the location(s). The florist needs to know the time and style of the wedding, wedding theme if you have one, your color preferences, the décor and sizes of the ceremony and reception sites, the type of reception service (seated dinner, buffet, or passed-tray service). You may not have all this information when you first talk, but give your florist the best descriptions you can. If he doesn't know the sites, provide floor plans and measurements; color photos will be a big help. Provide the names and phone numbers of ceremony and reception site managers, the caterer, and anyone else whom the florist may need to consult.

Installation and delivery. Do you want the florist to install all or some of the floral decorations, or do you need only delivery? Will flowers be delivered to one or several locations? When should deliveries be made? (For example, will flowers for a morning wedding remain fresh if delivered the night before?)

As soon as you can, provide the florist with complete delivery information: dates and times; address and directions to the site(s); precise information about site access and parking; names, addresses, and all telephone numbers for site managers, wedding coordinators, and anyone who will supervise deliveries and installations for you. If you are unable to be there and don't have a wedding consultant, try to have a parent, attendant, or someone else who's familiar with your plans at the site(s) when the delivery truck arrives.

Other floral needs. You may want your florist to handle floral gifts for wedding helpers, table arrangements for the rehearsal party, thank-you flowers for shower and party hosts, and welcome flowers for out-of-town guests staying at hotels. These items and delivery schedules should be included in your plans. Supply the florist with cards or thank-you notes to be included with floral gifts.

You might also include flowers and ribbons to mark pews, flower baskets for a flower girl, and decoration of the unity candle if you have one. If you will want fresh flowers on the wedding cake, your florist will need to coordinate with the caterer.

Flowers for the Ceremony

If your ceremony will be held in a house of worship, ask your officiant about any restrictions or limitations on the use of floral arrangements, greenery (including decorating the *chuppah*, or canopy, for Jewish ceremonies), and candles. Think about the place. Many religious sites are inherently decorative and need little embellishment; others are beautifully simple and benefit from arrangements that reflect that simplicity.

Whether the site is religious or secular, floral decorations are background and should not be so profuse or ostentatious that they overshadow the location or the wedding party. If your ceremony and reception are at separate locations, you may want the same colors and general floral theme at both, but the sites may be dissimilar in general appearance and require somewhat different treatments.

Flowers for the Reception

Again, you can have as many or as few floral decorations as you like, but consider what really suits the site. The following pointers can be useful as you plan your reception flowers:

➤ Guests need to be able to see across dining tables, so centerpieces should be low (below eye level) or elevated in tall vases (above eye level). Candles should be placed so that they don't interfere with the line of sight of seated diners. Flowers on buffet tables shouldn't impede food service.

➤ The bride's and attendants' bouquets can substitute for centerpieces on the bridal table(s). In addition to cutting reception costs, this charming custom enables guests to get a closer look at your flowers. Bouquets can also be placed around the wedding cake.

➤ Seasonal greenery can expand your decorations and stretch the budget. Swags, garlands, and sprays of greens lend natural elegance to staircases, arches, and doorways and can add volume to flower arrangements. Colorful autumn leaves can be used alone or mixed with seasonal flowers for spectacular displays.

➤ Potted plants can make attractive dining and service table arrangements. One idea is to use clusters of pretty pots, containing blooming plants or fragrant herbs, as centerpieces; each guest then takes a plant as a wedding favor.

➤ Hanging baskets filled with flowers and trailing plants add bursts of color and can be used indoors and out. Be sure there is strong structural support for baskets and other suspended objects.

Other Decorative Ideas

Flowers aren't your only option. There are numerous creative ways to add personal touches, especially to the reception.

Mood lighting. Indoors or out, you can supplement the basic lighting with romantic touches—twinkling fairy lights strung in trees, shrubs, and topiaries; hanging lanterns; and luminarias. The glow of candlelight is flattering, as long as there's enough electric light for people to see. In a reception hall or large room, the lights can be adjusted, so work with your site manager to get the right levels for special moments like your first dance. It's very important to have adequate lighting for late afternoon and evening weddings held outdoors; rough ground, steps, stone and concrete paths, and terraced areas can be hazards when poorly lit.

Table linens and fabrics. Traditionally, tablecloths and napkins are white for a formal reception. But more colorful fabrics are increasingly popular, and the colors of linens often carry out the color scheme of the wedding. Patterned and textured fabrics may add to the overall gaiety of the occasion—tartan plaid tablecloths for a Celtic theme or shimmering silver and gold table runners for a wedding near the New Year.

Themed decorations. If your wedding has a theme, you might include related objects in the decorations (for instance, using carved pumpkin centerpieces at a late October reception). It's best to avoid items that are too juvenile or simply too odd. Overdoing the decorations or using inappropriate items will distract from the real purpose of the occasion. If the reception is in a place of worship, consult with the officiant about all decorations.

Personal memorabilia. Some couples include photos of themselves and other personally significant items among the decorations. Displays of family photos and memorabilia might be arranged on the guest-book table or around dining table centerpieces. For a second marriage, including photos of the couple's children is a meaningful way to celebrate the creation of a new family.

Since items may be lost or damaged, it's advisable to use photocopies or replicas of your personal treasures. As with themed decorations, take care not to overdo it. You will be the undisputed stars of the occasion, so poster-sized enlargements of your favorite snapshots or slide or videotape reviews of your lives from cradle to wedding day would be excessive.

Music and Musicians

THOUGH MUSIC ISN'T A MUST AT A RECEPTION it can play several important roles: setting and maintaining the mood of the occasion; giving cues for specific ceremony and reception activities (the processional, the cutting of the wedding cake, and so on) and transitions (from cocktails to dinner, for instance); and providing a pleasant background for conversation.

When hiring musicians, audition before you make a commitment. If possible, you should see and hear the musicians—whether a soloist, a band, or a DJ—in a live performance. At the least, ask for a tape or tapes. Be sure that the performers are the ones

Gifts to the people who attend your wedding are not necessary unless part of your cultural tradition or local custom. A favor is intended as a remembrance of the occasion and need not be extravagant or expensive.

One popular favor—a wrapped or boxed slice of the groom's cake—derives from the old custom of giving unmarried guests a small piece of wedding cake. (Sleeping with the cake under their pillows was supposed to bring dreams of their future marriage partners.) Other ideas include small boxes of chocolates or mints, pots of flowers, and Victorian-style tussy-mussies (small bouquets of flower buds in cone-shaped containers of waterproof paper). During a holiday season, favors can be something appropriate like a Christmas ornament or a miniature flag for the Fourth of July. Making favors by hand can be time-consuming. Imprinting favors with your names and wedding date can add unnecessary expense.

Favors are usually set at each guest's place for a seated meal. At a buffet or passed-tray reception, favors can be arranged on a table near the exit, so guests can take one as they leave. Small bottles of wine are sometimes given, but a couple should be cautious. It's not smart to give alcohol to guests who will be driving. Avoid anything dangerous, such as sparklers or firecrackers.

Weddings

| 612 |

who will actually appear at your wedding. If the terrific soloist you heard at another wedding or on a tape has since moved on, you won't get the performance you expect.

Recorded music has greatly expanded the musical possibilities for receptions. Hiring a musician or musicians who can do double duty—playing for the ceremony and reception—can also ease the budget. Talented friends and family members might perform for the sheer delight of making your day special.

You should provide musicians, singers, and DJs with all the information they need, including size and shape of the space and its acoustical characteristics, availability of amplification systems if needed, and access to the site prior to the event. Some other issues to raise before you hire musicians or a DJ include the following:

All costs and methods of payment. Clarify payment deadlines, overtime and cancellation fees, and any extra charges such as travel expenses.

Repertoire. Review the musicians' and/or DJ's playlist. Is it sufficiently varied? Does it include the music you really want? If you plan to include ethnic music or songs in another language, be sure the musicians know the pieces.

Meals. You're responsible for meals for musicians who perform during lunch or dinner. (Meals for musicians and other hired professionals need not be the same as you serve your guests. Your caterer can provide good, hearty meals at a reasonable cost.)

Number and duration of breaks. For receptions, the general standard is one break of five to ten minutes per hour.

Special requests. Do you want music that reflects your wedding theme? Are the reception musicians familiar with numbers for special moments, including your first dance and dances with parents? Are they prepared to take requests from the guests?

Style of presentation. There's no real need for a bandleader or DJ to speak at a reception, beyond perhaps asking guests for silence for an invocation or toasts. A constant stream of amplified patter or joking from the bandstand can be annoying and sometimes distasteful. If you want the bandleader or DJ to act as master of ceremonies, be clear about the behavior and language you expect.

Ask for and check references. Study contracts carefully before signing, and be sure that everyone's responsibilities are crystal clear. Schedule a meeting with the musician, group leader, DJ, or their agent as soon as you've made your music choices and the wedding format is set. Provide a written list of your selections; work out the order of play; plan breaks and meals; and schedule any changeovers, as when the reception program switches from dinner to dance music or a live group is replaced by a DJ. Advise performers about whom to contact at the site, such as the event coordinator or audiovisual specialist at a hotel or the officiant or music director at a place of worship.

Music for the Ceremony

If you plan your ceremony in a house of worship, check with the officiant and/or music director about any restrictions on music. A growing number of religions and denominations are imposing rules and even banning all secular music (including the ultra-traditional "Bridal Chorus" from Wagner's *Lohengrin* and Mendelssohn's "Wedding March" from *A Midsummer Night's Dream*).

The house organist or other musicians affiliated with the site may be the best choice to play, since they already know the place and its acoustics, the organ or piano, and the timing of religious services. If you want outside musicians or singers, you must clear your plans with the officiant. Visiting organists and other musicians may need to coordinate practice time with officials of the wedding site.

Apart from specific religious requirements, the quantity of music is up to you. While it's traditional to have music for the procession and recession, intimate weddings are sometimes celebrated without musical accompaniment. You might dispense with the prelude and postlude. Today, the traditional musical components, listed below, offer a menu of choices.

Prelude. A program of music that begins a half hour before the wedding, the prelude can be played by an organist or other single musician or an ensemble and can include a choir or vocal soloist.

Processional. This music signals the beginning of the ceremony. It begins when the bride's mother is seated, the groom and best man enter, and the rest of the wedding party are ready to make their entrance. The same piece can be played throughout the procession, but many brides walk to different music.

Ceremony. Couples often include one or two hymns or songs in the ceremony. These might be solo or choral performances or sung by all the guests. If everyone joins in, choose a song that most guests are familiar with. You might include the words in the wedding program.

Recessional. The music played as a couple exits the ceremony site reflects the joy of their new union and might be accompanied by trumpets or ringing bells.

Postlude. Played as the guests leave the ceremony site, the postlude is a piece or short program that continues the joyful mood of the recessional.

At the Reception

Music, whether live or recorded, enhances the festive mood of any reception. The following guidelines should help you select music and musicians tailored to your occasion.

A midday or afternoon reception (lunch, brunch, or limited buffet). When dancing isn't planned, keep the music low-key, so guests can talk. A single pianist, harpist, violinist, flutist, or guitarist, or a small ensemble will add to the mood without being obtrusive. For recorded music, couples can indulge their romantic side and chose instrumental pieces that are light and lovely.

A cocktail reception. The music tends to lively, but not so loud that it drowns out conversation. A pianist, instrumental combo, or classical or jazz group are popular choices. You might match the music to your theme—a bluegrass band for a country

~ Just What Is Appropriate Music? ~

"Appropriate" boils down to music that is acceptable within your religious and cultural traditions, in keeping with the style and formality of the festivities, and comfortable for your guests. This doesn't mean stuffy or bland. Nor must the music be from the classical repertoire. If allowed, a favorite movie theme, show tune, or pop song might be adapted for your ceremony.

Reception music can be whatever you like. When you discuss music selections with the performers or DJ, be clear about what you *don't* want (such as endless repetitions of "Endless Love"). Think carefully about lyrics and avoid anything with strong sexual or violent content. Most people who react negatively to crude lyrics are not prudes; they simply know what's appropriate for a wedding.

Many couples choose a romantic tune for their first dance as husband and wife, but there's no reason to exclude a rousing piece. Just be sure that your selection fits the occasion and that, if you have a live band or orchestra, they can play the piece with agility.

Traditionally, after their special dance, the bride dances with her father and the groom with his mother, and then other guests join in. But when parents are divorced and there are stepparents to consider, it's fine to break with tradition if you decide that's best. You can ask parents, stepparents, and their spouses or partners to take the floor at a certain point.

wedding or strolling musicians who can move among the guests at an outdoor reception. In general, avoid vocal soloists because guests feel that they must stop talking to listen. But a musical interlude, during which guests gather to enjoy some bravura playing and singing, can be a treat.

A dinner dance. Your choices range from a dance band to a full orchestra to a DJ. The basic logistical concern is that the music suit the size of the reception area and the number of guests. An unamplified quartet will not be sufficient for a reception of three hundred in a grand ballroom but might be just right for seventy people in a smaller setting.

You want musicians or a recorded program that changes as the evening progresses from cocktail to dinner hours and then to the dance. For a large reception, a full orchestra can handle the musical mix, or you might have a band play through dinner and the first dances, and then switch to a DJ when the dancing gets lively.

Transportation and Travel Arrangements

UNLESS THE CEREMONY AND RECEPTION are held at your home, getting from one place to another requires planning. It isn't necessary to hire vehicles; you might do nothing more than spruce up the family car or cars. What matters is that everyone involved in the wedding gets where they need to be on time.

In general, the bride's family organizes transportation for the bridal attendants to the wedding and reception. The best man and/or head usher coordinates for the groomsmen and ushers. The best man usually drives the groom to the ceremony site, sometimes drives the newlyweds to the reception, and often organizes transportation for the couple when they leave the reception.

Wedding party members may arrange their own transportation, but they must know scheduled arrival times. If wedding participants drive themselves, you may need to reserve convenient parking for them—even for home weddings. Children in the wedding are usually brought to the ceremony site by their parents; they may go to the reception with the other attendants or the bride's parents, but it's fine if they want to ride with their families.

Be sure that wedding attendants have a ride home or to their lodgings from the reception. Ask the best man, head usher, or reliable relatives to see that every attendant has a safe ride and to stop anyone (attendants and guests alike) who has overindulged from driving.

Limousine Service

Working with a limousine service doesn't necessarily mean you must hire stretch limos. You may want less dramatic vehicles that are attractive and roomy enough for the people you will transport. Whatever your preference, begin interviewing reputable rental services as soon as your ceremony and reception sites are confirmed—limousine companies are often booked many months in advance for peak times.

The traditional complement of hired cars comprises:

➤ A car to the ceremony site for the bride and her father or escort (if the bride won't be dressing at the site)

➤ Cars from the ceremony to the reception for (1) the bride and groom (2) the bride's mother or both parents plus any children in the wedding party and/or bridesmaids, and (3) the rest of the bride's attendants

You'll need more if you provide transportation for special guests, grandparents, and other family members. On the other hand, you may want only one hired car for the bride and groom's drive to the reception.

When you arrange rentals, be precise about locations, determine exact times that drivers will be needed, and provide detailed directions to unfamiliar sites. Discuss drivers' attire so that their style of dress will be in keeping with the occasion. If you plan to decorate rented cars, ask about any restrictions.

How About a Horse and Carriage?

Maybe you want to arrive at the reception in a romantic horse-drawn or Cinderella carriage. Perhaps a caravan of taxis is just the thing to set a bright, fun tone for the celebration. The ideas are myriad, from hay wagons to classic vintage cars to motorcycles!

Sometimes, it's necessary to transport guests from parking areas to the ceremony and/or reception sites. Vans, buses, trolleys, even golf carts, can do the job. Arrangements to hire these vehicles and other novelty transportation must normally be made well in advance, just as for limos. Pay close attention to the qualifications of drivers. Check with your local municipal authorities about proper licenses for various vehicles and any legal restrictions on the use of public roads.

Travel and Accommodations

If members of your wedding party and guests are coming from out of town or you're planning a destination wedding, you have certain obligations.

For attendants and officiant. The couple and/or their families are financially responsible for accommodations for attendants, and for the accommodations and travel expenses of any officiant who must travel to the wedding location. Attendants usually make their own travel plans. When they arrive by plane, train, or bus, you or a family member or someone in the wedding party should meet them and transport them to their lodgings. (For advice about destination wedding travel, see Chapter 34, page 581: "Faraway Places.")

Though hotel/motel accommodations may be the obvious choice, you might have family members and friends who would be delighted to have an attendant or clergyperson as their houseguest. If attendants want to rent cars or to stay on after the night of the wedding, the cost of these extras is theirs.

For your guests. You aren't financially responsible for guest travel and accommodations, but you can help by providing information about hotels, motels, and inns in the area. (See Chapter 36, page 643: "A Mailing for Travelers.")

When there are a substantial number of out-of-towners, couples often arrange for a block of rooms to be available in one or two hotels or motels near the wedding location—sometimes the hotel that is the site of the reception. Guests receive a group discount, but the wedding hosts may be required to pay a booking deposit. There's usually a deadline for guests to make reservations in order to secure the lower rate. If you reserve rooms, be sure you understand your financial obligations, including any charges for late cancellations. Then inform your out-of-town guests as soon as possible and include the name or group code under which the rooms are reserved.

Sometimes, a couple or their families will pay for a guest's travel and accommodations—usually when this is the only way a valued friend or family member can attend. This generosity should be kept strictly between the hosts and the guest; to tell others might cause embarrassment for the person and hurt feelings if someone else feels the kind gesture is unfair.

Photos and Videos

BEFORE HIRING A PHOTOGRAPHER and/or videographer, couples need to consider several questions. Budget is primary, but almost as important is the type of visual record you prefer. Do you want the traditional album of posed wedding photos, mostly candid shots, or a mix of both? Do you want to record the entire event or just the ceremony or the reception? Do you really want costly videotaping, or are you feeling pressured because "everybody's doing it"?

Be honest as you discuss your feelings. Are you going to take great pleasure in looking at your wedding album and video for years to come? Or are they likely to

A number of our wedding guests will be staying at local hotels, and we want to give them something to say welcome when they arrive. Can you suggest ideas that are appropriate but not too expensive?

It's a nice touch to provide an arrangement of flowers or a fruit or food basket, but there are plenty of gracious ways to say "we're so glad you're here" without breaking your budget. How about a single flower and your personal note on the pillow? Or maybe a plate of cookies or small box of candy with a note? Or just a nice note together with a tourist map and a brochure about your area. It's a good idea to provide any details or instructions guests might need, such as the names of other wedding guests staying at the same place and directions from the hotel to locations of the rehearsal dinner, ceremony, and reception.

Don't forget to thank the hotel staff who put your welcome gifts in guests' rooms. Based on the number of rooms and amount of work involved, a tip may be in order, so consult in advance with the hotel guest services manager to determine what's appropriate.

gather dust on a shelf somewhere? (In the latter case, you might limit the professional picture-taking to basic posed photos and have friends take candid shots.) Ultimately, you should please yourselves, but don't overlook the following practical matters:

➤ Check with your officiant about any restrictions on photography/videotaping in the ceremony location or during the ceremony. If photography is prohibited during the service, you can probably stage photographs before or after.

➤ When you interview photographers/videographers, study their portfolios carefully. You don't have to be an expert to see when pictures and tapes are poorly framed, badly lighted, or fuzzy. Also listen to the audio on tapes and evaluate the sound quality.

➤ Ask about wedding packages and what's included: number and size of prints and options such as fewer but larger prints. Discuss any other items you want, such as formal engagement and wedding portraits, black-and-white prints for newspaper announcements, extra prints and photo albums, and extra videotapes.

➤ Talk about exactly what you want photographed or videotaped and in what style. Do you want color or black-and-white shots or some of both? If you want perfect still-life photos of the wedding cake and decorations, the photographer may be able to take them or to recommend a commercial photographer skilled in this type of work.

➤ Get all the details about costs, including taxes, overtime charges, and fees/expenses for travel time and pre-wedding inspections of the site.

➤ Find out how photos will be selected. Will you receive a completed album or can you select photos from contact sheets? Ask about copyright restrictions. Decide who will keep the negatives; if the photographer keeps them, ask how long they'll stay on file. If the photographer will be shooting digitally, can you get a disk of all the shots?

➤ If you plan to send a photo with your post-wedding thank-you notes, discuss the fastest way to get delivery of prints. Order photo note cards and envelopes. (Waiting for the pictures is not a valid excuse to delay writing.)

You and your photographer/videographer should feel comfortable working together. Few couples have the time or energy to cope with a prima donna at their wedding, so if you interview a photographer/videographer who seems very demanding, be aware that he or she may be difficult to work with. Professional photographers and videographers—whether they specialize in the traditional posed style or the spontaneous reportage approach—know to be unobtrusive. Still, their work will be easier when you are clear about:

➤ What photos or scenes you want and the settings you prefer for posed shots

➤ Whom to include (For candid shots, provide the photographer/videographer with a list of people you want in shots and assign an attendant or family member to help the photographer spot special people.)

➤ Approximate times of special activities (cutting the cake, first dance, etc.)

Finally, be considerate of your photographer/videographer's schedule. Yours may not be the only event he or she is doing that day, so don't expect extra time unless the photographer agrees. Remember that you must provide meals for the photographer/videographer and any assistants if they work through normal lunch or dinner hours.

Cameras for the Guests

Providing disposable cameras for guests can be great fun if everyone understands the rules. The idea is for guests to snap other guests in unposed moments and leave the cameras behind for the newlyweds. Problems arise because many guests think they are supposed to get photos of the couple, and the bride and groom can't take a step without a camera in their faces.

People need instructions, so provide written details with the cameras or have someone make an announcement. Keep the instructions simple and include the location of a collecting place for the cameras if they're not to be left on dining tables. If you're planning a wedding Web page, you might also provide the Internet address.

Chapter Thirty-six

Wedding Invitations and Announcements

THE MOST IMPORTANT MESSAGE of your wedding invitation is that you want to share the celebration of your upcoming marriage with people who are special to you and your families. Your invitation will tell guests not only when and where you will marry, but also the style and tone of your wedding. It will indicate the religious or secular nature of your service, and the formality or informality of the occasion.

Traditional invitation style and wording evolved to give invitees all the details in an instantly recognizable format. But times have changed, and today's couples are free to vary traditional forms or to design their invitations however they like. Yet from the most formal to the most casual—even when phoned, faxed, or e-mailed because a couple decide to marry on very short notice—all wedding invitations should honor tradition to the extent of providing the information guests need to plan their schedules, send their replies, make travel arrangements if necessary, and select their attire for the big day.

Timing for Orders and Mailing

WEDDING INVITATIONS ARE USUALLY MAILED six to eight weeks before the wedding date. To place your invitation order in time, count backward from your mailing date. As a general rule, plan on at least two months for printing and delivery of formal printed invitations, enclosures, and envelopes. The wait may be less for nontraditional invitations, but get a reasonable time frame from your stationer or supplier. Should you decide to laser-print or handwrite your invitations, you'll still need time to select attractive papers and envelopes and develop your design. In addition to preparation time, schedule at least an additional two weeks to address and assemble your invitations. If possible, add a few "just in case" days into your ordering and addressing schedule—just in case something unexpected delays your preparations.

Some Invitation Tips

Here are some good ideas that should make the invitation process proceed without stress and strain.

- ➤ Make sure that your supplier can deliver invitation envelopes to you as early as possible, so you can get a head start addressing them.
- ➤ Mistakes happen, so order at least a dozen extra invitations and envelopes or just the envelopes. Also order extras as keepsakes for yourself and your family.
- ➤ Since replies and gifts are normally sent to the return address on the envelope or with the RSVP, be sure that the person or people at that address—the bride, parents, the couple- -can keep track of responses and gift deliveries. Establish your system for recording all replies and gifts.
- ➤ For addressing, you need the full names and titles for all guests; be certain that spellings are correct. Make note of relationships ("Bob's mom's best friend," "Linda's fiancé") as you assemble your list; these details can be helpful when you greet guests whom you don't know personally, arrange table seating for the reception, and write your thank-you notes.

What's Your Style?

STATIONERS AND PRINTERS CAN PROVIDE catalogs and samples, and you will have an almost endless variety of papers, shades and colors, designs, typefaces, and extras to choose from. Whatever you select, the style of the invitation should reflect the nature of your ceremony and reception—the more formal the occasion, the more formal the invitation. (For information about engraving and other printing styles, see Chapter 17, page 225: "A Printing Primer.")

Traditional Formal Invitations

The formal wedding invitation has a precise form and style. It's printed on a heavy-weight paper of ivory, soft cream, or white. The paper can be flat or have a raised plate mark or margin. Formal invitations may be a large double sheet that is folded twice, a sheet folded once, or a single sheet.

The lettering style for a formal invitation is generally classic and conservative—a serif type such as Roman—and is printed in black or dark gray ink. If a family coat of arms or crest is included, it's printed at the top center of the page in the same color as the typeface. No other ornamentation is printed on the invitation.

Traditional Wording for a Wedding Invitation

Invitations are customarily written in third-person style, and the wording and spelling are governed by the following conventions:

➤ The words "honour" and "favour" ("the favour of a reply . . .") are traditionally written in the British style. But the American spellings, "honor" and "favor," are acceptable if a couple prefers.

➤ The phrase "request the honour of your presence" is correct for an invitation to a ceremony held in a house of worship and may also be used for formal and semiformal weddings in other locations.

➤ For invitations to a reception only, the wording is "request the pleasure of your company . . ."

➤ While traditional invitations use the phrase "*at* the marriage of," it's correct to alter the wording to make grammatical sense in a less formal invitation. For example: "invite you *to* the wedding of" or "hope you will join us *for* the wedding of . . ."

➤ When a Roman Catholic mass is part of the ceremony, invitations may include the phrase "and your participation in the offering of the Nuptial Mass" on a separate line below the groom's name.

➤ There is no punctuation except periods after abbreviations (Mr., Mrs., Ms.) and where phrases requiring commas appear in one line ("on Saturday, the ninth of December"). "Senior" and "Junior" may be abbreviated (Sr., Jr.), but "Doctor" and other professional titles and military ranks are written in full. (See page 636: "Correct Usage of Civilian and Military Titles"; Chapter 22, page 331: "Official Titles.")

➤ Names on invitations are written in full. Initials are not used. If someone prefers not to use his or her first or middle name, just leave it out.

➤ Numbers in the street address mentioned on the invitation are written in numerals: "3737 West End Avenue." But when there's just one number, it is spelled out: "Thirty West End Avenue."

➤ Half hours are written as "half after seven o'clock" (not "half past seven" or "seven-thirty").

➤ Numbers in the date of the wedding are spelled out: "the twenty-sixth of July."

➤ Dates on wedding invitations may include the year; although relatively new, this form is perfectly correct. The year is spelled out: "two thousand and four." The full date of the wedding, including year, is always used in a wedding announcement.

➤ When the invitation is to the wedding ceremony only, it does not include an RSVP.

➤ The invitation to the reception only or a combined ceremony–reception invitation does request a reply—either RSVP or "The favour of a reply is requested." (See page 627: "RSVP Etiquette"; Chapter 18, page 248: "Requesting a Reply.")

Traditional Invitation Examples

For the most traditional of formal invitations, the names of invited guests are written by hand, as in the first example below. You might use the services of a calligrapher, but this isn't necessary. If you laser-print your invitations, you can use a calligraphy font to simulate handwriting of the invitee's name.

You can adapt the following invitation examples for your own needs; consult the styles for wording on page 628: "Wording Invitations for Different Situations."

Most formal invitation with handwritten names of the invitees:

Doctor and Mrs. Thomas Wayne Fennessy
request the honour of the presence of

Mr. and Mrs. William Nygren

at the marriage of their daughter
Melissa Suzanne

to

Mr. Lawrence Frederick Mickelson
Saturday, the tenth of July
two thousand and four
at half after five o'clock
Community Presbyterian Church
Fort Worth, Texas

An entirely printed formal invitation from the bride's parents:

Mr. and Mrs. Vernon James Cooper
request the honour of your presence
at the marriage of their daughter
Katherine Charlotte

to

Mr. Charles Kent Adamson
Saturday, the eighth of May
two thousand and four
at half after three o'clock
First Congregational Church
Spring Hill, Minnesota

Semiformal and Informal Invitations

Semiformal and informal invitations are often written in a more intimate, first-person tone, though the information is the same as in a formal invitation. The paper and design might incorporate the theme of the wedding, and stationery manufacturers now offer a wide variety of color schemes, borders, and designs. Colored inks and contemporary typefaces are acceptable, so long as they are easy to read. Today's couples may prefer to design their invitations to reflect the nature of the occasion and their personal style.

The samples below illustrate how informal and formal wording can be integrated in less traditional invitations:

A semiformal invitation from the bride's parents (note that the names of the parents/hosts come near the end of this invitation):

∼ Please Save the Date ∼

Save-the-date cards, giving advance notice of an upcoming wedding, can be very helpful to guests who must make travel plans or when the wedding will be held at a time when there may be conflicts with other activities, such as on major holiday weekends. They are especially useful for alerting guests about a destination wedding. Save-the-date cards are also increasingly sent for other social events such as formal parties and charity balls.

Save-the-date cards are usually mailed from three to four months prior to the wedding or event, but may be sent earlier for a destination wedding at a distant location. Cards can be sent to all guests or only those who need more time to plan. Be sure that everyone who receives a save-the-date card also receives an invitation.

Printed on single, standard invitation-sized or postcard-like cards, save-the-date cards can be informal or formal to match the style of the upcoming wedding or event. The more informal ones might be colorful. The usual wording is as follows:

Please save the date of
Saturday, June 5, 2004
[*or, for a formal card,* Saturday, the fifth of June/two thousand and four]
for the wedding of

Angie Henrickson

and

Jim Marrero
[*or full names for a formal card*]

Invitations to follow [*this line optional*]
Mr. and Mrs. Byron Henrickson [*the hosts*]

We invite you to share our joy
as we celebrate the marriage of our daughter
Christine Joanne
to
Mr. Alfred José Diego
on Friday, the fifteenth of October
two thousand and four
at four o'clock
St. Xavier's Catholic Church
Nashville, Tennessee
Please join us after the ceremony for the reception
Richmont Country Club
231 Centennial Avenue
Mr. and Mrs. Samuel Riley [or Lucille and Sam Riley]
RSVP

An informal invitation from the couple to their at-home ceremony and reception:

Elizabeth Patton and David Kim
hope that you can be with us
for our wedding and celebration brunch
Saturday, April twenty-fourth
at half past eleven o'clock
113 Cedar Creek Drive
Bellingham
RSVP

Handwritten Invitations

Any type of wedding invitation can be handwritten, but this is a major undertaking when the guest list is lengthy. Generally, handwritten notes and invitations are suited for small weddings at which the guest company will be made up of family and close friends. Notes can be written by the bride and groom and/or their families, and each invitation can be issued by the person closest to the invitee. A note must convey the necessary information and can be as original and personal as the writer wishes.

> Dear Mr. and Mrs. Karlson,
>
> Donald Hambrick and I will be married on August seventh at two o'clock at the Skyline Plaza Hotel. We hope that you will join us for the ceremony and afterward for the reception.
>
> With love,
> Ruthie Miller

Invitations to the Reception

When all guests are invited to both the ceremony and the reception, you can combine the invitations as follows:

> *Mr. and Mrs. Harold Love Shillinglaw*
> *request the honour of your presence*
> *at the marriage of their daughter*
> *Gillian*
>
> *to*
> *Doctor Darren Henry Graves*
> *Sunday, March twenty-eighth*
> *at half after two o'clock*
> *Vine Street Methodist Church*
> *Savannah*
> *and afterward at the reception*
> *The Colony Club*
> *The favour of a reply is requested*

When the ceremony is small and private and a larger reception follows, the invitations to the wedding are generally issued orally, by personal note, or with a ceremony card (see page 628: "Ceremony cards"). The printed invitation is to the reception only. A traditional reception invitation would be worded as follows:

Mr. and Mrs. Roland Benjamin
request the pleasure of your company
at the wedding reception
for their daughter
Amy Claire
and
Mr. Mark Jerome Heinrich
Friday, the fourth of June
two thousand and four
at seven o'clock
The University Club
719 Eastside Boulevard
Cedar Rapids
RSVP

Reception cards. When the ceremony and the reception are to be held at separate locations or the reception is held several hours after the ceremony, a separate recep-

∾ RSVP Etiquette ∾

An RSVP—the abbreviation of the French phrase *répondez s'il vous plaît*, meaning "please respond"—or the phrase "The favour of a reply is requested" obligates invitees to accept or regret an invitation. Guests are not expected to reply for the ceremony, but they do reply to reception invitations, combined ceremony–reception invitations, or enclosed reception cards. Replies are traditionally mailed, and this remains the rule except for very casual invitations.

Usually the reply (personally written or indicated on a printed reply card) is sent to the return address on the invitation. When a different address is used for replies, that address is printed just below the RSVP or on the return envelope for the reply card. Do not include phone numbers, e-mail addresses, or individual names; don't include company names when replies are mailed to a wedding consultant's address. (If you have replies sent to a business, they are still addressed to the hosts of the wedding. Alert mail handlers that replies will be coming in, especially if the names of the addressees are not known in the mailroom.)

On a very casual invitation, you might include a phone number and/or e-mail address for replies—but only if your guests are used to informal communication. Provide a physical mailing address as well for guests who prefer to reply by mail.

tion card can be enclosed with the wedding invitation. The reception card includes the reply request (and mailing address if not the same as the return address on the invitation envelope); there is no RSVP on the wedding invitation. The card is simply worded, as illustrated here:

Reception
immediately following the ceremony [or at five o'clock]
Da Vinci's Restaurant
518 Lafayette Street
Lincoln, Nebraska
The favour of a reply is requested [or RSVP]

Ceremony cards. Ceremony cards are useful when the guest list for the ceremony is shorter than the reception list but too large for handwritten notes—as when a hundred people are invited to the wedding and an additional hundred to the reception. For those invited to the ceremony and reception, a small card is enclosed with the reception invitation. This card matches the style of the reception invitation, but it doesn't include an RSVP, since the reply is necessary only for the reception. The following illustrates formal wording for a ceremony card:

The honour of your presence
is requested at the marriage ceremony
Friday, the twelfth of November
at seven o'clock
Northside Baptist Church

Wording Invitations for Different Situations

ALTHOUGH INVITATIONS ARE TRADITIONALLY SENT by the bride's parents, family situations vary so widely that alternate wording may be necessary. The guiding principle is that the invitation is issued by the host or hosts of the wedding and reception. This may be a parent, parents and stepparents, the couple themselves, other family members, or friends. The examples in this section illustrate how formal invitations can be worded to reflect individual circumstances.

When the bride has one living parent
The invitation is normally issued in the name of the living parent.

Mrs. [or Mr.] James Prentiss Driscoll
requests the honour of your presence
at the marriage of her [or his] daughter ...

If the bride very much wishes to include the name of her deceased parent, it's important not to use wording that implies that the deceased is issuing the invitation. The special wording of this type of invitation overrides the issue of who is hosting the wedding, as in the following example:

Doreen Louise Michaels
daughter of Mrs. Marvin Gadsden Michaels and the late Mr. Michaels
and
Roger Leonard Simpkins
son of Mr. and Mrs. Horace Simpkins
request the honour of your presence
at their marriage ...

The same form is used if the groom wishes to acknowledge his deceased parent on the invitation, with his late parent listed below his name: "Roger Leonard Simpkins / son of Mr. Horace Simpkins and the late Mrs. Simpkins . . ."

When the bride's parents are divorced

If divorced parents are friendly, they may share wedding expenses and act as co-hosts. The wedding invitation is usually issued in both names, with the mother's name (and her current husband if she has remarried) appearing first and the bride identified by her full name.

Mr. and Mrs. Bryant Inman
and
Mr. Richard Cousins
request the honour of your presence
at the marriage of their daughter
Courtney Marie Cousins ...

If one of the bride's parents is not part of her life and isn't contributing to the wedding, the wording is similar to that for a deceased parent (see page 628: "When the bride has one living parent").

If the invitation is issued by the bride's mother only, her current name and title is used. The bride's name appears in full if her last name differs from her parent's.

Ms. Beatrice Kelly Quinlan
requests the honour of your presence
at the marriage of her daughter
Jean Marie Willingham . . .

When the bride has stepparents

When the bride has been raised by a parent and stepparent and her other natural parent is not co-hosting the wedding, the appropriate wording is as follows. The bride's full name is used if her last name is different from her stepfather's.

Mr. and Mrs. Kenneth Cummings
request the honour of your presence
at the marriage of his [or her] daughter
Olivia Carol [or Olivia Carol Stein] . . .

When the bride has been legally adopted by a stepparent or she regards the stepparent as if he or she were a natural parent, the invitation would read "their daughter," as in the following example. Again, the bride's full name is used if different from her stepfather's.

Mr. and Mrs. Kenneth Cummings
request the honour of your presence
at the marriage of their daughter
Olivia Carol [or Olivia Carol Stein] . . .

When the bride does not have parents

If both the bride's parents are deceased or have no part in her life, another family member may issue the invitation. Although the titles (Miss, Mrs., and Ms.) are not normally used for brides, this situation is one of the exceptions.

Mr. and Mrs. Grant Alan McIver
request the honor of your presence
at the marriage of their granddaughter
Miss [or Mrs. or Ms.] Emma Caroline Jackson . . .

I'm inviting many of my business associates to my wedding. The problem is that I'm known to them by my professional name. I'm afraid that people won't realize who I am if my invitations, which are formal, are sent in my real name.

Your problem is increasingly common in today's world, where businesswomen often use a professional name among colleagues. Fortunately, there's a simple solution. In formal and informal invitations, your professional name is printed in parentheses below your real name, as in this example:

Mr. and Mrs. Nicholas Von Schmittou
request the honour of your presence
at the marriage of their daughter
Theresa Abigail
(Teri Smith)
to . . .

If you and your fiancé are issuing the invitation, you would do the same:

Theresa Abigail Von Schmittou
(Teri Smith)
and
Charles Edward Geller
request the honour of . . .

Another option for a bride without parents is to issue the invitation in her own and her fiancé's names (see page 632: "When the couple issues the invitation").

When the bride is a widow or divorcée

If a widowed or divorced bride's living parents (or parent) issue the invitation, it can follow traditional form. The bride uses her current name, but her social title isn't used.

Mr. and Mrs. Winton Abrams
request the honour of your presence
at the marriage of their daughter
Sheila Abrams Constantine

[or, if she has resumed her maiden name, *Sheila Allison Abrams*] . . .

Widows or divorcées often choose to issue their own invitations (see page 632: "When the couple issues the invitation").

When the couple issues the invitation

There are many times when a couple wishes to send wedding invitations in their own names. The traditional formal wording is as follows (note the optional use of the courtesy titles):

The honour of your presence
is requested
at the marriage of
Miss [or Ms.] Deborah Anne Tillman
and
Mr. Naser Mahmud . . .

[or]

Deborah Anne Tillman
and
Naser Mahmud
request the honour of your presence
at their marriage . . .

A less formal version without social titles, like the following, is often preferred by older couples and couples who live together:

Constance Marcus
and
Timothy White Anderson
invite you to attend their wedding
on Saturday, the eleventh of September
at five o'clock
78-A Magnolia Terrace
Greensboro
and afterward at the reception
R S V P

When other relatives issue the invitation

When a bride's siblings or other relatives host the wedding, invitations are sent in their name or names (see page 630: "When the bride does not have parents").

If a couple's grown children host the wedding, the invitations can be issued in their names. The bride's children (and spouses) are listed first. The names appear in order of age, from oldest to youngest, in each family—as the following example illustrates:

Mr. and Mrs. Carlton Bennett /bride's oldest child and wife/
Miss Geneva Bennett /bride's middle child/
Mr. and Mrs. Hugh Sokolowski /bride's youngest child and husband/
Mr. and Mrs. Gerald Wilson Mosely /groom's only child and wife/
request the honour of your presence
at the marriage of their parents
Mary Geneva Bennett
and
Gerald Alexander Mosely . . .

When the bridegroom's parents give the wedding

If the bride has no family, her family lives far away and she is alone, or they refuse to take part in the wedding, the groom's parents (or parent) may host the wedding and issue the invitations:

Mr. and Mrs. Jay Harold Dobson, Junior
request the honour of your presence
at the marriage of
Miss Kesha Denise Watkins
to their son
John Harold Dobson . . .

When the bride's and groom's parents issue the invitation

In some religious and ethnic traditions, it's customary for both sets of parents to issue the invitation. These days, joint invitations are increasingly sent when the groom's family shares a major part of the wedding expenses. The traditional wording of the invitation would be as follows, with the bride's parents named first:

Mr. and Mrs. Anthony Cohen
and
Colonel and Mrs. Marshall Goodman
request the honour of your presence
at the marriage of
Sheryl Laura Cohen
and
Lewis Albert Goodman . . .

In some European cultures, a double invitation is used, with the bride's family's invitation appearing on the left side of the page and the groom's family's invitation on the right—a custom increasingly seen in this country.

Dr. and Mrs. Roberto Mendez	*Mr. and Mrs. Paul Knowles*
request the honour of your presence	*request the honour of your presence*
at the marriage of their daughter	*at the marriage of their son*
Maria Ines	*Justin Russell*
to	*to*
Mr. Justin Russell Knowles . . .	*Miss Maria Ines Mendez . . .*

If all the hosting parents are divorced, they and their current spouses, if they've remarried, are listed on the invitation in the following order:

Mr. and Mrs. Parker McAdams [bride's mother and spouse first]
Mr. and Mrs. Daniel Woods [bride's father and spouse second]
Doctor and Mrs. Arnold Zimmerman [groom's mother and spouse third]
Mr. and Mrs. Frederick Green [groom's father and spouse fourth]
request the honour of your presence
at the marriage of
Leslie Kay Woods
and
Theodore Leon Green . . .

When it's a double wedding

Double weddings usually involve sisters. The names of the elder sister and her fiancé come before the younger sister on the invitation.

Mr. and Mrs. Mitchell Travis Raines
request the honour of your presence
at the marriage of their daughters
Jessica Gale

to

Mr. Peter James Luckett

and

Mary Lynn

to

Mr. Angelo Ramirez . . .

∼ Six Invitation Mistakes to Avoid ∼

The beauty of the traditional invitation is that it's hard to get wrong. Still, mistakes happen, and the time to catch them is before anything is printed.

➤ Spelling errors can be avoided by checking, double-checking, and having others check your wording. Be particularly attentive to the names and addresses of ceremony and reception sites and the spellings of all names.

➤ Any mention of gifts or listing of gift registries is unacceptable. Also, don't include a notation like "No gifts, please."

➤ If you don't want children, don't invite them. Never add notations such as "No children" or "Adults only" to an invitation.

➤ Dress notations are not included on a wedding invitation unless the ceremony and reception invitations are combined. If it's essential to indicate "black tie" or "white tie," the notation is printed on the lower right corner of the reception invitation.

➤ References to food and alcohol service are not included on invitations, although food choices may be mentioned on reply cards (see page 642: "Reply cards").

➤ Invitations to B-list guests—people you want to invite when guests on your primary list decline—should be sent *preferably four weeks and no later than three weeks* before the wedding date. Any closer to the wedding is a dead giveaway that the invitee is on your second list; an extremely late invitation will probably be received as a personal insult.

When two good friends have a double ceremony, the order of the bride's names can be alphabetical, chronological by age, or the choice of the brides.

Invitations to Commitment Ceremonies

The formats for traditional wedding and reception invitations—and announcements—can easily be adapted for commitment ceremonies and celebrations, though couples often avoid the word "marriage" because it may confuse some guests about the nature of the union. Complete information about planning for and the etiquette of commitment ceremonies is provided in Chapter 42, "New Times, New Traditions," pages 732–739.

Correct Usage of Civilian and Military Titles

PROFESSIONAL TITLES ARE WRITTEN in full when used. Obvious examples are "Doctor" for physicians, veterinarians, and dentists and religious titles for clergy. Although many doctors normally identify themselves by their degrees (Raymond Lester, M.D.), the use of "Doctor" is appropriate for wedding invitations.

Educational degrees, professional certifications, and business titles are not included in wedding invitations and announcements. Lawyers may be entitled to have "Esquire" following their names, but since most Americans are unfamiliar with this term, it's best not to use it.

People who are customarily addressed by titles in daily usage may also use them in invitations—Judge *or* Justice Judith Wade; Doctor Andrew Cairns (for a university professor); Chancellor *or* President James Manly (a university or college head); Mayor Angelo Bentonni or Ambassador Rachel Waggoner (high elected or appointed officials). Professional and elected titles are not followed by any indication of the area of the person's employment or service.

When a woman holds a professional/elected title and her husband uses a social title, the wording for invitations and addresses is:

Senator Marilyn Wentworth and Mr. Russell Wentworth

It's also acceptable for people to use only their courtesy titles if they wish.

Military Titles

When the bride and/or groom and/or parents are members of the armed services or serving on active duty in the reserve forces, their military titles are used in invitations. All military titles are written in full—never abbreviated—on invitations and announcements and for mailing addresses.

The following information applies to United States military titles. If you're not sure about the correct use of titles for members of the wedding, consult Chapter 22, "Names, Titles, and Official Protocol," or check with a local office or a protocol officer of the service branch. For correct use of titles in the military of another nation, contact one of that country's consular offices or the embassy in Washington, D.C.

➤ Officers ranked captain or higher in the Army, Air Force, and Marines or commander or higher in the Navy and Coast Guard are listed as:

Major Amanda Riaz
United States Army

Commander Warren Stimson
United States Navy

➤ For junior officers, rank and branch of service are printed below their names. Students at U.S. military academies follow the same form:

Evelyn Ann Sweeney
Ensign, United States Navy

➤ In the Army, first and second lieutenants both use the title "Lieutenant." But in the Air Force and Marines, "First Lieutenant" and "Second Lieutenant" are correct.

➤ Noncommissioned and enlisted personnel use the name followed by rank and service branch or only the service branch on the line below. Grades are not included.

Neil Porter Ames
Staff Sergeant, United States Air Force

Or they may use their civilian names with social titles (Mr. Neil Porter Ames) and no indication of service.

➤ Members of the reserve forces who are on active duty are listed in the same fashion as members of the regular military.

Commander Francis McGill
United States Coast
Guard Reserve

William Hollingsworth
Corporal Specialist,
United States Army Reserve

➤ When a retired officer uses his or her military title, the status is indicated as follows:

Brigadier General Clarence Deluca
United States Air Force, Retired

➤ When an officer, on active duty or retired, is hosting the wedding, only the title is used. Retired officers may prefer to use civilian titles:

General and Mrs. Clarence Deluca
[or, if retired, Mr. and Mrs. Clarence Deluca]
request the honour . . .

If the mother is an officer who wishes to use her military title and the father is a civilian, she is listed first:

Colonel Martha McGee and Mr. Jerome McGee
request the honour . . .

➤ When both parents are on active duty, both are named by title or the wife may choose to use her social title. If both use titles, the higher-ranked officer is named first:

Commander George Nichols and Major Brenda Nichols
[or Commander and Mrs. George Nichols]
request the honour. . . .

➤ When military parents are divorced and they co-host the wedding, their names and titles (if appropriate) appear on separate lines with the highest-ranking officer listed first. If the parents are of equal or equivalent rank, the bride's mother is listed first:

Lieutenant Colonel Jeanne Gross Blanton
and
Commander Wayne Craig Blanton
request the honour . . .

In a traditional invitation to a military wedding hosted by the bride's parents, like the following example, only the bride's first names—with her rank and service—are used, unless her last name differs from her parents':

Major General and Mrs. Benjamin John Hodges
request the honour of your presence
at the marriage of their daughter
Victoria Susan
Lieutenant, United States Marines
to
Colonel Isaac Halliwell
United States Marines . . .

Envelopes and Enclosures

THE TRADITIONAL FORMAL WEDDING invitation is sent in two envelopes, and the paper and printing match the invitation. The outer envelope is addressed using full names and titles, and also carries the return address. The inner envelope includes only the names of the people for whom the invitation is intended.

Although inner envelopes are not required (it's perfectly correct to enclose everything in a single envelope), they can serve a useful purpose. The names on the inner envelope make it absolutely clear who is being invited.

For example, if you want a friend to bring a date if she likes, you would address the outer envelope to your friend (Ms. Gretchen Jones). But the inner envelope would be to "Ms. Jones and Guest." This tells your friend that she's welcome to bring someone to the wedding. But if you're not including guests, the inner envelope would read only "Ms. Jones."

Mailing Addresses for Invitations

The outside, stamped envelopes include the full names and addresses of invitees and your return address. The U.S. Postal Service prefers that return addresses on all first-class mail be written or printed in the upper left corner on the front of the envelope. You can have the return address embossed or printed on the back flap of the envelope, but flaps are often torn when opened and blind embossing (raised letters without color) can be hard to read. Without other instructions, invitees will send their replies and gifts to the return address on your envelope.

Wedding invitations are normally addressed by hand. You might use a laser printer font that simulates calligraphy, but it is relatively easy to distinguish between mechanical and genuine handwriting. Don't use stick-on labels for guest or return addresses.

Customarily, no words except courtesy titles (Mr., Mrs., Ms.) are abbreviated. (See also page 636: "Correct Usage of Civilian and Military Titles;" Chapter 17, page 228: "Addressing.") Initials are not used in names when addressing formal invitations. Addresses are written as "Street," "Boulevard," and so on. Although it's traditional to

Friends at the Post Office

Before making your final selection of invitations and envelopes, check with the U.S. Post Office from which they will be mailed. Postal workers can be very helpful—especially if you make a point to see them at a convenient time and not to complain about rules and regulations that your post office must follow. Take samples of your invitation, liners and tissue, enclosures, and envelopes (printers and stationers can supply sample sheets in the right sizes and weights). Have the postal clerk or postmaster check the size and bulk of your entire invitation package. Consult about postal regulations if you plan to use a large, small, or oddly shaped envelope or to enclose anything other than flat and folded papers. Look over the current stamp catalog. Many post offices don't keep large inventories of special stamps on hand but will gladly order them for you with advance notice.

write state names in full, the post office prefers the two-letter abbreviations with no comma between city and state (Boston MA).

Addressing Inner and Outer Envelopes

The inside envelope, if used, contains the wedding invitation and all enclosures. Inner envelopes are addressed to names only. The following information and examples should help you with most addressing questions, whether you use one envelope or two.

Close family and friends. While outer envelopes are always addressed with full names, it's fine to address inner envelopes with familiar names and titles for close family members and good friends.

Outer envelope	*Inner envelope*
Doctor and Mrs. Jeffrey Lentz	Aunt Sara and Uncle Doc
Miss Sally Webb Lentz	Cousin Sally [*or* Sally]

Married couples with young children. If you know the children, you can address the inner envelopes with their first names. Otherwise, use children's full names without titles. Generally, children's names are not included in the address on the outer envelope.

Outer envelope	*Inner envelope*
Mr. and Mrs. Oliver Jason Adair	Mr. and Mrs. Adair
	Lisa and Bobby
	[*or*]
	Lisa Adair
	Bobby Adair

If there are several siblings in the home, you can address the inner envelope to "The Misses Adair" (two or more sisters); "The Messrs. Adair" (two or more brothers); or both.

Teenagers in the home. Children aged thirteen and over really should receive individual invitations. If this isn't possible, include them in their parents' invitation as above. When courtesy titles are used, teenage girls are "Miss," but the title "Mr." is reserved for young men aged eighteen and older.

Different adults at the same address. It is always preferable to send separate invitations to each couple or adult who lives at the same address. You might address the invitation to "Mr. and Mrs. Vincent Marcos and Family" if you're inviting *everyone* at that address and it's clear that the invitation is intended only for people in the home, not other relatives.

Outer envelope	*Inner envelope*
Mr. and Mrs. Vincent Marcos and Family	Mr. and Mrs. Marcos
	Mrs. Edmund Ridley
	Miss Christina Marcos
	Ricky and Ginger Marcos

Couples who live together. As long as you *know* that two people at the same address live together as a couple, you can address one invitation to both. If you are unsure about the arrangement and can't find out, play it safe and send separate invitations to each.

Outer envelope	*Inner envelope*
Ms. Doris Rasmussen	Ms. Rasmussen and Mr. Colwell
Mr. Harrison Colwell	

If the couple has young children whom you're inviting, list them as you would the children of a married couple.

An invitee and guest. If you use an inner envelope, do not include "and Guest" on the outer envelope. If you use only one envelope, address it as follows:

Outer envelope (no inner envelope)
Ms. Penelope Denise McKey and Guest

Outer envelope	*Inner envelope*
Ms. Penelope Denise McKey	Ms. McKey and Guest

People with military and professional titles. On inner envelopes, treat military and professional titles as you would social titles. Titles are written in full.

Outer envelope	Inner envelope
Admiral and Mrs. Henry Jernigan	Admiral and Mrs. Jernigan
Colonel Marguerite O'Brian and Colonel Alex O'Brian	The Colonels O'Brian [*when husband and wife have the same rank*]
Judge Crystal Sims and Mr. Randall Sims	Judge Sims and Mr. Sims

Enclosures

There are a number of extra cards that can be enclosed with a wedding invitation. These are placed in the inner envelope, or the outer envelope if you use only one.

Reception cards and ceremony cards are discussed on pages 627–628. Other enclosures you might need are:

Reply cards. Although handwritten replies are always correct, the use of printed reply cards and envelopes has increased in recent times. Reply cards are actually for the reception—to give you an accurate guest count. Since the value of a reply card is convenience, make it as simple and easy to use as possible. Reply cards are printed in the same style as your invitation. The fundamental elements are a space for invitees to write their names and a space to indicate whether they will or will not attend.

Two basic reply cards:

M _____
[*space for the invitee's name and those of others included in his invitation*]
Will _____ *attend*
[*The invitee writes "not" in the space when regretting.*]

M _____
_____ *accepts [or will attend]*
_____ *regrets [or will not attend]*

The person returning the reply card should fill in the names of everyone included in the invitation. Don't use a line asking for "number of persons"; this can be confusing and may seem to indicate that invitees can bring other people.

A "respond by" notation (normally a date two weeks in advance of the wedding) may be included on the reply card.

M _____
Will _____ *attend*
The favour of a reply is requested [or RSVP]
before the twenty-ninth of May

If you include return envelopes with the reply cards, these are pre-addressed and stamped. But if you enclose the card only, it's a good idea to print the return address on the card, even if it is the same as the return address on the invitation envelope.

Caterers often ask for precise numbers for reception meals at which two or more entrées are served. Some reply cards now include a line such as "Do you prefer _____ chicken or _____ fish?" However, it's preferable not to include an entrée choice notation on the reply card; instead, choices can be offered or requests taken by the waitstaff at the reception (see Chapter 35, page 602: "Seated Meals").

Admission cards. These are used only to preserve the privacy of a ceremony in a popular wedding location or house of worship that attracts sightseers. Guests are asked to present this card when they enter. The card is in the same style as the wedding invitation and worded as follows:

Please present this card

at

St. Patrick's Cathedral

Friday, the eighth of October

Pew cards. Small cards printed with the words "Pew Number _____" or "Within the Ribbon" are sometimes included in invitations to family and friends who are to be seated in reserved areas. Guests with cards simply show them to the ushers.

Pew cards can also be sent separately, after acceptances and regrets have been received and the exact number of reserved seats needed has been determined.

∼ A Mailing for Travelers ∼

Out-of-town guests usually need to know more than can be included on a directions card, so you may want to prepare a separate mailing. This can include information about convenient hotels and motels, their rates, and instructions for making reservations. Even if you've organized blocks of rooms at one or two locations, it's thoughtful to include other options in a range of prices.

Couples can put together an attractive mailing without too much expense. You might include a city or area map as well as directions to the wedding site and other party locations. A list of restaurants can be very useful. You may also have tips for travelers, such as alternate routes to take during rush hours, rental car recommendations, and airport shuttle schedules. Travel mailings should be sent out after invitations but in plenty of time for out-of-town guests to make their arrangements.

At-home cards. Small name and address cards are sometimes included in wedding invitations and wedding announcements. They inform guests of your post-wedding address and phone number and when you expect to be "at home"—a convenient date after the wedding trip. At-home cards reflect the general look of the invitations or announcements they accompany.

Traditionally, an at-home card enclosed with a wedding invitation did not include the couple's married name, because they were not yet married at the time the card was received. But the custom has changed, and common sense says that you may include your married names if you want.

> Mr. and Mrs. Barry Morrison
> will be at home [or "At home"]
> after the thirteenth of August
> 1127 Stokes Lane
> Franklin, Arkansas
> (501) 555-9876

An at-home card sent with a wedding announcement always includes the couple's married names ("Mr. and Mrs. Barry Morrison / will be at home / . . ."). At-home cards may be printed with the bride's name—a good way to inform people if she will continue using her own name or if the couple will use a double name.

> Amelia Burns and Barry Morrison
> will be at home . . .

> Amelia and Barry Burns-Morrison
> will be at home . . .

Maps and directions. Maps and directions to the wedding and reception sites are helpful for guests unfamiliar with your area. You can include them in your invitations or send them later, when you receive acceptances. It isn't necessary to send directions to guests who already know the way.

You may be able to get maps from your ceremony and reception sites, but there's a good chance you'll have to order or design them yourself. You might find Internet maps that are easy to adapt. Written directions should be brief but precise.

When you enclose maps and directions in your wedding invitation, they don't have to be expensively printed, but try to keep them small so that they don't distract from the invitation, and conform them as much as possible to the look and style of the invitation.

Rain card. If you plan an outdoor wedding but have an alternate site selected in case of bad weather, you can enclose a small card worded like the following:

In case of rain, the ceremony and reception will be held
at the home of Mr. and Mrs. Sean Darnley
2121 Brookmont Circle
New Bedford

Tissues. In the past, tissue papers were included with invitations to keep engraving ink from smearing. Today's printing technology makes tissues unnecessary, but you can use them if you want. It's a matter of choice.

Stuffing the Envelopes

Organization is key to assembling invitations and enclosures. It's a good idea to lay out the pieces assembly-line style and stuff one envelope at a time. This method helps you avoid leaving a piece out—a real danger when you have multiple enclosures. Use the following guidelines to get every item in its correct place.

- ➤ Whether an inner envelope is used or not, the invitation is inserted faceup with its folded or left edge to the bottom of the envelope.
- ➤ An inner envelope is inserted into an outer envelope with its bottom side down so that the names on the inner envelope are visible when it is removed. The flap of the inner envelope is not sealed.
- ➤ When the invitation is not folded or has a single fold, enclosures are placed on top of the invitation so that the printed sides face the envelope flap.
- ➤ If the invitation is folded twice, enclosures are placed inside the fold with their printed sides up.

Enclosure cards are stacked in order of size, with large cards (reception or ceremony cards) directly on the invitation—over the tissue if you use one. Smaller cards are then layered. All cards are placed faceup. The reply card is slipped under the flap of its envelope, so the card face is visible and the addressed side of the envelope is down.

Stuffing the envelope: Once the invitation has been inserted, add the enclosures according to size, starting with the largest. Smallest item will be on top when the envelope is opened.

Postponement, Change of Date, or Cancellation

MANY THINGS CAN HAPPEN—an illness or death, an unexpected military deployment, even a serious business crisis—that force a change of wedding date after invitations have been printed. Reprinting the invitations is very costly, and there may not be time. If you haven't mailed the invitations and know the new date, you can either (1) neatly cross out the old date on the invitation and write the new one in ink, or (2) include a small printed or handwritten card with the message, "The date of the wedding has been changed from April eighteenth to May sixteenth."

If the wedding invitations have already been mailed and there's no time to print and mail announcements, the couple can notify invited guests by sending cards or personal notes. When time is very short, telephone calls and e-mails are fine.

If the wedding is postponed after the invitations have been mailed and there's time for additional printing and mailing, you can send a printed announcement:

Mr. and Mrs. Roy Kennon
regret that
the invitations to
their daughter's wedding [or wedding reception]
on Saturday, January tenth
must be recalled

[or]

Mr. and Mrs. Roy Kennon
announce that
the marriage of their daughter
Madison Gay
to
Mr. Stephen Wilhoite
has been postponed
[or, if the new date is known, *has been postponed to March sixth*]

If the couple issued their own invitations, the announcement might read:

The marriage of
Madison Gay Kennon
and
Stephen Wilhoite
has been postponed to March sixth

Cancellation

When a wedding is called off, invited guests must be notified as quickly as possible. A last-minute cancellation usually requires telephoning, and family and good friends should be ready to help. It isn't necessary to go into details, but if the cancellation is caused by the death of one of the couple, do tell people, since they may not yet have heard the sad news. (Guests should be considerate when learning of a cancellation: Don't ask the reason, and don't prolong a phone conversation.)

When there's time, the family can send printed cards. Cancellation notices should be sent to all invitees whether they have responded to the wedding invitation or not.

Mr. and Mrs. Hamilton Egerton
announce that the marriage of their daughter
Marian
to
Mr. Thomas Chou
will not take place

Wedding Announcements

WEDDING ANNOUNCEMENTS ARE NOT OBLIGATORY, but they're a nice way to share your happy news with people who were not included in your guest list—faraway friends, distant relatives, acquaintances, and business associates. Announcements are not sent to anyone who received a wedding invitation. Gifts are not expected; though some people may send gifts, this is strictly their choice.

Announcements are usually mailed a day or a few days *after* the wedding, but circumstances might delay the mailing, which is fine. (An announcement is a great way to let people know that families are happy about an elopement or sudden marriage.)

A traditional announcement is worded similarly to the invitation and is usually made by the bride's parents or by both sets of parents, as in the following examples. The year is always included.

> Mr. and Mrs. Frank Williamson
> have the honour of
> announcing the marriage of their daughter
> Judith Elaine
> to
> Mr. Pierre Michael Dumas
> Saturday, the seventeenth of January
> two thousand and four
> Oakland, California

> Mr. and Mrs. Frank Williamson
> and
> Mr. and Mrs. Louis Dumas
> announce the marriage of
> Judith Elaine Williamson
> and
> Pierre Michael Dumas . . .

Wedding announcements can be printed in the same style as the invitation. Handwritten announcements may also follow the traditional form or be more personal and informal. If the couple has an at-home card, it is included with the announcement.

Other Stationery Needs

THERE ARE A FEW OTHER printed invitations and paper products that you may want to include in your wedding inventory. Personalized cocktail napkins and other memorabilia are optional, but if you want them, you may be able to get these items from the supplier of your invitations.

Don't forget to order your thank-you notepapers and envelopes—the earlier, the better. You'll want to have your thank-you note cards ready when you begin receiving gifts, so be sure to order monogrammed or printed cards well in advance. (For more about thank-yous, see Chapter 38, page 674: "The Importance of 'Thank You.'" Monograms are discussed in Chapter 30, page 518: "Monogramming.")

Ceremony programs. Many couples have programs printed to help guests follow the order of a wedding service and to explain rituals with which guests may not be familiar. Programs for religious ceremonies sometimes include instructions for guests (when to stand, for example), translations of texts, and explanations of symbolic elements in the service. They may also include group prayers, refrains, and readings.

Programs generally list the officiant(s), participants in the ceremony (organist, musicians, readers, etc.), and members of the wedding party, but do not list wedding consultants, vendors, and suppliers. Don't include personal biographies. Although couples sometimes add an "In Memoriam" notation with the name or names of deceased parents or close relatives, the ceremony program is not the place for a lengthy tribute. A nice way to make a brief mention is: "We would like to remember . . ."

Programs can be a simple flat or folded sheet, or you might want a more decorative look. You might include a verse of religious text or poetry that suits the occasion. Just don't get carried away with ornate design or lengthy passages. Places of worship may be able to provide standard, blank bulletin forms that you can have written or printed and photocopied. Or use paper of your choice; normally programs are a standard sheet of 8½ × 11 inches, folded or cut in half.

Programs can be handed to guests by ushers or helpers, placed on pews or chairs, or placed in baskets by the entry to the sanctuary or ceremony area.

Place cards. Cards can be white or colored, plain or bordered or decorated. The main concern is that they are uniform in look: names written in the same hand. If you use a laser printer, choose a legible calligraphy font.

Hopefully, an invitee who brings a date or companion will inform you of the person's name in advance, and you will have a place card in his or her name. It's acceptable to write "Miss Gwinn's Guest" on the card if necessary.

Invitations to post-wedding receptions. Sometimes a wedding reception is held days, weeks, or even months after a wedding—following an elopement, for example, or when one or both of the couple must depart immediately for military service.

It's also common for parents or family members who live at a distance from the wedding site to host a reception for the couple after the honeymoon. Another nice tradition is for the mother and/or sisters and/or other close female relatives of the groom to hold a hometown luncheon or tea for the new daughter-in-law and invite family friends who were not included in the wedding guest list.

The traditional invitation form for a post-wedding reception is similar to a wedding reception invitation (see page 627), though the wording indicates that the honor guests are a married couple and there is no reference to the wedding. An RSVP is usually included.

Mr. and Mrs. Wayne Vandiver
request the pleasure of your company
at a reception
in honor of
Mr. and Mrs. Alan Scott Nelson . . .

Invitations to teas and other types of parties follow standard invitation formats (see Chapter 18, page 247: "The Basic Elements of Invitations"; page 256: "Informal Invitations"), reflecting the formal or informal nature of the occasion.

Chapter Thirty-seven

Wedding Attire

M ANY BRIDES-TO-BE begin shopping for their gowns as soon as they become engaged. But before you dash off to the stores, your first task is to determine how formal or informal your ceremony and reception will be, when and where they will take place, and how much money you're prepared to spend. (See Chapter 34, page 571: "The Major Decisions.") Religious and cultural considerations can affect your selections. So will your choice of attendants, since bridesmaids' dresses should be chosen with the women who will wear them in mind.

Most brides now purchase new wedding gowns, and it's smart to begin shopping as soon as the critical planning decisions are made. Special dress orders can take months—sometimes as many as ten months to a year for designer creations. If you're having your dress made, you need plenty of time to work with your designer or seamstress. Even off-the-rack dresses usually require alterations, so fittings will be part of your and your attendants' busy pre-wedding schedule.

Men's clothing is easier to select, but don't wait until the last minute. Many men rent formal, and sometimes informal, wedding outfits. Because formal-wear rental stores can run out of stock at certain times during the most popular wedding months, prom season, and holidays, you should investigate rental sources and place orders well in advance.

The following discussions and the dress chart at the end of this chapter apply primarily to traditional American wedding attire, but the basic guidelines and etiquette of selecting clothing for the wedding party are applicable to virtually every culture.

The Wedding Gown

WHITE IS JUST ONE of a rainbow of colors that brides wear, and though it has been the trend since the 1800s—boosted by the fashion for white gown and orange blossoms set by Queen Victoria at her 1840 wedding—it's not the only choice for today's women. In fact, until the late nineteenth century, most American brides wore their best dress, whatever the color, because the expense of a special gown was prohibitive except for well-to-do families. During the twentieth century, white came to signify joy rather than virginity (though traditionalists may hold to the older symbolism) and is now considered appropriate for all brides, including those marrying again and those who are pregnant at the time of the wedding.

Other colors—especially those drawn from non-European ethnic and cultural traditions—are equally acceptable. Although white, in all its many shades and pastel tints, is still the conventional choice for long formal and semiformal bridal gowns, the ultimate decision about color belongs to the bride.

Fabrics and Styles

As a general rule, the more formal the wedding, the more formal the fabric of the wedding dress. Fabrics are selected with the season in mind, as the general guidelines below indicate. But you have to take into account the weather in your area. In a cold climate, for example, velvet or brocade might be worn earlier in the fall and later in the spring than in temperate and hot zones.

Spring:	lace and tissue taffeta
Summer:	organdy, marquisette, cotton, piqué, linen
Fall/winter:	satin, brocade, taffeta, velvet, moiré, crepe,
	peau de soie, wool (informal)
Year-round:	silk, jersey, blends

Think about your comfort, and don't be guided by looks alone. Lace is beautiful but can be itchy over bare skin. Ball gowns of multi-layered or bead-encrusted fabrics can literally weigh a bride down after several hours of standing. Synthetic fabrics tend to be hotter than natural ones, so a blend might be the better choice. Since formal gowns may be boned and often require structured undergarments that women today are not used to, try on the dress with the correct undergarments to get a sense of its weight and ease of movement.

Your choice of style, or silhouette, is a matter of what is most flattering to you and most appropriate to the formality of the wedding. Floor-length gowns are usually worn for formal and semiformal weddings but are seen at less formal weddings, too. A long, summery, cotton or piqué dress might be just right for a casual garden or beach wedding. Style, length, and color may also be determined by the couple's cultural heritage. Many of today's brides, grooms, and their attendants wear full ethnic and national ensembles or adapt elements such as the Japanese marriage kimono, Turkish tunic, African *bubah* and symbolic patterned fabrics, and Chinese cheongsam.

Classic Wedding Gown Silhouettes

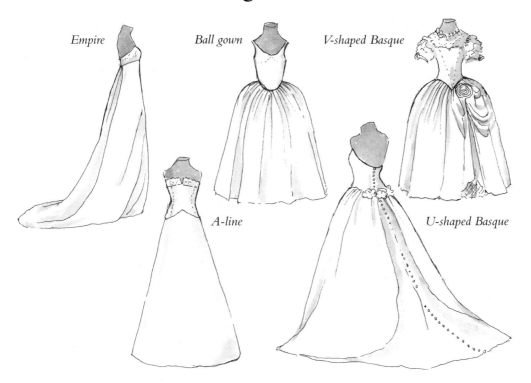

Empire

Ball gown

V-shaped Basque

A-line

U-shaped Basque

Empire. *High-waisted with the bodice cropped just below the bust*

Ball gown. *Floor-length "Cinderella" style with big, full skirt*

A-line. *In the shape of an "A," slimmer at the bodice and widening from the bodice down*

Basque. **V**- *or* **U**-*shaped waistline dropped several inches below the natural waist*

Neckline, sleeves, and back. Brides often ask how revealing their gowns may be. Your personal sense of decorum is generally paramount, but it's important to think about where and in what tradition the wedding will be held. For a religious ceremony, ask your officiant about any dress restrictions or expectations. (Are bare shoulders and arms acceptable? Is a face veil required? Do dress rules differ for religious services in a house of worship and at a secular location?) For an interfaith or inter-sect service, there may be several traditions to observe, so talk to each officiant.

There may be more freedom of choice for secular ceremonies, but issues of good taste and consideration for others still apply. If you will be married in a judge's chambers, for instance, respect both your officiant and the solemn civil office he or she holds by dressing appropriately.

Think about your guests. What is acceptable to your contemporaries may make older guests uncomfortable. While it's tempting to say, "My wedding, my way," a gracious bride would never deliberately shock or discomfort the people invited to share her wedding day.

Train. A train adds visual interest to the back of a floor-length gown, but it is by no means necessary. Trains may be sewn into the dress, and many sewn-in trains can be bustled, or gathered up, at the back, so the bride need not carry her train after the ceremony. Detachable trains are easily removed for the reception.

Sweep or brush train: drapes from the waistline to six inches on the floor

Court train: extends three to four feet from the waistline

Chapel train: extends five feet from the waistline

Cathedral train: extends 2½ to three yards from the waistline; very formal

Watteau train: drapes from the back yoke of the dress

Accessories

You have many options, from regally elaborate to charming simplicity. Accessories are best selected to complement your gown and the formality of the wedding, but your comfort is basic.

Veil and headdress. Historically, the bridal veil probably relates to the face coverings worn by unmarried and married women in many cultures as a sign of modesty and female subservience. But today's bridal veil is directly descended from French and English practice beginning in the 1500s and particularly from the nineteenth-century fashion for veiled headgear in all social situations.

Veils and headdresses may be a matter of religious custom but otherwise are strictly personal choices. Many of today's brides prefer nothing more than flattering hairstyles, perhaps enhanced with flowers, hair combs, or elegant barrettes.

Veils can be worn over the face or trail from the top or back of the head and are usually attached to or draped under a headdress. Veils come in a variety of semi-transparent materials, including lace and tulle, and lengths.

JUST COMMON SENSE

Rented and Borrowed

The average cost of today's new wedding gown plus headpiece and shoes is between $1,000 and $1,800, with designer gowns running into the multiple thousands. But brides have less expensive options, including renting and borrowing. Both routes are acceptable and sensible, especially if you want to save money and feel no real need to preserve the dress. Nor do you have to purchase your gown and accessories from bridal industry sources. You may find just the thing for an informal or casual wedding at your favorite department or clothing store.

Blusher veil: short veil worn over the face; may fall just below the shoulders

Fingertip veil: falls to the tips of the fingers

Mantilla: scarf-like veil that drapes over the head and shoulders

Sweep veil: touches the ground

Chapel veil: trails one to two feet behind the gown

Cathedral veil: trails one to three yards behind the gown

A face veil, worn for the processional and during the ceremony, is usually about a yard square and may be detachable. At the end of the ceremony, the face veil is either removed or lifted by the maid of honor when she returns the bride's bouquet or by the groom or the bride herself.

Bows, headbands, tiaras, Juliet caps, and floral wreaths can be worn with a veil or without. Fashion hats and headbands, with or without short veils, make attractive accessories with informal attire such as a wedding suit.

Undergarments. Your dress shop or dressmaker should be able to recommend bras and other undergarments. You should wear these for your fittings and make sure they complement your gown. Since women today are not used to wired, boned, or strapless bras or waist-length and full-torso undergarments, "practice" by walking around, bending, moving your arms, dancing, and generally getting comfortable in all new undergarments.

Shoes. The bride's shoes are traditionally satin (with a satin gown) or *peau de soie,* dyed to match her gown. Though pumps were once the only choice for formal weddings, sandal styles have become popular, particularly for warm weather weddings. Whatever the style, shop for comfort, avoiding stiletto-heeled shoes that can snag on a long gown, crinolines, or an aisle runner. Since comfort is so important, it's okay to change into attractive flat or low-heeled shoes for the reception and dancing.

Gloves. Wearing gloves can often enhance the look of a wedding dress, but is optional except for very formal weddings. Fabrics range from cotton and soft kid to satin and lace and should be in keeping with the wedding gown. A short, loose glove can easily be removed by the bride and handed to the maid of honor when rings are exchanged. Tight or long gloves are trickier. When it's difficult to remove a glove, you can snip open the seam on the underside of the ring finger before the ceremony and then slip off only that finger of the glove when you receive your ring. Finger-less gloves are another way to solve the ring-finger problem.

Jewelry. Traditional bridal jewelry is classic in design and neutral in color, such as a pearl or diamond and pearl necklace and earrings or simple gold ornaments. Colored stones are fine, too, and brides often wear heirloom family jewelry that is the gift of the groom. Very ornate jewelry is usually avoided if it will distract from the bride's overall look.

My mother has always hoped that I'd be married in her wedding gown. It's really beautiful and I'd love to wear it, but my mom is four inches shorter than I. She's petite while I'm more full-figured. She's offering to have her dress altered for me, but I'd rather get something new that really fits. How can I get out of this without hurting my mom's feelings?

Wearing an heirloom gown is a wonderful tradition, when it's practical. Because of the differences you describe, however, your mother's dress would probably need to be completely remade. When you talk with your mother, be sure she knows that you would really like to wear her dress if you could. (You aren't criticizing her taste.) Be respectful, but also be clear that you won't feel comfortable in a dress that doesn't suit you. You might also talk with a seamstress or tailor who can explain to your mom how extensive the changes would be. Then involve your mother in your dress selection; seeing you in a beautiful new gown is likely to cure her disappointment. If it's feasible, incorporate something from her wedding (a piece of her jewelry, some lace, or her veil) in your outfit—a loving way to show how much you appreciate your mom and to create a new family tradition.

Bridesmaids' Attire

BECAUSE ATTENDANTS GENERALLY PAY for their own dresses and accessories, the bride is obliged to carefully consider the cost of their outfits. It's also important to think about your bridesmaids' height and figures and look for styles that will be as flattering as possible for everyone.

Though the maid or matron of honor traditionally assists in the selection of bridesmaids' attire, try to consult with all your attendants. Unless someone requests that you order her gown, it's best to respect your attendants' privacy and not to ask for sizes and measurements. Try to let your attendants do their own ordering. Alterations are usually handled by the store where the gown is purchased, but inform your attendants if you have better sources.

Appropriateness

Bridesmaids' dresses should match the bride's dress in formality, though not necessarily in style or fabric. For example, if the bride wears satin, her attendants would wear a similar material, though not organdy or linen. As long as the dresses are complementary, the bride can wear a long gown while bridesmaids' dresses can be a shorter length. At very formal weddings, however, both the bride and her attendants traditionally wear floor-length.

Attendants' dresses don't have to be exact matches, so brides may offer their bridesmaids a range of styles—dresses in the same fabric and color (or range of colors) but of different cuts. Another option is to ask attendants to select their own dresses within general guidelines for fabric, length, color, and degree of formality. Maid or matron of honor's dresses and flowers may be of a different color and style than the other attendants'. Virtually all colors are acceptable today, including black and shades of white. If choosing white, be careful that attendants won't look like the bride.

Whatever you decide, the goal is to create a look for the entire wedding party that is harmonious and suitable for the occasion. Before selecting attendants' outfits, however, be sure to check with your officiant about any dress requirements.

Accessories

Attendants' shoes are usually the same type—pump or sandal—and color but need not be exactly the same shoe. Dyed fabric shoes are one choice. (If the bride herself will have all the shoes dyed, she should ask her bridesmaids to buy their shoes and deliver them to her in advance. The dying can then be done at one time to ensure that the colors are a perfect match.) Or you can ask your bridesmaids to wear dressy black or white shoes in the same basic style. When attendants are wearing street-length or midcalf-length dresses, you'll want to coordinate the color of panty hose.

Although the bride selects the headdress for her attendants, she should never dictate hairstyles. If you expect attendants to wear matching jewelry, you should provide it, perhaps as your bridesmaids' gifts. Otherwise, discuss jewelry with your attendants but leave the final choice to them.

Young Attendants

When children are included in the wedding, their parents are expected to pay for their outfits. The bride and groom or their families provide all the necessary accoutrements, including flowers, baskets, and ring cushions.

Junior bridesmaids and junior ushers wear the same clothing as their adult counterparts. A young bridesmaid's dress, accessories, and flowers are the same color and style as the other bridesmaids', through dress style can be adapted so that it is suitable for her age and size. A ten-year-old, for instance, could wear a strapped version of the bridesmaids' strapless dresses. A junior usher dresses like his elders, usually in a tux or dark suit and tie.

Flower girls. A flower girl traditionally wears a white or pastel dress of midcalf length, white socks, and party shoes like Mary Janes. The dress may be similar to the bridesmaids' gowns but should be appropriate for a young child. Headdresses include wreaths of artificial flowers or ribbons or flowers braided in the child's hair. (If headwear makes a child uncomfortable, it can be dispensed with.) Flower girls carry a small bouquet or a basket of flowers, but as a rule, they no longer scatter petals before the bride.

Ring bearers, train bearers, and pages. Very young boys wear white Eton-style jackets and short pants with white socks and shoes. Older boys usually wear navy-blue suits with navy socks and black shoes and a boutonniere.

I'll be a bridesmaid in a couple of months, but the bride is making all her attendants crazy with her instructions. She sends us lists with the color and brand of lipstick, eye shadow, and nail polish we have to wear. We're all supposed to have our hair and nails done at one, very expensive salon. Our shoes aren't open-toed, but she expects us to have pedicures. She's even asked one bridesmaid to have her ears pierced and another to get her hair highlighted. Is this normal? What can we do?

It's understandable that brides want their wedding days to be perfect, but some get carried away and obsess about details. Your situation could be worse. There are brides who have told attendants to lose weight, have teeth capped, hold off getting pregnant, or undergo skin treatments before the wedding.

You and the other attendants should meet with the bride now and talk about your issues. Be as kind as you can (she may not realize that her instructions are excessive), but let her know that you are united. Explain your objections clearly and rationally. Look for some compromises. You'll be glad to discuss makeup and hairstyles, but the final choice is up to each of you. You might bring up costs, but don't make it your main issue; if the bride says she'll pay, you will be back to square one.

For the discussion to go well, be prepared with positive as well as negative comments. A few well-deserved compliments can do wonders. If she reacts badly, give her time to calm down and think. If she still insists on having her way, you have two choices: go along graciously or get out (though, hopefully, it won't come to that point). Should you decide to "resign," avoid blaming or saying anything that could end your friendship. Good people can do very foolish things under stress, and your friend may someday regret her imperious behavior.

The Groom and His Attendants

THOUGH FORMAL AND SEMIFORMAL ATTIRE for grooms, groomsmen, and ushers hasn't changed significantly (aside from updating of cuts for trousers and lapels) for a century, today's groom does have more fashion choices, especially for informal and casual weddings. Even the traditional black or midnight-blue tuxedo can be paired with modern shirt and tie styles, and the ubiquitous dark suit or blazer and trouser combination offers room for variation. Clothing from other cultural or religious traditions can be worn for any degree of formality.

The point is to select outfits for yourself and your attendants that are appropriate to the style of the wedding and solemnity of the marriage service. The chart on page 662 will give you the specifics of daytime and evening dress for traditional formal, semiformal, and informal weddings, but the general guidelines are as follows:

Formal evening. Traditional evening formal attire includes black tailcoat and matching trousers, stiff white shirt, wing collar, white tie, and white waistcoat. Tuxedos are also acceptable.

Formal daytime. Worn for any wedding before six o'clock. Black or Oxford gray cutaway coat and black or gray striped trousers, pearl gray waistcoat, stiff white shirt, stiff fold-down collar, black-and-gray four-in-hand tie or dress ascot.

Semiformal evening. Black or midnight blue tuxedo and matching trousers, piqué or pleated-front shirt with attached collar, black bow tie, black waistcoat or cummerbund. For hot-weather ceremonies, a white dinner jacket and black cummerbund can be substituted.

Semiformal daytime. Suit-style dark gray or black sack (straight-backed) coat, matching trousers, soft shirt, and four-in-hand tie.

Informal day or evening. Lighter-weight suits or jackets and trousers, soft shirts with attached collars, and four-in-hand ties in a dark, small pattern. In warm weather, grooms and attendants might wear dark blue or gray jackets or blazers with white trousers, with either white or black dress socks and shoes. In hot climates, white suits can be worn.

There are basically two ways to organize attendants' attire. The groom might tell his attendants what he will wear and ask them to rent or purchase the same. Or it may be more convenient for the groom or best man to ask for sizes and measurements and then order all the outfits and accessories from a single rental source. (Formal-wear rental stores may offer discounts for multiple orders and normally provide alteration service.) Dress shoes can also be rented, and this is a good way to see that everyone is shod in the same style.

Except for boutonnieres (supplied by the groom), attendants are responsible for their rental and/or purchase costs. It's normally the duty of the best man or head usher to see that everyone is dressed appropriately.

∼ "Best Woman" and "Man of Honor" ∼

When the customary roles are reversed in the choice of attendants—a man as the bride's honor attendant or a woman serving as the groom's "best person"—the question of what to wear arises. The solution is surprisingly easy. A male honor attendant simply wears the same attire as the groom and groomsmen. A woman may wear a dress in the same color family as the bridesmaids, or she can choose a dress in black, gray, or whatever the primary color worn by the groomsmen. Her attire is in keeping with the formality of the wedding, but she wouldn't wear a tux, or dress like the groomsmen. A man wears a boutonniere, and a woman usually wears a corsage featuring the same flowers in the groomsmen's boutonnieres.

Don't forget comfort when selecting attire. Coats should lie smoothly across the back but give you freedom of movement. Coat sleeves should reveal a half inch of shirt cuff when your arms are straight at your sides. Trousers are hemmed even with the top of the back of the shoes and have a slight break in front, so the hem rests on the shoes.

Mothers and Fathers of the Wedding Couple

THIS WILL BE YOUR CHILDREN'S DAY, but you have the right to shine, too. Parents and stepparents should choose clothing in keeping with the style of the wedding. Comfort matters as well, since you're likely to be busy for the entire event, so select garments that feel and fit as good as they look.

Mothers

Fashionable mother-of-the-bride (and the groom) outfits—whatever the formality—are generally easier to find today than in the past, when even youthful mothers were expected to appear matronly. No one now expects mothers to look anything other than their age. Still, there are a few issues of dress etiquette to remember:

➤ Try not to wear colors that are the same as or very similar to the bride's and bridesmaids' dresses. If you want a light color, look for pastels and light or medium tones rather than white.

➤ It's preferable that mothers wear different colors, so consult with the other mother and/or stepmothers about color. Hopefully, everyone is on good terms, and you can discuss your plans so that each mother will be both distinctive and comfortable with her choice of attire.

➤ The length of your gown or dress is your choice, even for formal weddings. Long dresses and skirts are fine for any wedding from noon on. Mothers of the bride and groom do not have to wear the same length, though many do, feeling that the same length creates a more harmonious look, especially in wedding photos.

➤ Gloves and hats or headpieces are normally worn for formal weddings but are optional otherwise, so be guided by the bride's preference and any religious requirements. Gloves are worn for receiving lines but can be removed afterward and are always taken off when eating.

Fathers

When they participate in the ceremony, fathers and/or stepfathers almost always wear the same outfits as the groom's attendants. This is also the case for any man who escorts the bride down the aisle.

When the father of the groom doesn't have an active role, he can either match the formality of the male attendants or "dress down" a bit—choosing a tuxedo or dark suit instead of more formal attire. But if the groom's father is to be in a receiving line, his outfit will often conform to that of the bride's father or the groomsmen.

It's not uncommon nowadays to see all formal male attire classed as tuxedos, but in fact, a tux is a semiformal dinner jacket, worn with matching trousers to make a tuxedo suit. The man who started the fashion was Pierre Lorillard IV, of the tobacco fortune. Inspired by the traditional scarlet English hunt coat (and perhaps by the Prince of Wales, who reportedly had the tails cut from his coats while on a visit to India), Lorillard asked his tailor to make several black, tail-less jackets. The jackets were first worn by Griswold Lorillard, Pierre's son, and several young friends to a ball in Tuxedo Park, New York, in the fall of 1886—and a style was born. The tux got its name from the town, but "tuxedo" goes back to the Algonquin word for "wolf."

Griswold Lorillard and his friends wore scarlet vests under their daring new coats. But the cummerbund, most often worn with a tux today, owes its origin to an item of Hindu formal wear—the *kamarband*, or "loin band."

The Military Wedding Party

A MILITARY WEDDING can be anything from an informal service in a civilian setting to a full-blown, spit-and-polish affair complete with the American flag, unit standards, and the romantic Arch of Steel. The etiquette for military weddings varies somewhat from service to service, and members of the military should check their service manuals or consult with a protocol officer or base chaplain.

In general, brides and grooms in the service may wear either civilian clothes or their uniforms, as may their colleagues who serve as attendants. Depending on the formality of the occasion, everyday and dress uniforms are equally correct, since young and noncareer personnel often don't have dress uniforms. For commissioned officers, evening dress uniforms are the equivalent of civilian white tie, and dinner or mess dress is the same formality as a tuxedo. Noncommissioned officers can wear dress or everyday uniforms for formal and informal ceremonies.

Regulations vary by service branch, but as a rule, only commissioned officers in full uniform wear swords. Hats and caps are carried during an indoor ceremony, and gloves are always worn by saber or cutlass bearers. Flowers are never worn on uniforms, but brides in uniform may carry a bridal bouquet. Service members not in uniform and civilian members of the wedding party dress as they would for any ceremony. (For more on military weddings, see Chapter 35, page 599: "The Military Advantage"; Chapter 39 page 689: "Military seating protocol," and page 697: "A Military Wedding.")

Dress for the Wedding Party

This chart provides general dress guidelines for traditional American formal, semiformal, and informal weddings. Standards for dress are often different in other traditions,

	Most Formal Daytime	Most Formal Evening	Semiformal Daytime	Semiformal Evening	Informal Daytime	Informal Evening
Bride	Long, white dress, train, veil; gloves optional	Same as the most formal daytime	Long, white dress; short veil and gloves optional	Same as the semiformal daytime	Short afternoon dress, cocktail dress, or suit	Long dinner dress, short cocktail dress, or suit
Bride's attendants	Long dresses, matching shoes; gloves at bride's option	Same as the most formal daytime	Long or short dresses, matching shoes; gloves at bride's option	Dresses of same formality and length as bride's dress; gloves at bride's option	Same style as bride	Same style as bride
Groom, his attendants, bride's father or stepfather, and groom's father if in the service	Cutaway coat; striped trousers; pearl gray waistcoat; white stiff shirt, turndown collar with gray-and-black-striped four-in-hand tie or wing collar with ascot; gray gloves; black silk socks; black kid shoes	Black tailcoat and trousers; white piqué waistcoat; starched-front shirt, wing collar, and white bow tie; white gloves; black silk socks; black patent-leather shoes or pumps or black kid smooth-toed shoes (If tuxedos are preferred, see Semiformal Evening.)	Black or charcoal sack coat; dove gray waistcoat; white pleated shirt, starched turndown collar, or soft white shirt, with four-in-hand tie; gray gloves; black smooth-toed shoes	Winter: black tuxedo Summer: white jacket Pleated or piqué soft shirt; black cummerbund and black bow tie; black patent-leather or kid shoes; no gloves	Winter: dark suit Summer: dark trousers with white linen jacket or white trousers with navy or charcoal jacket; soft shirt with conservative four-in-hand tie Hot climate: white suit	Tuxedo if bride wears dinner dress; otherwise, dark suit in winter, lighter suit in summer
Groom's father and/or stepfather, if not participating in the ceremony*	Dark suit, conservative shirt and tie	Tuxedo if wife wears long dress; otherwise, dark suit	Dark suit, conservative shirt and tie	Tuxedo if wife wears long dress, or dark suit	Winter: dark suit Summer: light trousers and dark blazer	Dark suit
Mothers and/or stepmothers of the couple	Long or short dresses; hats or hair ornaments optional; gloves optional	Usually long evening or dinner dresses or dressy cocktail-length dresses; head coverings or hair ornaments optional; gloves optional	Long or street-length dresses; gloves and head coverings optional	Same as semiformal daytime	Short afternoon or cocktail dresses	Same length dresses as bride's

*If the father or stepfather of the groom is not among the attendants but will be taking part in the receiving line or wishes to dress formally, he may wear the same outfit as the groom and groomsmen.

and religious practice may affect decisions about head coverings, veils, and other clothing choices.

Flowers for the Wedding Party

THOUGH NOT LITERALLY ATTIRE, the flowers that you and your wedding party wear and carry will be your most striking accessories. Although you should wait until you've chosen your and your attendants' attire before selecting flowers, it's wise to begin interviewing florists as early as possible. As a rule, flowers that are in season locally are less costly than flowers ordered from distant suppliers, so ask about readily available flowers and greenery that are appropriate to the style and formality of your wedding. Even if you or friends will do your wedding flowers, it's a good idea to discuss ideas with a professional florist. (For more about hiring and working with a florist, ceremony and reception flowers, and who pays for the flowers, see Chapter 35, page 607: "Flowers and Decorations.")

Attendants' flowers can be of a different color or colors than the bride's, and styles can differ as well. (For example, bridesmaids might carry sprays, while the bride carries a traditional nosegay.) The maid or matron of honor might have a different color bouquet, or all the attendants' bouquets could vary across a color range (lighter to darker shades of pink, for instance).

In addition to the color scheme and style of the wedding and wedding attire, you should consider the individual physical characteristics of bridal attendants. The conventional nosegay has an eighteen-inch diameter, but that size can be overwhelming for a petite bridesmaid. The length of arm bouquets can be adjusted to suit bridesmaids of different heights. A considerate couple will also ask attendants about any allergies they may have; if there's a problem, you can substitute silk flowers for the offending blossoms.

Formal bouquets. Traditionally, formal bouquets are all white and can include one type of flower or several. The flowers are usually formal varieties, including roses, gardenias, lilies, and lily of the valley. Stephanotis, the symbol of marital happiness in the Victorian language of flowers, is a popular addition to formal and semiformal bouquets. Though usually shaped as a nosegay or cascade, a formal bouquet can be as simply elegant as a single calla lily or white rose. Formal bouquets might be trimmed with white satin ribbon, chiffon, or organza.

Semiformal bouquets. Usually shaped as nosegays or arm bouquets, semiformal arrangements are often colorful—either in mixed colors or shades of a single color—and can combine formal and informal varieties of flowers. White, semiformal bouquets are often accented with tinted ribbons to add soft color.

Informal bouquets. The shapes of informal wedding bouquets may be formal to very casual (such as a spray of garden flowers tied with pretty ribbon, a basket of fragrant heather, or an airy cloud of baby's breath). The range of colors and varieties is as wide as nature allows.

Tossing bouquets. If a bouquet toss is included in the reception plans, the bride's bouquet can be designed to include a "breakaway" bouquet that is removed from the main bouquet for tossing. Another option is to order a separate tossing bouquet that is similar to but not as elaborate as the bridal bouquet.

Flower girl's flowers. Traditionally, the flower girl scattered fresh rose petals before the bride. But petals tend to be slippery, so flower girls today usually carry small bouquets or baskets filled with firmly secured blossoms.

Flowers for the hair. Fresh flowers make charming adornments, whether pinned or braided in the bride's and attendants' hair, worn as a crown or head wreath, or attached to a headpiece. When a veil is gathered into fresh flowers, consult your florist about the best method to attach the flowers to the veil.

Boutonnieres. Boutonnieres are supplied for the groom, all groomsmen and ushers, the couple's fathers, stepfathers, and grandfathers, and perhaps for special male guests and helpers. A boutonniere is usually a single bloom or a small spray (like stephanotis) of a variety that doesn't crush or wilt easily. It may be wired with greenery, so long as it doesn't appear to be a corsage. The groom's boutonniere is traditionally a flower featured in the bride's bouquet. Boutonnieres for other male members of the wedding party needn't match the groom's in color or variety but should be complementary. (Boutonnieres can be dispensed with if you prefer the sleek look of unadorned male attire.)

Corsages. Corsages are normally given to the couple's mothers, stepmothers, and grandmothers, and sometimes to siblings who are not in the wedding and perhaps special female guests. When family or friends assist at the reception, the women often receive corsages both as gifts of appreciation and for the practical purpose of distinguishing them from other guests. Corsages complement the flowers of the wedding party but need not be the same color or flowers. You might not be able to consult everyone, but to avoid clashing with wedding attire, try to confer with female relatives about flower choices and colors.

Often the bride receives a corsage from her new groom to wear with her traveling outfit. But this is entirely optional.

Classic Shapes for Wedding Bouquets

Nosegays. *Dense, circular arrangements, approximately eighteen inches in diameter. Suited for long and short gowns. May include posies (petite nosegays of small buds) or tussy-mussies (buds in cone-shaped holders). A Biedermeier nosegay is composed of rings of flowers—one variety or color for each ring.*

Arm bouquets. *Crescent-shaped, curved to fit the arm. Larger than nosegays and best suited to long gowns.*

Sprays. *Flowers gathered in a triangular-shaped cluster. Sizes vary. Suitable with long or short gowns.*

Cascades. *Of any shape, the bouquet trails blossoms or greenery from its base. Best with long gowns.*

Chapter Thirty-eight

Wedding Gifts

WEDDING GIFTS HAVE A HISTORY that shouldn't be forgotten. In ancient cultures, whole communities celebrated weddings as times of renewal and hope for the future. Each union was greeted as the beginning of a new family, and families assured the survival of the community. Wedding couples were showered with symbols of fidelity, fertility, and prosperity. In many cultures, household items were given to help newlyweds establish their home and prepare for children.

In spite of what many critics regard as the overcommercialization of weddings today, the rationale for wedding gifts is still the good wishes of the "community" of family and friends included in the festivities. Gifts may be practical or fanciful, inexpensive or extravagant, but each one represents the giver's happiness for you. Whatever the gift may be, it is a symbol of hope for your future.

Gift Registry

BACK IN THE LATE 1800s, a bride's parents would place a notice in the newspaper shortly before her wedding date. This announcement, listing all gifts received so far, helped guests who had not yet selected presents to avoid duplications. Announcing soon evolved into registering with one or two stores in the community, and brides listed their patterns for traditional household gifts, including fine and everyday china, crystal, silverware, and linens. Wedding guests could select a place setting or serving piece within a couple's pattern, and experienced salespeople kept track of what was purchased. This kind of registry prevailed through most of the twentieth century.

During the late 1980s and early 1990s, the practice of registering many items at different types of department and specialty stores came into vogue, and couples can now register with stores specializing in items including hardware, garden supplies, and sporting goods. Computers enable national chains and catalogers to track gift purchases at all their outlets.

Today's gift registries remain a convenience for guests, especially those who don't know a couple's tastes, have little time for shopping, or live at a distance and can't shop at local stores. But many guests enjoy shopping for gifts and take pleasure in selecting "just the right thing," and no one is obligated to make purchases "on register."

When and What to Register

If you plan to register, do it as soon as you can, and complete the process before your wedding invitations are sent. You can register even if you're marrying on a short schedule, so guests can shop after the wedding.

Stores will do their best to see that you receive the gifts you want. The following suggestions should help you select registry items wisely and with consideration for your guests.

Think about what you need. A registry is a wish list but should be based on your real needs and lifestyle. If your style is casual, you may not be interested in fine china and silver. On the other hand, you may look forward to the time when your life is more formal and want to register more traditional gifts. Whatever you select, be sure that you and your spouse-to-be agree on the choices.

Register items in a variety of price ranges. Listing only expensive gifts is a discourtesy; it's up to your guests to decide what they'll spend. If your registry may also be used for shower gifts, include some moderately priced items appropriate for the type of shower planned.

Register with national chains and/or catalog services when possible. This makes gift selection easier for out-of-town guests. They can order through catalogs or local branch stores or use a chain's toll-free number or Web site. There's no limit on the number of stores where you may register, but be sensible.

Don't register for the same items at different stores. Since retailers do not coordinate information with other retailers, you might receive many more of an item than you want.

Don't abuse the registry for personal gain. Deliberately registering unwanted items in order to exchange them for cash or credit is unethical and an insult to those who give gifts. Many retailers are revising their return and exchange policies to stop registry abuse.

For a bride or groom to state or imply that only registered items are acceptable is the height of bad taste. Although guests may comply and use the registry, this behavior is never kind and rarely forgotten.

Getting the Word Out

The tried-and-true method of telling people about your gift registry is word of mouth. Once you've registered, provide your parents, attendants, and anyone else who is close to you with a list of your registry sources, their addresses, and how to contact them via phone and Internet. Most people know to ask a couple's close family and friends about registries. Don't hand out registry cards, even though store personnel may tell you that this is okay.

Do not include registry lists or information of any kind about gifts in your wedding invitations. There are stories of some couples mailing registry lists with their invitations, only to offend their guests with the emphasis on gifts seeming more important than joining them on their wedding day.

If a guest asks what you would like, it's courteous to respond by stressing that the *choice is hers.* You may tell her a bit about your wish list or where you're registered, but be sure to say, "Whatever you'd like to surprise us with would be wonderful." If the person asks where you're registered, tell her; just don't be the one to raise the subject.

Don't include registry lists in engagement party invitations, wedding announcements, or invitations to wedding-related social events. The one exception is shower invitations. Your hostess can include a registry list with the invitation if she wishes. Or you can supply her with a registry list or a list of items you'd like in a range of prices. She can then inform shower guests who wonder about what to give.

A note to shower hostesses and hosts: When guests consult you about their gifts, give them all the options. It's okay to provide guidance if you know what other guests are bringing, but well-mannered hosts are not insistent about what guests should give and won't pressure anyone to participate in a group gift.

Registry Alternatives

Not every couple is comfortable registering, and not everyone needs or wants tangible items. Alternatives like the following can fulfill your wishes, help your guests with gift selection, and may even spread your happiness in unexpected directions.

No registry. Couples do not have to register for gifts. If you plan an intimate wedding or your guests are all family and friends who know your tastes and needs, there may be no reason to register. Or you might register at only one or two locations for a limited number of items.

Charitable gifts. Couples who don't want gifts might steer guests to special charities and nonprofit services. Give close family and friends a list of the causes you consider worthwhile and ask them to inform other guests. Established charities will notify you of donations made in your name. It's advisable to avoid political or highly controversial causes. Some people may not hear about your desire or may prefer to give more traditional gifts, so be gracious if you receive traditional items.

Financial registries. Check with your bank or investment house about financial gifts; some now have registries for savings accounts, stocks, bonds, and other investment vehicles. There are even registries for couples who are saving for down payments on homes or automobiles. One caveat: If you want monetary gifts, let your family and friends tell others. Don't initiate discussion about your desire for funds or imply that money matters most to you.

Cash and checks. Cash gifts are perfectly acceptable, *if* the guest feels comfortable with the idea. (Although cash gifts are traditional in some areas and ethnic groups, some people just don't like to give money, and that's their prerogative.) If asked, a couple might say, "We're saving for living-room furniture, so if you like the idea of giving a check as a gift, that's how we will use it. Whatever you decide would be terrific!"

Honeymoon registries. Now available through many travel companies and agents, these registries allow guests to contribute to a couple's honeymoon trip fund.

All About Gifts

A GIFT IS, by definition, voluntary. Although gifts are customarily expected for some occasions, including weddings, this is a matter of social convention, and no one should regard a gift as an entitlement. Local and cultural traditions may influence gift choices and methods of delivery or presentation, but the following guidelines will help couples know when gifts are considered appropriate, what types suit specific occasions, and how to receive every gift with grace and gratitude.

Engagements

Except when part of a couple's culture, no engagement gifts are expected, regardless of whether there is an engagement party. If given, they are generally tokens of affection (for example, a picture frame, a guest book or photo album, a bottle of good wine, a set of guest towels) and not too expensive. If some guests bring presents to an engagement party, the gifts should be opened later so that guests who, correctly, didn't bring gifts are not embarrassed.

Gift Showers

Gifts fit the theme of the party (kitchen, bath, linen, etc.) and shouldn't be too elaborate or very costly. Handmade gifts such as monogrammed linens are traditional, but purchased gifts are more the norm today. A group gift, often organized by the host, is a popular way to give a more elaborate present, but no one should be forced to participate, and no other present is expected from people who do contribute. People who can't attend are not obliged to send a shower gift, though sometimes close friends or relatives do.

Conscious of the financial burden that shower gifts plus wedding gifts can place on friends, considerate couples today are coming up with clever, low-cost ideas like the following:

Book and CD showers. Reading and music make great themes for showers for a couple. A VHS/DVD shower might be perfect for movie lovers.

Recipe showers. An old custom revived, the presents are favorite recipes, usually written on standard recipe cards and collected in a recipe box or file.

Pantry showers. For couples who already have well-equipped kitchens, guests bring useful and often exotic pantry supplies—spices, condiments, coffees and teas, paper products, bamboo skewers, and the like.

Stock-the-bar showers. Guests needn't buy expensive vintages to help a couple acquire the basic bar components, including non-potables like measuring utensils, bottle openers, swizzle sticks, cocktail napkins, bottled garnishes, and tins of fancy nuts.

Best-wishes showers. Instead of things, guests bring sentiments—original writings, favorite quotations, humorous sayings. These expressions can be written on pages supplied by the host before the party, read aloud at the party, and then collected in an attractive notebook for the couple.

Your Wedding Gifts

As every child knows, receiving gifts is a thrill, and that childhood pleasure will bubble up again when your wedding gifts begin to arrive. It's especially delightful when couples open their gifts together, but circumstances don't always cooperate, as when the future bride and groom live some distance apart. Don't put off opening gifts; delays will hold up your thank-you notes and may cause red faces when you run into a friend whose unopened package you've squirreled away for a week or two.

Knowing the following fundamentals of wedding gift etiquette should increase the fun of every unwrapping and enhance your appreciation of the gift, the giver, and your own responsibilities as the recipients:

Is a wedding gift expected? Yes, with an exception. Following long-established tradition, everyone who receives a wedding invitation should send a gift whether they attend the wedding or not. But if you send invitations to casual acquaintances, business associates you don't know well, or people you haven't seen in years and they do not attend the festivities, then a gift is not expected.

Married couples and nuclear families generally send one gift, as do couples who live together. When you invite someone "and Guest," the person you invite is responsible for a gift, but the guest or date isn't. Group giving, when guests pool their resources to purchase a more elaborate gift, is fine.

How much should guests spend on gifts? People have tried to come up with formulas, but it is a falsehood that guests should spend an amount on their gifts that is equal to the per-person amount spent to entertain them at the reception. Expecting this kind of tit-for-tat exchange is impractical and thoughtless. A wedding gift is a social obligation, but the choice of the gift is based only on the giver's affection for and relationship to the couple and perhaps their families and on the person's financial capabilities.

When are gifts sent? Traditionally, gifts may be sent as soon as the wedding invitation arrives, and some may come earlier if people know for certain that they'll be invited. Most guests send gifts before the wedding, but gifts may arrive afterward, particularly when the wedding is held on short notice. It is pure myth that guests have up to a year after a wedding to send gifts. Gifts should be delivered as close to the wedding date as possible, but circumstances such as an invitee's illness may cause a delay, and couples shouldn't question a late arrival. Nor should couples ever ask why they didn't receive a gift from an invited guest. However, a guest who does not receive a thank-you note after a reasonable time—usually three months post-wedding—may contact the couple to learn if the gift was delivered.

When gifts are mailed or shipped, it's nice to call the giver and tell him that the item arrived. Regardless of whether you call, *every wedding gift must be acknowledged with a written thank-you note.* (See page 674: "The Importance of 'Thank You.'")

In some localities and certain ethnic and religious groups, it's customary for guests to take their gifts to the wedding ceremony or reception. In some cases, gifts in the form of checks are handed to the bride or groom in the receiving line or at another time during the reception. If gifts are brought to the celebration, they should be placed on a table set up for them. Newlyweds are not expected to open the gifts during the reception, but they should arrange to have someone oversee the packages and transport them to a safe place afterward.

How are gifts delivered? Gifts are usually sent by mail or delivery service. Traditionally, gifts are addressed to the bride and delivered to her or her parents' home before the wedding or addressed to the couple and sent to their home after the wedding. Today, gifts may be addressed to both the bride- and groom-to-be and may be sent to the groom or his family if that's most convenient. When gifts are being delivered to different people and different addresses, communication among the couple and their families is important, and you must keep an accurate record of what has been received and when gifts arrive.

Is record-keeping really necessary? Yes, absolutely. Gift cards can easily be lost or mixed up, and it's hard to remember who gave what. Keeping a record helps you associate specific gifts with the givers, so you can say something nice when you next see your guests and personalize your thank-you note. A detailed list also serves as a record for insurance purposes.

Most couples keep a written or computer-based log, recording information as soon as gifts arrive. This information should include:

> ➤ **The date the gift is received:** Also note how it was shipped in case there is damage or breakage.
>
> ➤ **A clear description of the item or items:** Writing "platter" won't help much if you receive three or four. Be specific: "18-inch pottery platter, sunflower design." Include the quantities of multiple items ("4 monogrammed pillowcases, pale blue").
>
> ➤ **The source of the gift:** Note the store, catalog service, and so on, if known.

➤ **The name and address of the giver or givers:** Save gift cards to double-check spellings.

➤ **A notation of when your thank-you note is sent.**

It's also a good idea to number the gifts in your log and attach the same number to the gift. If gifts are going to several addresses, be sure that everyone who might take delivery knows to jot down the date, delivery service, and other pertinent information and to attach a note securely to the package. If children might accept deliveries, instruct them clearly about how to handle and where to store packages. Another tip: Open deliveries as soon as you can. You may be expecting something from a store, but don't assume that the store's label on a shipping package means that it contains the item you bought. It could be a gift.

Gifts for the Wedding Party

Gifts are often exchanged among members of the wedding party, and gifts from the bride and groom to their attendants are considered especially important.

Bride and groom's gifts. It's traditional for the bride and groom to give a special gift of appreciation to each attendant. Usually the bride chooses the gift for her bridesmaids and the groom for his groomsmen and/or ushers, but a couple might give the same gift to everyone. (Glassware, picture frames, engagement books, and decorative boxes are typical of gifts that cross gender lines.) Gifts need not be expensive but should be a meaningful commemoration of the occasion. This is not the place for joke presents.

If you have children in your wedding, personal and age-appropriate gifts will be a special treat for each youngster.

Gifts to attendants are usually presented at the rehearsal dinner, the rehearsal if there is no party, or at bridesmaids' and groomsmen's parties. Sometimes gifts are presented at the wedding, but there's always the risk they could be mislaid or stolen.

Attendants' gifts. Wedding attendants often present gifts to the bride and groom, though this isn't an absolute. The expense of being in a wedding can put a serious strain on an attendant's budget, so couples need to be sensitive. If attendants host a prenuptial party or give shower presents in addition to their individual wedding gifts, a considerate couple will be clear that no other gifts are expected. (You might tell your honor attendants of your wishes, and ask them to speak to the other attendants.) Although costly gifts shouldn't be expected in any case, a group gift—bridesmaids to bride, groomsmen/ushers to groom, or all attendants to the couple—can be the ideal way to express love and best wishes at the least expense for each attendant.

Attendants' gifts are usually presented at bridesmaids' and groomsmen's parties, the rehearsal or rehearsal party, or possibly at the reception when other gifts are taken to the wedding.

Gifts to each other. Though it's not essential, couples often give one another personal engagement and wedding gifts, in addition to their rings. Gifts can range from jewelry engraved with the wedding date or a special sentiment to fun items to share in your new life together.

Gifts for family. Though not expected, gifts for parents, stepparents, and grandparents are a lovely tribute to the people who have cherished and supported you through thick and thin. Expense isn't the issue. A family gift can be as simple as a rose and a loving note placed on their seats at the ceremony or a small book of verse or meditations with a special, personal inscription.

Gifts are very important for the young and teenage children of either or both of the couple. Ideas for making children feel special at an encore wedding are discussed in depth in Chapter 41, page 725: "Making It a Family Affair."

Wedding announcements. Sent soon after the marriage to inform people who were not invited to the wedding, announcements are a courtesy and carry no obligation for a gift. Some people may send gifts, but you shouldn't expect them.

Gifts on Display

Whether to display gifts is your decision. Gift displays are for the home. Because of transportation and security problems, gifts are rarely put on view in hotels, clubs, restaurants, and reception halls. Security is always an issue; thieves search the newspapers for wedding days and times. If you're uneasy, you can hire a guard to watch the house when everyone is away. Also check with your insurer about additional coverage for gifts.

How to display. Gifts can be displayed during a home reception or for guests who are invited to stop by in the days before or after the wedding. Sometimes couples or their parents host a tea or cocktail event at which the gifts are on display—usually in a separate room from the party area. Normally, gifts are placed on a table or tables covered with cloths or sheets; the covering can drape to the floor so that boxes can be hidden underneath. Shower and engagement presents are not usually included in displays.

Tactful displays. Organize the table so that there's no visual comparison between the items. For instance, don't place a single piece of silver plate next to an elaborate sterling service. Sometimes, gifts are arranged by purpose: utilitarian items such as kitchen equipment or hardware on tables or areas separate from china and silver. With tableware, a single place setting (two if you have formal and everyday settings) is displayed rather than all the plates, utensils, and glasses you've received. If you receive multiples of any item, display only one.

Displaying cards. There's no rule about displaying gift cards. Some couples think that who gave what is a private matter. But showing cards can be a nice acknowledgment

We're having a small wedding (thirty close family and friends) in our apartment, and we don't expect many gifts. We both think it's nice to display what we receive, but my future sister-in-law says that with so few gifts, a display would be tacky. Who's right?

You are. If you want a display, go right ahead. With a small number of gifts, you can probably display them all and include gift cards if you like. Use an area apart from the ceremony location—a table in a bedroom or the dining room will be fine—for your display. Another option is to host a casual pre- or post-wedding get-together for your friends and put the gifts out for all to see.

and save you from the inevitable "Who sent that?" questions. You can place the cards with each gift or arrange them in a separate spot, overlapping cards so that the givers' names show.

Cards are advantageous when you receive large items that are difficult to display. On a folded card (small note size), write the item and the name of the giver or givers ("Gas Outdoor Grill" on the first line, followed by the names in the order they appeared on the gift card); then prop the card among the gifts on the display table.

There's one major problem with display cards: If you show one giver's name, you should show every name. People who do not see their names on your display may worry that their gifts never arrived or, worse, that you don't value their gifts. If you really want to include names, you might forgo cards and write all names, alphabetically, in a booklet left on the display table.

Displaying checks. The custom of displaying gift checks is waning, largely because financial gifts come in so many forms—certificates, cash, contributions to bank and investment accounts. Should you get financial gifts of different sorts, listing the givers, but not the amounts, in your gift book (above) may be the best approach. When checks are displayed, the amounts are never revealed. Checks are overlapped so that only the signatures are visible. Place plain paper over the top check to cover the bank name and the amount. Secure the checks to the table, so they can't be lifted or moved; a sheet of clear glass or acrylic over the checks should keep them safe and sound.

The Importance of "Thank You"

THERE ARE TWO FUNDAMENTALS of expressing gratitude. First, every gift—whether a tangible item, money, a social event in your honor, or a gift of time or talent—should be acknowledged in writing. And second, your acknowledgment should be prompt.

Personal, handwritten thank-yous remain the gold standard of courtesy in this age of cell phones, pocket computers, and instant messaging. Written notes demonstrate that the writer cares enough about the giver to compose an individualized message and put the words on paper. (See also Chapter 17, page 231: "Thank-you Notes.")

Respond in a timely fashion. Ideally, you'll write on the day you receive a wedding gift. If you put off all note writing until after the wedding, it can truly become a chore. For couples stymied by the large number of notes to be written, a good suggestion is to set a daily goal. Completing three or four notes each day doesn't seem nearly so impossible as writing a hundred notes within a month. The accepted standard: Your thank-you notes should be written and sent *within three months* of receipt of each gift.

Share the responsibility. The days when thank-yous were the sole duty of the bride are over. Today's brides and grooms share the responsibility, which greatly decreases the time involved, and each writes to the people he or she knows best. This makes it easier to tailor notes to the individual givers.

Include your fiancé/fiancée or new spouse in the thanks. Though you sign your notes with your own name, your message expresses gratitude from both of you. (See page 677: "The Perfect Note.") There may be exceptions (when someone does a favor or entertains specifically for one of you), but in general, people are giving to you as a couple.

Don't take shortcuts. Simply signing store-bought cards shows very little consideration. Likewise, writing virtually the same message to everyone is mechanical, and people quickly recognize a "fill-in-the-blanks" note. If you have a Web page, you might put up a general thanks to everyone for sharing your special day, but this is not an acceptable substitute for personal notes.

Whom to Thank

As you write notes, remember that not all gifts come wrapped in pretty paper. The following categories include both gift givers and the people who make a wedding special through their efforts and goodwill:

Everyone who gives you a wedding present. This includes people who literally hand you a present, no matter how effusively you thank them in person. You should write to each person or couple who contributed to a group gift. The one exception is a group gift from more than four or five coworkers. (See page 676: "People who entertain for you.")

Note: Thank-you notes are expected for shower gifts even though you thanked the giver in person when presents were opened. Written notes must also be sent to anyone who couldn't attend the shower but sent a gift.

What Kind of Stationery?

There's no single stationery required for thank-you notes, though you'll probably use a standard one-sided or single-fold note card and matching envelope. The paper can be plain or bordered, white, ecru, ivory, or a pastel color. Use ink that's easy to read; black ink is always legible.

Brides sign with their maiden names before the wedding, married names afterward. When using monogrammed papers, the notes sent by the bride before the wedding have the maiden-name initials; post-wedding notes have her married initials or the couple's last-name initial. (For more about monograms, see Chapter 30, page 518: Monogramming.)

Notepapers printed with "Thank You" or a short quotation or verse are fine, so long as you write your own note. But it's unacceptable to use a card with a pre-printed message.

Everyone who gives you money. Gifts of money—cash, checks, contributions to savings and investment accounts, donations to designated charities—must be acknowledged. You can mention amounts if you want, and doing so assures givers that currency arrived intact and account deposits were correct. Always include some indication of how you plan to use a monetary gift.

Anyone who sends you a congratulatory telegram on your wedding day. Though an old custom, sending a wedding telegram is still done and deserves a note of thanks. E-mail responses are fine for e-mailed congratulations.

Your attendants. In addition to thank-you notes for wedding presents, be sure to attach a card or note with a personal sentiment to the gifts you give your attendants. ("Thanks for everything, baby brother. You really are the *best* best man I could ask for. Love, Mitch.")

People who entertain for you. When there is more than one host for a shower or party, write to each person or couple. These notes should go out no later than two days after the event. The one exception is when a large number of people in your office or workplace host a shower or party in your honor and give a group gift. While it's preferable to thank everyone with an individual note, it is acceptable to write to the organizer or organizers only. Be sure your note includes your appreciation for everyone's participation. The person who receives your note should forward it to coworkers or post it in a common area. But if individual presents are given, write individual notes.

People who house and/or entertain your guests. When family and friends invite out-of-town guests or attendants to stay in their homes, you should write notes to the hosts and send thank-you gifts. The gift, with your card or note attached, might be an item for the home, such as a potted plant or a basket of soaps, or something special for the hosts, like tickets to a concert or a book by their favorite author. (For guest etiquette, see Chapter 26, "Hosts and Houseguests," pages 460–470. Friends who entertain your visitors—inviting them to dinner, taking them shopping, showing them the sights—deserve a note from you, though gifts aren't necessary.

People who do kindnesses for you. The neighbor who accepts delivery of your gifts when you're at work, the cousin who supervises guest parking at your reception—anyone who assists you during your preparations, during the wedding itself, and after the big event should be graciously thanked. It's also nice to send notes to your officiant and anyone else (the organist or music director, for instance) who worked with you on the ceremony, even though you've paid the customary fee.

Suppliers and vendors. You don't have to write everyone you hire for services, but anyone who exceeds your expectations will appreciate a courteous note of thanks.

The Perfect Note

While there's no formula for the perfect thank-you, the notes people remember are the ones that express real feeling. Think about the people you're thanking before you write anything. How would the conversation go if you were thanking them in person? Another hint: Look at the gift when you prepare to write; it may provide inspiration.

The first two examples below illustrate the difference between a note that gets the job done adequately and one that expresses thanks for a gift and real interest in the givers.

A simple note:

Dear Mr. and Mrs. Gresham,

Thank you so much for the lovely silver candy dish. It was so nice of you to think of Phil and me on our wedding day. I'm sorry you couldn't be with us, but we hope to be back in St. Paul at Christmas, and maybe we can all get together then.
     Thanks again for thinking of us in such a nice way.

Love,
Courtney

A livelier and more personal note:

Dear Mr. and Mrs. Gresham,

I'm looking right now at the lovely silver candy dish you sent and imagining how pretty it will be on our Thanksgiving table next month. (We're hosting Phil's family for the first time!) It really is one of my favorite things, and Phil and I are so grateful to you.
     We were both sorry that you couldn't come to the wedding, but I know your trip

to New Zealand must have been amazing. If all goes according to plan, we will be in St. Paul for Christmas, and we'd love to see you and the girls and hear about your travels.

Again, thank you so much for the candy dish and for the beautiful thoughts in your note.

Love from both of us,
Courtney

There's no reason for a note to be stuffy and formal. Write from your heart and the words will come—as they did in this warm and humorous example:

Dear Uncle Jim,

Well, you really saved the day—the Big Day—when my car conked out. If it weren't for you, I'd probably still be standing in front of Bartlett's, hanging on to my tux bag and trying to hail a cab in that downpour. Meg considers you our

～ Ten Do's and Don'ts of Thank-you Notes ～

This checklist should help couples avoid common missteps when expressing their gratitude in writing.

Do personalize your notes and make reference to the person as well as the gift.

Do be enthusiastic, but be realistic and don't gush. Avoid saying that a gift is the most beautiful thing you've ever seen unless you mean it.

Don't send form letters or cards with printed messages and just your signature; don't use e-mail or post generic thank-yous on your Web site in lieu of personal notes.

Don't mention that you plan to return or exchange a gift or indicate dissatisfaction in any way.

Don't tailor notes to the perceived value of gifts. No one should receive a dashed-off, perfunctory note.

Do refer to the use you will make of money gifts. Mentioning the amount is optional.

Don't include wedding photos or use photo cards if this will delay sending notes.

Do promptly acknowledge receipt of shipped gifts, either sending your thank-you within a few days or calling the sender and following up with a written note.

Don't use being late as an excuse not to write. If you're still sending thank-you notes after your first anniversary, keep writing.

Do remember that a gift should be acknowledged with the same courtesy and generous spirit in which it was given.

personal guardian angel. First you get me to the church on time, and then we arrive in Antigua and discover that you've treated us to three days of our trip! I'm enclosing a photo so you can see the incredible view of the ocean from our hotel.

We can't thank you enough for everything you've done. And I promise never to leave home without my jumper cables again.

Much love from your grateful, if forgetful, nephew,
Peter

Wedding Gifts

Chapter Thirty-nine

Your Day

AFTER SO MANY WEEKS AND MONTHS of planning and preparation, *your day* has finally arrived! What bride and groom don't look forward to a happy celebration with their families and friends? Though there may be a few problems along the way, there's no reason for occasional glitches to spoil your occasion. In fact, many couples look back on their wedding days and take pleasure and pride in memories of how well they handled things that went awry—hurriedly turning a table arrangement into a bridesmaid's bouquet when the florist's delivery was one short; drafting a friend to stand in when the best man fell ill at the last moment; arriving at the reception in an usher's old VW Beetle because the rented limo broke down on the expressway.

It would be unrealistic to say that a wedding day won't be stressful to some degree. But excessive stress (and venting one's frustrations on others) is often the result of unrealistic expectations of perfection. When couples keep the real meaning of the occasion firmly in mind; put the three C's of consideration, compromise, and communication first; and genuinely appreciate the efforts others make on their behalf, they're likely to achieve a kind of perfection that has little to do with dresses, decorations, and seating arrangements.

Getting Ready

REGARDLESS OF THE SIZE of your wedding, you probably won't have the time to check every detail on your day. This is where friends and family members can be extremely helpful. Try to have someone at the site(s) to check on deliveries, especially the flowers, special decorations, the wedding cake, and any equipment that must be set up or installed. (The bride's father and/or brothers traditionally supervise wedding-day logistics, but this may not be possible, so couples often turn to reliable relatives or family friends.) Make sure the person is fully informed about delivery times and where and how items are to be placed. If tipping of delivery people is expected, provide your helper with cash and instructions about how much to tip.

Your helper(s) can also check the wedding and reception sites before you or the wedding's hosts arrive. Provide a list of items that should be in place, such as ceremony programs, pew decorations, guest book, place cards, table favors, and so on. Express your sincere gratitude and let helpers know how important their contributions are to your day.

Dressing

Plan enough time to dress with as little hurry as possible. You might dress at your home, a friend's home, or the ceremony site. Many wedding locations provide well-equipped dressing rooms, and a bride might decide to arrive at the site early to complete her dressing.

If you don't dress at home, take everything you'll need to the site. Conduct a full inventory of your clothing, makeup, and other supplies a day or two before the wedding day, to avoid suddenly discovering that you've left something important behind.

If you will change into "going away" clothes, be sure they're packed and ready to take to the reception location. It may be possible to deliver these items earlier on the wedding day if the site provides secure, locked storage. Otherwise, someone must take your departure attire to the reception site after the ceremony and deliver it to the right place.

Leaving for the Ceremony

No one wants to be late to a wedding, so it's important to anticipate potential problems. Provide everyone in the wedding with a timetable of all wedding-day activities (such as hair appointments and picking up rented attire), arrival times, and exact locations where they're to go when they reach the ceremony site. Someone—perhaps an attendant if you don't have a wedding coordinator—should have a list of who will ride with whom as well as phone and cell phone numbers for all drivers and/or car services. Be sure everyone has the phone number(s) of your transportation "point person."

Deciding when to leave for the ceremony depends on how long it takes to get to the site, so it's smart to time your drive in advance—taking problems like congested traffic and inclement weather into account. Be alert to events like a big football game or a community festival that can delay traffic.

The following guidelines should help you plan arrival times for all members of your wedding party:

Bride and bridesmaids. The bride and her attendants should be ready at the site at least fifteen to thirty minutes before the start of the ceremony. Traditionally, the bride who dresses at home goes to the site with her father or escort, and her attendants travel with her mother. Children in the bridal party may go with the mother of the bride or be brought to the site by their parents. But transportation arrangements depend on individual circumstances.

When the bride's attendants will come from different locations, be sure that they have transportation and know precisely when they're expected to arrive. Professional dressers and hair and makeup stylists must also know when to arrive and have clear directions to the site.

Groom and best man. Generally, the groom and best man are dressed and ready at least an hour before the start of the ceremony—earlier if their drive to the site will be lengthy. This should give them time to attend to last-minute necessities (see "Don't Forget These Essentials!" below) and get to the site no later than fifteen minutes before the ceremony. Typically, the groom waits in a private room; the best man gets his and the groom's boutonnieres and then waits with the groom until they are signaled that the ceremony is about to begin.

Ushers. However they travel to the site, the ushers usually arrive about an hour before the ceremony. The best man or one of the ushers is responsible for seeing that the other ushers have transportation to and from the ceremony—which may involve booking taxis or car services in advance.

Out-of-town officiants. If your officiant has come from out of town, you are responsible for seeing that he or she has transportation to the ceremony and the reception. If the person has a car, provide clear directions to the sites.

Don't Forget These Essentials!

Several items are absolutely essential—the license, the wedding rings, and payments for the officiant and others involved in the ceremony. Traditionally, the best man is responsible for seeing that all these indispensables arrive safely.

Fees for officiant(s), organist and other musicians, and others who help with the service should be prepared in advance and placed in plain, sealed envelopes with the recipients' names on the outside. (The couple can also include a nice note of appreciation.) The best man delivers the envelopes before or just after the service. Generally people who participate in the service are not tipped, but you might increase the amount of the fee payment if you choose.

Tipping. Tipping of professionals—wedding consultant, photographer, florist, site manager, caterer—is not expected, though the couple might want to add an extra amount in their final payment or send a bonus check and a thank-you note to any vendor or supplier who has provided superior service.

Contracts with caterers and limousine companies generally include gratuities (ask if you aren't sure). If not, the couple should tip waitstaff, bartenders, table captains, and hired drivers. Tips are also appropriate for valet parking attendants, coat check and powder room attendants, and delivery truck drivers. The general standard is $.50 to $1 per guest, but amounts may vary in your area.

At the reception, have someone check that there are no tip jars or baskets set out at the site. (You don't want guests to feel obligated to tip, particularly when you're already doing so.) Some gratuities are given in advance. When tips are presented during the reception (to musicians, for example), determine the amounts beforehand and place cash in sealed envelopes. Conventionally, the host or best man distributes tips at the end of the reception.

A wedding day "emergency kit." Professional wedding planners know to prepare an emergency kit chock-full of things that might be needed at the ceremony. Taking a cue from the pros, you might include the following items in your own "just in case" kit: needles, threads in the colors of the wedding party's attire, adhesive tape, scissors, safety pins, hairpins, extra pairs of panty hose and black socks, nail polish and files, a lint remover, and whatever else might come in handy. Don't forget any medications, such as allergy relievers. Contact lens wearers might bring an extra pair plus solution.

Before the Ceremony

SINCE THE WEDDING DAY is usually crowded with activities, it's wise to review everyone's responsibilities at the rehearsal.

Duties of the Ushers

Should ushers ever doubt their importance as members of the wedding party, they need only look over the following duties, some or all of which they are expected to perform:

Aisle carpet. Check that the aisle runner, if one is used, is available in a convenient place, usually at the front of the site. After the guests are seated and just before the entry of the attendants and the bride, the runner—a white or red carpet or canvas strip—is unrolled down the main aisle from the front to the back of the room. Ushers should practice the maneuver at the rehearsal or before guests arrive for the ceremony.

The site. Take a few minutes to check the surroundings. Is the room temperature comfortable or does the thermostat need adjusting? If it feels stuffy or drafty, it may be necessary to open or close windows or doors. Before guests begin to arrive, ushers should see that seating areas are clean of any papers and other debris. Ushers should be familiar with the location of telephones, restrooms, coatrooms, and umbrella stands.

Pew ribbons. The use of pew ribbons is a custom not followed so often these days, but it can be helpful to control the exit of guests at a large or very formal wedding. After the mothers of the couple have been seated, ushers lay a wide white ribbon across the end of each row of guest seating—but not the reserved seating area—along the main aisle or aisles. (The ushers see that the ribbons are folded and left on the last seats in the reserved section before the guests arrive.) The ribbons remain in place throughout the ceremony and until the families have been escorted from the site after the re-

An elopement today is unlikely to fit the stereotypical image of a couple secretively slipping away in the dead of night. Modern elopements tend to be more like destination weddings, but without the advance planning. Sometimes family members and/or friends accompany the couple to the wedding location, or the wedding may be for the couple alone.

There are many reasons to elope: It's inexpensive. It's relatively private, for those who dread the spotlight of a traditional wedding. It's easy to organize. And it's exciting in a romantic way. But before you head off to the wedding chapel, there are a few very important considerations.

➤ Is the decision mutual or will one of you be truly disappointed not to have a conventional wedding? Compromise is one of the essential ingredients of marriage, so there may be another solution (such as an intimate service just for close family) that will satisfy both partners.

➤ How will your parents and family take the news? It may be easier for close family members when you've been together as a couple for some time and your family knows and values your partner.

➤ Do you have children, and do you really want to spring such a life-altering event on them without warning? Can you include the children in your wedding plans?

If eloping is right for you, think carefully about how you will announce your marriage to family (if they don't already know) and the larger world of friends, acquaintances, and business associates. Allowing parents to entertain for you relatively soon after the marriage may be a good way to salve any disappointment caused by their inability to stage the wedding. Parents might send wedding announcements (see Chapter 36, page 648: "Wedding Announcements") and the marriage might be announced in your newspapers. You can also ask close friends and colleagues to spread the news.

Whatever you do, *don't* cause anyone to worry about your safety. Before or as soon as possible after you take your vows, call the people who care about you and tell them about the marriage. Let them know where you are and when you'll return. If the news is a shock, stay calm and respectful. People who love you may say unkind things or ask prying questions when they first learn about the elopement, but *you* surprised them, and tolerance at this point can preserve relationships that are very important to you.

cessional. Then the ushers remove the ribbons, going from the front to the rear of the site, indicating that the rest of the guests can depart.

Special seating. Review seating arrangements for family members and special guests and check that ribbons and/or flowers used to mark pews or rows of seats are in place. Some couples send pew cards to close family members and friends, indicating that they are to sit in reserved seats near the front. When these cards have "Within the Ribbon" printed on them, ribbons are draped across the reserved pews or seats, and ushers lift the ribbon so that special guests can get in—replacing the ribbon after the guest or guests are seated.

Seating guests. An usher's primary duty is to greet guests and show them to their seats. Conventionally, the usher asks guests he doesn't know whether they wish to be seated on the bride's side (the left) or the groom's side (the right). When guests have no preference, ushers should try to seat people so that the audience is more or less evenly divided.

A male usher can offer his arm to a woman. When escorting a couple, he gives his arm to the woman, and her male companion follows behind. When escorting a group of women, the usher can give his arm to the eldest. Or ushers can simply lead all guests to their seats—a good plan when there are male and female ushers. But offer an arm to anyone, male or female, who needs assistance.

Even in a religious site, there's no reason for ushers to be silent and somber. Ushers should smile warmly and can converse pleasantly as they take guests to their seats.

Flowers and candles. Ushers are responsible for presenting corsages and boutonnieres to designated guests—usually the parents, stepparents, grandparents, and special helpers. If possible, assign this task to an usher who knows the recipients by sight. If a special guest is seated before she receives her corsage, an usher can present it to her at her seat. Some couples leave a flower or a note on their parents' seats before the ceremony, and ushers should check that such items are in place. When ushers light the candles, decide who will handle this duty, and don't forget to bring a lighter.

A reminder: A boutonniere is pinned, with the stem end down, at the buttonhole of the left lapel. When worn at the shoulder, corsages are pinned so that the stems are down. Since corsages can also be worn at the waist or on a purse, women generally attach their own, unless they need assistance.

Programs. Ceremony programs, when used, can be distributed in several ways:

➤ The ushers can hand programs to guests when they arrive or as they are seated.

➤ Programs can be placed on each seat before guests arrive.

➤ Programs can be put in a basket or pretty container and placed on a table or tables at the entrance to the site, so guests can take one as they enter.

➤ Special helpers might be asked to give out programs. If so, ushers should be watchful to ensure that every guest receives one.

Late arrivals. After the bride's mother is seated, guests are generally not seated from the center or main aisle; instead, they may be led down side aisles or to balcony seating. After the wedding party assembles to enter the sanctuary or ceremony room, guests are not seated until the processional and any opening remarks or prayers are

When there are more than two or three ushers, it's wise to have a head usher who will supervise. The duties of a head usher typically include:

➤ Ensuring that all ushers arrive on time (arranging transportation as necessary) and are correctly dressed

➤ Assigning specific duties and checking that all pre-ceremony tasks are completed

➤ Familiarizing the other ushers with seating arrangements for family members and special guests

➤ Being sure that all the ushers know the location of restrooms, coatrooms, telephones, and so on (perhaps conducting a quick site tour for the ushers before guests begin to arrive)

➤ Seeing that the site is cleared after the ceremony and taking charge of any lost items

Sometimes the head usher also acts as a general troubleshooter—the "go-to" person for other ushers, the wedding party, and suppliers and site managers. It's a good idea for him to have a cell phone and a list of phone numbers for everyone he might need to contact.

completed. Ushers should indicate where latecomers are to stand until they can enter. It may be possible to quietly slip guests in via a side door, but only if this won't be a distraction. Once the ceremony begins, it's a good idea for at least one usher to remain on duty to assist late arrivals.

After the ceremony. Traditionally, when the wedding party has completed the recessional, the ushers go forward to escort family members and special guests from the site and then remove pew ribbons, if used. The other guests leave unescorted. But there are many variations—especially at less formal weddings. Parents and family may prefer to mingle with their guests, or there may be no formal processional as the couple greet and chat with the guests. Whatever is planned, ushers should see that disabled or infirm guests are able to exit without difficulty; provide directions to the reception when asked; and help gather the wedding party for photos or the receiving line if there is one.

Once the site is cleared, ushers usually help clean the area by disposing of programs and other debris, checking for lost belongings, extinguishing candles, closing windows, rolling up the aisle runner, removing pew decorations, and gathering items such as floral arrangements that will be taken elsewhere. Even if there is a professional cleanup crew, the ushers should be sure that the place is spruced up and that nothing is left behind.

Duties of the Bridesmaids and Groomsmen

The attendants of the bride and groom provide both moral support and hands-on assistance. On the wedding day, bridesmaids may be asked to help the bride dress, attend to last-minute chores like getting their and the bride's bouquets, and assist with young children in the wedding party.

Very often, groomsmen also serve as ushers, and they will perform both sets of duties. Groomsmen (whether or not they are also ushering) might be responsible for picking up and delivering rental items, helping ready cars for transportation to the reception, taking deliveries at the wedding site, and keeping an eye on junior attendants.

After the ceremony, attendants (or a family member or friend) might be asked to clear out on-site dressing areas and check waiting rooms for anything left behind. If photos are taken, attendants must be on time for their shots; they should chat with guests but be ready to assemble when summoned.

Minding the Children

When young children are in the bridal party, someone must supervise them at all times. While this might be a bridesmaid, the mother of the bride, or a babysitter hired for the occasion, it may be best to ask parents to supervise their children. The presence of a parent can soothe a child who's nervous or overly excited. Parents can entertain their children while the attendants and mother of the bride tend to other necessities. Whoever minds the children should stay with them until the processional is formed and help them understand and follow directions.

Junior attendants usually don't need supervision, but they can use some attention. When the other attendants make preteens and teens feel included, it can help settle nerves and ease any stage fright.

Your Day

A QUESTION FOR PEGGY

Can I see my fiancé on our wedding day? Everyone says it's bad luck for the groom to see the bride.

Unless seclusion is part of your religious or cultural tradition, then there's no reason not to see your fiancé. If fact, many modern couples plan a few quiet moments together before their ceremony. It's also common for engaged couples to be entertained together on the wedding day—at a brunch or luncheon preceding an evening wedding, for example—so seeing each other is a social must. Many brides, though, prefer not to reveal their full wedding regalia until the processional begins; it's a matter of choice, not luck.

Seating the Families and Special Guests

THE FRONT ROWS of the ceremony site are traditionally reserved for the bride's and groom's immediate families, and their parents are honored with front-row seats. The bride's family members are seated on the left side of the room (facing the ceremony area) and the groom's family on the right. This order is easy enough for intact nuclear families, but since today's families take many forms, couples often need to plan seating arrangements carefully. It's not always easy, especially when parents are divorced and not on good terms. A seating plan won't mend family feuds, but it is possible to make seating decisions that will alleviate much of the stress.

The following seating guidelines reflect the traditional American wedding and can be adapted for your particular circumstances.

Parents. Parents of the bride are seated in the front row on the left side facing the altar or ceremony area. The groom's parents sit in the right front row. If there are two aisles, both sets of parents are seated in the middle section—the bride's parents on the left side of the front row (next to the left aisle) and the groom's parents on the right side of the same row (next to the right aisle). The parents are usually joined by members of the couple's immediate families (grandparents, siblings, aunts and uncles, and sometimes cousins).

Widowed parents. Widowed parents may wish to have someone sit with them, and this is perfectly correct. The companion might be a family member, a friend, or the parent's fiancé or fiancée. Unless the companion is engaged to a parent or is hosting the reception, he or she generally doesn't take part in other wedding activities such as the receiving line or formal photos.

Divorced parents. When divorced parents and stepparents have good relations, there's no reason why all cannot sit together in the front row, with the mothers and their spouses or companions nearest the aisle.

However, when relations are not so friendly or when a divorced parent has a large family, it's usually best to separate the families. The following order is customary for both the bride's and the groom's divorced parents and families:

➤ Front row: the mother of the bride or groom and her spouse or companion, plus the mother's parents and siblings. The bride's or groom's siblings who are not in the wedding party are also seated in the front row. Note: If the bride or the groom is estranged from her or his mother, the father would be seated in the front row, with the mother seated behind him.

➤ Second row: other members of the mother's immediate family (These family members may require an additional row of seating, but it's best not to occupy more than two rows.)

➤ Third row (or the row behind the mother's immediate family): the father and his spouse or companion and his family. If the divorced father is escorting the bride in the processional, he will sit in this row—not the front row—after he leaves the bride. The family of the father may require an additional row.

By separating the families of divorced parents, this arrangement can work even if the bride's stepfather escorts her down the aisle.

Same-sex parents. Same-sex couples who have parented the bride or groom together are seated in the first row. (Both parents might escort the bride and then take their seats in the front row alone or with other siblings and/or grandparents.) A same-sex partner who has not been in the bride's or groom's life may be seated as a companion in the front row if this is comfortable for everyone. But if the seating will cause dissension (as it might if the bride's or groom's parents are divorced and one is now in a new relationship), the parent's partner can be seated farther back.

Siblings. Siblings of the couple who are not in the wedding party, their spouses or partners, and their children generally sit with their parents or in the row behind with other immediate family members.

Grandparents. Grandparents and great-grandparents traditionally sit in the row behind the parents of the bride and groom. But they can also be seated with the parents in the first row, as can elderly aunts and uncles.

Special guests. Sometimes seating is reserved for special guests, such as honorary attendants, close family friends, or wedding helpers and their spouses or companions. This would be the last row in the reserved section. But since it's best to keep reserved seating to a reasonable minimum, special guests can just as well be in the general guest seating.

Military seating protocol. Attention to rank is very important in a military wedding. A special place is reserved for the bride's and/or groom's commanding officers and spouses (in the first row if parents are not present, or with the family). Officers of the rank lieutenant colonel and above are seated directly behind the families for the ceremony and also given places of honor at the reception. Since arrangements vary by branch of service, consult with your protocol officer or base chaplain. Make certain that ushers are instructed in the correct seating arrangements. (See also page 697: "A Military Wedding.")

The Ceremony

THE LAST CHORDS of the prelude die away, and the assembled guests still their conversations. Throughout the room, a sense of expectation permeates the air. The big moment has arrived; the ceremony that will unite two people in marriage and mark the beginning of a new family is about to begin.

Cautions for Feuding Families

Whatever the nature of family relationships, a wedding is no place to air personal animosities and grievances. Couples should be able to invite everyone they love to celebrate their marriage—without having to worry about how their relatives will behave. No matter what a family member may think of another guest, there's no excuse for any display of ill will: no frosty greetings, no snide remarks, no turning one's back or changing assigned seating, no whispered gossip. Everyone should be particularly conscious of the impact that harsh words and discourteous actions can have on younger family members.

Frankly, anyone who cannot control his tongue or temper for the few hours of the wedding should probably not attend. (Send your regrets, but don't imply that the couple was wrong to invite someone you don't like.) When negative feelings are likely to surface at a wedding, then staying away may be the kindest gift anyone can give to a couple he or she cares about.

Weddings

[690]

The Traditional Processional

When the attendants, the bride, and her escort have gathered and lined up at the entrance to the ceremony room or site, a signal is given and the officiant, followed by the groom and the best man, go to the ceremony area. The signal can be given by an official of the place of worship, a wedding coordinator, or someone you ask to notify the officiant that all is ready. Some sites have a buzzer or bell system. Or the opening bars of the processional music may alert the officiant, groom, and best man.

The best man stands at the left and slightly behind the groom, and they face the congregation. At this point, the procession begins.

The following is the traditional order of procession for Christian and many secular services, illustrated on page 691.

1. Groomsmen (ushers), walking in pairs and often ordered by height
2. Junior bridesmaid or bridesmaids, singly or in pairs
3. Adult bridesmaids, singly or in pairs and often ordered by height
4. The maid or matron of honor
5. The ring bearer
6. The flower girl (When the ring bearer and flower girl are very young, they often walk together and might hold hands.)
7. The bride and her father or escort. The bride enters on either the left or right side of her father, depending on religious practices and personal preference.

When the site has a double aisle, the wedding party can proceed up one aisle or use both aisles, with the groom's attendants entering on the right and the bride's attendants, including ring bearer and flower girl, on the left. Sometimes the entire wedding party proceeds via one aisle and leaves by the other.

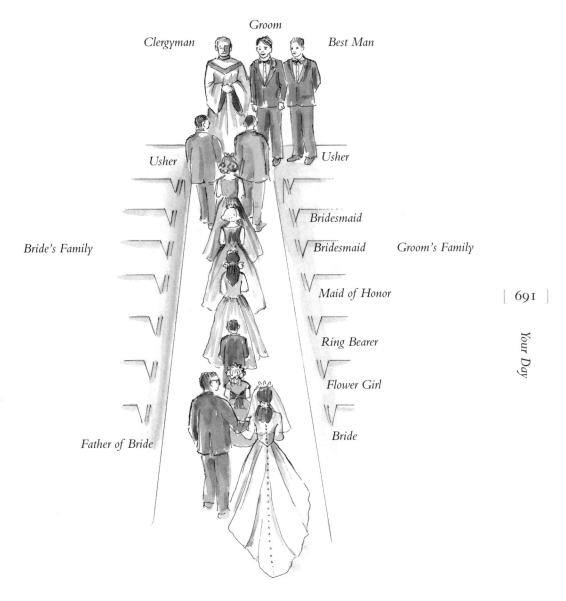

Traditional processional for a Christian wedding

The arrangement of the attendants in the ceremony area can vary. One plan is for all the bridesmaids to stand on the bride's side, and all the groom's attendants on the groom's side (as seen on page 692). Another arrangement is for the groom's attendants and the bridesmaids to divide when they reach the ceremony area, men and women standing on both sides.

When the bride arrives, the groom and best man turn to face the officiant. The best man remains next to the groom (now at his right), with the ring bearer at the best man's right. After the bride's father sees that she is joined by the groom, he either remains with her until the ceremony begins or goes to his assigned seat. (See page 693: "During the Ceremony.") The maid or matron of honor stands to the left and slightly behind the bride (or below if there is a step or raised platform). The flower girl stands at the maid of honor's left, then the bridesmaids.

Christian ceremony, at the altar

All these arrangements will depend on the specific religious nature of the service, the composition of the wedding party, and the physical layout of the ceremony site. In Jewish weddings, both the bride and groom are escorted by their parents in the procession and gather, with the honor attendants, under the *chuppah*. (See page 694: "The Jewish Ceremony.") For Muslim ceremonies, the bride and groom are usually seated apart, often at opposite ends of the room. In Hindu tradition, the couple is seated under a *mandaps*, or decorated canopy, at the beginning of the ceremony. There is also wide variation among Christian churches. In Eastern Orthodox tradition, for example, the service begins with the betrothal and blessing and exchange of rings, after which the couple is led to the wedding platform by the priest. Interfaith weddings often combine elements from the couple's faiths.

An important element of the wedding rehearsal is to work out the specific organization of the wedding party's entrance and exit, and their positions during the ceremony. Everyone should practice what he or she is to do at specific points in the ceremony, whether religious or secular. Even a small wedding party can benefit from at least one run-through of the entire ceremony.

During the Ceremony

In most traditional Christian and many secular ceremonies, when the bride and her escort reach the altar or ceremony area, she gives her right hand to the groom. The groom may place her hand through his left arm, but couples may prefer to hold hands or just stand side by side.

The father or escort remains at the bride's side until he responds to the officiant's question ("Who gives this woman?" "Who represents the families in blessing this marriage?" etc.); then he goes to his seat. If the couple chooses not to have any question-and-response, the father or escort simply takes his seat when the wedding party is in place.

Just before rings are exchanged, the bride hands her flowers to her maid of honor. Usually the maid of honor holds her own and the bride's bouquets until the end of the service, but if the flowers are very heavy or cumbersome, she might place her own bouquet on a small side table or stand and retrieve it after she returns the bride's bouquet.

The Traditional Recessional

After the couple have been pronounced "husband and wife," they may kiss (though this isn't an absolute) and the officiant may introduce them to the guests (again, a matter of the couple's choice). The maid of honor hands the bride her bouquet and, if necessary, straightens her dress and train before the couple start their walk.

The flower girl and ring bearer follow the bride and groom; then come the maid of honor and best man. The other attendants then exit, either singly or in pairs. It's up to the couple to decide whether male and female attendants leave in the order that they entered or pair up for the recession.

Note: When very young children serve as flower girls and ring bearers, they may sit with their parents or the couple's parents after the procession, rather than stand throughout the ceremony. If the children become tired or agitated, they need not walk in the recessional.

∾ Taking the Long Walk ∾

The old "step-glide" or "hesitation" processional walk for the wedding party has been largely replaced by a more natural gait and pace. Attendants are not expected to start on the same foot. What's important—in both the procession and recession—is to walk at a moderate speed and maintain roughly the same distance (about four paces) between attendants. The walk into the site will be slower than the walk out, and the music is often the best guide to the pacing. If possible at the rehearsal, have attendants practice walking to the processional and recessional music. (You may be able to get a tape from the organist or other musicians who will play, if they can't attend the rehearsal.)

Once the wedding party has left the room, the ushers go forward to escort the families out and remove any pew ribbons, indicating that other guests may exit.

Bridesmaid		Usher
Bridesmaid		Usher
Maid of Honor		Best Man
Flower Girl		Ring Bearer
Bride		Groom

Traditional recessional for a Christian wedding

The Jewish Ceremony

The processional for a traditional Jewish ceremony is led by the rabbi and the cantor. The groom's attendants, then the best man, follow. The groom is escorted by his parents—mother on the groom's right and father on the left. They are followed by the bridesmaids, maid of honor, and finally the bride, escorted by her parents. Another option is for the groom to be accompanied by both fathers and the bride by both mothers.

The bride's and groom's grandparents may also be included in the procession. They follow the rabbi and cantor and are seated in the front rows as the rest of the party approaches the ceremony area.

The bride, groom, their parents, honor attendants, and perhaps the rest of the wedding party gather under the *chuppah*, or canopy, and the ceremony begins. (At the rehearsal, the rabbi will help determine how many of the wedding party can be accommodated under the *chuppah*.)

The recessional is led by the newlyweds, followed by the bride's parents, groom's parents, attendants, and the rabbi and cantor.

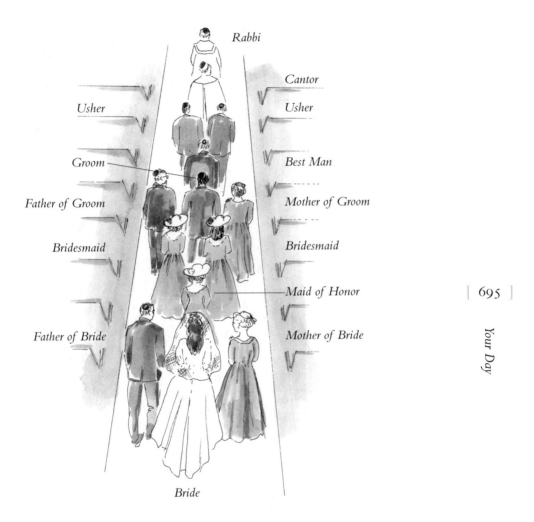

Jewish processional for a Conservative or Orthodox ceremony

Conservative or Orthodox Jewish ceremony under the chuppah

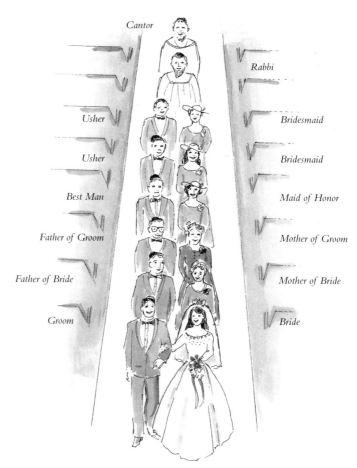

Jewish recessional

A Military Wedding

A full military wedding integrates contemporary trends with centuries of military custom. Though the ceremony is conducted in the couple's religious tradition or as a secular service, there are several key differences, listed below. Traditions vary by branch of service and the rules can be complicated, so service members should closely consult their service manuals and talk with their military chaplains and/or protocol officers when planning the specifics of their ceremonies and receptions.

➤ Brides and grooms have the option of wearing their uniforms or civilian attire, but if some of the wedding party are in uniform, all service members normally are. The choice of dress or everyday uniforms depends on the formality or informality of the wedding. When full dress uniforms are worn, nonmilitary attendants wear attire (usually tuxes or tails and formal gowns) equivalent to the standards of the uniformed attendants.

➤ Service members in uniform do not wear boutonnieres or corsages, though a bride and her attendants in uniform can carry traditional floral bouquets.

➤ If the groom is wearing a sword or saber, the bride stands on the side opposite the blade.

➤ The U.S. flag and the flag or flags of the couple's service branch(es) and/or unit(s) can be displayed in the ceremony site and at the reception (behind the receiving line if there is one). Miniature flags can be used in table decorations. It's also appropriate to have the song(s) of the couple's branch(es) played at the reception.

➤ The Arch of Steel (see Chapter 40, page 716: "The Arch of Steel") may be formed after the service by an honor guard composed of officers who are qualified to wear swords or sabers when in full dress uniform. All saber or sword bearers wear white gloves.

➤ Seating of military members at the ceremony and reception is governed by rank. Since the rules of protocol vary by service, it's important to talk with a protocol officer or chaplain. Carefully instruct ushers about seating arrangements at the ceremony.

➤ If one or both of the couple can wear swords, they may cut their wedding cake with the sword. (See page 703: "Cutting the Cake.")

Double Weddings

A double wedding may be double the fun, but it also requires extra attention to the details of the ceremony. A double wedding usually involves two sisters, two cousins, or two best friends. When sisters are brides, the elder sister enters first, on her father's arm. The younger sister enters second, usually escorted by an uncle, brother, or another male family member. The processional order for cousins or friends is determined by the participants.

The usual order of the procession is:

1. Grooms' attendants (half attending one couple; half, the other)
2. Bridesmaids and then maid or matron of honor for the first bride
3. First bride and her father or escort
4. Bridesmaids and then maid or matron of honor for the second bride
5. Second bride and her escort

In the ceremony area, the first couple stands to the left (facing the officiant) and the second couple to the right. If the brides are sisters, their father may give each in marriage, then go to his seat. The wedding service and responses are performed twice. In the recessional, the elder sister or the bride who entered first leads the walk up the aisle with her new husband, followed by their attendants. The second couple and their attendants follow in the same order.

Post-ceremony Activities

Now you are husband and wife, and your guests will want to greet you and extend their congratulations. Couples frequently mingle after the ceremony, but another option is a receiving line. This can be organized outside the ceremony site or in the vestibule. Often a receiving line immediately after the service is fairly informal, but it can be formal if preferred (see page 699: "The Receiving Line"). It might include some or all of the wedding party or just the couple, their parents, and anyone else who is hosting. Whether you have a receiving line at the site depends in large measure on the number of guests and the space available. If photos will be taken immediately after the ceremony, it may be best to schedule any receiving line for the reception; this way, guests don't have to wait so long before going on to the reception site.

Check with the officiant about other events scheduled at the site after your ceremony. If another wedding or activity is planned, you may have to hurry the meeting and greeting along. Weather may also be a factor. If you plan a receiving line in the courtyard of the place of worship, for example, rain might force a move indoors or a delay until the reception.

Regardless of your plans, cars for the wedding party should be waiting at the entrance to the ceremony site (unless the reception is at the same site). The best man

~ Sign on the Line ~

If you and your officiant and witnesses haven't signed the necessary legal documents before the wedding ceremony, don't forget to complete this essential step before going to the reception. Some couples use this as an opportunity to be alone together after the signing—taking a few minutes of private time just for themselves.

helps the couple into the first car. The bride's parents traditionally ride together and may be accompanied by the flower girl and ring bearer. The bride's and groom's attendants usually leave in the same cars in which they arrived.

On to the Reception

THE RECEPTION HOSTS and the couple should get to the reception as soon as possible. This may mean that parents and perhaps attendants will precede the newlyweds if photos are taken at the wedding site after the ceremony. (You can plan the photo session so that the shots including parents, other family members, and attendants are taken first.)

If there's a long lag between the arrival of guests and the wedding party, you can have special helpers at the reception site to greet guests, make necessary introductions, and see that guests are offered drinks and hors d'oeuvres. It's nice to have music (live or recorded) to set the mood.

People do expect some delay, but any longer than thirty to forty-five minutes becomes excessive, unless your invitation included a later starting time for the reception. What is not acceptable is for the wedding party to disappear, whatever the reason, while reception guests are left to cool their heels and wonder when the reception will begin. If there is likely to be a considerable delay, be sure that guests will be served beverages and hors d'oeuvres while they await your arrival.

If a receiving line is planned, it should be formed as soon as possible after the couple reaches the reception site. Couples may choose to dispense with the formal receiving line, especially if the guest list is relatively small and the couple and their families know most of the guests well. In this case, the newlyweds and their parents should make the effort to circulate, chatting with as many guests as possible. It's courteous to first greet older family members and anyone who must depart early.

One important caveat: If photos are taken just before the reception starts, the session should be as brief as possible. Organize carefully so that everyone in the photos knows exactly where to go and what pictures will be taken. If you have a receiving line, it may be advisable to take photos after the line is finished or to take some shots before the receiving line and finish the photo shoot later. You may need to politely remind the wedding party to be punctual.

The Receiving Line

A receiving line is a great way to greet all your guests, especially if your wedding is large and you may not have the chance to speak personally with everyone during the course of the event.

Must there be a receiving line? No, but it's often a wise choice. A rule of thumb: It's helpful to have a receiving line if you have seventy-five or more guests. If you forgo it, be sure to greet each guest at some time during the reception.

Where should the receiving line be? The best location should be worked out in advance, with the reception site manager. You might choose a spot where guests can enjoy refreshments as they wait their turns. Another option is a location that leads into the main party area. To accommodate guests who eat and drink while waiting in line, see that a small table for used glasses, plates, and napkins is placed near the beginning of the line. (No food or beverages should be carried through the line.) You might also want servers to offer drinks to guests as they leave the receiving line.

Who stands in the receiving line? The traditional line includes the couple, their parents, the maid of honor, and perhaps the bridesmaids. The basic order of the line is: the wedding host(s)—traditionally the bride's parents (her mother first, then her father); the groom's mother and father; the bride and groom; the maid or matron of honor; the bridesmaids. Fathers are not required to stand in line; they might handle other hosting duties while the line is in place. But if one father participates, the other should as well. In a military wedding, it is protocol for a groom in uniform to stand before his bride.

| Mother of Bride | Father of Bride | Mother of Groom | Father of Groom | Bride | Groom | Maid of Honor | Bridesmaids |

Receiving line

The best man and perhaps the groom's attendants can be included, if the wedding party is small. Sometimes the children of the couple participate, if they are mature enough to stand still and greet people. Ushers, flower girls, and ring bearers are not included, nor are siblings who are not members of the wedding party. If a widowed or divorced parent is engaged, his or her partner may stand in the line if this is comfortable for everyone.

If people other than parents host (the adult children of the bride, for instance, or an aunt and uncle), they would be first in the receiving line—before the bride's parents or the couple.

Where do divorced parents stand? Divorced parents and their spouses generally do not stand side by side. The parent and stepparent who host the reception or are closest to the bride or groom usually stand in the line. But situations vary so much that you have to work out an arrangement that is the most sensible for your family.

When relations between divorced parents and their current spouses are amicable, they may all be in the line—but separated by the other set(s) of parents to prevent confusion or embarrassment for guests. When all the parents are divorced and remarried, the order can be as follows: (1) bride's mother and stepfather, (2) groom's mother and stepfather, (3) bride's father and stepmother, and (4) groom's father and stepmother. The same alternating order can be followed for single divorced parents.

To avoid a very long line, the different sets of parents might take turns standing in line. Or you could include only the maid of honor (and let the other bridesmaids go on to the party).

Traditionally, the parent (and stepparent) who hosts the reception stands first in the line. But when divorced parents are friendly, it is perfectly acceptable for the bride's mother to have first place regardless of whether she pays the bills—especially if she was the custodial parent and this is agreeable to everyone. But if there is serious discord between parents and stepparents, it may be best to forgo the formal receiving line altogether.

What about the greetings? Keep your remarks gracious but brief. Greet guests warmly and acknowledge their congratulations. Try to steer anyone who is particularly talkative along before the line is bogged down. ("I really do want to hear about Don's school days, Mrs. Mulgrew. I'll look for you after dinner, and you can tell me all about it.") Make introductions if the next person in line doesn't know a guest. Complete an introduction before greeting the next person in line. (Mannerly guests should know not to push themselves forward and also to introduce themselves in case you forget.)

∾ The Guest Book ∾

A guest book, while not obligatory, provides a nice memento of your wedding and the people who celebrated with you. Usually the guest book is placed on a small table near the entrance to the ceremony site or reception room, or at the end of the receiving line. A special helper stands at the table and asks guests to sign. When the guest book is placed at the ceremony site, the ushers ask guests to sign before they enter for the service. But if you're inviting more guests to the reception than to the ceremony, the reception is the best location. Some people may not sign the book, so it isn't an exact record. Also, don't expect the helper to stay at the guest book table after the party gets under way. You can leave the book out for people to sign and ask someone to retrieve it at the end of the reception.

Do we have to kiss everybody? There will probably be some close family and friends whom you want to kiss on the cheek, but there's no need to kiss or hug everyone. The normal gesture is to shake hands when guests extend theirs.

How long does the receiving line last? Basically, as long as it takes for every guest who is in line to go through. This is why it's so important to politely move guests forward and save lengthy conversations for later.

Toasting the Newlyweds

Champagne is traditional for toasting, but you can substitute any drink. At a seated dinner, the champagne is poured as soon as everyone is seated. At a buffet with tables, it is poured after everyone has gone through the receiving line. But these aren't hard-and-fast rules. Drinks for toasts can be passed at cocktail receptions. They might be served at tables just after dessert or during the cake cutting if toasts are to follow. The point is to schedule a time for toasts and coordinate with your site manager or caterer.

Usually, the best man gets everyone's attention and then offers the first toast. This can be the only toast, or other members of the wedding party may want to add their best wishes. The couple may want to make a toast, and their parents might toast their children and add their welcome to all the members of the new families. Telegrams or special messages are read by the best man; if there are many messages, they can be intermingled with toasts.

If guests are seated, everyone rises for toasts—except the person or people being toasted. When, for instance, there's a toast to the bride, the groom rises while she remains seated, and vice versa. Whether standing or sitting, no one drinks a toast made to him or her. (For sample toasts, see Chapter 28, page 489: "Wedding Toasts.")

Dancing

If there is dancing, it follows dessert at a seated dinner, but at a buffet reception, it might start after the receiving line or photo session. At an afternoon reception when the meal is served later, guests might dance before the bridal party goes to their table.

In many traditions, the bride and groom dance the first dance. Even if you don't consider yourself a good dancer, a couple of minutes on the floor will provide great pleasure for your guests.

For the second musical number, traditionally the father of the groom dances with the bride, and then the bride's father cuts in. The groom dances with his new mother-in-law and then his mother. Then the groom's father might dance with the bride's mother and the bride's father with the groom's mother, while the groom dances with the maid of honor and the bride with the best man. At this point other guests usually join them on the dance floor.

But when family relationships are more complicated, everyone can join the couple after their first dance. The newlyweds should then make a point to dance with all parents and stepparents at some time during the reception.

We're planning our daughter's wedding reception, and a question has come up about saying a blessing before the dinner. Not all guests belong to our faith, so is this appropriate? And if so, whom should we ask to say grace?

A blessing before the wedding meal is certainly appropriate. Anyone you choose—a family member, a friend, or the officiant—can say the blessing. Be sure to ask the person in advance, so he or she can prepare. When the time comes, the best man, emcee, bandleader, or DJ can ask for everyone's attention.

Usually the best man makes a brief introduction; the person you've asked offers the blessing; and then the best man thanks the person, signaling to guests that the meal should begin. If the best man is uncomfortable with this role, you might ask a family member to do the introduction and thanks. Guests who are not religious or are of other faiths can simply lower their heads and remain respectfully silent during the blessing.

Cutting the Cake

Customarily, the wedding cake is on display when the reception begins—on the bridal party table, in the center of the buffet table, or on a separate smaller table or a cart. But sometimes, the cake is dramatically revealed only when it is about to be cut; the room lights are lowered, the music is hushed, and the cake is brought to the middle of the room under a spotlight where the wedding party or all guests gather around for the cutting ceremony.

At a seated dinner, the cake is cut just before dessert is served. At buffets or passed-tray receptions, the cake cutting usually takes place nearer the end of the reception. When the couple and their attendants gather at the cake, guests know that the time has arrived. Be sure to give your caterer or site manager and your photographer an approximate time for the cutting.

The tradition is for the bride to hold the cake knife; the groom places his hand over hers. Together they cut a small slice, which is put on a plate. Using dessert forks, the groom feeds his bride the first bite, and she feeds him the second. (This custom symbolizes the couple's commitment to share with and support one another, so stuffing a partner's mouth with cake is out of place.) The newlyweds usually kiss after their first bite. Sometimes they cut additional slices for their parents—the bride serving the groom's parents and the groom serving the bride's. The cake is then quickly removed to be cut and served. Or helpers can cut the cake at the table and pass plates to guests.

In a military wedding when either of the couple is a commissioned officer, the cake may be cut in dramatic style. At a command, the officers who performed the Arch of Steel following the ceremony enter the reception area in formation. They repeat the saber or cutlass arch, and the bride and groom walk under to stand before the cake. The couple cuts the first slice of cake with their hands together on the sword. The sword cutting is often done without the arch of sabers.

Traditional Tosses

If you include a bouquet and/or garter toss or other cultural customs, these are usually scheduled near the end of the reception. Wedding party members should gather together for these activities, and other guests should be alerted, whether they will join in or just watch the fun.

The Newlyweds Depart

The couple might make their departure wearing their wedding attire or change into "going away" clothes. In the latter case, the couple go to separate changing rooms; the maid of honor assists the bride, while the best man attends the groom. The newlyweds are often joined by their families for a private farewell. It's the best man's responsibility to see that the departure car is ready at the exit.

When the couple is about to leave, the wedding party and guests form a farewell line and might shower them with rice, rose petals, or birdseed as they dash for their car. When something is tossed, guests are provided with a small amount—say, a scant half-handful. The goal is to honor an ancient wedding tradition, not to create a mess.

These days, however, many couples do not make the traditional departure and continue to party with their guests until the end of the reception. In this case, guests may begin leaving after the cake cutting or first dance. Though the party goes on, the couple and the hosts should be available to say good-bye to their guests.

Off for the Honeymoon

A honeymoon is the romantic start of your married life, but don't forget to be practical. Write down instructions for people who will be caring for your home, pets, and children. Leave your travel itinerary and phone numbers where you can be reached with anyone you've left in charge, as well as parents or other close relatives. (You might supply prepaid phone cards for people who are house-sitting or minding children.) Details matter, so have your newspaper delivery stopped and your mail held until you return, pay bills that will come due during your absence, and stock up on supplies, like pet food, that helpers will need.

If you have children, be sure that caretakers have complete instructions and can contact you at all times. Check in with your children when you arrive at your destination and throughout your trip. Teens as much as younger children need to hear your voices to be assured that you are safe, sound, and missing them as much as they miss you.

Chapter Forty

A Guide for Wedding Guests

A N INVITATION TO A WEDDING IS AN HONOR. Think about it . . . two people want you to be with them as they take one of the biggest steps of their lives. A wedding is not just another party. It's a piece of history—recorded in law and cemented in ceremony—and you will be part of its celebration. That's quite an honor, and it entails some obligations.

The bride and groom are the stars of the event, but guests also have a role to play—to witness the formation of a new family and to celebrate their union joyously, graciously, and with utmost consideration for others. Unlike most parties, a wedding usually brings together people of several generations, and it's important to be understanding and solicitous of people whose view of "proper" conduct may differ from your own. A wedding may be your introduction to a tradition or culture, and good guests will adapt to and respect customs that are new to them.

Whether the wedding is held in a cathedral or a backyard, whether the guest list includes a mere handful or several hundred, every guest should behave in a way that will make the day happy for everyone—an obligation that actually begins with the arrival of the invitation.

Prompt Responses

A GUEST'S FIRST DUTY is to respond to any wedding invitation that includes an RSVP request or a reply card. Check your schedule, consult with anyone else included in your invitation, then make your response as soon as you can. The reasons for a prompt reply are simple. The hosts of the wedding need the most exact count of guests in order to plan for catering, guest seating, and so on. If you regret, the couple will have time to invite someone in your place if they wish.

Many wedding invitations come with a reply card and pre-addressed return envelope. You need only fill in your name(s) and indicate whether you will attend. (See also Chapter 36, page 642: "Reply cards.") Although some casual invitations have no request for a reply, it is considerate to call the hosts if you will not be able to attend.

When the invitation is addressed to you "and Guest," you must decide if you want to take someone. When you accept, let the hosts know if you will be bringing a guest. Ideally, you can write the name of your guest on the reply card or include the name in your written response. If you don't know yet who that will be, accept for you "and Guest" ("Ms. Janna Abernathy and Guest"). Once you know whom you'll bring, it's thoughtful to let the hosts know your guest's name—prior to the wedding day, if possible. If you reply only for yourself, don't show up at the wedding with a date or companion.

Written Responses

When an invitation includes an RSVP but no response card, be guided by the information on the invitation. If there's an address below the RSVP notation, write to the hosts at that address. When there is no address on the invitation itself, respond to the return address on the mailing envelope.

In some cases, there may be an address and a telephone number, and you can reply either in writing or by calling. Invitations to very casual weddings might include an e-mail address; otherwise, reply either by written note or by phone.

Written responses are written by hand, normally on plain or bordered notepaper or monogrammed stationery. When you regret, excuses are not included, but in a personal note, you might explain your absence if you want. There are three basic types of response, illustrated below.

Formal response. Written in the third person, this reply follows the wording of a formal invitation:

> *Mr. and Mrs. Harold McGuigan*
> *accept with pleasure [or regret that they are unable to accept]*
> *your kind invitation for*
> *Saturday, the nineteenth of June*

～ Are Children Included? ～

Your children are invited *only* if their names are on an invitation. No one should ever ask the couple or the hosts to include children—or anyone else—who hasn't been specifically invited. It is rude to ask a couple to make "an exception" for children or to subject them to the embarrassment of having to say no to such a request.

Occasionally, children are invited to a ceremony but not to the reception or vice versa. But whether children are excluded altogether or included in only one of the wedding-day activities, the invitation will arrive in more than enough time for you to arrange for child care on the wedding day.

Informal response. Written in the first person, these replies reflect, but don't mimic, the phrasing of a formal or informal invitation:

*We are happy to share your joy
and look forward to attending
the marriage of your daughter
Anna Karen
on Saturday, the nineteenth of June.*

*I sincerely regret
that I cannot attend
your wedding
on Friday, the second of April.*

Jack Saunders

Meredith and Harold McGuigan

Personal note. Usually written to hosts you know well, a personal note should be brief but sincere:

Dear Ann and John,

*Rob and I are delighted to accept
your invitation to attend Margaret
and Tom's wedding on
June nineteenth.*

*Yours sincerely,
Britany Ellis*

Dear Agatha,

*I am so sorry that I can't
join you and Max for your wedding.
I have to be in Chicago on business,
but you two will be first in my
thoughts on your special day.*

*Love to you both,
Dottie*

Cancellations

If something unforeseen happens and you cannot attend a wedding after you've accepted the invitation, you should call the hosts immediately. This is very important because the hosts will, in most cases, be held financially responsible for all or a substantial percentage of any catering expenses for no-shows. If a couple is paying $50 per person for the wedding dinner and ten people fail to attend, that could mean a needless $500 expense. Also, alerting the hosts that you can't come may give them time to invite someone else.

Choosing and Sending Gifts

APROPOS OF WHAT TO GIVE and how much to spend on wedding gifts, there's an old saying that should probably be dusted off and given more prominence today— "It's the thought that counts."

Gift selection isn't really about buying. Nor is it a competition. Choosing a gift is a matter of *deciding* what you believe will give pleasure. Thinking about someone else is one reason why people who hate to shop for themselves quite often enjoy shopping for others. Still, guests do have questions about gifts, and the most frequently asked include the following:

Guests to a destination wedding are invited months in advance, particularly if the location requires extensive travel. This can be a problem if your schedule is uncertain or if you're unsure that you can afford a trip. A long weekend of wedding festivities in Barbados may sound fantastic, but take some time to consider before accepting. The couple is responsible for accommodations (but not travel) for their attendants; other guests pay for their own transportation and lodging. Can your budget bear it? Also, will you be able to get the time away from your job? If children are not invited, can you make child-care arrangements? Do you have other obligations that must be honored—military reserve service, for example? What you want to avoid is a last-minute cancellation that disappoints your hosts and costs you financially.

Do I have to choose something from the bridal registry? No. The registry is a convenience for guests, not a mandate. However, checking a couple's registries may give you a better idea of their taste and needs, even if you purchase "off-registry."

Am I supposed to buy a gift that costs as much as the families spend on each person at the wedding? No. This modern myth causes considerable anxiety for guests, but it is false. The amount you spend is strictly a matter of your budget and what you think is an appropriate gift. Even if someone is brash enough to indicate how much is being spent on the wedding, you are under no obligation to spend more than you can afford.

Is it tacky to send money? Not at all. Money gifts have been traditional in a number of cultures for quite some time; more and more these days, they may be just right for couples who have already established their households or are saving for something special. A monetary gift is usually presented in an envelope addressed to the couple or to the bride or groom, and is accompanied by a personal note. Deliver currency in person; otherwise, send personal or cashier's checks. (For more about financial gifts, see Chapter 38, page 668: "Registry Alternatives.")

Can I send something I already own? Yes, as long as it is in good condition—*not* a castoff—and you are confident that the couple will like the item. You might send something you never used if it's still in mint condition and in its original packaging. Or you might wish to give an heirloom piece, such as a silver tray or a crystal vase, that is valued for its age and history. Heirloom jewelry is often passed on in families; just don't insist that the bride or groom wear Aunt May's brooch or Grandfather's cuff links with their wedding attire.

Don't I have up to a year after the wedding to send a gift? No. This is another myth. Gifts should be sent before the wedding or as soon after the wedding date as possible. But late is better than never, so if you have an unavoidable delay, send your gift when you can.

Can I take my present to the wedding? You can, but don't do it unless this is the tradition in the couple's religion or community. In most cases, it's best to send or hand-deliver gifts to the bride's or the couple's home.

How do I know if my gift arrived? A thank-you note from the couple is your best guarantee. You can also ask for delivery confirmation on gifts sent by mail or commercial delivery service.

What do I do if I don't receive a thank-you note? Give the couple a reasonable amount of time to send their thank-you—three months post-wedding. Then you're free to ask if the gift was received. You can check with the couple or with a parent you know well. Be sure to inquire in a tone of concern, not confrontation.

What if I learn that my gift was returned or exchanged? Say nothing. Once you have given any gift, the recipients may do as they like with it. Returns and exchanges are common when a couple receives more than one of the same item.

Guest Attire

DESPITE THE GENERAL TREND toward casual attire, many people look forward to weddings as opportunities to dress up and look their very best. But a wedding is different from a gala party or opening night at the theater. Guests' clothing should be appropriate to an occasion that is, at its heart, a serious ceremony and, in many religions, a sacred rite.

Suitable for the Occasion

The wedding invitation and the time of the wedding will be your best guide to the formality or informality of the occasion. A formal invitation to an evening wedding indicates that you will definitely dress up. An informal invitation to a noon wedding tells you the affair is either informal or casual.

Other factors will also influence your dress choice.

The nature of the service. Is it secular or religious? Does the religion or the culture of the bridal couple require head coverings? Would bare shoulders and arms or open-toed shoes be offensive? Note: If head coverings for women and/or men are required, they will usually be provided at the site for people who do not have them.

I've received a wedding invitation from someone I knew in high school. She was a friend back then, but I haven't seen or heard from her in fifteen years. She lives halfway across the country, and I have no intention of going to the wedding. Would it be terribly rude not to send her a gift?

In your situation, you need not give a gift, but you should send your regrets and best wishes immediately. Your case is a reasonable exception to the "rule" that the receipt of a wedding invitation carries the obligation to send a gift, whether or not you attend the wedding. This is because you have really lost touch with each other, and it's unlikely that you would be reviving your friendship at this point. However, instead of simply checking a reply card or writing a formal response, it would be thoughtful to send your friend a personal note, saying how nice it was to hear from her after so many years and wishing her your very best.

If you want to renew the friendship, you could give her some brief information about what you're doing now and express interest in future contact. Even if you don't want to keep up, thank her for thinking of you at this very special time in her life. Your prompt, gracious note of regret will be an acceptable substitute for a wedding present.

The attire of the wedding party. No guest should dress in a manner that will outshine the bride or groom.

Local custom. Some parts of the country are more conservative than others. For instance, in some areas, men wear tuxedos to formal weddings after six o'clock regardless of whether women wear long or short dresses.

Season and weather. Wedding attire tends to be lighter, both in weight and color, in summer and in tropical and subtropical climates. In cold weather, coats and outerwear should complement your wedding attire if possible. (A sports parka would not be the best look over an evening gown.) If rain is in the forecast, take an umbrella.

The listing below includes general recommendations for formal, semiformal, and informal guest attire, but if you're unsure, check with someone who knows—parents, wedding attendants, good friends of the couple, or the couple themselves. (The information in Chapter 37, page 661: "Dress for the Wedding Party," may also help with your clothing choices.)

	Formal Daytime	Formal Evening	Semiformal Daytime	Semiformal Evening	Informal Daytime	Informal Evening
Women	Street-length cocktail or afternoon dresses; gloves optional; head coverings optional unless required	Depending on local custom, long evening dresses or dressy cocktail dresses; gloves optional; head coverings optional unless required	Short afternoon or cocktail dresses; gloves and head coverings optional unless required	Cocktail dresses; gloves and head coverings optional unless required	Afternoon dresses; gloves and head coverings optional unless required	Afternoon or cocktail dresses; gloves and head coverings optional unless required
Men	Dark suits; conservative shirts and ties	Tuxedos (if women wear long dresses or if invitation indicates "Black tie") or dark suit	Dark suits	Dark suits	Dark suits; in summer, light trousers and dark blazers	Dark suits

These guidelines also apply to teenagers. Younger guests wear party clothes to formal and semiformal weddings. Nice school-type outfits—dresses or skirts and jackets for girls; pants, sport jackets, and ties for boys—are appropriate for informal and casual weddings.

∽ Women in White? Pantsuits? ∽

In the past, no female guest would dare to wear white—the bride's traditional color. Today, that rule is no longer in effect, and you may wear white, with caution. Whatever the shade of white, the outfit should in no way distract from the bride's or her attendants' dresses. A creamy white, street-length sheath or tailored silk suit might be just fine, but not a full-skirted, white evening gown. If you have any qualms, wear another color. Black is also acceptable, as long as your outfit is in keeping with the formality of the wedding. You might want to add a bright accessory if you're concerned that you would otherwise look too funereal.

Pantsuits are also acceptable, and nowadays, women of every age may be seen in dressy trousers with jackets or soft, flowing tops. But be conscious of local customs; if wearing a pants outfit will make you stand out like a sore thumb—or violate any religious restrictions—then wear a dress.

An invitation to a wedding outside your faith is an opportunity to experience the rituals and customs of others. It's normal to be a little anxious about what to do in an unfamiliar setting, but as long as you don't wait until the last minute, the couple and their families should be happy to give you guidance.

When deciding what to wear, the best course is to dress conservatively. Don't wear jewelry with symbols of other religions. At the service, you won't be expected to take part in rites and rituals that aren't part of your faith, but you should observe the traditions of others respectfully. For example, you can stand with a congregation and remain silent during prayers or singing.

The following brief survey points out some major differences you may encounter but is by no means definitive. For detailed information, you can call the house of worship where the ceremony will be held or speak with someone of the faith.

Christian. The traditional Christian ceremony is described in Chapter 39, page 689, "The Ceremony." There are variations among denominations, and traditional services may include elements specific to the couple's national and ethnic origins and local customs.

➤ **Roman Catholic.** Traditional Roman Catholic weddings may include a nuptial mass followed by communion; this precedes the final prayer and nuptial blessing. Generally, non-Catholics don't take communion. In Italian tradition, the priest may greet the couple and their families at the church door.

➤ **Orthodox (Eastern Orthodox).** The service consists of two parts: the betrothal and blessing of the rings followed by the ceremony at the altar. During the latter, crowns or garlands are exchanged three times over the couple. No vows are said during the service. Female guests wear clothing that covers their arms, with hems below the knee. A Greek Orthodox reception may include the traditional breaking of plates, symbolizing happiness and endurance, and guests usually participate.

➤ **Church of Jesus Christ of Latter Day Saints (Mormon).** If the marriage is held in a temple, only members of the church attend. Weddings may also be held at local meeting houses. The traditional reception is an open house, though it may take any form. Guests often bring their gifts to the reception, but sending gifts is fine.

➤ **Mennonite and Amish.** A wedding is a worship service and may be part of a larger service. Guests stand with the congregation and may join in hymns and readings. If communion is offered, other Christians may take part. Attire is conservative; women's dresses should cover their arms, and hems should be below the knee. There may be music at the reception, but no dancing; alcohol isn't served.

➤ **Quaker.** Conducted as a regular meeting, a wedding may be held in the meeting house, at home, or in another location. There is no officiant; the bride and groom exchange vows and sign a religious certificate. The reception might include light refreshments or a full meal and may be a potluck; no alcohol is served. There may be music and dancing. Some couples request gifts in the form of charitable contributions.

Jewish. The traditional Jewish wedding is described in Chapter 39, page 694: "The Jewish Ceremony." Male guests wear a *yarmulke* or *kippah* (head coverings supplied at the site for non-Jewish guests). Head coverings may be required for female guests. In Orthodox tradition, conservative dress is traditional. Only Jewish guests wear a prayer shawl. Otherwise, wedding attire is often very festive. Foods at the reception may be kosher.

Islamic. Marriage is a sacred contract, but not a sacrament. The contract (*aqd-nikah*) is signed in the presence of witnesses and then publicly announced. The officiant can be any practicing Moslem and may be an *imam* (prayer leader). The bride and groom sit apart during the ceremony and at the reception. The service often takes place in a mosque but may be held in the bride's home. The post-ceremony banquet (*walima*) is hosted by the groom, his family, or the couple. Alcohol is not served. There may be dancing if the *walima* isn't held in a mosque. Female guests should wear clothing that covers their arms, hems below the knees, and a head scarf. Gifts are often presented at the banquet. By tradition, women congratulate the bride, and men congratulate the groom.

Hindu. A Hindu wedding is a holy sacrament. A priest officiates and may provide explanations of rituals during the ceremony. The most important rite is the Seven Steps—seven symbolic rituals. The ceremony may take place in a temple, house, or an outdoor site under a canopy. Receptions, at which traditional Indian foods are served, may begin before and continue after the ceremony. Gifts are often brought to the wedding.

Baha'i. There is no standard service or officiant. The couple say their vows in the presence of two witnesses (approved by the local spiritual council). The wedding may be as simple or elaborate as the couple desires, at a location of their choosing. No alcohol is served at receptions, but there may be music and dancing.

Buddhist. There is no standard ceremony, and some Buddhist weddings are similar to Protestant ceremonies. The service is generally brief, with a minister or priest presiding. It can be held in a temple or outdoors, and seating may be on meditation cushions. Guests should never enter during meditation. Wedding gifts are not normally expected. No alcohol or meat is served at the reception.

Sikh. The *arnand karaj* (ceremony of bliss) may be performed at the place of worship (*gurdwara*) or the bride's home and is often scheduled before noon. The officiant may be a priest or any Sikh approved by the families. Guests sit around a central platform on which the Holy Book is placed. Men sit to the right and women to the left. The ceremony concludes with prayer, a hymn, and the sharing of sweet food by all the guests.

Native American. There is no single marriage service, but traditionally, a Native American wedding is a community event. It may be religious or secular in nature, and the service and reception often integrate modern customs with ancient tribal rituals. The reception may include a full meal, and gifts may be presented at the reception.

Guest Fashion Faux Pas

Even for the dressiest wedding, it's usually best to err on the conservative side when selecting attire. Out of respect for the bride, groom, and their families, guests should have no difficulty avoiding the following fashion blunders:

➤ Clothing that is too skimpy or overtly provocative (Save the plunging necklines and bare backs for other occasions.)

➤ Costumes except when you've been expressly asked to dress to the wedding theme (Leave the Klingon battle gear at home unless you've been asked to dress à la *Star Trek*.)

➤ Blue jeans (unless the wedding is very casual and you *know* that the groom and his attendants will be in jeans) and T-shirts

➤ Any jewelry or symbols of another faith worn to a religious ceremony

➤ Baseball or sport caps; large fashion hats that block other guests' view of the ceremony

➤ Casual shoes or boots with formal or semiformal outfits

➤ Sunglasses worn indoors (except for a legitimate medical reason)

On the Wedding Day

ANYONE WHO HAS EVER PLANNED a wedding knows how quickly the hard work can seem for naught if guests (including members of the wedding party) behave badly. The stereotypical "bad guest" is one who drinks too much and becomes loud and unruly. But the truth is that seemingly small discourtesies, such as arriving late for the ceremony or shifting a few place cards in order to sit next to a friend at the reception, can be just as disturbing.

Wedding guest etiquette is not so different from the manners for any social occasion. The information that follows will, however, alert guests to some matters specific to weddings today.

At the Ceremony

Punctuality is essential. A wedding usually begins at the time stated on the invitation, and you should arrive at least twenty minutes to a half hour early. There may be meeting and greeting with friends in the narthex (or vestibule) or forecourt of the ceremony site, but it's best kept to a minimum.

Let an usher show you to your seat. At a casual wedding, guests might seat themselves, but remember that the front two or three rows are usually left free for family and special guests. If a program is provided, look it over and familiarize yourself with the order of the service. Programs may include helpful instructions for guests of other faiths and traditions.

After you're seated, low chatting is permissible, but the entrance of the groom's and bride's mothers is a customary signal for guests to wrap up their conversations. All talking should cease when the groom and groomsmen enter.

Here are a few other basics of good ceremony manners:

➤ Avoid loud greetings in the sanctuary or room.

➤ Be conscious of people with physical problems that make seating difficult and make room for them to take aisle seats.

➤ Do not save seats for late guests.

➤ Turn off cell phones, beepers, and any other electronic devices that can disrupt the service.

➤ Don't use a flash camera and don't videotape unless you have been asked to record the event by the couple.

➤ Stay where you've been seated throughout the service. (If there's a likelihood that you must leave early, take an aisle seat in an inconspicuous location near the rear.)

➤ If your children become disruptive in any way, leave immediately and don't return unless they are calm and quiet.

➤ Respect traditions that are unfamiliar to you, and avoid commenting on the service. You can ask questions later.

Late arrivals. If you arrive to see that the wedding party is already assembled in the foyer, stay out of the way. Hopefully, there will be an usher or ushers to assist you, and there may be a side door you can enter quietly. Do not enter during the processional or a prayer. If there is no usher present, wait until the service has begun; then slip in and take a seat at the rear. Be conscious of what is going on in the service and tiptoe if you must; high heels and heavy-soled shoes can make a terrible clatter on uncarpeted floors.

〜 JUST COMMON SENSE 〜

Bride's Side or Groom's Side?

Strict seating rules are not so often observed these days, but family members are generally seated on the bride's or groom's side of the sanctuary or room, and specially assigned seating areas are usually marked off with ribbons. Other guests may be asked if they prefer one side. If you are a friend of both the bride and groom or if you see that one side of the room is emptier than the other, you can leave the seating choice up to the usher. Be willing to sit on either side if you're asked to help to even out the seating.

Standing and kneeling. There are usually points in a religious service when the congregation stands and perhaps kneels. As a general rule, guests of other faiths stand at the appropriate times but are not expected to kneel. You don't have to say prayers, refrains, or creeds outside your faith. If communion is offered, it may be limited to those of the religion of the service or open to the entire guest company, but you don't have to participate if this rite is not part of your faith.

The end of the service. The ceremony's conclusion may be marked with a kiss or an introduction of the newlyweds to the guest company. Some couples now end the service with their own ritual, such as the lighting of a unity candle. Whatever is done, guests should be observant and not make a move to leave until it is clearly time.

In a traditional wedding, the bride and groom lead the recessional, followed by the wedding party and family members. Then guests depart by rows, the rows closest to the front of the room emptying first. But the etiquette of departing really depends on the situation. In a variation on the traditional recessional, the newlyweds might stop at each pew or row of seats to greet guests. (In this case, guests should limit their comments to offering best wishes and not delay the couple with conversation. Wait until the wedding party has exited before leaving.) At informal and casual weddings, there may be no formal recessional, and guests simply disperse, often going forward to speak to the couple and their families.

If there's a receiving line at the site, go through quickly; introduce yourself to the first person in the line if necessary and keep all comments brief and complimentary. Should there be a gathering for photos outside the ceremony site, just make your way around it, out of camera range. Unless you can't attend the reception, you'll have plenty of time to congratulate the newlyweds later on.

Clapping. Religious and secular ceremonies sometimes end with the guests clapping for the couple when the officiant introduces them to the guest assembly. The applause

∼ The Arch of Steel ∼

Undoubtedly the most romantic sight at a military wedding is the raising of sabers or cutlasses to form an arch under which a couple passes at the end of the service. The arch ceremony, which symbolizes the couple's safe entry into their new life together, may be performed inside or outside the ceremony site, sometimes both. The formation varies slightly by service branch and is a tradition rich in history and meaning. Whether the arch is formed by commissioned officers who are members of the wedding party or by a special honor guard, a command will be given ("Draw swords" or "Arch sabers"). Only the couple and perhaps their attendants participate. All other military guests should stand at attention, and civilian guests honor the tradition by standing still and being quiet.

This is really embarrassing to admit, but I made a fool of myself at my best friend's wedding last weekend. Too much champagne. My friend's new wife will probably never forgive me. Is there any way to make amends?

People are often tempted to send a nice gift and a short "I'm sorry" note in these situations, but a face-to-face visit is better. Your friend may never raise the subject, so it's up to you to arrange to see the couple as soon as possible. A heartfelt apology, made without excuses will probably earn forgiveness. Your friendship may require some extra nurturing for a while, but isn't it worth it for your best friend and his wife?

should be initiated by someone who knows the couple's preference, and the guests can follow that lead. Otherwise, don't clap.

On to the Reception

It's time to celebrate! There may be some lag time before the reception gets under way, and this is a good chance to greet friends, meet guests you don't know, and sign the guest book if there is one. Hors d'oeuvres and drinks may be served immediately, but if not, don't ask.

The following fundamentals are specific to wedding receptions, but if you want to brush up on your party manners and dining etiquette, you can refer to Chapter 23, "Table Manners," and Chapter 25, "The Dinner Party."

- ➤ Move quickly through a receiving line, and don't monopolize anyone's time. Don't carry plates or drink glasses while in the line.
- ➤ When there's no receiving line, be sure to greet the couple and their families at some time during the festivities.
- ➤ As you mix and mingle, introduce yourself to guests you don't know.
- ➤ Never move place cards if there's a seated meal. Respect your hosts' seating arrangements, and don't ask anyone to change places with you.
- ➤ Be gracious to guests at your table, and be sure that everyone is introduced. Don't abandon anyone at a table.
- ➤ Ask guests without partners to dance. (This isn't a requirement, just a very nice thing.) Customs vary, but generally the first dance is reserved for the couple and their parents.
- ➤ Pay attention to the needs of elderly or infirm guests. Also, be attentive to children—just a smile and a few words can make them feel special.

Usually for scheduling reasons, guests may be forced to take a lengthy break between a ceremony and the reception. There's always some delay, particularly when the reception is at a different location. But what do you do if the ceremony ends at three-thirty and the reception doesn't start until six o'clock? You'll be able to tell from the invitation that there's going to be a break, so plan ahead. If you live in the same locality as the wedding, you can just go home and put your feet up. You might even invite some of the out-of-town guests to join you. Other possibilities include taking in a movie, enjoying a bit of sightseeing, or shopping. While it's advisable to avoid heavy food and alcoholic drinks, a little hospitality can turn the downtime into a fun occasion for you and for guests who are a long way from their homes.

➤ If asked to make a toast, be prepared and keep it brief, clean, and appropriate to the occasion. No embarrassing anecdotes about the newlyweds. (See Chapter 28, page 489: "Wedding Toasts.")

➤ Participate in activities if you can. No matter what your feelings about a bouquet toss, for instance, don't leave the bride standing alone.

➤ Don't overwhelm the band or DJ with special requests.

➤ Don't take centerpieces, favors, or anything else that is not clearly yours. If the hosts give you a centerpiece or decoration, take it only after tables have been cleared or at the end of the reception. And don't ask for a doggy bag for leftover food.

Respecting reception customs. These days, you are more likely than ever to be invited to weddings in traditions outside your own. Even the most traditional celebration may include innovative customs with which you are unfamiliar. A mannerly guest will observe others and go with the flow. It's fine to ask necessary questions but very rude to make negative remarks or comparisons.

When to leave. It's customary for guests to remain at a reception at least until the couple cuts their wedding cake or after their first dance, if there is dancing. Many guests remain until the bride and groom depart. When there is dancing, the party may go on very late, with the newlyweds staying to the end; in this case, guests may leave when they think it's appropriate. In any event, do not exit without thanking the couple and their parents. If you haven't done so already, take a few moments to offer congratulations to grandparents and other family members before leaving.

The type of reception will give you a sense of its probable duration. An evening or midday reception that includes a seated meal or full buffet is likely to last longer than an hors d'oeuvres–and–cake affair. An afternoon reception is often briefer, but guests should probably plan on at least a three-hour commitment even for very intimate weddings and receptions.

Tipping. Since gratuities are usually included in wedding costs, guests have little need to tip anyone. But if you wish, you can tip a coatroom or parking attendant.

Chapter Forty-one

Remarriage

A N ENCORE WEDDING—when one or both of the couple have been married before—is almost, but not quite, like a first wedding. Gone are the days when couples were expected to solemnize second (or third or fourth) marriages with as little fanfare as possible. Today's couples are free to celebrate their unions in whatever style they like, and encore weddings range from classic traditional to highly individualized and creative events.

Encore couples, however, have to consider how their wedding will affect other people. It is especially important for the couple to think carefully about the impact their marriage will have on the lives of those whom they love.

The differences between encore and first-time weddings arise chiefly from these two factors:

➤ When one or both of the couple have children, the marriage is the joining not only of two people but also of pre-existing nuclear family units. Other family members, former spouses, and former in-laws will also be affected.

➤ Encore couples are usually older than first-time couples and are often fairly or entirely independent (financially and emotionally) of their parents.

In other words, an encore couple may be wholly responsible for wedding planning and expenses, yet every decision they make is likely to have an enormous impact on other people. When there are children, the wedding will begin the formation of a new family and bring changes (not all of them welcome) in the children's established relationships and routines. For other family members and friends, the happiness of a remarriage may be tempered with memories of sad or difficult times.

Encore brides and grooms have certain advantages because of the perspective gained through past experiences. They tend to be more mature (in their thinking if not actual age) and more aware of potential stumbling blocks of wedding planning and marriage itself. Having been through it all before, they're usually familiar with some of the essentials of wedding etiquette and are often better prepared to take problems in stride.

The decision to marry again is a powerful commitment to the ideals and values of love and family, and it deserves to be celebrated. Honoring responsibilities to others is a major part of that commitment, but it's also important for couples to make time for themselves and share the satisfaction of planning a wedding that expresses their love for each other and their hopes for the future.

Planning an Encore Wedding

WHETHER A PREVIOUS MARRIAGE or marriages ended in divorce or the death of a spouse, at least one of the encore couple will have gone through a wedding. For a number of reasons, including respect for the new spouses, the remarrying bride and groom will want to avoid an exact duplication of the earlier celebration. Thus, encore weddings are often planned in a more relaxed style and tone than first weddings.

However, if the bride has not been married before, she may want a traditional formal or semiformal wedding complete with long white gown and veil, multiple attendants, and a full-scale reception. This is perfectly acceptable, as long as the couple is in complete agreement. If, however, a first-time bride thinks she wants an elaborate wedding but her initial ideas remind her fiancé of his past marriage, then honest discussion is called for. As the couple work to reach a compromise that's acceptable to both, their mutual goal should be a joyous occasion, free of painful associations and resentment.

An encore wedding marks the beginning of a brand-new partnership, so couples should think carefully, talk candidly, and make decisions in tandem. This is a time to consider all your options and be open to doing things differently.

Fortunately, your options are plentiful. A welcome trend for today's encore weddings is personalization, with encore couples integrating personal touches in every aspect of the celebration. This can mean anything from writing your own vows and including your children in the ceremony to hosting your wedding at your dream destination. (For more ideas, see Chapter 42, page 734: "Wedding Trends for the Twenty-first Century.")

The Engagement

Before telling anyone else that you're getting married, you must inform all the children—whatever their ages—from previous marriages. Ideally, each parent will talk with his or her own children privately and in person. A telephone conversation may be necessary when it's not possible to get together, but don't resort to letters or e-mail unless there is literally no other choice.

The news of a parent's remarriage may be expected, but it can still be unsettling, particularly for younger children and teenagers. No matter how fond they are of a future stepparent, children often feel torn, seeing the remarriage as a test of their loyalty to their other natural parent. Many children of divorced parents harbor the hope that their parents will reunite, and a remarriage puts an end to their dreams. Children may worry about how their new family will function, especially if they will soon share their parent with stepsiblings, and how much control the new stepparent will have over their lives. Very young children may not know how to react and will need your help to understand what is happening.

The following list should help couples plan and stage encore weddings that become happy memories for the bride, groom, and those they care about. While many of these basics apply to any wedding, some are specific to encore weddings.

➤ Work together; the decisions about an encore wedding should be shared.

➤ If you have children, tell them first—no matter what their ages.

➤ Be realistic about budget. Even if you can afford to be extravagant or you have financial assistance from family, determine early what you can afford and stick to your limits.

➤ Plan your celebration around traditions and interests that are significant to you and have positive associations for your children, family, and friends.

➤ Talk with your officiant about ways to include your families. Review the wording of traditional services and texts for appropriateness.

➤ Be sure that all legal, financial, and emotional issues are finalized and put to rest. Discuss any prenuptial legal agreements carefully, and be sure that you have settled matters from previous marriages.

➤ By the time you begin planning your wedding, put away engagement and wedding rings from past marriages. You can save them for the next generation or have stones reset into other jewelry. Widows and widowers should no longer wear rings from an earlier marriage, even on their right hands.

➤ Register for gifts if you want. Even if you don't expect gifts, many guests will want to give them. Registries are helpful to those trying to select something that a couple would like to have. Be sure to register in a range of prices.

➤ Avoid publicly resurrecting the past. An encore wedding celebration isn't the place for remarks about ex-spouses or even heartfelt references to deceased partners.

➤ Thank everyone—in person and by note—who helped make the wedding a success.

Talking first with your own children, without your fiancé/fiancée present, gives them the opportunity to be candid without fear of hurting the other person. It will also give you insights into your children's real concerns, so you and your future spouse can work together to alleviate fears and doubts before the wedding. Use the engagement period to lay the solid foundations of mutual respect, understanding, and affection on which your new family unit will be constructed.

Also be sure to tell your former spouse of the engagement, especially if he or she is a custodial parent. You might want to inform your ex before talking with your children, so he or she can be prepared to react appropriately. When divorced couples are on reasonably good terms, the first concern should be helping their children adjust to the new family arrangement.

After you tell the children, inform your parents, siblings, and other close relatives before making a public announcement. Though you may no longer be dependent on the people who raised you, make the effort to tell them of your plans before they hear it from someone else.

Announcing the news. In general, an encore engagement is publicly announced in much the same way as a first-time engagement. (See Chapter 33, page 560: "Making It 'Official.'") You may agree to an engagement party hosted by family members or friends. Although couples don't normally host their own engagement parties, you might want to hold a family get-together and make your announcement to your extended family.

It's fine to invite friends who attended your first engagement party. But be aware that if your divorce was acrimonious or only recently finalized, people who remain friends with your ex-spouse may feel uncomfortable attending. Throughout your engagement and wedding, be sensitive to the feelings of others. Never put anyone in the awkward position of appearing to choose between you and your ex.

If you don't have a party, take the time to inform others in person or by a phone call. The news will spread, of course, but good friends and family members will appreciate being contacted directly. You can also announce your news in personal notes.

Newspaper announcements are often made for encore engagements and/or weddings. Announcements sometimes make general reference to the previous marriage of the bride or groom, without naming ex-spouses: "The bride's previous marriage ended in divorce." The wording of the announcement will be determined by the publication.

Whom to Invite

The guest list may play an especially significant role in the size and style of an encore wedding. The size of the guest list is up to you (and your budget). But whom to invite can be problematic if a previous marriage ended in discord and you retain mutual friends with your former spouse. If friends sense that attending the wedding means choosing sides between you and an ex-spouse, they may legitimately feel trapped between a rock and a hard place. In this instance, you might decide on an intimate wedding with only close family and friends in attendance. Another option might be a small ceremony and a larger, informal reception.

If you include guests who attended your first (or most recent) wedding, it's usually best to plan a ceremony and reception that will not invite comparisons. Instead of the formal, evening church wedding you had last time, you might host an informal midday service and brunch reception at home.

Inviting your former spouse and in-laws? It's not a good idea to invite an ex-spouse to an encore wedding. Friends can feel awkward celebrating a new marriage when the former husband or wife is there. Even if you and your ex are on good terms, there are other family members to consider, and there's no reason to open old wounds when it can be avoided.

The idea of a prenuptial agreement can be difficult to raise, but if you feel one is needed, discuss it as soon as possible after you decide to marry. Prenups can be very important for encore couples who bring assets to the marriage and have children from former relationships.

A prenuptial, or premarital, agreement is a binding legal contract that becomes enforceable only after a divorce or the death of a spouse. The usual elements in a prenup include the following:

➤ Division of financial assets and property (individual and marital)

➤ Waivers of claims to the other spouse's individual property (enabling children from former marriages to inherit as you wish)

➤ Custody of children in case of a divorce

Because of changes in state laws regarding inheritance and disposition of assets, which can sometimes override the provisions in wills, prenuptial agreements have become much more commonplace. Today, prenups are not just for the very rich, nor do they represent any lack of faith in one's future spouse. In fact, they serve to protect both partners and their children.

If you aren't familiar with prenuptial agreements, it's wise to do some basic research first; the Internet and your local library can be excellent resources. Be tactful when you raise the subject with your future spouse. This is a decision you should make together, so avoid presenting your fiancé/fiancée with a completed document. If one or both of you are unsure about the provisions and implications of a prenup, you may want to consult an attorney experienced in family law to learn about the fundamentals—although legal experts recommend you have separate lawyers when your actual agreement is drawn up. Whether to discuss the agreement with others (adult children, for example) is your decision.

Most important, consider your new spouse and any children you both bring to your marriage. It can be difficult and confusing for them to celebrate your new family if your former spouse is present. Even if you and your ex are friendly, it's best to leave him or her out of the festivities.

Former spouses should not expect to be invited, but if there is an issue, keep the discussion between you and your ex. Do not draw your future husband or wife or your children into any conflict. If you are marrying someone with a "problem ex," don't try to intervene or negotiate.

Widowed and divorced people who remain close to their former in-laws may certainly invite them. But be conscious of their feelings; your new marriage may be bittersweet for your former spouse's parents. It's a good idea to talk with them personally and tell them how much you would like them to attend. But also let them know that you understand if they choose not to.

Invitations

Just as for first-time weddings, invitations to encore weddings reflect the nature of the occasion—formal, semiformal, informal, or casual. Invitations to small weddings are often made in phone calls or personal notes.

Parents may issue the invitation, especially if the bride is young. Or the invitation can be sent in the names of both sets of parents, with the bride's family listed first. These options are correct even though parents may not be paying for the wedding.

When the couple have been living independently, they often issue the invitation themselves. The following example is a traditional invitation from the couple. The use of social titles is optional.

The honour of your presence is requested
at the marriage of
Clara Miller O'Connor
and
Arnold Neumeyer
Friday, the twenty-seventh of August
at half after four o'clock
The City Club
San Antonio
And afterward at the reception
RSVP

For more examples of invitations for encore weddings, see Chapter 36, "Wedding Invitations and Announcements," pages 620–650.

When adult children host. It's particularly nice when grown children host their parents' wedding and/or reception. On the invitation, the children (and their respective spouses) are listed as hosts, with the bride's children named first. Each set of children is listed by age, from eldest to youngest.

(For an example of an invitation issued by adult children, see Chapter 36, page 633: "When other relatives issue the invitation.")

Making It a Family Affair

IN THE PAST, children were by and large ignored at a parent's remarriage—almost as if they were expected to be "seen and not heard" during the actual ceremony. But the proliferation of encore marriages has brought recognition that children *need* to feel included. It's estimated that a quarter of all marriages today involve children, and each of these children will have a profound effect on the success of the marriage.

With the growing popularity of the "family wedding," many officiants—religious and civil—are now able to advise couples on meaningful ways to include children in the service. Your children themselves may have good ideas, and they will appreciate being consulted.

The following are some ways that today's encore couples are reaching out to make their weddings into genuine family affairs.

Children as attendants. This is practical when there aren't too many children or children too young to take an active part. To avoid any appearance of favoritism, if one younger child or teen is included, all should be. Equal treatment is extremely important to youngsters and teens, so try to assign each child a role that is significant to him or her. For example, if the bride wants her teen daughter to be a bridesmaid, then it's advisable to ask the groom's teen daughter as well.

If the bride has more than two children, it's usually best not to have them all escort her down the aisle. Since girls as well as boys can be ushers, this can be a responsible role for older children. Children who are comfortable before an audience might present a reading. Just be sure that each child is happy with his role, whatever it is.

A family addition to the service. After the couple are pronounced husband and wife, the children can be asked to come forward to join them. The officiant then addresses a special message to the children. A family prayer is often included in religious ceremonies. This brief part of the service usually emphasizes the creation of a new family, and the children are mentioned by name.

A candle-lighting ceremony. After the ceremony, the children and perhaps the parents of the bride and groom come forward, or the couple can go to where the family members are seated. Candles are lit by everyone as an expression of the union of the families.

(For more on unity ceremonies, see Chapter 42, page 733: "Unity candle.")

Special remembrance gifts. The couple might present all the children with something unique to the occasion, such as an engraved medallion, picture frame, or photo album. Include the children in wedding photos. Be sure your photographer knows who they are and gets them in plenty of candids as well as formal photos.

Flowers. Small tokens can mean a great deal. Whether they take part in the ceremony or not, be sure that each child has a boutonniere or flowers. Corsages are fine for girls, but a particularly memorable idea is a small nosegay including the same flowers as the bride's bouquet.

A Few Family Do's and Don'ts

As you work with your children—and former spouses—to plan a family-oriented wedding, the following guidelines should help you maintain family harmony:

Do consult each child individually to determine if he or she would like to be in the wedding. Avoid simply expecting them to participate. Respect the wishes of a child or teen who doesn't want to take part, but also leave the door open for a change of heart.

Don't question your future spouse's children about their other parent. Your interest may be benign, but questioning children may be seen as prying and can undermine the children's trust in you.

Do answer children's questions about your previous marriage. You can be honest without being explicit.

Do speak respectfully about former spouses. If you demean an ex-spouse, your future stepchildren may conclude that you will talk the same way about their mom or dad after the wedding.

Do consult your former spouse to schedule events involving the children, especially if wedding activities may conflict with regular visits. Set the pattern now for cooperation with ex-spouses.

Don't use wedding-related activities as an excuse for missing your regular visits and special events with the children.

Frequent Encore Wedding Questions

SINCE THE DIVORCE rate began to rise in the 1950s, the etiquette of remarriage has changed and evolved significantly. Along the way, some old-fashioned restrictions have been tossed aside, and the emphasis has shifted from what is "socially proper" to what is comfortable for the couple and considerate of their families and friends. Including a couple's children in the wedding, discussed at length above, is an excellent example of today's new encore wedding etiquette.

But changes can sometimes be confusing, so this section offers answers for some of the questions most often asked by encore couples.

May we have a big wedding? The size and style of an encore wedding is entirely up to the couple, and if you both want to pull out all the stops, feel free to do so. If an earlier wedding was small or an elopement, the encore couple may want a big event. Common sense and tact are the best guides, and encore marriages generally do not repeat past performances. But if you missed the excitement of a big celebration in the past, you can have it now.

Is it all right for the bride to wear white? And what do her attendants wear? Yes, the bride may wear white. In the past, white symbolized purity or virginity, but this is no longer the case, even for first weddings. Today, white signifies joy and celebration. An encore bride may wear white if she chooses, or any other flattering color that's appropriate to the occasion.

Regardless of color, the bridal gown, dress, or suit should fit the formality, theme, and location of your wedding. Select an outfit that compliments your age and figure. Whatever the length of the dress, mature women often prefer tailored styles—leaving more fanciful and frilly looks to younger brides.

Whether the bride selects her attendants' outfits depends on the situation. The bride may prefer that her attendants dress alike. But often, an encore bride will simply give her attendants a description of her clothing, including color, length, and general style, and let the attendants select attire that coordinates with hers.

Unless the wedding is very formal, younger children in the wedding party normally wear party clothes. The groom, his attendants, and ushers dress as they would for a first wedding. (See Chapter 37, page 661: "Dress for the Wedding Party.")

Is it okay for the bride to wear a veil? Encore brides may wear veils, and some religions require them. It's best to avoid long or overly frilly styles, so many encore brides select short, simple veils that are part of or attached to fashion hats or other headpieces.

The blusher veil (worn over the face) is still reserved for young, first-time brides and is not worn by encore brides. Orange blossoms, either in headpieces or bouquets, are also traditionally reserved for first-time brides.

∾ When Future Stepsiblings Meet ∾

If you both have children from previous marriages, you'll want to get them together before the wedding, but try to make first meetings as casual as possible. A ball game or a movie-and-burgers night makes for a lot less stress at first meetings than a formal family dinner or an engagement party. It can be hard, but work at dividing your attention equally among all the children. Avoid remarks such as "I know you're going to be great friends" or "Isn't it wonderful that you're going to have a big brother now?" Kids are naturally curious about and wary of new stepsiblings, so let them take early meetings at their own pace. If their manners aren't the best, you can let minor missteps slide.

It's vital to discuss discipline issues with your future spouse before you get the children together. Anticipate problems or conflicts that might arise, so you can present a united front. If your child is deliberately rude or hostile, take him or her aside to correct the behavior. Chastising one child in front of the others can only breed resentment at this point.

Adult children also need some TLC. Give your grown children opportunities to meet, if possible, before the wedding, but don't try to force relationships. Adult stepsiblings may never become close, but they should always treat one another—and you—with respect and courtesy.

If your children are young, sooner or later they are likely to ask, "What is a honeymoon?" followed by "Can we go?" Whether they raise the subject or you do, be very sensitive to their feelings.

An encore wedding followed immediately by a honeymoon trip can be like a one-two punch for children. The disappearance of their parent and new stepparent right after the wedding may cause very young children to fear that their natural parent will not return. Older children may feel hurt or angry at being excluded, especially if they worry that your remarriage will relegate them to second place in your affections.

Children tend to live in the present moment. They may not really grasp why you are going away after the wedding—no matter how well you explain. If children are genuinely troubled or upset, there are alternatives that couples might consider.

➤ Dividing the honeymoon into two parts—for example, several days devoted to the children followed by time on your own as a couple.

➤ Delaying the wedding trip. Give the children some time to settle into their new family life (and perhaps new home) and also to adjust to the idea that you and your new spouse will be going away on a trip by yourselves.

➤ Forgoing the honeymoon. This might be an option when both spouses have children who will live with them. Devote the weeks or months following the wedding to integrating the families and establishing stable routines. Once the children are secure in their new lifestyle, they'll probably have no problem with their parents taking off for some "alone time."

"Who gives this woman?" Just as in first weddings, it is always appropriate for the bride's father, an older male relative, her mother, or both her parents to escort her down the aisle. Encore brides without parents might ask their eldest son, daughter, or both to accompany them in the processional. Brides may make the processional walk without an escort, or the couple might walk down the aisle together.

Because a divorced or widowed bride has already been "given" in marriage at least once before and many encore brides are totally independent of their families, the traditional wording ("Who gives this woman?") is often altered to reflect reality. When teens or adult children serve as escorts, it is considered inappropriate for them to "give" a parent who raised and supported them. An escort who isn't related to the bride (a best friend, for instance, or a foster parent) obviously cannot "give" her away.

Although the giving of the bride is not considered a fundamental part of the marriage service itself, couples should consult their officiants about acceptable language in their faith. A variation on the traditional question and response might be:

Officiant:	"Who presents this couple?" *or*
	"Who blesses this couple?"
Escort:	"We do" *or* "Their families do."

Another approach is for the officiant to ask, "Who joins me in supporting the union of . . . ?" The response ("We do") is voiced by the families or the entire guest company.

Some couples simply dispense with any "giving away." The bride's escort walks her to the altar and then goes to his seat when she is joined by the groom. But a young encore bride who is living with her parents might want her father or both parents to follow tradition and "give" her, which is just fine in this situation.

What is the polite way to say, "No gifts, please"? Technically, gifts are not obligatory for encore weddings, and many couples don't want them. However, guests who were not invited to a previous marriage—and some who were—often want to express their best wishes with gifts.

Do not refer to gifts in any way on your wedding invitation or enclosures. Even the notation "No gifts, please" implies that presents are somehow equal to the importance of the marriage ceremony. The best approach is to tell family, attendants, and good friends that you don't want gifts and ask them to spread the word.

If someone sends a gift anyway, receive it graciously and acknowledge it with a thank-you note. (Gifts are not returned to senders unless a wedding is cancelled by the couple.)

Should we register for gifts? It's actually a thoughtful thing to do. Even though many encore couples have little need for china, silver, and other traditional gifts, registering at one or two stores can be helpful for guests. If you decide to register, think

---

A QUESTION FOR PEGGY

After my divorce, I kept my ex's last name and all the monogrammed wedding gifts, including the sterling flatware. Now I'm remarrying, and I wonder what to do with these things.

Many encore couples dispose of monogrammed items like towels and table linens—either giving them away or passing them on to children from their earlier marriages. But something as costly as sterling flatware can be another matter entirely. You might sell the sterling and replace it with a set you both choose. Or if your future husband agrees, you could continue to use it. Nowadays, people collect silverware that has been engraved with many different initials, so setting the table with your monogrammed flatware may hardly be noticed. Just be sure to discuss the options with your fiancé and make the decision together.

about your interests. Sporting goods, hardware, garden tools, books and CDs, video-tapes and DVDs—you can register for items that are both useful and inexpensive. (See also Chapter 38, page 668: "Registry Alternatives.")

Can I have a wedding shower? While it can be fun to be honored at a shower (see Chapter 34, page 590: "Showers), encore couples should think carefully. Since encore couples often acquire new friends after their earlier marriages, a shower is appropriate when the guests are mostly people who were not included in the past. But people who attended showers for the bride's or groom's previous marriage are not expected to bring presents.

If a shower is given, provide the hostess with a list of people who you think would enjoy coming. (You can include close family and friends even though they may have attended showers for your previous wedding and therefore are not expected to bring presents.) You might also tell the hostess about any items you really need, so she can share your wish list with guests who ask for ideas. Remember that shower gifts are not supposed to be expensive. (For ideas about alternative shower themes and gift ideas, see Chapter 38, page 669: "Gift Showers.")

Showers are not the only way people can entertain for you. If a friend or coworker offers to hold a shower, you might suggest a luncheon, afternoon tea, or after-work gathering instead—without presents.

Is a rehearsal dinner necessary? Not at all, but it's a nice idea when you want to bring everybody in your wedding party and your immediate families together. Instead of a full-scale party complete with toasting, encore couples might host a dinner at a favorite restaurant, or friends might throw a night-before-the-wedding cocktail buffet. It's not unusual for a couple who live together to invite friends to their home for a casual evening.

If one or both of the couple have children, the rehearsal and a low-key family gathering afterward can ease some of the stress children may feel about how to behave (with you and new stepsiblings) on the big day. Including your children at the rehearsal—whether or not they are in the wedding party—should help to increase their overall sense of involvement.

Chapter Forty-two

New Times, New Traditions

WEDDINGS IN THE EARLY DAYS of this country tended to be simple occasions. Americans were building a nation, and few had the time or money for exhaustive planning or elaborate displays. But our ancestors were very conscious of weddings as hopeful events confirming the continuation of the community. They incorporated customs from their Old World cultures and adapted them to the frontier. They created new rituals that expressed their individualism and pioneer spirit. And that spirit survives in surprising measure.

Today's weddings are full of traditions. At the same time, personalization is one of the most visible trends in contemporary weddings. Brides and grooms now enjoy the freedom to fashion weddings that are unique to them. They have the best of both worlds—new and novel ideas and timeless traditions. Couples of different ethnic, national, and religious heritages are likely to plan weddings that blend and honor their individual cultures. Personal interests can provide inspiration for wedding themes and elements of the ceremony and reception. Increasing attention is being given to same-sex unions and the emerging etiquette of commitment ceremonies. This chapter provides an overview of such trends as well as ways to adapt wedding plans with sensitivity to the feelings of the wedding party, family members, guests, and wedding professionals.

Weddings are more full of happiness when couples are careful not to let the details overwhelm their feelings for each other and for those around them. Couples who are true to the underlying principles—respect for one another, consideration for others, and honesty in all their dealings—should have little difficulty achieving the wedding of their dreams.

Traditions in New Contexts

MOST GUESTS will enjoy unconventional weddings, but their enjoyment will be greater if they know what to expect. When you include elements such as the following, the objective should be a pleasant surprise for guests—not a shock. The ceremony program is a good place to include explanations of customs and rituals that are likely to be unfamiliar. Or the officiant or members of the wedding party can explain specific rituals to the guests during the service.

Discuss the inclusion of religious rituals and/or readings from other religious texts with your officiant. Some faiths do not allow deviation from their standard services, but it may be possible to include other rituals either before or after the ceremony or at the reception.

Unity candle. A fairly recent addition to many marriage services, the lighting of a single candle symbolizes a couple's unity. Usually, the bride and groom each hold lighted candles and set a third candle alight together. The individual candles can then be extinguished, but some couples keep them lit throughout the service as a sign that they remain individuals within their union.

The unity candle ceremony is easily adapted. Family members may be included, and parents and stepparents can participate if everyone agrees. Sometimes, the bride's and groom's mothers light the candle. A unity candle lighting is also a good way for an encore couple to involve their children in the service. The ceremony can take place at any point in the service, but if more than the couple are involved, it's often staged after the exchange of vows.

Customs from other faiths and cultures. In religious and secular services, today's couples may adopt and adapt elements from faiths other than their own. One example is the Jewish tradition of having mothers and fathers in the processional. Some couples have adapted the Greek Orthodox crowning, or wreath, ceremony (see Chapter 40, page 712: "Wedding Customs in Many Faiths") as a symbol of their unity. Another gracious addition to some American weddings is the Chinese tea ceremony, during which the couple offer cups of sweet tea to each other's families. Native American ceremonial sand painting has inspired sand-blending rituals to signify the mingling of two individuals and their families into a single family.

Secular readings. Including nonreligious poetry and prose readings in marriage ceremonies enables couples to express their commitment in words that have special significance for them—and also allows personalization of the service by couples who do not compose their own vows. Couples may ask family members and friends to be readers. Religious and secular officiants might suggest sources for readings, and an Internet search will yield many ideas. Appropriateness and brevity are important, so discuss your options with the officiant early in the planning process.

Musical mixes. Maybe you'd like to open your ceremony with the ringing of a Tibetan gong. Or walk up the aisle to the sound of Scottish bagpipes. Or include Balinese dancing at your reception. Music provides innumerable ways to personalize (and internationalize) wedding celebrations. Ask your officiant about any restrictions on secular music. Musical selections are usually listed by title and composer in the ceremony program, and a very brief explanation can also be included.

Trends don't always become traditions, but the following current wedding customs seem to have real staying power.

Personalized weddings. Today's marriage ceremonies often include elements that have special meaning for couples, and perhaps their families. Many couples make concerted efforts to "fight the hype": Lavish might be in, but so is intimate and individualized.

Sharing the costs. Wedding expenses are frequently shared by the couple, as well as the bride's, and sometimes the groom's, parents. More couples pay most or all of the expenses. With wedding costs so high, "Who pays?" is often one of the first conversations that engaged couples have.

Weddings and high tech. The Internet plays a growing role in registries, gift selection, and shopping for supplies and vendors; wedding-oriented chat rooms and bulletin boards enable couples to share information and advice. Couples can create wedding Web sites, but e-mailing invitations and thank-you notes is still an etiquette no-no.

Encore and family weddings. Nearly forty-five percent of today's weddings are "encore" events, meaning that the bride, groom, or both have been married before. More couples are hosting "family weddings" that actively involve their children. (See Chapter 41, page 725, "Making It a Family Affair.")

Involved grooms. Grooms are now as likely as brides to participate in planning and decision making. Couples often take mutual responsibility for everything from financing to writing thank-you notes.

Celebrating different religious traditions. Interfaith ceremonies often combine elements from both faiths. Services may include several officiants.

Including parents. Mothers as well as fathers can escort their daughters in the processional, and brides may ask both parents to accompany them on the walk down the aisle.

Honor attendants. A bride may have a male friend as one of her attendants or a groom might include a female as one of his. When serving as "maid of honor" or "best man," these friends are called "honor attendants."

More wedding attire choices. Wedding dresses and accessories can include colors, designs, and fabrics that reflect the bride's culture or ethnic heritage. Attendants' outfits are often chosen with consideration for future use, and many brides select dresses in different cuts to flatter each bridesmaid. Black and shades of white are no longer "out" for bridesmaids or women guests. (See also Guest attire, page 709.)

Variations in color. Color is blooming in bouquets and floral arrangements, brides' and grooms' attire, invitations and announcements, reception decorations and table linens, wedding cakes, and gift wrappings.

Destination weddings. More couples and their guests are traveling to distant locations for their big day. Guests often turn the trip into a longer vacation.

Jumping the broom. This custom, most often associated with African–American weddings, is done to honor the slaves who were not allowed to marry legally, but who did marry and form strong families. The ritual is said to symbolize the establishment of a new household and is usually performed just after the wedding service or at the reception. The broom (a regular house broom is fine) is decorated with ribbons, flowers, and perhaps special trinkets. The broom is laid on the floor, and guests gather around. On the count of three, the newlyweds, hand in hand, jump over the broom and into their new life as husband and wife. (In the pre–Civil War era, the broom was held above the floor, behind the couple, and they jumped it backward!)

Handfasting. A custom most associated with pagan Celtic tradition, handfasting is now being included in some religious as well as secular services. During the service, the couple's hands are ceremonially tied with rope or cords to symbolize their union. Though the Celtic handfasting ceremony probably originated as a contract between a couple to stay together for a year and a day (if the arrangement worked, the contract was renewed), handfasting today signifies the enduring nature of the marriage commitment. It may be the source of the phrase "tying the knot."

The shared cup. In many traditions, both religious and secular, the bride and groom share a cup of wine during the wedding ceremony—a custom unrelated to Christian communion services. In Chinese tradition, the couple drink wine and honey from goblets tied together with red string. In Japan, couples who wed in the Shinto tradition take nine sips of sake, as do their parents, to symbolize the new bonds of family.

Sharing a wedding cup is also a reception custom in many cultures. French couples drink wine from a *coupe de marriage*, or double-handled cup. Irish guests gather round the newlyweds, and toasts are made over cups of mead, a fermented drink made from honey, malt, and yeast.

Marrying to a Theme

Themed weddings can carry personalization into nearly every aspect of planning, from the look of invitations to the shape of the wedding cake. Themes should be meaningful to both of the couple—and not so far out that guests won't get the idea. A theme shouldn't be an imposition on guests, as acquiring period clothing would be. It's also important to consider budget; a themed wedding complete with costuming for the wedding party and staff at the reception, elaborate decorations, and complicated menus can be very costly.

But themes—whether carried through the entire occasion or just the reception—can be great fun and a satisfying outlet for creative thinking. The following categories and examples are provided as idea starters for themes that are both practical and memorable.

> *The season or the month of the wedding:* An October wedding might be the inspiration for autumn colors, country dances, even a hayride to the reception site.

A favorite place: A couple who met in Paris, Nairobi, or Hong Kong might theme their reception around the foods and music typical of that place.

A historical period or era: The spectacle of ancient Egypt, the romance of medieval courts, the sleek style of 1930s Art Deco—history is a treasure trove of ideas.

A shared interest: A mutual love of Shakespeare might suggest an Elizabethan theme with sonnets as guest favors. A couple devoted to water sports or camping could create a nautical or outdoors theme.

The wedding location: A floral theme might be perfect for a wedding in a beautiful garden. The reception for a beach or lakeside wedding could be just right for a clambake, luau, or barbecue.

The honeymoon: A couple planning their dream trip might stage their reception as a bon voyage party with a travel theme.

Commitment Ceremonies

CEREMONIES CELEBRATING the partnerships of gay and lesbian couples are planned much the same way as heterosexual weddings. The current, nearly universal lack of legal status affects some aspects of the engagement and ceremony—notably the absence of a marriage license, mandated health testing, and a marriage certificate signed by a licensed officiant and witnesses—but in no way limits the joy of the couple and those who share their happiness.

There isn't any one-size-fits-all formula for telling family and friends about an engagement and impending union ceremony. Each situation is personal, and couples have to be guided by their knowledge of the people involved. Reactions can range from unfettered delight to concern about the public nature of a ceremony (even when families approve of the relationship) to rejection and outright hostility. But patience is a virtue to be cultivated; a negative initial reaction may be transformed when family and friends have time to consider their true feelings. There may be people who never accept the union, but couples should try to give their loved ones the opportunity to come around.

The first people most couples should inform are their parents, but if either partner has children from a previous marriage, they should be told even before the couple's parents. This is particularly important for young children and teenagers whose lives will be directly affected by the union. However, before speaking to parents or children, some gay and lesbian couples may prefer to tell supportive friends. This is often the case when family members are not likely to accept the union or may be uncomfortable with the idea of a same-sex wedding. By telling friends first, couples can enjoy the lift of sharing their news with people whose approval is certain—a morale-builder prior to family discussions that are likely to be difficult—and get advice from friends who have had their own commitment ceremonies.

It's wise not to attribute every negative response to prejudice. People who love you may be worried about issues including your choice of partner (Is he or she the right person for you?) and lifestyle changes that the union may bring about (How will career or education goals be affected? Will you be moving far away?). Listen carefully to any objections before assuming motives that may not be real.

Planning Same-sex Unions

Gay and lesbian couples today are creating their own traditions but also following some of the steps of traditional wedding planning. A couple's first major decisions involve guest list, budget, the date and time for their ceremony, and style of the celebration. (See Chapter 34, pages 571–582: "The Major Decisions.") After these choices are made, it's time to get down to the brass tacks of putting together your big day.

Same-sex ceremonies can be religious or secular, and couples are free to plan the kind of occasion that is meaningful to them. They might consult friends who have celebrated their own unions. Gay and lesbian organizations can often provide information about ceremonies, officiants, and local vendors and suppliers. Internet searches might provide links to resources in the immediate area.

While most of the etiquette in the "Weddings" section of this book applies directly to or can easily be adapted for commitment ceremonies, there are some specific guidelines that can help same-sex couples plan their big events.

Attendants. You can ask as few or as many as you like—or none at all. Just be certain that attendants understand that they will not be legal witnesses, except where same-sex unions are recognized by law. Attendants are often called "honor attendants," especially when they stand with someone of the opposite gender. Children can be included as junior attendants, flower girls, and ring bearers.

A QUESTION FOR PEGGY

I asked my best friend from college to be my matron of honor for my commitment ceremony. Although she said yes and has been supportive, I can tell that she's not really comfortable with the idea. Should I let her off the hook by taking back my invitation?

You need to talk openly with your friend. Let her know that you sense her discomfort, but don't say anything that implies prejudice on her part. Be tactful and listen carefully to what she says. She may have problems you don't know about, such as difficulty with her family, financial constraints, or simple nerves at being in the ceremony. Whatever the issue, you can tell her that being your attendant is her choice and that you won't be hurt or offended if she opts out. If she decides not to serve as an attendant, you might talk about another way she could be involved in the ceremony. Maybe she would give a reading. Or perhaps she won't participate but will be comfortable attending as a guest. Whatever her decision, you'll keep a good friend by showing your concern for her feelings.

Officiants. A licensed officiant isn't required except where gay and lesbian unions are legal. Couples can ask friends, family members, or respected mentors to officiate. You might want several people to conduct the service. Some couples have no officiant, choosing to exchange vows themselves and perhaps to include readings and musical contributions by friends.

Couples who want a religious service might consult their own clergy. A number of faiths and sects today allow individual congregations to determine policies about gay and lesbian ceremonies. Even if a clergyperson cannot perform the service, he or she may be able to refer the couple to someone who can. Churches including the Metropolitan Community Church, Universalist Unitarian, and Universal Life Church, as well as some Reform Jewish and mainline Protestant congregations, welcome same-sex couples. Ethical Humanist organizations offer spiritual but nonreligious services for couples regardless of orientation.

When you first contact a member of the clergy, clarify the exact nature of the service and your relationship—that you are a gay or lesbian couple and you want to

~ A Few Tips for Guests ~

If you're invited to a same-sex ceremony and have not previously attended one, it's natural to wonder what is expected of guests. The answer is simple: Guest etiquette is the same as for a traditional wedding celebration. The following points address some concerns, but common sense is always the best guide:

➤ Reply to the invitation as soon as possible. If you must regret, there's no need for excuses. Invitees who are genuinely opposed to or upset by same-sex unions would be wise to decline graciously rather than risk dampening the happiness of the couple.

➤ Whether you can attend or not, the invitation obliges you to send a wedding gift.

➤ When choosing attire, be guided by the time of the ceremony and the nature of the invitation (formal, informal, or casual).

➤ Follow the order of the service in the ceremony program if one is provided. Otherwise, take your lead from the wedding party and other guests. Chances are, the ceremony and reception will be similar to other weddings you've attended.

➤ Go through the receiving line if there is one. All the traditional expressions of congratulations are appropriate, except references to "bride and groom" or "husband and wife." If there isn't a receiving line, be sure to extend best wishes to the couple and their families at some point during the party.

➤ Refrain from making comments and asking questions that might be perceived as negative. This won't be hard if guests bear in mind that the ceremony, while it may not be legally sanctioned, honors the lifetime commitment of two people in love.

arrange a commitment ceremony. In addition to being courteous, full disclosure at the outset can save time; if the person doesn't perform same-sex services, you can ask for recommendations and then get on with your search.

Locations. Even though couples may not have a house of worship in their area that permits same-sex ceremonies, there are many location options. Your own home or a family member's or friend's home; a hotel, club, or restaurant; a civic or historic site; a park or beach setting; a fabulous resort destination—the choice comes down to what you want and can afford. If you plan to rent a space, inform the management about the nature of the event. An increasing number of commercial sites have experience with same-sex ceremonies, but if you sense discomfort or antagonism in your initial contact, it's probably best to find another spot. If a clergyperson will officiate, you'll need to co-ordinate with him or her. (See also Chapter 34, page 579: "The Officiant.")

Part Eight

You and
Your Job

Chapter Forty-three

Life in the Workplace

Lᴇᴛ's ғᴀᴄᴇ ɪᴛ. Even if you're in love with your job, many of the obstacles you confront at work spell stress with a capital S. In the corporate world, your company might have reengineered to the point that you're doing the work of two, even three, people. In a small business, the boss may reign as a feudal lord, with you feeling very much the serf. In a machine shop, you might have to suffer a backstabber who's doing his best to keep you from being promoted.

Some workplace problems you can do something about, and others you simply cannot. What you can *always* do is conduct yourself in such a way that you contribute to a harmonious atmosphere, do your part to see that justice is done, and help keep things on an even keel—from cordial interpersonal relationships to clean and orderly surroundings. That means calling on your better qualities and putting manners into play.

Office or Not?

ɪғ ʏᴏᴜ ʜᴀᴠᴇ ᴀɴ ᴏғғɪᴄᴇ with a door, real walls, and maybe even a window, remind yourself to be modest when interacting with workmates who don't. In other words, don't flaunt it.

How an office-dweller handles his door is key. Keeping it closed is a stark reminder of the inequity between you and any cubicle-bound workmates, so shut your door only when you must: when you need quiet to concentrate, you're meeting with a visitor, or you're discussing a confidential matter with an employer or coworker. (A closed door doesn't give you the license to make personal calls all day long or to complete personal tasks. As much as it feels like your home away from home, your office and its equipment are the property of your employer.)

No slamming! If you're bothered by a conversation going on outside your door, get up and shut the door as softly as possible; the chatterers will no doubt catch on.

A Little Humility, Please

When someone who works from a cubicle comes into your office, don't play the big shot who puts his feet up on the desk and surveys his domain. While the inequities may not bother your visitor in the least, you can de-emphasize them by either standing up and leaning on the edge of the desk or taking a chair near to him. No matter who the visitor or what the situation, any time you leave your desk and sit near someone, you set the stage for a more relaxed discussion. The behind-the-desk position is formal and emphasizes that this is your turf.

Open-office Courtesies

Workers in cubicles or common work spaces are so visible that they seem always to be available to one another and everyone else. Remind yourself that they're not. However compact and noisy the arrangement, open-office workers have the right to expect visitors to respect both their time and their space. A worker's assigned space is as much his territory as the CEO's corner office is hers.

Just as you wouldn't barge into anyone's office through a closed door, it's better to enter a cubicle by asking, "May I come in?" Workers who interact for much of the day are exempted from this courtesy, but anyone else who arrives unexpectedly should ask permission in one way or another.

For the same reason, keep the practice known as prairie-dogging—standing up or hanging over the wall to speak to the person in the neighboring cubicle—to a minimum. If you want to show your disapproval of prairie-dogging, choose your words with care: "Mary, I know it's easier to talk over the wall, but would you mind coming around? Or I could come see you in a minute." Such a request serves as a reminder to both you and your neighbors that there's no substitute for communicating face-to-face.

An unfortunate by-product of cubicle life is the ability of those around you to hear everything you say—and vice versa. It takes a strong-willed person to tune out the voices around him, which is often impossible. Improve your lot (and your neighbors') by trying the following:

> ➤ Gently dissuade coworkers from loitering or socializing around your cubicle. A polite "Larry, I'm working on something so complicated that I really have to concentrate" should get the message across.

> ➤ When hosting visitors, meet in a common area or a conference room so that you won't disturb your neighbors.

> ➤ Be discreet—a cubicle is not the place to spread office gossip, so discuss confidential matters in a private place.

> ➤ Whenever you don't want a phone call to be overheard, try to find an unused office with a working phone, use a pay phone or cell phone in the lobby, or wait and make the call after hours.

➤ If you walk up to someone in a cubicle or an office and he's talking on the phone, don't hover and wait for him to hang up. Try again later.

Who Rises, and When?

Male or female, courteous people rise when their boss, any other person of senior rank, or someone elderly enters their work space. You also stand for clients and customers. It's even nice to stand to greet any workmate who hasn't dropped by your office or cubicle for a while. Rising isn't an empty gesture done for the sake of "rules" but a quiet way of showing respect.

At most other times during the workday, you can remain in your chair. Assistants and other people who come and go with regularity would find it strange if you popped up every time they walked in.

Sharing Equipment and Space

COMMUNAL OFFICE EQUIPMENT, which has a way of needing repair more often than it should, is a lightning rod for the "it's not my job" attitude among workers. Even if machine maintenance isn't technically your responsibility, take care of things if you can. If a fax machine, printer, or copier needs toner or has a paper jam, either do the job yourself or call whoever is in charge of machine maintenance right away. This applies twice over in a small business, where everyone—including the boss—should pitch in.

Copiers

Copying machines run at different speeds, with some processing thirty pages in half the time of an older machine. But even the use of state-of-the-art copiers requires remembering the needs of others.

The most obvious courtesy is for someone who's got a large copy job—twenty pages or more—to allow anyone who has only two or three pages to interrupt (or if you got to the machine at the same time, to go first). It's another matter if you've set the machine for finishing (sorting, stapling, enlarging) and you need four copies of a forty-page manuscript. In this case, give anyone who's waiting an estimate of how long it will take. A newcomer who sees that someone has just set the machine for a major job should be the one to defer.

Jobs of any real magnitude are best done early in the morning or just after quitting hours, when the machines are freer. An alternative is to do the job on a copier that's off the beaten path. Another reminder: After any large job, check the paper drawer and refill it as necessary.

If you work for a business with a "no personal copies" policy, always abide by it or ask special permission from your boss. Better yet, make your personal copies elsewhere, regardless of your workplace policy.

If you're a manager, remember that you have as many obligations to your subordinates as they have to you. The world is full of bad, even abusive, bosses—but despite the questionable success of some major-league brutes, showing concern and respect for the people you manage will benefit you as well as them. You're a gold-star boss if you . . .

Make yourself available. Strike the right balance between paying attention to your subordinates and leaving them alone. Dropping by the office to ask about any concerns or to give feedback can motivate employees; overdoing it intrudes on their time.

Communicate clearly. Make sure a worker understands the duties outlined in her job description and that any instructions for a specific task are crystal clear. Use plain English; jargon and euphemism, often used to sound more "businesslike," will only muddy the waters.

Remember the small courtesies. Saying "please" and "thank you" when you speak to anyone in a subordinate position is a pleasant reminder that the bedrock civilities of human interaction are something you and your employees share.

Praise a job well done. Complimenting a subordinate shows that you understand the skill that a task required and that the worker was up to the job. Just don't start handing out compliments too freely, which could cheapen the value of your praise. Compliments work best when they're sincere and well deserved.

See things coming. Prevent conflicts between workers by making sure everyone clearly understands who is responsible for what. Drop into offices now and then, keep your ear to the ground, and sense any blowups that might be in the offing. You can't keep a volatile situation from boiling over unless you know that it's brewing.

Accept responsibility for your mistakes. Blaming another person, another department, or "circumstances beyond your control" not only marks you as a buck-passer but could also raise questions about your integrity.

Don't delay delivering bad news. Layoffs, a poor earnings report, or even the start of a project that will require considerable overtime—it's preferable to deliver bad news of this kind in a meeting than in a memo. Be prepared to answer the inevitable questions.

Fire gently. Lessen the blow to someone being fired by doing it in private, delivering the news quickly and straightforwardly, and not rushing the person out of your office.

Fax Machines

When faxing, abide by the office rules. Some companies allow fax machines to be used only for business, not personal, communications; others don't mind, although you'll show consideration by sending personal faxes after hours. If your workplace policy falls somewhere in between, ask permission from a supervisor whenever you want to use the office fax for personal correspondence.

Unlike a copying job, a fax transmission can't easily be interrupted, and sending faxes of twenty pages or more can tie up the machine for what seems an eternity. Follow the same "who goes first" rule that applies to copiers. Or try to send a fax early in the morning, just after closing time, or when most people are at lunch. Better still, before blindly dumping a job in the fax machine, check with the intended recipient to see if an e-mail attachment is an option. In big cities, a messenger service is another option for a large job being sent locally.

Most offices keep in and out boxes near the fax machine. If you spot a newly arrived fax for a coworker, you aren't obligated to put it in her mailbox or let her know it has arrived. But if it's no trouble to drop it off as you pass by her office, by all means do.

Printers

Don't print out lengthy jobs on a printer that you know to be heavily used. If your job is for 8½" × 11" paper, direct it to a laser printer that handles that size only, leaving the other printers free for 11" × 17" and 8½" × 14" printouts.

∼ The Privacy Problem ∼

Privacy is a concern regardless of the nature of your workplace. One problem is people's propensity to snoop, and snooping seems to know no bounds.

Faxing and copying. Communal office machines yield ripe pickings for the snoop, so use them with care.

➢ As you sift through a fax in-box or remove someone else's just-transmitted document from the machine, look only at the cover sheets.

➢ If you open the lid of a copier to find someone has left an original sheet, don't get curious if it has the look of something private.

Eavesdropping. Try not to listen to your neighbor's phone conversations. If despite your efforts, something obviously private or intimate catches your ear, *keep it to yourself.* Many a rumor has started because of something overheard.

Prying. The particulars of a coworker's love life, finances, divorce, problem teenager, or health should be volunteered by the person himself, if he wants—not asked about by you. Even if the person broaches the subject, don't dig for more information.

If a printing job hasn't been picked up, either place it face-up where it can easily be seen or put it in a space designated for finished jobs. As with faxes, it would be thoughtful to drop off a job if it's obvious who printed out the pages, but there's no need to go far out of your way.

Furniture

Treat your desk and any tables in the reception area, conference rooms, or kitchen as you would your own furniture. With wooden furniture, put soda cans and sweating glasses on napkins or coasters to avoid leaving rings.

Think ahead: Your office furniture will more than likely be used by someone else down the line. As a favor to those who inherit it, don't wipe your greasy fingers on a fabric-covered chair or leave spills on your work surface so long that they might stain. Clean up snack crumbs to prevent stains and grease spots on carpets.

In the Kitchen

The kitchen can be the messiest room on the floor, so be thoughtful and do your part to keep it clean.

- ➢ If you spill something—on the counter, in the fridge, on the floor—*wipe it up.*
- ➢ Don't leave your dirty dishes in the sink.
- ➢ As necessary, wipe down appliances (including microwaves and toaster ovens) after you use them.
- ➢ Refill an ice cube tray if you've emptied it.
- ➢ Refill a communal coffeemaker if you pour the last cup.
- ➢ Don't leave milk or leftovers in the refrigerator until they start to smell.
- ➢ Avoid foods that smell while cooking, including cabbage and fried fish.

∼ The Food Thief ∼

Little is more frustrating than finding that the ham sandwich you brought for lunch has mysteriously disappeared from the office fridge. Then there's the pilfering of milk (a splash here, a splash there) by other coffee drinkers who think of it as "borrowing just a little." Personalizing your brown bag by labeling it with your name—thereby announcing to one and all that it's *not communal*—may deter a thief, but don't count on it.

It's almost impossible to catch a food thief. Your best bet is to post a note on the fridge door—something like "To the person who took my lunch on Monday, January 12: Thievery may not be a capital offense, but it's seriously disrespectful to your coworkers. Was a ham sandwich really worth it? [Signed,] An angry coworker."

In the Restrooms

Restroom etiquette is simple:

> ➤ Dispose of paper hand towels and any personal hygiene products.
> ➤ Wipe the washbasin clean of any toothbrush suds, makeup spills, or shaving cream.
> ➤ Don't have conversations from a stall.
> ➤ In a unisex restroom, don't leave the toilet seat up.
> ➤ If you're the hygiene-minded type who arranges toilet paper on the seat, dispose of it when you leave instead of leaving it to litter the floor.

Requesting and Offering Help

THE BEST way to get help in the workplace is to give it. For instance, if you see an officemate working through lunch to collate a large client packet and you pitch in to help, your generosity will likely be returned in kind. Whenever you voluntarily help out around the workplace, your reward is a coworker's gratitude, not extra pay. The person who is genuinely willing to help is one who doesn't demand favors in return.

When you receive a helping hand, a thank-you is always in order, no matter how small the favor. If a coworker gives up his lunch hour to help you, you could reward him with a funny card, a little gift, or an invitation to lunch. When possible, compliment helpful coworkers and subordinates to their supervisors.

Help for Newcomers

Do what you can to help newcomers. New employees may have crackerjack skills, but they will have a lot to learn about how your business works—names to remember, places to locate, policies to master, reporting relationships to understand.

Be helpful and forgiving within reason. Try to recollect how you felt when you were first employed and what information you needed. Give them answers, even if the questions haven't been asked yet: "Ms. Guzman wants those weekly reports in a folder, but Mr. Kenny prefers a memo." Or "If you have a doctor's or dentist's appointment, tell Mrs. Shepard, and she'll clear your schedule." Just remember that "help" doesn't include clueing the newcomer in on the latest office gossip; she has the right to make her own judgments about coworkers and bosses.

The Gofer Question

Not so very long ago, it wasn't unusual for assistants to perform personal services for their superiors—fetching coffee, picking up dry cleaning, even shopping for an anniversary or birthday present. While the practice may be less common today, it still hangs on in some places.

The management of a company of any kind should always make clear whether a support job entails performing services that have nothing to do with actual work. It isn't fair to blindside a new assistant with duties she may resent. By taking the job, she entered an agreement that she'll aid her supervisor professionally, not personally. Any respectful manager does his part by abiding by that agreement.

If you're asked to perform nonbusiness tasks or run errands, start by asking yourself some questions. Are the tasks honestly eating into your work time? Are the things you're asked to do the kind you would be doing anyway, since you simply enjoy helping? Only if the tasks are clearly inappropriate or frequent enough to be disruptive do you really have grounds for complaint.

The Temp

When temporary employees arrive at your office, welcome them and be ready to help. Assume that temps are both skilled and ready to learn (temps are often very accomplished people who take on short-term work so they can pursue other interests or look for rewarding full-time jobs), and consider them as deserving of professional treatment as permanent employees are. Since temps often receive chilly receptions, do your part to show them the ropes and introduce them in a positive way to the company.

If it's standard procedure to take a new employee to lunch in the first week, try to do the same for a temp. Also include him in normal office socializing, but don't draw him into office debates about company policy or subject him to your complaints about work—especially in an attempt to elicit his sympathy and support.

When You're the Temp

When starting your tour of duty, dress conservatively and take your measure of the place. You'll quickly peg the office style on the casual-to-formal scale, both in dress and behavior. Also, try not to judge your new coworkers too harshly if they seem cold. You may be arriving in the wake of a downsizing or reorganization, and temps are easy targets for the resentments of longtimers who sense that their jobs are in jeopardy.

Respond graciously when someone makes a friendly overture—say, an invitation to lunch in the cafeteria. It's also a good idea to accept offers of assistance, even when you don't really need the help; accepting shows collegiality and respect for the knowledge and experience of the permanent employees.

When chatting with permanent employees, never discuss salary or benefits, because comparisons will inevitably be drawn between theirs and your own. Another major concern is confidentiality. The fact that you have two bosses—the agency employing you and the company contracting with it—makes staying tight-lipped doubly important.

If you decide to complain about nonbusiness tasks, first request a meeting with your boss. Then couch your complaint in terms of efficiency: "It's not that I mind shopping for gifts for your daughter. It just makes it harder to keep up with my workload. Besides, running errands really isn't part of my job description." If there's an existing agreement that personal assistance is inappropriate, politely remind him of it. After you've talked, you can only hope that he sees the error of his ways. If he doesn't, you may have to take it to a higher level (see also page 753: "Going Over the Boss's Head").

Lodging Complaints

COMPLAINTS ABOUT WORKPLACE CONDITIONS can involve anything from excessive overtime to disgustingly messy restrooms. Some gripes are touchier—those about coworkers and supervisors. Complaining effectively is something of an art, and you can avoid some common pitfalls by asking yourself the following questions:

Is my complaint worth my boss's time? Before going to the boss, calmly examine the problem in the light of common sense. Is the problem persistent and serious enough to warrant intervention? Also choose the right time; if the issue isn't urgent, wait until your boss isn't busy with other obligations.

Am I the right complainer? The best complainer is the person who's best positioned to make a solid case. For example, if you've been reprimanded for tardiness, you'll be on shaky ground complaining about a coworker who habitually takes long lunch hours. Let Miss Punctuality handle the job.

Should I make my case in person? Bosses are usually either listeners or readers—the former preferring to talk it over in a private meeting, the latter wanting to learn of complaints and other matters in a well-prepared, confidential memo.

Have I documented the problem? It's important that you have support for your complaint, especially when your boss may have to take the issue to higher levels. Serious accusations, including office theft and sexual harassment, require proof (suspicions and gossip don't count). Keep a journal or diary of events, assemble paper evidence, and find others who can back up your claim.

Do I have solutions in mind? Be ready with suggestions for solving the problem. But let the boss take the initiative; you don't want to look as if you're usurping his problem-solving role.

Complaints About Conditions

Before lodging a gripe about workplace conditions, know whom to approach: the boss, the boss's assistant, the office manager, your coworker, or, if you're a union member, your steward. Then determine how to best present the problem. Minor problems such as a malfunctioning copy machine or chair can be covered in a brief memo or e-mail. More serious complaints (an unreasonable share of work or the schemes of a rumor-mongering colleague) call for a meeting. Report potentially dangerous problems (the presence of a stranger on the premises, a locked fire door) as quickly as possible and by the fastest means available.

Problems such as excessive overtime and short staffing are trickier. Don't jump to the conclusion that the boss is at fault; she may already be working to fix things. If not, inform her in a polite, conciliatory manner. You may get the results you want if you frame the complaint in terms of productivity—for example, instead of saying that you're overworked, tell the boss that the lack of staff is causing missed deadlines and errors.

If conditions don't improve, it may be time to rally the troops and meet as a group, which can be made up of department representatives or the whole department. The advantage of a group complaint is that numbers can impress even the most insensitive supervisor; most bosses want to avoid serious and widespread morale problems. If group complaining doesn't work, you may have to appeal to a higher authority (see also page 753: "Going Over the Boss's Head").

Complaints About Coworkers

You and your coworkers can often work out difficulties among yourselves, but at other times you'll want the boss to step in—especially if the problem is serious or has legal implications. Sexual harassment, racist remarks, theft, lying, fighting, threatening behavior—these are examples of serious problems that can affect the entire company, and your direct supervisor needs to know about them.

Be sure that any complaint is valid and not a mere personal issue. Arrange a private meeting with your boss instead of writing a memo (and never complain via e-mail, which in effect makes your words public property). In your meeting, be calm and focus on the troubling behavior, not the person: "Henry leaves a half hour early at least three days a week, and we're having a problem getting his time sheets" is far better than "Henry is irresponsible and deceitful." Be as objective as you can, and don't be tempted to express moral judgments.

Like it or not, sometimes you must simply tolerate difficult people whose value to the business outweighs their quirks. The conceited saleswoman who is always the top producer, the ill-tempered art director who wins the most coveted awards, the sharp-tongued secretary who can quickly master the most complex computer program—they may irritate your boss even more than they bother you. But remember that bosses have the responsibility to balance any shortcoming of the individual against the general good.

I work in an office that has three employees from Italy. They all speak flawless English but use only Italian among themselves—sometimes even when the subject is work-related. Am I wrong in thinking this rude?

It is rather rude, given that they seem to be purposely excluding everyone around them. However, it's really not your concern if your coworkers choose to communicate in their native tongue. If the habit is simply annoying but not detrimental to the work at hand, just do your best to ignore it. If, however, it is interfering with business, you have every reason to inform their supervisor and ask if she will take up the matter.

Going Over the Boss's Head

If you have to go over or around a boss for any reason—say, he stubbornly refuses to consider a project you know to be worthwhile or, worse, he is abusive to employees—remember that your objective is positive change for everyone, including the boss himself. In fact, if your company has an experienced human resources staff, they should be able to help you decide on the most strategic approach.

In any case, you must inform a boss (preferably face-to-face) if you are going to meet with one of his superiors: "Richard, I hope you'll understand, but I've decided to show Miss Parsons that proposal from Ned Croom. I honestly feel we're missing out on a great opportunity if we ignore it." Blindsiding a boss will only make matters worse between the two of you, regardless of the outcome of your dispute. (See also Chapter 44, page 766: "About Sexual Harassment.")

The Trouble-free Meeting

MEETINGS MAY BE one of the most effective tools for getting things done in the workplace, but ill-planned and badly managed ones are notorious time-wasters. No matter the type—a weekly department meeting, a videoconference, a hastily called crisis session—respect for people's time will make the meeting more efficient and ultimately more successful.

Meeting Invitations

Many companies provide employees with computerized scheduling programs that simplify issuing and responding to invitations. Even so, certain considerations will benefit all meeting participants:

Schedule carefully. Give thought to the time of day. If workers are busiest in the morning, meet in the afternoon. Even the day of the week can matter. Friday afternoon meetings are often a bad idea; many of the participants' minds will have already left for the weekend even though their bodies remain in the chairs.

Give plenty of advance time. Give invitees as much advance notice as possible—at least a week for informal in-house meetings, two to four weeks for more important, formally structured meetings.

Plan and distribute the meeting agenda ahead of time. At the very least, advise those invited of the general topics to be covered.

Segment when possible. Try not to make people who need to be there for only part of a long meeting sit through the whole thing. Segment the meeting with breaks so that those who are no longer needed can make a graceful getaway.

Accepting and Declining

It's courteous to respond to all meeting invitations, whether attendance is compulsory or not. As soon as you receive a notice, check your schedule to make sure there's no conflict and then make your reply. Even if your invitation doesn't specifically ask you to respond, do it; either e-mail or a quick phone call will suffice.

If you're called to a last-minute meeting, remember that "spur-of-the-moment" doesn't mean "unimportant." If you can't attend, include in your regrets a request for a report of the meeting.

The Politics of Seating

Traditionally, the meeting leader sits at the head of the table at the end farthest from the door; the seats opposite the leader are for guests or visitors, senior management, or the leader's assistants.

High protocol applies only to very important meetings, such as when the guests are representatives from an overseas company. In that case, the senior representative of the visiting company sits at the center of the length of the table facing the door, with his staff seated alongside (the short ends of the table are left vacant). The executive of the host company and her staff sit directly opposite.

Meeting Manners, Briefly

Meeting leaders and attendees can make things run more smoothly by observing a few courtesies. The first is punctuality. A leader who starts a meeting late shows not only that he's disorganized but also that he has little respect for the attendees' schedules.

Late arrival by attendees is equally disrespectful. There are times, however, when being late is unavoidable. If you've been invited to a meeting and know you'll be unable to get there in time, tell the leader as soon as you can; he may be able to revise the agenda if your participation is needed at a certain point. In any case, enter a meeting in progress as unobtrusively as possible. Walk in, apologize briefly without interrupting anyone (hold your excuses for later), and take your seat. Don't disturb by rattling papers, snapping a briefcase open and shut, getting coffee, or whispering to your neighbors.

Other points of politeness:

➤ Turn off cell phones, watches with timers, and anything else that might make noise. (If you must take or make a cell phone call during the meeting, let the leader know in advance. When the time comes, step outside the room to conduct your call.) If you're prone to stomach rumbling, save yourself embarrassment by having a small snack before the meeting.

➤ Don't argue with anyone over an issue that is better discussed one-on-one.

➤ Don't engage in finger-pointing. If, say, you're reviewing a joint effort and feel a fellow team member made a wrong decision, don't sound accusatory. Instead, offer an alternative and say why you think it is stronger.

➤ In a question-and-answer session, don't drag out the meeting by asking unnecessary questions. Sometimes, people pipe up just to be noticed, causing restlessness in those who are eager to get back to work.

➤ Stick to the agenda. Ensuring that this is done is really the meeting leader's responsibility, but all attendees can help by avoiding wayward discussions.

A QUESTION FOR PEGGY

A manager in my department holds meetings that almost always run at least twice as long as they should. For one thing, he often goes to great lengths to explain details that are already clearly laid out in his handouts. How can I let him know that we feel our time is being wasted—but not offend him?

First of all, he'll probably get the message better if you approach him with a coworker who feels as you do. Then try to couch your complaint in positive terms: "Chris, your handout did such a good job of explaining the new business unit that we didn't think you needed to elaborate." In any further conversation, try to gracefully suggest that the shorter your meetings, the more time you all have to devote to your work.

Meeting leaders can get their act together by drawing up an agenda, setting time limits for each item (and sticking to it), calling on people to speak in turn, and forbidding interruptions. By doing so, they are in fact practicing good manners: Smart planning and staying in control = efficient meetings = showing respect for the participants' time.

Videoconferences and Teleconferences

In a world grown smaller, videoconferencing is more and more common. This doesn't mean, however, that conference calls via the telephone are a thing of the past. To proceed without a hitch, both types of electronic meetings have requirements that ordinary meetings don't.

First, a few guidelines that apply to videoconferences alone:

➢ Dress as you would for a face-to-face meeting.

➢ Make eye contact with the camera, but don't lean in too close.

➢ Don't leave the room unless you absolutely must.

➢ If you're the leader, use nameplates to identify the attendees if necessary, test the equipment in advance, and have a contingency plan in the event of a technical problem.

Participants in either kind of electronic meeting—video or telephone—should keep the following in mind:

➢ Speak more loudly (in a teleconference, only if a speakerphone is being used).

➢ When directing a question to a specific person, use her name.

➢ Don't speak over people or interrupt.

➢ Keep background noises to a minimum—no rustling of papers, snapping briefcases shut, or whispering to a colleague.

➢ Don't eat during the actual conference, even if snacks have been set out.

➢ Keep cell phones and pagers turned off.

➢ If you're the organizer, issue a clear agenda, let all participants know who will be present, introduce all participants, and begin and end on time.

Office Appointments

MEETINGS IN YOUR WORK SPACE are different from group meetings, but they can be highly productive if you observe a few courtesies.

Places to meet. First evaluate your private space. Is it comfortable physically and psychologically? If not, reserve a meeting room for your appointments.

Early arrivals. If a visitor arrives more than ten minutes early and you're not ready, try to keep her from feeling awkward. If you work in a small company without a receptionist proceed as follows: Come out of your office, greet the visitor, accept her reasons for arriving early, offer her an available chair, and ask if she'd like something to read while she waits. If your workplace has a receptionist, ask him to make the visitor comfortable and to tell her you'll be out as soon as possible.

Late arrivals. If a visitor arrives so late that you won't be able to see her, graciously accept her apology and arrange another meeting. Or, if it's impossible to tell her in person, ask the receptionist or an assistant to explain that you waited as long as you could and that you'd like to reschedule.

Keeping someone waiting. Never keep a visitor waiting more than five or six minutes past the appointed time. If you have no choice but to do so, walk out and apologize in person (your concern means more when it comes firsthand). Offering a cup of coffee or a magazine is a nice gesture. If something's come up that will delay your meeting for more than fifteen minutes, apologize for taking your visitor's time and ask whether she prefers to reschedule.

Office Meeting Courtesies

When someone from outside your workplace arrives for a meeting, there's more to getting off on the right foot than just a pleasant greeting. If she has a coat, offer to hang it up; then ask her to be seated. Remember that sitting behind a desk (especially an imposing one) can seem less personable than taking a chair near the guest. If you want the meeting to remain private, close your door. If you're in a cubicle, go to a common area or conference room (reserve the latter in advance).

Have all the necessary meeting materials at hand so that visitors won't have to wait as you sort through piles of files. If coworkers are participating, arrange for them to be present when the guest arrives, then make introductions all around.

If you have a do-not-disturb feature on your phone, activate it; it's generally bad form to answer the phone when a visitor is present. If you have an assistant and he considers an incoming call important enough to interrupt your meeting, use your intuition to gauge whether your visitor will mind.

When the meeting promises to last a half hour or more, you might offer the visitor a beverage. Keeping a coffeemaker, tea bags, and a couple of cups nearby simplifies things, since orders from outside could arrive at an inopportune time. (Note: Using real china instead of mugs or paper cups adds a nice touch.)

If a visitor overstays her welcome, you can politely end the meeting by saying that you'd like to talk more, but duty calls: "I wish we had more time to discuss this, Joan, but I have another appointment. Shall we make plans to talk later?"

Seeing Visitors Out

Be sure to walk the visitor back to the reception area, or, if you're unable to, arrange ahead of time to have someone else escort her. (Visitors should be shown out even if there's no maze of corridors to negotiate.) A few parting pleasantries are in order, but if your visitor keeps chatting, you could always plead a pressing duty.

These days, cards come in many varieties and don't necessarily follow any traditional format. Your main concern is that your card is easy to read and projects professionalism. It's best to present the necessary information as clearly as possible, including the following: the company name and address, your name and title, your telephone numbers (direct line and, if applicable, cell phone), fax number, and most likely your work e-mail address. Business cards also often include the company's Web site address and logo.

A business card should carry the name by which the person is known in the business world. People who use nicknames may either use their full names or their nicknames; a full name often sounds more professional, so it's fine to say, "Please call me Kathy, not Katherine" when handing out cards.

Titles, including Mr., Ms., Mrs., Miss, and Dr., are not used on business cards, although credentials may follow the name: "Katherine Thompson, J.D." An exception is when the person has a name that could be either male or female (Dana, for example); in such a case, placing Ms. or Mr. in front of the name is useful.

Following are a few do's and don'ts for handing out business cards:

Do keep your cards in perfect condition. Carry them in a business-card holder to prevent smudging and creasing.

Do keep your cards handy in an easy-to-get-to place. You don't want to fumble around for them.

Do bone up on business-card protocol of the countries you'll be visiting before traveling abroad. Customs can vary widely from country to country.

Don't put a business card you've just received into your pocket or wallet without a glance. Taking a moment to look at the card demonstrates your interest.

Don't offer your card up front to someone who outranks you. If the person doesn't ask after a while, you can present yours and ask for his or hers. With businesspeople of equal rank, don't hesitate to initiate the exchange.

Chapter Forty-four

The Social Side

Tᴴᴇ sᴏᴄɪᴀʟ sɪᴅᴇ ᴏғ ᴡᴏʀᴋ is the grease that keeps the wheels turning smoothly. Handle it badly, however, and it becomes the wrench in the works. In fact, the skill with which you interact and socialize with your workmates can mean the difference between advancing in your field of work or being left behind. Minding your p's and q's when dealing with people at work is not only the right thing to do but also an essential part of your job.

Being sociable doesn't require a perky, fixed smile and constant hellos or high-fiving; forced friendliness quickly grows tiresome. The best kind of sociability is effortless, and it's based on respect and thoughtfulness. It's the small gestures, like these:

> ➤ You're working late into the night and the cleaner arrives in your office. You say hello and exchange a few pleasantries, a simple act that lets the cleaner know he's not intruding and that you appreciate the work he does to keep your workplace tidy.

> ➤ You've witnessed a coworker defuse a tense situation between two other employees. Later, in private, you compliment him on his role as peacemaker.

> ➤ A coworker is the subject of a rumor you know to be false. You do your part to set the record straight and politely inform the source of the rumor (if you know who it is) that she was wrong.

> ➤ You unofficially take under your wing a newcomer, who is faced with names to remember, places to locate, workplace culture and policies to master, and hierarchies to understand.

> ➤ During a staff meeting, you sincerely praise a coworker's work on a project.

Office Courtesies

MANNERS AT WORK begin with greetings and small talk and extend to, among other things, respecting territory and privacy, handling conflicts, exchanging gifts, and knowing how to behave at office parties and other social occasions. Every workday will inevitably go better if workers show a modicum of respect and consideration for everyone they encounter, from front desk personnel to coworkers to supervisors.

Greetings and Small Talk

BEING COURTEOUS doesn't mean having to say hello every time you pass someone; a preoccupation with what you're doing is expected when you're busy and shouldn't be taken as an affront. You'll want to greet coworkers the first time you see them with "Good morning" or "How's it going?"—but as the day goes on, a quick smile or nod will do. More important is what *not* to do when passing people in the workplace: staring straight down at the floor with a sour look on your face.

Small talk with workmates is an inevitable part of the workday, but be careful what you say: Criticism of a coworker, a too-vivid account of a hot date, or remarks about the eccentricities of your boss are easily overheard in work environments, especially the kind without walls. Following are a few small-talk guidelines (see also "The Good Conversationalist," pages 279–294):

➤ When initiating small talk, be attuned to the other person's receptiveness. If he seems distracted or unresponsive, take the hint and back off.

➤ Even when the person is willing to chat, don't overstay your welcome. Visiting shouldn't get in the way of business.

➤ During even a short hallway chat, *stand to one side* so that you won't block traffic—an obvious courtesy, but one too often ignored.

➤ If other people want to join in, make an effort to include them. In some cases, this might mean switching topics to something that everyone can discuss.

➤ Be aware of the impact of small talk on those working around you. Keep your voice down; then read the body language of anyone nearby to judge whether to keep talking or to take your chat elsewhere. Just whispering may suggest gossiping or secretiveness.

➤ End the conversation pleasantly (not abruptly) with a remark like, "Well, I think it's time I got back to work," or "This was really interesting. We'll have to talk again."

➤ If a coworker who feels like chatting interrupts your work, suggest another time. "You've caught me at a bad moment. Can we wait to touch base after I've finished these letters?" If *you* interrupt, be sensitive to the other person's reaction. If she says she can't take a break, take no for an answer and don't feel rejected.

Respecting Rank

Rank is power, so be conscious of the position of the person with whom you're talking. Just because you're chatting with your boss about last night's baseball game

One of my coworkers is a chronic interrupter. A group of us will be discussing something, and she'll walk up to one of us and say, "I just have to ask you this one thing," then launch right into a new conversation. How can I let her know this drives me crazy?

The occasional interruption for an emergency is fine, but your coworker's constant interruptions should be squelched. The best option is to speak with her privately. Without getting personal (avoid the word "rude"), focus on the situation. Say something like "You probably don't even realize this, but when you jump into the middle of a discussion, it really gets us off track. You always have interesting things to say about our projects—but if you could wait until one conversation is over before starting a new one, it would be more productive for us all."

Alternatively, confront her on the spot, a tactic that can be awkward but is often effective. Just as she's about to jump in, hold up your hand as you calmly say, "Carla, just a minute, please. We're talking about the proposal." Then continue as she waits quietly, joins in, or decides to leave and speak later.

doesn't mean you can dispense with the common courtesies. Maintain a respectful conversational distance and avoid backslapping, nudging, hugging, elbowing, or other touching that implies a close friendship.

These days, most offices operate on a first-name basis—for employers and employees alike. If this isn't the case in your company or any you happen to visit, you should address your boss and other senior people as "Ms. Jackson," "Mrs. Oliva," and "Mr. Wells" unless they ask you to use their first names.

Giving and Accepting Compliments

NATURALLY, YOU AND YOUR WORKMATES need occasional pats on the back. Paying compliments whenever they're due is a kind of day-to-day justice. Saying "well done" or "good job" to someone not only raises her spirits but communicates that you're a thoughtful and observant person, capable of giving and sharing credit when it's deserved.

Receiving compliments graciously is difficult for many people. Taught from childhood not to be show-offs, their first impulse is to negate positive comments by saying why the compliment is undeserved. ("Oh, it was nothing" can make it sound as if the person extending the compliment is wrong.) In fact, a momentary burst of genuine gratitude plus a little immodesty ("Thanks so much! I'm really pleased") is preferable to rejecting a sincere pat on the back.

Two little words can solve all compliment dilemmas: *Thank you.* Unless you are receiving a trophy and a full-blown speech is requested, those two words, delivered with a smile, are always up to the job.

Personal Issues

SQUABBLES, GOSSIP AND RUMORS, offensive comments—sooner or later, you'll likely find yourself at loggerheads with a coworker or dragged into someone else's quarrel. Drawing on your social skills will help defuse such problems and show your mettle as a mature adult.

Dealing With Conflicts

You're certain that an extra day per week should be built into a project schedule, but the project manager refuses. Or you find yourself having to defend a coworker whom another worker unjustly demeans. Conflicts such as these can happen in virtually any workplace, and the first rule for handling them is to do it *in private.* Then follow these steps toward a resolution:

Stick to the subject. Don't allow a disagreement to wander into nongermane issues. And avoid referring to old conflicts; just because you were proved right in the last argument doesn't mean you're automatically right this time.

Be open to compromise. Although you may not get everything you want, some resolution is better than lasting hard feelings. Be sure to document the outcome of the disagreement; if it's business-related, you should confirm the final resolution with a memo to your "opponent." Documentation and confirmation are important if it becomes necessary to take the matter to a higher-up.

Don't make it personal. Stick to the situation and steer clear of criticizing. The moment you call Jonathan a dunce for preferring to file alphabetically rather than by invoice number, you may have won the battle—but Jonathan has just won the war.

Know when to postpone. There are times when disputes are integral to the work process—during a brainstorming session, for example, or a policy meeting. In such situations, state your case clearly and engage in debate if necessary, but don't be stubborn. Pay attention to the reaction of others. As soon as you sense resentment or annoyance, bring the conversation to a close; otherwise, it could degenerate into personal attacks. "Actually, I think it would be better if we talked about this later" is one way of defusing the situation. Or you could try, "Let's take this up when we can get [the supervisor] to help us figure out the direction the company wants to go."

Don't gloat. Avoid the temptation to say, "I told you so." If everyone recognizes that you were right, gloating will make you look petty.

Ways to Win Friends at Work
(or What *Not* to Do)

Staying on good terms with your coworkers largely depends on what you *don't* do during the workday. Petty annoyances come in all guises, some more serious than others. Three areas in particular are problematic: noise, smells, and offensive language.

Sounds

➤ Many tend to unconsciously talk louder when they're on the phone, so keep that in mind even if it requires posting a reminder on your desk.

➤ Use a speakerphone only when you must—ideally in a closed office and only when more than two people are on the line. Turn off the speaker when dialing, lest you create noise that is most unnecessary.

➤ Never shout a request or response to someone in a nearby office or work area. Walk over, pick up the phone, or e-mail instead.

➤ If you must listen to music, use headphones. Then again, if your neighbors find the music from your favorite classical station soothing, play it but keep it low.

➤ No clicking the clip of a pen while talking on the phone! Nor should you noisily tap your nails while phoning or reading.

➤ If you chew gum, do it quietly; a gum-chewer who cracks his gum can drive nearby workers up the wall.

Smells

➤ Always test a new scent before wearing it to work, since body chemistry can intensify the power of fragrances. Apply perfume or cologne lightly and keep spritzing to a minimum.

➤ Practice good personal hygiene so that you won't offend with body odor, bad breath, or smelly feet.

➤ When eaten at your desk, smelly foods like fried fish, onions, and cabbage-family vegetables will include your coworkers in your meal whether they like it or not.

➤ If you're a smoker, try to brush your teeth a few times during the workday.

Words

➤ The workplace stance on profanity is grounded in company culture, but bigoted and sacrilegious comments are intolerable, especially when aimed at individuals.

➤ Be careful what you post on your walls. Never put up materials that are offensive, are obscene, or have sexist or racist undertones. Remember that pinning any anti-company articles to your walls will do you no favors with management.

Gossip and Other Offenses

GOSSIP IS INEVITABLE in the workplace, but suspicion and speculation about who's trying to snow the boss, who's taking credit for someone else's work, or who's going to the movies on their telecommuting days can belittle the person in the eyes of coworkers and result in serious, job-threatening consequences.

If you become the focus of false gossip or rumors, you'll want to uncover the source. Begin by talking to the person who clued you in, explaining that the story is untrue and that you want it stopped. If you promise confidentiality, there's a good chance you'll be told who originated the falsehood.

Talk with the gossip in private. Adopt an attitude of concern, not anger: "Vince, I hear you told a couple of people that I'm looking for a new job and I've been meeting with a headhunter. The truth is that I had lunch last week with my old college roommate, and she happens to work for an employment agency. I am *not* job-hunting, and having people think I am could make things pretty awkward for me here." Even if the gossip denies spreading the tale, he'll be stung because he's been caught—and might think twice before spreading rumors again.

To avoid becoming the subject of office gossip, keep information about yourself close to your chest. Seemingly innocuous questions about your age, income, personal relationships, sexuality, and politics can set you up for gossip and innuendo. You don't have to answer or discuss details about your personal life, no matter how hard anyone tries to pry.

Just *listening* to the latest gossip makes you an active participant, even if you don't spread the story. Gossip can be hazardous. (You never know who's chummy with whom, and you could wind up covered in mud if you dish dirt about the wrong person.) If you feel a colleague is trying to draw you in to gossiping, be tactful but firm: "I make a point of not speculating about anyone's private life." Then politely refuse to listen: "Oh, that sounds interesting, but I'd just rather not know." If he won't change the subject, excuse yourself and leave.

Offensive Remarks

What do you do when a coworker makes blatantly sexist or racist remarks, calls you or someone you know to be trustworthy a liar or a cheat, or treats coworkers and subordinates with extreme disrespect?

First, you have an obligation to yourself and your company to confront or report offenders, just as you would a thief. If you just sit back and listen, you become something of a collaborator. Also, your company can be held liable for the hateful remarks of employees, and as long as you're in its employ, you owe your loyalty to the greater good.

If you can talk with the offender in private, do so. Frame your statements as criticism of the remarks, not the person himself, and be specific: "You probably didn't realize it, but that comment you made to Jill about her legs was really suggestive and could get you in big trouble." Because people who repeatedly offend or degrade others rarely take hints, they're more likely to cease and desist when they think their reputation or job is at stake.

Some remarks require immediate and public response. Be direct, but remember to confront the remark rather than the speaker. Stay calm and take care not to sound patronizing. For example, if a coworker's subject is racial office politics, try something on the order of, "People are treated fairly here, Steve, and I know that Harold got his job because of his talent, not his race." If you can, give the person a graceful way to retreat: "Don't you think we talk too much about race here, Steve?"

Small Embarrassments

Spinach stuck in the front teeth, an open fly, an unbuttoned blouse—when they happen to you, all you can do is laugh and blame bad luck. When they happen to a coworker, step in and help. Discreetly (and privately, if possible) tell the person and, if need be, assist her to repair the damage. If you're a woman and too shy to tell a male colleague that his zipper is undone, get another man to do it. When a coworker alerts you that there's a blob of mustard on your tie or something in your teeth, don't take offense. Be thankful that a friend has saved you from an embarrassing moment.

Some imperfections should just be left alone. If there's a problem that can't be fixed right away, don't mention it. Why make the person feel uncomfortable during a meeting if she's unaware of the tear in her sleeve, which she wouldn't have time to repair anyway? Also, certain problems—dandruff, for instance, or an ill-fitting hairpiece or outlandish eye makeup—don't affect the workplace in any serious way and are really nobody else's business. It's up to the person with the problem (or her supervisor) to realize that it may negatively affect her chances for advancement. Only if you're close to the person should you discreetly bring up the subject, and then in the spirit of help.

A QUESTION FOR PEGGY

A friend who was laid off a few months ago just heard about a job in my office and wants me to recommend her. The problem is, I don't think she's qualified. How honest should I be with her?

Even if she's in dire straits, you need to be up front with your pink-slipped pal. Tell her you think the world of her but don't believe this job is the right fit. Then give her a specific (and true) reason why, such as "They expect five years of experience in customer service for this kind of position." Finally, offer to help in some concrete way—redesigning her resume, say, or calling her with any leads you hear about in her field.

Relations Between the Sexes

FLIRTING AND ROMANTIC RELATIONSHIPS are inevitable when workers spend a large part of the day together, but in many workplaces, they're a potential minefield. Questions of conflict of interest, distraction from work, and the unpleasant ramifications of a fling's sour ending are very much on the minds of workers and employers alike.

The trick is to approach an attraction to another person with the same principles that underpin good manners—respect, thoughtfulness, and honesty. Also remember that relations between the sexes can have serious consequences, given heightened concerns about sexual harassment. (See also Chapter 6, page 75: "Dating and the Workplace.")

➤ If you ask a coworker out and she declines more than twice, stop asking—unless she seems genuinely disappointed she can't accept. Persisting after repeated turndowns may get you into trouble with management if the person reports the incidents.

➤ If you decline invitations, be honest without causing offense. A white lie will be exposed if you go out with another coworker later.

➤ Keep in check any public displays of affection, which are especially inappropriate in the workplace.

➤ Learn the company policy about dating superiors or subordinates and abide by it.

➤ Don't gossip about an office romance that isn't out in the open. At the same time, don't pry into one that is.

➤ Calling someone "sweetie" and "honey" can sound condescending or suggestive even when said out of affection, and such terms are particularly out of line in a work environment.

About Sexual Harassment

An executive offers an employee a promotion or a raise in return for a date or sexual favors. A middle manager threatens negative consequences if his or her advances aren't succumbed to. A worker makes suggestive comments about a coworker's appearance and accompanies them with lewd gestures. Sexual harassment comes in many forms, but conduct such as the following identifies it as such:

➤ Conduct that creates a hostile environment. This includes aggressive flirting, inappropriate comments, touching, and lewd gestures or language.

➤ Quid pro quo ("this for that") conduct, when promotion or firing is based on the employee's submission to, or rejection of, someone else's sexual overtures.

Flirting is one thing, and unwanted advances are another—and sexual harassment falls in the latter category only. Before going so far as to accuse someone of harassment, tell the person that you object to his or her behavior. A straightforward explanation might put a stop to it: "David, your constantly asking me out makes me uncomfortable. I'd prefer to keep my business and personal lives separate." It's possible that there's been a simple miscommunication that you could clear up with frank and open discussion.

If the behavior continues, keep a record of your encounters with the person (complete with what was said and done), any witnesses, and specific times and dates. Then speak with your supervisor (or, if he's the offender, your supervisor's boss) and supply the encounter record in memo form. (Note: Because employers are now held responsible for sexual harassment that occurs in their companies, the executives you turn to will probably come to your aid at the start, making official complaints unnecessary.)

If the problem remains unsolved, speak to the human resources (HR) director and take a copy of your memo and any new documentation. Members of the HR department should intercede for you; it is their place to warn, or even fire, the offender. They can also file a complaint with the Equal Employment Opportunity Commission (EEOC) in your area. If the HR department is unsuccessful in putting an end to the harassment, you have the legal right to file a complaint with the EEOC yourself.

Taking Children to Work

WHEN TAKING A NEW BABY or a young child to work, remember that a little goes a long way. The gaggle of workmates emitting oohs and aahs shouldn't cause too much consternation to those not taking part, as long as the meeting is very brief. Gatherings that last more than two or three minutes, however, should be taken to an empty conference room or any other room where the cooing can continue behind closed doors. In small workplaces, workers should bring babies and young children only when they have been invited.

Under no circumstances should you let a toddler or preschooler run free. Your coworkers will no doubt greet your child if he happens to poke his head in their doors, but a disruption is a disruption, no matter how cute the offender.

If you must breast-feed or pump milk, find a women's lounge, a clean restroom, a closed office, or another private space. Some offices have special areas where mothers can tend to babies' needs.

Lunches and Parties

PURELY SOCIAL GET-TOGETHERS at work include lunches (whether in the company lunchroom or the coffee shop down the street) and parties that range from holiday banquets to a send-off for a new retiree or a shower for the mother-to-be.

Communal Lunches

Having lunch together is a great time to get to know your coworkers. More important, it's a great time for them to get to know *you*. The quality of your small talk and table manners makes you someone who's a pleasure to be around. Avoid sensitive work topics, since people at other tables may overhear. Also bypass topics that are too personal—details of your love life, health issues, or trouble you're having with your child. Lunch is a time for relaxing and taking a break, not the place for conversation that would be better conducted after work, if at all.

If you bring your lunch and always eat at your desk, becoming too much of a creature of habit may make you seem unsociable. If a coworker sometimes drops by and asks if you want to go get a bite, appreciate the gesture and try to join him.

Office Parties

Today's office parties have matured, by and large, into calmer occasions that serve as much to build morale and showcase the company as to share camaraderie. (If that proverbial drunken partygoer with the lampshade on his head hasn't retired, he's probably been forced out by now.) Office parties also provide employees with the chance to become better acquainted and even to forge the bonds of real friendship.

First, give thought to how you dress. At a party held after work in the workplace, both men and women usually wear the clothes they've worn all day. Or they might change to fancier dress in anticipation of the event. Although over-dressing (like under-dressing) is generally out of place, some people dress up their office wear with jewelry, a new tie, a silk scarf, or other accessories.

At an office party held outside the office, both men and women might change from work clothes into dress clothes. Just remember that clothing too dressy for the occasion or too revealing is in poor taste. Err on the side of conservatism. Wearing high-tops or a T-shirt with your tuxedo may get a laugh from coworkers but not necessarily from your boss. If unsure about proper dress, check ahead of time with a colleague who's attended similar events in the past or with one of your coworkers who has helped plan the event.

At business functions attended by people from other businesses—and at conferences and conventions, for that matter—name tags are often necessary. The tags are usually worn on the right side because that's where most people look when they first greet each other with a handshake.

You don't have to wear a name tag if its adhesive or clasp might damage your clothing. If pinning, clipping, or adhering a badge is likely to pull threads, cause puckering, or damage delicate fabrics, you might attach the label to your purse or handbag strap or your briefcase (or, alternatively, just be ready to introduce yourself frequently). Necklace-style ID tags are increasingly popular because they're easy to see, durable, and not hard on clothing.

People who drink too much at office parties or other business gatherings risk doing serious harm to their careers. Sloppiness and lack of self-control become obvious to superiors, who will probably think twice about giving a big drinker future responsibilities. Even relatively benign behavior under the influence of alcohol—laughing too loudly, talking too much, acting giddy, becoming quietly morose—will be remembered.

Another real danger is becoming too intimate with colleagues or superiors. In the spirit of seasonal abandon, men and women who've had too much to drink often place themselves in compromising positions, of which actual sex is just one possibility. Excessive flirting, inappropriate soul-bearing, too-eager touching, maybe even those little kisses under the mistletoe—amorous adventures in all forms lose their romance in the clear light of the office workday. The safest way to avoid embarrassment and regret is to be well aware of the dire consequences that can result. Stay in control, starting with strict limits on your drinking. And take heed: Company cultures range across the spectrum, but illegal drug use (or even possession) at the office or a business-related social function is grounds for both instant dismissal and legal action at most businesses.

After-hours Activities

After hours, don't be too quick to let your hair down with coworkers. In a relaxed atmosphere, tongues are loosened and defenses are dropped, especially if alcohol is consumed. Don't make the mistake of believing that a conversation held off the premises is off the record. If you pass on a rumor, take potshots at an absent coworker or boss, or reveal a workplace confidence, you can bet what you said will get back to the office, sometimes faster than you.

Socializing or Traveling With the Boss

In earlier times, becoming a buddy with your boss was ill advised. These days, there are so many permutations of the boss–employee relationship that this idea has more or less bitten the dust. But it's generally up to your boss, not you, to initiate any socializing. That doesn't mean that you can't suggest an occasional lunch together, but it does mean that you should do so only if you and your boss have established a comfortable rapport and your lunch invitation seems natural. You don't want to force your friendship on your boss, since there's deference due to rank to consider. You also don't want to buddy up in an effort to become her favorite, a tactic that won't go unnoticed by your workmates.

What about traveling with your boss? Whether she's of the old school or new, you should stay respectful and deferential, without being obsequious. Such polite acts as offering to give her the more comfortable seat or letting her initiate conversation shows you as not only courteous but also as someone who understands your respective ranks. Unless your boss insists on doing them herself, take charge of various tasks—hailing cabs, making restaurant or theater reservations, and tipping service providers. Stay on your toes in every way. You've been handed the opportunity to get to know your boss better and to make a lasting, positive impression.

Exchanging Gifts

WHEN YOU'RE PRESENTING A GIFT to either a coworker or a business associate from outside, your gift choice should depend on the occasion, your relationship to the recipient, and your position in the company. Moreover, *whether* to give or accept a gift from outside depends on the policy of the organization; some have hard-and-fast rules regarding gift giving.

A "professional" gift—something to be used in the workplace, such as a reference book or calendar—is appropriate for someone you don't know very well. A "personal" gift is one given out of knowledge of the recipient's likes and dislikes (say, a nice garden tool for a gardener or a subscription to a biking magazine for a keen biker). Just don't let personal business gifts cross the line into inappropriate: jewelry, clothing, and anything with romantic overtones (perfume, roses, lingerie).

Acknowledging your workmates' birthdays, weddings, and other milestones shows you respect their lives outside of work. This doesn't mean showering them with presents, but some occasions call for at least a card. While chipping in for a group gift is fine, you might also want to send a separate card to someone to whom you're especially close. Following are some guidelines (see also "Giving and Receiving Gifts," pages 514–528).

Birthdays. There's no reason to give something to a colleague every time her birthday rolls around, but it's a good idea to recognize a significant one, such as forty or fifty. Even then a card is sufficient from all but her closest friends, who most likely will want to give a present.

Weddings. For the wedding of a coworker, send a gift if you've been invited. If you haven't been invited, the choice of whether to send a gift is yours. (For more about wedding gifts, see Chapter 40, page 707: "Choosing and Sending Gifts.")

New babies. If you're close to the new parent(s), you'll probably want to give a gift. Sometimes coworkers give a joint gift, in which your participation is optional. But if you attend a baby shower for the new parent (either at work or off the premises), you're obligated to give a baby present or contribute to a group gift.

Illnesses. A get-well card is usually an adequate gesture when a workmate or business associate is ill or in the hospital. If you have a close relationship with the person, consider a gift as well.

Deaths. Whether to send a separate, rather than group, condolence note or gift depends entirely on how close a friendship you've had with either the person who died or a member of his family. A handwritten condolence note is preferable to a pre-printed card.

Accepting and Declining Gifts

When receiving a gift in your workplace, it's fine to open it right away; usually, the giver will want to see your reaction and to be thanked on the spot. However, if other coworkers aren't taking part in the gift exchange, it's polite to present and open gifts in private.

At a shower or retirement party, the opening of presents is part of the fun. If the occasion is formal, however—a wedding or an official ceremony—any gifts are generally put aside, then opened later.

If you have to decline business gifts, it is usually because the gift (1) came from a business associate outside the company and the cost is over the limit your company allows or (2) is too personal. In the first case, there's no need for embarrassment; in effect, it is the company, not you, that is declining. A note clearly stating so is all that's needed, as long as you say that you appreciate the person's thoughtfulness.

A gift with romantic overtones can also be a problem. You don't have to return a dozen red roses, but you could let the sender know (either in person or by note) that while you know he meant well, sending such gifts is inappropriate in light of your business relationship.

If you receive a sexually provocative gift, such as lingerie, return it on the spot. (Don't keep such a gift "just to be polite.") Tell the giver you cannot accept the gift because it is inappropriate. It would also be wise to reiterate your objection in a

A QUESTION FOR PEGGY

I'd like to give a Christmas present to my boss, who went out of his way to look after me during my first year at work. Would that be inappropriate?

A thoughtful, yet simple, acknowledgment such as some homemade cookies would be fine. But giving a gift to your employer is indeed inappropriate unless he has been your boss for several years and the two of you have worked closely together. A handwritten note expressing your appreciation of your boss's attention during your first year should do just as well.

On the other hand, joining with other employees to present a gift for a holiday, birthday, or anniversary is always a nice gesture to any supervisor. A group gift also has the advantage of not looking as if it were given to score points.

brief note, making a copy for your file. (See also page 766: "Relations Between the Sexes.")

Where to Draw the Line?

Here's a quick guide to the appropriateness of exchanging gifts with the people with whom you work. In every case, you should avoid gifts that are too expensive or too personal.

With coworkers. Exchange gifts privately with coworkers so that other workmates won't feel left out. Don't choose a gift with too-personal an overtone, such as perfume, unless you're romantically involved with the recipient.

With supervisors. Group gifts for the boss are always fine, as are small individual gifts when the two of you have had a long-standing business relationship. Even if you're certain it's fine to give the boss a gift on your own, an expensive one could look like an attempt to curry favor.

With business associates from outside. Company policy usually dictates whether you can give or receive gifts from outside and, if gifts are permissible, sets cost limits (typically $25). If you plan to give a gift to a customer or client, check his company's policy first. Token gifts from business associates are generally within bounds, especially during the holidays; but if you receive a gift that violates company policy, it's essential that you return it—and without embarrassing the giver.

With your employees. While as a manager you can accept both group gifts and small gifts from employees with whom you've worked for a long time, you're better off giving a gift to your subordinates as a group, not just the select few. Gifts can range from cakes and doughnuts set out in the conference room to T-shirts or caps bearing the company logo.

With your support staff. Some companies provide annual holiday gifts for employees, but as a manager you may also want to reward your assistant(s) yourself. The gift choice depends on length of service, with long-term employees receiving more generous gifts (around $35 or $40) and anyone who's been there less than five years, or so, receiving something worth $25 or less.

Office Collections

OFFICE COLLECTIONS FOR BIRTHDAYS, weddings, the birth of a baby, or charities are acceptable but can make workers feel they're being nickel-and-dimed to death. Before you ask for donations, consider how often employees have been solicited in recent months. If it's more than two or three times, you may want to solicit only those who always seem eager to give.

If office policy allows collections, they should be organized so they don't get out of hand. Some official guidelines are a good idea. In many workplaces, a "celebration kitty," to which each employee contributes a small amount ($5 or $10) once or twice a year, has dual benefits: It supplies enough funds while keeping the donors happy.

When You're Asked

If you can't chip in for one more birthday cake, don't feel guilty, no matter the reason. Simply say, "Oh, I'd love to, but I'm afraid it's impossible for me to contribute this time." As for charitable donations, if you've already contributed to one organization and a workmate asks you to contribute to another, explain that you can give only so much each year and that you hope she understands why you must decline.

If the frequency of collections still doesn't let up, you could adopt a policy of giving only for certain events, like showers. Don't refuse across the board, or your workmates could make negative assumptions about your generosity.

∽ Volunteer Work ∽

For many, volunteer work is a meaningful part of their lives. However, some people volunteer for a position with the notion that "if you don't get paid, it's not a regular job"—and as a result don't hold themselves to the same work ethic expected in the world of business. Unless you're really *ready to work*, think twice about applying.

Be sure to follow up once you've offered your services. If you've waited for a week or two for a call from a nonprofit you've applied to, call back. Those in the organization are probably simply busy and would likely be pleased to know of your real interest.

Some people have mixed motives for volunteering: not only doing something useful but also strengthening their skills or meeting people. While there's nothing wrong with growing professionally as you provide services to others, volunteering *only* for your own personal gain is less than admirable.

It's also time to be realistic about your expectations. In business, if you see things aren't working well and try to set them right, you usually get results. In a nonprofit, it's sometimes trickier. Don't get frustrated about the way things are done and simply assume ineptness on the part of the organization's managers. The fact is, they often have to make what seem like poor business decisions because they lack financial resources.

If you have ideas for improving things, don't wait to be asked. Your input will probably be quite valuable. Just be sure not to push your suggestions too hard, and don't be hurt if nothing comes of your effort.

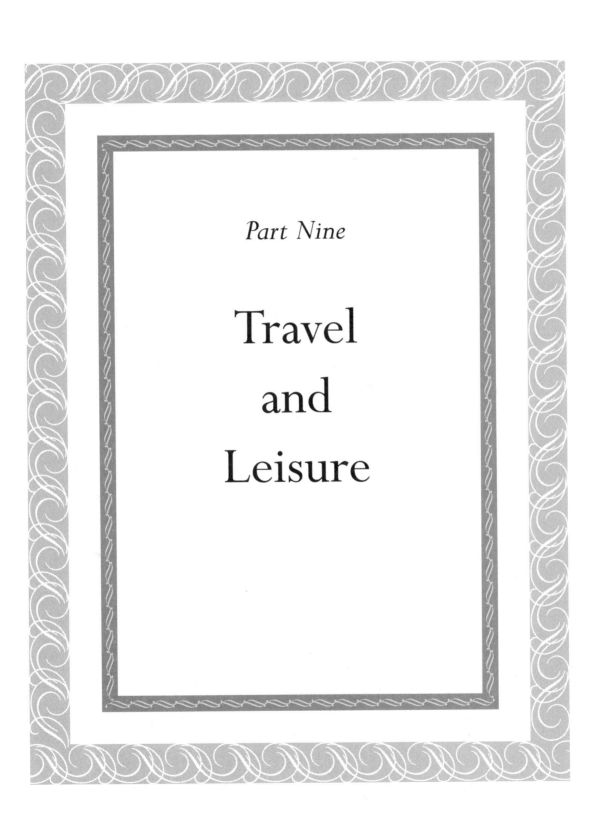

Part Nine

Travel
and
Leisure

Chapter Forty-five

Traveling Near and Far

THE JOYS OF TRAVEL ARE MYRIAD: escaping from your routine, broadening your horizons. realizing your dream of visiting an exotic place, sharing unique experiences with family or friends, enriching your memory bank—or simply grabbing the chance to rest.

But, will your trip live up to expectations? With a little luck, it will—and your chances are all the better if you handle any problems with grace and civility. (This is equally true for business travelers, who account for a huge percentage of trips taken.)

Getting to the resort hotel only to find that the "sweeping view" from your room is of the parking lot is only one of the glitches that might come your way. Although you have no real control over some of the difficulties you may encounter, including delayed or canceled flights, you *can* control how you react. That's where manners come in. Travel etiquette boils down to three key courtesies, whether you're driving to another city for a round of business meetings or cruising the Caribbean:

Put respect in the forefront. Treat respectfully and courteously the people with whom you're traveling, those you meet, and those who serve you.

Keep your requests reasonable. Asking to switch hotel rooms is fine. Making a scene when all the rooms with an ocean view are booked is not.

Don't "leave your mark." At your travel destination, you're a guest of sorts. Avoid leaving anything unpleasant behind, from litter in a public park to the sting of a confrontation to the impression that you think things are "better back home."

This chapter charts the traveler's territory, addressing such practicalities and concerns as preparing for a trip; traveling in groups or with children; traveling by plane, train, and automobile; hotel etiquette; cruise ship etiquette; and traveling overseas. (For boating, camping, and beach etiquette, see Chapter 48, pages 832, 833, and 836; for tipping while traveling, see Chapter 46, pages 805–809.)

Before You Leave Home

BEFORE TRAVELING, it's sensible to try to *prevent* trouble. How to start? Put family and friends at ease by telling them how to get in touch with you. Write down your itinerary and, whenever possible, the names and phone numbers of hotels—then leave the list with your parents, your children, and anyone else who might need it. It's also smart to cancel all deliveries to your home or apartment, and to put your valuables in a safe place.

To get the most out of your travels—especially if you're going someplace for the first time or traveling to a foreign country—learn as much as possible about the places you plan to visit; try your local library or on the Internet (see page 791: "Traveling Overseas"). Plan early and carefully, which entails devising an itinerary that's not too crammed and keeping records and confirmation numbers of reservations and agreements. (See also page 791: "Passports and Other Practicalities.")

Be courteous when you deal with reservationists, travel agents, or anyone else in the travel industry. Whether discussing your plans over the phone or in person, gather all the necessary details beforehand so you won't waste time. If you're having trouble getting the air fare, lodging, or service you need, calmly ask for alternatives instead of sounding angry or annoyed. "Could you keep looking, please?" is more likely to reap results than a "I refuse to believe there are no hotels in that price range!"

Road Trips

THE "GREAT AMERICAN ROAD TRIP" isn't a thing of the past. Legions of families and friends still cruise the highways and back roads of the fifty states for an up-close look at our national treasures. But being in a car together for hours on end can quickly take its toll—so it's imperative for everyone to go to special lengths to keep the peace and make everything run smoothly.

Whether you're the driver or a passenger, think about the other riders' comfort. If someone wants to nap, be quiet. Be flexible when it comes to setting the air temperature, opening (or closing) windows, and choosing music. Passengers should be careful not to distract the driver, particularly when in heavy traffic or when driving conditions are difficult.

When You're the Driver

Because the driver's first responsibility is safety, build some extra time into your schedule so you won't be tempted to speed. When you do get held up by slow traffic, don't complain so often that you cast a pall over what's meant to be a good time.

Drive at the speed limit, turn on your blinker before changing lanes, use the low-beam headlight setting at night, and refrain from tailgating. As an incentive, remember that speeding and tailgating run the risk of angering other drivers—an eventuality

Traveling With Friends

Traveling with another person (or people) you know is a true test of friendship. Human nature decrees that being cooped up together in a plane or hotel room can easily lead to friction. To help stave off tensions, make sure you and your traveling companion have two things in common:

Similar tastes. If you prefer picnics in the country and simple country inns, don't travel with friends whose idea of heaven is a Paris nightclub.

Synchronized body clocks. If you like to be up and on the sightseeing bus by 8:00 AM, don't travel with people who prefer to sleep until noon.

There's no law that says you and your companion have to do everything together. If you decide you'd rather spend an afternoon at a museum while your friend explores a park, you'll be able to share and enjoy each other's experiences over dinner that night.

The question of sharing expenses may have a simple solution. Each traveler (or couple) puts in the same amount of money at the beginning of the trip and replenishes the kitty with equal amounts as necessary. All food, liquor bills, and any other agreed-on items are paid for from the kitty, with whatever's left over divided evenly at the end of the trip. However you handle the costs, work out an equitable plan before you head off on your journey.

[779]

to be avoided at all costs in the era of road rage. (See also Chapter 3, page 26: "Road Rage.") If you have to make a call from the car, pull into a rest area. Using a cell phone while driving is a dangerous distraction and is also illegal in some states and municipalities.

Some additional tips:

➤ Simply *understanding* that you should cruise in the right lane and use the left only for passing is different from actually *doing* it. Unless you stay to the right, you'll create a bottleneck. If anyone behind you is driving over the speed limit, let them pass so you'll be out of harm's way. (Chances are, you'll later spot him by the side of the road, collared by the highway patrol.)

➤ On two-lane roads, practice give-and-take with other drivers. If a car behind you wants to pass, slow down a little, then signal for the driver to go ahead and pass when you're sure that the road ahead is clear.

Driving While Drowsy

While the biggest "do not" for motorists is drinking while driving (*never* do it and never let anyone who has overindulged get behind the wheel), driving while drowsy is also a growing concern in an age when few people get a good night's sleep. In 2003, the National Highway Traffic Safety Administration estimated that driver fatigue caused at least 100,000 car crashes each year in the United States. Some states have passed legislation allowing a driver who's gone without sleep for more than twenty-four hours and is involved in a fatal accident to be charged with vehicular homicide.

Falling asleep is only part of the problem; a sleepy driver's judgment is impaired to the point that one highway safety expert called driving while drowsy the equivalent of having downed five drinks.

Up, Up, and Away

TODAY'S AIR TRAVELERS have to face the reality of flight delays and cancellations, anxiety about flying, rigorous new security procedures, and reduced or no meal service. How to cope? You might start by lowering the bar on your expectations; then, when the worst doesn't happen, you'll be pleasantly surprised!

It's futile to get upset about things over which you have no control. And take note: If ever there were times when directions must be followed, it's when you're at an airport or in the air. We're all too familiar with passengers who break the rules and end up delaying or disrupting flights.

At the Airport

So that you won't be in for any surprises after your bags are packed, check with the airline about size limits for carry-on luggage and the number of pieces allowed. Get in the habit of jotting down a checklist before you leave for the airport: wardrobe items, toiletries, personal or business documents, and—at the top of the list—your photo ID.

Be alert when going through security. To keep the line from slowing down, take off your shoes and remove as much metal as possible from your person before reaching the screeners: change, jewelry, and other small items that can be put in a pocket, retrieved quickly, and dumped into the plastic tray.

Take your laptop computer out of its case so you won't have to fumble with it on the spot. If a screener gives you a thorough wanding or goes through personal items in your bag, don't get huffy. Remind yourself that a minor inconvenience is a small price to pay for safety and peace of mind.

When checking in. Have your ticket and ID ready to hand over so you won't hold up the line. Another lining-up concern: Many passengers holding boarding passes unwittingly stand in line at the gate when there's no need to, slowing things down. When in doubt, ask an airline employee whether getting in line is necessary.

Even if your flight is delayed or something went wrong on your way to check in, maintain a pleasant demeanor; the counter agent isn't responsible for the bad weather that caused the delay, the security issue, or the plane's mechanical problems. Experienced travelers know that showing common courtesy to airline employees results in better service (and less anxiety) in the long run.

As you wait to board, place luggage on the chairs next to you only if there are plenty of seats to spare. Even if several are vacant, don't take up the best seats—those facing the window, for example—with your carry-on luggage. This is also not the time for long and lengthy cell phone calls. (See also Chapter 22, pages 306–308: "Using Your Cell Phone.")

When boarding. Stand clear of the gate while waiting for the boarding call; crowding together slows things down for everyone. Board the plane only when your row or group number is called—the more closely passengers follow instructions, the more quickly everyone will be settled in a seat.

As you walk through the jetway to the plane, never push ahead of others, and be particularly patient with elderly or infirm passengers; remind yourself that they aren't being slow by choice.

Switching seats. You're all settled, when a passenger asks you to swap seats. Must you comply? You don't have to agree, though switching is admirably unselfish—especially if a parent and child make the request. If you decline, do so politely. Being tall gives you an easy out: "I would, but I need this space for my legs." Otherwise, just say "I'm sorry, but I'd like to stay where I am." The length of the flight also enters

∾ Baggage Battles Averted! ∾

In a time when some people will go to almost any lengths to avoid checking a bag, you'll win friends by practicing good "luggage etiquette." Start by holding your carry-on or shoulder bag in front of you, not at your side, as you walk down the aisle of the plane so that you won't accidentally bump passengers in aisle seats. Backpacks and suitcases on wheels require precision navigation as well.

Problems can usually be averted if you carry on only one piece of luggage and board only when your row is called. Then quickly put the bag into the overhead bin over your seat or one nearby, taking care not to squash other people's belongings. If you're next to a passenger who's having trouble lifting a suitcase, offer to help if possible; it will not only speed things up for those waiting in the aisle but count as your good deed for the day.

When it comes to those overhead bins, it's first come, first stowed—so if you can't find space, either stow your bag under your seat (if it's small enough) or ask a flight attendant for help. If need be, calmly accept that your bag must be consigned to the cargo hold.

into your decision. A married couple who won't be able to sit together on the fourteen-hour flight from Los Angeles to Sydney have more reason to request a swap than the pair taking the shuttle from New York to Boston.

If you want to switch seats because you don't relish the thought of being wedged into a middle seat or subjected to a seemingly endless conversation going on nearby, move to an empty seat in another part of the plane. Before moving, wait until the plane doors are shut and you're certain that the available seats aren't assigned. Excuse yourself to any seatmate you must slip past, and don't make it obvious to the bothersome passengers that you're escaping them.

In the Air

Once you're aloft, the real test of your civility begins. Every frequent flier can recall a long list of annoying, rude, and even dangerous acts he has witnessed in the cramped space of an airplane. In recent years, the behavior of some passengers has qualified as a threat to safety, with alcohol often to blame.

As for minor incivilities, you have little choice but to grin and bear them. If you don't respond angrily to boorish behavior—the mother who lets her child scream at will, the couple who engages in a nonstop argument—your trip will at least *feel* smoother. Any truly unacceptable or suspicious behavior, however, should be reported to a flight attendant.

Airplane Etiquette 101

Here are some basic plane manners that apply under any circumstances:

➤ If you have an aisle seat, keep your elbow or foot from protruding into the aisle. Aisles in some airplanes are so narrow that you're lucky if there's an inch to spare.

➤ If the person in the aisle seat is sleeping and you need to get out of your row, softly say, "Excuse me," and if necessary, tap him lightly on the arm. It's perfectly okay to wake someone as long as you do it gently.

➤ Be understanding if a passenger in your row repeatedly asks you to let her out; it's possible she has a medical condition that means frequent trips to the lavatory. You might want to switch seats for her comfort and yours.

➤ Keep any work materials you're using from overflowing into the space of the passenger next to you.

➤ Don't snoop by surreptitiously reading the work sheets or laptop screen of the person beside you.

➤ Keep noise to a minimum, whether talking with a passenger or reading a book to a child. Being heard over the noise of a plane requires raising your voice, but some people literally shout. If you or your child plays a video/computer game, turn the volume as low as possible.

Bad behavior is magnified in the confines of an aluminum tube rocketing through the air at 35,000 feet, and there are five things in particular to avoid:

Treating attendants shabbily. There's no excuse for making unreasonable demands of attendants, treating them as if they were servants or failing to say "please" and "thank you." Flight attendants deserve a friendly and respectful attitude.

Schmoozing in the aisles. Passengers who stand in the aisle next to friends and have lengthy conversations (encountered most often on long flights) can become nuisances when they hover over other passengers and block traffic.

Drinking too much. Drunkenness has been at the root of most instances of purported "air rage," possibly because alcohol hits the drinker harder at high altitudes. Also, business travelers who have to attend a meeting soon after touchdown should think twice about arriving with their breath smelling of alcohol.

Offending the nose. Some passengers forget the importance of personal hygiene. Others bring strong-smelling food on board and make the plane smell like a greasy-spoon diner. Then there are those who remove their shoes and subject their fellow travelers to foot odor. Worst of all is the parent who changes a baby's soiled diaper in a seat, not the lavatory.

➤ Don't stay too long in the lavatory; the full makeover can wait until you've landed. Leave the premises neat and clean—surfaces wiped, paper towels disposed of, the sink drained.

➤ Try not to block the view of those who are watching the movie or other entertainment. If you must stand to retrieve something from the overhead bin, be as quick as possible.

➤ If you have a bulkhead seat, don't prop your feet against the bulkhead—even if you've taken your shoes off. The wall might be covered in carpeting, but it's not a floor.

To chat or not? You're not in the mood to talk, but the passenger in the seat next to you is warming up for a marathon conversation. To nip things in the bud without offending, smile and answer any questions with a simple yes or no. If that doesn't work, be direct but polite: "I'd like to chat, but I really need to use this time to read. Thanks for understanding." Then bury yourself in a book, magazine, or your work.

An even more effective way to discourage conversation is to don earphones as soon as you're seated, whether you're eager to listen to music or not. Whatever tack you take, be gracious to your fellow traveler. Chatting is usually just a friendly gesture or perhaps a way to allay a person's fear of flying. Later in the flight, you might even welcome some conversation.

Seat etiquette. Your airline seat is about the only thing you have any control over in an airplane. At the same time, it can spell trouble, with its cramped space, movable back, and shared armrests.

Whenever you have to get out of your seat, it's natural to steady yourself by grabbing the back of the seat in front of you—but for the person sitting (or sleeping) there, it's a rude surprise. Try to use your armrest or your own seat back for the purpose. Another jostle alert: When you unlatch or secure the meal tray on the seat back in front of you, try not to push too hard.

On some planes, reclining your seat all the way will cause no problem for the person behind you. On others, it may mean that his meal tray is almost touching his chest. The simplest and nicest approach is to turn around and ask the person whether he minds if you recline your seat all the way. If you're the one being squeezed, politely ask the person in front if she could move her seat up a little.

Then there's the armrest, that small but coveted space passengers often have to share. Ideally, your and your seatmate's elbows will alternately occupy the armrest without causing trouble. But if your seatmate has other ideas, you could propose a compromise: "How about if one of us takes the front half of the armrest, and the other the back half?" An air traveler in the middle seat faces double trouble over armrests. In the spirit of fairness, polite passengers in the aisle and window seats will cede the center armrests to the person in the middle.

Babies and children. Kids are part of the air travel package, whether frequent fliers like it or not. Nevertheless, parents need to do all they can to keep babies quiet and toddlers under control.

> **When you're the parent.** Aside from walking a crying baby in the aisle, trying to soothe him when seated (and, in the case of ear pain that comes with flying, applying a hot towel to relieve pressure on the eardrum), there's little a parent can do to stop the noise. The important thing is to be seen trying to calm the child. Often, other passengers don't resent the crying as much as the thoughtless parent who makes no effort to control it.
>
> There are a few pre-trip ways to help prevent a crying jag. First, have your baby's ears checked by a doctor and ask about ways to relieve pressure on the ears. *When* you schedule your trip can also make a difference: A short trip during the baby's regular naptime means he's more likely to sleep. And some parents plan off-peak flying so that the crying will disturb fewer people.
>
> To lessen the chances of toddlers' misbehaving, let them work off energy before boarding by walking them down the corridors or letting them play in the airport's children's area. Then take them to an airport restroom so they won't need to go again before the seat-belt light goes off. Once on board, introduce your children to the passengers seated around you; if the children become unruly or cry, the passengers may be more sympathetic.

Bring not only snacks, comfort items, games, books, and small toys but also a "bag of tricks" from which you pull surprises—crayons and coloring books, notebooks and stickers, finger puppets, and other items that may keep kids occupied. Walking your child in the aisle is another distraction, so long as it doesn't disturb others. If despite your best efforts your children still act up, the passengers will at least know that you're the kind of parent who tries.

➤ **When you're a bystander.** Don't embarrass the helpless parents of a crying child. When a noisy infant or restless youngster disturbs you, leave your seat and see if a vacant seat is available. If you find crying babies intolerable, stash ear plugs in your carry-on bag. When a child behind you is kicking your seat, address the child or parent politely: "Excuse me, but my seat is being kicked." Most likely, the parent will apologize and put a stop to the behavior before you can return to your reading.

Disembarking

After the plane touches down, and the seat-belt lights go off and everyone jumps up, remind yourself to be patient. Once you're able to open the overhead bin to collect your carry-on, offer to remove the belongings of any seatmates in your row who might need help, if you're physically able.

Don't push yourself past people in the aisle. And if someone elbows past you from behind, let him pass; commenting on his rudeness could lead to more unpleasantness. If you have to meet a traveling companion from whom you've been separated, connect with her in the terminal instead of waiting for her in the jetway and possibly impeding traffic.

If you need to get off quickly because you have to make a connection, tell a flight attendant before the plane makes its final descent; he or she might be able to seat you closer to the front. If not, inform the people around you that you have to make a connection and ask if they mind letting you go first. Then be considerate of others who are in the same predicament.

Train and Bus Travel

THE TENETS OF COURTEOUS AIRPLANE travel apply equally to travel on a train or bus, whether for a business trip or a family vacation.

Seats and Seatmates

Except on certain trains, train and bus seats aren't reserved. Still, your seat stays yours for the trip once it's chosen. It is a good idea to place a magazine on the seat when you get off at rest stops to show that it's taken.

Hogging space is a major breach of etiquette on trains and buses. Don't put a suitcase on the seat next to you to keep another passenger from sitting there; the overhead racks are there for a reason. Space-claiming ploys (including pretending to be asleep after you've loaded the adjoining seat with your stuff) are obvious to most people, so think twice about trying to get away with them.

Although you may be sitting for hours with a seatmate, don't spend the trip chatting unless the person is clearly interested. (See also page 783: "To chat or not?") If you use a lavatory on a train or bus, don't forget to toss towels into receptacles so that the sink will stay uncluttered.

Cell Phones and Headphones

Unlike airline passengers, people on trains and buses are usually able to use cell phones. But in response to complaints from customers, a growing number of train and bus lines are posting notices discouraging cell phone use. Some train services have introduced "quiet cars" where cell phones and other noise-making devices are prohibited.

While cell phones are a boon when you need to advise others of delays and changes in travel plans, calls should be brief. Even then you'll do everyone a favor by conducting your call quietly or at the rear of the train car. When traveling by bus, try to make your call during a rest stop.

Also use headphones with care. The tinny, scratchy overflow and thumping bass from headphones can be especially annoying, so make sure the volume isn't high enough to disturb anyone nearby.

Other Hints and Tips

Here are a few other do's and don'ts to remember when traveling on a train or bus:

➤ If you sit at one of the tables in the club car of a train, don't monopolize it. Eat your meal, but don't settle in with the newspaper and keep the table to yourself for too long.

➤ When you have a snack at your seat, eat only things that don't have a strong smell and that aren't likely to spill or make a mess. Then be sure to clean up after yourself.

➤ When walking down the aisles, keep to the right if others are walking toward you. When you can, step into a vacant row when someone else tries to pass.

➤ For the benefit of other passengers, travelers who take a smoking break at a train station or bus stop should try to keep their clothes from smelling of smoke. Smoking in an open-air space, preferably with a fresh breeze, is preferable to puffing away in an enclosed one.

➤ Control your children. Don't let them run about or bother other passengers.

At Hotels and Other Accommodations

NO MATTER HOW WEARY you feel, be gracious as you check into your hotel or motel. When you make any special requests during your stay, a polite demeanor will get you further than a brusque one. If, for example, there's something about your room you don't like, call the front desk and ask calmly for a change, giving the reason—the room is too noisy or too near the elevator, or the heater or air conditioner is on the fritz. Most hotels will try to accommodate your requests, depending on availability.

Dealing With Hotel Staff

Large hotels have full-service staffs to assist their customers. Although staff members may be very deferential and willing to handle most requests, treat them with respect and don't skimp on your tipping. Word spreads about rude or difficult guests, who may then receive less attention. (See also Chapter 46, page 807: "At Hotels.")

The doorman. This may be the first hotel employee you encounter as you step out of your car. Besides greeting you, a doorman can help you with directions and will hail or call taxicabs, for which he should be thanked and tipped.

～ Taking Your Pet? ～

Depending on their temperament, some pets may be better off left with friends, relatives, or in a kennel when you travel. Many places (national parks included) prohibit pets; if you can't bear to leave home without Fido or Whiskers, call to ask if your hotel, or motel, allows animals. (The smaller your pet, the better your chances.) Beyond that, most guidelines for traveling with pets apply to dogs.

Even if your dog is perfectly well behaved, he may make other people apprehensive, so keep him on a leash when on the street or in buildings. Some hotels have designated pet walks; if not, walk your dog off the property. Also be sure to take a pooper-scooper or plastic bag then *use* it.

In hotels, it's a bad idea to leave your dog behind when you leave your room, even if the management allows it. The best-trained dog can damage furniture and carpeting, and the barking of a lonely dog can drive nearby hotel patrons to distraction. When you have no choice but to leave your dog, put out some toys and turn on the TV as "company."

When you're not in the room with your dog, put the "Do Not Disturb" sign on the door so that housekeepers who might be wary of dogs won't face an uncomfortable—even frightening—situation.

The parking attendant. An attendant may take your car to the garage every time you pull up to the hotel. When you tip, keep in mind that the parking attendants rely on tips as part of their salary.

The concierge. Large hotels have a concierge's desk to provide information and services—directions, ordering theater tickets, suggesting restaurants and making the reservations, and even ordering flowers to send your mother on her birthday. Tip the concierge for a special service either on the spot or when you check out.

Front desk personnel. Like concierges, the personnel at the front desk are a source of help—for directions, information about the city, and restaurants. Just don't distract them from their main job, which is checking guests in and out.

The bellhop. The bellhop takes your luggage from the car to the front desk, then from there to your room. Unless you have a light bag or the hotel is especially busy, don't deprive him of his tip by taking your bags yourself. If during your stay you have to ask the front desk a favor, such as having a package picked up, a bellhop will be sent to run your errand and should be tipped.

Housekeeping. These staff members handle complaints or requests about your room—supplying towels, for example, or an ironing board or other equipment. If you need service of any kind for your room, call the housekeeping department (not the front desk) number on your room telephone. Then greet whoever delivers the items and give a small tip for any special service.

Room service. If there is no room service menu in your room, ask about prices before you order; they can be sky-high. Don't worry about wearing a bathrobe when

A QUESTION FOR PEGGY

I know the little bottles of shampoo and such that you find in hotel and motel bathrooms are meant as "gifts," but what about monogrammed towels? My husband insists that hotels think it's fine to take them because they consider them free advertising. Is he right or wrong?

He's wrong. The hotel doesn't mind if guests take the small toiletries stocking the bathroom (in fact, they're meant as a gift of convenience), but towels are another matter. Just as restaurants constantly have to replace stolen flatware, hotels have to replace towels and linens—but that doesn't make pilfering any less a misdemeanor. Remind your husband of this. If he wants to buy towels or the bathrobes found in luxury hotel rooms, they're usually available in the hotel gift shop.

you open the door to servers, who are used to seeing guests in something other than street clothes. After the waiter has brought your order, sign the check. If the tip isn't included and noted on your bill, add it. When you've finished eating, call room service to let someone know your tray is ready to be picked up.

At Bed-and-breakfasts and Inns

Bed-and-breakfasts, or B&Bs, are generally large private houses with rooms provided for a minimal number of guests. Guests are treated as friends, sharing a family-style breakfast with other guests and the owner, who often serves as cook, maid, and tour guide. Unless previously arranged, other meals usually aren't provided. Country inns, on the other hand, often have more rooms and guests, but the manners observed in an inn and a B&B are much the same.

Make every effort to be both thoughtful and neat. Remember that noise carries easily in most old houses, so keep your voice down. If you plan to stay out late, ask the owner for a key so that you can let yourself in; the last thing you want to do is wake anyone.

In communal rooms, always pick up after yourself and don't leave shopping bags or personal items lying about. In some B&Bs and inns, guests share a bathroom; each time you use it, leave it just as you found it. (Also be sure not to monopolize it.) (For tipping at B&Bs, see page 809: "At Bed-and-breakfast Establishments.")

On Cruises

IN MANY WAYS, a cruise ship is a world apart, with an etiquette all its own. In other ways, basic good manners are all that's required—especially when you're at sea for days with hundreds (or even thousands) of people you don't know.

Cruise manners start when you're at the dock waiting to board. You should never cut in line (talk about getting off on the wrong foot!), nor should you save space in line for a small army of well-wishers who come to see you off. As you wait to board, you might want to strike up a brief conversation with a few of your fellow passengers; it's never too early to start meeting.

Cruise Dress

Cruise ships have dress codes, which are usually outlined in the pre-cruise printed material and in the daily programs. Depending on the ship and the type of cruise, attire can range from supercasual for a luau to black tie for a formal event. What to wear is also a consideration when you take a shore excursion. Unless the information has been provided, ask at the excursion desk about appropriate dress.

Recreational Activities

Swimming pools, shuffleboard courts, hot tubs, gyms—most cruise ships offer the lot.

➤ Deck chairs are available for sunning and reading, but that doesn't mean they're yours to do with as you wish. Don't save a deck chair for later use, since they are usually in much demand. Arriving first thing in the morning and piling a chair high with magazines and suntan lotion to make it look occupied is unfair, especially if you don't show up for hours.

➤ Keep children under control, and make sure they don't venture into the casino or other places where kids aren't allowed. Take special care to monitor their behavior at the swimming pools, explaining to them that having fun doesn't mean shouting at the top of their lungs.

➤ When using exercise equipment, don't hog it. Limit your time on exercise bikes, treadmills, and other equipment to twenty to thirty minutes when others are waiting. It's also not only polite but necessary to wipe down any equipment you've used.

➤ If you're a jogger, run only when the rules allow. Passenger cabins often lie beneath the jogging deck, and you don't want to keep someone from sleeping or napping.

➤ Limit hot-tub time to fifteen or twenty minutes unless no one else is waiting. The usual number of hot tubs on a ship is four, and sharing is essential when there are 2,000 passengers aboard.

Meals and Entertainment

Both the meals and shows on cruise ships can be fantastic, but passengers' behavior can make or break the experience.

➤ You'll most likely dine regularly with an assigned group of passengers. Decide in advance how the wine for a meal will be paid for. The usual way is for the tablemates to take turns buying the wine, but you could also agree to split the bill each time.

➤ Don't hold seats in the entertainment lounge or theater for anyone but your traveling companion. Seats are usually at a premium, and it's more than unfair to take up more than your share by holding several for a group. Here, it's first come, first seated.

➤ Don't talk loudly or try to talk over the entertainment.

Quiet, Please!

A cruise is a time to get away from it all, and peace and quiet comes with the package—so be as quiet as you can in the appropriate places and at the right times. For instance, make sure your door doesn't slam when you enter your room late at night. (Most ships have self-closing hinges on cabin doors to prevent smoke from spreading in the event of a fire.) And don't be so loud on a private balcony off your stateroom that you disturb the neighbors.

If you want to complain about noise, dial security so that you won't have to confront the offender yourself. Ship security officers deal often with this complaint.

Traveling Overseas

NEVER HAS IT BEEN more important to behave with friendliness and humility when going abroad. Being critical or disrespectful of the customs, landmarks, beaches, foods, or bargains of a foreign country— especially in front of its people—marks you as a poor representative of your country. There's no need to fawn, but you should always behave with courtesy and respect.

A short, self-taught history lesson, whether on-line or from books, will enhance your understanding of the country's culture and its citizens. Moreover, it's difficult to fully appreciate a picturesque chapel or even a great cathedral without some knowledge of the culture that created it.

Here's what you should know at the very least:

➢ A little something about the nation's history

➢ Whether there's a national religion and, if so, what it is

➢ The form of government (constitutional democracy, monarchy, theocracy) and what it means (whether political leaders are elected, for example)

➢ The significance of any national holiday that falls during your visit

➢ A few words and phrases in the native tongue (see page 792: "Language").

Passports and Other Practicalities

Lack of attention to passports, visas, and money can disrupt your visits and cause hassles both for you and others. In a nutshell, be sure your passport is valid, check to see whether you need a paper visa or electronic visa (or any at all) to enter the country to which you're traveling, and confirm any reservations well ahead of time. (Tip: Your airline can secure an electronic visa for you.)

While the ability to draw cash from your bank account virtually anywhere in the world is great for small amounts of cash, traveler's checks are without doubt the better bet for large amounts of money because you'll get your money back if the checks are lost or stolen. Be sure to record the account numbers of credit cards and traveler's checks in case you have to report a loss or theft.

Depending on where you're going, it's wise to check out the travel section of the State Department's Web site (www.state.gov/travel/), which provides useful information, including entry regulations, warnings of political unrest, and driving conditions.

When you sign up for a specialty tour—whether the kind of adventure travel that calls for mountain climbing, a spirited music tour of Branson, Missouri, or a quieter eco-tour of a world heritage site—you're likely to have more in common with your fellow travelers than you would in most groups of strangers. Here's how to keep everybody as happy as possible:

➤ Show interest in the other travelers. Introduce yourself at the start of the tour and exchange a few friendly words. In later conversations, don't focus on yourself but rather on what you've been experiencing together.

➤ When you have to be somewhere at a designated time, don't be late.

➤ Don't complain. Whining casts a pall over the trip for others. Also don't criticize what you're seeing; leaders of the group are often locals, who could find your remarks hurtful.

➤ Pay attention to the tour leader's descriptions and explanations. Talking over the leader or conversing with someone else is rude.

➤ Make an effort to include a single or elderly tour group member, inviting him to join you in conversation or for some meals.

➤ Thank the tour organizers at the end of the trip, and tip as generously as you see fit. (See Chapter 46, page 806: "Charter Buses and Bus Tours.")

Language

The American who walks up to a stranger and blurts out "Do you speak English?" without so much as a hello is doing herself and her country's image no favors. What Americans see as directness can sound demanding to others. Tone is everything. Common sense says that "Excuse me—could you please direct me to the Piazza Bellini?" will be better received than a brusque "Where's the Piazza Bellini?"

If you don't know the native tongue, a small phrase book will smooth your path in any strange land. Carry it along to consult as necessary; it's also smart to memorize a few words and phrases:

➤ "Hello," "Good-bye," "Good morning," "Good evening," "Good night"

➤ "Please" and "Thank you"

➤ "Yes" and "No"

➤ "I don't speak [language]."

➤ "I don't understand."

➤ "How much does it cost?"

➤ "Where is . . . ?" and "How do I get to . . . ?"

- "Ladies room" and "Men's room"
- "More, please" and "No more, thank you"
- "The check [or bill], please."
- "Beautiful," "wonderful," "nice," "kind," and other complimentary words that will show your admiration or appreciation

When attempting to communicate in English, do all you can to be understood. Speak slowly, though not as if you were speaking to a child, and enunciate with care. Dispense with idioms and colloquialisms: The likes of "dead as a doornail," "in the same boat," and "lock, stock, and barrel" can stop a conversation cold. Watch the expression of the listener to gauge whether he's grasping what you say, and don't be afraid to repeat your words as often as necessary.

Body language is another important consideration, since certain facial expressions, stance, and gestures can be easily misunderstood by others. An example: In the United States, looking directly at the speaker's face shows you are paying attention; in Asia, making direct eye contact is considered impolite.

Gestures, too, can be misinterpreted. Beckoning with a curled index finger is considered offensive in many countries. Three gestures in particular—thumbs up, the "okay" sign (thumb and forefinger held together in an O), and V for victory—should be avoided unless you're certain they have the same meaning in the host country. In some countries, waving your hand (arm raised) in greeting or to get someone's attention is seen as meaning "no."

The distance you stand from others matters as well. North Americans and Northern Europeans are comfortable standing some three to four feet apart. Asians expect more space, while Latinos and Pacific Islanders expect less.

What about handshakes? In Asia and the Middle East, the firm American handshake can be interpreted as aggressive; in Islamic countries, offering your hand to a woman is highly offensive. In Japan and some other Asian nations, the bow is the equivalent of the handshake. In India and Thailand, some people place their hands together at the chest, prayerlike, as a form of greeting, although the handshake is now more prevalent in both countries.

Then there's touching. Latin Americans and some Europeans engage in casual touching more than North Americans do, so if someone touches your arm in conversation, don't take offense. In Arab, Southeast Asian, and Pacific Island nations, a man may even find a male friend taking his hand as they walk. Don't misconstrue these gestures, but don't try to copy them while touring the country, either.

Basic International Courtesies

BESIDES FAMILIARIZING yourself with the history, government, religion, and language of any country you visit, the following basic courtesies will smooth your way when you travel internationally.

➤ Greet others appropriately. Be prepared to shake hands frequently in Europe and to bow when in Asia.

➤ Pay close attention to your grooming and the standards of dress in the country. In general, conservative is better.

➤ Be open-minded. Don't criticize customs in the host country, and never express frustration that things aren't done "the American way."

➤ Ask someone "Do you speak English?" only after you've greeted him, and in a polite (not demanding) tone.

➤ Become familiar with gift-giving customs, which vary greatly from country to country. A common rule is to have any gift beautifully wrapped.

➤ Allow for greater formality. Titles are often used, and you shouldn't immediately call a person by his or her first name.

➤ Respect the dietary customs of the country. If someone is hosting you, don't request food or drink that may be contrary to his practices.

➤ Understand the currency so that you can use money without making remarks or asking questions.

➤ Refrain from being loud in speech and attention-getting actions and dress.

➤ Stand to show your respect if you happen to be present when the national anthem of your host country is played.

Adjusting Your Cultural Lens

CULTURAL SENSITIVITY TO LOCAL CUSTOMS is a must for overseas travelers. Whenever tourists behave politely, show respect, and express interest in a country and its people they show themselves and their own country in the best light.

The observations that follow are intended as nutshell descriptions of differences in attitudes and customs between North Americans and people in other regions of the world. The wise traveler will search out books listing behavioral do's and don'ts for particular countries. The Internet is also a good resource: Start by searching under the name of the country plus the word "etiquette."

Latin America

Latin Americans are warm, effusive, and very polite, so be prepared to be greeted with a friendly handshake. Male friends embrace in what is known as an *abrazo*, or a warm hug; close female friends will greet each other with a light kiss on both cheeks, accompanied by a light touch on the arm.

Courtesy titles are important to Latinos, so use them when greeting or introducing someone. Remember, too, that most Latinos have two surnames—the first from their father, the second from their mother. Use the first when addressing a person (e.g., greet Señor Eduardo Perez Montaldo as Señor Eduardo Perez).

When conversing, Latinos like to stand close, and backing away will only draw them nearer. While you may not feel comfortable in such close proximity, you should maintain solid eye contact at all times.

Many countries in Latin America, particularly in Central America, have suffered years of political unrest—so it's wise not to discuss politics. And because Latin America is overwhelmingly Catholic, don't treat religion lightly. If you're casting about for a congenial topic, look no further than sports. Most Latinos are avid sports fans and are passionate about soccer and baseball.

Western Europe

Twenty-five countries across the length and breadth of Europe now belong to the European Union, yet it remains a diverse amalgamation of histories, cultures, and temperaments. At the same time, there are common traditions of polite behavior that hold fast throughout Western Europe.

Public behavior and dress alike tend to be more formal than in the United States, especially in Austria and Switzerland. Whatever seems mildly sloppy to an American—chewing gum, slouching in a chair—is a serious breach of etiquette in Western Europe. Two examples: A Frenchman would never dream of conducting a conversation with his hands in his pockets. An Italian would be appalled by a hearty slap on the back unless he's your closest friend, yet he might grasp you gently by the arm.

A great dividing line between north and south is the matter of personal space. Northerners conduct conversations from a distance of about four feet, and anything closer is seen as an invasion of privacy. For Southern Europeans, the distance shrinks to about two feet.

The standard greeting for both men and women is the handshake, though you should wait for a woman to extend her hand first. Many Western Europeans (women in particular) are likely to greet friends of either sex with a kiss on both cheeks.

Chocolates or flowers are appreciated as a gift in most Western European countries, but red roses usually signal amorous intent.

Eastern Europe

Like their Western European cousins, easterners tend to be more formal than Americans and should always be addressed by their titles and surnames unless they've requested otherwise (only good friends refer to each other on a first-name basis). Handshakes are the typical form of greeting. For Hungarians, Poles, and Czechs, the handshake is the extent of physical contact. In Russia, on the other hand, good friends greet each other with hearty bear hugs or kisses on both cheeks. Like Americans, Eastern Europeans typically stand three to four feet apart when conversing.

Eastern Europeans generally love to entertain. Hungarians, for example, will fete foreigners with lavish meals that go on for hours. Poles enjoy staying up late socializing. (When being entertained in Eastern Europe, guests often notice an abundance of alcohol—especially vodka.) Being invited to a social occasion in a private home is considered an honor in most Eastern European cultures, and guests should take a gift of flowers, chocolates, or the like. Avoid yellow flowers, however, which many Eastern Europeans associate with mourning.

The Middle East

The Middle East is a study in contrasts, with a diversity of ancient cultures.

Israel. A warm handshake is the standard Israeli greeting, though local Arabs may hug or kiss. Informality is the standard here. Many Israeli men wear slacks and open-necked shirts to work. Women favor conservative suits or dresses. (If you are planning to visit a synagogue or mosque, make sure the dress covers your elbows and knees, and bring a scarf in case you need a head covering.) A gift of flowers or candy is appropriate when you're invited to dine at an Israeli home. If your host follows dietary laws, be sure a food gift is kosher.

Israelis with European or American backgrounds tend to be more forgiving of social lapses. Still, it's best to avoid discussions of regional politics and religion in general.

Arab nations. Arab peoples are warmly outgoing, proud, inquisitive, and very polite. Arab men greet each other with elaborate compliments, often embracing and exchanging cheek-to-cheek kisses. In conversation, they gesture and touch but never point, which is considered impolite.

Religion is a dominant fact of life, with Islam the primary religion. Even in a secular state such as Turkey—where people drink wine, women dress in European style, and government is nonclerical—the culture of Islam predominates. In traditional societies like Saudi Arabia, it touches every corner. Prayers are said five times each day: dawn, midday, afternoon, evening, and night.

Arabic names sometimes mystify westerners, but the formula is simple. The given name comes first, then usually the father's given name followed by the family name; in between come syllables indicating the relationship. Thus, Abdul bin Khalid al-Saud is Abdul, son of Khalid, of the Saud family.

Asia

As varied as their countries may be, the people of Asia hold one trait in common: a rigorous, deeply ingrained sense of courtesy. The forms of social correctness vary from place to place, yet their underlying principles seldom change: respect for the elderly, personal humility, subordination to the group, regard for authority, and meticulous avoidance of controversy or confrontation. Nothing must disturb the harmonious flow of proper social intercourse. Throughout Asia, it is also good manners to address people by their business or professional titles: "Doctor Shiga," "President Chan," "Chief Engineer Mehta."

Central and Eastern Asia. In Japan, be prepared to bow from the waist, arms straight by your sides. Close friends in Pakistan commonly embrace. People in Hong

Certain customs must be observed by travelers to countries with large Moslem populations—all the gulf states, Turkey, Egypt, Indonesia, Malaysia, India, Pakistan, and the countries of East and West Africa.

➢ Avoid using the left hand, which is considered symbolically unclean, when shaking hands or eating.

➢ When seated in a chair, keep both feet on the floor and never show the soles of your feet.

➢ Don't touch anyone on the head, which is considered sacred.

➢ Do not ask a Moslem man about his wife or daughters.

➢ Wear only long pants or skirts.

➢ In public places, don't kiss or hold hands with your traveling companion.

➢ When visiting a mosque, remove your shoes before entering and leave them outside. Do not cross in front of someone who is in prayer, and never enter the mosque's main hall.

➢ If you want to present someone with a gift, avoid giving pictures of people or animals; Islam frowns on realistic images of living creatures. Don't give a present of alcohol or anything made from pigskin.

Kong shake hands both on meeting and leaving. Indians love to talk, and they do so with expansive eloquence; they also make little effort to hide their opinions.

Southeast Asia. The Western handshake is common throughout Southeast Asia, but there are many other ways of greeting, from placing the palms together and inclining the head (Thailand) to a preceding nod or bow (Indonesia). For this reason, it's best to wait for locals to initiate a handshake. Outside of a tourist resort, dress modestly—no short shorts, short skirts, or exposed chests, navels, or shoulders. In areas that are predominately Buddhist (parts of Thailand, Vietnam, and Laos), approach everything in a gentle manner; anger of any sort will earn much disapproval.

Africa

Africa is a vast and complex continent, home to many distinctive and disparate cultures. Arabic and Islamic culture prevails in northern countries such as Egypt and Morocco, while the 250 ethnic tribes of Nigeria make this nation a rich cultural stew. South Africa's customs reflect the influences of three hundred years of Dutch and English settlements.

In much of Africa, English is spoken, but people will be most impressed if you learn a few words of the local language. A gentle handshake is the accepted form of greeting; in most countries, however, men do not shake a woman's hand—but they will if she is from the West and extends her hand first. In former French colonies, the greeting often includes kisses on each cheek.

African people are very courteous, friendly, and giving, and they love to entertain. If you are asked to dine in a private home in a rural area, however, be prepared to eat with your hands; many traditional households, in the countryside, do not use utensils. Your hosts will be happy to show you the proper way to eat by hand.

When visiting the countries of Africa, keep your dress conservative; it is acceptable for women to wear pants in most areas, but always dress modestly.

Oceania

Australia and New Zealand, where Americans will feel more at home than in any place other than Canada, are the southern anchor of the travel destinations of the Pacific. Spread northward across the vast ocean are the island cultures that increasingly depend on tourism to bolster their economies.

Australia. It's said that the Aussies love the Yanks, and vice versa. It's hard to make a faux pas here unless it's to put on airs. In a parallel to the United States, the warmer the climate, the more casual the people seem, whether in the rate of their speech or their clothing. (Down Under, the farther north, the warmer the zone.)

The southern Australian cities of Melbourne and Adelaide are decidedly more formal than free-spirited Brisbane, the capital of the northern state of Queensland, and remote Darwin (capital of the Northern Territory at the part of the continent known as the Top End). Sydney, the largest city, falls somewhere in between.

Egalitarianism is much in evidence in Australia, so much so that a sole taxi passenger is expected to sit in the front seat with the driver. Most Australians also move quickly to the use of first names.

Australian greeting customs are so akin to those in the United States that any missteps are unlikely. While Australians regularly shake hands, women rarely shake hands with one another.

New Zealand. Although New Zealanders are somewhat more reserved than Australians (calling attention to oneself in any way, such as talking loudly or backslapping, is frowned on), they readily take to Americans. They also expect you to understand that their country isn't an annex to Australia. Trusting and hardworking, New Zealanders reflect their English heritage.

The American handshake is firmer than what is necessary here, so be sure not to grip too tightly. Women shake hands with women, but a man should let a woman extend her hand first.

Pacific Islands. Geographically, the islands of the Pacific are classed as Micronesia (north of the equator and comprising such tiny islands as Guam and the U.S. Trust Territory); Polynesia (including Samoa, Tonga, and Tahiti); and Melanesia (including Fiji, Vanuatu, and the Solomon Islands).

Tourists who venture from the modernized cities to the villages are expected to dress modestly. Men shouldn't wear shorts, and women should avoid halter tops and bare shoulders. Hats should be left behind, since covering the head is seen as a sign of disrespect. Always remove your shoes before entering a private house. And speak softly, since raised voices are interpreted as expressing anger. Show respect, but be cautious with praise: If you show too much liking for an object, many islanders will feel obliged to give it to you as a gift, whether they can afford to or not.

799

Traveling Near and Far

Chapter Forty-six

The Finer Points of Tipping

A N IMPORT, tipping was brought home by free-spending Americans who traveled to Europe in the late nineteenth century. Given its medieval beginnings as a way for lords of the manor to show appreciation to their minions by allowing them a few extra coins, it's hardly surprising that the custom was slow to arrive in the Cradle of Democracy. Nor should it come as a shock that tipping was a subject of angry debate in its early years in the United States as it began to move from the rarified realm of wealthy private homes, where tips were a reward for servants, to restaurants and hotels.

Today tipping is an entrenched part of our culture, partly because so many people in service industries must depend on tips to earn a decent wage. In fact, tipping is so prevalent that it's all too easy to lose sight of it as a reward—a way of saying, "I appreciate what you do."

Be that as it may, a tip should *always be merited*. Whenever service falls somewhere between indifferent and deliberately rude, reduce the tip proportionally. By rewarding good service generously—and calling attention to bad service by reducing the tip—we do our part to help raise the standard of service.

While tipping augments the incomes of those who serve and rewards them for a job well done, treating the person who's served you with respect is every bit as important. No amount of tip money makes up for treating someone dismissively. Furthermore, praising the person himself—and, when you can, commending him to his supervisor—will please everyone concerned.

Just How Much?

RECOMMENDING PRECISE AMOUNTS for tips is easier said than done. Tipping is also situational. If not exactly on a sliding scale, it varies according to the establishment (from upscale hotel to coffee shop) and the service you've received, from the mover who hauls your armoire up three flights of stairs, to the waiter who brings the menus and then vanishes for half an hour.

Still, some guidelines for tipping are straightforward:

- When in doubt about tipping, ask in advance. If a department store has scheduled delivery of your new sofa, call and ask someone in the furniture department whether tipping is customary; in a hair salon, ask the receptionist. In other cases, ask how much to tip and even whether you should tip at all; in some situations, tipping is not only discouraged but could be seen as demeaning. Taking time to find out what's expected can spare you an embarrassing moment.

- Tip on the pre-tax amount of the bill, not on the total.

- Tip discreetly. Tipping is a private matter, so don't play the big spender who likes to flash bills.

- Money is the tip of choice in most cases, but sometimes a small gift, usually given during the holidays, can be substituted. A gift is also a good way to "top off" the tips you've given over the year—to your hairdresser or barber, for example. (See also pages 816–817: "Holiday Tips and Gifts Guide.")

At Restaurants and Bars

DIFFERENCES IN TIPPING RATES vary less by region than by whether you're in a large city, small town, or rural area. If your tip to a waitress in a barbecue restaurant in a Southern capital is twenty percent of the bill, it would be closer to fifteen percent in a small town off the Interstate, even though the menu offerings are the same.

Waiters and Captains

The minimum standard for acceptable wait service in restaurants anywhere in the United States is fifteen percent of the bill *before* tax, not on the sum total. In New York, San Francisco, Boston, and other major cities, fifteen to twenty percent is standard. Exceptions to the fifteen-to-twenty-percent range include the following:

∼ The Ubiquitous Tip Jar ∼

In the 1990s, the mental disconnect between tipping and exceptional service found a symbol in tip jars, blooming on retail countertops like weeds after a spring flood. But does their omnipresence mean you should tip when the salesperson has merely taken your money and bagged your quart of milk?

Whether to pocket your change or to drop it into the jar is your choice. You might choose to tip because the salesperson provides a little something extra—she notices a leak in the carton and replaces it or she's particularly cordial. Still, you are under *no obligation to leave a tip in a countertop tip jar*. Unlike waiters and waitresses who provide table service and pay taxes calculated on their base pay plus tips, workers at counter-service businesses normally receive sufficient base salaries. Besides, the purpose of a tip is to reward; the gesture should come from the giver, not from the inanimate equivalent of an outstretched palm.

When the restaurant is self-service. At a buffet restaurant, ten percent of the bill is customary, since the waiter isn't serving your meal. Your tip is a thank-you for providing beverages, clearing the table, and answering any questions.

When the waiter has been especially accommodating. If a waiter was particularly helpful—asking the chef to adapt a dish to your needs, bringing crayons to your child, or cleaning up a mess—you might want to top your tip off with an extra $2 to $5.

When a gratuity has already been added to the bill. Check the bill for a built-in gratuity, or service charge—usually fifteen percent. Such gratuities are common overseas, but in the United States they're usually built in only at major resorts and in certain locales (Miami's South Beach, for one) or when a table has been booked for groups of more than six people. If a gratuity is added to your bill, you can leave an additional tip when you think it's well deserved.

When your stay at a crowded restaurant is lengthy. Most restaurants depend on turning the tables fairly regularly every night, and hogging a table can mean both lower nightly receipts for the owner and less money for waiters. Tacking on an extra ten to fifteen percent will express your thanks for being allowed to linger.

When your meal costs far less than the restaurant's average. When you're in the mood to eat light, your taste for nothing but an appetizer and a side salad might mean a lower day's take for your waiter. The same happens when you use a coupon ("Buy one entrée and get the other at half price"). Thoughtful diners will leave a tip commensurate with a full-course meal.

What if your bill includes a line for a captain's gratuity? Almost all high-end restaurants with captains (also called headwaiters) pool diners' tips, with seventy-five percent of the total going to the waiter and twenty-five percent to the captain. If a separate line for the captain appears on a credit card bill, you can usually ignore it and compensate by increasing the tip.

Hosts, Hostesses, and Maitre d's

Tipping the host or hostess who greets and seats you—often called a maitre d' at upscale restaurants—is not the norm in North America. Usually, tipping is a concern only for frequent patrons, who offer the host $10 to $20 every once in a while for extra service—remembering their favorite wine, for example, or seeing that they're seated promptly or at a favorite table.

When you're not acquainted with the host, a tip is in order only if he's gone out of his way to find a table for you on a busy night when you've arrived without a reservation. (Offer him $10 to $15 *after* he's shown you to the table.) If your dining party is large, double or triple the tip, depending on the number of people.

Offering a host you've never seen before a "$20 handshake" to get a table on a busy night may be seen as an insult; petty bribery is a distasteful activity anywhere. And charging to the front of the line and flashing a large bill only compounds the problem, earning you the contempt of the people you've pushed past.

Bartenders

How much you tip a bartender depends in part on whether you're waiting at the bar for a table in the adjoining restaurant or you're at a bar for its own sake.

> ➤ As you wait for a table, you can either pay for drinks as you order or ask the bartender to run a tab, which will be added to your dinner bill. In either case, leave a tip for the bartender when you're told that your table is ready. One dollar per drink is standard. In small towns, fifty cents (or a little more) per drink should be fine.

> ➤ If you're at a bar simply to have a drink, tip between fifteen and twenty percent of the total; tip at the higher end if the bartender has run a tab for you. If he's thrown in a free drink or two, add a couple of extra dollars to your tip.

Wine Stewards

A wine steward (in upscale restaurants, the *sommelier* if a man, *sommelière* if a woman) is tipped fifteen to twenty percent of the wine bill, but only if he or she was especially attentive. If the steward merely took your order and poured your first glass of wine, you might leave ten to fifteen percent, though no tip is required.

Customers usually tip a wine steward in cash at the end of the meal, but in some restaurants you might find a wine-tip line on the credit card bill. And take note: When tipping a wine steward, tip your waiter only for the food portion of the bill.

Checkroom and Washroom Attendants

Washroom attendants are tipped at least fifty cents for doing nothing more than handing you a paper towel. If they brush off your jacket or whip out a needle and thread to mend your falling hem, leave $2 or $3. A small dish of coins is usually on display, and the tip is placed there instead of in the attendant's hand. If washroom attendants do nothing but stand there biding their time, no tip is necessary.

Valet Parkers

Tip the parking attendant $1 in smaller cities and $2 in larger cities. Give the tip when the car is brought to you, not when you arrive.

Busboys

Busboys are not tipped, with two exceptions: If you spill a drink and the busboy cleans it up, you might tip him $1 or $2 when you leave. When the busboy in a cafeteria carries your tray to a table, fifty cents to $1 is in order.

Musicians: Play It Again, Sam

In the classic film *Casablanca*, how generously Rick Blaine (aka Humphrey Bogart) rewarded Sam, the piano player, for indulging his repeated requests to play "As Time Goes By" is anybody's guess. In 1943, when the film was set, he might have tipped Sam a dime, request or not. If he requested one song, he would have doubled the tip. If Sam played the song a total of, say, six times, a polite Rick should have added an extra ten cents per play, for a total of $2.70—the equivalent of about $30 in 2004.

Why the incremental increase? Because Rick wanted Sam to veer from his usual repertoire when he might rather have played "Harbor Lights." Rick's generosity illustrates how tips for musicians—or anyone else, for that matter—increase as the situation warrants.

It's another story in upscale establishments with steep cover charges: Refrain from tipping in such places unless you see a tip jar in the vicinity of the piano, unlikely as that may be.

When you tip musicians, keep the sliding scale in mind:

➤ Sometimes, expressing appreciation to a pianist is more important than a tip—especially when few patrons are acknowledging her efforts. It's thoughtful to tip $2 to $5 on leaving, even if you've made no request; receptacles for tips are usually in clear view. If you *have* made requests, add an extra dollar or more for each tune.

➤ For strolling musicians who serenade you at the table, the basic tip is $1 per musician, $2 for a party of two; a total of $5 is usually sufficient for a group. If you make a special request, add an extra dollar to each musician's tip.

You needn't stop eating when musicians perform tableside. Just smile and thank them as you tip when the musicians finish.

When to Tip Less

A multitude of things can go wrong: The music in a restaurant is so loud that you have to shout over it to be heard. The rare steak you ordered is served well done. You spot a worm inching its way across your salad plate. Or you wait so long for the dessert menu that you wonder if the pastry chef went home early.

Whether you convey your dissatisfaction through your tip depends on how well the waitstaff addressed the problem. If there was a successful resolution, tip the full amount. If your waiter got only so-so results but doesn't deserve all the blame, you might reduce the tip to ten percent.

If the problem wasn't taken care of or your waiter was surly, tipping eight percent is the "fairest" monetary expression of your dissatisfaction. (According to the Internal Revenue Service, most restaurants report eight percent of their take as waitstaff income, so reducing the tip any further actually *costs* the server.) Leaving no tip (a drastic step, in most people's eyes) may cause your server to think you forgot—and your point will be lost. To leave a penny, as a few do when they want to make a statement, is to comment on ineptitude with nastiness.

In Transit

EXCEPT FOR COMMUTING to and from work, travel generally requires keeping a pocketful of dollar bills handy. From curbside check-ins at the airport to taxi or limousine rides, you'll be doling out tips for any number of services.

At Airports

Airline personnel who staff the counters at the terminal, the gate, and the information booths at baggage claims are not tipped, even if they do you a favor—escorting you back to the plane to retrieve your reading glasses, for example. Unlike airline workers, airport personnel are given tips for their services:

> **Curbside baggage checker, skycap, or airline porter.** The standard is $1 to $2 per bag—a little more if the bag is very heavy.
> **Wheelchair attendant.** A $2 to $5 tip is standard. If the attendant goes the extra mile, such as pushing the wheelchair from one end of a large airport to the other, tip on the higher end or even more.
> **Hotel shuttle bus driver.** If the driver helps you with your baggage, tip no less than $1 per bag.
> **Workers in airport restaurants.** Tip as you would tip servers in other restaurants.

On Trains

On an extended train trip, you're expected to tip a number of railroad employees. The amounts below are standard, but tip a bit more if the service is special.

> **Dining or club car waiter.** Fifteen to twenty percent of the bill (never less than a quarter)
> **Waiter delivering to sleeping car.** Fifteen to twenty percent of the bill
> **Redcap, or train porter.** $1 per bag, plus $1 added to the total
> **Sleeping car porter.** $2 per person per night

In Taxis, Private Cars, or Limousines

A tip to a taxi driver is generally about twenty percent of the fare, but in large cities you should tip a minimum of $1. If a taxi driver helps with your luggage or packages, a slightly larger tip is always in order; in general, add fifty cents for each bag. Try to avoid using big bills, especially during short rides or shift changes, when drivers are likely to have less change.

For car and limousine services, the easiest way to tip is to tell the service to add the gratuity to your bill; do it when you request service. In larger cities, the standard tip is about twenty percent; in smaller cities, fifteen percent. When a gratuity is included in the fee, there's no need to tip more.

Charter Buses and Bus Tours

Tip a guide on a short bus tour ten to twenty percent of the cost of the tour; give it to her when you say good-bye. (Do *not* tip tour guides at national parks and other government sites.) On a prolonged tour with no built-in gratuity, the guide and a separate driver are each tipped $5 to $10 per passenger, depending on the length of the tour.
Charter- and sightseeing-bus drivers are tipped in certain cases:

➤ When drivers double as guides, passengers generally tip $1 per person per day.

➤ When a driver has been particularly amiable, the person in charge of a private charter sometimes asks each passenger to contribute $1 (and sometimes more) to a tip pool.

On Cruises

MOST CRUISE SHIP OPERATORS anticipate passengers' confusion about tipping on ocean cruises, with some providing tipping guidelines and envelopes for tips. Other cruise lines add a substantial service charge to the fare, in which case only extra-special service calls for a tip.

To be sure you know what's expected, discuss tipping amounts and procedures with the travel agent or cruise line agent who books your trip. Tipping customs can differ depending on the nature of your trip, but in general tips will add ten to twenty percent to the cost of your cruise.

Tips at Sea

A good general rule for shipboard travelers is to allow approximately fifteen percent of their fare for tips. Divide about half of this allowance between the cabin and dining-room stewards and distribute the rest to others who served you.

➤ Cabin stewards, dining-room stewards, and waiters should receive $3 per day minimum. Put tips in separately addressed envelopes and hand them to each person at the end of the cruise, with a note of thanks if you wish.

➤ Lounge and bar stewards are tipped fifteen to twenty percent of your bar bill at the time they render service. It's preferable to pay and tip order by order—but if you run a tab and pay periodically, you tip when you pay.

➤ The wine steward should receive fifteen percent of the total wine bill each time you use his services.

➤ Hairdressers, manicurists, and other service people are tipped at the same rate as on land.

> Like train and airport porters, dock porters are tipped $1 per bag at the time of service.

On Long Cruises

For a trip of two weeks or more, tip weekly—generally on Friday evenings. (This enables shipboard personnel to have cash during stops in ports.) The rate will vary according to whether you're traveling first class, cabin, or tourist class:

Tips to . . .	First Class	Cabin	Tourist
Cabin steward	$25 per week	$20 per week	$15 per week
Deck steward	$20 per week	$15 per week	$12 per week
Dining-room (DR) steward	$25 per week	$20 per week	$15 per week
Chief DR steward	$20 per week	$15 per week	$12 per week
Assistant DR steward	$10 per week	$ 7.50 per week	$ 6 per week
Busboys (tip shared among them)	$ 6 to $8 per week	$ 5 to $6 per week	$ 4 to $6 per week

Who Not to Tip on a Cruise

Never tip the ship's officers, but *do* thank them for their courtesy if you cross paths with them near the end of the trip. Also don't tip the ship's doctor if you've consulted her while on board. You'll probably receive a bill for medical services; if not, wait until the end of the cruise to give the doctor a dollar amount commensurate with that your own doctor would have charged.

You aren't expected to tip a bridge instructor, children's activity director, aerobics instructor, or similar ship personnel, although doing so is perfectly okay.

At Hotels

LIKE RESTAURANT WORKERS, hotel staff depend on tips to augment their salaries, so arm yourself with dollar bills before you check in. Another consideration: To assist their customers, large hotels have a full-service staff, who should always be treated respectfully no matter how deferential they may be. Be courteous and tip as generously as you can.

Doorman. A doorman is not tipped for opening the door for you (a smile and a simple "thanks" will do) but is given a small reward for other tasks. Depending on the room rate of the hotel, tip him $1 to $4 when he takes your bags and hands them to a bellhop; when he hails a cab for you (add $1 if it's raining); when he asks the garage to bring your car; and when he takes your luggage from the bellhop and loads it into a vehicle.

Bellhop. To a bellhop who carries or delivers your luggage to your room, tip $1 a bag—never less than $2 in all. A bellhop who takes your bags and points out facilities in the lobby and your room should receive $1 to $2 more. In some luxury hotels, someone from the manager's office may show you to your room; he isn't given a tip, but do tip the bellhop who follows behind with your luggage. Each time a bellhop does something special, such as bringing an item you've requested to your room, tip $2 to $3.

Concierge. A concierge is generally tipped $5 to $10 for each special service she performs—say, recommending a restaurant and making dinner reservations. Extra-special service, including making multiple reservations and obtaining hard-to-get tickets for the theater, a sporting event, or a concert calls for $15. Another way to tip for tickets: Give ten to twenty percent of the cost of each one. Tip a concierge when she performs the service; if you wait to tip until the end of your stay, she may not be on duty. If the concierge fails to get what you want but you know that she made a real effort, tipping shows appreciation for her hard work. For tickets that were impossible to obtain, for example, tip five to ten percent of what they would have cost.

Dining-room staff. Tips for dining-room staff are the same as in any other restaurant—fifteen to twenty percent of the bill. If you stay in an American-plan hotel (meaning that meals are included in your total bill), tip as usual unless a service charge is included. (See page 802: "When a gratuity has already been added to the bill.") At the end of your stay, give an additional tip to a maitre d' who has been particularly helpful—from $10 to $15 for a family or group of four people staying the weekend, to $20 to $30 for a longer stay or larger group.

Room-service waitstaff. When food from room service is delivered, check the bill to make sure the gratuity isn't included; just don't confuse a gratuity with a room-service charge, which you'll also see on the bill. If the gratuity isn't included, tip the room-service waiter fifteen to twenty percent of the bill—but not less than $2.

Housekeeping staff. When you stay for one night or more, tip the chambermaid $3 to $5 per night per person in a luxury or upscale business-oriented hotel; $2 per night per person in a less expensive hotel. Guests often leave their gratuities for the housekeeping staff in their rooms at the end of their stay, perhaps with a thank-you note. Or you can put the money in a sealed envelope marked "Housekeeper" or "Chambermaid," write your room number and dates of your stay on the envelope, then leave it at the front desk when you check out. Tipping daily rather than when you check out ensures that the tip goes to the chambermaids who actually worked in your room, not those whose shift begins on the day you leave. Another option is to tip in person if you see the chambermaid, adding a "thank you."

Valets. Valet services are added to your bill, so there's no need to tip for pressing or cleaning. If you're in your room when clothing is delivered, tip $1 for the delivery for one or two items, $2 or $3 for several items.

Other hotel staff. Barbers, hairstylists, manicurists, massage therapists, and other personal service providers are tipped as they would be outside the hotel. Drivers who shuttle you between the airport and hotel should be tipped $1 to $3, especially if they've helped with your bags.

Pool, beach, or sauna helpers, fitness club assistants, and other special service attendants receive tips only if they perform a special service. For example, if an attendant sets up a beach chair and umbrella for you, tip him $1 per item. For a large group, tip him $1 for every two or three items.

At Bed-and-breakfast Establishments

The owners of a bed-and-breakfast are not tipped, but if they give you especially attentive services, you may want to thank them with a small gift and a note. Employees of the B&B (usually limited to the manager, cook, chambermaid) should be tipped $2 to $3 each for every day of your visit.

At Private Clubs

Usually, members of private clubs (including country clubs and members-only social clubs) are requested to contribute to a holiday fund for club employees, so the waitstaff and bartenders in the formal or casual dining rooms aren't tipped when they provide service. At most clubs, however, members tip those who provide personal attention—washroom and locker-room attendants, golf-bag-storage attendants, and so on. These tips generally range from $2 to $10, depending on the type of club and the amount of service. Caddies get more—often a tip in the $30 to $40 range.

Overnight guests who stay a couple of days at a private club are not expected to tip. For longer stays, tip as you would at a first-class hotel unless a service charge is added to your bill. When in doubt, ask at the club's office about the norm for tipping housekeeping staff and other club personnel.

∼ JUST COMMON SENSE ∼

Tipping at Motels

Tipping is of less concern in a motel because fewer people serve you. For a short stay, no tips other than those normally given to a bellhop or bartender are necessary. For longer stays, it's polite to reward the people who serve you in any capacity, which usually means a $1 or $2 tip per night for the chambermaid. You normally don't tip the manager, but if he performs the service of a hotel concierge tip him accordingly (see page 808: "Concierge").

At Beauty Salons, Barber Shops, and Spas

THE CUT-AND-STYLE a hairdresser or barber delivers can either make your day or ruin it. Adjusting your tip (normally fifteen to twenty percent of the bill) to send a message—from "I'm thrilled" to "I'm very upset"—is up to you, but leaving no tip merely makes for bad feelings. If you're unhappy with the results but the hairdresser can do nothing to remedy the problem, reduce the tip to five to ten percent; if she can and does, tip as you normally do.

Beauty Salons

When you're attended by several beauticians, use the totals for each service on the bill as the base for tips. The following percentages and sums are standard:

Hairdresser. Fifteen to twenty percent
Separate colorist. Fifteen to twenty percent
Separate shampooer. $2 to $3, depending on whether you've had special conditioning or extra latherings
Manicurist. Fifteen to twenty percent, with a $2 minimum
Coat-check person. $1 per clothing item

Salon owners who cut hair usually accept tips (the standard fifteen to twenty percent), but those who charge more for cuts may not. When in doubt about tipping an owner, ask the salon receptionist. (See also pages 816–817: "Holiday Tips and Gifts Guide.")

Barbers

Fifteen to twenty percent of the bill (but not less than $1) is standard for a barber, even if other people performed additional services. Shampooers and shavers are tipped $1 to $2, manicurists $2 to $3. (See also pages 816–817: "Holiday Tips and Gifts Guide.")

At Spas

At a spa, ask the receptionist what percentage of the total cost is customary for a tip for all services performed; it's usually fifteen to twenty percent. If the total equals $80, say, you might want to give the largest tip to the person who spent the most time with you, then divide up the rest.

Facial, makeup, waxing, or other personal service. Fifteen to twenty percent of fee
Massage therapist. Fifteen to twenty percent of fee
Changing room attendant. $1 to $2

Health Care Providers

THE QUESTION OF WHETHER to tip nurses may arise when you or family members are hospitalized, and the answer is *no*. It's proper, however, to bring a box of food (cookies, fruit, candy) that can be shared by all the staff caring for the patient.

Because hospitals usually have three shifts, bring three of the gift items and mark them "first shift," "second shift," and "third shift." (A gift of only one box of candy will likely be eaten by the nurses and caregivers on duty when the gift is received.) Leave the packages, along with a note to the effect that "this is for all of you who have been so nice," with the nurse on duty at the nursing station.

Health care aides, doctors, lab technicians, and dietitians are not tipped. Private home nurses on prolonged duty are given tips by some families at holiday time, while other families prefer to give both a gift and a tip.

Nursing Home Employees

Nursing home personnel are not tipped individually. Instead, a Christmas or holiday fund is usually established, and relatives of residents are asked to contribute whatever they can; the proceeds are then divided among the employees. It's fine, however, to give a gift (perhaps accompanied by a card signed by both the resident and a relative) to special caregivers during the holidays or after an extraordinary act of kindness.

Home Deliveries

HOW MUCH—AND EVEN WHETHER—to tip for deliveries, installations, and help around the house and garden isn't always cut and dried. The tip for a delivery, for example, depends on the volume of the goods and how difficult your house or apartment is to reach. A delivery carried up five flights of stairs usually warrants a bigger tip than one delivered to the front door of a suburban home at street level.

Company policies vary. While pizza deliverers receive a good portion of their income from tips, a cable company service employee might be forbidden by his employer to accept tips. When you're especially pleased with how the delivery or installation has been handled but aren't sure whether to offer a tip, go ahead and try; the person will either accept the tip or say that company policy doesn't allow it. You can also check with the company in advance.

Movers

Tip a mover when the job is complete. The head mover is tipped between $25 and $50, and the crew members between $15 and $30 each, depending on how much they've moved, the difficulty of the move, and the care they've taken with your possessions. If they packed your belongings, increase tips by a few dollars.

An alternative is to give a lump sum to the whole crew; the members will split it among themselves. Calculate the tip per mover based on the criteria below, then give the whole amount to the head mover.

Large and difficult jobs. Jobs with challenges as varied as several flights of stairs, small elevators, narrow doorways, unwieldy furniture and appliances, and particularly large and heavy boxes call for tips of $20 to $50 per person.

Small jobs. When fewer than ten items and boxes of regular size are moved, tip $10 to $20 per person. If some of the items weigh more than twenty pounds, tip a little more.

Furniture and Appliance Deliveries

Traditionally, department store deliverers aren't tipped unless they uncrate and set up the items. But you might call the store in advance to see whether tips are expected. (Better safe than embarrassed and seemingly ungrateful!) When deliverers uncrate, assemble, or install an item, each receives between $5 and $20, depending on the amount of work performed. An especially large, heavy, or difficult delivery calls for increasing the tip by ten percent or so. When the deliverers remove an old piece of furniture or an appliance and take it away, another slight increase is called for. An exception is when the removal of the existing goods is part of the work agreement.

Take-out Food Deliveries

For take-out food delivered to your door, tip ten percent of the bill. For especially quick or courteous service or if the deliverer walks up more than one flight of stairs, tip fifteen percent. (For a pizza, $2 is adequate if the bill is between $10 and $15. A tip for a larger order may be between $3 and $5, depending on the number of pizzas.)

A delivery charge on your bill usually goes to the owner to help cover delivery costs, so a tip of ten percent ensures that the deliverer gets his due.

Newspaper Deliveries

Newspaper deliverers you know—be they neighborhood children, teens, or working moms—can either be tipped $1 or $2 whenever they collect (if weekly, you can tip monthly) or be tipped at holiday time. Holiday tips range from $10 to $20, depending on the region, frequency of the deliveries, and quality of service. If you regularly tip the deliverer when he collects, a smaller tip during the holidays is appropriate.

If you live in a large city and your deliverer is anonymous, tip only in the holiday season; many deliverers leave a holiday greeting card and a self-addressed envelope. If you're pleased with the service, tip the equivalent of one month's bill—usually between $10 and $30. If you don't receive a card but want to tip, send the equivalent of one month's bill to the newspaper service, who will then give it to the deliverer. If the service has been terrible, you needn't tip at all.

Miscellaneous Deliveries

When taking delivery of items such as the three below, tip a bit more if the service has been especially courteous or the deliverer had to brave bad weather or climb several flights of stairs.

Groceries. No less than $2
Flowers. $1 to $2
Dry cleaning. $1 to $2

Other Home Services

FOR MOST PEOPLE, "hired help" refers to the babysitter, the cleaning person who comes in occasionally, or the neighbor's son who mows the lawn. (See also Chapter 12, page 147: "Tipping and Gifts.")

Part-time domestic workers. Rather than being tipped each time they work for you, a regular cleaning person (who usually comes weekly or every other week) is typically tipped at holiday time with an extra one-job payment. For babysitters, a small tip (say, $5) is appropriate for each sitting in some communities, but you may also tip her a larger amount at holiday time and include a small gift chosen by your child.

Live-in domestic workers. Cooks, housekeepers, and chauffeurs are tipped over the course of the year only when you've asked them to provide services well beyond their usual duties. Otherwise, each is usually given the cash equivalent of a month's salary at holiday time, accompanied by a small gift—perhaps a book or an item for their rooms. A nanny is usually tipped on a sliding scale, between the cash equivalent of a week's and a month's salary, and is given a small gift by the children in her care.

Houseguests and tipping. Whenever you visit friends who have household help, do not tip the workers unless they perform a service outside their normal duties; and even if they do, check with your hosts before tipping. If they don't object to your tipping, follow these general guidelines:

Maid. Leave $10 to $15 if she's performed such personal services as cleaning, unpacking, ironing, or bringing meals to your room.
Chauffeur. When he drives you and your hosts, no tip is given. If he runs personal errands for you or drives you to the airport, you might give him $5 to $10, depending on the amount of time he has expended—even if the service was at the behest of your host.
Gardener. If the gardener has provided you with daily fresh flowers or another special service, leave $5 to $10.

Yard Maintenance Workers and Gardeners

The person who regularly tends your yard—whether to cut the grass or to also prune shrubs and take care of other garden tasks—doesn't have to be tipped after each work shift. But if she works throughout the year, you might tip her at the end of the season or during the holidays. Amounts vary from $20 to $50 or more, depending on the amount and quality of the work and the tipping standard in your area. Workers from a professional gardening service usually aren't tipped, but it's a good idea to call the company and check on its tipping policy.

Carpet Installers

When the job of carpet installers entails removing old carpeting, installing new carpeting, and cleaning up, the standard tip is between $10 and $15 for the crew boss and from $5 to $10 for each worker.

Trash Collectors

If your municipality provides garbage collection, check to see whether you would be violating the rules by tipping the sanitation crew. If not, or if service is provided by a private company, holiday tips range from $10 to $20 per crew member.

Dog Walkers

Tips for dog walkers—either the cash equivalent of a week's pay or a gift—are typically given during the holidays. Many dog walkers have dogs of their own, and a bag of dog treats is an appropriate gift.

Tipping Residential Building Personnel

HOW MUCH TO TIP RESIDENTIAL building employees during the holidays—the usual time to reward them—depends on the custom in your town or city, the type of building, the size of the staff, and the amount of time they spent helping you over the year. Employee seniority and any special services performed at a resident's request are also taken into account. If you tipped employees throughout the year—each time the doorman hailed a cab for you or received your dry cleaning, for example—then your holiday tip can be smaller.

Following are holiday tipping guidelines, each depending on the size and type of the building and the amount of service provided by the employee:

Superintendent. Give $20 to $80 to live-in supers who take care of your deliveries, make repairs, help you carry heavy packages, and so on. Superintendents in luxury buildings might receive the higher amount or more for such services, particularly if they aren't tipped throughout the year. If the superintendent lives off-premises and provides few services, a tip of around $20 is the norm.

Doorman. Give $35 to $80 each to the most helpful doormen and $20 to $30 to those you rarely see. Special services like feeding your cat or holding your mail when you're away can be either rewarded each time or remembered in the holiday tip.

Elevator operator. It's standard to give $15 to $40 to each operator, with tips on the larger side going to operators who performed any special services.

Handyman. It's your choice whether and when to tip a handyman. If you don't tip at the time the work is done ($5 to $10 is sufficient for most jobs) and he regularly helps you out, you might give a holiday tip in the range of $15 to $40 or more.

Note: On departure, guests who have stayed at a friend's apartment for more than a few days may tip any member of the building staff who's been especially helpful.

∼ Party Hires ∼

If you're throwing a party so large that you need to hire help and possibly even entertainment, tips will likely be in order. The method of paying temporary help for a party varies from region to region and also depends on the policy of the caterer or employment agency. Some caterers include gratuities in their total price; others send a bill indicating that you may add a tip.

If your help has been hired by an employment agency or by you personally, pay them before they leave at the agreed rate, adding a fifteen-to-twenty-percent tip. Catering company employees are usually tipped $10 each, but if there's only one server, the tip is doubled. (If friends help you out as a favor, a small gift presented at the end of the evening is a nice token of appreciation.)

The important thing is to establish the method and amount of payment at the time the help is hired so you can head off any embarrassment or unpleasantness later. A party, after all, is all about good feelings.

Entertainers hired for a party range from a piano player to a children's-birthday-party clown to psychics and palm-readers. Musicians are generally tipped twenty percent of their fee. A clown or magician hired for a children's party is tipped fifteen to twenty percent of the fee, depending on the length of the performance and how hot the weather on the day of the show (costumes can be like ovens). Other entertainers are generally tipped between ten and twenty percent of their fee, depending on the importance of their contribution. Just be sure to check contracts with performers to see if a gratuity is built in.

Out-and-about Tipping

AN OCCASIONAL TIP IS LIKELY to be called for as you go about your daily routine—usually when shopping or parking your car.

Grocery Loaders

Tip $1 for a normal number of bags taken to your car and loaded in the trunk, and $1.50 to $2 for a large number of bags. Check with the grocery manager first to make sure tipping isn't prohibited by the store or state regulations.

Car Wash Attendants

Tip $1 for the basic service at a car wash. Sometimes a tip jar, which serves as a kitty shared by the car washers and detailers, is placed in clear view. If this is the case, deposit your tip in the jar. For a car that has had extra service—anything from waxing to careful detailing—the standard is to tip ten to fifteen percent of the charge.

Garage Attendants

If you've parked your car in a garage for only a few hours while out shopping or going to dinner, tip the attendant who brings the car $1. If you pay a monthly rental, however, there's no need to tip each time the car is delivered. Still, service may be faster (and your car better cared for) if you give each employee $5 periodically, then reward them with holiday tips. The latter can be given to the employees individually or in one lump sum to the manager for distribution. Base the amount of holiday tips on your satisfaction with the service and the customary tip rate in your area (often an amount ranging from a half-month's to a full month's rent).

HOLIDAY TIPS AND GIFTS GUIDE

When the holiday season arrives, it's customary to thank those who have regularly served you throughout the year. Whether and how much to tip varies widely, depending on the quality and frequency of the service, where you live (amounts are usually higher in large cities), and your budget. If you've regularly tipped at the time of service, either forgo a holiday tip or cut back on the amount. Try to get your child's input when deciding on any gifts for teachers, day care providers, nannies, and babysitters.

Every situation is different so let common sense, specific circumstances, and holiday spirit be your guides. The tip amounts in this chart are typical.

Au pair	A gift from your family (or one week's pay), plus a small gift from your child
Babysitter, regular	One evening's pay, plus a small gift from your child
Barber	Cost of one haircut and possibly a small gift
Beauty salon staff	$10 to $60 each, giving most to those who give most to you, and possibly a small gift

Child's teacher	Gift, not cash—check school's policy; possibilities: classroom supplies, book, picture frame, fruit basket or gourmet food item, or joint gift with other parents and their children
Day-care providers	$25 to $70 each, plus a small gift from your child; if only one or two providers, consider higher-range amount.
Dog walker	One week's pay
Fitness trainer, personal	Cost of one session
Garage attendants	$10 to $30 each, to be distributed by manager
Housekeeper/ house cleaner	One day's pay
Letter carriers	U.S. government regulations permit carriers to accept gifts worth up to $20 each
Massage therapist	One session's fee
Nanny	One week's to one month's salary based on tenure and customs in your area, plus a small gift from your child
Newspaper deliverer	$10 to $30
Nurse, private	Gift, not cash
Nursing home employees	Gift, not cash
Package deliverer	Small gift if you receive deliveries regularly; most delivery companies prohibit cash gifts
Pool cleaner	Cost of one cleaning
Residential building personnel	
Doorman	$10 to $80
Elevator operator	$15 to $40
Handyman	$15 to $40
Superintendent	$20 to $80
Trash/recycling collectors	$10 to $20 each, for private service
Yard and garden worker	$20 to $50

Chapter Forty-seven

Performances in Public Places

WHETHER IT'S A BROADWAY SPECTACULAR, a rock festival in an open field, or the high school choral society in concert in the school auditorium, truly enjoyable performances depend to a degree on the behavior of the audience. Patrons' courtesy to others in the audience and to the performers engenders attentiveness, and by being attentive, the people on both sides of the footlights can open themselves to the magic of words, music, and movement that transcends everyday experience. But how can you concentrate on the stage or screen when the woman in the next seat pokes you repeatedly with her oversized bag, a cell phone rings in the row behind you, and somewhere nearby, thoughtless parents refuse to take their crying child outside? Multiply such disturbances by hundreds, sometimes thousands, of patrons, and it becomes clear why good manners and consideration for others are essential to the success of every public performance.

The General Courtesies

SOME OF THE MOST COMMON PROBLEMS associated with public performances can be prevented with advance planning and awareness of the policies of the event location. The obvious place to start is knowing when the performance will begin.

Be Punctual

Arrive in plenty of time to park or navigate the crowds, buy tickets if you haven't already, meet friends, purchase refreshments, get to your seat, and still leave at least five minutes to settle in before the performance begins. Experienced performance goers know to count backward from the scheduled start of the event and to allow extra time for unexpected delays.

An accident delayed traffic for a half hour. The boss asked you to handle a last-minute task. Whatever the reason, you arrive after the concert or feature film has started. You may be able to slip in and stand or find a seat in the back of the theater; some establishments allow only back-of-the-theater sitting or standing until intermission. Before trekking down the aisle, take a few moments to adjust to the low light; then scan for a convenient seat. Other patrons will appreciate your not stumbling over them. If there's an usher, allow him or her to seat you. For live performances, theaters often have a policy of not letting anyone enter except during a scene change, a break between musical numbers, or intermission. These rules are intended primarily for the benefit of the performers.

Tickets, Please!

When you must stand in line for tickets—whether purchasing in advance or just before the performance—good manners make the process more pleasant. Be prepared. Have your money or credit card ready. If there's a choice of seating, know approximately where you would like to be. If you're in line at the cinema multiplex, notice what's playing and have an alternative in mind just in case your first choice is sold out when you reach the ticket window. (When other people are waiting for tickets, it's rude to expect the cashier to give you the basic plot line of every movie on show.) Some venues have a separate window for reserved tickets, so noticing signs can save wasted time in the wrong line. If you have a ticketing problem—not unusual in these days of computer glitches—seek out a manager and let the line move forward.

Courteous people never break in line and are cautious about saving places. A person who has been in line for some time will be rightly angered by a patron who suddenly allows five people to jump ahead. When a group of people are purchasing separate tickets, everyone should wait in line or delegate one person to buy all the tickets. If you must save a place, tell the person behind you that someone else is coming.

Once you have your ticket, keep it handy for presenting to ticket-takers and ushers. Hang on to the stub; that bit of paper can save time and frustration if you must leave and reenter a theater or performance hall or if there's a dispute over correct seating.

Tickets for Guests

Inviting friends or colleagues to the theater or a concert is a nice way to entertain, and a few ticket etiquette tips can help.

> ➤ If everyone is entering together, the host or hostess should present all the tickets to the ticket-taker and identify the members of the group. The purpose

is to expedite the process; whether the host enters first or last depends on the particular situation.

➤ If the host leaves guests at the entrance before parking, he should give the tickets to a member of the group—keeping one for himself in case he's late. Do the same if a guest is parking; give her a ticket.

➤ When guests and hosts are not arriving together, designate a place to meet. Be specific ("beside the marble fountain") if the lobby or forecourt is large or normally crowded.

➤ If a guest or guests are likely to be late, the host can either deliver their tickets in advance or leave the tickets, in an envelope clearly marked with the guests' names, at the ticket office.

Taking a Seat

When there are ushers, it's normally best to allow them to guide you unless you know exactly where your seat is located. Ushers know how seats are numbered and, when seating is not assigned, where seating is available. They are also prepared to help with special needs such as aisle seating or wheelchair spaces for the handicapped.

Entering a row full of people is always inconvenient, but you can minimize the hassle. Begin by saying "Excuse me" to the person on the aisle and then down the line, and "Thank you" to anyone who moves or stands to let you pass. Face the front or the stage. This means showing your backside to the people in your row, but should you trip or stumble, it's easier to regain your balance (and maintain your dignity) by falling forward against a seat rather than into someone's lap. A sort of semi-shuffling gait enables you to move forward without stepping on feet. Proceed as quickly as you can, and be sure to hold purses, cases, backpacks, and coats high above the people around you. Be very careful with umbrellas and canes.

If you must leave a row during a performance, repeat the process but whisper your thanks and apologies. If returning to your seat will inconvenience people yet another time, it's often best to sit or stand at the back of the hall until intermission and then get back to your place before others return to your row. Anyone who may be summoned away during a performance should try to get a seat on or near an aisle, as should parents with young children.

When you're the one being passed in a row, it's often possible to clear space by remaining seated and turning knees in the direction the person is moving. Standing may be easier if seats fold up, but it's better to move knees than to stand (thereby blocking the view of those seated behind) when the performance is under way.

Box Seating

You may be part of a group of box subscribers for an opera, symphony, dance, or theater season. The etiquette among subscribers is to alternate seats for different performances so that everyone gets a chance at the best views of the stage.

When box seating is for a single performance and seats are not numbered, first-comers get their choice of seating. Still, gracious patrons will adjust, if seats can be moved, so that everyone has as clear a line of sight as possible.

When the House Lights Go Up

Intermissions are opportunities to get the kinks out, visit the restroom, or enjoy a refreshment and some chat. Leaving a performance should be a steady, measured departure. Neither intermission nor departing should be a stampede to the doors.

Intermission. A good strategy is to look at your watch as soon as the intermission begins and resolve to head back to your seat five minutes before the end of the interval. (Twenty minutes is the normal length of intermissions, but check your program to be sure.) This lets you avoid the general rush when the warning lights or bells signal patrons to return to their seats. If you linger in the lobby or restroom after the intermission, don't expect people to forgive you for climbing over them to reclaim your seat. If you want to stay in your seat during intermission, be courteous and leave your seat until others have departed the row.

Exiting. When the show ends, go with the flow. It's rude and sometimes dangerous to push, shove, or demand to get ahead of the crowd. Don't block the aisle by stopping to chat with anyone; wait until you're outside to use your cell phone. It is discourteous to leave a few minutes before the end of any entertainment. Patrons who feel compelled to get a head start to the parking lot have ruined many a punch line or surprise ending for others.

Audience Etiquette

TODAY, WITH SUCH A WEALTH of entertainment offered in widely differing settings, it's impossible to pinpoint every expectation for gracious audience members. But the following fundamentals of good public manners are highly adaptable to virtually any situation you might encounter.

∼ Row D, Seat 7 ∼

When seating is assigned by row and seat number, there's no room for debate. Yet an unfortunate trend among some people today is to take the seat they want and hope the seat holder doesn't appear. Bolder interlopers try to bluff and argue when the real ticket holder appears and may hold out until the house lights dim and the legitimate patron is driven away.

If this kind of thing happens to you, don't make a scene. Check your ticket; then get an usher or manager and let him take over. Mistakes do happen, so be courteous if it's clear the person took your seat in error.

No talking, unless audience participation is requested by the performers. If something must be said, whisper it quickly. Shushing a talkative neighbor can be just as disturbing, so if the talk doesn't stop, try tapping gently on the person's arm or shoulder and using the finger-to-lips signal for silence. Or wait for an usher to intervene. If the person beside you begins to snore, wake him.

Use good posture. Sit up straight and keep feet on the floor. Auditorium seating is often arranged so that the person in the seat behind can see between the two seats in front, so slumping sideways or lounging on a partner's shoulder blocks the view. Feet or knees shouldn't touch the seat in front. And don't hog the armrests.

Remove hats, unless they are head-hugging. Also, forgo bouffants, Mohawks, and other towering hairdos.

No rattling of candy boxes, shaking popcorn containers, slurping drinks, rattling ice in cups, or opening cellophane wrappers. Remove and dispose of any cellophane wrappers *before* the performance begins. There should be no food or drinks taken into a classical music, ballet, theater, or opera performance.

Control coughing. If you might need cough drops or mints, bring them unwrapped in a soft container, such as a plastic sandwich bag. Muffle coughs and sneezes with a handkerchief, and leave if you can't stop the attack. If you have a cold or an allergy and are inclined to cough, try to get an aisle seat near an exit so you can beat a hasty retreat at the first tickle.

Turn off cell phones, beepers, watches that chime, and any other sound-making gadgets in any performance setting. If you need to stay in touch with the outside world, use a vibrating ringer or pager. Don't use headphones during a performance; the sound leaks and can be as irritating as a buzzing bee to the people on either side. If you must use a cell phone during intermission, find a secluded place. Some venues provide an emergency number for physicians and others who expect calls during a performance; to be summoned, provide the number to your service and then inform managers and ushers of your name and seat location.

Avoid other sounds that can disturb the people around you and the performers. Munching noisily, smacking or cracking gum, rattling the pages of programs, tapping feet or drumming fingers, humming or singing along, wearing leather or vinyl that crackles against metal or plastic seats and rubber-soled shoes that squeak on flooring, opening and closing zippered or Velcro closures on bags, popping metal clasps on purses—these are just a few of the seemingly limitless ways people can drive others crazy.

Smoke only in designated areas. When the environment is totally smoke-free— as most indoor and many outdoor performance venues now are—you should leave and find a place outside the venue if you must smoke.

Don't take photos or roll the videocam during live performances. This isn't an absolute, so check the policy of the performance venue, but the point is to do nothing that will distract the performers and disturb other patrons. A clicking, flashing camera and a whirring videocam will do both.

Dispose of trash, including chewed gum, in waste containers. Tell an usher or attendant if anything was spilled; you may save the next person who has your seat the discomfort of feeling stuck to the floor.

What to Wear?

The subject of appropriate dress can spur heated debate, especially when audiences show up in everything from tuxes and evening gowns to jeans and T-shirts. Some contend that dressing more formally is a sign of respect for performers and the special nature of the occasion. Others hold that dress is of little matter compared to polite audience behavior and that the price of the ticket entitles audience members to wear whatever they like.

As a general rule, the style of dress is determined primarily by the nature of the event—an outdoor rock festival being very different from an Easter performance of Handel's *Messiah*—and the general standards in the community. For example, people still tend to dress up for opening nights at the theater but choose casual attire for matinees. Clothing at concerts on college campuses is often very informal, and older patrons frequently "dress down" for these events. Sometimes, style is dictated by before-and after-performance plans, as when you are attending an informal concert but going on to an upscale restaurant for supper.

When you aren't sure what to wear, ask someone who will also be attending or has attended similar performances. If you're to be someone's guest, talk with your hosts and be guided by their preference. If you can't get reliable advice, you will probably

Performances in Public Places

A QUESTION FOR PEGGY

My husband and I recently spent our vacation in England, our first overseas trip. We attended several plays and movies, and at the start, the audiences stood and sang "God Save the Queen." As Americans, we weren't sure what to do.

Just as when "The Star Spangled Banner" opens an event in the United States, a guest in another country stands in respect, and men remove their hats (and women their sport caps) when the anthem of that country is performed. Normally you wouldn't sing, place your hand over your heart, or salute. If a statement of national loyalty similar to our Pledge of Allegiance is offered, stand respectfully but don't say the words.

be fine in business attire—suit and tie, jacket and skirt or dress. There are, however, a few basics that apply regardless of fashion:

> When the seating is close, avoid bare arms and bare legs that can brush against the stranger seated next to you. A jacket or sweater to cover bare skin is a worthwhile accessory.

> Be conscious of personal hygiene, and use scents sparingly or not at all. Even in an air-conditioned theater, body heat in tight quarters will intensify odors and fragrances.

> Don't wear jewelry or accessories such as metal chain belts that clank or jingle.

> If the venue has a coatroom, check heavy coats and rainwear, hats, umbrellas, book bags and backpacks, briefcases, and anything else you don't need during the performance. Take a small purse.

Expressing Yourself

Every performer wants approval for good work, and hand clapping is the convention in the United States. (See page 826: "Performance Specifics," for more on the etiquette of applause.) How long and how hard to clap is determined both by your pleasure in what you've seen and heard and by the general audience reaction. Standing ovations and cheering are usually reserved for the end of the performance.

Thankfully, we've come a long way since the time when audiences expressed dissatisfaction by pelting performers with rotten vegetables and storming the stage. Polite but unenthusiastic clapping often registers an audience's disapproval with deadly effectiveness when it's general. Knowledgeable art patrons sometimes indulge in low hissing and booing that, while not exactly courteous, is still part of the theater tradition and intended as serious criticism. However, most people who feel that a performance wasn't up to par will simply not clap and remain seated. Leaving early is also an option, but do so between acts or at intermission when you won't inconvenience other audience members.

Addressing performers in any way while they are performing is not acceptable, and heckling is tacky. Voicing complaints loudly to the people seated around you is just as bad. (They may not share your opinion.) Save harsh remarks until after the show, and try to get a sense of other people's ideas before carping too much. Don't spoil someone else's enjoyment because the performance failed to meet your standards.

Outdoor Etiquette

Many outdoor performances and open-air film presentations have a relaxed, laissez-faire atmosphere, but not so easygoing that good manners can be forgotten.

Be quiet. Audience members don't have the right to drown out the performance with their shrieking, catcalls, and ear-popping whistles. Outdoor concerts, plays, and

For a number of reasons, including appropriateness of content and children's short attention spans, it's generally best not to take a child under age seven or eight to any performance intended for adult audiences. No matter how bright, younger children simply don't have the social maturity for adult fare. Happily, there are excellent family-oriented entertainments available today—from young people's concerts to outdoor festivals to circuses and other traveling productions. With so much to choose from, parents can introduce their children to a variety of cultural experiences, without subjecting the youngster to boredom or other adults to a fidgety, whining, disruptive child. As for movies, pay attention to the age ratings and read reviews. Most adults who attend G (all ages) and PG (parental guidance) films tend to be accepting of the ways of children. The ratings also provide guidelines for parents of adolescents, and you're well within your rights to limit their viewing.

Of special concern for parents of preteens and teens are *all-ages* concerts and clubs—venues where liquor is prohibited so that underage patrons can attend. The danger is what goes on *around* these locations, even though the performance itself may be well supervised. Parents should be aware that drug sales and other illicit activity may be taking place outside. Check out the place with your Better Business Bureau chapter and local police before allowing underage kids to go without an adult escort.

movies are not karaoke, so don't sing along (unless the performers encourage you to) or repeat dialogue.

Control children and pets. Know where they are at all times and, if necessary, clean up after them.

Use common sense about outdoor seating. Blankets, folding camp stools, and low lawn chairs are fine at many outdoor events. But a truckload of outdoor furniture, including chaise lounges and drink coolers the size of garden sheds, isn't—especially near the stage or in a pedestrian traffic area. Place seating and accessories that can block others' view or cause congestion as far from the center of the crowd as possible.

Be very careful with food and drinks. No one should have their clothes damaged by another person's sloshed drink. The food served at outdoor events can be messy, so don't wave that slice of pizza or mustard-slathered hot dog around. Wipe up spills, especially on surfaces where others may sit or eat.

Smoke away from the crowd. If you must smoke and it's permitted, head for the fringes where the smoke is less bothersome and you're unlikely to bump a lighted cigarette into strangers.

Clean up. Municipalities and private event organizers often spend thousands or hundreds of thousands of dollars for trash disposal after outdoor events, and eventually the money comes out of your pocket (either in higher taxes or ticket prices).

Performance Specifics

DIFFERENT TYPES OF presentations and even different performers often evolve their own etiquette. The event-specific courtesies included here benefit everyone—performers, crews, organizers, and their audiences.

At the Theater, Opera, and Ballet

At the ballet, opera, and sometimes musical theater, the orchestra conductor is applauded when he or she enters, before the curtain goes up. Although enthusiastic audiences often applaud stars at their first appearance or exit from stage or after a memorable part of the performance—and most performers are prepared for the interruption—this custom is disruptive. It's good manners to hold clapping until the end of each act. At the appropriate times during a performance and at the final curtain, you can clap and cheer as enthusiastically as you like, but when the performers have taken their final bow, it's time to leave.

Going backstage to congratulate performers is a matter of being invited. Autograph-seekers should wait at the stage door exit and exercise restraint. A scrawled, illegible autograph isn't worth mobbing a star performer; you're more likely to get results by writing your favorite performer a polite letter.

At Classical Music Performances

People who are classical music novices often worry about when to clap at performances. The appropriate times for applause are:

When the conductor, concertmaster, and guest artists walk on stage. When the conductor steps on the platform and raises his or her baton, all clapping ceases, and the audience becomes silent. At performances by ensembles and soloists, watch the performers carefully; they signal by gesture and mood when they are ready to begin.

At the end of each entire piece. It's sometimes hard to know a piece has ended because there's usually a pause between movements and you may think the piece is over. One suggestion is to count the number of movements listed in the program and applaud only when the last movement is completed. The conductor may turn immediately to the audience, but some don't, so if you aren't sure the piece is over, follow the audience's lead. The audience may not always be right, but at least you won't be clapping by yourself.

At the end of the concert. The conductor will turn to the audience and bow and may point out members of the orchestra for recognition. Guest artists and occasionally composers will come to the stage for more applause. Don't rush for the exit at intermission or the end of the performance; remain seated until the clapping begins to die down and the people around you start to move. (See page 821: "Exiting.")

Although the mood and manners are less restrained at pop concerts and audience participation is often part of the program, the concert manners above still apply.

At Other Music Events

People nowadays seem to expect hard rock concerts and clubs to be rowdy. But the trend toward rude audience behavior has invaded jazz, country-western, and even the gentlest of folk music presentations. The vast majority of patrons are thoughtful and civil, but a few seem to believe that their tickets are license to do whatever they like. It only takes a few rotten apples to destroy everyone's good time.

Crowd control and safety isn't always top priority with event organizers, so it's up to participants to mind their own manners, be attentive to the needs of others, and observe these do's and don'ts:

➤ *Don't* use drugs or become intoxicated. In addition to risking arrest and hospitalization, inebriated people are a pain to be around. If alcohol is sold at an event and you're of legal age, be responsible and know your limit. Do not offer alcohol or any kind of narcotic to anyone. If you need an excuse to behave responsibly, volunteer to be the designated driver.

≈ Do You Mosh? ≈

Moshing is uninhibited and uncontrolled physical activity—jumping, bumping, flailing, body slamming, head banging—that takes place spontaneously among audience members at rock performances and other kinds of concerts. It often includes crowd surfing, or passing people above the audience, and diving at the stage. To the uninitiated, the pit—the moshing area usually near the stage—may resemble the depths of Dante's *Inferno*. The average mosher is a male in his teens or twenties, though some young women do participate. Those who do it more than once say that it's exhilarating and wear their cuts and bruises with pride. But medical professionals, public officials, and even a few performers and organizers are increasingly expressing concern about the dangers, which have included broken bones, head and spinal injuries, paralysis, and several deaths.

Believe it or not, there is an etiquette for moshers. Rule 1: Watch out for others in the pit. This includes not slamming into or dropping others, calming down if you see someone who has fallen or been hurt, getting help for anyone in trouble, and not dragging unsuspecting bystanders into the action.

> ➤ *Do* stay seated unless everyone stands. The music may be telling you to "get up and boogie," but common sense says that the people whose view you block will be really bothered.

> ➤ *Don't* throw things. Although tossing lightweight objects like beach balls is fairly common at some music concerts, don't heave anything, such as half-empty cola bottles and beer cans, that can cause injury. Don't toss food or candies. Be very careful about waving flags and placards, especially those mounted on poles or sticks, and lit cigarette lighters to show your approval of the performance.

> ➤ *Do* be alert for anyone who needs assistance. Help if you can, but report to authorities any problem or potential danger—physically or verbally aggressive patrons, threats of violence, fighting, sexual harassment or assault, the presence of weapons of any sort—that is more than you can handle. It's common decency to get medical assistance for someone who is hurt, ill, or clearly drinking or drugging himself into oblivion.

At the Movies

Movie theater etiquette tends to be a bit more relaxed than that for live performances. Whispering, coughing, and opening candy wrappers won't disturb on-screen performers, but excessive noise and movement can drive other patrons batty. Considerate moviegoers adhere to the basics of performance etiquette—and instruct any children they may have charge of to be thoughtful of others.

Probably the most recent annoying movie audience trend (along with loud cell phone use) is talking and yelling back at the screen—a popular pastime among many young people and some of their elders. Shushing raucous teenagers is nearly impossible, and movie theater proprietors are sometimes reluctant to take action. So the moviegoer who wants to hear every word of dialogue is advised to exercise some common sense. Sit toward the rear if you can see clearly; shouters and screamers often take the front seats. If the noise is intolerable, complain to the management and ask for the return of your ticket money. Better yet, avoid the opening weekend of the latest action film, sci-fi blockbuster, or teen flick; young people often want to be the first to see a movie; then they move on to another diversion.

At Parades, Street Festivals, and Street Performances

From the smallest rural hamlet to the largest cities, people still gather in and along their streets for entertainment and celebration. Usually, street events have no entry fees, and many are publicly funded. Virtually anyone is welcome; visitors can spend money as they please and follow their own schedule.

While police and security personnel are often present, maintaining order depends on the good natures and manners of the people who attend. In addition to the guidelines for outdoor performances (see page 824: "Outdoor Etiquette"), responsible people will pay attention to direction signs, respect barriers, and observe the general pattern of foot traffic. Be sure to hold young children's hands or keep them in strollers, and don't allow older children to wander. If police or an event official asks for your cooperation, give it without question.

When stopping to enjoy a street or subway entertainer, be especially aware of the people around you. You'll probably want to drop a tip (roughly one to a few dollars) in the hat or instrument case and move on quickly if the attraction is blocking sidewalks, doorways, or access to turnstiles and train platforms.

Chapter Forty-eight

Sports and Recreation

WHEN WE DEVOTE LEISURE TIME to sports or recreation, fun and pleasure should be the goal. Boating and camping let us get away from it all and soak in the beauty of nature. Golf, tennis, even a pickup basketball game, allow us a little friendly competition and a chance to hone our athletic skills. And sitting in a stadium and cheering on a football, baseball, or any other sports team is a time-honored pastime for young and old alike.

In a time when the idea of sportsmanship seems to have lost some of its sheen and competing can too often mean winning at all costs, manners are more essential than ever as we enjoy the great outdoors or play sports. To keep things in perspective, look no further than the roots of the words. "Recreation" is from the Latin verb *recreare* ("to restore and refresh"), while "sport(s)" comes from the Old French *desporter* ("to divert, amuse, please"). In today's hectic world, a little refreshment and amusement free of heated competition can be a real boost to us all.

This chapter offers pointers for ways to keep things on an even keel as you enjoy both the great outdoors and recreational activities at home. It begins with etiquette on wilderness trails and at campgrounds; proceeds to manners for boaters, beachgoers, skiers, golfers, and tennis players, then moves on to behavior at spectator sports—an arena of growing concern.

Ah, Wilderness!

RESPONSIBLE HIKERS, horseback riders, mountain bikers, and cross-country skiers know not to disturb the flora and fauna of the wilderness. If you're a novice, follow their lead. First, observe and follow all posted signs. Second, take care not to damage any trees or shrubs and leave those wildflowers for the next visitors to enjoy (no picking!). Third, try not to startle the wildlife with sudden movements or noise. Also refrain from "doing the animals a favor" by feeding them; squirrels, raccoons, bears, and birds can become dependent on humans and unable to survive naturally.

Be considerate of everyone else using or living along the trails, greeting them with a friendly hello. Stay to the right, pass on the left, and yield the right of way to uphill traffic unless you're a downhill or cross-country skier (in which case traffic should yield to you). Leave gates as you found them, and don't climb fences.

Do not smoke on the trail, and tend any fires you build with utmost care (see also page 832: "Happy Campers"). To learn whether you're allowed to build a fire, check burning and campfire regulations before leaving home.

Hiking

Whether you're a day hiker or a backpacker, make a point not to dawdle while hiking with others; a group moves only as fast as its slowest member. Also watch where you walk: Stick to the trail, since taking a shortcut around hillsides or obstacles could contribute to an increase in erosion. In alpine areas, try to walk on rocks whenever possible so as not to compact soil.

Don't take a dog on the trail unless you can keep it under control. Dogs that run free or bark can deprive other hikers of enjoying wildlife by scaring other animals, not to mention hikers themselves. Obey any leash laws, fit your dog with an antibark collar if necessary, and dispose of dog droppings as you would on a city street.

Horseback Riding

Make sure any trail you plan to ride allows horses. Then check the trail system signs, stay on designated trails, and do your best not to damage trailside vegetation.

Because riders sometimes can't see the whole trail when it ascends or descends, it's a good idea to tie a small bell to the horse's bridle so that its tinkle will warn people and animals that you're coming. When riding in groups, maintain a distance of at least one horse length between animals; when going uphill, at least two horse lengths; and on downhill trails, at least three horse lengths.

Never gallop on public trails! Walking is the preferred trail gait, since the point is to savor the great outdoors. When passing another rider, let her and her horse know by saying, "Trail, please"; the rider should then move her horse as far right on the trail as possible or simply stop the horse in its tracks. Then thank the other rider as you pass.

When greeting hikers or entering a camp, dismount and lead your horse. Also ask anyone you're greeting to approach the horse from the front.

Mountain Biking

Mountain bikers should always announce their approach to hikers and anyone else on the trail. The best way to do so? With a greeting or a handlebar bell—and remembering that others haven't seen you until they look your way. Thank anyone who yields the right of way to you, including other bikers. Other bikers have the right of way when they're going uphill, have children along, or are traveling in a group.

Don't tailgate another mountain biker. It's also important not to startle other bikers as you approach. When you want to pass, say "On your left" or "On your right" once you're within speaking distance. (The usual phrase for racers is "Track, please!") Then follow with a "thanks" as you pass.

Happy Campers

When you're at a public or private campground, you're essentially renting the space. So it stands to reason that you leave your campsite pristine for the campers who will follow. Following are a few essential do's and don'ts for campers.

Do abide by all campground rules. "That's obvious," you say, but legions of campers break rules regarding pets, trash and cigarette disposal, speed limits, and quiet hours.

Do leave the trees alone. Don't chop wood to use as firewood and never drive nails into the trunks or branches when hanging lanterns or hammocks; tie them on instead. Even dead trees are home to many critters, and destroying them can upset nature's balance.

Do bring your own firewood. If the campground doesn't sell it, you'll more than likely find bundled firewood at gas stations, supermarkets, or home stores in the area.

Do put cigarette butts in the firepits. Think of the firepit as your one and only ashtray. Smart campers who are smokers know to save the butts of cigarettes on the trail and dispose of them in the firepit when they return to camp.

Don't cut through other campers' campsites on the way to the showers, toilets, trails, or anywhere else on the grounds. Their space may not have walls, but it is private nonetheless.

Don't put metal, glass, or plastic in the firepit; wood and paper are the only two things that belong there. Aluminum cans and foil won't burn, beer bottles and other glass can shatter and cause injury, and plastic will merely melt and give off noxious fumes.

Don't disturb the peace. Loud music or laughter robs neighboring campers of the very thing they came for—peace and quiet. Besides, noisy groups risk being evicted from the campgrounds.

Don't let children play in the shower rooms. Sound is magnified in cinderblock or concrete rooms, so exuberant shouts are all the harder on the ears. Like everyone else, children should use the rooms only for showering.

Don't leave any traces of your stay. That means no beer bottles or bottle caps in the firepit, no bits of toilet paper in the woods (it should have been used only in the toilets anyway), and no food scraps, paper plates, cups, or other detritus overflowing the trash bins. Food scraps can attract bears and other animals and put campers in real danger.

If you encounter a horseback rider going either way on the trail, slow down, announce your presence, and ask if it's all right to pass. Once the rider says it's safe, thank him as you proceed slowly. In some cases, it may be necessary to dismount, remove your helmet (so as not to frighten the horse), and perhaps step off the trail to let horse and rider pass. In any case, stay quiet so the horse won't be spooked.

The Joys of Boating

AS CAREFREE AS A DAY on the water should be, boaters must adhere to long-standing customs and traditions. Whether taking to the water in a canoe, a power boat, or a sixty-foot yacht, the boater's first concern is safety, rules and regulations for which can be obtained from, among other sources, the United States Coast Guard Auxiliary at www.cgaux.org. State and local boating commissions can provide information on an area's waterways, tides, and the placement of depth markers and other buoys.

One of the most important things for boaters to remember is the effect their wake has on other boats. When passing a slower boat or a small fishing boat at anchor, avoid rocking it (and, in the latter case, scaring away the fish) by slowing your speed and giving the boat as wide a berth as possible. Another point of politeness: Don't hold up other boaters waiting at the dock when you launch your boat into the water. Get organized and take care of any maintenance in advance so you can get your boat into the water and out of the way as quickly as you can.

At the Marina

The marina is a place you literally don't want to make waves. Unless you enter an anchorage or mooring at very slow speed, you'll create a wave that could send another boater's drink or dinner plate scooting. Also be careful not to anchor your boat in close proximity to others, since a sudden change in the wind can cause boats to bang against one another and anchor lines to tangle.

If you plan any nighttime activities, anchor well downwind from your neighbors. Many boaters plan early departures and go to bed early, and voices, music, and the sounds of children's play—all of which carry exceptionally well over water—can keep them from getting a good night's sleep. The smoke from a barbecue can also be unpleasant for neighbors anchored upwind of your boat.

Here are some other considerations for the courteous boater:

> ➤ Don't warm up engines more loudly (or for longer) than necessary when leaving the dock early in the morning. Likewise, if you have a dinghy and want to use it at night to go ashore, preserve the peace by using oars instead of your outboard.

> ➤ When rowing around the anchorage, be friendly but not intrusive. If you decide you'd like to say hello to strangers on deck, approach their craft on the starboard side and stay about six to ten feet away. If you start a conversation

and they don't seem all that interested in continuing it, politely bid them good day and move on.

➤ When you stop for fuel, make sure you're not jumping ahead of any other boaters who are waiting. Tie up your boat securely, follow proper fueling procedures, pay the bill, and leave. Leaving your boat to run errands on shore is a major no-no.

➤ If you see another boater docking or undocking and no dockmaster or other helper is around, offer to help with their lines.

➤ Keep the dock area just outside your boat clear. Roll up and stow hoses and power cords so as not to trip passersby, and don't leave tackle, buckets, mops, and other items strewn around the dock.

➤ After using communal equipment like carts, immediately put them back in their proper place so that the equipment will be accessible to others.

When Hosting Guests

Whether guests are joining you on board for the day, a weekend, or much longer, show them the ropes beforehand, especially if they're inexperienced. If they need to handle lines or perform any other duties on board, teach them how if necessary.

Once guests are on board, take a few minutes to demonstrate how things work, from the toilet to the galley sink. Also inform them of safety and emergency procedures and any rules of behavior that must be observed on board—no smoking, for example.

If on an extended sail you'll be visiting foreign ports, let your guests know in advance which documents they should bring. Also tell them of any local customs they should be aware of.

Once the trip is under way, be the first to rise every day. You're the one in charge, and your guests will be more comfortable if you make that clear.

Angler's Etiquette

When fishing by boat, pay special attention to the rules of no-wake zones. Also, never anchor right next to other fishers who are catching; it's not fair to take advantage of their good luck. Follow all boating and fishing regulations.

Anglers who fish the surf at popular beaches should cast their lines far away from swimmers, or fish at dawn or dusk when the beach is clear of bathers. Anyone who fishes from piers should always reel in his line when a boat approaches.

Thoughtful behavior is also expected of anglers who cast from the shore of a stream, a river, or a lake, be they fly-fishers or bait fishers. The main concern? Giving others as much space as possible to make sure that, for one thing, you don't risk hooking other anglers with your line when you cast. Also remember to refrain from shouting and to keep any noise to a minimum so that the fish won't be scared away.

Spending time aboard a boat requires more than just showing up and hoping for a good tan. The special circumstances of being a guest on a small craft demand that you bone up on a few courtesies in advance:

➢ Take the minimum amount of clothing you'll need on board and on shore and pack it in a canvas bag—not a hard suitcase, which will be almost impossible to stow. (Most captains keep foul-weather gear on board, but you should ask beforehand whether you should bring your own.)

➢ Wear rubber-soled, nonskid shoes, which will keep you from slipping and sliding on deck.

➢ Have your gear stowed and be ready to leave in every other respect well in advance of the departure time set by your host.

➢ Abide by your host's hours, rising and retiring as he does.

➢ Ask your host if you can bring a cooler of beverages or anything else to contribute toward a meal on board.

➢ When sailing for several days, offer to chip in for expenses—paying for gas when refueling, treating for a meal on shore, or replenishing beverages or other staples.

➢ A thank-you gift for the host is appropriate but should be given afterward so that there's one less thing to stow on the boat.

Water-skiing and Personal Watercraft

Operators of boats towing water-skiers should be on constant lookout, making sure their lines don't cross in front of other boats. Beyond that, the regular rules of the waterways apply.

Jet Skis are another matter. These personal watercraft resemble snowmobiles and are propelled forward by a pump that pushes out a powerful jet of water. Their noisiness, rolling wakes, potential for accidents, and ability to travel in shallow water (and the resultant effect on wildlife habitats) have led to their banishment from national parks and in waterways from Puget Sound to Maine.

In waters where Jet Skis are allowed, the following considerations are paramount:

➢ Never leave a wake in a no-wake zone.

➢ Don't travel on the water with large groups of others using Jet Skis, which can cause excessive noise and wakes.

➢ Watch out for boaters and follow every safety guideline.

➢ Don't race around in circles or jump waves or wakes.

At the Beach

FOR THE SAKE OF OTHERS at the beach, stay relatively quiet (no loud radios or shouted or raucous conversations) and keep children under control. Having fun is in no way prohibited, but activities that disturb others should be avoided. Be sure not to litter either!

Avoid other acts that could be deemed offensive: smoking (especially of cigars), steamy public displays of affection, ball and Frisbee games that encroach on others' space, changing a baby's diaper in full view of others, feeding seagulls that in turn could bother other beach goers, and leaving big holes in the sand (dangerous if unnoticed).

Sunbathing

When you choose a place to lay down your mat or towel, don't crowd other sunbathers. A good rule of thumb: You're too close if you cast a shadow on other sunbathers or you can't shake out your towel without getting sand on them. Also try not to block their view of the water.

How much skin to reveal is determined by the nature of a particular beach. In other words, women shouldn't sunbathe topless unless doing so is common custom. Nude or nearly nude sunbathing is permitted only on specified beaches—so always check first.

Don't save beach chairs by piling books, towels, or lotions onto them so they appear to be occupied. At some resorts, "claim-stakers" (many of them arriving at the beach at the crack of dawn) load up chairs for friends or family members who may or may not show up. The problem has gotten so out of hand at some resorts that the management directs beach boys to carry a guest's chair to the desired spot and then retrieve it once the guest leaves.

Surfing

The worst displays of behavior at surfing beaches grow from the "no outsiders" mindset of local surfers. Needless to say, getting defensive surfers to change their tune is beyond the scope of this book, but even at tension-free beaches there are a few rules to observe, with these three among the most important:

➤ When you paddle out, go around (not through) waves to avoid collisions.

➤ Give the right of way to the surfer who's closest to the pocket of the breaking wave.

➤ When you wipe out or crash, hang on to your board to keep it from becoming a missile that could injure others.

Skiing and Snowboarding

MOST OF THE ETIQUETTE GUIDELINES for skiers have grown from the need for safety. The same goes for snowboarding, which has brought more and more people to the slopes. Specific rules are based on common sense and should always be obeyed.

When waiting in the lift line, be patient, don't complain, and be careful not to step on others' skis with your own. Be willing to ride up with others even if you don't know them, particularly if the line is long and you're riding the lift alone. Remember to thank the lift attendants for their help.

Prior to hitting the slopes, check the trail map to locate trails for your level of skiing. If you're a novice, give the better skiers in your group the chance to take some of their own runs by not expecting them to spend the day waiting for you at the bottom of the trails. By the same token, if you're an expert skier, avoid poking fun at beginners. Be patient with those who are slower, and don't push less skilled skiers into accompanying you where they'll have trouble.

Always ski in control, remembering that it's your responsibility to avoid objects and other people. Skiers ahead of you have the right of way, and when entering a trail or starting downhill, you should yield to others. When stopping, make sure that those above can see you and that you don't obstruct the trail.

Cross-country skiing. Learn the symbols indicating trail difficulty, and ski within your abilities so you don't become a hazard to yourself and to others. When approaching another skier, keep to the right and yield to anyone coming downhill. If skiing on a snowmobile trail, stay as far right as possible when a vehicle approaches. Whenever you stop for any reason, be sure not to block the trail. If you fall, take a moment to repair damage to the trail. (Note: All of these guidelines apply to snowshoers as well.)

Snowboarding. Snowboard riders need to be particularly sensitive to the fact that their equipment is noisy; skiers and other riders can easily be intimidated when they hear a board bearing down on them. Remember, too, that people downhill from you have the right of way. Give others on the slopes plenty of room. Jumps and speedy maneuvers obviously need to be carried out with safety in mind, and that means being aware of skiers and riders at all times. Looking before leaping and staying in control are the smart ways to go because they're not only safe but considerate.

Dealing With Falls

Always use braking devices to help prevent runaway equipment. After a fall, quickly move off the trail, if you can, to prevent collisions and to allow other skiers and riders to pass. If you're unable to exit the slope, you or someone else should plant your skis or poles in a vertical, crossed position—the signal that alerts other skiers that someone is down on the slope.

If for any reason you accidentally knock another skier or rider down, stop, apologize, and make sure the person isn't injured before you continue down the hill. Never try to move an injured person. If the skier is unable to get up or is in pain, stay with him until another skier arrives. One of you should then immediately seek the help of the nearest ski patrol while the other stays with the injured skier.

Most skiers and riders are quick to lend a helping hand to anyone in trouble. If you see that someone has fallen, ask if she needs assistance—then, as above, either seek the help of the nearest ski patrol or ask someone else to do so. Don't be the kind of skier or rider who blithely zooms by someone who has fallen without so much as a glance.

To Tip or Not?

Tips aren't mandatory for ski or snowboard instructors, but most people tip if they are pleased with the lesson. (Even if you've had a group lesson, a small monetary thank-you is always appreciated.) The amounts vary. A tip is given either as a flat amount (say, $10 or $20) for a one- or two-hour lesson or as a percentage of the lesson's cost. Skiers and riders who have had a full-day lesson costing $200, for example, typically tip fifteen to twenty percent ($30 to $40) or more. Some treat their instructors to a meal in addition to—or in lieu of—a tip.

Many instructors rely on tips to augment their incomes, since much of the lesson fee goes to the ski resort company. Customs vary from region to region, so it's a good idea to inquire about local custom regarding tipping at the ski resort you're visiting.

Golf Etiquette

GOLF ETIQUETTE IS A COMBINATION of respecting safety, understanding the rules, and being thoughtful. In fact, manners are an integral part of the many aspects of the game. With the increasing popularity of golf meaning that courses are now crowded with beginners, knowing golfing etiquette is more important than ever.

A shout of "fore!"—the golfer's warning call of an errant shot—is one of the few times you'll hear loud noise on a golf course. During most of the round, regular conversation is the norm except when someone is taking a shot. The rest of the time, the camaraderie of the players is one of the things that makes golf so appealing.

Safety First

Safety is of paramount importance. Accidentally hitting another player with a ball or club is the last thing a golfer wants to do, and here are three ways to prevent it:

➤ When taking practice swings, make sure there is no risk of hitting anyone with your club or with any stones, sticks, or turf propelled by your club.

➤ Wait to tee off until those in the group ahead of you have hit their second shots and are outside of your range.

➤ When making a blind shot, send a caddie or ask another player to scout the area where your ball is expected to land. If other golfers are within your range, the lookout can signal for you to wait until the landing area is clear.

Because concentration is key, never speak, rattle your clubs, or move when another player is taking a shot. Even if your fellow players don't seem to mind noise, keep your voice down.

So that the game will move right along, plan your shot before it's your turn. Then take only one practice swing (if any) before hitting the ball. And don't fall too far behind the group ahead of you. On a crowded course, make sure you don't leave a whole hole open ahead of you. If you do, you've fallen behind—and being slow is one of golfing's cardinal sins.

Another way to speed things up is for the group to agree to play "ready golf." This allows a player who's ready to go ahead and hit, even if he's playing out of turn. Naturally, golfers playing ready golf should keep track of what the other players are doing so they don't end up hitting at the same time.

When using a golf cart, follow the course's rules. Don't drive the cart too fast or in places where carts aren't allowed, and watch out for other golfers. Carts should be kept off the greens and tee areas, and most courses post signs showing where you can and cannot park.

Playing Through

To the thoughtful golfer, asking the group behind you to play through is the polite (and right) thing to do. But certain conditions apply. The United States Golf Association (www.usga.org/rules) publishes specific rules of etiquette for playing through, the essence of which follows.

Unless special rules apply, threesomes and foursomes are obligated to allow a twosome to play through, but only if there is an empty hole ahead. If you sense that the group behind you wants to play through, first determine whether the next hole is open. If it is, ask them if they would like to play through. If they take you up on the offer, stand aside as they play, then resume play once they are out of your range.

What if you're part of a group that is being slowed down by the players ahead of you? Asking to play through can be touchy, so go about it in the most courteous way. First, make sure that the group ahead isn't waiting for those in front of them to move on. Second, don't imply that the group you're asking is dawdling. If the group agrees to let you play through, don't waste time. If your ball disappears after a bad shot, just drop a ball near where yours was last seen and play on. Then thank the group for accommodating you before moving on to the next hole.

Course Maintenance

Always repair any divots after your shot. When leaving a putting green, put the flagstick back in the hole and repair any marks made by your golf shoe spikes or a ball where it hit the green. After playing a shot out of a bunker, rake the sand to erase your footprints and the hole made by your club. Also keep any wrappers, tissues, or other trash with you or toss it into a waste receptacle.

In a time when more than a few professional athletes alternately grandstand and sulk, the word "sportsmanship" almost seems old-fashioned. But it's not! When you take to the course, court, or field, you can do your part for basic civility. (See also page 846: "A Word to Parents.")

➤ If you're so proficient that you could practically go pro, keep it to yourself. Your performance will speak for itself—and nobody likes a braggart.

➤ Don't gripe about lapses in your own performance (and, naturally, *never* your opponent's).

➤ Watch your expletives. A foul word that may not offend close friends is nonetheless inappropriate—and it might be overheard by others.

➤ As important as being a good loser is being a gracious winner. When you come out on top, compliment your opponent on his skill and say that luck just seemed to be on your side.

➤ Treat a sports ground of any kind as you would your own backyard. Pick up litter, stretch the tennis net tight after your game, repair any marks you left on the green, and return equipment to the locker room as necessary.

Tennis Etiquette

SOMETIMES TENNIS ETIQUETTE has as much to do with sharing a public or private court as it does with interacting with your opponent and your partner during the match.

➤ If you've reserved a court and arrive at your appointed time to find a match still going on, tell the players you don't mind waiting until they finish the game in progress. Then wait patiently without pacing, bouncing balls, or appearing miffed.

➤ If players who have overrun their time limit refuse to leave until they finish the set, it's wiser to ask a tennis center staff member to intervene than handle the matter yourself.

➤ If you and your opponent are the players occupying the court and your allotted time is up, finish the game you're playing and then leave the court—even if you're near the end of the set.

➤ At a public court with a first come, first served policy, it's perfectly fine to ask those ahead of you for an estimate of how long they expect to play—but only when the ball isn't in play.

➤ When playing on an unreserved court, don't play on endlessly. Instead, tell new arrivals how long you plan to play and then try to finish your set within an hour. (Note: generally, assigned public court time is 1 hour for singles, 1½ hours for doubles.)

➤ If you have to cross behind someone else's court to get to your own, wait until they change sides before venturing forth.

The Match

Etiquette starts with knowing the rules of the game and following them. It's advisable to purchase and read the U.S. Tennis Association book of rules or to go to the organization's Web site (www.usta.com/rules/).

Even if you're not playing well, act as if you're having fun. The game will be better for you, your partner (if you're playing doubles), and your opponent if you think positively—and you'll probably improve your play while you're at it.

There are certain things you want to avoid, no matter the quality of your play: complaining about your bad shots, losing your temper or angrily slamming a ball (or, worse, your racket) onto the court, sulking when losing, and using foul language.

If you're playing in a tournament, never question the ruling of the linesman or referee. Even if you think your ball has landed *in* by a foot but the official says it's *out*, you should accept the official's decision as final.

Some other important points to remember:

➤ The server, not the receiver, calls out the score before serving so that there will be no dispute about how many points have been scored.

➤ Balls should be readily accessible. Servers will keep from wasting time by keeping balls in their pockets or against the fence behind the center mark.

➤ When served balls have obviously been hit out, the receiver should refrain from returning the balls over the net.

➤ When there's doubt over whether a ball was in or out, the player receiving the ball makes the call. Unless the receiver clearly sees that it was out, the ball should be called good.

➤ Change sides every other game, on the odd game—starting after the first, then continuing after the third, fifth, and so on. Changing courts in this fashion is a requirement in tournament play and a courtesy in a friendly match.

➤ If your ball bounces into a neighboring court, wait until the players have finished their point before asking them for their help in retrieving it.

➤ While white used to be the required color of tennis clothes practically everywhere, this is no longer the case—although some places still adhere to the "tennis whites" rule. When invited to play at a private club, ask your host if whites are required; if you're the host, be sure to tell your guest whether white must be worn.

➤ At the end of a tennis match, it's a courteous tradition to shake hands with your opponent and congratulate him on his win or thank him for an excellent match if he's the one who lost.

Running, Biking, Etcetera

ON PARK ROADS and other thoroughfares frequented by cyclists, in-line skaters, joggers, and walkers, it's important to stick to the lanes designated for your mode of transportation; failing to do so is not only rude but dangerous. If you're moving more slowly than others sharing your lane, be sure to stay to the right.

Then there's the all-important issue of safety. Although pedestrians have the right of way, cyclists and skaters stay watchful and alert on the assumption that not everyone knows this rule. Walkers and runners should face oncoming automobile traffic when moving down a road, and anyone out for some road-based exercise after dark should dress in brightly colored or reflective clothing or use a clip-on flashing light. It's also smart to carry an ID (name, phone number, and contact person) when exercising, just in case there's an accident.

Running and Walking

There are two big don'ts for runners and walkers: (1) staying in the middle of the lane and (2) hogging the lane by moving along with two or three people abreast. Besides those reminders, consider these:

> ➤ In neighborhoods, try to jog where both foot traffic and automobile traffic are light. Choose sidewalks you're sure will be sparsely traveled, then run or walk in the street only when having to dodge an obstruction.

> ➤ If you're running on a circular track with several lanes, leave the inside lanes for faster runners who might be doing timed sessions.

> ➤ When you come to an intersection, don't put yourself in danger by trying to beat traffic or dodge it. Your stride won't be broken if you just jog in place until the light changes. You could also use the break to stretch.

> ➤ If a motorist or pedestrian makes a smart-alecky crack about you jogging through his neighborhood, just smile and continue on your way. If he has a point, however, then maybe you should consider taking his advice and look for a new route.

Cycling

The first rule for cyclists is to *obey stop signs and traffic signals*. Racing through red lights and stop signs could end in disaster—for both you and an unwary driver or pedestrian. The second is to stay focused on the road and everything around you at all times, whether pedestrians, potholes, or parked cars. Ride in a straight line, keep a consistent pace, and feather (don't slam) your brakes whenever you need to slow down. It's also a good idea to use hand signals when you need to turn.

When cycling on roads with a group, ride single file. Riding two or more abreast not only horns in on automobile drivers' territory but could cause an accident if the cyclist to your side swerves toward you for any reason.

Yes, that charity-sponsored footrace or marathon is for a noble cause, but that doesn't mean you can let your manners off the hook when you take part. Runners should exhibit the "right stuff" from the moment they line up for the race.

The first consideration? Where to position yourself. So that the slower participants (walkers included) won't delay the faster runners' break from the pack, everyone should position themselves according to their predicted finishing times. (Besides, starting up front will in no way get a slower-paced runner to the finish line more quickly.) There's also the matter of safety: Slow runners and walkers clogging the road at the start of the race increase the dangers that come with any tightly packed group of moving people—pushing, tripping, and trampling. Likewise, if parents choose to share the thrill of racing with their stroller-bound infants or young children (or pet owners enjoy running with Fido), then they should plan on staying toward the back of the pack to avoid crowding or getting in the way of others.

It's important to rehydrate and refuel during a footrace, especially when running long distances or in extreme heat. Drinking on the run is made easier by race organizers and volunteers handing out paper cups or bottles of water or flavored sport drink along the course. Some runners drink the water while others cool down by pouring it over their heads. If doing the latter, take care not to splash others with your water. (Wet running shoes not only are uncomfortable but increase weight and the risk of blisters.)

Wondering what to do with the paper cup (or gel-pack remnants, banana peel, or other food packaging) once you've finished? For some, it's common practice to throw the used items on the ground, leaving them for the volunteers to clean up. The better option is to dispose of your trash by placing it in one of the receptacles provided along the racecourse and typically found near the water stations. If you still choose to throw your trash on the ground, be sure to thank the volunteers whose job it is to clean up after you. Note: Even if you throw your own trash away, it's a good idea to shout out a general thank-you to the volunteers working the water station on your behalf. Your kind words are likely the only payment they'll receive for their time.

In-line Skating

When it comes to following traffic regulations, in-line skaters should consider themselves as having the same obligations drivers and cyclists do—stopping at traffic lights and stop signs and not going the wrong way on one-way streets. Expert skaters should also be tolerant of learners (especially children) and other less proficient skaters—giving them the "you're getting in the way" glare is offensive to people who are out for a bit of fun and exercise. All skaters would be wise to wear a helmet, wrist protectors, and elbow and knee pads, but such safeguards are a must for beginners. The International Inline Skating Association (www.iisa.org) is a good source of information on the sport.

At the Fitness Center

EXERCISING ON YOUR OWN is one thing, but doing it at a health or fitness club calls for considering the needs of those around you. Here's how:

➤ Only a novice at a health club would be unaware of the number-one etiquette concern: wiping sweat off mats and machines. That's one of the reasons you keep a towel with you. No one wants to sit or lie in someone else's sweat (yours included) and will no doubt wipe down the equipment himself—but it's your responsibility to do it for him.

➤ Don't leave loose weights and dumbbells on a bar or machine. Otherwise, the next person who uses the equipment may have to spend time removing them or finding someone to help him do so. Likewise, replace dumbells in their storage racks instead of leaving them scattered on the floor.

➤ Don't hog the weight machines. When others want to use them, agree to rotate your sets.

➤ If all the treadmills or any other cardio machines are full, limit your time to give those who may be waiting a chance. Some gyms limit treadmill time to twenty minutes.

➤ If you're into flirting, don't be a pest. Flirt only if the other person is receptive; if you try to strike up a conversation with someone you find attractive and he or she gives you the brush-off (no matter how politely), drop your overture then and there.

➤ A quick and friendly hello is one thing, but chatting to a fellow gym-goer who's working out could interrupt his routine.

➤ Comply with the fitness center's rules, such as wearing correct workout shoes (black soles can mar vinyl floors), not using cell phones, and signing in at the front desk.

➤ Be aware of the smell factor: Arrive clean, remember to apply deodorant, and lay off the perfume and cologne, which get stronger as you work up a sweat.

➤ Be punctual for personal training sessions and group fitness classes.

➤ Do your part to keep the fitness center area neat: Keep your towels, water bottles, and fitness logs with you at all times so that they are out of the way of others.

➤ Pitch in for a tidy locker room by keeping your clothes and other personal items stored in lockers. Clean up after yourself in the showers, at the sinks, and in the changing areas. Deposit used towels in their receptacles.

Cards and Other Games

CARD-PLAYING AND BOARD GAMES are in a league of their own, but the rules of good sportsmanship apply as much to these tabletop pursuits as they do to games of exertion played outdoors. Whether playing bridge, poker, Monopoly, or Scrabble, you'll want to watch your p's and q's.

When it's your turn, don't slow down the game by waiting too long to make your move. You also want to avoid two more time-wasters: leaving the table unnecessarily and talking too much about other things. Even if chatting is the norm, pay attention to the game. It's rude to let your mind wander in the thick of even the friendliest competition.

When hosting a party, don't make guests feel that they must join in a game, whether charades or cards or Clue. Then group the willing players by how seriously they take the game and the level of their skills.

Games of Knowledge

Don't propose playing Trivial Pursuit, Botticelli, or similar games to your friends just so you can show how smart you are. And even if you're a veritable Einstein and get every answer right, never brag or gloat.

Trivia nights in bars are popular in some places, and those who play should keep three things in mind—especially if the beer flows freely and inhibitions are lowered. First, don't name your team anything obscene or offensive. Second, when the leader (or emcee) asks a question, don't yell out (or even hint at) the answer. Third, don't argue with what the emcee says is the correct answer, though a friendly or joking objection isn't out of bounds.

At Spectator Sports

TIME WAS WHEN a disruption at the ballpark was rare. But in recent years fan behavior has taken a decided turn for the worse, with catcalls ringing through the stadium, beer bottles thrown, and even the overenthusiastic supporters of the winning team running riot.

Such acts are unquestionably out of place, of course, but even the best-behaved spectator in the stands might need to brush up on a few good-sport guidelines:

➤ Be patient as you walk to your seat, taking care not to jostle or shove anyone. Walk slowly with the crowd, not through it, when arriving and leaving.

➤ When vendors are hawking sodas and snacks in the stands, raising your arm to signal you want to buy something is preferable to shouting, "Over here!" If you're in the middle of a row and have to ask others to pass your money and food, be sure to thank those who did the passing.

Little did Emily Post know when she wrote in the 1945 edition of *Etiquette* just how apt her words would remain all these decades later: "The quality which perhaps more than any other distinguishes true sportsmanship is absence of temper . . . not temper brought along and held in check, but temper securely locked and left at home."

Poor sportsmanship on the part of parents has become epidemic. Taunts rain down on the referee of a Little League game from some parents in the stands. A mother stalks onto the field to protest a move by the coach. Two fathers come to blows over perceived slights in a soccer or hockey match. A referee who quit doing the job he loved put the problem succinctly when he said that there used to be respect for the official, for other people, and for the game, whereas today "all anyone thinks about is themselves."

Psychologists theorize that parents project their fears of failure onto their children and that today's society engenders a "winning is everything" attitude. Obviously, overzealous parents do more harm than good by being poor role models, sapping the fun out of the games, and embarrassing young players. To keep from crossing the line at a game, parents should do the following:

Leave coaching to the coach. Shouting negative comments and instructions at the adult in charge will confuse a young child. (Which adult is she supposed to listen to—you or the coach?) Aggressive sideline coaching sets a bad example for all children, undermines their confidence, and can actually harm performance.

Don't criticize referees and judges. When disagreeing with a referee's calls, keep the criticism to yourself. Even if you think the referee was completely off base, don't convey your hostile feelings to your child. You can discuss a decision with your child, but stick to the action itself ("I don't think the ref saw Josh touch home plate") and don't indulge in personal insults.

Compliment the opposition. If the other team is playing particularly well, remark on team members' skills. Showing your appreciation for other children is not a betrayal of your own youngster but simply an essential part of sportsmanship and good manners.

Steer clear of tantrum-throwing parents. You can't reason with a furious parent, but if you know the person, you may want to speak with him about the behavior at a calmer time. Then again, if a parent is throwing things or seems physically threatening, get the authorities immediately instead of taking on an out-of-control spectator yourself.

➢ When a large group of spectators rises and blocks your view, go with the flow and stand. If only one or two people are standing in front of you, be polite: "Get down in front!" will raise hackles, while "Would you mind sitting so that we can see?" usually won't.

➤ Watch your language. Obscenities in public are by nature offensive, no matter how free-spirited the atmosphere. Remember, referees and coaches are people, too. Avoid being downright nasty if you don't agree with a call or decision.

➤ Cheer your heart out after a play that goes your team's way, but don't be so loud or engage in so much horseplay that your behavior becomes obnoxious.

➤ At events where quiet is expected—a golf tournament, a tennis match, a game of billiards, or even a game of chess—don't utter so much as a whisper when the players are trying to concentrate.

Sports and Recreation

Index

Index

Index

EMILY POST

JAMES MONTGOMERY FLAGG

Emily Post 1873 to 1960

Emily Post began her career as a writer at the age of thirty-one. Her romantic stories of European and American society were serialized in *Vanity Fair, Collier's, McCall's,* and other popular magazines. Many were also successfully published in book form.

Upon its publication in 1922, her book *Etiquette* topped the nonfiction bestseller list, and the phrase "according to Emily Post" soon entered our language as the last word on the subject of social conduct. Mrs. Post, who as a girl had been told that well-bred women should not work, was suddenly a pioneering American career woman. Her numerous books, a syndicated newspaper column, and a regular network radio program made Emily Post a figure of national stature and importance throughout the rest of her life.

"Good manners reflect something from inside—an innate sense of consideration for others and respect for self."

—Emily Post